The Life of
ARCHBISHOP
JOHN IRELAND

Most Reverend John Ireland, d.d.

The Life of
ARCHBISHOP
JOHN IRELAND

by James H. Moynihan

HARPER & BROTHERS PUBLISHERS NEW YORK

46587

MA5
Ir2 M

Library of Congress catalogue card number: 53:5003

TO HIS EXCELLENCY

THE MOST REVEREND JOHN GREGORY MURRAY, S.T.D.

ARCHBISHOP OF ST. PAUL

THIS WORK IS DEDICATED IN GRATITUDE

AND IN REVERENCE

CONTENTS

Illustrations

FOREWORD

In his introduction to *The Church and Modern Society*, which was the title of a collection of lectures and addresses he had given over a period of a quarter of a century, Archbishop Ireland set forth his conception of his responsibilities as a churchman in the following terms: "As the priest and as the citizen I held it my duty to contribute my mite as opportunity permitted to the pleasure or the improvement of my fellow-man, to the welfare, passing or permanent, of country and society. I hope I have been right; I crave indulgence if I have been wrong."

In harmony with this conception of his duty he embraced all men in the field he sought for service. His view could not be limited to his own country or to any particular group within his own sphere of jurisdiction.

Educated from early youth away from the associations of home, he learned to adjust himself to companions who spoke a language other than his own and live a life unadorned with the comforts of American standards.

Immediately after his ordination to the priesthood he became the chaplain of the very first regiment in the United States to respond to the call of Lincoln for the defense of the Union and the termination of servitude under the American flag.

Stricken ill on the fields of battle, he reluctantly was invalided home from the young men to whom he had consecrated himself in every need both spiritual and temporal.

Called by his bishop to become his coadjutor, he immediately organized a colonization bureau to empty the slums of the eastern shores of the United States of the helpless, hopeless immigrants who had neither means nor opportunity to help themselves and to settle them on the rich soil of Minnesota where hundreds of thousands of acres were placed at their disposal.

Elevated to the rank of Metropolitan and thereby made a participant in the counsels of the hierarchy of the United States, he became the most stimulating force in the organization of the educational and welfare activities of the Church in this country, a role he played for more than thirty years.

The record herein set forth may well cause one to marvel at the courage displayed in creating opportunity rather than awaiting its fortuitous event, the breadth of vision in seeking the solution of problems resulting from the repudiation of Christ in Christendom while entertaining the vain hope of preserving its heritage, the fidelity to principle in an atmosphere where principle is dethroned and expediency is exalted, the unselfish consecration to the dominant motive of his life as it was the favorite theme of all his discourses: Jesus Christ, yesterday, and today, and the same forever. (Heb. XIII, 8.)

✠ JOHN GREGORY MURRAY,
Archbishop of St. Paul

PREFACE

After the death of Archbishop Ireland in September, 1918, all available material was given to his intimate friend and school companion, Bishop Thomas O'Gorman of Sioux Falls, South Dakota, who intended to write the Archbishop's life, but who outlived him by only three years. In 1923, Monsignor Humphrey Moynihan, who had been at one time secretary to the Archbishop and who had always enjoyed his confidence, undertook the project. After collecting considerable material, he contributed to the *Catholic World*, to the *Irish-American Review*, and to *Acta et Dicta* articles on the life of the prelate, on the Spanish-American War, and on colonization. Much to his sorrow, however, the toll of years and failing health prevented the prosecution of the work. In 1948, in preparation for the celebration of the Centenary of the Archdiocese of St. Paul, His Excellency, the Most Reverend John Gregory Murray, assigned to me the task of completing the life, a task which because of lack of training in historical technique and of acquaintance with many of the problems involved, I accepted with considerable trepidation. Fortunately, I have had the advantage not only of the four published articles and the many detached notes left by my brother, all of which I have felt free to use, but also of the vast amount of correspondence, which, contrary to widespread impression, had not been destroyed. It is unfortunate that Monsignor Humphrey Moynihan was unable to complete the work, as no one knew the mind of Archbishop Ireland as well as he. It was he who, when a student at the North American College, Rome, drew up the memorial which the Archbishop presented in 1892 in defense of the Faribault plan, who edited in 1896 and 1905 the discourses contained in *The Church and Modern Society*, and who attended to much of the Roman correspondence. It may be said without false humility that to him must be attributed much of whatever value this work possesses. For the inefficiencies and the ineptitudes I alone am responsible. I am happy in the privilege of being able to present the story of one who, if not without peer in the American hierarchy, is undoubtedly the most colorful and dynamic of those prelates who are the glory of the Church in the United States.

I have not attempted to give complete histories of the three great controversies, dealing with them only so far as they reflect the life of the Archbishop. If I have quoted widely, my excuse is that any attempt to paraphrase the speeches and letters of Ireland would only rob them of their color and force. It is to be expected that in the career of one, most of whose life was involved in heated controversy, expressions will at times occur, excessive in their frankness. Their reproduction, after due deliberation, has been motivated by the conviction that to omit them would be to give an incomplete picture of the mind and heart of the prelate. The desire to contain the life within the scope of one volume has necessitated the omission of some details, which, however, I felt would contribute but little to my purpose—to indicate the vision, the courage, and the myriad activities of "the Apostle of the West," as well as the contribution which during half a century he made to Church and State.

I gladly acknowledge indebtedness, first of all to His Excellency, the Most Reverend John Gregory Murray, without whose unfailing encouragement and sympathy this work would not have been produced; to Monsignor James M. Reardon, who, while engaged in preparing a history of the archdiocese, took time to read the manuscript; to Father Patrick Ahern, who made many valuable suggestions; to Father John Tracy Ellis, who was at all times helpful; to the Right Reverend John M. A. Fearns of St. Joseph's Seminary, Yonkers, New York, and to Father Jeremiah J. Brennan, archivist of the Archdiocese of New York; to the Most Reverend Francis P. Keough, Archbishop of Baltimore, and to Father Paul L. Love, archivist of the archdiocese; to the Most Reverend Peter L. Ireton, Bishop of Richmond, and to Fathers Robert C. Hickman and Justin D. McClunn of the Chancery Office; to Father Thomas T. McAvoy of the University of Notre Dame; to Fathers Joseph I. Malloy and Joseph McSorley of the Paulists; to the librarians of the Minneapolis and St. Paul public libraries, the State Historical Society, the St. Paul Seminary, St. Thomas College, the Catholic University, the Library of Congress, the Biblioteca Nacional of Madrid, the Bibliothèque nationale of Paris, the Central Catholic Library of Dublin; to my assistants, Fathers Harry Towey and Jerome Quinn; and to the ladies of the parish of the Incarnation who assisted with the typing of the manuscript.

JAMES H. MOYNIHAN

The Life of
ARCHBISHOP
JOHN IRELAND

Chapter 1

PREPARATIONS FOR PRELACY

❖❖❖❖❖❖❖❖❖❖❖❖

1. THE IMMIGRANT

Half a dozen miles from the cathedral town of Kilkenny, a city of importance in medieval days, the seat of parliaments and once the Confederate capital of Ireland, a city which knew its hour of victory when Owen Roe O'Neill rode proudly at the head of the United Irish army in defense of King Charles and the faith, but which tasted the bitterness of defeat when Cromwell stood battering at its walls, a city whose cathedral church of St. Canice and Castle of the Ormands still speak of faith and valor, and whose ether still vibrates with the clashing echoes of Berkeley's idealism, Swift's savage realism, and Congreve's mocking Muse, lies the sleepy hamlet of Burnchurch in the parish of Danesforth. There, on September 11, 1838, John Ireland received the waters of Baptism. His father, Richard Ireland, an artisan of better education than his social standing would indicate, was a man of unusually fine physique, impulsive, tenacious of his convictions, and of indomitable will. His mother, Judith Naughton, was a woman of deeply religious character who left the stamp of her piety on her two sons and four daughters.[1]

It was a bleak picture which presented itself to the youthful eyes of John Ireland—a land of poverty and hunger, of injustice and oppression. In the long story of the world's inhumanity no country ever suffered so cruelly and so continuously from war, famine, and pestilence as Ireland suffered. English rule, and what Lord Clarendon called "felonious landlordism" with its merciless rack rents, left nothing but a precarious crop between the people and starvation. Irish industries had been crushed out of existence by English law in the interest of England's factories. As Bishop John Lancaster Spalding said, "Famine was the terrible prerogative of the Celt in his native land." John Ireland was hardly seven years of age when the Great Famine of 1845 struck the land and continued to devastate it for three years.

1

The imagination boggles at the picture which the countryside presented, and which Father Thomas O'Herlihy has depicted:

Gaunt and drawn faces, eyes that stare and a body that sways with unsteady gait, diseased and delirious beings, human things falling down faint and writhing in pain, corpses about with mouths discoloured by grass or nettle leaves, mangled remains found here and there torn by dogs and wild animals; all that does not describe the horrors of famine; it is some of it; but not all. The pain and anguish of a slow death is something more. . . . Add to that the open pits, growing daily by the accumulation of dead, the wretched paraphernalia of funerals where there are no mourners, the squalor of that hinged coffin that evacuated so many dead on its cruel mission from house to house and thence to the graveyard; it is all stereotyped because there is no one to mourn, for all are in desolation.[2]

It is small wonder that Lord Brougham, speaking of the sufferings of the Irish people, said: "They surpass anything in the pages of Thucydides, in the canvas of Poussin, in the dismal chant of Dante."

In the spring of 1849, abandoning the hopeless struggle for a decent livelihood for himself and his family, Richard Ireland, accompanied by his sister, Nancy, crossed the sea in search of a new home, taking up his residence in Burlington, Vermont. In late 1850 Mrs. Ireland and the children set out to join the father, who met them in Boston. The family remained in Vermont until the following year, when it was caught up in the tide of western migration and made the long jolting journey to Chicago. There, while the girls attended the Academy of the Sisters of Mercy, John went to St. Mary's School. A chance meeting on a Chicago street in 1852 of Richard Ireland and his old friend John O'Gorman resulted in their decision to settle in Minnesota. At the time there was much exploitation of a steamboat line between Galena and St. Paul. Minnesota was being advertised as a health resort as well as an agricultural paradise, and immigration was getting under way. After considerable thought the two decided to try their luck in the new territory.[3]

The only means of long-distance transportation was by prairie schooners, four of which were hired to take the families to Galena, Illinois. There they took the *Nominee* for St. Paul, arriving at the foot of Jackson Street in the first week of May, 1852. Richard Ireland, a carpenter by trade, constructed a rude shack at Fifth and St. Peter streets to shelter the two families, and a little later built a more commodious dwelling a short distance away. As they settled in this frontier village, it was just emerging from the log-cabin stage. Here young John was thrilled at the newness of the life which greeted him. Here he saw *voyageurs*, boatmen and raftsmen and Indian traders, who spoke French chiefly—in those pioneer days French was heard as much as English. Here he saw many Indians—the Indian village, Kaposia, Little Crow's village, then occupied what is now a suburb of South St. Paul. Fine specimens of humanity, these Sioux, with their peculiar ease and grace of bearing, their litheness and nonchalance, their pride in their rifles and gay blankets, their numerous pouches and trinkets. Here he saw the little log chapel which Father Lucien Galtier had erected in 1841, and which he called "the basilica," so poor that it recalled the stable at Bethlehem. Here he heard how only in the preceding year bands of Sioux and Chippewas had fought a battle on the spot where now Wabasha and Third streets meet. Here he saw the first church of St. Paul worthy of the name in process of completion on the corner of Wabasha and Sixth streets. At the first Mass which he attended, the congregation was being urged to contribute to the finishing and plastering of the building. And yet, even in those early years—the population was twelve hundred—the air was full of forecasts of the wonderful future in store for St. Paul. Soon the wilderness would blossom like a rose; Atlantic and Pacific would be bound by long slender lines of steel, and trains would be speeding from St. Anthony to the Gulf. The fame of Minnesota, with its forests and loamy prairies, its broad-bosomed rivers and countless lakes, was spreading far and wide, and to Minnesota, as to a land of promise, families were pouring in from all parts to seek their fortune on a virgin soil. In those days almost every public address echoed the well-worn lines:

> I hear the tread of pioneers
> Of nations yet to be,
> The first low wash of nations where soon
> Shall roll a human sea.

Richard Ireland resumed his trade to provide for his wife and six children, one of whom, Richard, died soon after arriving in St. Paul.[4] Of the family Bishop O'Gorman once said:

If Richard Ireland had the advantages of early education, he would, I think, probably have been an even greater man than his son. The son has his father's strong personality, his gift of quick decision, his interest in a very wide variety of subjects. And he has the gentleness, the softness, which particularly characterized his mother. But his most unusual characteristic—the one which has doubtless been his greatest practical asset in life—is the faculty of being mentally quick and mentally deep at the same time.[5]

2. THE STUDENT

On July 19, 1850, at the request of the Council of Baltimore, St. Paul was erected into a diocese, and, on January 26, 1851, the Reverend Joseph Cretin, a French missionary of the Diocese of Dubuque, was consecrated its first bishop by Bishop Devie of Belley in France. Bishop Cretin was among those priests who answered the call of Loras for missionaries. In 1838 he quitted Ferney and the college whose foundation he had just laid and came to Dubuque. When the vast Diocese of Dubuque was dismembered and the Diocese of St. Paul established, it was he who was called upon to organize it. Bishop Devie, in his desire to assist the newly consecrated Bishop in his apostolic work, informed him that he would be pleased to educate free of charge any boys manifesting signs of a vocation whom Cretin might find in his diocese.[6] As the first Bishop of St. Paul at once cast about him for vocations, the intelligence and piety of John Ireland and Thomas O'Gorman speedily marked them out as desirable candidates for the priesthood. On an April morning in 1853—it is Bishop O'Gorman who told the story—Bishop Cretin called them and led them before a statue of the Blessed Virgin in the Cathedral, and as they knelt reverently there, he raised his hand over them, saying: "I bless, in its first pupils, the Seminary of St. Paul." He then confided them to the care of Father Augustin Ravoux, Vicar General, who accompanied them to the College of Meximieux in the Diocese of Belley. In those days the diocese had its theological seminary at Bourg, the capital city of the department of Ain, in which theology and branches pertaining to the *grand séminaire* were taught. It had also two preparatory seminaries, the one at Meximieux, the other at Belley. The former was founded in 1802 by Father Ruivet, a native of the city, who after being a confessor of the faith and a faithful missionary in that country during the dark days of the French Revolution became pastor and donated his paternal home as the beginning of a Latin school. When Joseph (now Monsignor) Guillot entered it in 1867, it had three hundred students.

After the completion of their course the two students passed on to the scholasticate of the Marist Fathers at Montbel, near Toulon.[7]

Meximieux left an indelible impression on John Ireland, as the number of letters which he sent to his old teachers testifies. Among them is one which he wrote in 1891 to Canon Theloz, Rector of the Seminary, on the occasion of the publication of the Life of Abbé

Robelin, and which at once expresses his affection for the school and illustrates how facile and generous were his emotions. He spoke of the joy in his labors and the solace in his sorrows which he found in the memory of his school days. It reawakened in his soul peace and happiness; "in its light and inspiration all restlessness of spirit vanished, discouragement ceased, and refreshed and rejuvenated I retake the road of life with renewed ardor." He had visited many institutions but knew of none he would prefer to Meximieux. Those who presided over the seminary were masters of men, venerable names:

Tarlet—the ideal superior, great in his diginity and his sacerdotal gravity, edifying in his piety, tender in his affection for his pupils, how we hated to displease him; Robelin, the saint and the father; Ballufin, a learned and profound man; Monfat, the distinguished litterateur, able to inspire a taste for what was good and a love of serious studies; Pasquier, the untiring workman, a living encyclopedia with an answer for every question; Perrier, precise, clear, sparkling in mind, eloquent in speech, with ideas new and original. Had they been called to higher spheres, to more eminent posts, they would have become historical personages.[8]

He followed its career with intense interest, and when in 1907, as a result of the Law of Separation, the community was driven out by the military, he wrote to Canon Laplace, the Superior, that the expulsion of the professors and students made his heart bleed. He spared no effort in his attempt to save it.

Nor was his loyalty confined to the Petit Séminaire. In June, 1913, he wrote to Canon Perretant, Superior of the Grand Séminaire, who, on the Golden Jubilee of his ordination, had been made a domestic prelate. He must have brought great joy to the Canon's heart as he said:

What a wonderful career you have had, a half-century spent in the holiest, most divine of works, the formation of the priest. What a wonderful picture opens before your eyes—the priests of the beautiful diocese of Belley, so devoted, so on fire for the things of God and of souls, almost all the result of your zeal and your spirit. I envy you. As for me, I have missed the calm, the peace so valuable for personal welfare. With me it has been bustle, the violent rocking of the waves, contact with the world; little or none of that peace of mind which draws and keeps the voice of heaven. With Father Marechal, but for entirely different reasons, I say the *"Miserere."* I am on the great highway where rest is impossible, where I must either run or fall. But whether I wish it or not, the end is coming.[9]

He also kept in touch with the old students, writing in March, 1915, to Archbishop Jean-Augustin Germain of Toulouse that he hoped to see France crowned with victory, Alsace-Lorraine spared, and Belgium enriched with the spoils of the enemy, for otherwise he would not have the courage to put foot on the soil of the country of his youth.[10] And when America sent its soldiers to Europe, he wrote in August, 1917, to Stanislas-Arthur-Xavier Touchet, Archbishop of Orleans, to assure him that although the United States was slow in entering the conflict it would never quit in defeat. He told of his meeting with the members of the French Commission in Washington and of his conversation with "M. X." (Viviani), to whom he spoke very frankly about the need of religious peace in France and of the renewal of diplomatic relations between France and the Vatican. "He showed himself," he said, "with regard to me altogether the gentleman, and I believe that you and other bishops of France would profit if you remained close to the men of State and especially to 'M. X.' "[11]

3. THE CHAPLAIN

On the completion of his theological studies, John Ireland returned to St. Paul, and after his ordination to the priesthood by Bishop Thomas Grace on December 21, 1861, he was appointed assistant at the Cathedral. He arrived to find the country in the throes of war. For months rebellion had been brewing in the land, and on April 14, the day after the fall of Fort Sumter, Lincoln called for 75,000 volunteers. On the same day, Governor Alexander Ramsey offered the Secretary of War 1000 men. Realizing that a vast army would be required, Lincoln called for a fifth regiment from Minnesota, muster beginning on December 19, 1861. In March, 1862, when the last company of the Minnesota Fifth was mustered in, Ireland, who had lost no time in volunteering, received his commission as chaplain. His regiment was sent to the South, forming part of the army under General Rosecrans, who was withstanding the Southern Army under Generals Van Dorn and Sterling Price, seeking to break into the North. For months he shared the hardships of the soldier's life, winning the heart of the regiment. After much hard service, the regiment saved the day at the battle of Corinth. On the morning of the third of October, 1862, the regiment, which had been sent out to guard a bridge across the Tascumia River, was lost sight of in the excitement and confusion of the battle. Seeing the blunder, Lieutenant William B. McGrorty hastened to Rosecrans, who ordered the regiment to return to Corinth. Before daybreak on the following morning, the Confederate guns opened on the town, and shells began to drop near the campfires of the

Fifth. After some hours of fighting, the Union lines were broken and Federal troops poured pell-mell into Corinth, hotly pursued by the Confederate soldiers. It was at this point that the Fifth swung into action and by their withering fire, followed by a vigorous charge, closed the lines once more and practically brought the battle to a conclusion.[12] The picture of the battle of Corinth in the Minnesota state capitol depicts that charge and deservedly gives Ireland a place of honor, for, during the battle, when the cry was raised that the ammunition was failing, he was seen hurrying down the line, heedless of the bullets flying around him, carrying a supply of ammunition and crying: "Here are your cartridges, boys, don't spare them." When the last shot had been fired and the enemy had retreated, the soldiers looked for their chaplain, wondering what had happened to him. They found him at last—tending the wounded and dying. Ireland gave an interesting account of the battle when he delivered a eulogy at the burial of General Lucius Hubbard on April 8, 1913, and he also wrote a report from Corinth on October 23, 1862.

Many stories attesting to the respect and admiration for him were vouched for by those who took part in the engagement. Colonel John Arkins, who served from December 19, 1861, to the end of the war, told of the first sermon Father Ireland preached and of the rude altar which the boys built for him "with a sort of little canopy covering all, of green bushes and little saplings gathered from a neighboring wood." In three years' experience with soldiers, this was the first and last attempt of its kind, witnessed by the writer, where such preparation was made for a chaplain. Ireland did not make any wearying preparation for his sermon, which was a sort of talk for the boys, but went right at it in a soldierly way, and before he had proceeded five minutes he had gotten an audience together under a burning Mississippi sun. The men, who had spread their blankets in the shade of the neighboring trees to play chuck-a-luck, abandoned their games, gradually pressing forward to hear what the young priest had to say, and, when he closed, the veterans cheered him as he descended from his brush pulpit.[13] Dr. J. C. O'Connell wrote that Ireland was one of the most popular officers in the regiment, always ready to drop a kind, encouraging word to this soldier, a smile and a nod of recognition to another, words of cheer to everyone. He was, he said, of a cheerful, happy disposition, and, like the sun, he cast his rays of sunshine all around and won the hearts of all, officers and soldiers alike. It was cheering to the sad and homesick youth to see this good father gather the soldiers around him and seek to divert their thoughts from the thousand and one trials they had to encounter through their love for the fatherland. He was a good chess player, too, and always carried with him his little set of chessmen and board. After camping for the night and taking his supper of bacon and crackers, washed down by water or coffee, he was ready to give battle with his chessmen on his rubber blanket board to any of the men, no matter how rough or polished, ragged or otherwise.[14]

The *Herald* of Utica, New York, quoted the reminiscence of a veteran of the Civil War who lay on the battlefield of Corinth wounded and, as he thought, dying, when a man came to him, knelt down beside him, made him drink out of his flask, and never left him until he had dressed his wounds. He asked the name of his benefactor, which, he said, he would never forget, for he had saved his life. It was John Ireland.[15] Similar incidents were narrated by Major I. R. Holcomb in a description of the battle which he wrote for the St. Paul *Pioneer Press*. Years afterward when Ireland met Rosecrans in Washington and asked him if he remembered the Fifth Minnesota regiment, the General replied, "How could I forget it? It saved the day at Corinth." Without the victory at Corinth, the Middle West might, at least for the time being, have been lost to the Union.[16]

Captain McGrorty, in a letter written to his daughter from Camp Van Burgesrode, told of the hardships which Chaplain Ireland was enduring. He spoke more truly than he knew, for Ireland, broken in health, was forced to return to St. Paul.[17] In the G.A.R. reunions no name was more warmly cheered than that of the Minnesota chaplain, and it was also an open secret that the old soldiers had no more powerful friend in the Pension Department at Washington. One of the most beautiful tributes paid to him was written by the Reverend Robert J. Burdette, pastor of the Temple Baptist Church in Los Angeles:

My dear Archbishop Ireland—For you are my Archbishop, aren't you. I was a private soldier in C company, 47th Illinois regiment in the 60's, when the entire brigade called you its Chaplain. And time and promotion has not moved you from the place you then held in a soldier's heart. There was a boy's love and reverence then, there is the reverence and love of a man today. This is your birthday anniversary. God make it beautiful with the memories of yesterday, splendid with the faith of to-day, and glorious with the fruition of tomorrow.

Always affectionately yours,
Robert J. Burdette.[18]

4. The Pastor

On his return from the war, Father Ireland took up his work at the Cathedral, serving under Father Louis Caillet, its pastor. There he showed the qualities which marked him all through life. He threw himself with eagerness into the routine of parish life, interested in every phase of its activity, devoted to the people, and in turn readily received and loved by those to whom he ministered. No labor was too hard, no journey too arduous. Sometimes his duties took him to neighboring towns and involved considerable hardship. One of the pioneers describes his visit to Watertown:

There were no means of travel but to walk, with poor roads or no roads most of the way. But Father Ireland did not stop at that; he took his suitcase and the things that were necessary for saying Mass, and walked from St. Paul to Watertown and four miles farther to the Madden homestead, a total distance of forty-four miles. He had reached the town as night was falling. As he left for the homestead he lost his way, and after wandering through ploughed fields, reached a house. There was only one bed, which was offered but refused. And so a bed was arranged on the floor, with his coat as a covering. The next morning he arose at an early hour, and continued on his way to his destination, where he heard confessions and said Mass.

His sincerity and frankness, his democracy and affability, his sense of the pathos that lies in things, his fellow feeling for the joys and sorrows of the flock—all quickly made him a welcome figure as he went about the parish. Early he manifested that magnetism which drew people to him and made the work of conversion easy. His interests were not confined to purely spiritual matters but embraced every aspect of the life of his people. When on July 28, 1867, on the resignation of Father Caillet, he succeeded to the rectorship, he sought ways and means of improving the social, intellectual, and religious condition of his flock. He made clear at an early date his interest in temperance, education, and the Indians. While still a young priest he petitioned the Board of Education regarding the proposed use of parochial schools by the city and received a favorable answer. The proposal submitted was that the Cathedral and Assumption schools be transferred to the supervision and control of the Board, that the buildings be supplied free of rent during school hours, and that the Board be relieved of any risk or responsibility arising from fire or other cause. To this proposition the committee found no legal or educational objections.

The concession of the school board, however, brought a protest from the St. Paul *Press*, which said that the Catholics, in return for the free grant of the buildings, were demanding that the sexes be taught separately and that Catholic teachers be employed.

The reply of Father Ireland is interesting inasmuch as at such an early period of his priesthood it shows the same qualities which were so conspicuous later on—his confidence in his own judgment (what the French call *courage de tête*), the clearness of his vision, and the air of authority with which he spoke. After pointing out how Protestant the schools were in their teachers, their children, and the type of Bible read, as well as in their furthering of Sabbath schools and their slurs on Catholicism, he said:

You will strive, you say, to have the atmosphere neither Protestant nor Catholic. Do not attempt moral impossibilities. Were you to succeed, the matter would be still worse. The atmosphere would be infidel, atheistic. I have often listened to well-intended declarations that, in schools, the general principles of Christianity would be inculcated with satisfaction to all denominations. I would be pleased to know one general principle of Christian faith upon which all agree.

He then answered another allegation made by the *Press*, that the Catholics are aliens, the blind subjects of European monarchies:

Oh shades of Christopher Columbus, Charles Carroll, Lord Baltimore. The Catholics aliens to America. Were they aliens, those Catholics, whom, illustrious Washington, you thanked for their persevering energy to free you and their country? The Catholics—I repeat it with pride—were first in America, first in Minnesota, first in St. Paul. It is rather late in the day for the repetition of those old calumnies that Catholics are opposed to a republican form of Government; that they wish to uproot all the institutions of the land.[19]

Protestant opposition, however, prevailed, and at the next meeting of the Board Father Ireland's proposition was rejected by a vote of ten to four.

He waged a campaign for Catholic rights in state institutions in Minnesota. The inmates of the Reform School and other penal institutions found difficulties thrown in their way in the practice of their religion. A priest could not address a word to the children of the Reform School, except in the presence of one of the officials. Liberty of Conscience bills were twice introduced into the legislature only to be defeated. After a strenuous election campaign, the bill was passed by an overwhelming majority, only to be vetoed by Governor

Horace Austin. Finally, in 1874, Governor Cushman K. Davis affixed his signature, a triumph for the cause of freedom and of equal rights, which led, in other states, to the bursting of bars that deprived any section of the people of full religious liberty. It was to Father Ireland that the victory was due.[20]

Father Ireland also had the great privilege of attending the Vatican Council as a representative of Bishop Grace, who was ill. On October 18, 1869, he sailed for Rome in company with Bishop James Gibbons, Archbishop Martin Spalding, and other prelates. Prior to his departure from St. Paul, a committee of Catholic laymen presented him with a purse for the expenses of the journey. In Rome, although in his role of Procurator he could not take part in the discussions, he was able to attend all the meetings of the Council. There also he made the acquaintance of some of the foremost figures of the universal Church.

He left no reminiscences of the Council but we can easily imagine how his youthful mind must have been impressed by the great leaders of the Church, as well as by the freedom of thought and discussion which prevailed on the question of the timeliness of the promulgation of the Doctrine of Infallibility, and in particular by the opposition of such American prelates as Archbishop Peter Richard Kenrick and Bishop Edward Fitzgerald. The three months he spent in Rome gave him invaluable experience and a conception of the world-wide activities of the Church.

There was an aftermath to the Council in the following year, when Father Ireland sent a communication to the St. Paul *Press* on the subject of Döllinger, whose opposition to the Doctrine of Papal Infallibility had been a favorite theme for editorial comment in that paper. He denied the assertion that Döllinger was a scholarly theologian, and he characterized him as "somewhat of a historian, who wrote history from preconceived notions."[21]

In the pursuit of his parochial duties Father Ireland soon found that heat, cold, exposure to the elements, and wearisome journeys were the smallest of his crosses, and that there were other and more trying problems to face. He realized that, as the supernatural is built on the natural foundation, he must first make men good citizens before he could leave upon them a spiritual impress. He saw that in this work his greatest stumbling block was going to be intemperance, which was brutalizing and pauperizing many of his people. Like many another frontier town, St. Paul had been cursed with intemperance almost from the time the first steamer had landed. Nor was his pride in the land of his birth exalted as he discovered that most of the saloons were owned by Irishmen. The sight of a people, naturally keen, blocked by drink from the progress and preferment to which their talents entitled them, filled his soul with pity, and he resolved to uproot the evil. His plans to combat it received fresh impetus when late one evening in the winter of 1869 three men, evidently under the influence of liquor, called upon him at the Cathedral residence and presented a crumpled piece of paper on which were written the words: "For God's sake, organize a Temperance Society." It was signed by seven men, including a saloonkeeper.[22]

The Total Abstinence Society which was organized the following Sunday was the beginning of a nation-wide movement against the drink evil. From hut to hut he went, from hamlet to hamlet, from city to city, preaching and teaching that drink had brought greater calamities upon the world than war, famine, and pestilence combined. This was the work which lay nearest his heart, and the one which brought him into universal favor with all classes of men and women who regarded the home as one of the sacred spots on earth and intemperance as its greatest peril. With zeal as untiring as that of his great prototype, Father Mathew, with a thoughtful intelligence which made no mistakes, and above all with a love that never slept, he waged a lifelong war against drink. To his personal efforts probably more than to any other cause was due the awakening of the conscience of the Catholic world to the crying evil of intemperance, and there were thousands of clean, prosperous and happy homes, the salvation of which from utter ruin was directly traceable to his labors. No man who, like himself, had come up from the ranks of the common people of scant means and of as scant opportunities for intellectual training, and who had been blessed with his perspicacity and vision, could lose sight of the great truth that the first essential to moral as well as to material elevation on the part of the poor or the unlettered is abstinence from the use of intoxicating drink.

5. THE PRELATE

Father Ireland must have made a deep impression at the Vatican Council, for on February 27, 1875, a cablegram from Rome to the New York *Freeman's Journal* announced that he had been chosen Vicar Apostolic of Nebraska. Bishop Grace, however, who did not wish to lose the services of one who had served him so faithfully and loyally, immediately set out for Rome to appeal to the Holy Father not to remove his friend from St. Paul. Later Father Ireland sent him his own petition to be presented to the Pope, together with the un-opened Bull of Appointment. These, however, never reached him, as the steamer which carried them was shipwrecked. When, long after-wards, the mail pouch was recovered, the documents were returned to St. Paul and now rest in the archdiocesan archives. The Pontiff harkened to Bishop Grace's request, canceled the assignment, and in July appointed Father Ireland Bishop of Maronea and Coadjutor Bishop of St. Paul. The consecration took place in the Cathedral on December 21. From an early hour crowds thronged the streets ad-jacent to the church, manifesting their happiness at the joyful event about to take place. The church, which was filled to overflowing as soon as the doors were open, was completely festooned in evergreens and pendent floral ornaments; from the galleries were draped the banners of the many temperance societies of state and city as well as the papal and American flags. High above the main altar extended the motto: *Dies Tuos in Sua Pace Disponat,* and a brilliant star jetted its rays from myriad tapers.

Bishop Grace was celebrant and consecrator; the co-consecrators were Bishop Heiss of La Crosse and Bishop Seidenbusch of St. Cloud. Surrounding the new Bishop were his close friends, some of whom were later to be raised to the episcopate: Father Augustin Ravoux, Assistant Priest; Father Louis Caillet, Deacon of the Mass; Father James McGolrick, Subdeacon; Father Augustine Oster, Master of Ceremonies; assisted by Fathers John Shanley and Joseph Cotter. Father James Trobec was Ecclesiastical Notary.

The sermon was preached by Father Thomas O'Gorman, who, tak-ing as his text "Going, therefore, teach all nations," treated of the powers of the episcopate. In his conclusion he referred to Bishop Ire-land's ordination fourteen years before in the same cathedral and to his coming to Minnesota in 1852. He spoke of Bishop Grace, "whose right arm you have been and who now bestows upon your more vigorous youth a share of his responsibilities and labors, and transmits to you the mantle of Joseph Cretin of revered memory." Then turning to the newly consecrated Bishop, he said: "Child and heir of such saintly ancestry, take up your father's mantle. Assume the burden Heaven imposes upon your shoulders. Grasp your crozier and rule the flock committed to you. Before you is opened a field worthy of your energies and your zeal. Labor like a good soldier until the moment when the jeweled mitre shall be transformed into the crown of eternal glory."[23]

The administration of Bishop Grace was long and successful. To meet the demands of immigration he built many churches, schools, and convents; he brought into the diocese Dominicans, Benedictines, Franciscans, as well as several sisterhoods, and he founded the Convent of the Visitation. At the celebration of his Silver Jubilee on July 25, 1884, Bishop John Lancaster Spalding preached the sermon. At the banquet which followed, Father O'Gorman contrasted the twenty-seven priests and the thirty-one churches of Cretin's time with the 150 priests, the 250 churches, and the hospitals, schools, academies, and asylums of the present. Bishop Ireland spoke of the intimate relations existing between him and Bishop Grace, of their unity of hearts, minds, and labors. He compared his own life to a streamlet gladly mingling its waters with the great river and lost in it unseen. "Our plannings and methods for the extension of God's kingdom have been the same," he said, "and if in the execution of the work a seeming separateness appeared visible, it was only thus far that the physical effort may have at times fallen to me, the inspiration and the direction being always the fruit of his generous love and his matured thought."

In the same issue of the diocesan paper which described the celebration a letter appeared from Bishop Grace, announcing his retirement.[24] Long before he actually did so, he would have resigned in favor of Bishop Ireland, but the latter protested against such a step whenever it was suggested, and it was not until the jubilee observance that he would listen to the thought of succeeding his friend. Bishop Grace, who was appointed titular Bishop of Mennith, continued to reside at the episcopal residence until 1890, acting as Vicar General and giving co-operation and counsel to his successor. On September 24, 1889, he received the title of titular Archbishop of Siunia. He died on February 22, 1897.

When, in 1886, Bishop Ireland went to Rome in the interest of the Catholic University, negotiations were started for the erection of the Archdiocese of St. Paul. Bishop Martin Marty of the Vicariate of Dakota had written to Cardinal Giovanni Simeoni, Prefect of Propaganda, on November 16, 1886, requesting that the Vicariate of Dakota be divided into two dioceses and incorporated into a new Province of St. Paul, on the grounds that he lost too much time going to Milwaukee, that he did not find there either knowledge of the situation or sympathy, and that his confreres east of the Mississippi had nothing in common with him. He suggested as the line of separation between the two proposed dioceses the forty-sixth degree of latitude.[25] Bishop Ireland also wrote to the Cardinal, giving as his reason for corresponding directly with him the fact that Archbishop Michael Heiss of Milwaukee had ignored the request of Bishop Marty that a provincial synod be summoned and had vehemently opposed the efforts of Bishop Grace to make St. Paul an archdiocese. If his request were granted that the vicariate be divided and the archbishopric erected, Milwaukee, he said, would still have three suffragans and St. Paul four, namely, the Vicariate of Northern Minnesota, two dioceses in Dakota, and another see to be chosen.

In June of the following year, Monsignor Denis O'Connell, Rector of the North American College, Rome, informed Bishop Ireland of correspondence which Monsignor Donato Sbarretti, Secretary of Propaganda, had had with Heiss, who had expressed the opinion that it would be better to have the Provincial Council of Milwaukee approved first, as otherwise the decrees would not bind in the new province.[26] Three months later O'Connell wrote that the Propaganda was committed to the approval of the decrees, that it was likely that division and approval would take place together and then the question of promulgation would have to be considered by the new province.[27] In March of the following year he wrote:

You have every reason to congratulate yourself. I do not know if you could have had things more according to your desires. The new province is created. You are the archbishop; Minnesota and Dakota are the territory. Two dioceses are to be erected in Dakota and a diocese in Northern Minnesota, but, later on, the see of Northern Minnesota is to be erected after the resignation of the present Vicar Apostolic. A new see is also to be erected at Winona.[28]

In July Bishop Ireland notified O'Connell that the ceremony of conferring the pallium would take place in September and that immediately afterwards he would send on names for the two new sees. He said: "Bishop Seidenbusch is home. He tells me that Cardinal Simeoni asked him to resign. He took care, he adds, not to go up that stone stairway a second time."[29]

At the celebration of the Golden Jubilee of Father Edward Sorin's priesthood at Notre Dame, on August 15, 1888, the solemn Mass in the newly consecrated Church of Our Lady of the Sacred Heart was celebrated by Cardinal Gibbons; the sermon was preached by Bishop Ireland. In the evening, after supper, Bishop John J. Keane of Richmond extended to the Cardinal the pallium which had been brought from Rome for the new Archbishop. After the Cardinal had bestowed it, the Archbishop responded with a short address, promising even greater effort in the cause of the Church.[30]

The formal conferring took place in the St. Paul Cathedral on September 27, 1888. From early morning there was a procession of people of all faiths, wending their way to the church. Five thousand tickets had been issued, but these did not suffice for the crowds that sought entrance. The interior of the Cathedral presented a lovely sight. The high altar was ablaze with lights and redolent of flowers. Wreaths hung from the galleries; windows and niches were filled with potted plants. The throne had been newly decorated in rich plush, and on its top rested a bank of many-hued roses. A feature which attracted much attention was an oil painting of the first log-cabin chapel suspended high above the altar. The long rows of prelates, representing dioceses from one end of the country to the other, and the crowds of people rejoicing in the honors conferred on one whom they admired and loved made a stirring sight. The appearance of the venerated Bishop Grace, now bearing the burdens of the years, as he placed the pallium on the shoulders of him who had always regarded him as a father, deeply moved the emotions of the audience. At the Mass, at which Bishop Marty pontificated, the sermon was preached by Bishop John J. Keane, who dealt with the parable of the mustard seed. After tracing the beginnings of the Church in the Northwest, and outlining the struggle of the masses to secure freedom, he pointed to the New World as a refuge for oppressed humanity, a land of opportunities as boundless as the country itself for the development of all that is noblest in human energies and for the use of them for ends the wisest and best that humanity can aspire to.[31]

Meanwhile a problem had arisen which called for solution. In 1856 the Benedictine Fathers had come to Minnesota from St. Vincent's Abbey, Pennsylvania, at the call of Bishop Cretin. In the course of time a priory was established with Father Rupert Seidenbusch as its first Abbot, who in 1875 was named Vicar Apostolic of the newly established Vicariate of Northern Minnesota. Father Alexius Edelbrock succeeded him as Abbot, the ceremony of his induction taking place in the Church of the Immaculate Conception, St. Cloud, on October 14, 1875, the same year in which Bishop Ireland was consecrated. Bishop Grace was present in the sanctuary and Bishop Ireland preached.

Bishop Seidenbusch and Abbot Alexius made notable contributions to the development of the Church in the Northwest. The Abbot, a man of amazing vitality, with a genius for building, was not content with developing St. John's Abbey and College, where he constructed buildings which still function, but he also extended his labors throughout the Northwest, establishing branches in Duluth, Bismarck, and St. Cloud. Some members of the Community, however, felt that his new activities were not in keeping with the traditions of the order or with the purposes for which the Benedictines had come to Minnesota, that he was placing too much stress on external growth at the expense of the monastic spirit, and that his lack of tact, his aloofness and arbitrariness had a tendency to alienate. Finally a group of dissatisfied monks received enough support from members of the hierarchy to secure a hearing before Cardinal Simeoni, Prefect of the Propaganda.[32] Bishop Ireland, who was aware of the situation, wrote O'Connell that, although he personally was in no position to intervene in the dispute, he felt that religion was suffering and that strong action was in order.[33] O'Connell suggested that if Ireland could not secure the resignation at once without exerting strong and risky pressure, he should use the matter as a means of carrying through his other plans of putting the right men in Dakota and the new dioceses of the province of St. Paul. He felt that the Vicariate Apostolic of Northern Minnesota would yield to him on those points, as they had said that they did not wish to erect the new diocese of St. Cloud before the resignation. The suspicion in Rome was that the Benedictines were opposed to the Vicar's resignation. He also informed him that on the resignation of Bishop Seidenbusch he would be charged with the investigation of the Benedictine trouble.[34]

Abbot Alexius resolved to go to Rome and face the charges brought against him. After an audience with Archbishop Ireland, who informed him of the nature of the criticisms, and who agreed that most of them bore little weight, he set out on his mission in June, 1889. A long letter from O'Connell gives a history of the Abbot's experiences, his indecision as to the mode of acting, the conviction of Prior Adalbert that the Abbot was innocent and that the attacks were begotten by a few malcontents, and the Abbot's ultimate resignation.[35]

The Archbishop, appointed Visitator, visited St. John's Abbey and came away much impressed by the splendid buildings and the progress that had been made. When Abbot Alexius resigned in November, 1889, St. John's Abbey still continued under the apostolic visitation which the Archbishop had begun in March. In his visit in November Ireland relieved the Prior, Father Norbert Hofbauer, and the Subprior, Father Peter Engel, of their offices and appointed Father Peter as lawful superior *ad interim*, until such a time as the monks should be authorized to elect a successor to Abbot Alexius.[36]

The resignation of Bishop Seidenbusch opened the way for the establishment of the new dioceses. When Monsignor O'Connell spoke at the Propaganda of Ireland's success in the vicariate, Archbishop Domenico Jacobini said, "Ireland will do well anywhere." O'Connell wrote of Zardetti's expectancy to receive one of the new sees and of the promise of Sbarretti to have everything ready for September, 1889. The only difficulty urged against the division of the Northern Vicariate was that it would leave St. Cloud too poor. After Propaganda had requested and obtained maps showing the boundaries of the dioceses, it approved of the project.[37] In due time the appointments arrived: Father James McGolrick to Duluth, Father Joseph B. Cotter to Winona, and Father John Shanley to Jamestown, North Dakota.

The consecration of the three prelates was unique in the history of the country. Although once before, in 1853, three bishops had been consecrated on the same day, never before had three been consecrated for three new dioceses. On December 27, 1889, Archbishop Ireland, assisted by Bishops Grace and Marty, and in the presence of fifteen bishops and archbishops and a large crowd of clergy and laity, had the happiness of elevating his three close friends. The shadows of Americanism made their appearance in the sermon preached by Father Walter Elliott, C.S.P., who said:

Here in America the ideas of manhood are not loyalty, obedience, uniformity, but worthiness to be free. Law has a high place here, but freedom is higher, and all agree that to be free men should be virtuous. Liberty and intelligence are what our institutions exist for. The mines of the old world send their metals here, where a fiery life melts them all into one; nationalities are here fused and mingled into one, and this is a new nationality. Bronze is made of tin and copper, but is neither one nor the other, but a new metal. So our population is made up of the races of the old world, but it is itself a new race, and its aspiration is towards progress and intelligence and liberty, the dignity of man and his capability to govern himself.

Hence it is the duty of all who love both God and country to show that Catholicity is a religion based upon the dignity of human nature. Freedom of will is an article of Catholic faith. It is the duty of all Catholics in high place to show forth this parallel of Church and State in America. Church and State should not be united here, but they must be parallel in their onward march if they both make for human happiness. It is right that we should hate heresy, apostasy and rebellion of Catholics against their Church. But we Catholics should also hate bribery and corruption in office, trading in votes, and all the vices of low-grade politics. How we should hate intemperance and saloons, how we should loathe obscene literature, foul pictures and statues, and lewd plays! How, on the other hand, we should cultivate the natural virtues which make men good citizens, kindly neighbors and successful men in business! Without the natural virtues Christianity is of little force in this age. There is no more contemptible creature alive than a Catholic huckster.

At the dinner in the Ryan Hotel, the Archbishop proposed the toast "Pope Leo XIII," to which Monsignor O'Connell, who had brought the briefs, responded. On the following day the new prelates were the guests of the St. Thomas Seminary and heard addresses delivered by Mr. (later Monsignor) John A. Ryan. The sermons at the installations were preached by the Archbishop.[38]

Such is the brief outline of the early career of Archbishop Ireland. A man of abounding vitality and of positive convictions, he had hardly succeeded to the archiepiscopate before he was plunged into the midst of controversies, which were to occupy his attention during much of his life. In order to treat these important phases of his career as a continuous whole, I have thought it well, after weighing the relative merits of the chronological and essay types of historical narrative, to use the latter form, which lends itself better to my purpose.

Chapter 2

THE ARCHBISHOP AS COLONIZER

✦✦✦✦✦✦✦✦✦✦✦✦✦

1. THE IMMIGRANT AND HIS PROBLEMS

Behind the movement of colonization in Minnesota lay two motives: to afford relief to the unemployed and to offer a home to European immigrants, who were fleeing from famine and oppression. Bishop Ireland sought a remedy for the great suffering in the larger cities of the United States. The problem of finding relief for the unemployed occupied his thoughts, and he saw that if the unemployed in the cities could be brought back to the land their lot might be vastly improved. "The problem in this country," he said, "is different from that of Europe. In this country, there is such a thing as unemployed labor, but it bears no comparison to the amount of unemployed land. When the question of the solution of the labor problem is discussed, it will not do to keep out of view the almost limitless treasures of wealth that are hidden only by the grass of our western prairies." He saw that if the suffering poor of the cities could be placed upon the land, the labor question would be, to a large extent, disposed of. And so he decided to offer the opportunity to locate upon rich free lands or cheap railroad lands on long terms, together with supplies to last the settlers until they had raised a crop. In addition, there was the large influx of Irish immigrants, for whom provision had to be made. The United States Census of 1850, the first to take account of the nationality of citizens, numbered 961,000 Irish-born in the population of the country, 44 per cent of the entire foreign-born population of the nation. During the ten following years, another million fled from Ireland, and the preponderance of the Celtic element in our population reached its height.

Of the vast numbers of immigrants fleeing from their native land, hundreds of thousands settled down in the cities of the seaboard. "They helped," Professor Adams writes, "to make New York the first city of the country by swelling the urban population and digging the Erie Canal." In the eastern states they found employment; there also they found parishes well established, and the Irish have always been wistfully dependent upon their priests. But while they staved off starvation, their lot was all too often a miserable one. Their lack of training left them unfitted to compete with skilled labor, and so they were hewers of wood and drawers of water, working in factories and mines, living in tenements or in shanties by the railroads and canals they built, the natural prey of the saloonkeeper and the petty ward politician. The mortality rate among them was, at times, fearful. Professor Adams states: "During the great famine it was said that one-third of the Irish died within three years after reaching this country, and longevity of the Boston Irish was fourteen years." "Mines and factories," wrote Archbishop Ireland, "have literally devoured our race." Fearful, especially, was the mortality rate among the children; no wonder the first charitable institution erected by a diocese in those days was always an orphan asylum. In many instances the immigrants escaped the serfdom and starvation of their own country only to become the slaves of industrialists in a land which, in their dreams, was flowing with milk and honey.

In Bishop Cretin's days, Archbishop Hughes—he was appointed first Archbishop of New York in 1850—assumed a puzzling and regrettable attitude toward the question of Catholic colonization. While he showed himself favorable to the ambition of individual families to make their homes in the West, he distrusted and discouraged all organized movements to promote westward migration. The man who in his day could have done more than any other man in the country to foster Catholic colonization openly denounced the efforts of D'Arcy McGee and others to place the movement on a solid basis. His opposition was disastrous to the growth of the Church in the West. Speaking at the unveiling of the statue of General Shields in the Capitol, St. Paul, on October 20, 1914, Archbishop Ireland said:

It is today beyond a doubt that had the enlightened views of D'Arcy McGee and those who took part with him in the famous Buffalo colonization convention of 1856 been duly encouraged and pushed to a favorable issue, the Catholic Church would be immensely more prosperous in all the Western States than ever again she can hope to be, and tens of thousands of Catholic families would have gained happy homes and an honorable competence upon the land, instead of having gone down to ruin in the fierce maelstrom of large cities.

Others, also, there were who frowned on the movement, emphasizing the loneliness of prairie life and stressing the danger to the faith in a wilderness where churches were few and far between.

We have but little information of a definite character concerning Irish settlements in Minnesota in the fifties. In a letter written in 1867, by Dillon O'Brien to John P. Maguire, reference is made to an Irish settlement at Jessenland as early as 1854. It was on a small scale, and little or nothing is known about it.

General James Shields, who was a resident of the state in 1857, and who saw the great possibilities which the West offered to settlers, through the columns of the American Catholic press invited Irish Catholics in search of homes to come to Minnesota. He selected as the suitable site of a Catholic colony the district of Rice County now known as Shieldsville. In June, 1879, there were in Shieldsville 250 Catholic families, "as sober and as prosperous a community as the West could boast of." As an aftermath of General Shields' work, colonists continued to arrive even after the Shieldsville lands were entirely taken. It was these colonists who settled the surrounding townships and formed the parishes of Erin, Montgomery, and Kilkenny.

On May 12, 1864, the Minnesota Irish Emigration Society was launched in St. Paul under the auspices of Bishop Thomas Grace, successor to Bishop Cretin. It had for its purpose to establish Irish emigrants "in homes in lieu of those from which they had been compelled to flee." It had for president Father Ireland and for secretary Dillon O'Brien. Although Dillon O'Brien worked in the East in an effort to further the development of the organization, and in the 1869 convention tried to infuse new life into the long-neglected subject of Irish emigration, no records of the society are extant, and only a faint recollection of its existence lingered among the survivors of pioneer days. It comprised twenty-five active members and nine honorary members, including Ignatius Donnelly and Honorable Thomas Wilson of Winona.

2. THE CATHOLIC COLONIZATION BUREAU

At last, in 1876, Bishop Ireland established an organization which was destined to promote Catholic colonization in a systematic and efficient manner. It was called the Catholic Colonization Bureau of Minnesota, and in April of the following year the Catholic Colonization Land Stock Company was officially organized.

Bishop Ireland always attached the highest importance to the formation of companies which by the sale of stock could command sufficient capital for carrying on the great work of colonizing, deeming the establishment of such companies throughout the country to be the one truly effective method of promoting Catholic colonization. The files of the *Northwestern Chronicle* contain appeal after appeal for funds to be raised in this fashion—appeals, however, which evoked only a pitiful response.

The first meeting of the Board of Directors of this colonization company was held on April 10, 1877, for the purpose of drafting a constitution and bylaws and of preparing a form of stock certificate and corporate seal. Emphasis was laid on the fact that the company was in reality a charitable savings bank. Stock was issued at ten dollars a share, and within a month 215 shares had been subscribed. At no time, however, did the company succeed in raising more than a few thousand dollars by the sale of shares.

In January, 1876, Ireland announced in the columns of the *Northwestern Chronicle* that through the kindness of George L. Becker, president of the St. Paul and Pacific Railroad, he had secured the control of all the railroad lands in Swift County for the term of two years, during which period no one would be allowed to purchase an acre without his permission. It was a vast tract, comprising 117,000 acres, in the vicinity of DeGraff, a tiny village named after Andrew DeGraff of St. Paul, a railroad builder.

Besides the railroad lands in Swift County, there was about the same amount of government land available for settlement under the pre-emption and homestead acts, and Bishop Ireland, with his characteristic sagacity, foresaw that the Catholic colony would attract many settlers to the adjoining government land.

Immediately settlers began to flock into Swift County. On January 26, the first prospective settlers, thirty-two in number, had selected their lands, and over nine thousand acres were taken that day "for new homes in the broad acres of God's domain." Less than three months later Ireland gave warning that no Minnesota farmer would be admitted into the Swift County colony, which, the Bishop declared, was reserved for the poor and homeless.

In every colony which he founded, the Bishop invariably began by placing on the spot a priest whose duty it was to advise and help the colonists as well as to minister to their spiritual needs. Next he arranged for the erection of a church around which the life of the colony would center, and also for the building of an immigration house which would afford temporary accommodations for the families of settlers while they were selecting their farms. Needless to say, the saloon in every case was banned.

On September 16, 1876, he reported to the president of the Board of Colonization of the Irish Catholic Benevolent Union that up to date eight hundred entries had been made by the people on government land, and about sixty thousand acres of railroad land had been occupied.

Special mention should be made of Father F. J. Swift, the first pastor of DeGraff, who will always be remembered for his self-sacrificing services to the Swift County settlers, and of Monsignor Anatole Oster, whose name will always live in the story of Clontarf as the beloved pastor who devoted the best years of his life to the service of his people.

As to the mode of purchase, one plan required the settler to deposit one year's interest and to pay the principal in ten installments with 7 per cent interest. The price of land varied from five to seven dollars an acre, depending on its location. Another plan, of which the settlers availed themselves on a generous scale, allowed them to pay for their farms by railroad land certificates. As these were selling considerably below par and were accepted at their face value in exchange for land, the actual cost did not, in many instances, exceed $1.50 an acre.

Among the difficulties involved in colonizing was the grasshopper plague. In the very first year of the DeGraff colony, on July 9, 1876, there suddenly appeared swarms of these pests. We read that on July 10, 1877, they disappeared as suddenly as they came. The harm wrought by them did not discourage new settlers from casting in their lot with the colony.

The region of the Toqua Lakes in Big Stone County was, in early days, a famous hunting and camping ground for Indians. In the sixties it was the scene of a flourishing fur trade; in 1870, we read of Barse and Company dealing with the Indians and shipping a vast number of skins. In 1874, Colonel Dunlap entered claims around the lakes and erected buildings on them. The richness of the soil, equally adapted to tillage and to stock raising, offered tempting advantages to settlers which did not escape the notice of Bishop Ireland. In 1878, Colonel J. R. King, a practical surveyor, purchased for the Bishop a soldier's claim of eighty acres, as a town site, and also 120 acres to the west, the property of Colonel Dunlap. Colonel King laid out on the northeast side of the East lake a town which was named Graceville in honor of Bishop Grace. Immediately settlers coming from various parts of America and Europe began to throng into the newly founded colony.

As much of the land of Graceville belonged at that time to the federal government, settlers were located on the lands under the homestead or tree-culture laws. During the months of March and April, 1878, a great number of claims for Catholic colonists were entered in the United States Land Office, and before any of the settlers took possession of their land Bishop Ireland had shipped in five carloads of lumber for the erection of a church. The church was completed in the rough in about three weeks. The first pastor, Reverend T. Ryan, was very active in organization, and within three months of the opening of the colony, over 150 comfortable cabins were erected within a radius of six miles of the little village of Graceville.

Bishop Ireland, seeing that the colony would ere long require more lands than were available to homestead settlers, made an arrangement with the St. Paul, Minneapolis and Manitoba Railway for the control of about fifty thousand acres of land near Graceville, known as indemnity lands. According to this agreement, he obtained the sole and exclusive right until December 31, 1881, "to place settlers upon and to make sales or agreements of sale to parties desiring to settle upon or purchase" certain specifically described tracts of land selected as applied for by the railway company. The minimum price was fixed at four dollars per acre. As the company had not acquired full title to the lands in question, a new contract was entered into between him and the commissioner of the company on March 30, 1883, in terms identical with the original agreement. About one hundred families arrived the first year, erecting little houses, putting in crops on a small scale, and preparing for the planting of the great staple of the country, wheat, in the following year. As the years went by, Graceville developed and became one of the largest and most prosperous parishes in the diocese. In September, 1880, it numbered four hundred families.

In 1880, Father Nugent, whose name was long a household word in Liverpool as a friend of the poor, was working to alleviate the lot of the victims of the famine in Ireland—for once more famine was scourging that unhappy land. He offered to provide for the passage of a number of families from the wilds of Galway to America if arrangements could be made to place them in homes on the prairies of the West. The hovels in which they dragged out a miserable existence in Connemara were in a district so frightfully congested that their pastor wrote to Father Nugent: "This locality is not fit for human habitation. Not more than a third of the present population could live in any sort of comfort on the land." Ireland, working with Father Nugent, promised to take care of the emigrants on their arrival at Boston and to defray the expenses of their overland journey to Minnesota. On June 11, 1880, the "Connemaras," 309 in number, not one of whom probably had ever put his hand to a plow, embarked on the *Austrian* at the port of Galway, and landed at Boston on June 22. Never were strangers in distress more kindly received. From the moment of their arrival care and sympathy were lavished on them. On June 26, they reached St. Paul, where people of all creeds vied in helping them. For several of the young men and the young women employment was provided in St. Paul, and also for some families in the neighborhood of the city. Thirty families were sent on to Graceville.

Mr. William J. Onahan, who took care of them in their passage through Chicago, has left his impression of them in words that throw light on their subsequent history and its regrettable concomitants: "The famine was visible in their pinched and emaciated faces, and in the shrivelled limbs—they could scarcely be called legs and arms —of the children. Their features were quaint, and the entire company was squalid and wretched. It was a painful revelation to all who witnessed it." The improvidence of the Connemaras quickly roused the ire and indignation of the Graceville colony and alienated sympathy from the newcomers.

When the winter of 1880 swooped down in all its bitterness on the Graceville colony fully six weeks before its usual time, reports began to emanate from the neighboring town of Morris that "horrid suffering existed among the Connemara settlers." A Morris bigot published a report which was meant to discredit "the great institution," as he derisively called the Church, and his efforts were ably reinforced by newspaper correspondents who were on the lookout for what was startling rather than for what was true. Bigotry and jealousy exploited the native cunning of a group of dependent mendicants who, unmanned by serfdom and a lifetime of want, now felt themselves entitled to a living in Minnesota even if they did not bestir themselves to earn a livelihood by the toil of their hands. When lumber was given them for the erection of houses they refused to put a hand to the work, saying, "The Bishop brought us here and he must care for us." In the course of an investigation made into their condition it was shown that they would conceal food and clothing with which they had been provided, and plead want of the necessities of life. However, despite the lying on the part of the little group of Connemaras and the facile credence of certain correspondents of papers aching for what was sensational or for evidence hurtful to Catholic colonization, the facts of the case eventually came to the knowledge of the public. The *Pioneer Press* of St. Paul, which had ample opportunity of learning the true story, did much to dissipate the false impressions that had been put in circulation. In the undesirable prominence attained by this insignificant group of born beggars the public at large seemed to overlook the existence of hundreds of happy homes dotting the prairies for miles around Graceville. That the disastrous record of the Connemaras caused untold pain and humiliation to the best benefactor Catholic colonists had in America need not be emphasized. Indeed, Archbishop Ireland regarded the incident as the greatest grief of his life.

The Bishop finally arranged to distribute among neighbors the cattle assigned to the Galway immigrants, and also undertook to bear the expense of the removal of the families to St. Paul. The final scene in the Connemara drama was their last-moment effort to recover their cattle and return to their cabins.

In September, 1877, Ireland announced that he had secured the control of seventy thousand acres of railroad land in Nobles County, in the southwestern corner of the state. In addition to the railroad lands there were also some government sections still available for settlers. The county, by reason of the fertility of its soil, the number and beauty of its lakes, and the fine class of people who were pouring into its settlement, offered many attractions to Catholic colonists. When Reverend C. J. Knauf arrived at the little village of Adrian on September 20, 1877, he found that it consisted of a wayside station and three houses. Fifteen months later he had sold 22,000 acres of land to the settlers, and the village had sixty-eight houses, including three hotels, a mill, a public school, a Catholic church, and stores of various kinds. In September, 1877, there was not a Catholic in the colony; in December, 1878, there were sixty Catholic families, and Father Knauf had on his books the names of a hundred families who had secured land in the colony, had already done a good deal of breaking, and intended to move to their new farms in the spring of 1879. Lands sold at the time from five dollars to $7.50 per acre, with a discount of 20 per cent for cash. The colonists were German and Irish settlers, among them a large group from Boston.

While Bishop Ireland was devoting his time and his energies to the colonies which were his first foundations, he was keeping in view the splendid possibilities awaiting the establishment of a Catholic colony in the northwestern part of Lyon County in western Minnesota. The land was some of the finest in the state; watercourses were numerous; the scenery was picturesque. In July, 1879, announcement was made that 45,000 acres in the vicinity of the village of Minneota, founded two years previously, had been placed under the control of the St. Paul Colonization Bureau. The purchase terms were made very attractive to prosperous colonists.

The first settlers arrived in the spring and summer of 1880. It may be interesting to quote again from the pamphlet of the Catholic Colonization Bureau of that year estimates of expenses set before settlers: "A very cheap house, 16 x 18 feet, built of single boards and sodded on the outside as deeply as the owner wished, could be erected at a cost of $38.75; furniture could be purchased for $43; cattle and farming implements for $198. The cost of living was estimated at $100."

Late in the summer of 1880, Canon Van Hee, a Belgian priest of the Diocese of Liverpool, accompanied by his brother, Angelus, visited Minnesota with the view of preparing the way for the coming of a group of their countrymen. After having surveyed the prospects offered by various locations, the brothers selected the colony in Lyon County as the most desirable of all and purchased for Belgian immigrants land near the village of Grand View, six miles east of Minneota. In the following year they were followed by the rest of the family —the vanguard of the Flemish colony. The first Canadians to join them arrived in the autumn of 1882. Hollanders and Germans also came from time to time. In deference to the Flanders farmers, Bishop Ireland and Father Cornelis effected the change of the name of Grand View to that of Ghent. In the first report which the pastor, Father Jules Devos, turned in to the Bishop he gave an account of his administration of the three missions of which he had charge— Ghent, Marshall, and Currie, comprising respectively forty, seventeen, and nineteen families.

In April, 1878, Ireland obtained control of 52,000 acres of railroad lands, around Avoca in Murray County, and, although at this time of the year the breaking season was over, thousands of acres were sold by the following December. The price of the land varied from five to six dollars an acre, and unusually easy terms of payment encouraged settlers of modest means to avail themselves of an opportunity to secure desirable farms. By arrangement here, as well as in other colonies, a prospective settler of small means could have a certain number of acres broken before leaving his own home, and take possession when all was ready for the planting of a crop. Reverend Charles Koeberl not only assisted settlers to select farms but also saw to it that orders for breaking a number of acres were faithfully carried out. At the end of the year he reported to Bishop Ireland that this colony promised to be a great success, that since June, when the land sales commenced, 9,850 acres had been sold, that forty-five Catholic families were prepared to move in the next spring, and that immigrants would have in the village of Avoca a building where they could leave their families till they had put up their houses, and also a boarding house and store.

When a party comprising Father Nugent, Mr. James H. Tuke, and some other distinguished visitors from England and Ireland visited the colony they interviewed various settlers, and the information gathered from the farmers throws a flood of light on the whole colonization scene as it existed in 1879, especially on the extraordinary rapidity with which settlers passed from poverty and uncertainty of life to comparative prosperity and the comforts of happy homes. In 1880, the temporary church of Avoca was already entirely too small for the congregation and plans were in progress for the erection of Catholic churches at Iona, Fulda, and also in the northeast part of the colony.

Far different was the aspect which the colonized districts presented in those years from that which they present today. There were no roads in the ordinary acceptance of the term—just prairie trails—and oxen were used for farming as well as for traveling. In some places the howl of the wolf and the yelp of the coyote were familiar sounds; cranes and pigeons would cover the ground in vast flocks; wild geese and ducks and prairie chickens in huge numbers made every colonist a hunter, and the lakes were full of fish.

Life on the prairie was a life of hardship. Many of the settlers' shanties consisted of two rooms and a garret—only a slab board standing between the occupants and the elements. It was often difficult, if not impossible, to procure a sufficient supply of coal and wood for the long months of the Minnesota winter. Now and then a blizzard would rage for days at a time, so fierce and so dense as to render even the trip from the house to the barn a hazardous adventure without a guiding rope. People on their way home from town would suddenly find themselves in the grip of a furious snowstorm that would force them to take refuge in the nearest house and remain until they could see their way homeward.

At Avoca the awful winter of 1880 is yet remembered by the old inhabitants. Snowdrifts were as high as the eaves of the settlers' homes, and more than one colonist barely escaped with his life from the rage of the blizzards and the pangs of hunger. In these days slough hay and flax straw twisted into the form of the figure eight were commonly used as fuel; indeed, of one family a pioneer narrates to the present day that for fourteen years it used nothing else to heat its home. In the winter of 1880, furniture was burned, and even some shanties were torn down to save neighbors from death by freezing.

Besides the hard work, the lack of amusements, and the inconveniences incident to the primitive prairie, the colonists were only too often hampered by their entire lack of acquaintance with farm ways. The sense of isolation and of loneliness to which mothers of families, especially, more easily fell victims brought its own discouragement. Many a time Archbishop Ireland was sorely grieved to see his settlers go back to the glare and glitter of the cities which they had left for a more promising future in the open spaces of the West.

When we have recounted the labors of Archbishop Ireland in establishing the colonies that form the theme of this sketch, we have by no means told the full story of his service in the cause of Catholic colonization. First, the whole movement, using, as it did, the Catholic press of the country as well as the activities of agents in the East promoting migration to the West, by familiarizing multitudes with the advantages of family life on the prairies, profoundly influenced many of those who were eking out a miserable existence in the slums of crowded cities to seek homes on lands in various states.

Second, when in 1880 Mr. John Sweetman, a wealthy Irishman, resolved to devote himself and his means to bettering the conditions of his countrymen by colonization, it was to Archbishop Ireland he turned, and from the Archbishop's experience drew not only inspiration but also the practical knowledge necessary for his philanthropic schemes. In an article on Mr. Sweetman's colony at Currie, Miss Alice E. Smith, writing in *Minnesota History* for December 28, 1928, says: "Through the interest and help of Bishop Ireland, arrangements were made to erect an imposing church and parish house in Currie, a ten-acre tract being donated by the town for the purpose. A priest arrived from Ireland to take charge, and the church building was completed and dedicated with elaborate ceremony in the fall of 1883. Early in 1881, Bishop Ireland wrote to Sweetman, 'With the present year I will conclude with my colonies to make way for your work and cooperate more freely with you to the best of my ability.'"

3. The Irish Catholic Colonization Association

No account of Catholic colonization in the West would be complete which ignored the part Archbishop Ireland played in the founding of the Irish Catholic Colonization Association of the United States. A few words about this organization will not be out of place.

The beginnings of the association must be traced back to a meeting of the St. Patrick's Society in Chicago on January 20, 1879. This society, of which Mr. William J. Onahan was president, acting on the request of the principal organizations promoting Irish colonization with the concurrence of several bishops and priests, planned a national conference to deal with Irish Catholic colonization and designated March 17 of the same year as the date of the conference. It issued invitations to various societies interested in Catholic colonization and bespoke the presence of several bishops. The convention formed an Executive Board of seven bishops and seven laymen "to adopt such measures and perfect plans as may seem to the members of the board most wise and practicable for the promotion of Catholic colonization in Western States."

It would take us too far afield to trace *in extenso* the history of the Irish Catholic colonization of the United States. Suffice it to say that it was on Bishop Ireland's insistence that Bishop John Lancaster Spalding of Peoria, who subsequently, as president of the society, was to render such splendid service in the cause of colonization, was nominated to a place on the Executive Board; that Bishop Ireland threw all his energy into the project of raising $100,000 by the sale of certificates of stock issued by the association—this project he always deemed "the crowning stone in the work of colonization"; and that Bishop Spalding and he toured eastern dioceses in a strenuous campaign designed to arouse interest in the colonization scheme and to secure funds for its realization. Moreover, in February, 1880, he transferred to the association the control of eight thousand acres of land in the Adrian colony which the association purchased from the railroad and sold to incoming settlers.

In the long and laborious life of Archbishop Ireland, among all the enterprises that within the span of his episcopacy built up one of the great dioceses of the country there was none that so cruelly taxed his energies as did the colonization movement, none that caused him so much anxiety of soul. No sketch such as is here presented could give the faintest picture of the days and years of toil and thought that initiated and carried that great undertaking to its beneficent consummation. While faithful priests ably co-operated with him, and while men like Dillon O'Brien devoted themselves heart and soul to carry his farseeing plans into execution, he it was who, with his grandeur of personality, his resourcefulness in difficulties, his power of inspiring confidence, scattered thriving villages and happy homes over hundreds of thousands of acres of the prairies of Minnesota.

Chapter 3

DEFINING THE ROLE OF THE
CATHOLIC CHURCH IN
AMERICAN LIFE

❊❊❊❊❊❊❊❊❊❊❊❊❊

1. BALTIMORE ADDRESSES

The Third Council of Baltimore, which was opened on November
10, 1884, was a turning point in the history of the Church in America.
It also marked a turning point in the career of Bishop Ireland. The
occasion was a memorable one. Leaders in whose hands lay the destinies of the Church were assembled in council. Bishop Ireland was
invited to deliver an address and, with the judgment he always
showed in fitting his theme to the time, selected as the subject of his
discourse "The Catholic Church and Civil Society." "I do not, I think,"
he said, "mistake my fellow countrymen when I ascribe to them on
the occasion of the Plenary Council holding session in Baltimore the
wish that a statement be made as to the attitude of the Catholic
Church in her teachings and in her history toward the form of civil
society which obtains in the United States of America." It was the
theme demanded by the occasion, and the eyes of America were on
the Council of the Catholic bishops of the country. The foundations
of authority in eternal law, the origin of society in the ordinances of
God, the mutual relations of liberty and authority—subjects vital to
the nation's welfare—he expounded with the fire and the force of his
impassioned eloquence. For a people who regarded the Church as
the foe of liberty, or looked askance upon her as wedded irrevocably
to obsolescent institutions, he painted an arresting picture of the
Church as the true guardian of liberty through the ages.

"There is," he said, "no conflict between the Catholic Church and
America. I could not utter one syllable that would belie, however re-
motely, either the Church or the Republic, and when I assert, as I now

33

solemnly do, that the principles of the Church are in thorough harmony with the interests of the Republic, I know in the depths of my soul that I speak the truth." He expounded the principles of Catholic theology relating to civil authority, refuted the theories of Hobbes and Rousseau, established liberty upon the eternal principles of divine truth, which live with the life of Mother Church whose noble progeny they are. "To bid her to be silent," he said, "when faith is opposed or morals violated by subjects or by rulers, is to make the State supreme no less over mind than over body, and to consecrate despotism most absolute." He showed how through the ages the Church had fought for liberty, liberty for herself, personal liberty against slavery and serfdom, civil liberty against the encroachments of sovereigns. "Strange fortune of the Catholic Church," he cried. "She battled for centuries in giant warfare, and saved Europe to liberty, and today she is accused of befriending despotism and crushing out free institutions." He concluded with this moving peroration:

Republic of America, receive from me the tribute of my love and of my loyalty. With my whole soul I do thee homage. I pray from my heart that thy glory be never dimmed. *Esto perpetua.* Thou bearest in thy hands the hopes of the human race, thy mission from God is to show to nations that men are capable of highest civil and political liberty. Be thou ever free and prosperous. Through thee may liberty triumph over the earth from the rising to the setting sun. *Esto perpetua.* Believe me, no hearts love thee more ardently than Catholic hearts, no tongues speak more honestly thy praises than Catholic tongues, and no hands will be lifted up stronger and more willing to defend, in war and in peace, thy laws and thy institutions than Catholic hands. *Esto perpetua.*

It was a new and lovely vision of Catholicism that began to dawn on men's minds, and they who listened to the voice from the West declaring the imperishable principles from which government derives its authority and laws their sacredness went home with a new insight into the truth that the Church is the strongest bulwark of the nation. As he unfolded the teachings of the Church in accents ringing with power, in language whose rugged beauty was all his own, men realized that a new leader had arisen in America, a man whose words would henceforth carry weight in the councils of Church and State.[1]

And the impression which Bishop Ireland produced at the Third Plenary Council of Baltimore was deepened by the address which he delivered at Baltimore on November 10, 1889, the hundredth anniversary of the establishment of the Catholic hierarchy in the United States. This address must be read in the light of contemporary events if it is to be understood as it should be understood. The inspiration of it came from the conviction that "the greatest epoch of human history, if we except that which witnessed the coming of God upon earth, is upon us, and of this epoch our wisdom and our energy will make the Church the supreme mistress." A panegyric of the present age, it was remarkable not only for eloquence and freshness of thought but also for the admission that the Church must adapt itself to the requirements of the day. An epoch-making pronouncement, it was a vision of democracy struggling toward a higher plane of social and intellectual life. In the presence of nearly the entire body of bishops and many laymen gathered from far and near, Bishop Ireland proclaimed with dramatic boldness the task of Catholics in the new century that was opening. He then went on to outline the work which divine Providence demands from Catholics. It was twofold: to make America Catholic and to solve for the Church universal the all-absorbing problems with which religion is confronted in the present age. To make America Catholic, all that is needed is to love America and to love the Church. "The Catholic Church," he said, "will preserve as no human power, no human church, can preserve, the liberties of the Republic. If we are loyal to duty, the record of our second century will tell of the wondrous spread of Christ's Church over the United States."

He spoke of the change which had come over the world, of the revolution in the ideas and the feelings of men, of the new watchwords of the age—reason, education, liberty, and the amelioration of the masses—in the name of which war was declared against the Church. It was the duty of Christians to maintain in the world the supremacy of the supernatural, and to save the age to the Church. It should be possible to reconcile them, for the American people are not hostile to the Church, and America is at heart a Christian country. He pleaded for a more sympathetic attitude toward the age, a discernment of what was good in it from what was bad. The age was eager for the gifts which the Church alone can bestow, for "it was the religion of Christ that first whispered into the ears of the world the sacred words: charity, brotherhood, liberty. It was the religion of Christ that took to its bosom bleeding, agonizing humanity, warmed it with divine love, healed its sores and breathed into it health and vigor. And only under the blessed guidance of the religion of Christ can humanity proceed on the road towards greater progress." He urged that the gifts of the Church be revealed to the age. "Whisper in tender accents to liberty," he said, "that religion cherishes it. Go down in sympathy to the suffering multitude, bringing to them charity, and, what is more rarely given, justice. Let labor know that religion will ward off the oppression of capital, and will teach capital that its rights are dependent upon its fulfillment of duties." Catholics should realize the happy conditions under which they live and the liberty they enjoy. And they must be more aggressive. "Laymen need not wait for priest, nor priest for bishop, nor bishop for Pope. The timid move in crowds, the brave in single file. The Church must regain the scepter of science which she wielded for ages. To sing lovely anthems in Cathedral stalls and wear copes of broidered gold while no multitude throng nave or aisle and while the world outside is dying of spiritual and moral starvation—this is not the religion we need today." Priests must speak to men not in stilted phrases but in burning words that go to their hearts as well as to their minds. Religion must be popularized; the appeal must be to the masses. This implies an abiding and active interest in the social questions that torment humanity. He spoke of the dreadful social injustices which were so common—men, made in the image of the Creator, viewed as pieces of machinery or beasts of burden, the moral instincts ground out of them. Until their material condition is improved, it is futile to speak to them of supernatural life and duties. He upbraided Catholics for their inaction. They say their prayers, they preach, they listen to sermons on the love of God and on resignation in suffering, but if they venture at all into the arena, it is at the eleventh hour, when others have long preceded them, and public opinion has already been formed. These are the days of action, days of warfare. It is not the age of the timid and fugitive virtue of the Thebaid. "Into the arena," he cried, "priest and layman. Seek out social evils, and lead in movements that tend to rectify them. Speak of vested rights, for that is necessary, but speak, too, of vested wrongs, and strive by word and example, by the enactment and enforcement of good laws, to correct them."[2] We hear much of Catholic action today; if we go to the writings of Archbishop Ireland and study what he did, we shall understand what Catholic action in the highest and truest sense of the word means.

Again, four years later, on October 18, 1893, at the observance of the twenty-fifth anniversary of the episcopal consecration of Cardinal Gibbons, we find this apostle of the new age expounding his views on the role of the Church in the twentieth century. The orator of the day, he took for his theme "The Church and the Age." Again he emphasized the necessity of adapting the measures and methods of the

Church to the changing needs of the time. Again he insisted that the age called for a new race of men, saying: "The need of the world, the need of the Church, today as at other times, but today as never before, is men among men, men who see farther than others, rise higher than others, act more boldly than others"—words which characterize himself. The mission of the Church is the same throughout the ages, but the world changes, and to conquer the world to Christ, the Church must herself be new, adapting herself in manner of life and in method of action to the conditions of the new order. "Today," he said, "routine is fatal; today the common is exhausted senility. The crisis demands the new, the extraordinary, and with it the Catholic Church will score the grandest of her victories in the grandest of history's ages."

He spoke of the conflict between the Church and the age, as both are portrayed by their representatives. Rightly understood, they are not at war. He blamed the age, which, elated with its material and intellectual successes, exaggerated its powers and imagined that the natural is all-sufficient. He blamed the Church, or rather its leaders, many of whom were too slow to understand the new age and to extend to it the conciliatory hand of friendship. The age has its sins, but these are the accidentals. The Church, too, has her accidentals and her essentials. While jealously guarding the latter, she must be ready, as circumstances of time and place demand, to abandon the former. To hold that she cannot change is to make her rigid and unbending, incapable of adapting herself to new and changing surroundings. After giving examples from history of the flexibility of the Church and of its power of adaptation, he exclaimed:

What! The Church of the Living God, the Church of ten thousand victories over pagans and barbarians, over heresies and false philosophies, over defiant kings and unruly peoples—the great, freedom-loving, truth-giving, civilizing Catholic Church—this Church of the nineteenth century afraid of any century, not seeing in the ambitions of the nineteenth century the fervent ebullitions of her own noble sentiments, and in its achievements for the elevation of mankind the germinations of her own Christlike plantings, this Church not eager for the fray, not precipitating herself with love irresistible upon this modern world to claim it, to bless it, to own it for Christ.

I preach the new, the most glorious crusade. Church and age! Unite them in the name of humanity, in the name of God.

He reviewed the characteristics of the age. It demands knowledge. The Church proclaims that all truth is from God, and therefore between reason and revelation there can be no contradiction. This is an age of democracy. The Church has no fear of democracy, "this flowering of her own most sacred principles of the equality, fraternity and liberty of all men, in Christ and through Christ. The whole history of the Catholic Church is the record of the enfranchisement of the slave, the curbing of the tyranny of kings, the defense of the poor, of woman, of the people, of all the social entities that pride and passion choose to trample upon."

He concluded by appealing for understanding hearts: "We desire to win the age. Let us not, then, stand isolated from it. Our place is in the world as well as in the sanctuary. Do not, I pray, lose time in thinking of opposition that may come to you. If you dread opposition, you are not of the seed of those men by whom salvation is brought to Israel."[3]

These three great discourses of Archbishop Ireland were a trumpet call to Catholics everywhere that went reverberating over the land— and far over the seas also it went reverberating, rousing from their lethargy those who "in utter oblivion of the living world behind them sat at the gates of cemeteries, weeping over tombs that shall not be opened." They shed a new light on the role which the Catholic Church was destined to play in the age that was dawning on the greatest democracy in the world. For the first time millions of the American people saw the Church as it really is, the mightiest power for good that ever entered the cycle of human affairs. For those millions Archbishop Ireland was the Catholic Church, and in Archbishop Ireland they came to understand what they had never before understood.

In these discourses and in others kindred in theme and tone, Archbishop Ireland stirred the Catholics of America to a consciousness of their duties and opportunities, and he brought the country to a new realization of the value of the Church to the nation. He did in America what Lacordaire and Schlegel and Wiseman had done in Europe —showing the necessity of the Catholic religion to the modern world, and pressing its claims by arguments that carry weight with men of a practical age. And he did it "with a master's hand and prophet's fire," in addresses vibrant with intensity of feeling, striking in their boldness and candor of expression, and starred with truths of lasting wisdom. The growing reverence for the Church among all classes and creeds told how well the work was done. The Archbishop declared that the Church could win the age, and he himself was living proof that the world is a rapt listener to a spokesman of the Church who appeals to it in a language it understands. In these days of ours, when anchors are lifting, and men are putting out to sea, neither knowing nor recking what is before them, we can realize how fateful are the principles which the Archbishop brought home to the mind of the country.

Ireland was the moving spirit behind the two Congresses of Catholic Laymen held in Baltimore in November, 1889, on the occasion of the Centennial of the Establishment of the Hierarchy, and in Chicago in September, 1893. In the latter, on September 5, Archbishop Satolli, the representative of the Pope, was received with thunderous applause as he mounted the platform accompanied by Archbishop Ireland. Here, with much majesty and with his mentor, Ireland, on the lower chair beside him, the Delegate, with his eyes aglow, measured the throng before him, while Judge Morgan J. O'Brien, the presiding officer of the Congress, delivered an address of welcome, and the sea of spectators scanned eagerly the massive-jawed, firm-mouthed, dazzling-eyed man who had been sent by Leo as his mouthpiece. Satolli addressed the audience in Italian, and his words were translated by Ireland. He recalled the first great social congress, the ideal and model of all others, in which Christ laid down the vital principles for the solution of human problems: "Seek ye first the kingdom of God and its justice, and all other things shall be added to you." He regarded America as the key to the future, and he brought the audience to its feet with his closing word: "Go forward. In one hand bearing the book of Christian truth, the Bible—and in the other the Constitution of the United States. Christian truth and American liberty will make you free, happy and prosperous. They will put you on the road to progress. May you ever persevere on that road."[4]

2. THE COLUMBIAN EXPOSITION

One of the many remarkable things about the life of Archbishop Ireland was the extent of his interests. Convinced as he was that the Church should be in the foreground of every worth-while movement, he allowed no opportunity to pass in which he might demonstrate the contribution which it could make to American life. It is not surprising, therefore, to find him taking a lively interest in the Columbian Exposition, in which he was the initiator of the activity of the hierarchy. It was he who secured the invitation of the United States government to the Pope, and also the Pontiff's co-operation.[5] It was he who not only arranged for an invitation to the Cardinal of Baltimore but also suggested to him the type of prayer—"an invocation over the future century and over the World's Fair." After Gibbons and Secretary of State Foster had drawn up a letter to the Pope, the Archbishop expressed his dissatisfaction with it and suggested that a supplementary letter be written which would make it clear that the Pope's representative would be welcomed at the opening exercise. The correspondence which passed between the Cardinal and the Archbishop is interesting in showing the contrast in temperament between the two prelates—the inhibitions of the one and the ability of the other to master a situation.[6]

The Archbishop was in constant communication with the officials of the Exposition—in particular with the president of the World's Congress Auxiliary, Mr. Charles Bonney, with the vice-president, Mr. Thomas B. Bryan, whom he had met in Rome and for whom he had arranged an audience with the Holy Father, and with Mrs. Potter Palmer, who enlisted his services in obtaining from the Pope a letter endorsing the proposed exhibit of the work which Catholic women were doing all over the world.[7] He also suggested the thoughts for a letter which the Pope addressed to the president of the European Commission of the exhibition, and of which he said that it demonstrated Leo's willingness to accept all that was good in the new age and to break with traditional, but obsolete, forms. It was, he said, another manifestation of the Pontiff's high esteem and warm love for the United States, where he saw the perfect blossoming of the rational liberty which he so ardently desired for all nations.[8]

In the afternoon of September 17, at the dedication services for the opening of the World's Congress Auxiliary, the Archbishop was chosen to explain its plans and purposes. He sketched the work of the various departments—the physical and social sciences, the arts and religion. "The sole lesson which I inculcate," he said, "is that the earth is the footstool of man, and that material progress in its grandest flights fails unless man retains throughout his higher nature and is made by it a greater and a better being." The department of religion he called the crown of other departments, perfuming them with the fragrance of heaven.

There is, he said, no progress deserving the name where no provision exists for the growth of man's spiritual nature. Without God's love inspiring and God's justice rewarding, men's hearts are warped, souls are chilled, enthusiasm is transient sentiment. The fatal enemy of the spirit of sacrifice and of self-control, from which springs all moral and social progress, is the cold positivism which unbelief seeks to substitute for the religion of a living God.

He spoke of the spirit of the age and of his hopes for the future. The world was in one of those momentous cycles of history when humanity was casting around for new pathways and girding itself for unusual manifestations of its energies. It was an age of unrest, of searchings and dreamings. Past achievements had but whetted the appetite. Science was more restless in its inquiries into cause and effect than when it made its first step beyond the borderland of guessings.

He was confident that the moral and social forces which so profoundly agitated the world would work into an increase of goodness and happiness among men. "The future," he said, "will bring no millennium. There will be no rosebush without thorns, no day without the nearness of evening shades, no life without the menace of death. There will be inequalities among men, and passions will disturb the peace of souls. But I do believe there will be more mercy in the world, more justice, more righteousness."

The intellectual phase of the Exposition was developed in the Congress Auxiliary, whose device was: "Not matter, but mind." In all, over one hundred congresses were held.

In the evening of the same day the Archbishop spoke again, choosing as his theme "Human Progress." He began by saying that the greatest of things is mind, which is the causative power in all orderly results. Whatever of beauty, goodness, and progress there is in the universe, outside the workings of the First Cause, comes through man, who, within the limits of God's creation, is a second creator. He then went on to say that the discovery of America marked a new era for mankind, and that, since the preaching of the Christian religion, nothing of such import had happened for the human race. Asking what should be in future history the record of the commemoration, he replied that it inaugurated another era of progress for the world. Great as were the treasures of earth and sea brought to Chicago, something else was needed—mind, "the thinkers, the workers, the scholars, the apostles of action, the men who have rendered possible or have produced the marvels which will be displayed; the men whose dreams make for the building up of humanity, and whose arms reach out to the improvement of men along all the lines of progress."

He also delivered three other addresses, one in June, 1893, before the World's Social Purity Congress, another in September before the

Labor Congress. In the first he said that the religion of Christ differentiates itself from all other religions in demanding the complete triumph of the spiritual over the animal in man. So zealous was Christ for social purity that "He wreathed His own personality in its most translucid beauty, holy virginity—He was born of a virgin Mother."[9] In the second address he expounded the Pope's encyclical on labor, showing the fallacy of Adam Smith's "Economic Man" and stressing the work of religion in protecting labor.[10] Writing of these addresses, Monsignor O'Connell said:

> My heart went out to you when I read your grand orations at Chicago. You are back in your element, doing good away from intrigues, and mean little dishonesties. What a man you would be if you were untrammeled, and what benefits your great big heart could pour out on humanity. That's your field, and every seed you sow there grows. I told all to Rampolla, and he says the Pope will be delighted.[11]

In his third address, which was delivered before the World's Temperance Congress, he paid tribute to Cardinal Manning, who had recently died and whose place he took.[12] He also contributed an article to the *Illustrated World's Fair.*

One feature of the Chicago Exposition is interesting in itself and in its aftermath—the Parliament of Religions. Religion had been excluded from all previous fairs because of the probability of discords, but the directors of the Chicago Fair felt that any attempt to cover the chief departments of knowledge would be incomplete without consideration of it. They therefore invited representatives of all the great historic faiths to present the tenets of their beliefs, to call attention to the teachings of their sacred books, and to indicate the effects of their religions upon their peoples. The representatives were to meet in friendly conference without controversy and without compromising their individual convictions. The purposes of the Parliament were "to deepen the spirit of human brotherhood among religious men of diverse faiths, to indicate the impregnable foundations of theism and the reasons for man's faith in immortality, to strengthen the forces adverse to materialism, to throw light on the problems of the age, and to bring the nations of the earth into more friendly fellowship."[13] It was in reality a comparative study of religion.

The question of participation was brought up at the Third Annual Conference of the Archbishops on November 16-19, 1892. After a letter of Bishop John J. Keane, outlining the project, was discussed, it was resolved that Cardinal Gibbons should request him in the name of the board to make arrangements to have twenty Catholic speakers, selected by the Bishop, to expound Catholic doctrine at the Exposition.[14] Although Satolli looked askance at participation, Gibbons was favorable, as also was Ireland, at whose urgent solicitation Keane had entered into it.[15] The Cardinal informed the Papal Secretary of State that, although Catholics did not originate the plan, it was thought well to accept it in order to offset dangers; that the bishops were aware of the possibility of the evils of latitudinarianism and indifference, but that these dangers were less probable in Chicago than in Europe.[16] Archbishop Ireland was also well aware of the objections to such a project, but he felt that there was no ground for apprehension, that the Church had nothing to lose by comparison, and that "they who hold the truth need not fear."

The Parliament lasted from the eleventh to the twenty-seventh of September. Addresses were delivered by Cardinal Gibbons, Archbishops Redwood of New Zealand and Ireland, Bishop John J. Keane, Monsignor Seton, Fathers Walter Elliott, Thomas O'Gorman, James M. Cleary, John Gmeiner, and others. John Henry Barrows, the moving spirit of the project and the chairman of the General Committee, rhapsodized on the spectacle which the Parliament presented, orthodox Christians greeting with cordial words the representatives of alien faiths which they were endeavoring to bring into the light of the Christian gospel, the religions of the world brought together not for contention but for conference.[17] His enthusiasm, however, was not shared by the Pope, who wrote to Satolli:

> But although these promiscuous conventions have unto this day been tolerated with prudent silence, it would, nevertheless, seem more advisable that the Catholics should hold their conventions separately, and that, lest the utility of these conventions should result simply to their own benefit, they might be called with the understanding that the admittance should be open to all, including those who are outside the Church.[18]

Asked by a representative of the St. Paul *Pioneer Press* for an expression of opinion concerning the Pope's letter, Ireland said:

> The words of the Pope are in no manner a condemnation of Parliaments of Religion. He merely prescribes the methods or conditions under which Catholics may take part in them. He deems unadvisable the promiscuous assembling of Catholics with men of all forms of religion. He fears that from such gatherings the impressions go out into the public mind that all forms of religion are looked upon as of equal value and equal sufficiency. The Catholics who participated in the Chicago Parliament of Religion were not without their misgivings as to the peril of impressions of this

kind, but they satisfied their consciences that all things would be made right by their emphatic and repeated declarations that the principles of the Catholic faith remained intact and that nothing done or said should be taken as placing other religions on the same footing as the Catholic.[19]

The Parliament of Religions was something of which both Ireland and Keane were destined to hear much in days to come. Many a time it would be thrown in their faces as an example of their liberalism.

Abbé Felix Klein, who had taken a great interest in the Parliament, hoped that a similar one could be arranged for the Paris Exposition of 1900. He succeeded in interesting in the project such men as Brunetière and Goyau. Unfortunately he allowed information concerning his plans to reach the ear of Abbé Victor Charbonnel, a priest of ultraliberal opinions and later an apostate. When the project began to be severely criticized by such papers as *La Croix* and *La Vérité*, and also by the Archbishop of Paris, Charbonnel became contumacious, continued his activities, sent communications to the press, and wrote an insolent open letter to the Archbishop of Paris. L'Abbé Moreau, Vicar-General of Langres, expressed the real mind of the Church when he said:

It is well and good to invite Protestants, Jews and Orientals, but the Catholic Church has no place there. The supporters of the project think that it will bring about tolerance, but tolerance in matters of dogma is heresy. The Catholic Church, which alone possesses truth, has nothing to learn from others, and has no concession to make. It may be well and good for other religions, but the Catholic Church is excluded by the very principle on which it lives.[20]

Neither did Cardinal Guillaume Meignan favor the Parliament. He said: "America is not France. Neither her people nor her clergy are like those in France. The fact that something succeeded in the New World does not guarantee its success in France."[21] On the other hand, Ireland hoped that it would take place. "It will be a pity," he said, "if, when other religions are vocal, the Catholic will keep silent and appear before the nations as dead. It is only the dying who do not love the noise of action."[22] He held Charbonnel responsible for much of the unfavorable reaction. He wrote to Klein: "L'Abbé Charbonnel has given a good kick to the Congress of Religions. I feel that the project will survive with difficulty. We are not prepared in France for American projects, and, when our friends show themselves too enthusiastic, instead of advancing, the cause is completely lost."[23]

A final attempt was made to arrange a Parliament for the St. Louis

Exposition, concerning which Cardinal Satolli expressed his mind to Paul Carus of the Open Court Publishing Company: "It is my conviction, which I frankly dare to express, that such a Parliament would only lead to scepticism and to naturalism. I must declare that no Catholic, whatever his condition or rank in the Church might be, should be allowed to take part or even sympathize with your work."[24]

3. His Love of Country

Archbishop Ireland was not only a lover of the Church; he was also passionately devoted to the land of his adoption. It is not too much to say that no man in public life extolled the glory of patriotism with such power as did he. In a country where the Church was in many quarters regarded as a menace, as a foreign institution, whose members waved their foreign flags, and spoke their foreign languages, and cherished their foreign traditions, and owed allegiance to a foreign authority whose laws overrode those of American lawgivers, in a country where periodically there was an outburst of venomous bigotry against Catholics, a Catholic bishop was heard proclaiming: "Next to God is country, and next to religion is patriotism. Patriotism is a Catholic virtue. I would have Catholics be the first patriots of the land." He termed patriotism the vital spark of national life, the fount of the nation's prosperity, the inspiration of the historian, the orator, and the poet.[25] Proud of his American citizenship, he regarded the United States as a providential nation, whose mission is to prepare the world by example and moral influence for the reign of human liberty and human rights, to teach the nations of the earth man's just relation to man. Hence American liberty must be preserved as the one thing of earth most sacred, for "when it is quenched, there is no other ray of light toward which common man may turn his face."[26] And because in the last analysis national life is what the manhood of the nation makes it, the first and fundamental attribute of good citizenship is the private honor, dignity, and independence of the citizen. If democracy is to remain sound, the people must be sound. "The citizens of America," he said, "are her monarchs. No country deserves so well of its people as America, and none is so dependent upon them."[27]

A determined enemy of all that saps the vitality of political institutions, he constantly raised his voice against the too prevalent view that judgment in questions of politics can be left to others. He often reminded his people that there are no rights without obligations, that the man who refuses to vote merits disfranchisement or exile, and that the American boasting of his political indifference proclaims his shame.[28] He also stressed the need of an educated citizenry, holding that as a rule the man who does not read and write intelligently cannot vote intelligently.[29] He inveighed against the caucus and the primary, by which a few men are able to impose their candidates upon the whole party, and he favored the total elimination of the liquor power from politics.[30]

A patriot of the old-fashioned type, a man who loved his country with the passion of enthusiasm, he always showed in his attitude and his utterance the affection of one who glorified in being part of a great nation. If *Civis Romanus sum* was once a proud boast, prouder still is *Civis Americanus sum*, for "never another title meant for its possessor such a copious well of rights and privileges." The essence of the American Republic is, he said, manhood suffrage, a recognition of the dignity of manhood in all men. In its foundation this government was an act of supreme confidence in man, a confession, such as never before had been heard, of human dignity. Its creation was a bold experiment, the bravest political act recorded in history. Liberty had never been really understood until it was caught up in a human embrace and embodied in a great and abiding nation. This liberty he defined as "exemption from all restraint, save that of the laws of justice and order, exemption from submission to other men, except so far as they represent and enforce these laws."[31]

In his day the hierarchy was not without a voice. Whenever important issues arose, whenever points of morality or religion were involved, whenever patriotic sentiment demanded an eloquent spokesman, he could be found in the public forefront. Naturally the moral and religious aspects of patriotism engaged his attention, and again and again he stressed the fact that materialism and unbelief are fatal to liberty and social order, that a people without belief in God and in a future life will not long remain free, and that for its protection an age of democracy must be an age of religion.[32]

Running through all his addresses is a heartening note of optimism, of faith in democracy and in the good sense and wisdom of the American people. "Clouds may cross the heavens, but a burst of sunlight soon dispels them. Menacing social and political evils, however formidable, go down before the tread of an indignant people."[33] But at the same time he knew the perils of democracy, the dangers that come from lack of care and vigilance.[34] If the greatness of America is her democracy, the peril of America is also her democracy, for danger can come from human passions, from mere reliance on physical force, from the inefficacy of laws. Hence it cannot be abandoned unprotected to struggle for existence amid the passions of the race; it needs the best that men can give it.[35] He knew too well the dangers of corrupt morals, dishonest voting, lax observance of the law. How pertinent to our day are his words: "The one menace to republican institutions is political corruption, which covets for self or awards to others places of trust in the nation with a view to private gain, and subordinates public to personal interest. There will always be men who do not refuse to tear down the commonwealth if only they be lifted upon its ruins, and the multitude lulled to dangerous slumber by perfidious cajoling, or by their own somnolent dreamings."[36] He denounced the initiative, the referendum, and the recall, praying especially that no sacrilegious hand be laid upon the courts, impairing their independence or lowering their majesty.[37]

Between the Catholic Church and the free institutions of America there is, he said, perfect sympathy:

> I can truly say that my Catholic heart and my American heart are one, and I am delighted to say that the free air of America has cheered the soul of Leo XIII, and that he has not been without guidance from our institutions. When the question is asked, "Do you put Church before country or country before Church?", I say that one is not to be put before the other. They are in different spheres altogether, and so far as principle goes, the Church tells me that service to the State and country is a solemn, sacred, religious duty. I do not think that anyone is fit to enter the kingdom of heaven who is not capable of taking care of, so far as the opportunity affords, this magnificent kingdom given to us here, the republic of America.

At Archbishop John Hennessy's Jubilee in Dubuque, on October 18, 1891, responding to the toast "Church and Country," he said:

> Church and Country; soul and body; the one is necessary to the other, and there is no distinction between the love we owe to the one and that which the other demands. Church and Country; nature and grace; and grace demands as its soil a thorough and well prepared field, and a field made thorough and beautiful by nature is enhanced when the dews of supernal grace fall on it.

From the pulpit of his Cathedral he gave sound advice to Catholics, reminding them that, in contrast with conditions in other countries, the Church in the United States enjoys fullest liberty. Hence Catholics should be models of Americanism and of personal righteousness.

He refused to regard as a serious menace bigots who seek to deprive
Catholics of political and civil rights, for "being un-American in
thought and purpose, they cannot thrive upon the land of America."
When the attack upon the Church proceeds from malice, the one
plan to be followed, he said, is to ignore it. Where ignorance is at the
bottom of it, it is proper to dispel it by peaceful and dignified methods, but to defend the Church by unworthy means is to dishonor it.
Catholics should not seek a fight by the formation of organizations to
oppose anti-Catholic propaganda or by noisy public discussions. Nor
must they pose as martyrs and attribute all their misfortunes to a
persecution of their faith, nor be boastful when a Catholic comes into
prominence, nor undertake to pull the Church with them into any
party. Like De Tocqueville, a writer for whom he had the highest
admiration, Ireland believed that the power of religion in America
and the surest guarantee of its permanent hold upon the people depends on its absolute divorce from political parties.[38] But Catholics
should be, in the best sense of the word, American, loving America,
loving its institutions, devoted to its interests, chary in blaming,
ardent in defending it.[39]

At a time when the Guardians of Liberty, the A.P.A.'s and the
Know-Nothings were active, the ringing patriotic addresses of the
Archbishop freed the minds of millions of Americans from prejudice
based on the belief that the Church is a political organization under
the control and direction of the Pope. The remark of the Chicago
Tribune that "the Catholic Church in this country is more American
today than it has been at any time in the last forty years and is becoming more so every day" was prompted by an address Ireland had
given a day or two before in St. Paul, in which he had cut the ground
from under the A.P.A.'s by adopting their principles.[40] In an address
before the Union League Club of Chicago on Washington's Birthday,
1895, he urged the necessity of fully assimilating all who come here
seeking an asylum. If no encouragement should be given to political
organizations which perpetuate in this country foreign ideas and
customs, neither should Americans be permitted to become foreign-
ized by importing foreign fashions and seeking foreign titles.[41] This
address Cardinal Gibbons regarded as, next to the one in Baltimore,
the happiest effort of the Archbishop's life.

At the banquet of the New York Commandery of the Loyal Legion
on April 4, 1894, Ireland protested against discriminations and segre-
gations on lines of birthplace, race, or language as un-American and

wrong.[42] The address brought approving comments from newspapers all over the country, the Chicago *Times* saying that it should be placed in the hands of every schoolboy of the land.

In his address in the Milwaukee Auditorium on August 11, 1913, he thrilled his large audience by recounting an incident of the battle of Gettysburg, when, at a crucial moment, Father William Corby, leaping to the top of a large boulder, cried out: "The Catholic Church refuses Christian burial to the soldier who turns his back to the foe or deserts his flag." In the same address he was asked: "Is America to be Catholic in religion?" "Fain would I make it so," he replied. "Need America fear the spread of the Gospel of Christ?" No harm, he insisted, can come to America from the spread of Catholicism, which brings to its institutions elements vital to their life and growth. Salvation for the social organism is in the name and the power of the ever-living God; the potent agency to preach God and uphold His authority is the Catholic Church.[43]

There were times when Monsignor Denis O'Connell influenced not only the thought but also the oratory of the Archbishop. Writing from Rome soon after the unsuccessful attempt to prevent the war with Spain, the Monsignor told him that over there sympathies were entirely Spanish; that two ideas summed up the situation as they understood it: the right of Spain, the highhandedness of America, and that all said about humanity was pure hypocrisy.[44] This must have been in the mind of the Archbishop when he spoke at the Peace Jubilee in Chicago in October, 1898, and paid tribute to the American people, who believed that only through war could they acquit themselves of the sacred duty of rescuing others from their sufferings, and whose impelling motive was the sentiment of humanity and not sordid ambition or pecuniary gain. A little later O'Connell felt that the time had come for America to take her proper place among the nations and give up her isolation. The old nations of Europe would no longer lead. God has passed the banner to the hands of America, who could not evade her duty to humanity.[45] This lofty concept of the role of the United States found its echoes in the same address, in which Ireland expressed the hope that America would be conscious of its dignity and power and take her proper place among the nations of the world.[46] She was now a world power, to whom no world interest could be alien. She owed it to humanity to spread her two great ideals: democracy and liberty.[47]

Although his sympathies in the days preceding the declaration of war against Spain were largely with that unfortunate country, which, he felt, was drawn into an unnecessary conflict against the wishes of the President, nevertheless, once war was declared, he gave whole-hearted support to the government, and he gloried in the manifestation of unity among the people, of thousands animated with one ambition—service to their country.[48]

Again, when war was declared in 1917, he called on the people to remember that they were Americans, and he put his eloquence and energy at the service of the nation in his appeals for military training, the purchase of Liberty bonds, and war relief. In an eloquent funeral oration in the Cathedral over the body of Josiah R. King, the first man to answer the call of President Lincoln in 1861, he made a strong plea for preparedness and characterized as a shame and a disgrace to humanity the man who shirked his duty. He said: "No nation can be weak today in preparedness and strong tomorrow in efficiency. We must be so strong that no nation shall dare to raise its hand against us."[49]

He gave little consolation to pacifists. On October 17, 1898, in company with President McKinley and ex-President Harrison, he spoke in the Auditorium, in Chicago, at a benefit for suffering soldiers and sailors. Beginning with an apostrophe to peace, and a picture of the horrors of war, he insisted that there are times when war is necessary,[50] that more horrible than war is the destruction of social security, the disruption of the nation, its enslavement to foreign power, the robbery of its territory, or the possible lowering of its flag through disgrace abetted by cowardice.[51]

Archbishop Ireland was a patriot both in theory and in practice. Hardly were the sacred oils dry on his consecrated hands before he became a hero. When the Union was in danger, and the call went forth summoning all valiant men to its defense, he did not hesitate. Again, in 1908, when the country was in danger from pacifists, who were making their influence felt among the people, he stood before the House committee and begged for preparedness in words which have a message for our time: "I have always believed that the best way to have peace is to be ready for war. A good deal is said now-adays against the army and against the spirit of war. The idea of universal peace is very good, but to make it a gospel is a mistake." One of the last acts of his life was to greet the men of Minnesota who were about to leave for war and to say to them: "It is a privilege which is now given you to be soldiers of America, to suffer to defend its flag, to carry it far and wide without stain or reproach." He took every opportunity of expressing his love for America, its institutions and its ideals. He could be found speaking at the erection of a monument in memory of Major George Quincy White, member of the Loyal Legion of Minnesota; delivering a eulogy at the funeral of General Bishop; paying tribute to the memory of General Lucius Hubbard, who had saved the day at the battle of Corinth.[52] He loved to contemplate the painting in the Minnesota Capitol, which depicts the Fifth Minnesota charging the invading Confederate column—a painting which brought back many a memory. At a time when the Grand Army of the Republic was regarded with suspicion by some members of the Church, he accepted membership in it, frequently attended its meetings, encampments, and campfires, and was elected Chaplain-in-Chief in 1906. He was proud of his membership in various patriotic societies and was elected Honorary Member of the Veteran Corps of the 69th Regiment, composed of members of that regiment, the Irish Legion, and the Irish Brigade. At the funeral of Major White he said that the veterans of 1861, by preserving America as a nation, had made possible all future victories.[53] He was never more happy than when greeting the old soldiers, and he took an especial pride in his companionship with those who were privileged to wear the Medal of Honor.[54] In New York, in October, 1899, he congratulated them on their spirit of tolerance in disregarding distinction of race and creed, at the same time taking occasion to characterize the introduction of religious prejudice into politics as a "boomerang which returns on him who launches it." When with bared heads the age-worn survivors of Minnesota's veteran regiments received their bullet-scarred battle flags from the government, bore them to the newly erected state capitol, and placed them in the keeping of the governor, the Archbishop was deeply moved and expressed his emotion in the following apostrophe:

Dear old flags, tattered and shattered, storm-beaten and bullet-bored, our hearts go out in sweetest love, in fondest embrace. The tear-drops bedewing our eyelids bespeak the deep emotions welling within our souls. Dear old flags, receive our salute most sincere in its tenderness, most plenary in its effusiveness. Precious and sacred the memories you evoke; meaningful the lessons you impart.[55]

The *Post Express* of Rochester, New York, characterized the address a masterpiece of emotional eloquence, which would become a part of the war literature of the nation.

Abbé Felix Klein, who attended a meeting of veterans in Washington on October 14, 1907, on the occasion of the unveiling and the dedication of a monument to General Sherman, gives an account of the reception which followed:

Once more the Archbishop became again the old chaplain of the Fifth Minnesota Volunteers. Former companions in arms thronged around him, and they dwelt on reminiscences of which I knew nothing. The Army of the Potomac, whose reception we were attending, resolved for this night to form a junction with the Army of the Tennessee, which was bivouacked at another hotel. So, about half-past nine, to the strains of martial music, off we set, marching two by two, as solemnly as you please. Archbishop Ireland and an old officer headed the line, setting the step for us and looking positively war-like. The Archbishop, in fine spirits and full of vivacity, proudly wore his military medal.[56]

The Archbishop loved not only America but also the human beings without distinction who composed it. That is why he was so much at home with the veterans, with mixed groups of Protestants and Catholics. It is said that at these meetings he did not wish to be called by them "Your Grace," preferring the title "Archbishop," and that he did not like to have the members of his old regiment kiss his ring—"It is not American," he said. His true catholicity of spirit prevented the overaccentuation of denominational difference, as was shown by the beautiful address which he prepared to be read at the memorial service of Bishop Gilbert of the Episcopal Church. He never hesitated to give honor where honor was due. His compassions were strong and whole-souled, and they were without bias. He appreciated goodness and greatness wherever he found them.

Only on rare occasions were his statements criticized. Speaking before the New York Commandery of the Loyal Legion on April 4, 1894, he said that it was not easy to see what could be more effective than war in electrifying the nation's patriotism,[57] a remark which called for a later statement that war is not to be brought on for the mere purpose of intensifying patriotism. A similar assertion concerning war and arbitration made before the Loyal Legion of St. Louis resulted not only in a critical editorial in *Harper's Weekly*, which said that his position on public questions was determined not alone by accident of birth, but by remote ancestral influences, but also in all kinds of comment in Rome.[58]

The Archbishop's discourses delivered before the New York Commandery of the Legion on April 4, 1894; his address on American citizenship before the Union League of Chicago on Washington's Birthday, 1895; his address on the American Republic before the Marquette Club of Chicago, October 7, 1899, in the presence of President McKinley; his address on Abraham Lincoln before the Lincoln Club of Chicago, February 12, 1903; as well as those delivered in Sioux City, Omaha, Boston, St. Louis, and other cities—all throbbed with the purest patriotism. No wonder that when a visiting minister at a certain church in St. Paul preached on the Catholic Church as the enemy of America he was reminded by leading members of the congregation that "the biggest Republican" in America was Archbishop Ireland.

The message of Archbishop Ireland was not for his day alone; it still retains its force and its lesson. America can always profit from his pleas for loyalty and tolerance:

America demands that all who live on her soil and are protected by her flag be Americans, and she cannot do less than to demand this: beyond this, she proclaims the sacred right of liberty. The individual who does not in his own name and from his own heart proclaim this right of liberty for his fellow citizens is no true son of America. American loyalty and fitness for office—these must ever be, and these alone, the conditions which determine an American's vote.[59]

The fears so often expressed today that "the Church is a foreign institution" find their answer in his words:

Yes, if the Savior of the World is a foreigner, and the Bishop of Rome as His vicar is a foreigner. The Catholic Church is extra-American, supranational, begotten for all nations—a foreigner on no spot of the earth's surface. Catholics demand no special power—merely equal rights for all. The rights of Catholics are the rights of the personal conscience of the Catholic citizen. It is not the Catholic Church in its official name that comes into issue—it is the American citizen, whose religious faith is the faith of the Catholic Church. Not to know one's rights is lowmindedness; not to defend them is cowardice.[60]

Chapter 4

RESISTING NATIONALISM IN THE CHURCH

❧❧❧❧❧❧❧❧❧❧❧❧❧

1. THE PROBLEM AN OLD ONE

Few questions stir greater passions than those of nationalism, and the foreign problem in the Church in the United States was from the beginning a source of contention. As early as 1833, Archbishop James Whitfield of Baltimore wrote a quaint letter to Dr. Nicholas Wiseman, Rector of the English College in Rome, in which he expressed his views on Irish bishops and priests. He referred to Bishops John England and Francis Patrick Kenrick as warm-headed Irishmen who had strong predilections in favor of Irish bishops and Irish discipline, and who had placed on the list for Cincinnati the names of three Irish priests. He objected especially to the *agitating* disposition of Bishop England, who, he said, "would be restless in proposing changes in our discipline untill [sic] it were reduced to the standard of Ireland or reformed according to his republican notions." He rejoiced that there were only five Irish clergymen in his diocese and that the dismissal of some whom he had received from his predecessor and the refusal of others had contributed much to the peace, whilst New York and Philadelphia, where the clergy were almost entirely Irish, had trouble and disunion. Acknowledging his English prejudice against the Irish, he hoped that Propaganda would be on its guard in dealing with England, who at the time was in Rome, and of whom he said: "He is very glad to come to Baltimore and is more pleased here than at home, but I wish him well at Charleston, and am never quite at ease as long as he stays preaching and debating here." He also refused to follow the advice of the Bishop of Charleston to invite promising students from Maynooth and Carloue (sic), whom the bishops offered. For Cincinnati he favored "Mr. Dubuisson, S.J." rather than Mr. Purcell, who, he felt, would be led by England. He objected to

54

"Mr. Power of N.York," whom he should be much griefed (sic) to see a bishop in any part of the United States. From England's regulations in Charleston and from his conversation in Council, he received the impression that he wished to assimilate some religious and charitable institutions and even the temporal affairs of the Church "to the form of our republican governments." He concluded by hoping that the contents of his letter might not reach Irish ears, "Otherwise it will soon be echoed into mine."[1]

Two years later Bishop England, in a letter to one of his friends, said that he was more and more convinced every day that the genius of the nation and the administration of the French (clergy) were not easily reconcilable, and that one of the strongest prejudices against our religion was that it was foreign, not American. The Irish, he said, mixed easily with Americans; their principles, dispositions, statecraft, ideas of government, and appearance became American quickly; on the other hand, the language of the French, their love of *La Belle France*, appearance, ideas, bearing, way of dressing, and manner of speaking of their religion were all foreign. As a result, they made the Catholic religion appear exotic.[2]

Thus did coming events cast their shadows before, and half a century later the same charge of foreignism and the countercharge of liberalism were freely hurled. Early in his episcopal career Archbishop Ireland came face to face with the national question and became involved in a controversy, the first of a series which absorbed much of his attention throughout most of his life. In December, 1886, while he and Bishop John J. Keane were in Rome, commissioned by the American episcopate to lay before the Roman authorities a proposal to establish a Catholic University at Washington, they learned that a certain Father P. M. Abbelen of the Archdiocese of Milwaukee, posing as the representative of the German bishops of the United States, was at work endeavoring to secure for German Catholics legislation which would enormously increase the power and enhance the influence of the German element in the United States, giving them the position of favored sons, but at the same time hindering seriously the progress of the Church. To effect this, Father Abbelen, who two years previously had written to the Propaganda a letter embodying the views of fourscore St. Louis priests, presented a memorial[3] bearing the approval of Archbishop Michael Heiss of Milwaukee. The memorial, dated September 28, 1886, asked that German parishes be altogether independent, so that the rectors of "Irish" parishes could exercise no rights over the Germans. It stated that the opinion prevailed everywhere that the "Irish" rectors were the lawful pastors of all those born in America, enjoying, as it were, a high dominion over them, while German priests were merely regarded as necessary for the care of Germans who spoke the German language, and as being, therefore, of secondary importance. Ineptly dividing American priests into Irish and German, it asked: "Are the Irish so much better than the Germans that they should have greater privileges? In the number of their parochial schools, charitable institutions, religious societies, in domestic virtues, etc., the Germans can hold their own." It contained expressions of which we are destined to hear much in later days: "Americanization," the devotion of Germans to parochial schools— expressions which were to be anything but conducive to the peace of mind of Ireland. It concluded with proposals which, had they been granted, would in his opinion have definitely stamped the Church in the United States as the Church of foreigners. These were: equality among Irish and German foreign parishes, equal consideration shown in the appointment of irremovable rectors, the assignment of emigrants and their children to churches of their own language, permission of the rector of the parish or of the bishop required for those who wished to pass over to English-speaking parishes, admonition to bishops and priests not to try to suppress foreign language or customs, the administration of mixed parishes by priests who knew both languages, the obligation placed on bishops ruling over mixed dioceses to appoint a German vicar-general in addition to the "Irish," the fair division of German parishes whenever English became more necessary than German. How irritating the memorial was to Ireland and Keane may be judged by the latter's remark: "A more villainous tissue of misstatements I have seldom read."

2. Ireland Meets the Issue of Disunity

Ireland, whose whole life was characterized by a contempt for cabals, was quick to see the danger to Church unity and also the peril of accentuating the taint of foreignism already attached to it. He saw that acceptance of the memorial meant the establishment throughout the length and breadth of the land of parishes and schools on a purely foreign basis—foreign bishops, foreign priests, foreign churches, foreign schools, foreign colonies set up in the heart of American democracy. He was not without experience, for he knew that this was not the first time that the question had been raised. Not only had Bishop Thomas Grace of St. Paul written to Archbishop Martin Spalding[4] of Baltimore concerning a request from some Germans for the establishment of their own cemeteries, but, in 1878, he had also attempted to place John Lancaster Spalding in Milwaukee so as to break the German hold on that diocese. Moreover, he had always urged on Ireland the necessity of fighting nationalism.[5]

Ireland and Keane, still in Rome, lost no time in presenting a counter memorial, and in cabling to Cardinal Gibbons to acquaint him with the situation and to ask the help of the hierarchy. This action they followed with a letter telling of Abbelen's activity and the intent to secure special legislation in favor of the Germans and of their own success in obtaining copies of the memorial. They had, they said, no objection to the first petition, which asked for equality of German and English parishes, but this was accompanied by various accusations against the non-German clergy, and by certain demands the granting of which would be disastrous to the Church of America. They were convinced that there was a widespread, well-organized conspiracy against English-speaking bishops and priests, as was shown by the charges of persecution and discrimination with which the consultors and the cardinals of the Propaganda had been filled.[6] This letter of the two bishops and their demand for immediate action resulted in a meeting of the archbishops in Philadelphia on December 16, 1886, and in the sending of a protest to Rome.[7]

The memorial[8] which Ireland presented in rebuttal and which shows his skill as a controversialist, as well as his sincerity, frankness, and fearlessness, began by stating that the American bishops of English language and even some American bishops of the German language had no knowledge of the presence in Rome of Father Abbelen and would be indignant when they learned of it. It objected to the wording of the petition: "The Question in the United States between the German Catholics and the Irish Catholics." It should have been, "The Question between the English tongue, the language of the United States, and the German tongue, which emigrants from Germany have brought and are bringing over to America." It protested against the insinuation that there was a conflict of races in America between the Germans and the Irish. There was no attempt, it said, to establish an Irish Church or Irish parishes. There are parishes of the English language, composed of Catholics who are not of the Irish race, or of Irish ancestry, but they are never called

Irish. Emigrants of other nationalities would demand the same concessions as the Germans, leaving the Church a *"moles informis et
indigesta,"* without unity, life, or power. The rank and file of the
Germans were not interested in this question, only a clique, whose
estimate of the number of their priests, bishops, laymen, and religious
he rejected. But among these nationalities there was a definite movement toward the English language. Many of the children had a very
imperfect knowledge of German and, therefore, never acquired a
thorough knowledge of their religion, and later could not answer objections against the faith when those were presented to them in
English.

The memorial also told of the attempt of Germans to get a Cardinal
Protector; of the action of Bishop Michael Heiss of La Crosse in choosing the German Church for his Cathedral and thus making German
the official language of his dioocese; of the Cathedral in Green Bay,
in which a sermon in English was never heard; of Fort Wayne, in
which the English-speaking priests were reduced to a dozen; of
parishes in these and other German dioceses which, although almost
entirely English, had German pastors who spoke indifferent English,
to the distress of the parishioners, who "grow weary of bad sermons
in worse English" and gradually absent themselves. The boast of
Bishop John Henni of Milwaukee that no bishop of Irish nationality
would ever sit on his episcopal throne, the preponderance of German
professors in the seminary of that diocese to the great dissatisfaction
of the English priests, the exclusion of English students from the
seminary at Cleveland—these and other instances were quoted to
show the determination of Germans to Germanize the Church.[9] The
ill effects upon the people were pointed out: the tendency to regard
the Church as an alien stepmother, the refusal to send their children
to Catholic schools, the gradual alienation from the Church, the
lack of hope for the conversion of Protestants, many of whom were
well disposed, the charge that the Church in the United States was a
foreign institution. Then the memorial said:

> The Church will never be strong in America; she will never be sure of
> keeping within her fold the descendants of immigrants until she has gained
> a decided ascendancy among the Americans themselves. She must be
> presented in a form attractive to Americans. The great objection which
> they have until now urged against her—an objection which at certain
> periods of her history they entertained so strongly as even to raise persecu-
> tions—is, that the Catholic Church is composed of foreigners, that it exists
> in America as an alien institution, and that it is consequently, a menace
> to the existence of the Republic.

The charge that Germans were neglected was denied, the bishops having done all in their power to meet the needs of German parishes, often supplying to mixed parishes priests who could speak both languages. There were four major foreign nationalities often mixed in one parish, and "unless for the gift of Pentecost, some of them would be dissatisfied." The very people who insisted on German in the Church were satisfied to transact their business affairs in English. Only those ought to be bishops in America who know well the language of the country, who well understand the needs of the Church in the country, who can crush in their hearts foreign national- ism, and who see in their new charges opportunities for serving the Church.

The memorial then took up, clause by clause, the petitions of Father Abbelen. It showed that parishes of the German language had the same rights as those of the English, and that the same applied to the establishing of irremovable rectors. As to the demand that German emigrants and their children be regarded as subjects of German parishes, this system already prevailed, but the formal approbation of the demand would mean that German pastors would reserve to themselves the right to baptize and to bless marriages, and would prevent their parishioners from ever sending their children to English-speaking Catholic schools, or from renting pews in English churches. The demand that descendants of Germans who wish to join English churches must procure the permission of the German pastor was a matter of too small importance to become a subject of general legislation and could best be handled in each diocese. The demand that a bishop who did not speak German appoint a German vicar-general in addition to the Irish vicar-general was unreasonable because of the multiplicity of nationalities; all would also demand one of their language.

The memorial concluded by requesting a delay in the determina- tion of these matters until the bishops could be heard.

Archbishop Ireland felt that the Germans had not acted in good faith in sending a secret embassy to Rome and that they had broken the union which should exist in the episcopacy. They had the op- portunity of making their complaints at the Council of Baltimore and at provincial and diocesan synods but had not done so. Abbelen's letter was signed by Archbishop Heiss, although when Ireland had attended the synod of the Province of Milwaukee only eight months ·before and had expressly asked for a discussion of difficulties arising from the use of the German language all discussions had been refused as unnecessary. Abbelen visited Ireland in Rome and told him that the question referred to the Propaganda was the granting to German parishes the rights granted to English. He repeated the same statement in a letter contributed to Columbia on September 1, 1887, in which he denied that he had asked for special privileges.[10]

Propaganda gave its answer on April 5, 1888, granting the unimportant petitions—things which the Germans already enjoyed—and not only rejecting the main clauses, which dealt with transfer from parishes, admonition to the bishops, and preaching in both languages, but also declaring that the "Sacred Congregation of the Propaganda will never consider these petitions."[11]

The rebuke administered by Propaganda to Abbelen did not put an end to the national question, which continued to crop up in 1890, 1891, and even as late as 1910. Ireland called attention to its revival by sending to Monsignor Denis O'Connell, Rector of the North American College, Rome, a copy of the reply he had made on August 6, 1888, to Father Casimir Hueppe, O.S.F., who had requested him to grant permission and to obtain the papal blessing for a meeting of German societies at Chaska, Minnesota.[12] This request the Archbishop refused at first, because he felt that it really emanated, not from the Minnesota societies, but from the German-American Katholikentag (meeting of German societies) held in Chicago in the previous year, and also because he did not approve of the manner in which the blessing had been secured for that meeting. Only a few weeks before, he had heard from Bishop Camillus Maes of Covington all about the Chicago blessing. Father William Tappert had requested it from Cardinal Giovanni Simeoni, and Maes had approved of it, but now the Bishop complained that Tappert had not observed the conditions laid down by the Cardinal—that the assembly be held under the leadership and approbation of the episcopate. Maes also said that many prelates had complained that the Chicago assembly and the one following, which was to be held in Cincinnati in September, were all simply organized by a clique of German priests, that their prevailing spirit was dangerous, and that their purpose was to counteract the wise efforts of the bishops to create gradually a single homogeneous Catholic people in the United States, without at the same time encroaching on the rights of the various national groups. Moreover he felt that the spirit which had marked the actions of the two most ardent propagators of German ideas, in opposition to purely American ideas, was something less than a spirit of submission to the authority of their bishops. "I know no Bishop," he said, "who has approved the idea which it is said prevails in all their actions, namely, that of uniting the Germans in order to make a breach in the American Catholic idea, and to perpetuate German, cost what may, even to making second the best interests of the Church in the United States."[13] Ireland, therefore, urged O'Connell to use all means to block the granting of a blessing for the Cincinnati convention of the following year, "as it would be taken as the approving seal of infallibility set upon German tricks." This mission O'Connell finally accomplished, although at first he received little encouragement from Propaganda, which was afraid it might be taxed with inconsistency. "Cardinal Melcher's Secretary," he wrote, "told me you had worked as hard as you could against the general meeting of the German Catholics. In that quarter, you are pretty well written up, but you have your Pallium now."[14]

A short time later, Ireland sent to Bishop Richard Gilmour of Cleveland an editorial from his diocesan paper entitled "Nationalism in Religion," with the hope that he could keep him in the front ranks. "Providence wills," he said, "that you meet the foe on your own ground. They adjourned in Cincinnati to meet next year in Cleveland. I have thanked God for this. Of all places in America, where I would wish them to meet, Cleveland is my choice."[15]

In spite of his objections to certain parts of the Chaska program as showing a spirit of ultranationalism not consonant with Catholic unity, Ireland did consent to attend after some changes were made. He delivered an address in which he directed his remarks not only to the Germans but also to all English-speaking groups. While paying tribute to the cultural and religious value of the German language, he reminded his hearers that English is the language of the country, and that the political unity of the United States, the economic future of their children, and their religious interests demanded its maintenance. Americanization, he said, does not mean the sudden extirpation of foreign languages and cultures, nor the forgetting of the old land to the setting aside of previous traditions and inspirations, but rather the filling up of the heart with love for America and her institutions, so that immigrants will not be as strangers in a strange land. "It is," he said, "the knowing of the language of the land and failing in nothing to prove our attachment to its laws, and our willingness to adopt as dutiful citizens all that is good and laudable in its social life and civilization." He regretted that in certain German-

American newspapers the word "Americanization" was held up as an opprobrious term, synonymous with tendencies most dangerous, to be deplored and avoided. "To me," he said, "all Catholics, whencesoever they have come, are Catholics and nothing else. The motto of the diocese, chosen by the first bishop, is 'All to All,' and I pray that my tongue be stilled, and my arm fall nerveless, if ever I am not true to it." He would adapt his services of religion to the several nationalities in the diocese so far as it might be necessary or useful for the good of souls to do so, but he would not encourage movements or tendencies, the outcome of which would be injurious to national or religious unity. He deemed dangerous, he said, the efforts made through conventions held in Chicago and Cincinnati to gather into separate groups by themselves, isolated from other Catholics, those of German origin, as if they had no interests in common with their fellow Catholics. He saw nothing but chaos if all nationalities had their separate clerical unions and conventions. He did, however, regard favorably the Chaska convention, which was organized for the special and well-defined work of the societies.[16]

This address won the approval of Archbishop William Elder of Cincinnati, who thanked him for setting forth so clearly and forcibly the true Catholic view on the whole subject; particularly for drawing so accurately the lines between what is to be encouraged and what is to be opposed in regard to foreign languages and national traditions and usages. He also asked him if it would not be well to have a clear statement given of those changes in the program of his convention which made it acceptable to him. It would furnish a guide for others, and the example ought to be set forth somewhat strongly with all praise to the parties who gave it.[17]

Archbishop Elder had always regretted the spirit of nationalism, which he regarded as the source of the greatest evil among Catholics and the cause of prejudice among Protestants. He felt that special legislation on behalf of the Germans would lead to similar demands from other nationals and also to requests for a Cardinal Protector at Rome. He said, moreover, that while the German language is often a help to religion, it is also sometimes an instrument of irreligion and sensuality among German infidels, instancing their action in Cincinnati in opposing Sunday observance.[18]

Both Ireland and Gibbons were as much opposed to distinctively Irish agitation as they were to the German. On several occasions the Archbishop warned the Irish that they must not set themselves up as a class apart, for it was their duty to become completely identified with American spirit and institutions. The Cardinal hoped that the Irish Benevolent Society would drop the first prefix,[19] as also did the Archbishop, who felt that such action would be an example to the Germans. "My conviction grows daily," he said, "that the Church cannot prosper in America so long as she seemingly persists in draping herself in foreign un-American garbs."[20] How different the attitude of Archbishop Michael Heiss of Milwaukee, who, in August, 1887, spoke of the need of more German bishops.[21] As Archbishop William H. Gross, of Portland, Oregon, said: "Heiss makes every bishop in the United States to be an Englishman, Frenchman, Irish, German or Belgian—there is not an American among us."[22]

Ireland continued to keep a watchful eye on the national problem, calling, in March, 1890, the attention of Bishop John J. Keane to the fact that the old question had been revived, that Abbelen had published a pamphlet containing both documents, his own memorial and an introduction in which he stated that he had the full approval of the Archbishop of Milwaukee, but that he had been defeated by the representations made against him. The translation of the document, Ireland said, was poorly made and often incorrect. Abbelen had also printed the reply of the Congregation in mutilated form, retaining the answers to the first three propositions, leaving out those unfavorable to him and giving the impression that, on the whole, he had gained his point. As these documents and also articles in the German press were doing harm by their misrepresentations, the St. Paul prelate recommended the publication of a pamphlet which would call attention to the mutilations, and the sending of copies to Rome and to both German and non-German clerics.[23]

3. THE CONTROVERSY WITH CAHENSLY

The next manifestation of the German movement introduced the man after whom it has been called—Peter Paul Cahensly, General Secretary of the St. Raphael's Society, which had been founded for the protection of German emigrants, a member of the Prussian House of Representatives and of the Reichstag. Following the international congress of the Society in Lucerne in December, 1890, he presented in April, 1891, a memorial which asked for the establishment of separate churches and parochial schools for the immigrants of the various nationalities, the assignment of priests who could speak their languages,[24] the appointment of bishops on the basis of population, and instruction of school children in the language of their parents. A series of Associated Press cablegrams, which purported to come from Rome, Brussels, and Berlin, on May 8, 26, and 27, but which really originated from Monsignor O'Connell and Monsignor Eugene Boeglin, a correspondent for Vatican news, gave further details, bringing from the *Northwestern Chronicle* the assertion that German priests in the United States were behind the movement. The last cablegram, on May 27, also associated with it Herr von Schloezer, German representative at the Vatican, the famous Dr. Windthorst, Premier Henri Mercier of Canada, and the Austro-Hungarian Ambassador to the Holy See—strange bed-fellows indeed.[25]

Immediately Ireland, who was approached by a representative of the Associated Press, accused Cahensly of working to harness the Church in America into the service of German immigrants. He expressed his amazement at "the impudence of the man in undertaking to meddle under any pretext in the Catholic affairs of America," as well as his own conviction that American Catholics would treasure up the affront for future action. While accusing a German clique in America, he absolved the mass of German-speaking Catholics from any part in plots and intrigues. He felt that the American bishops could take care of the situation and that Rome, whose policy was to trust the hierarchy of each country, would turn a deaf ear to Cahensly. In proof of this he quoted the words which Leo XIII had addressed to himself: "The bishops should see that all can practice their religion in the language they understand, but, when this much is done, let the work be toward amalgamation and union." He charged that the promoters of German foreignism in America were certain journalists whose trade was gone if the German language lost its hold, and certain priests who on coming to America in advanced years never learned much English and scarcely knew that there was in America a country outside the German village or quarter surrounding their parsonage.[26] He enlarged on this in a second interview, in which, while admitting that some of Cahensly's demands, such as German parishes and German schools, were quite admissible, he regarded as singular malice his attempt to represent the Catholic Church in America as Irish. In still another interview he said:

It is strange news for American ears that the Austrian and Prussian ambassadors in Rome had been instructed by their government to bring on the Vatican their influence in favor of Cahensly's plan. The Prussian ambassador, von Schloezer, declared that he viewed the appointment of Bishop Katzer of Milwaukee as favorable to German interests.

M. Mercier, the Minister of the province of Quebec, who met Cahensly in Rome, rushed to the Vatican to urge the appointment of Canadian bishops in the United States.

Though the Deutsch-Amerikanischer Priester Verein or German Clerical Society disclaims all knowledge of or cooperation in the Cahensly memorial, the Cahensly memorial is nearly word for word the document which the German priests of St. Louis, founders of the Verein, sent to Rome in 1886 by Rev. Abbelen of Milwaukee.[27]

Ireland saw that if Herr Cahensly succeeded in his scheme of appointing "national" bishops the manifold elements composing the Church in America would become so many foreign colonies, living in weakness and isolation, shut off from one another by the barrier of language. He at once enlisted the aid of Cardinal Gibbons, to whom he wrote a letter which in its outspokenness reveals the happy warrior, who had the courage of his convictions, the boldness to trust his reason, carelessness of opposition, and scorn of consequences. He said:

Is there no protest to be made by us as regards what has been so aptly called the "Lucerne conspiracy"? Is Mr. Cahensly, Herr Schlosser [sic], Premier Mercier etc., to go on telling Rome how the Church in America is to be ruled, with our silence and apparent approval? Are we, by saying nothing, showing ourselves worthy of the trust which our people put in us? Will not Rome herself deem us worthless men, whom she need not consult on this or any other matter, in which we are concerned? I am reading the late book of "Drumont" in which you are quoted as the model bishop because of your courage to speak out in the case of the K[nights] of L[abor]—your action being in contrast with that of the Cardinal of Paris, who is by nature all submission, and who is, in consequence, utterly ignored by Rome. The American Church has been deeply insulted. We look to you as our leader to invite the Archbishops to meet with you and counsel with you. The time fixed for our November meeting is too distant. By that time the whole value will be lost to our protest.

I know your delicacy of sentiment, which might tempt you not to act, lest jealous minds complain. I honor this delicacy. Yet, it must at times yield before stern duty. Ask the Archbishops to meet you, if convenient to them, and, if not, to write to you. A certain number will come—sufficient to take action. You will say I am hasty and need to be repressed. Not so, this time I think. We are American bishops; an effort is made to dethrone us and to foreignize our country in the name of religion. The question will not be as to quarrels between us and Germans—or Canadians in America —that is a home question. But it will be as to men daring to rule us from Germany or Canada. Our non-Catholic fellow-citizens can well call us traitors if we are silent.[28]

Meanwhile O'Connell, who had a flair for the sensational, sent frequent communications, sometimes every few days. He told Ireland that no one had any idea of the extent and perfection of the German scheme, that all the most notable men in Europe were involved in it, that Rome was in their favor and had no intention of consulting the American episcopate. The opposition of the "Irish" was assumed and disregarded.[29] He also conveyed the interesting news that Rome regarded the Archbishop of St. Paul as the leader of a dangerous set of liberals that must at any cost, but prudently, be put down; the Germans as the only reliable Catholics, the only ones in favor of parochial schools, and therefore to be patronized. Moreover, since the American government would remain indifferent, the "Irish" had no strong power behind them, whereas the Germans had the patronage of a powerful government. He instanced the case of the Irish episcopate, whose influence could not compare with that of the English government. He evidently had in mind the condemnation of the Land League agitation. When he spoke to Rampolla of the indignation of the American bishops, he made no impression upon him, but when he said that the American government would settle the matter for itself without Cahensly, the Cardinal changed his attitude.[30]

Fuel was added to the fire in June, when a second memorial appeared. It was written by Cahensly and Marchese Battista Volpe-Landi, an Italian lawyer and a member of the St. Raphael's Society, in response to a request from Cardinal Rampolla for further information on matters of emigration. It stated that more than sixteen millions of emigrants had lost their faith owing to lack of priests and bishops of their own nationality, want of societies to protect them, and the influence of public schools. It gave as a reason for the granting of their requests the fact that by it "the sweetest and most cherished relations of the fatherland would be constantly brought to the emigrants." It went on to say that the question affected the interests of the countries from which emigration took place, that, through their emigrants, the nations were acquiring in the United States an influence and an importance by which they would one day be able to profit. These nations were so well aware of this that they did everything possible to have those of their nationalities settling in the United States develop and strengthen themselves in every respect.

Such remarks led Archbishop Ireland to suspect that the whole movement had an international political angle, and that forces in

Germany were attempting to influence the Vatican. His suspicions were borne out by an interview O'Connell had with Cardinal Rampolla, in which he requested that no encouragement be given to the petition. To this the Cardinal replied that the Vatican could not refuse to see those who were protecting the interests of their co-nationalists, and that, moreover, such influential men as Windthorst were deeply interested in the matter, a statement which brought from O'Connell the retort that public sentiment in America was offended by the attitude of immigrants who still considered themselves under the control of the government of Prussia.[31]

When Ireland received a copy of this second memorial from O'Connell, who referred to it as "the whole cancer in a nutshell," he gave it at once to the Associated Press, together with an introduction of his own. To the Monsignor he wrote:

Well, I gave to the Associated Press the Second Memorial. We are in war, & we must use all our powder. . . . I think we have the country well worked up now, & we will be able to begin reaping our harvest. . . . I sent an "alarming" cable to you yesterday. You may be able, I thought, to show it around.[32]

He also sent a copy of the memorial to Gibbons, pointing out the calumnies against the whole Church of America, the insults to the Republic, and the influence over her affairs promised to foreign powers, as well as the sympathetic reception of the document in Rome. After expressing his satisfaction at the news that the Pope would write to the Cardinal his assurance that he would not grant Cahensly's requests, he asked:

Are we, however, to stop there? . . . Have we no duty toward our fellow-citizens in the way of assuring them officially and formally that we are Americans? Are we satisfied to let base calumnies go out to Rome against us, our priests and people, without refuting them? Ought we not take this opportunity to assert ourselves before Rome and compel her to have in the future some regard for us? Do you not owe it to yourself to speak out before Rome, unitedly with the leading prelates, and make her remember that you are on the watch tower?[33]

He told of distressing news from O'Connell that the American episcopacy was being driven out of favor in Rome by determined foes. He felt that a crisis had come in which bishops must sink or swim, and that at home they were surrounded by spies and traitors.

Rome's first tendency was to maintain a neutral attitude in the controversy. As Rampolla expressed it to O'Connell: "Unfortunately there are two parties in the United States and the Holy See cannot favor either of them."[34] However, the counsel of Ireland and his friends prevailed, and in July the Cardinal Secretary of State indicated to Gibbons that the Holy See approved of neither Cahensly's propositions nor the rumor that the hierarchy planned to consider the matter in special meetings. He urged him, together with his brother bishops, to work for the restoration of peace, assuring him that the Head of the Church was not inclined to accept any of the proposals which could provoke even the slightest misgivings.

This advice Gibbons followed, when, on the occasion of the conferring of the pallium on Archbishop Katzer of Milwaukee, August 20, 1891, he made a plea for greater unity and harmony. At the same time, however, he warned:

Woe to him, my brethren, who would destroy or impair this blessed harmony that reigns among us. Woe to him who would sow tares of discord in the fair fields of the Church in America. Woe to him who would breed dissension among the leaders of Israel by introducing a spirit of nationalism into the camps of the Lord. Brothers we are, whatever may be our nationality, and brothers we shall remain. We will prove to our countrymen that the ties formed by grace and faith are stronger than flesh and blood. God and our country—this our watchword. Loyalty to God's Church and to our country—this our religious and political faith.[35]

The Cardinal's brave plea for harmony, however, often fell on deaf ears, and how bitter were the emotions which the controversy produced may be seen in the charges and recriminations which so often found their way into the pages of rival publications—the *Northwestern Chronicle*, the *Catholic Review*, the *Western Watchman*, on the one hand, and the St. Louis *Amerika*, the Rochester *Katholischen Volkszeitung*, and the Illinois *Staats-Zeitung*, on the other. Not infrequently were personal attacks made on Archbishop Ireland. He was, however, by no means alone in his opposition to Cahensly; he had the active support of Cardinal Gibbons, Archbishops Williams, Ryan, Elder, Bishops Keane, Foley, Maes, Moore, Gross, Gilmour, Brondel, and, at first, of Archbishop Corrigan.

How united was the episcopate in its opposition to Cahenslyism is manifest from the second Annual Conference of the Archbishops of the United States, held in St. Louis on November 29, 1891, a conference at which all the prelates were present. Cahensly's petition was taken up and discussed. Two points were marked for special censure: (1) the exaggerated and unjustifiable statements as to the losses to the Church of foreign-born Catholics, owing to their neglect by the bishops of the country; (2) the interference by subjects or governments of foreign countries in the direction of ecclesiastical affairs in America. The resolution was unanimously adopted that a letter be sent to the Holy See respectfully and firmly protesting against all such foreign interference in the affairs of this country as had been threatened in the Cahensly memorial, and also against the utterly false representations made in this and other documents to the effect that the losses to the faith in the United States had been during the century enormous in size.[36]

Ireland went to Rome in January, 1892, in support of his Faribault school plan, and while there did not, in the words of Gibbons, "allow any grass to grow under his feet" either in defense of the plan or in opposition to Cahenslyism. Zest was added to his efforts by his knowledge of the activities of his opponents. As he wrote to his Vicar-General, Father Louis Caillet: "Our enemies—the Germans & the Jesuits—watch all details and send word at once to the Roman authorities, so as to prejudice them against us. The plea is—have nothing to do with the State. It is Protestant, it is infidel. Indeed the cry practically is—have nothing to do with the American people."[37] With the aid of Cardinal Rampolla, "the dead enemy of the 'Triplice aleanza,'" his efforts were rewarded, and before he left Italy he was able to tell Gibbons that Rome had decided that bishops must be in touch with their country, as otherwise there would be no hope for the Church, and that it was determined to put down "intransigents, reactionaries and men of backward movements."[38]

The decision was announced in May, 1892, in a letter which Cardinal Mieceslaus Ledochowski, Prefect of Propaganda, addressed to the American hierarchy—a letter called by a great Roman authority "perhaps the strongest political document that has ever been issued from Rome." In this letter, which was known to express the personal views of the Pope, the Cardinal said:

Whenever an episcopal see is vacant in America, clergy and people become excited, different factions discuss possible candidates in meetings, and, through the public press, seek all means to advance their favorites. The chief cause of these divisions is that Catholics, dividing on national lines, demand bishops from the ranks of their several nationalities, instead of keeping solely in view the welfare of the Church. This welfare is the sole guide of the Holy See in naming bishops for all countries, and especially must the principle be followed in the case of the United States, whither populations go from various European countries, to the end that they build

up there for themselves a new *"patria,"* where they must coalesce into one
people and form together one nation. This principle shall be kept steadily
in view by the Holy See, which, in consequence, will, in the number of
bishops, adhere strictly to the rules of the Baltimore Council.[39]

It is not surprising that the controversy attracted the attention of
the government. It formed the subject of a conversation between
Cardinal Gibbons and President Benjamin Harrison in July, 1892.
The President said that he regarded it "as a subject of deep importance to our country at large, one in which the American people are
much concerned. Foreign and unauthorized interference with American affairs cannot be viewed with indifference."[40] It also made its
appearance in the halls of Congress, where Senator Cushman K.
Davis declared that "there is more matter for profound concern in
the attempts of Herr Cahensly last year to denationalize American
institutions and plant as many nations as there are people of foreign
tongues in our midst, than in all the Chinese questions which have
arisen since 1858." In the course of his address he took occasion to
praise highly Leo XIII as "the greatest Pope since Ganganelli
[Clement XIV]." He told Ireland that his remarks had attracted unusual attention from the senators and that he had received many
thanks from very conservative members of both parties for his discussion of the matter.[41]

There is little doubt that Davis' action was inspired; Ireland wished
to counteract the influence of the German government by that of
the United States. As O'Connell wrote to him: "It is my opinion that
the only way to convince officials here, once for all, that all this excitement was not false thunder, is if the Government were to speak.
Then no doubt would remain about the mind of Americans."[42] For
his statement Davis was bitterly attacked at the national convention
of the German Benevolent Society in Dubuque in September.[43]

The other side of Cahenslyism appears in a letter which Bishop
Sebastian Messmer of Green Bay wrote to the *State Gazette*, saying
that Cahenslyism as set forth by Ireland was a bugbear and never
existed, merely a phantom called forth from its dark hiding place for
a purpose and by constant misrepresentation still kept before the
public; that the continued cry of a "Luzern Conspiracy," or of "foreign
political interference" in ecclesiastical affairs, or of a "double or
multiple jurisdiction" according to the various nationalities, or of
the preponderance of "foreigners" as against "Americans" in the
hierarchy was the utterance either of a man suffering from hallucina-

tion or of an evil mind. The memorial presented to the Holy See (not to the Triple Alliance) by the St. Raphael's Society was, he said, nothing more than an attempt to provide with the help and approval of the highest ecclesiastical (not political) power more ample and efficient measures for the spiritual and religious care of Catholic emigrants.[44]

This, however, was not the view of many of the bishops, who were quite outspoken in their estimate of its danger. Bishop John Foley of Detroit wrote of the tremendous excitement caused by "that scoundrel Cahensly, who by his infamous lies has done immense harm to religion in this country," and of the violent attacks made on him in the press.[45] Bishop John Brondel of Helena regarded Cahenslyism as "the greatest insult that could be made to the Church in the United States."[46] Archbishop William Gross of Portland, Oregon, referred to "the horrible move initiated by Herr Cahensly," and to "that disgusting and diabolical nationalism hatched in Milwaukee, which already has done grievous mischief."[47] Bishop John Moore of St. Augustine told O'Connell that the president of the German Catholic Union made the prophecy, at their meeting in Toledo, that in fifteen years the Germans would control the political parties in this country and that they would remain German in language and manners, in spite of the Anglo-American bishops, who would have them become one with the American people. "Evidently," he said, "we did not misinterpret their sentiments."[48]

In his interview with a representative of the Boston *Pilot* in Rome, after telling of the determination of the Vatican to maintain the hierarchical unity of the Church in America, which, he said, did not prevent constant renewal of efforts, Ireland stated that Canadian bishops were urging that they be given charge over their nationals in New England, because the faith of the latter was being imperiled there; that a Polish movement was on foot in Rome to gather the Polish Catholics in the United States into one religious party distinct from existing ecclesiastical groupings; that Monsignor de Concilio of Jersey City was writing pamphlets deploring the neglect of Italian nationals in America, and that even the Greek Catholics were trying to secure national bishops in the United States.[49]

The charge was made, and received some credence in Rome, that Archbishop Ireland was purposely keeping alive the national question for his own ends and using it as a red herring to divert attention from his difficulties in the school question. O'Connell told him that in Rome he was regarded as the man who made all this hollow thunder, using false telegrams of the Associated Press for that purpose, that no one saw all the reasons for preoccupation that Ireland saw, and that it was considered simply an effort to frighten the Holy See and the Germans and to keep them from their share of the places. He was represented as opposed to the Germans on account of his total abstinence and his favor of the public schools. "But," the Monsignor added, "the authorities here never read nor thought of reading the tide of indignation that flowed through the American Press."[50]

The charge, however, is not easily substantiated, and it would appear that no one regretted the resurgence of the controversy as much as Ireland. In August, 1892, he wrote: "Another misfortune, Conway [the editor of the diocesan paper, the *Northwestern Chronicle*] has written for the *Review of Reviews* a scathing article on Cahenslyism. He brings up all the old cablegrams about Von Schloesser's interference in Katzer's nomination and accuses the Verein of un-Americanism, naming right and left Zardetti, Wigger." When Katzer told the Archbishop that he would appeal to Rome, Ireland replied that he would join him so as to know what could be done with Catholic writers who attacked bishops, as he had suffered immensely from Katzer's official German paper. "I am thinking," he said, "of sending off Conway; he is reckless, erratic, and I'm accused of what he writes in spite of me."[51]

Moreover, Ireland in his interviews to the press, his addresses to German societies, and his sermons was careful to separate the material from the spiritual aspects of the question, to disclaim any hostility toward people of foreign origin. He also took advantage of the opportunities afforded him by his episcopal visitations at a meeting of German societies at Chaska, Minnesota, and at the consecration of Bishop Trobec of St. Cloud, to defend himself against charges of prejudice and of interference in the teaching of German, and also to point out to the German people that in his opposition to Cahensly he was consulting not only the interests of the nation but also those of their children.

What Cahenslyism would have meant for America is well brought out in a letter which the Archbishop received from Father John Murphy, C.S.Sp., later Titular Bishop of Mauritius and Superior of the Fathers of the Holy Ghost. Father Murphy felt that an article in the *Moniteur de Rome*, in March, 1892, which had referred to the attack on Ireland as a perfidious campaign, "one of those Machiavellian strategies which the history of the Church has so often witnessed," did not go to the bottom of the malicious hostility directed against him. It was sad, he said, to see the torrents of venom which the German clique continued to pour out against him. Yet his policy was the only logical one for the Church and for the Germans themselves. If the Church were split up into foreign factions, it would lose its influence and court hostility. If the present policy of German-born priests had its way, German Catholics would be practically excluded from their legitimate sphere of influence in the nation, or they would drift into religious indifferentism. Even German parents would not long tolerate that their children be brought up in practical ignorance of that English language which alone would supply them their bread and butter. Nor would they long tolerate foreign parochial schools. The Italian priests in Pittsburgh were already making provision for the ultimate replacement of Italian.[52]

In this, as in subsequent controversies, the fine hand of the Archbishop of New York is apparent. Numbered among the resolute opponents of Cahenslyism, he seemed to subordinate his opposition to it to his jealousy of Archbishop Ireland and to his desire to thwart him at every point. In a letter to him dated October 31, 1892, Cahensly quotes with approval an attack on Archbishop Ireland made by a friend in Paris, which referred to the Archbishop's "dangerous and rationalistic ideas." In Cahensly's mind, the question at stake was "whether in the United States the principles of the Church [as represented by Cahenslyism] would gain the victory over the liberalism of Ireland and his colleagues." He felt that "at the next meeting of Catholic Archbishops it would not be very difficult to your Grace to convince your Most Reverend brother Bishops of the dangerous and, to the Church, so pernicious tendencies of Monsignor Ireland, so to effect his isolation."[53] Corrigan maintained correspondence with Cahensly, and also with Monsignor Joseph Schroeder and Dr. Joseph Pohle of the Catholic University, who addressed the Congress of German Catholics at Mainz, Germany, praising the work of Cahensly. The New York prelate addressed a German congress in Newark, New Jersey, in September, 1892, expressing his conviction there there was nothing political in Cahenslyism, which was intended solely for the spiritual welfare of the immigrant.[54] He must have forgotten that it was he who in December, 1886, not only had suggested a meeting of the archbishops to draw up a protest, and drafted the letter, but also had written sharply to Cahensly in July, 1891.

The contention of Archbishop Ireland that other nationalists would demand the same privileges as the Germans is borne out by a letter from Bishop Edward Fitzgerald of Little Rock, who said that a petition signed by forty-three French priests of New Orleans was sent to Mlle Lucie Faure, daughter of the French President, with the request that she present it in Rome through the Minister of Foreign Affairs, M. Haniteaux, and that she go to Rome and personally use her influence for the appointment of a French archbishop. He felt that if such action were permitted by the archbishops, European governments would claim the right of "Presentation" to dioceses in the United States, and thus the American Church would become the object of political intrigues in the courts of Europe.[55] The Polish priests in Chicago also demanded that Polish bishops be appointed to look after their fellow countrymen in the United States, one of them going so far as to urge President Cleveland to plead their cause in Rome.[56]

The charges of the Germans that "Irish" bishops and priests were shutting out from their episcopal lists the names of Germans were met by counterassertions on the part of the "Irish" that in such dioceses as Milwaukee and Cincinnati "Irish" priests received no consideration. Again, the formation of such clerical unions as the Deutscher Verein prompted similar unions among the English-speaking clergy. And thus the Church was constantly torn apart by dissensions and robbed of that unity which was so sorely needed.

The controversy developed bitterness which was to follow Archbishop Ireland during most of his life. Reverend Henry Tappert, in an address which was aimed at Archbishop Ireland and which shows the interrelation of nationalism, the school question, and Americanism, said to the General Convention of German Catholics at Cologne at their session of August 26, 1894:

Since our enemies kept up their sorry courage to concentrate their criminal attacks on a man from the Centre, who had been highly useful to the German Catholic emigrants, you will permit me to explain our attitude towards the ecclesiastics and religio-political questions which have so prominently occupied the Catholic mind recently in the United States. Our great enemy is liberalism, the denial of the social kingdom of Christ on earth. This great heresy of our time is three-fold; first, avowed unbelief; second, social rationalism; last, but not least, an ecclesiastical liberalism which here and there blocks our way. It holds sway over certain Catholics who have inscribed on their banner: "Union of the Church with the Age, with modern ideas, with Americanism." Hence the extolling of modern liberties, not as a requisite for a justified tolerance, but as the ideal of political and ecclesiastical wisdom, hence the more than sparing attitude of this third kind of liberalism towards the secret societies; hence the unreasonable breaking away from sane Catholic tradition in the temperance and liquor question; hence, finally, that coquetting with a more or less general all-embracing Christianity to which a far-reaching expression was given at the Chicago religious parliament of unholy memory. From the same source originate those fulsome praises for the public schools, and that ridiculous boastfulness about Americanism, which is not ashamed to reproach foreign-born co-religionists with an attachment to the language and customs of their fathers, and brand them publicly as being opposed to the English language, and devoid of love for country.[57]

It is no wonder that Father William McGucken, S.J., remarked: "Catholic critics seemed to dip their pens in gall when they attacked Archbishop Ireland."[58]

Three years later, O'Connell, who was convinced that the cause of Americanism was suffering from the antagonisms and passions aroused in former controversies, advised Ireland to take the ground from under the small clique of Germans in the United States who, chafing under their defeat in the national question, tried to represent him as waging war on all Germans. He reminded him that he had many friends not only among the German people in Europe and America but also among the Jesuits. He instanced the enthusiasm manifested for him by the leaders of the congress at Freiburg.[59]

Accepting his advice, the Archbishop preached in St. Patrick's Church, Washington, on March 26, 1897, a sermon which was a reply to his adversaries. Using the term "refractaires," the word which Pope Leo used of those who refused to follow his French policy, he said that they were to be found where least expected—in America. Divisions among Catholics in America were not in strict matters of faith, but in tendencies and movements, in adaptation of action to modern circumstances—the policy of Leo. Loyal Catholics and refractaires are confined to no race, language, or color. "I would scorn," he said, "to draw distinctions among Catholics because of race or language. I am, I must be, as Catholic as is God's Church. I differ from men, I war with men on account of ideas, not on account of race."[60]

This address Monsignor O'Connell regarded as one of the Archbishop's best. It was, he said, a throwing down of walls which the refractaires had erected against them; it prevented them from making capital out of pharisaical orthodoxy and won many friends in Germany.

Catholic America has reason to be grateful to Archbishop Ireland. Although the vast majority of the bishops felt as he did, he alone bore the brunt of the controversy, he alone had to withstand the attacks of the adversary. If it were only that he saved the Church from embarrassment and suspicion in 1917, when the United States entered the war against Germany, Catholics owe him a debt of gratitude. And if the Church in the United States was saved from European influence, and if the various national groups were ultimately fused into a compact whole, throbbing with vitality, conscious of power that comes from absolute unity, and presenting an unbroken front to the world, it is in large measure due to the man who could see further than other men, and who saved the Church and the country from foreignism. As the New York *Times* pointed out, about twenty-four million immigrants had come to America, many of them from Germany, Austria-Hungary, Italy, and Poland (the actual statistics show 25,985,237 between 1820 and June 30, 1907). Adding the children and grandchildren of Catholic immigrants, one can grasp some measure of the *Imperium in imperio* which would have been firmly rooted here at the outbreak of the European war in 1914 if the tide had not been checked at its source. As the *Times* said:

The Cahensly movement was a direct outgrowth of Pan-Germanism. Cahensly and his associates had succeeded in allying with themselves Italian Catholics under the leadership of Marchese Volpe-Landi and French Catholics whose champion was Abbé Villeneuve. Many who recall the struggle in the eighties and early nineties do not hesitate to say that it is due to Ireland and Gibbons more than to any other men in the United States, that the country went to war with so great a degree of solidarity against the government of one of the great peoples from which the American nation sprang.[61]

Cahenslyism struck at the very life of the country as a compact whole and would have set up innumerable factions prejudiced against one another and ignorant of the principles of the government under which they lived. It would have set up an episcopacy within an episcopacy and thus opened the way to jurisdictional disputes. It would have deferred indefinitely the unification and Americanization of the Catholic population and caused grave suspicions about its loyalty.

The legislation enacted by the Holy See in the question of parochial jurisdiction was designed to solve the problems arising from the care of various groups, viz.:

1. Decree of the Sacred Congregation of the Propaganda issued April 26, 1897, and communicated by the Apostolic Delegate to the Bishops of the United States May 12, 1897. As published in the *American Ecclesiastical Review*, Vol. XVII, July, 1897, page 87:

    I. The children of parents not born in America, speaking a language different from English, are not obliged when they attain their majority to become affiliated with the quasi-parish to which their parents belong, but enjoy the right to unite with the parish in which the language of the country, namely English, is used.

    II. Catholics who have not been born in America but know the English language have the right to become members of that church in which the English language is in use, nor can they be obliged to submit to the jurisdiction of the Rector of a church established for a people speaking the language of their own country.[62]

2. Canon 216, Code of Canon Law (May 19, 1918):

    The territory of each diocese shall be divided into distinct territorial sections, and each section shall have its own church to which the Catholic population of the district shall be assigned. The parts or sections of a diocese are called parishes.

    Without special permission from the Holy See parishes may not be established that are not divided by territory but by the difference of language of the people in the same town or city. It is likewise forbidden to establish purely personal parishes for certain classes of people or parishes for certain families. As to already established parishes of this category nothing shall be changed without consulting the Holy See.

Cahenslyism, as Archbishop Ireland said, is dead, but the bitterness lingers on. Like all controversial matters it is difficult to evaluate, because passions ran high on both sides and both were guilty of excesses. Although Cahensly wrote bitterly of Ireland's so-called "liberalism" and grossly exaggerated the losses in the Church, there seems to be little doubt that he was a man of fine character, who enjoyed the respect not only of the German episcopate but also of Archbishop Ireland in later years. When he came to the United States in 1910, he and Ireland co-operated in the newly formed Catholic Colonization Society. At that time he insisted that he was finally doing what he had advocated in 1891—placing immigrants in colonies where they would not lose their faith. He told Father Max Groesser, S.A.C., Secretary-General of the Raphaelsverein, that on his visit in 1924 he was informed by Archbishop Messmer that both Gibbons and Ireland had admitted that they had made a mistake in regard to him. Messmer also publicly made this declaration at the 67th Convention of the Central Verein in Milwaukee. Archbishop Antonio Agliardi, when Papal Nuncio to Germany, told Cahensly of the sympathy of the Holy Father in what he was suffering; Leo XIII blessed his work in 1902, as also did Pius X in 1904.[63] It was unfortunate that his name became somewhat of a fetish and a war cry in the fight over nationalism. But if he suffered from the exaggerations of his opponents, so did Ireland, to whom a German-American Catholic Congress held in Dubuque, Iowa, in September, 1892, paid tribute and referred as "the much misunderstood and misrepresented prelate of St. Paul." When Ireland completed fifty years in the priesthood, Archbishop Messmer sent to him these gracious words:

Permit me on this occasion to say how sorely disappointed I was at the news that the dignity of Cardinal had not been bestowed upon you. I made no secret of my deep regret & I am glad to say that in these sentiments I am not the only one among German-American bishops in the U.S. Bishop Fox of Green Bay is quite strong in his expressions. While for many years, as you are well aware, German-American Catholics had not very much love for the Archbishop of St. Paul, I am only too happy to state that that sentiment has changed very much of late. There are more than one reason for that. I have spoken with a number of German-American priests and laymen who were unanimous in expressing their disappointment that the red hat had not landed in St. Paul. I, for one, will hope for the happy event in the not far future.[64]

Chapter 5

THE SCHOOL QUESTION

1. THE ARCHBISHOP STATES HIS POSITION

In July, 1890, the National Education Association of the United States held its annual convention in St. Paul. The address[1] which Archbishop Ireland delivered on the occasion, dealing with State and parochial schools, gave rise to a controversy that extended far and wide through the United States, aroused keen interest in European countries, and required Vatican action to bring to a close. The Archbishop began by laying down as a fundamental principle not only the right but also the necessity of the State school to exist. "The child," he said, "must have instruction and in no mean degree, if the man is to earn for himself an honest competence and acquit himself of the duties which, for its own life and prosperity, society exacts from all its members." While pointing out that the care of the child's mind as well as of its body is committed to the parents by divine appointment, he emphasized the fact that tens of thousands of children would remain uninstructed if the task of their education rested solely on the parents. Without State action universal instruction would have been impossible in any country; hence the necessity of free schools. "Free schools!" he exclaimed. "Blest indeed is the nation whose vales and hillsides they adorn, and blest the generations upon whose souls are poured their treasures." "No task," he declared, "is more legitimate than that which is levied in order to dispel mental darkness and build up within the nation's bosom intelligent manhood and womanhood."

The Archbishop then proceeded to declare his faith in compulsory education, for "instruction is so necessary for the sake of the individual and of society that the parent who neglects to provide it sins against the child and against society and should be punished by the State." All this the Archbishop emphasized while conceding that instruction is primarily the function of the parent, who, he said, "possesses the right to educate his child in the manner agreeable to

79

himself, provided always that the education given in this manner suffices to fit the child for his ulterior duties to society." Compulsory instruction he restricted to circumstances where children do not attend other schools known to be competent to impart instruction. Indeed, he found fault with compulsory laws recently enacted in certain states as objectionable in some clauses.

Because of the value of the instruction imparted by the American State school, he hailed it as the pride and glory of the country. "The Republic of the United States," he said, "has solemnly affirmed that within its borders no clouds of ignorance shall settle upon the minds of its children." Then came the words which, especially when torn from their context, brought such a storm of criticism on the Archbishop: "The free school in America. Withered be the hand raised in sign of its destruction."

Having paid tribute to the public schools, he proceeded to formulate in no uncertain terms his grievance against them on the ground that they made no provision for instruction in religion, but rather tended to eliminate it from the minds and hearts of the youth of the country. The school dealt with immature, childish nature, upon which silent facts and examples make deepest impression. It treated of land and sea but not of heaven; it spoke of statesmen and warriors but not of God and Christ. Fireside lessons in religion or attendance at Sunday school could never make up for the lack of religion. Indeed, he pointed out, "the State school crowds out the Church." And so great multitudes of children are growing up without religion. And while the children of the masses are learning no religion, that of thousands of adults is the merest veneering of mind and heart—"not the religion that built up our Christian civilization in the past and that will subjugate passion and repress vice. It is not the religion that will guard the family and save society." He likewise deplored the inability of the public school to teach morals, for it is from the principles of religion that morals derive vitality.

Next came the question to which the Archbishop's address naturally paved the way: Ought we not to have religious instruction in connection with the school? "It is manifest," he declared, "that dissatisfaction exists with the State school because of its exclusion of religion. This dissatisfaction, founded on conscience, will continue until the cause of it is removed."

At this point he launched into a denunciation of the injustices to which Catholics are subjected. It was no honor to America, he said, that ten millions of its people were forced by law to pay taxes for the support of schools to which their conscience does not give approval; that they were, furthermore, compelled by their zeal for the religious instruction of their children to build schools of their own and to pay their own teachers. It was no honor to the American Republic that she, more than any other nation, was eager to keep religion away from the schools. No nation went in this direction as far as ours. It was a terrible experiment upon which we had entered; the very life of our civilization and of our country was at stake.

For the first solution of the school problem in the United States the Archbishop directed the attention of his audience to the plans adopted in England, where the secular education given in denominational schools is paid for in whole or in part from public funds. In this way "every pupil passing the examination before State officials and in full accord with the State program would secure to his school the cost of the tuition of a pupil in the State school."

As a second solution he proposed the so-called Poughkeepsie plan —a plan in vogue in many cities throughout the country—according to which the school board rented parochial schools during school hours, paid the salaries of the teachers, and conducted examinations of teachers and pupils, "the door being always open to superintendent and members of the board."

In conclusion, he protested vigorously against the charge that the schools of the nation had their enemies among the Catholics. "Catholics," he said, "demand the Christian State school and, in doing so, prove themselves truest friends of the school and of the State."

2. REACTION HERE AND ABROAD

So violent was the attack launched against the address from various quarters that the rumble of the war it stirred up reached Rome. One of the first of Ireland's statements to cause comment was his advocacy of compulsory education. On this point he explained his real position in a telegram sent to Father Keough of Milwaukee, in which he said that, while he favored compulsory education, he did not have in mind compulsory education in State schools; he wished the rights of parents to choose the mode of education to be sacredly guarded. It was, therefore, he averred, incorrect to say that "he favored the public school system, whilst the highest Roman authority was opposed to the common schools." He favored State schools, in which the State controls and pays for secular education, provided that they offered religious instruction. Hence it was false to say that he disagreed with his superiors in the Church. He protested against the Catholics who had done as much as some non-Catholics to misconstrue his words, and he asserted that he was speaking only about conditions in Minnesota and did not refer to the situation in Wisconsin, where the Bennett Law was causing much indignation.[2]

The first intimation of trouble in Rome came to the Archbishop from Monsignor Denis O'Connell, Rector of the North American College, who wrote in August, 1890: "Now you have a little case yourself before the Propaganda—a little case of doctrine, your last speech. It was sent from America to the Congregation of the Council, and thence to the Propaganda, and Sbarretti is translating it *'per un po di esercizio pure di lingua inglese'* into Italian for the priests that make up the Congresso or maybe for the *Padri Cardinali*." O'Connell explained to the Cardinal Prefect the nature of the address, saying that the only difference between Ireland's utterance on the public schools and utterances of others in the Church was that he did not inveigh against them. It was the fashion of some priests to denounce them as "hotbeds of vice" and "sources of corruption," language which offended American sentiments.[3]

O'Connell kept his friend constantly informed on the situation and on the reactions of the leaders of the Church. When Cardinal Simeoni, Prefect of Propaganda, told him of the protests that continued to come in against the address, the Monsignor said that this was merely an indication of a serious state of affairs, and that Ireland understood better than many other bishops in the country that the burden of the parochial schools was crushing the pastors.[4]

In a later interview Archbishop Domenico Jacobini, Secretary of Propaganda, informed the Rector that the "writers of the protests were not those who usually write—Corrigan, McQuaid, Chatard— but rather some Germans and some priests." He also expressed the opinion that it might be *"fatale"* to act on these protests against a bishop like Ireland, particularly in view of the acquiescence of the other bishops.[5]

O'Connell must have been much perturbed, because he informed Cardinal Gibbons that Simeoni seemed greatly troubled over the address, and that a prelate "whom you know" referred to it as a very delicate matter that required immediate attention, as some of the Cardinals were wildly excited over it.[6] Gibbons, in turn, expressed his regret for the severe handling which the Archbishop had received from some Catholic papers, as he was really a power in the country, had more public influence than a half-dozen of his neighbors, and had done more than any other prelate to elevate and advance the Catholic religion in the United States. "Protestants," he said, "regard him as a fearless and uncompromising champion of the Catholic faith, and Catholics venerate him as a grand and eloquent exponent of their religion." He had built up the Province of St. Paul as hardly any other man could have done. "Had he been a dumb dog," he said, "no whelps would have barked at him here."[7]

Ireland thanked the Cardinal for "extending over him at the first sign of danger the shield of his powerful influence," at the same time regretting that "some of our own men are so ready to slay the bishops."[8]

Matters were finally brought to a head by a request from Cardinal Rampolla to the Cardinal of Baltimore asking his opinion of the address.[9] Gibbons immediately communicated with Ireland, who promised to put his discourse into French and to expose the real meaning of it.[10] This he did in December, telling his reasons for making the address—to indicate the cause of Catholic opposition to State schools and to allay angry feelings between Catholics and non-Catholics which were due to exaggerations on the part of one and prejudice on the part of the other. He showed how the meaning of some of his statements which had been severely criticized had been distorted. His statement, "Free schools! Blest indeed is the nation whose vales and hillsides they adorn," was taken to mean that he regarded the free schools as perfect, whereas he was speaking of free schools in the abstract, free instruction for all. He pointed out that he had devoted two-thirds of his discourse to his reasons for dissatisfaction with the public-school system. His expression, "I repeat my regret that there is the necessity for its [the parish school] existence," was taken to mean that he was opposed to it, whereas he meant that if the State school were properly organized and if it granted to Catholic children all that was needed for the protection of the State there would be no need for the parish school. The Church was not established to teach writing and ciphering but morals and faith. He then indicated what he demanded of the State school—positive Catholic dogmatic teaching. This was the really important part of his discourse, but one totally ignored by his opponents. He was also criticized for saying that he did not wish to see in America the ground which Protestantism occupied exposed to the devastating blast of unbelief.

But in this he had the support of Manning and Newman, who believed that factional Christianity is better than materialism. He regretted denunciation of the public schools, and he said that in places where bishops were severe against them their parish schools had done more harm than good. The system which he favored was the Poughkeepsie plan, the Irish system in vogue for forty years. He concluded by offering to explain or, if necessary, withdraw any statement which Rome might criticize.[11]

Using the material contained in this letter, Gibbons wrote to the Holy Father, telling of Ireland's zeal for education as manifested in the number of parochial schools in his diocese, in the development of his Seminary, and in his furthering of two Catholic congresses. He did not regard the campaign conducted against Ireland as founded alone on a disinterested love of truth or on pure zeal for sound doctrine.[12]

The state of mind in some quarters in Rome was indicated by O'Connell, who reported that Archbishop Domenico Jacobini had said to Monsignor Boeglin that there were eight archbishops in the United States, all liberals, with Ireland at their head; that three were very obedient to the Holy See, the so-called *Intransegenti*; that he must not encourage the liberals, or attack them, for they were most powerful, especially Ireland.[13] This news surprised Ireland, who had always regarded Jacobini as a friend.[14]

When Gibbons learned from O'Connell that all was well, he expressed the hope that the Pope would approve Ireland's course, as a rebuke to those who questioned the soundness of his views.[15] Reassured that there was no further need of apprehension, the Archbishop expressed his joy at the outcome, giving grateful appreciation to Gibbons but, at the same time, hoping that the Pope would be cautious in his language and not awaken the old fear of Roman interference which lay deep in many an American breast. He had been disturbed by rumors of certain suspicions in Rome, and he regretted that bishops had to assume an attitude of subservience. "Well," he concluded, "principle and conscience will stand by us."[16]

The school question might have been forgotten had not two incidents given it new life—the Faribault plan and Dr. Thomas Bouquillon's pamphlet on education.

The Archbishop had implemented his educational theories by making an arrangement with the school boards of Faribault and Stillwater by which, in consideration of the nominal sum of one dollar per year, the parochial school building, during the hours devoted to secular knowledge, was to be regarded as a State school, preserving its character as a parochial school before and after school hours. On August 26, 1891, Father James Conry, pastor of the Church of the Immaculate Conception, Faribault, submitted to the Board of Education of that city a letter embodying the proposal outlined. The proposal was accepted, and in this manner the parish was relieved of the burden of supporting the school, which retained its own teachers and its Catholic tone. The children heard Mass and received religious instruction. Outside of Father Conry's letter, there was no formal arrangement, merely a tacit understanding. A similar arrangement was made in Stillwater in October, 1891.[17]

The plan was an attempt to solve one of the most serious problems besetting the Church in America. Of the 2,200,000 Catholics in the country, not more than 725,000 were enrolled in Catholic schools; in New York only 42,000 out of 150,000. How could a million and a half Catholic children be brought under religious instruction, into contact with priest and nun? How could our people in poor parishes be relieved of the heavy burden of building and maintaining schools? In many dioceses, in fact in ten states, a similar plan had been in operation for years. It was only when it was set up in Minnesota that it raised a storm of opposition. It met opposition from two quarters— Protestant ministers, who saw in it a plot to secure a subsidy for sectarian schools, and Catholics, who felt that it would undermine the parochial-school system. The Archbishop could not hope to generalize the plan, but he could hope that in favorable conditions, such as existed in Stearns County in the Diocese of St. Cloud, many struggling parishes might, without sacrificing any Catholic principles, receive the State aid to which, in justice, they were entitled.

The experiment only added fuel to the fire and intensified the controversy, which was the subject of editorials in the Catholic press, such papers as the *Freeman's Journal* and the *Northwestern Chronicle* favoring the plan, the Baltimore *Catholic Mirror* and the Milwaukee *Catholic Citizen* opposing it.

The Archbishop found himself in a singular predicament. He was between two enemies—one Catholic, the other Protestant. If he stated all the concessions made to Catholic schools, he would bring upon himself the wrath of anti-Catholic bigots; if he defended his plan against Protestants, Catholic extremists would become alarmed.[18] The truth was, as Maurice Francis Egan said, that Ireland was years ahead of his time.

If the Archbishop's address before the National Education Association convention aroused clashing comments in educational circles, the storm which it provoked was only a gale in comparison with the tempest of denunciation which a pamphlet—the first of three—entitled *Education, to Whom Does It Belong?* [19] published by Dr. Thomas Bouquillon, Professor of Moral Theology at the Catholic University, brought down upon its author. His position may be summarized as follows: Every man has the right to communicate truth after the fashion that is most efficacious and best adapted to those who wish to receive it. If the right belongs to individuals, it belongs also to individuals collected in legitimate association and fitted to teach. Such a right is, of course, subordinate to the action of legitimate authority, civil and religious. Among all who have a right to teach, parents hold by nature the right of giving education to their offspring, of developing their children's physical, mental, and moral faculties. This right is, like that of individuals, limited and subject to the control of authority, civil and religious, so that the possibility of deleterious training be completely eliminated.

The civil authority also has the right to teach, because, for the promotion of the common good, knowledge is a prime necessity. Indeed, it has not only the right but the duty to teach, and it can compel parents to fulfill their duty in the matter of educating their children. It can even make education compulsory, although it cannot make its own schools obligatory if the parents choose other schools.

As to the Church—she has received from her Divine Founder the mission to teach supernatural truths, but her duty of imparting merely human science is indirect, a work of charity when human science is insufficiently taught by others, a work of necessity when it is opposed to supernatural truth and morality. She has to do with the teaching of letters, sciences, and arts only in so far as they come in contact with faith and morals. Dr. Bouquillon summed up his position in these words: "Education belongs to the individual, physical and moral, to the family, to the State, to the Church; to none of them solely and exclusively, but to all four combined in harmonious working, for the reason that man is not an isolated but a social being."

Bouquillon's pamphlet evoked expressions of approval from various writers, who pronounced it "a splendid specimen of reasoning."[20] But, while its clarity of thought and diction, adorned with erudite quotations from the writings of such great authorities as St. Thomas and Suarez, stamped it as an ideal presentation of an essential case, it also soon summoned from the press pamphlets and articles that strove with a vast semblance of learning to refute the claims made for the right of the State to educate. *The Parent First*, a bitter reply by the Reverend René Holaind, S.J., was rushed into print with breathless haste by its author, because he feared that Bouquillon's pamphlet would influence the archbishops of the country, who were about to hold their annual meeting at St. Louis in the month of December, 1891.[21] But the prelates took no notice of it. Neither did they say a word of criticism of the Faribault plan which Archbishop Ireland presented to them when asked by Cardinal Gibbons. As the Cardinal wrote to O'Connell: "After Ireland's explanation and his answers, not one of the Archbishops offered a word of blame; many were explicit in approval."[22] Bishop Spalding said that the right of the State to see that all acquire the rudiments of letters was "so plain a case that argument becomes ridiculous."[23]

The campaign launched by Father Holaind was continued by other Jesuits, who regarded Bouquillon as the one serious advocate of State control in the United States, whose principles would work irreparable harm to the Catholic school system. As we read articles and pamphlets written by Father E. A. Higgins, S.J., Father J. Conway, S.J., and Father D. T. Sullivan, S.J., and as we read the two rejoinders in which Dr. Bouquillon criticized the endless attacks made upon him, we realize how reasonable was the remark made by Father James J. Loughlin of Philadelphia: "To me, the whole discussion looks like a raging tempest in a very diminutive teapot. There is just the faintest appearance of the ridiculous coming to light in the accumulation of pamphlets and rejoinders."[24]

Although Dr. Herman Heuser's *Ecclesiastical Review* manifested its animus in several articles, the journal that poured the most vitriolic poison on Bouquillon and that showed itself the bitterest enemy of Ireland was the *Civiltà Cattolica*, the most prominent Jesuit organ in Europe. Only a few months before Bouquillon published his first pamphlet it hailed him as one of the great thinkers of the age, giving him the title *"sommo maestro."* In his famous *Theologia Moralis*, which won such praise for him, he had formulated precisely the same principles which, when presented in his first pamphlet, called forth unpardonable acrimony from the *Civiltà Cattolica*. In the December, 1891, and the January, February, and April, 1892, numbers of that organ, seven articles appeared, maintaining that in condemning him it reflected the universal voice of Catholics and of sensible thinkers, whose hearts were profoundly wounded by the events narrated. In a long article slashing the Faribault plan, it stated that the Sister Superior of the Stillwater school was removed by the Board of Education and that forty children of the Faribault parish school had been removed among the public schools to receive lay instruction, not from the sisters but from Protestants and infidels—both items absolutely false.

Not all the Jesuits were on the side of the opposition. Father Walter Hill, who admired the Archbishop, wrote to Mr. Charles Hardy, pointing out that some writers were misquoting the encyclical *Sapientiae*, inserting a clause which was not found in the encyclical, and misusing the word "education." Some writers rambled far from the true issue, so that it was not surprising that, with much pains, they proved what Dr. Bouquillon did not deny and refuted what he did not assert. Civil education, he averred, is not included among "divine things" but is in the class of human things. Every civilized nation from the earliest period of history has claimed and exercised some authority over the civil education of its citizens. Such concurrent judgment of nations concerning a natural duty of civil government is not erroneous.[25]

In December, 1891, Cardinal Gibbons told O'Connell of the meeting of the archbishops in St. Louis, which was attended by all the prelates from the thirteen provinces, and of his request to Archbishop Ireland to explain to them the Faribault system. He recounted the willingness of the Archbishop to discontinue the plan if his colleagues so advised. After Ireland had answered the questions which were asked, no one advised his abandoning the experiment. In fact, there was a triumphant vindication of his course.[26]

As accounts of the growing bitterness of the controversy continued to reach Rome, the Pope wrote to Gibbons asking more complete details of the meeting. The Cardinal repeated the account which he had given to O'Connell, adding that many of the prelates were most explicit in their approval of the system. This, he said, was particularly true of Archbishop John J. Williams of Boston, who congratulated Ireland on the results obtained and expressed the wish that he could install a similar arrangement in his diocese.

The experiment, he said, was not new; it was already in vogue in several dioceses. No objections had been raised against the others, but now Monsignor Ireland's enemies were bitterly attempting to ruin his prestige in Rome. The Cardinal felt that the silence of the Holy See on this question would be interpreted as a virtual condemnation of Monsignor Ireland, which would excite the national sentiment and might lead to harassing measures against Catholics in school questions. He hoped, therefore, that the Holy Father would show to the American public his confidence in the Archbishop of St. Paul.[27]

After an article had appeared in the New York *Herald*, on December 13, 1891, professing to give the inside story of the meeting of the archbishops, the Archbishop denied that Holaind's pamphlet had been discussed, at the same time paying his respects to it as a collection of all the antique and un-American notions he could get hold of. He denied that the Faribault plan was a surrender of Catholic principles, and he said that the Protestant ministers who sought to prevent the Church from protecting the faith of its children would be much better employed in securing religious instruction for their own. Father Holaind, "who could not distinguish between education and instruction," and who held that it could not be proved by natural law that parents can be compelled to give their children a knowledge of the three R's, he regarded as a source of danger to the Church in that Americans might take his utterances as a statement of Catholic doctrine.[28] Archbishop Ireland's ability to hit hard made him a very effective controversialist, but unfortunately it also made him many bitter enemies. He had now definitely thrown down the gage, and the war would be fought to a finish.

Because of the many attacks, O'Connell urged the Archbishop to come to Rome and plead in person his cause, "to confirm this new turn of events and pull up the old by the roots."[29] Ireland accepted his advice, but before leaving, he took a page out of the book of his adversaries and showed that two could play the game. Through Monsignor Eugene Boeglin, Catholic correspondent, and O'Connell he arranged that a cablegram from Berlin would appear in the press, reviewing the policy of the Church toward State schools in the principal countries of Europe, showing that it recognized the right of the State in primary education and did not refuse the Sacraments to parents who sent their children to public schools in which their faith and morals were protected, and that, moreover, the Continental system had the approval of the Catholic citizens.[30]

He sailed for Europe on January 16, 1892, and after a visit to the social congress at Liége arrived in Rome only to be presented with a list of charges made against him. These he later answered in the memorial he presented.

The Archbishop kept his friends informed on his progress in Rome. To Father Louis Caillet, his Vicar-General, he wrote of the action of the Holy Father, who, taking the matter out of the routine of the Congregations, appointed for its consideration a special commission of five cardinals, who gave decision favorable to the Faribault plan. While they were in session, the Pope sent word that he desired their decision to be brought to him at once, interrupted his audiences, approved it, and expressed his joy that the Archbishop had been sustained. There must have been many anxious moments, for Ireland told of the powerful opposition of the Jesuits, who threw their whole strength against him. He said: "They say all round that in the memory of man no bishop has come to Rome who was able to triumph against such fearful odds. I give all to God—something to friends and to hard labor on my part, and much to public American sentiment, which Rome understands well is back of me."[31]

To Cardinal Gibbons he wrote of his audience with the Pope, who was most affectionate, eulogistic, and familiar, and who discussed with him social questions in which he was much interested, especially his encyclical on labor, which, fortunately, the Archbishop knew almost by heart. He told of his efforts to protect Bouquillon, of the notes which he sent to the Holy Father in his defense, of the friendship of Cardinal Rampolla for himself and Bouquillon. He said:

He is the dead enemy of the "Triplice aleanza," [the Triple Alliance]— the dark advance of which over America I pictured to him in Cahenslyism and its allies. All the papers owned or controlled by Jesuits in Italy are writing against Dr. Bouquillon and myself. Miss Edes watches, and whenever she finds a number steeped in gall, she puts it into Propaganda.[32]

In Rome, Ireland submitted a memorial[33] in his own defense. Shaking himself free from all the theoretical aspects of education, he declared that what was at stake was simply an act of his administration in his diocese which his judgment and conscience assured him to be of the greatest benefit to education in the two towns. He alluded to the St. Paul address and set forth its main ideas. He disclaimed any intention of setting the pace for other bishops. Painting, in a few sentences, a sketch of Minnesota, he presented at length the condition of the parishes of the two towns—their population, finances, etc., especially their difficulties in maintaining their church and school.

He emphasized the fact that the state of the schools was far below the standard required by the Council of Baltimore, and he averred that in his conscience he deemed the proper support of a parochial school impossible. Hence a compromise by which he sought to save the schools by arranging with the State that the teachers would receive support without compromising the position of the School Board on the one hand or losing the religious teaching of the children on the other.

Next came an account of the enemies of the plan: Protestant bigots, certain Catholic clergymen, and some foreign Catholics, who were bent on guarding their native languages in their primary schools and who, on that account, were hostile to him because he deemed it advisable for the interests of the Church to train all the Catholics of the country in the language of the country. "They thought it my intention," he said, "to have it applied everywhere to the detriment of their language, and they sought an opportunity of ruining me at Rome." The same class of opponents also declared that the Faribault plan was out of keeping with the mind of the Council of Baltimore, that the system of parochial schools was growing in strength and favor every day, that a recognition of the Faribault system would dampen the ardor of Catholics for parochial schools, and that ere long the government would recognize the denominational school system and endow it with part of the public funds.

In reply to these objections, the memorial laid stress upon the fact that, according to official statistics, only 26 per cent of the Catholic children were in parochial schools; it maintained that parochial schools, to be successful, should be gratuitous, on a par with public schools—a requirement rendered impossible by the poverty of the parishes; it emphasized the fact that "the Government school with its unlimited endowments is increasing in every perfection that money can command," while the Sacred Congregation of the Propaganda required the parochial school to be at least not inferior to the schools of the State.

In reply to the assertion that the American people were giving indications of a willingness to endow in the near future Catholic confessional schools, the Archbishop declared that "we are further today from State aid for purely confessional schools than ever we were before." This, he explained, was due to the fact that the American Republic is composed of a vast mass of heterogeneous elements poured into the country from all parts of the civilized world, bringing with them the customs and traditions and political feelings of their different fatherlands. To amalgamate these people and their children, to assimilate their minds to republican institutions, to identify them in political thought with the body of the people, was conceived in the public mind to be the office of the public school. Hence the improbability that the State would approve and encourage the system of denominational schools.

Concerning the alleged danger of admitting the State into the domain of the Church, the reply was that public opinion demanded that the government be nonsectarian. "The Government in the United States," he said, "is not a group of apostate Catholics banded by masonry in hatred of the Church. In fact during the past fifteen years the entire episcopate of the United States has labored to induce our Government to accept the control of all our Catholic schools for the education of our Indians, and hitherto our success has been rather incomplete."

The closing pages of the memorial dealt with objections arising from so-called practical difficulties. (1) Opponents of the Faribault plan protested against the separation of religious instruction from the teaching of secular branches. This objection, the Archbishop pointed out, was applicable not only to Faribault and Stillwater but to the schools of other dioceses based upon the same plan. Moreover, the same objection could be raised against all the Catholic schools in England and Ireland, in which "it is absolutely forbidden to teach religion during the official hours of school or to exhibit on the walls thereof religious emblems of any character whatever." (2) The objections that the concessions made to the Church are illegal, and that the superintendent of the schools in Minnesota said that the State cannot bind itself legally to hold religious ideas in consideration in the selection of teachers, were, the Archbishop said, scarcely worth refutation. (3) Other objections were of similar nullity: that the sisters be required to have their diploma of the State, that teachers could be removed at will, that all the children must frequent the school assigned to them in their own district, that dangerous books could possibly be introduced, that great danger arose to faith and morals from the mixing of children of different sex and religion. These objections were easily refuted. So also was the objection that next year the Protestant Bible might be read in the schools in question. Particularly false, as the memorial explained, was the charge of the *Civiltà Cattolica* that Sister Hyacinth was removed from the parochial school.

The memorial closed with "supplementary remarks": (1) that the Faribault system had already been put in operation by many bishops of the United States; (2) that, while assailed by bigoted Protestants and Catholics, the Archbishop had the approval of nearly all the American archbishops; (3) that he and his action were submitted to an intolerable and invisible system of espionage that rendered life almost unbearable; (4) that the *Civiltà Cattolica* had published various articles against him—articles evidently written in bad faith. He said that he was regarded as the representative of the party of the American Church in favor of the government, his opponents as those who would combine foreigners into a danger for the Republic. Catholics numbered only one in eight, and in Germany a larger proportion than that did not prevent a *Kulturkampf*.

Cardinal Gibbons congratulated him on not having allowed the grass to grow under his feet in Rome, told him of the sensation caused throughout the country by the long, favorable article in the *Moniteur de Rome*, expressed indignation at the attempts of the enemy to minimize its importance, and wished that the *Ecclesiastical Review* had received a more crushing rebuke for its partisan spirit, for which it should have made a public apology.[34] He also expressed to O'Connell his satisfaction with the decision, for, as he said, it was not the Faribault school that was on trial but the question whether the Church was to be governed by men or by children—by justice and truth or by diplomacy and intrigues.[35]

When the Archbishop was in Rome, attacks upon him and rumors concerning the purpose of his visit were multiplied. The *Amerika,* a German paper of St. Louis, issued a statement purported to have been made on the authority of Archbishop Satolli that Ireland had been ordered to Rome. This the Delegate declared was the work of an enemy, and he took the opportunity of expressing his profound respect and admiration for the practical wisdom and untiring zeal of the Archbishop.[36] These attacks also served to elicit many a tribute to Ireland's personality and character, such as that of the *Moniteur de Rome,* which told of his efforts to extend the influence of the Church, to follow Catholic tradition in not allowing himself to be impeded by forms and abandoned notions, to place religion above party politics, and to win souls to the Church.[37] In the mind of Dr. Thomas O'Gorman of the Catholic University, this article was inspired by the

Pope,[38] a statement borne out by a letter from the Archbishop to his Vicar-General, in which he said that the Pope had the article written under his own eyes and, after revising it, sent it directly to the office with instructions that it should be printed *"tel quel"* (as it was).[39]

Dr. O'Gorman came to the defense of his friend, contributing to the *Educational Review* an article explaining the Archbishop's purpose in the Faribault plan—to bring under religious instruction the large number of Catholic children attending the public schools who never came in contact with the catechism and Catholic priests.[40] Nor was he alone in his defense. Bishop John J. Kain of Wheeling, West Virginia, wrote to Cardinal Simeoni that the Jesuits, who had started a campaign against Ireland, were allies of the Germans, who resented his opposition to their anti-American spirit.[41] So strong was his letter that Ireland said that if it did not set him right in Rome the case was hopeless.[42]

The formal decision of the Holy See was announced on April 30, 1892, in a letter sent by Cardinal Ledochowski to the Archbishop, praising his action in submitting his case to the Holy See and announcing that the plan could be permitted (*tolerari potest*). He also sent a communication to the bishops, reminding them that there should be a parochial school in every parish, making a plea for concord, and urging them to make provision for Catholic children attending public schools so that they might be protected from any dangers inherent in them.[43]

In reply, the Archbishop expressed his joy and gratitude for this act of the Holy See, which, he said, was indeed a work of light and wise opportuneness and answered admirably to the new needs of the Church in the United States. While the decrees of the Council of Baltimore were a clear expression of the efficacious love and tender solicitude of the bishops for the children, they only traced out the rule for general circumstances, whereas the decision of the Holy See would serve as a practical code for particular conditions. To be able to hold in view the decision of the cardinals wherever the establishment and maintenance of an independent parish school was impossible or very difficult, to guard all the purity of the divine deposit and all the inflexibility of the decrees of the Council of Baltimore, and, at the same time, to be placed in the enviable position of multiplying centers of educational influence and of providing religious instruction for a larger number of children—this, he said, was the favor with which Rome now enriched the Church of America, and for which he congratulated himself for having come to Rome to see Peter. The papacy had given unity of devotion and action, and restored peace and harmony. It was to be expected that in the young and vigorous Church of America, where each day brought new forms of civilization and complex questions, there would be divergency of opinions in the application of principles and practical methods, but a lasting disagreement would be a great misfortune to the people, resulting in the division of hearts and the scattering of forces. He was grateful for the high trust reposed in him, which would guide his apostolate and inflame his zeal for "all the great causes of which Rome is in the world the personification and the protectress." He concluded with these words:

Most eminent Sir, if it be permitted to a humble witness of the American Church to express all his thoughts, I would bless God and the Holy See for having put at the head of the ministry of missions a prince of the Church who possesses your light, your wisdom and your experience.[44]

The Cardinal was not to be outdone in praise and courtesy. He thanked him for his gracious words, hoped that passions would be appeased and that the inexact and unmeasured comments of some journals would have no effect in the presence of the *legitimate interpretation* contained in his official letter, "*faithfully reproduced* in yours."[45]

The decision was not altogether a surprise to the Archbishop, for three months earlier he had written to Father Louis Caillet that he was confident of victory, that the Holy Father was his friend and understood the situation, and that Cardinal Ledochowski was a man of superior mind and keen judgment.[46]

Exultingly Ireland wrote to Bishop John J. Keane: "Victory over the Dreibund. The matter is summed up in the Faribault plan being allowed. Dr. Bouquillon's pamphlets shall certainly not be examined. Moreover, the whole theological world of Rome is coming over to him—outside the Jesuits."[47] Keane congratulated him on the glorious news, urging a clear and unmistakable pronouncement from the Pope, which, while reasserting Catholic principles and thus closing the mouths of those who asserted that the Church was committed to a false policy, would give the country clearly to understand that the Church, recognizing and admitting civil rights, was ready to cooperate fairly in education as in all wise that concerns the public welfare. "Dear me," he said, "what a brewing is going on in the caldron from which the future is to emerge. Thank God, it is not 'the witches' but your own good self, who is seeing to it."⁴⁸ And to Cardinal Gibbons he wrote: "Thanks be to God for the good news about Ireland. There must have been a good deal of consternation in the ranks of the enemy. From my soul I cry out: *'Exsurgat Deus, et dissipentur inimici ejus. Domine, non praevaleat homo.'* "⁴⁹ Father Walter Elliott, of the Paulists, expressed his joy in these words:

To say that I was amazed and really half frenzied with joy at what you write is not an exaggeration. You have whipped them. And you have done it where they can alone be thoroughly routed. Like all men who trust mainly for guidance to approvals and condemnations or disciplinary authority, the enemies of a Living Church whom you have routed are adepts at intrigue. They are whisperers by profession. You could easily vanquish them before the public conscience of the Church or in a regular court of Canon Law. But in the mazes of the Roman Congregations and in the ambushes of the Roman Monsignori you were likely to encounter such pitfalls as would ruin you. But you have whipped them in Rome.⁵⁰

The rigors of the controversy served but to draw closer the bonds which united Ireland and Gibbons, who could hardly express his sense of relief and exultation. He told of the reaction of Archbishop John J. Williams, who had been visiting him, and whose advice to Ireland was that now that he had conquered he could afford to be magnanimous, should do nothing to wound or irritate his adversaries, and should make no public statements which might be turned against him. The Cardinal, who on more than one occasion had had reason to fear the Archbishop's outspokenness, wrote to him, "Fear not. Be prudent and conservative in words and writings. With regard to alleged attempts at alienating Baltimore from St. Paul, that effort will never succeed until Baltimore becomes so blind as not to see and admire honor, virtue and heroism."⁵¹

But unfortunately Ireland had spoken already. He wrote a letter to a St. Paul priest which found its way into the press and served to increase the bitterness. After telling of all the kindness he had received in Rome, he said: "The so-called Faribault plan is now formally allowed, in spite of Germans and Jesuits."⁵²

3. Complications and Aftermath

A flood of commentaries followed the papal decision, Ireland's opponents attempting to interpret it as a virtual condemnation. Condé Pallen, editor of *Church Progress,* was one of the most vocal leaders of the opposition. Archbishop Corrigan, the *Civiltà Cattolica,* Father

Joseph Jerge, Assistant Provincial of the Jesuits, Monsignor August Zeininger, Chancellor of the Archdiocese of Milwaukee, and others were all glad to accept the view that the Faribault plan had been condemned; Dr. Thomas O'Gorman, Father Bouquillon, and Father Phelan of the *Western Watchman* that in the plan, which was intended only for exceptional cases, there was no sacrifice of Catholic principles and that in this view the Archbishop had been sustained in Rome. Their opinion received confirmation from Father Palmieri's interpretation of the *"tolerari,"* which, he said, was not always applied to what is evil, often excludes the notion of wrongfulness in an action, and is equivalent to a declaration that such course of action is licit.[53]

On March 6, 1892, Ireland wrote to the editor of the *Civiltà Cattolica*, requesting him to publish a letter which Cardinal Gibbons had written to Monsignor O'Connell concerning the meeting of the archbishops in St. Louis. This the *Civiltà* did, but at the same time it accused the Archbishop of lack of good faith in publishing a letter written three months earlier, which, because of later occurrences, such as the removal of crucifixes from the Faribault schools, had lost its value.

The accusation of bad faith was very far-fetched and in no way interfered with the Cardinal's support of the Archbishop, to whom Father Magnien wrote:

We are all highly pleased with your success in Rome, but at the same time I fear with you that the war is not at an end. In Rome the *Civiltà* is fierce, and this gives strength to the enemies here; they publicly boast that this magazine expresses the mind of the Holy See and that the *Moniteur* has no weight whatsoever.

He also told of the plotting of Archbishop Corrigan, who had induced the Jesuits to go into the fight, had requested Father Holaind to write his pamphlet and financed it, had forbidden the *Catholic World* to write a word in favor of Bouquillon's views, and was constantly asserting that the *Civiltà* represented the mind of the Holy See.[54] The Archbishop, already incensed by the bitter antagonism of the Roman paper and by its perverted interpretation of the decision of the Propaganda, decided to settle the matter once for all. He wrote to Cardinal Rampolla, protesting against one of its articles, which had already been announced in the United States as containing the official interpretation of the decision.[55] The Cardinal denied that the articles of the periodical were submitted to the revision and approval of the Holy See, or that the Vatican had anything to do with the article of which he complained. As a matter of fact, he said, when rumor had reached the Pope of certain articles on the school question which were in course of preparation for the *Civiltà*, he had made known to the directors that the publication of such articles would be unbecoming while the matter was before the Holy See for judgment.[56] To Cardinal Gibbons the Archbishop said that Rampolla's letter had surprised Europe, ruined the prestige of the paper, and dealt the Jesuits the greatest blow they had received in a century.[57]

However, when Pius IX was in exile and felt the need of defenders, he appealed for writers to come to the support of the Catholic religion, an appeal which the Jesuits answered. He erected the Jesuit writers of the *Civiltà* into a College of Writers and paid tribute to their work, which brought so much benefit to the Church. It was not, therefore, surprising that Cardinal Rampolla should, a little later, write to the *Civiltà* an expression of his pain at the attacks made on the paper in some Catholic journals. Such action, he said, was hostile to the Catholic faith, fomented discord in the very bosom of the Church, and calumniated those who had been her unwearied defenders.[58] This letter seemed, at first sight, to neutralize the Cardinal's former statement, but, as Eugene Veuillot of *L'Univers* pointed out to the Archbishop, although praising in general the work of the *Civiltà* it did not touch at all upon the school question.[59]

The controversy produced some strange developments, into which, however, it is not necessary to go in detail, as they have been treated elsewhere. There was the letter which Archbishop Corrigan addressed to the Pope, accusing Archbishop Ireland of warning against the danger of a *Kulturkampf* if the school plan were condemned,[60] a charge which the Holy Father denied.[61] Of the Pontiff's reply Ireland said: "It was a lesson to Corrigan and a justification of myself."[62] Monsignor Boeglin called it a *capo lavoro* (a masterpiece); "he put them all in a sack so gently and so effectually." Connelan, the representative of the *Pilot*, regarded it as the strongest he had ever seen leaving Rome for any Bishop; Abbot Bernard Smith felt that now nobody could attack Ireland without attacking the Pope; Monsignor Della Volpe averred that Ireland had left Rome crowned with laurel.[63]

There was also the attempt of His Grace of New York to persuade many of the bishops to unite with him in a protest, some of whom, according to Father Magnien, were entrapped into signing an equivocal document, the full meaning of which they did not see.[64] Cardinal Ledochowski told Ireland that he understood it at once. For him it was the protest of one, who beguiled others into it—and, he added, were it the protest of seven, he would prefer to them Cardinal Gibbons and the Archbishop of St. Paul.[65] Father Magnien felt that Corrigan, in his attempt to weaken the influence of Gibbons and Ireland, was directly attacking the Holy Father himself. He said: *"Quem vult perdere Deus, prius dementat.* Somebody was telling me in Baltimore that Archbishop Corrigan, after he has made a *faux pas,* is bound to make a second one, and this seems really to be the case."[66]

Archbishop Ireland regarded the opposition of Archbishop Corrigan and Bishop McQuaid as based on reasons other than the Faribault plan, for in the dioceses of both a similar plan had been in use for years. Moreover, the experiment was too insignificant to call forth such animus as the former displayed, and his constant efforts to enlist the co-operation of Judge Dunne, Bishop Zardetti, Fathers Holaind, Fulton, Conway, and other Jesuits, as revealed in their correspondence.[67]

An account of "the romance" of Archbishop Ireland's memorial appeared in the *Northwestern Chronicle* on March 4, 1893, giving the Archbishop's reasons for not accepting Corrigan's challenge to publish it. He "deemed it a prudent piece of war tactics to permit his adversaries to entangle themselves in the difficulties which its possession was weaving for them." The difficulties were the suspicious manner in which copies of it had disappeared in Rome.[68]

It is interesting to note that not long before his death Archbishop Corrigan was heard to deplore the fact that hardly more than 50 per cent of the churches in his archdiocese had any parish school. In the city of New York, at the close of the administration of Archbishop Hughes, despite the poverty of the people, twenty out of thirty-six parishes had established parochial schools. In 1902, nearly forty years later, a statement was published by the Committee of the New York Catholic School Board which showed that in the number of parochial schools New York ranked twenty-second among all the dioceses.

Nor was the controversy without its humorous side, such as the remark of McQuaid to O'Connell that if Ireland would stay at home a little more and mind his own diocese the latter would be the gainer. "He is away from his diocese," he said, "only a little more than Cardinal Gibbons."[69] After the *Osservatore Romano* had published a defense of Ireland, Archbishop Corrigan wrote to Bishop McQuaid that the article was written by the secretary of Cardinal Rampolla, Monsignor Della Chiesa, "a gentleman without any influence whatever in theological circles, and whose name consequently if published would carry absolutely no weight with it. I have direct and reliable information that Mgr. Della Chiesa wrote the article, and the estimate of his standing is also beyond question." As this was the later brilliant Benedict XV, His Grace of New York was not a particularly good judge of ability.[70]

When Ireland was informed by O'Connell that the Vatican was seriously thinking of asking him and Katzer to go to Rome to present both sides of the school question, he replied: "Imagine the insult to myself and to the Republic—to be brought to argue with Katzer, a man who knows as little of America as a Huron."[71] When on another occasion he was told of a Roman who had translated his discourse with a view to attacking him, he exclaimed: "The scoundrel! But I think that Phelan [editor of the *Western Watchman*] will ventilate him."

Archbishop Satolli came into the controversy in November when, after a month's visit to St. Paul, he attended a meeting of the archbishops held in New York on November 17, 1892, and submitted fourteen propositions. While reaffirming the provisions of the Council of Baltimore and urging the erection of parish schools comparable in efficiency to public schools, the establishment of normal schools, and the securing of teaching certificates, he granted the right of attendance at public schools whenever dangers to faith or morals were removed and provision could be made for religious training. His action, while encountering considerable opposition and leading to further tension and controversy, gave great joy to Archbishop Ireland,[72] who said that now there could no longer be room for the old-time accusation that the Church was opposed to instruction or deprecated the efforts of the State to remove ignorance. Archbishop Corrigan, who never relaxed his efforts, made a last desperate attempt by sending a note in Italian to Archbishop Satolli, stating that in his interview in the New York *Herald* of the previous December Ireland had declared that he intended to make the Faribault system general, that only the previous day he had confessed to the Archbishops of Philadelphia and San Francisco that no such interview had ever taken place, that he had merely written it himself and given it to the press, and that he had also asked the secretary of the meeting to note that he stood alone on the school question against Cardinal Gibbons, Archbishop Williams, and all the other prelates.[73]

The Holy Father, who would not allow the authority of his Delegate to be questioned, addressed a letter to the archbishops on May 31, 1893, which, as far as Rome was concerned, brought the controversy to an end. After speaking of the mission of the Delegate to settle the school question, of the decrees of the meeting, of the excited controversies which had started afresh, and of his request for reactions, he referred to the apprehensions of some who seemed to think that the propositions partially abrogated the Baltimore decrees. Pointing out that Satolli's principal propositions were taken from those decrees but that he left it to the judgment and conscience of the Ordinary to decide, according to circumstances, when it was lawful to attend public schools, he regarded it as unbecoming and unjust so to explain his later utterances as to make them disagree with the preceding ones, especially since the Delegate's meaning was not at all left obscure.[74]

The Pope's letter did not surprise the Archbishop, who "could scarcely believe that he would go back on Satolli's propositions." However, such pressure and unfair arguments had been brought to bear on Rome that nothing would have astonished him.[75] Annoyed by misrepresentations in the French press, he wrote to *L'Univers* protesting against statements that the pontifical letter was a condemnation of all his opinions on the school question, that the favor shown to him in Rome in the previous year had been withdrawn, and that a monitum had been addressed to him, enjoining him to abandon his former position and to restrict the decision of the *tolerari potest* to the schools of Faribault and Stillwater. All this he denied, stating that he was extending the system to other parishes in his diocese, and vindicating his action as in keeping with the spirit, if not the letter, of the Council of Baltimore, a distinction which the Pope had clearly indicated in his letter. He concluded by saying: "I feel the duty to give this explanation to the Catholics of France, to whom I am attached by bonds which go too deeply into past life to be ever broken; I could not endure calumny in the country which was the cradle of my education."[76]

Before Ireland had left Rome, he had received from Father Louis Caillet word of trouble in Stillwater, and when he reached home, on July 15, 1892, he learned that the arrangement in both towns had fallen through. In Stillwater, the Board of Education had rejected the application of five nuns as teachers and thus prevented the renewal of the contract. In Faribault, a new school board, unfriendly to the system, had been elected. Father Conry appeared before the Board of Education on September 14, 1893, and said that the Catholics of Faribault could no longer consent to the assignment of two Protestant teachers to the old parochial school. Professor Willis West, Superintendent of Education, gave as reasons for the failure Protestant opposition to the dress of the sisters, neglect on the part of the board to inform the people on all that had been accomplished, and the placing of Father Conry's name on the election ticket in the place of Mr. Keeley, which made the Protestants suspicious. The Archbishop, who laid the blame on Father Conry, attempted, without success, to save the situation.

The Faribault plan, which had such ephemeral success, was, as the Archbishop declared, a measure of internal administration, intended to meet a difficulty in well-defined and well-understood circumstances. It was never meant to supplant the Catholic school system as it existed within and without the borders of Minnesota. Now that the Archbishop's career is before us in its fullness and that we may scan the whole tone and trend of his life and thought, it is superfluous to say that to no man did he at any time yield in love for the Catholic school and in solicitude for its safety. Never for an instant did he change his views on a question so vitally bound up with the Church's existence, or deviate from the position which he held on Catholic education from the first days of his priesthood. On this point there can be no lingering misconception in the minds of those who knew him.

Unfortunately, the controversy, like many of the others, fell into the hands of reporters who made of it a field day. They spoke of the war between the "conservatives," represented by Archbishop Corrigan and Bishop McQuaid on the one hand, and the "liberals," led by Cardinal Gibbons and Archbishop Ireland on the other. They sought interviews with the spokesmen of the two parties and succeeded in making it into an *opéra bouffe*. There were claims and counterclaims, charges and countercharges, stories of documents stolen from the offices of the Propaganda, rumors of paid agents pleading the causes of both parties in Rome, until the whole matter became a source of grave annoyance to the Vatican and of scandal to the faithful. Perhaps the explanation of it is to be found in the clash of positive personalities and in the youth of the Church in this country. It was a lusty youngster, characterized rather by vigor and enthusiasm than by the culture and tolerance which only age can bring. One can hardly conceive of such a situation's arising today.

The controversy was complicated by the enmities remaining from Cahenslyism, the establishment of the Catholic University, and personal jealousies. How close was the connection between the controversy on Cahenslyism and that on the school question may be seen from a pastoral of Archbishop Katzer, in which he attempted to characterize the position of the Archbishop:

Liberalizing opinions, always injurious to the true Catholic interests; sentimental phrases of closer communion with our separated brethren, appeals to a false and unreal American patriotism, lying charges of foreign and disloyal nationalism, highflown and indiscriminate praise of the public school system together with a scornful and unfair criticism of our parochial schools, a hypocritical sympathy with the poor "double-tax" ridden Catholics, even the silly spectre of a conflict with the political powers—all this was brought into play to make the Catholics of this country understand that parochial schools, Catholic schools, were no longer opportune.[77]

The Faribault plan did not have much success; in Faribault and Stillwater it was soon discontinued. Today it would excite little comment. The school problem is still with us. A large proportion of our children still attend public schools, and we attempt, with minor success, to solve the problem through release classes.

Chapter 6

THE FATHER HECKER CONTROVERSY, OR "AMERICANISM"[1]

++++++++++++

To form some idea of the forces leading to the condemnation of Americanism, which shocked the leaders of the Church in the United States, one must recall the conditions which prevailed at the end of the nineteenth and the beginning of the twentieth century. It was an age of agnosticism, liberalism, and subjectivism; of false notions of the development of dogma; of misdirected attempts to reconcile science and religion and to bring the Church into harmony with the intellectual, moral, and social needs of the times; of the extension of evolution to the domain of theology; of the infiltration of Protestant liberalism, of the "religious experience" of Schleiermacher, Harnack, and Sabatier, of the higher criticism and the study of historical origins; of the growth of neo-Catholicism with its desire to recapture primitive Christianity without, however, its dogmas; of the overflowing of democracy into socialism. How serious was the situation may be judged from the number of those who were either condemned or suspected, among whom were Lamennais, Mivart, Tyrrell, Loisy, Schell, Muller, Rosmini, Fogazzaro, Père Hyacinthe (Loyson), Houtin, Charbonnel, as well as d'Hulst, who was removed from his chair in the Catholic Institute of Paris, Von Hugel, who was suspect, and even Duchesne, one of whose books was placed on the Index. Add to this the reflection of the spirit of the age in literature, the *fin de siècle*, in which the excesses of romanticism, the combination of a bizarre mysticism and eroticism in Huysmans, Verlaine, Rimbaud, and Baudelaire, the writhings and posturings of the aesthetics and decadents, unrestrained individualism, uncurbed emotionalism, Satanism, sadism, and sensationalism—all expressed the morbidity and unhealthiness of the time. It is no wonder that the Church was

104

apprehensive and on its guard. But, as so often when the State is in peril the disloyalty hunters only too frequently accuse the innocent, so too when the Church is in danger the heresy hunters suspect defection where it is not. And as happens in both instances, some individuals and groups take advantage of the opportunity of satisfying personal or racial spleen. Such was the case of Americanism.

Few priests were so well known in the United States in the past century as Father Isaac Hecker, founder of the Congregation of St. Paul. Born on December 18, 1819, he was compelled by the loss of his parents' fortune to leave school when eleven years of age and to take up work in his brothers' bakery. However, even at this early age his passion for study triumphed over difficulties which would have discouraged less ardent spirits. His biographers paint a picture of him studying Kant's *Critique of Pure Reason,* the volume fixed before his eyes while he was kneading dough. Even in his teens his voice was often raised in the streets of New York in behalf of the workingman, the victim of injustice. He inherited from his mother a profoundly religious spirit—indeed, he was "with a fatal gift of introspection" a born mystic, dreaming dreams and beholding visions, guarding the innocence of life as only a saint guards it, eager to devote himself to poverty, solitude, and sacrifice. Brownson, whose acquaintance he had made in those youthful days in the course of his social crusade, suggested that he join the Community at Brook Farm. This he did, but in the course of a few months realized that it did not meet the needs of his restless heroic nature. Brownson's conversion, however, influenced young Hecker, who felt himself drawn more and more to the Catholic Church—drawn by his own study, his own thinking, and by the passion for spiritual perfection which he came to see could be realized only in the Catholic Church with its Communion of Saints. In August, 1844, he received Baptism at the hands of Bishop McCloskey at New York and, in the following year, entered the novitiate of the Redemptorist Community at St. Trond in Belgium. How he lived the life of an ascetic, how he encountered in his studies difficulties which in one less saintly would have barred him from the priesthood, how in his eagerness to found a Community which would devote itself to the work of converting non-Catholics he incurred the displeasure of his superiors, how he was dispensed from his vows by Pius IX and was authorized by the same Pontiff to organize a Community to do missionary work in the United States, we need not linger to tell in detail. Neither does our present purpose call for an extended account of the work of Father Hecker as organizer and Superior of the "Missionary Society of St. Paul the Apostle." Suffice it to say that his lectures, his apostolate of the press, especially his founding of the *Catholic World*, supplemented by his three volumes, *The Aspirations of Nature, Questions of the Soul, The Church and the Age*, likened him to Cardinal Newman. Indeed, the Cardinal's words on the occasion of Father Hecker's death happily expressed the part he played in the Church in the United States: "I have ever felt that there was a sort of unity in our lives, that we had both begun a work of the same kind, he in America and I in England."

Father Hecker's life and work speak for themselves. He devoted himself to winning to the Church the confidence of the American people, very many of whom looked with suspicion upon it as a foreign institution. He strove to win acceptance for Catholic principles and practices among a people who, with their Puritan background, profoundly distrusted them. In a word, he tried to do in the United States what Newman did in England. Though a mystic from the dawn of consciousness, whose profoundest conviction seems to have been the indwelling of the Holy Spirit, he was also a man of action, emphasizing the active virtues in contradistinction to those of the solitary ascetic. The timid listlessness of Catholics in Europe he deplored, regretting the absence of individual activity without which religion would not emerge from its routine ways to stir the country at large to a conviction that in the Catholic Church alone lay the hope for the future.

And yet, it was the life of this saintly priest that led to the famous controversy on Americanism, a controversy so fierce and so bitter, arousing national and theological passions, that it required an apostolic letter of Leo XIII to put an end to it.

The English edition of *The Life of Father Hecker*, written by Father Walter Elliott, bore an Introduction from the pen of Archbishop Ireland. It was not strange that the Archbishop would be called upon to write it, for there was much in common between them. Both realized the democratic and social needs of their age and had little patience with those clerics who were tied up to a monarchy; both favored individual action and the social virtues. They were at one in their devotion to America, their passion for liberty, their war on intemperance as the great evil which interfered with the progress of the Church in America, their conviction that between the Church and the American Constitution there existed genuine harmony and that therefore Catholics should be second to none in their devotion to the Republic, their sensitiveness to the charge of foreignism so often brought against the Church, their feeling that the sterility of the Church in Europe and the loss of souls was to be attributed to the isolation of the clergy from the people and to a type of asceticism which found little response from the masses. Both were men of strong convictions for which they were ready at all times to give battle. Indeed, as the Archbishop acknowledges in his Introduction, it was to Father Hecker that he was indebted for most salutary impressions. He saw in him the providential man who traced and realized in his life the ideal of the priest of the new future of the Church.

The Life of Father Hecker caused little stir in America, although Archbishop Ireland knew that some of the views he and Father Hecker held in common might be criticized. He wrote: "I do not expect that my words will receive universal approval, and I am not at all sure that their expression would have been countenanced by the priest whose memory brings them to my lips. I write as I think, and the responsibility must be all my own."[2] And so, while the Church had no more loyal or obedient son than Isaac Hecker, there are in his writings some passages which express more than his conception and which left him open to criticism.[3] He felt that in the sixteenth century, in order to counteract Protestantism, which threatened the destruction of the principle of authority, the Church had to condemn the excesses of individualism and to place before everything else the idea of authority. The victory was gained by the sacrifice of certain human qualities. But a new period had opened to the Church, and it was now to be the individuality, the personality of souls, their free and vigorous initiative under the direct guidance of the Holy Spirit dwelling within them, which was to become the distinctive Catholic form of action. He insisted on the practice of the natural virtues as preceding any practical move toward the higher life. He began with the natural man and made every supernatural force in the Sacraments and prayer aid in establishing and increasing natural virtue as a necessary preliminary and ever present accompaniment of spiritual progress.[4]

The Life of Father Hecker has been called one of the most striking and suggestive biographies published since Newman's *Apologia*. Indeed, Canon William Barry did not hesitate to write that in actual interest it does not yield to that famous volume.[5] Archbishop Corrigan not only gave it an *Imprimatur* but, in his early days, was a disciple of Father Hecker and even proposed joining the Paulists.[6]

A French translation of the *Life*,[7] bearing an introduction by the renowned Abbé Felix Klein, was first greeted with acclamation by several priests and ecclesiastical journals. *L'Ami du Clerge, Le Peuple Français, L'Enseignement Chrétien* gave it favorable notices, as also did the Benedictine *Review*, the Jesuit *Etudes*, and even *La Vérité*. Sympathetic reviews appeared in *Le Temps, Le Journal des Debats, L'Univers,* and many others. But the book also became the object of scrutiny by theologians who questioned its orthodoxy.

The first mutterings of the coming storm were heard at the Fourth Scientific International Congress held at Freiburg in August, 1897, at which Monsignor Denis O'Connell, former Rector of the North American College, Rome, took for the subject of his address "Father Hecker's Americanism, What It Is and What It Is Not."[8] The idea embodied in the word "Americanism," he said, shone throughout the pages of *The Life of Father Hecker,* giving to the volume its impress and the reason for its existence. The word has a twofold signification— political and ecclesiastical. Political Americanism has its origin in the Declaration of Independence, proclaiming the equality of all men, their rights which are safeguarded by governments deriving their authority immediately from the people and ultimately from God. In it law is the supreme power—law imposed by the dignity of the citizenry. He contrasted the American system with that of ancient Rome, showing that in one the State had only such rights as were accorded to it by the people, while in the other the sacred rights of humanity could be outraged by those in power. He recalled the praise given by the Holy Father to the Constitution of the United States, adding that no one eulogized the Constitution as did Cardinal Satolli, who recommended the Gospel and the American Constitution taken together as the complete rule of human life.

Taking up the ecclesiastical conception embodied in the word "Americanism," Monsignor O'Connell quoted the amendment to the Constitution forbidding Congress to establish any State religion or to prohibit the free exercise of religion. He adverted to the fact that if any religion were at any time established by the State in America it would be Protestantism. The amendment, therefore, banned the establishment of Protestantism as the religion of the State and guaranteed to Catholics the absolutely free exercise of theirs. The Church lives entirely under her own laws, the relations of the bishops with the Holy See are unfettered, the exercise of the authority of the Pope is in no way controlled. Nowhere is the action of the Church more free; nowhere is the exercise of Pontifical authority less subject to interference. Hence Father Hecker's enthusiasm for a Constitution based upon the rule of God and the natural dignity of man, and at the same time furnishing a splendid basis for the work of the supernatural. He added that however true or beautiful may be in theory the doctrine of the legal union of Church and State, in practice it unfortunately too often results in serious injury and loss to the Church. Americanism stands for nothing more than the loyal devotion of American Catholics to the principles on which the government is founded, and their deep conviction that these principles offer to Catholics valuable advantages for the promotion of the glory of God, the development and expansion of the Church, and the salvation of souls.

The great majority of the Congress applauded the generous and liberal ideas of Father Hecker. Monsignor Charles Turinaz, Bishop of Nancy, did not, however, share the opinions of the others. The individualism of the founder of the Paulists, he maintained, and his theory of the direction of souls by the Holy Spirit smacked rather of Protestantism than of Catholicism. Abbé Klein in reply quoted pages from *The Life of Father Hecker* which affirmed that the more a soul is guided interiorly by the Holy Ghost, the more it filially submits to the Church and her representatives.[9]

Outside the Congress, the war against Americanism was actively taken up by the Jesuits, and particularly by Abbé Charles Maignen of the Congregation of St. Vincent de Paul. Early in November, 1897, in the churches of Saint Sulpice and Sainte Clotilde in Paris, two Jesuits, Père R. P. Coubé and Père Gaudeau, preached on what they asserted were the evils of the time—the Parliament of Religions, Brunetière's article on science, the philosophy of Georges Blondel, and Hecker and his Americanism. Abbé Klein, who was present at these two sermons and who later learned that they were followed by a third at Sacré Cœur, concluded that they were not accidental, but rather part of an organized campaign.[10] The following year Maignen began in March a series of attacks, which he later collected in book form under the title *Le Père Hecker—Est-il un Saint?* (*Is Father Hecker a Saint?*). It was this book which more than any other gave fullest impetus to the controversy. Maignen began by identifying Americanism with two tendencies, which, he declared, were observable among the young clergy and educated laymen belonging to the State-directed universities:

> The first looks with disfavor on the doctrines, methods, and institutions of the past, and attributes all the conquests made by error to the way in which truth has been defended; the second accepts with confidence and propagates with vigor all kinds of rash ideas, risky methods, and doubtful institutions.[11]

He lost no time in indicating the real target of his attack, for he went on to say that the visit of Archbishop Ireland to Paris in 1892 "greatly contributed to spread and accelerate the movement." Against Cardinal Gibbons there was only a vein of insinuation, but Archbishop Ireland was the future head of the schismatical American Church, and Archbishop Keane was a rationalist, who threw all dogma over to modern ideas.[12] As for O'Connell, his views were denounced as among those which had resulted in grave injury to religion.[13] "The Ireland party," he said, "is full of doctrinal audacity; it allies itself shamelessly with the Protestants against Catholics, and it has the support of the American government."[14] He criticized O'Connell's definition of Americanism as being in opposition to the union of Church and State, though nowhere did the latter deny that the union is the ideal condition of things. O'Connell was concerned only with America, where the Constitution "interdicts the institution of a State religion," and "leaves the whole domain of religion to the authority of the Church." One would think that any French priest would envy the freedom enjoyed by the Church in America and refrain from remarks derogatory to it. For those who knew these prelates, the identification of Americanism with the tendencies described by Maignen is a source of amusement; for those who knew them not, the logic of the Abbé arouses wonder.

Abbé Maignen was famous for his hatred of democracy. In a brochure which he published in 1892, he set himself to prove that "the sovereignty of the people is a heresy." Indeed, he stood out as the most prominent figure among those theologians of France who waged war on republican tendencies and institutions. He incurred a sharp rebuke at the hands of the Archbishop of Paris for a vile attack on Count de Mun, who enjoyed the confidence of the Holy Father.[15] He had also been dismissed by the Superior General of his Congregation from the direction of the Cercle Catholique de Montparnasse because of a regrettable letter of his published by *La Libre Parole*.[16] He had been refused permission to publish his book on Americanism by the Archbishop of Paris. And this was the man whose book had for its purpose to discredit Father Hecker and to show that the Americanism of the most respected prelates of the American Church "may be fairly considered one of the greatest dangers that threaten the Church."

Among all his attacks none created so much disgust, none reveal the senseless bitterness of the Abbé as that based on an article written by "Romanus" in the *Contemporary Review*. This article, which attempted to eliminate divine agency in the institutions of the Church, stirred horror in the breast of every Catholic who read it. Maignen termed it an "explosion of infidelity and rationalism." It was, he said, a summary of the ideas of Americanism. Sounding as if it were taken from the pages of Renan or Loisy, it reflects, we are assured, the views of Archbishop Keane, who in his lifetime was Bishop of Richmond, Rector of the Catholic University, a member of various Roman Congregations—especially the Congregation of the Propaganda—and ultimately Archbishop of Dubuque.[17]

Like the other European critics of Americanism, Maignen was characterized by a bitter hatred of everything American, a hatred based on crass ignorance of the country. His views of the United States as a nation "not even in swaddling clothes, yet to be born, in which hostile races are meeting and clashing within its walls, like Esau and Jacob in their mother's womb, a land of uptorn populations of immigrants, who wander over the vast American continent without finding a place of rest,"[18] and his weird tales of golden staircases, each step of which cost twelve thousand francs, would be amusing were they not so ridiculous and impertinent.[19] As a specimen of reckless reasoning impregnated with *odium theologicum*, it would be difficult to find a work that surpasses *Père Hecker, Est-il un Saint?* The calmness and fairness that one would expect to find in a book written by a clergyman are lamentably absent—indeed, there is hardly a page which is not reeking with bitterness.

As this was the book which directed the heaviest fire against Americanism, so also was it the book which drew upon itself the most scathing criticism. An article entitled "The Genesis of Americanism" in the *North American Review* of May, 1900, which bore the signature J. St. Clair Etheridge,[20] but which Abbé Klein assures us was really written by Archbishop Ireland,[21] tore it to pieces in this trenchant statement:

Maignen is an adept in all the devices of the heresy-hunter. He puts upon the rack the thoughts of the simple priest whom he is pursuing, and strives to extort from them by hook or by crook matter for the condemnation of the Inquisition. He wrenches passages from their context and bases upon them charges that are refuted in the very chapters from which the sentences are torn. He makes one of the most pious prelates of the American Church speak the language of Welhausen and Harnack. Worst of all, M. Maignen has been repeatedly convicted of downright dishonesty. He accuses Father Hecker—a priest known to all as a man of exalted piety— of lacking in the fundamental devotion of the Catholic religion, and when from pages of surpassing beauty a score of thrilling tributes to the Incarnate Word are quoted to him as words of the man whom he assails, he is reduced to savage but impotent silence.[22]

But Maignen was by no means alone in his campaign. He was ably abetted by L'Abbé Henri Delassus in France, Jules Tardivel in Canada, Father Salvatore Brandi in Rome, as well as by Monsignor R. P. Péchenard, Abbé George Périès, Father J. A. Delattre, S.J., Father David Fleming, O.S.F., and Father Monsabré, O. P. Delassus, in his *L'Américanisme et la Conjuration Antichrétienne,* represented Archbishop Ireland, Cardinal Gibbons, and other American prelates as working with Jews and Freemasons to hasten the triumph of Anti-Christ and the overthrow of the Church.[23] Tardivel, who shared with Maignen a hatred of America, and whose gullibility would have delighted the soul of Ben Jonson, characterized in *La Vérité,* of Quebec, the American government as "the eldest daughter of Freemasonry and its people as atheistic and interested only in money.[24] Paying his respects to this production, the Archbishop said: "The entire book is a foul and contemptible calumny on America. As one reads it, one is forced to ask, Why is it that all the men who 'discovered' Americanism and then clamored for its condemnation are, without exception, slanderers of America?"[25] Of Brandi's fulminations in the *Civiltà Cattolica,* the organ of the Jesuits, he said:

This Italian journal has done immense harm to the best interests of religion by the narrowness and intolerance of its views. Its bigotry, political and theological, its truculent methods of controversy, and its impatience of liberty and progress in every form are contributing much to alienate the intellectual element of Europe from the Church. The *Civiltà Cattolica* has always been the enemy of democratic institutions, and hence of America and of all the principles which America represents.[26]

If Maignen could see in America only a chaos of unformed immigrants, Péchenard, Rector of the Catholic Institute of Paris, could discover there "a certain bending in the matter of dogmatic affirmation, a separatist tendency with respect to the central ecclesiastical authority, a claim to a larger independence, and a minimizing in the practices of the Christian, and especially the religious life."[27] In *The Passing of Americanism* he rejoiced with quixotic enthusiasm at the demise of a heresy which never existed—at least in the United States. Referring to this article, the Archbishop said that he regretted the passing of Monsignor d'Hulst, his predecessor, "who would never have suffered that great seat of learning to become the ally of men who attempted to blacken the fair name of the American Church." "Father Fleming," he said, "was formerly highly respected at Rome as an exemplar of large-mindedness. Recently, however, in obedience to the edict of his order, he has become the exponent of English reactionary views, and he is rapidly atoning by his zeal in his new cause for his theological escapades of former years." The celebrated Dominican preacher, Monsabré, lost no time in assuring Maignen that the only fault of his "excellent work" was that it treated American prelates and their doctrines with *"trop de douceur."*[28]

A sermon which the Archbishop preached at the consecration of Bishop Thomas O'Gorman on April 19, 1896, in the presence of Cardinal Satolli, was hardly conducive to winning the support of the orders. He earnestly commended to the care of the episcopate the diocesan priesthood. Yielding to none in his recognition of the orders, he felt that, formed to meet extraordinary emergencies and subject directly to the Supreme Pontiff, they were taken from the jurisdiction of the bishop, who could not depend upon them for diocesan work and who had nothing to say about the formation of their priesthood. In his mind the diocesan clergy had been neglected, having to do the rough and ready work and lacking leisure for study. He protested against the false notion that less growth of mind and soul was expected from them than from the religious. They should be conscious of their dignity. They are the normal clergy for a diocese, and, as they grow and work, so will the diocese prosper.

Speaking of the episcopate, he said that government by priests is abnormal, and he averred that had the successors of St. Francis Xavier in Japan quickly petitioned Rome to appoint bishops and prepare the way for a diocesan clergy, persecutions would not have obliterated the Church there. This, he said, was the view of Cardinal Manning and of distinguished historians. Then he piled Pelion on Ossa when he asserted that had Father Parsons, the Jesuit, and his abettors made no opposition to the appointment of bishops in England during penal times many of the people would have retained the Catholic faith.[29]

This typically bold and frank expression of his mind caused much comment and helped to complicate his problems. Father John A. Zahm of Notre Dame told of the excited comment aroused by the reference to the Jesuits. People were asking "What next?"[30] Father Cuthbert, however, writing in the *Franciscan Annals,* defended the Archbishop against the charge of antagonism to the orders, characterizing the accusation as misleading and mischievous. The Archbishop, he said, had emphatically stated to him: "I have never been opposed to them, I esteem and admire them." No man, Cuthbert insisted, ever breathed so frankly honest and outspoken. Nevertheless he regretted the Archbishop's remarks, which, he felt could have the effect of setting against him the strongest force in the Church.[31]

How formidable was the opposition which the Archbishop had to face may be gauged by the influence wielded in Rome by the religious orders, especially by those which Delattre, Fleming, and Monsabré represented—Jesuits, Franciscans, and Dominicans—by the royalists in France, who never forgave him for his discourses in Paris in favor of the Republic, and by the friends of Spain. Those who labored to fasten the charge of heresy upon American Catholics he characterized as "the ecclesiastical allies of all the political reactionaries of the Old World, who would fain blot out from the continent of Europe every vestige of democracy—the theological scriveners of all who chivalrously and foolishly cling to lost causes and regimes of olden days." Their hatred of republican institutions was shown by Maignen, who openly resisted the Pope's policy for France and who was so insubordinate that the papal representative in Paris closed the doors of the nunciature against him.[32]

Add also the support of some members of the Sacred College, notably Cardinals Mazzella, S.J., and Satolli. Mazzella was said to be the author of a brochure entitled *L'Americanismo*, which criticized Father Hecker. In the light of the close friendship which once bound Satolli and the Archbishop, Satolli's position was indeed strange. On more than one occasion he had expressed his admiration for the Archbishop and paid tribute to the Constitution; yet, on the publication of an English edition of Maignen's book, he wrote to the author expressing his very great satisfaction with the translation, "which puts the work in greater harmony with its subject, its aim, and the well-known need which it fills," and he hoped that "the Good God will aid in stopping this deadly pest whose contagion spreads over two worlds."[33] The words of the Archbishop: "Since his return to Rome, he has maintained an attitude of sullen hostility to America and everything American," do not give a satisfying explanation.[34]

Not that the Archbishop was without his supporters. While, on the one hand, views of the grossest ignorance were commonly presented in France concerning the Church in America, on the other hand, calmer and more impartial spirits, such as Abbé Naudet, editor of *Justice Sociale,* drew attention to the fact that the detractors of Ireland were those who fought the efforts of the Pope to orientate French Catholics toward the Republic.[35]

Neither did Abbé Klein escape criticism, the London *Tablet,*[36] an archivist named Coppinger,[37] and Monsignor Eugene Boeglin,[38] newspaper correspondent, stating that he had distorted Father Hecker's thought. Even Ireland seemed to approve Coppinger's brochure, for in September, 1898, he wrote:

> In a few trenchant statements you vindicate thoroughly the name and the life of good and great Father Hecker from the vile attacks of ignorant and vengeful bigots. You serve much the cause of truth by calling attention to the mistranslations in Abbé Klein's book and in exposing the *"mauvaise foi"* of Abbé Maignen. Your book has put all America under obligations to you.[39]

Perhaps, however, it would be fairer to say that the fault was due not to the translation but rather to differences in phraseology. As Boeglin pointed out on another occasion, the words "democracy," "individualism," and "liberalism" are often synonymous in the United States; in Europe they not merely have a different sense but are opposed to one another. In the United States they signify government for and by the people, strong and broad action, high and generous conceptions of the things of the world; in Europe, individualism and liberalism are at once a philosophical system and a social theory. The system and the theory are the antipodes of democracy; they stand for the rule of the individual in opposition to the State—the aristocratic idea of society. Liberalism in philosophy and politics is an antireligious conception of society.[40] This, too, was the view of Dr. William Barry.[41]

All the while the controversy raged, Monsignor O'Connell and Bishop Keane kept Ireland informed on the situation in Europe and particularly in Rome. Throughout 1897 they gave many indications of the beginning of trouble. O'Connell told of Cardinal Satolli's remark to Archbishop Chapelle that there was none of the supernatural in the Church in America, of his intimacy with Cardinal Mazzella, of his refusal to attend a lecture delivered by Keane, and of the comment of "a very eminent person" that such refusal made a bad impression, as it showed that Satolli must be engaged in something that made his presence incompatible.[42] Bishop Keane, who had heard of some expressions purported to have emanated from the Pope, protested to him against the idea that there existed among the "Americanists" any disaffection toward the Holy See. The Pope replied that he had always said to those who spoke to him that he was sure there could be no danger of schism in the United States, and he alleged the example of a Mexican bishop who had left the Church but who had been powerless to draw others after him. Whence he argued that, if even a similar thing should happen in the United States, there would be no following there either. This reply, Keane said, showed clearly to what extent misrepresentation had gone.[43] He also informed the Archbishop that, when he had heard that Cardinals Satolli and Mazzella had opened "a new and fierce war in the Vatican against Americanism," he had handed to Cardinal Rampolla a full memoir of American conditions, which, he hoped, would antidote their poison.[44]

Throughout 1898, in spite of his preoccupation with the Spanish-American War, the fate of Americanism absorbed more and more the attention of Archbishop Ireland. In January Bishop Keane wrote hopefully from Rome of an article in the *Civiltà Cattolica*, which suggested that a republic would be a better form of government for Italy than a monarchy, and which evidently expressed the private opinion of the Pope. This, he thought, would prove favorable to Americanism.[45] He also told of the urgent desire of the Holy Father and of Cardinal Rampolla that the Archbishop come to Rome as soon as possible, but he did not know their motive in so wishing. On his own part, he advised him to come, as, he said, "your presence here would have a powerful influence in spreading right ideas and averting mischief."[46] In June he gave a history of Maignen's book, of Lepidi's *Imprimatur*, and of his protest against it to Rampolla, who "professed himself astonished, sorry, indignant—and assured me that due action would be taken at any rate upon receiving the protests to the Pope which he expects from you and Cardinal Gibbons."[47] Writing in July from France, on his way home, he impressed upon the Archbishop the seriousness of the situation, which had now reached a crisis. The Pope was, he said, at the mercy of influences, and the Jesuits were openly in the field, using Delattre, their best man. He also asked for a united protest on the part of the hierarchy, and once more urged Ireland to come to Rome, as he was *the only man who could speak so as to be heard and heeded.* "Run to Rome," he begged, "talk and act as you alone can, crush the vipers and avert danger."[48]

Letters from O'Connell told of his visits to Lepidi, who, while admitting that neither in Hecker nor in Ireland was there anything contrary to faith or morals, felt that in the former there was too great a *"souffle"* of individualism and democracy, and in the latter an exaggerated form of expression. When O'Connell offered to amend any doubtful expressions in the *Life* of Hecker, Lepidi seemed to acquiesce, and later asked him to draw up a list of the points he had made in his conversation, as "his heart was torn by the hate he saw raging in the controversy." Great was O'Connell's amazement to find his statement later published in *La Vérité*, much garbled, omitting his protests against the calumnies spread about Americanism, and so construed as to constitute a repudiation of the movement on his part.[49] He, too, warned Ireland that the crisis had come and that the decisive battle of the war must be fought. He had heard that the *Life* of Hecker had been put on the Index, and that an opportune moment was awaited for the publication of the sentence—probably at the conclusion of peace in the Spanish-American War. He strongly urged an immediate protest from the hierarchy of the United States as the one hope of saving the situation.[50]

Nor were Keane and O'Connell the only ones who hoped that the archbishops would enter a protest. Dr. Thomas Bouquillon, Professor of Moral Theology at the Catholic University, felt that a formal and energetic appeal should be made to the Pope as well as a request for protection to the Pontiff, who, he pointed out, had written at least twenty times that "his first duty was to see that the divine authority of the bishops be held sacred." What in Bouquillon's mind increased the scandal was the fact that *La Vérité*, in which Maignen's articles originally appeared, had repeatedly been censured by Cardinal Rampolla in official letters and in private conversation. The complaint should be both individual and collective on the part of the hierarchy. He was convinced that not only the Jesuits but also a group of the Dominicans were hostile, and that the latter were especially powerful, since they held three important offices—that of Secretary of the Index, of Master of the Sacred Palace, and of Commissary to the Holy Office.[51]

In due time the protests came. In August, 1898, Cardinal Gibbons wrote to Cardinal Rampolla:

> Knowing that their main author, Fr. Maignen, was a worthless individual and little appreciated in his own country, I paid no attention to the articles. But the situation is completely changed today. The *imprimatur* granted that libel by the Master of the Sacred Palace gives it the importance of a serious and trustworthy piece of work.[52]

In reply to Archbishop Keane's protest, Lepidi expressed his regret for the pain caused him but tried to defend himself by asserting that the publication of Maignen's book would stimulate discussion of Americanism and result in good by clarifying doctrines which lent themselves to false interpretation.[53] To this Keane made the obvious reply, that on the contrary the book could only do harm, because the approval was an odious attack on respectable prelates.[54] In his protest to the Papal Secretary of State Keane made a similar declaration, reminding him that the "refractaires" both in America and in France would take advantage of it, and that the priests and people of the United States would ask him whether Lepidi's reply expressed the mind of the Holy See. He knew, he said, that the General of the Dominicans was hostile to the United States because of the Spanish-American War but that the ten million American Catholics would not be happy that they were judged by such men. Americanism was neither a doctrinal program nor a propaganda; the picture of it presented by Maignen was infamous; that by Lepidi, distorted. He returned to the subject again, pointing out how far matters had gone, and saying: "It has come to this that they accuse us of wishing to give heretics a new Church without any of the traits of the true religion. And this calumny has been published with the approval of the Vatican."[55]

Archbishop Ireland, who wrote a nine-page letter to the Cardinal Secretary of State, was especially outspoken in his protest:

> I have read Maignen's book, carrying the approval of Lepidi, which in the eyes of Europeans and Americans means the almost official approval of the Vatican. American papers announce "Americanism condemned, the Paulists are Anathema, Gibbons, Keane, Ireland and their Friends are under Papal Censure." The lay journals are amazed and imagine a new war is announced—the war between Rome and America.
>
> The names of the authors of the book reveal malice and bad faith. Maignen is well known; the other, Périès, a former professor of Canon Law at the Catholic University, who left unpleasant memories in America. The book is full of calumnies, palpable exaggerations. Corrigan gave the Imprimatur to the Life of Hecker; Gibbons praised the French translation.

In the United States there are no more devoted ecclesiastics than the Paulists. The announcement that Rome suspects their orthodoxy will be terrible for the American people, Protestants and Catholics. I am said to be the head of a movement which is called one of the most dangerous of modern times. The visit of Mgr. Martinelli last December is called an official inquest. Sinister motives are imputed to the advances which I made at your invitation to the President of the United States in the interest of peace in Spain. I am a terrible bishop, on the point of starting a schism.

Does Your Eminence advert to the great harm the book can do? For the American people the word Americanism is sacred, a symbol of everything they hold dear, their civil and political institutions. And Americanism is cursed with the Imprimatur. If Maignen wished to irritate the American people and strengthen their prejudices against the Church, he could not have chosen a better word. He gives as partisans of the Americanism which he condemns, Cardinal Gibbons and other prelates whom the American people hold in their affection because of their loyalty and attachment to the United States.

Then, the American people will say: our institutions are condemned in Rome; Rome is opposed to America. The Bishops who work with all their might to show that the Catholic faith is compatible with the civil duties of a citizen are put under censure; the Church and America cannot therefore live in harmony. America will soon decide the fate of twelve million Catholics in the old Spanish colonies. The time is badly chosen. We are accused of wishing to invade Rome and conquer with our ideas the government of the Church. What dreams of crazy brains! The Bishops who are attacked have only one system—that of the Holy See; have only one kind of ideas—that of the Holy See. They obey the least word that comes from Rome. In what instance have we not followed the wish of the Pope?[56]

To this letter Cardinal Rampolla replied urging calmness and patience. The Archbishop, he said, should not pay too much attention to the controversies, as the Holy Father in his own time would pass judgment.[57] This advice the Archbishop accepted, at the same time, however, pointing out that the situation created by Maignen's book was day by day becoming more painful, since a translation into English bore another Vatican *Imprimatur*.[58]

It had been hoped that at the meeting of the archbishops a united protest would be sent to Rome, but this hope was frustrated. Bishop McQuaid warned Archbishop Corrigan that the "Paulists must not be made scapegoats to cover Ireland, Keane & Co."[59] Archbishop Keane told the outcome of the meeting to Archbishop Ireland, who was unable to be present, detained by engagements at Loretto, Pennsylvania. He wrote:

What a pity that you were not here last week. The Cardinal told me after the Archbishops' meeting that what he foresaw as to the impossibility of getting a protest from them was fully realized. Corrigan with much trepidation and deprecation presented a protest from the Paulists. He argued that they had better keep out of the controversy—so did Feehan—so did Ryan—so did Katzer—*so did Williams*. And so it was dropped. No strong voice there for truth and justice.[60]

One would expect that under such circumstances Archbishop Ireland would feel again, as after the school controversy, that he was much alone. But, finding "comfort in himself and in his cause," he wrote to Father Elliott in November:

I regret very much that I was not to be there [at the meeting]—as I was anxious to break a lance against all comers in defence of Heckerism. You heard how your cause was treated. No voice bellowed out in the name of justice—and all was over. It is as well. I like to fight—and conquer with few allies. You owe nothing, or but little, when the victory is won.

We are going to win—the last letter I have received from Cardinal Rampolla, written on the field itself—in the Vatican, is most encouraging. Besides I shall soon invade Africa, and either Lepidi or Ireland will go into winter quarters. I expect to be in Rome about Christmas.[61]

As might be expected, the Paulist Fathers followed the controversy with keen interest. Father Walter Elliott, their Superior, feared the power of the Jesuits but was reassured by Cardinal Gibbons, who expressed his high regard for Father Hecker, referring to him as one who had been an instrument of Providence for the spread of the faith and who had done immense good in winning non-Catholics and in lessening prejudices. His spirit, Gibbons said, was that of an obedient child of the Church, truly Catholic in every sense of the word, adorned with all the fruits of piety, and able, by his apostolic zeal, to attract Protestants without sacrifice of orthodoxy.[62] Elliott also prepared an abridged version of Hecker for translation into Italian, convinced, as he was, that Lacordaire, Montalembert, Ozanam, and their movement were of a piece with that of the founder of the Paulist Congregation, even though time was needed to assimilate him. He was unable to understand why the Jesuits objected to the Paulist mode of life. "Do I object," he said, "to a Jesuit burying himself in 'methods'? Not the least. But why can't he let me try to fight without so many obediences, resulting, as they too often do, in really less actual obedience?[63] He told Klein of the meeting of the archbishops in October, 1898, and of their failure to take action, because Gibbons had received reassuring words from Rome. He paid tribute to the American Jesuits as "fine men, full of peace and goodwill," and he felt that the knowledge of Hecker would be advanced by the controversy. "Rome," he said, "will not strike him dead. We in America and you in France will be allowed some means of placing all the essence of his mission before the Church, eliminating the matter (or rather the apparent matter) which has been hateful to our present antagonists."[64] He gave his enemies a lesson in Christian charity when he wrote: "I know not if I have passed a single day for many months without earnestly praying for the Abbé Maignen, especially during the Holy Sacrifice. Also for the men who have worked hardest against us in Rome."[65]

The mood of Ireland and his friends alternated from hope to despair according to the good or evil reports they received from O'Connell, the watchman on the tower. At one time he told of a dinner at the home of Bishop Francis Mourey, the Auditor of the Rota for France, at which the two Vannutellis, Archbishop Keane, the Bishops of Laval and Perpignan, and the Chargé d'Affaires for France were present. When the conversation turned on the *Life* of Hecker, Mourey spoke of him with eulogy, saying, however, that as the Paulist had never made a regular course in Catholic theology he did not always understand the technical way of stating his opinions. He urged O'Connell, therefore, to bring out an Italian translation with annotations added by Father David, the Definitor of the Franciscans, to explain what probably the Italians might not understand. He also suggested that Ireland's Introduction, since it was the work of an archbishop, should remain untouched, but that Klein's Preface should be remodeled, as it put into too high relief the very point of Hecker's life which the Italians most feared.[66]

At another time O'Connell told of the visit to Rome of Bishop Sebastian Messmer, who had said so much against Heckerism to the Pope, the cardinals, and the Jesuits that the Monsignor feared lest the Congregation of the Index take action. Moreover, Maignen's book was being translated into English right in Rome, the Pope was sick and weak, and now Brandi and Company felt that their opportunity had come.[67]

To Father Elliott, who had given him distressing news, Ireland wrote: "I have read your letter with sadness that things are as they are; with resolve never to be defeated. I have written two terrible letters to Rampolla. I think we must agree on a vigorous campaign. You know I am 'a veteran,' ever ready for re-enlistment."[68]

The ex-Rector of the American College, whose information was not always accurate, must have been in touch with an authoritative source, for, only a short time before the decision of the Holy Father, he informed Klein that there was to be no condemnation of Hecker's *Life* or of the Abbé's Preface; that the treatment of the entire question would be reduced to the publication of a letter addressed to Gibbons, which would treat of (1) the relations existing between Church and State in America, which, though good in themselves, did not represent the type for the entire Church; (2) the need of an external director, since, for example, his agency is essential for the Sacrament of Penance; (3) insistence upon the doctrine of St. Thomas that a solemn vow made to God is an act of dignity and heroism. Thus the papal pronouncement, he said, while falling short of all that could be wished, would also fall short of what the enemy desired and expected.[69]

Keane also knew what was coming, for Cardinal Serafino Vannutelli had told him of his audience with the Holy Father, who had said:

"They [without saying who] have been urging me to be severe with the Americans; but I am convinced that gentle measures will do more good." Then he gave him the points of the encyclical now being prepared: (1) Church and State, (2) individualism, (3) vows. As to each only the familiar warning not to represent the contingently useful as the ideal.[70]

Archbishop Ireland maintained his characteristic optimism to the very end, lulled into a tragic sense of security by the consciousness of his own integrity and his conviction that he enjoyed the good will of the Holy Father and Cardinal Rampolla. He felt that the Vatican was disposed to regret the *Imprimatur*, for Rampolla had written to express the Pope's "*vivo desiderio*" that he do what he could for the protection of Catholic interests in the countries lost to Spain's domination and, moreover, to reiterate his assurance that the Archbishop might very safely leave the Maignen book to the Pope, who, in his own good time, would speak and act.[71]

The Archbishop's enemies were not all on the other side of the water. The old antagonisms resulting from the founding of the Catholic University, the national and school controversies, were carried over into Americanism. The most active and also the most secret of his opponents was Archbishop Corrigan, who, as Archbishop John Hennessy once said, "never acted directly, but always through the medium of others."[72] He was in constant touch with Father Brandi, who kept him informed on the progress of the controversy, and who gloated over the coming action of the Holy Father.[73]

Although Archbishop Ireland's enemies accused him of opposition to the religious orders and to the Pope, of threatening America with a schism by his liberalism and laicism, and of combining with Archbishop Keane to found a new Catholicism in America, he maintained throughout his attitude of contempt until rumors were spread that he would be called to Rome to suffer the same fate of deposition as Archbishop Keane. He then wrote to the editor of *L'Univers* that there was not a word of truth in all the stories recently published about his relations with the Vatican, and that not a single word had come to him from Rome to indicate the least change in the sentiments of good feeling which the Pope and his close counselors had always shown him.[74]

Finally but tardily Ireland hearkened to the advice of his friends and set out for Rome. He arrived there on January 27, 1899, only to find that the matter had already been given to the Congregation of the Index, had later been withdrawn and entrusted to a Committee of Cardinals, said to consist of Cardinals Mazzella, Satolli, Ledochowski, Ferrata, and Vincenzo Vannutelli. Although in his interview with the aged Pope he had, in some manner or other, received the idea that no letter would be sent to the bishops, the document was already prepared and on its way. One needs little imagination to picture the anguish that possessed the soul of Ireland during those days in Rome or the anxiety with which he went from one influential door to another in a desperate attempt to save the situation. Like Dante he knew the bitterness of climbing as a suppliant inhospitable stairs, of receiving empty phrases of reassurance, of hoping when hope was gone. He could almost hear the mocking accents of his adversaries as again and again was flung in his face a letter of congratulation to Lepidi from His Grace of New York, proof that the American hierarchy was divided in its attitude.[75] And to crown it all, there appeared on the streets of Rome a scurrilous sheet, *The True American Catholic*, making contemptible personal attacks and characterizing Americanism as "evidently inspired by Satan," a pamphlet so vile that he was forced to protest to the Minister of Public Instruction.[76] It is no wonder that he later exclaimed: "Mon Dieu, what a sad visit mine was to Rome. I wish those three months were blotted out of my life's story."[77]

Brandi was evidently in close touch with the whole situation, for on January 2 he informed "New York" that the encyclical was ready at last and might be sent in a few days. There had, he said, been great difficulties to overcome, and every possible means had been used to prevent its publication. He also averred that when Ireland had signified to Rampolla his intention to come to Rome, the Cardinal wrote to him that he had better stay at home, for his presence in Rome *"nelle presenti circostanzi"* might give rise to false reports and interfere with the settlement of ecclesiastical affairs in the new colonies of the United States,[78] a statement difficult to reconcile with Archbishop Keane's earlier assertion that both the Holy Father and the Cardinal were emphatic in asserting their desire that he come.

Ireland tried in vain to see a draft of the letter; he had to wait until its appearance in the *Osservatore Romano* on February 21. To Father Deshon he wrote:

All that giant will could do was done by me to prevent its publication. It had been signed, sealed and printed before my arrival. The forces against us were enormous—Jesuits, Dominicans and Redemptorists fought for very life.

Rampolla gave me to understand that after the letter had been signed and printed—he, in deference to my words, had it softened "in the beginning and in the end." I believe a second printed edition was made. Rampolla says that the words of the letter allow us to say that the things condemned were never said or written in Americanism, not even by Hecker—but were set afloat in France as Americanism at the occasion of the Life and especially of its translation and of interpretations given in foreign languages, and he added that I should do my best to spread this view. Small comfort—but we must make the most of it. Read the letter carefully and you will see that the Americanism condemned is Maignen's nightmare, v.g. who ever preferred natural to supernatural virtues? Who ever taught that the practice of natural virtues was not to be vitalized and supernaturalized by divine grace? Who ever taught that in hearkening to the Holy Spirit the Christian was not to be constantly guided by the visible magisterium of the Church? Fanatics conjured up an Americanism and put such before the Pope. Lepidi and Mazzella wrote the body of the letter—I cannot pray that God forgive them.[79]

In his letter, entitled *Testem Benevolentiae*, the Holy Father referred to the Preface of the French translation of *The Life of Father Hecker* and examined certain opinions contained therein, the basis of which was, he said, that, in order to make converts, the Church should adapt herself to the age and relax her rigor as regards the rule of life and the deposit of faith, and should minimize certain doctrines or give them a new meaning. But faith, he pointed out, is not a doctrine for speculation, and in place of bringing converts into the Church, such a process would rob Catholics of their Church. The rule of Christian life may be modified according to differences of time, place, or national custom, but such modification must be made by the Vicar of Christ, not by individuals. He then took up the consequences of such opinions. It is wrong to say that spiritual direction is less needed in our day, and it is presumptuous to place natural virtues above the supernatural. From such quasi disdain of the passive virtues follows a scorn of the religious life and of religious vows, and of those who engage in works of prayer and penitence. Hence, he said, he could not approve of the opinions called by some with the name of Americanism, unless by that name is signified the characteristic gifts which reflect honor on the people of America or the customs and laws of America.[80]

Assured by the Pope that the *Testem Benevolentiae* did not touch him, Archbishop Ireland lost no time in acknowledging the letter:

Most Holy Father: Immediately on reading the letter which Your Holiness has just addressed to his Eminence Cardinal Gibbons and to other members of the American episcopate, I hasten to thank Your Holiness for this act of esteem and love toward the Catholics of the United States as well as our entire American nation.

New Light has come; misunderstandings are no more. Now we can even define the errors which "certain ones" have wished to cloak with the name of "Americanism" and define the truth which alone Americans call "Americanism."

Moreover, so clear and precise are the distinctions and explanations given in the Apostolic letter that the danger which was not understood by all the people of the United States—a danger which I myself, I confess, did believe might arise—is no longer possible.

Seeing the astonishing confusion of ideas and the subsequent controversies started, especially in France, about the book, "Vie du Père Hecker," the extent of which can be measured by the Apostolic letter, I can no longer be blind to the fact that it was a necessity for the chief Pastor to raise his voice to enlighten and pacify men's minds.

Assuredly, with all the strength of my soul, I repudiate and condemn every opinion which the Apostolic letter repudiates and condemns, all those false and dangerous opinions to which, as the letter says, "certain persons give the name of Americanism." I repudiate and condemn those opinions without any exception, literally, as Your Holiness repudiates and condemns them, and I repudiate and condemn them with all the greater readiness and heartfelt joy because my Catholic faith and my understanding of the teachings and practices of the Holy Church never for a single instant permitted me to open my soul to such extravagances. The whole episcopate of the United States in their own names and in the names of their people are ready to repudiate and condemn those errors. We cannot but be indignant that such an injury has been done us—to our Bishops, to our faithful people, to our nation—in designating by the word "Americanism" as certain ones have done, such errors and extravagances as these.

Most Holy Father, it is the enemies of the Church in America and the faithless interpreters of the faith who "imagine" that there exists or that some desire to establish in the United States a Church differing in one iota from the Holy and Universal Church which other nations recognize, and which Rome itself, infallible guardian of the revelation of Jesus Christ, recognizes or can recognize.

Begging Your Holiness graciously to accept this expression of the sentiment of my love and devotion and to bestow upon me the favor of the Apostolic blessing, I have the honor to be your Holiness's devoted son.

John Ireland, Archbishop of St. Paul[81]

This letter was followed by others from Cardinal Gibbons, Archbishop Keane, and Father Deshon. The Cardinal wrote: "I do not think that in the whole country could be found a single bishop or priest or even a well-instructed layman who had ever put forward such extravagances. No, that is not, has never been and will never be our Americanism."[82] Archbishop Keane called God to witness that he had never taught or maintained any part of what the Pope had reproved.[83] Father Deshon wrote for the Paulists, expressing their adhesion to the doctrine laid down in the pontifical document, their joy that the Pope had not condemned Father Hecker, but rather interpretations of his opinions. He also promised that they would not sell or give to others copies of the *Life* until the corrections judged necessary by the Holy See should have been made.[84] This last statement did not please Archbishop Ireland, who wrote to Deshon: "No one asked you to withdraw the book from circulation; no one expected this of you, and by so doing you give rise to the belief that the book itself is somewhat condemnable."[85]

Abbé Klein sent his adhesion to the letter, announced the withdrawal from sale of the French edition, and said:

If unwittingly I have fallen into the errors condemned by your Holiness, I eagerly and gratefully seize the opportunity of rejecting them all, without exception or reserve, and in the natural sense in which they are condemned by your Holiness, only too happy that I am able to clear myself of suspicion, and to profess once more my sentiments of absolute submission to the divine authority of the Church and her visible Head.[86]

Later, the Abbé regretted his withdrawal of the *Life*. He felt that his friends in Rome should have informed him of the nature of the replies of Archbishops Ireland and Keane, and of the reactions to them, so that he might have modeled his reply on theirs. Had he known them, he would never have withdrawn a book which had "withstood the thunders of the Index, which had the approval of Cardinal Gibbons and Archbishop Ireland, and which had not only fostered fervor in Christian souls, but had also disposed unbelievers towards the Faith." He realized more and more that the condemnation of Rome had fallen not on the ideas of the "Americanists" but on those attributed to them.[87]

Bishop Thomas Byrne, who was in Rome before the *Testem* was published and who knew that Mazzella had composed it, told the Pope that it should not be sent. The Pope replied that he had been given to understand that Father Hecker taught the inspiration of the Holy Spirit without the Sacraments and the authority of the Church, and that, anyway, minds had been so much disturbed in France that it was necessary for the sake of French Catholics to write the letter.[88] Bishop John L. Spalding also said that in his visit to Rome he told the Pope that no such errors existed in America, that he knew Father Hecker, who never believed or taught such doctrines.[89]

Such, however, was not the opinion of the prelates of the Archdiocese of Milwaukee, who thanked the Holy Father for "calling the erring back to the right way of thinking, at the same time expressing their indignation that some who proclaimed their detestation of such errors, also protested that hardly anyone in America held them."[90] The letter from the Archdiocese of New York, which was sent in the name of all the bishops of the province, much to the surprise of two prelates who knew nothing of it, avowed that the errors were widespread but that the germs had been killed just in time.[91]

Archbishop Ireland's letter did not altogether escape criticism. On the one hand, Father Zahm, Archbishop Keane, and others praised it highly. Zahm exclaimed: "What a magnificent coup Ireland's letter was; it saved the situation completely. That is the general verdict here. It was a Quixotic tilt against wind-mills that the 'refractaires' got the Pope into. They feel that themselves, and are saying little about the condemnation of Americanism."[92] Father Alphonse Maignen felt that the Archbishop had struck the right key and taken the wind out of the sails of his enemies.[93] The London *Times* said that the Archbishop's reply was "rather a cleverly-worded *fin de non-recevoir* than an act of humble submission. As a French writer observed, one looked through it in vain for any note of contrition."[94]

On the other hand Dr. Frederick Rooker wrote to O'Connell:

While we on the inside could understand the hidden meaning of that letter, the country at large has completely misinterpreted it. It has been universally accepted as an abject recantation and an acknowledgment of defeat. There is news that the Pope is tickled to death with the Archbishop's letter and has given it himself for publication. This, instead of appearing here as an approval of the hidden meaning of the Archbishop's letter, is taken as confirming the opinion that it was a recantation. Then comes the Archbishop's interview in which he seems to throw down the gauntlet and to make a plain open issue on which he frankly declares war.[95]

Before Mr. Taft went to Rome to arrange for the settlement of Philippine affairs, William Curtis, correspondent for the Chicago *Record*, wrote for him a series of notes in which he gave his impressions of some of the leading ecclesiastics with whom Mr. Taft would come in contact. Referring to Monsignor O'Connell he said:

O'Connell does not approve of all that Archbishop Ireland has done, particularly the alleged retraction of his views. Ireland says he did not retract, O'Connell says he did, induced by hope of the cardinalate. O'Connell feels quite sensitive on this subject. He thinks Ireland got out from under and left him (O'C) to endure all the odium of the liberal policy of the Church in America.[96]

The letter of the Holy Father met with mixed reactions. By European adversaries it was hailed with joy and exultation. In the words of Father Péchenard: "The French clergy uttered a cry of relief and joy; they welcomed with transports of joy the papal decision which had just dispelled all uncertainties." They were, however, taken aback and scandalized by the reactions of some of their fellow clerics as expressed in such papers as *L'Univers* and *La Justice Sociale*. In the latter journal l'Abbé Naudet wrote:

The Pope, after having condemned a collection of propositions which are not found in Father Hecker, or in Cardinal Gibbons, or in Mgr. Ireland or Mgr. Keane or in works of other American theologians, orators or philosophers recently attacked, adds these words: "We cannot approve these opinions summed up under the name of Americanism." The Pope is careful not to attribute to our brothers beyond the seas what owed its birth to the prolific imagination of writers who take their orders from *La Vérité*.[97]

Writing in the *North American Review*, Archbishop Ireland said:

More interesting for us is the reception accorded by the American Episcopate. Five archbishops and their suffragans, while condemning what the Pope condemned, respectfully defended that American Church against the charge of heresy. These prelates are Cardinal Gibbons of Baltimore, Archbishop Williams of Boston, Archbishop Ireland of St. Paul, Archbishop Riordan of San Francisco, and Archbishop Kain of St. Louis. To these may be added Archbishop Ryan of Philadelphia and his bishops, who informed his Holiness that scarcely any among the souls committed to their care held the false principles so justly condemned. From Chicago and Dubuque came no reply, the archbishops of these provinces being then ill. The archdiocese of Santa Fe was vacant. The Archbishops of Portland, Cincinnati and New Orleans did very little more than acknowledge with reverence the receipt of the Pontiff's letter. Out of the fourteen archdioceses of America two only—those of Milwaukee and New York—reported the presence of Americanism. This had been expected. The letter from the ecclesiastical province of Milwaukee represented the views of four German bishops; and although the friends of these prelates defend their action on the ground that not one of the good pious men had ever read the "Life of Father Hecker," it should by no means be overlooked that Milwaukee is the pet preserve of Cahenslyism—it is a miniature American Germany, more carefully barred than the Fatherland itself against the influx of American ideas. As to New York, it is said with much show of reason that had there not been of old serious friction between that See and those of Baltimore and St. Paul, Archbishop Corrigan might not have so suddenly detected the smell of heresy. This is rendered probable by the fact that the "Life of Father Hecker," from which the heresy was supposed to have been extracted, actually bore the imprimatur of Archbishop Corrigan himself. Be this as it may, it is now more than an open secret that the letter which his Grace of New York sent to Rome in the name of his suffragans did not represent the views of at least some of the bishops whose signatures it bore.

The Archbishop then takes the *Civiltà Cattolica* to task for reproducing the letter from the archdioceses of New York and Milwaukee and keeping silent about the letters of those prelates who protested against the imputation of heresy; also for ignoring the chorus of repudiation of the Catholic press of America. He challenged Péchenard to produce any evidence which would support his charges that American Catholics are guilty of "a certain bending in the matter of dogmatic affirmation, of a separatist tendency with respect to the central ecclesiastical authority, and of a minimizing in the practices of the Christian and especially the religious life." He concluded with these words: "In Europe Americanism was cradled as well as entombed; in America, it was unknown until it was condemned."[98]

If the controversy over Americanism produced no other results than this gem of polemical discourse, with its constant play of sarcasm, innuendo, and ridicule, it almost justified its existence.

The Archbishop expressed his own reactions to the papal letter as follows:

This letter, hailed by the enemies of America as a triumph, is in reality the only bright page in the history of Americanism. As we read it, we feel that we have passed from the atmosphere of sordid strife, where men with motives live and squabble, into the august presence of one of the great

Pontiffs of the Church. Every line of the document breathes respect for the Church in America, and of that Church, no member, be he bishop, priest or layman is censured or condemned. "Certain opinions concerning the methods of Christian life," which are sometimes included under the name Americanism and "which have been brought in" (by some persons not named) are false and dangerous and to be repudiated—such is the sum and substance of Leo's decision. The Pope not only carefully guards himself against imputing to American Catholics the errors sometimes included under the name Americanism, but even signifies his incredulity that such errors are held by Americans. "If, indeed, by that word (Americanism) is meant qualities of mind which distinguish the people of America as other nations are distinguished, and in so far as the expression applies to the constitution of your States and laws, there is not, assuredly, the smallest reason for us to think it should be rejected. But if it is used not only to describe but also to justify the errors we have already pointed out, what doubt can there be that our venerable brethren, the Bishops of America, will be the first to reject and condemn it as injurious to themselves and the whole nation."

To a representative of the *New Era* of London, who visited him, Ireland said that American Catholics proclaim no thesis which might be applicable to other nations or other times. They take what exists in their own country, they are satisfied that this is for them the best that could be in the circumstances of their country, and they are absolutely and unhesitatingly loyal to those conditions; nor in this positive and unreserved cohesion do they believe that they offend in the least any principle or dogma of the Holy Catholic Church. So there is an Americanism in America to which they adhere, and there is an Americanism spoken of in Paris of which they know nothing, and which they repudiate as an insult to their country.[99] To a representative of the London *Chronicle* he explained the importance he attached to the natural virtues, saying that temperance and truthfulness in the clergy cannot be replaced by devotional fidelity. He also protested against the charge of hostility to the religious orders.[100]

In spite of the reassurance of the Holy Father that the letter did not touch him, the Archbishop was depressed and indignant. How deeply the iron had entered his soul may be judged from his letters to O'Connell. From Naples he wrote: "Life has become too serious for me to allow me to find employment. I have made up my mind to say nothing in defence until after Orleans. Then I will speak and denounce my calumniators."[101] Difficult as it must have been for him to concentrate on the address which he was preparing for the Joan of Arc festivity, it at least served to relieve his mental anguish. From

Turin he wrote: "I am rested—resigned to my lot—working. Only you and Archbishop Keane know and will know my inmost thoughts. C'est la triplice—and I swear to it eternal allegiance."[102]

But, as in the fitful skies of his "sweet Kilkenny," the sun came bursting through the plangent cloud of depression, and he quickly recovered his spirits. In a short time he was in France, meeting his old friends and giving interviews. Bishop O'Gorman found him in the best of spirits, determined to go his way and do his work regardless of consequences. He was angry at the injustice done to him by the complacency of the Vatican with attacks on Americanism and himself, also at the refusal to make reparations, but "his anger had passed into contempt."[103] Abbé Klein said:

Three months after the *Testem* he returned to Europe, and, as if nothing had happened, he could be heard speaking with complete success in France, Belgium, England and Ireland. And everywhere the applause of the elite drowned out the protestations, the reproaches, the abuse which his disconcerted enemies continued to hurl at him and which he ignored.[104]

On his return home, Archbishop Ireland expected action at the meeting of the archbishops but was disappointed. As he wrote to O'Connell: "We had a stormy meeting at Washington. San Francisco, St. Louis, Portland, St. Paul tried to get a joint protest against the idea of existence of errors. Philadelphia almost joined it, but Baltimore cried 'peace, peace—death even for the sake of peace,' and nothing was effected."[105] The official account of the meeting is as follows:

Archbishop Riordan, having called attention to the letter of the Holy Father, referred to the letter of the Bishops of the Province of Milwaukee in which the existence in this country of the condemned errors was admitted and in such manner that those who deny their existence are now branded as Jansenists. This he considered a matter of grave importance, being a direct charge of heresy against some of ourselves. Archbishop Kain spoke on the same lines and expressed his opinion that some action should be taken in protest against the charge implied in that matter.

Archbishop Ireland followed, and, tracing the development of the charge of erroneous teaching in the Church of America and deprecating the letter of the Milwaukee Prelates, he moved that the Most Rev. Secretary be instructed to write to all the Bishops of America and ask them an expression of their opinion on these two questions: first—"Whether these errors do exist in their Dioceses or in other parts of America," and, second—"If they do, then to specify where they exist and by whom they are held." The Archbishop of New York strongly deprecated the adoption of the above resolution, because he thought it would be disrespectful to the Holy

Father. Archbishop Ryan also objected to the resolution and offered the following substitute: "That the Prelates here present do all they can to induce all the Bishops, who have not written to the Holy Father, in response to his letter to Cardinal Gibbons, to write to him." The substitute was lost by a tie vote. The original resolution was then put and defeated by a vote of four ayes to five nays—His Eminence casting his vote against it.[106]

The effectiveness of the campaign of the enemies and the impression left on the mind of the Holy Father by the letters from New York and Milwaukee may be seen from the following incidents. On March 18, 1899, receiving in audience the Superior of the Congregation of the Brothers of St. Vincent de Paul, the Holy Father said to him: "Fr. Maignen should be satisfied with my letter on Americanism. Submission has been made, but we must be vigilant."[107]

When he sent the documents appointing Monsignor Keane Archbishop of Dubuque, he enclosed together with the brief a personal letter exhorting him to bear in mind his letter to Cardinal Gibbons on Americanism, in which he showed that *"multis de causis, quas ibi attigimus, fidelium pietatem in discrimen vocari"* (for many causes which we mentioned there, the piety of the faithful was endangered). And he went on to say that these dangers must be combated by every means, especially by fostering Catholic schools. He concluded with the words: *"Nec dubitamus quin ad gliscentes istic errores discutiendos et animarum conjunctionem cum hac infallibili veritatis Cathedra fovendam, sis adlaboraturus."* (Nor do we doubt that you will strive earnestly to suppress the errors spreading there and to promote the union of souls with this infallible seat of truth.) Keane wrote bitterly to Ireland: "He simply reiterates the assertion made in the Encyclical—and this at the very time when he was virtually apologizing to you for it, and saying it was needed only in France—for his letter to me is dated August 18th. It made me sick—and it was a painful blow to the Cardinal too."[108]

It was surprising how many people took the productions of Maignen and Delassus seriously. When Cardinal Serafino Vannutelli told Rampolla of his visit to the Pope, who had indicated his intention of publishing a letter favorable to the Americans and of tranquilizing them, the Secretary of State drew himself up and, looking at Vannutelli with surprise, asked, "But, Eminence, have you read Maignen's book?" On receiving a negative reply, Rampolla said, "You must read it, for it is important."[109] Again, when Countess Sabina di Paravicino, of Milan, a warm admirer of Ireland and a translator of some of his discourses into Italian, saw a news item which seemed to indicate that Cardinal Andrea Ferrari approved of Delassus's book, she wrote to him in protest, reminding him of the keen displeasure his action would cause the Archbishop and of the "exquisite courtesy your Eminence showed him during his visit here."[110] The Cardinal replied that he had merely thanked Delassus for the gift of the volume and for the good will he showed in manifesting his desire to comment on the Pope's words. He repeated to the Countess what he had written: "Americanism is not a system of its very nature localized as to doctrine and method; all novelty which has reference to it is not without interest even in Italy, and the letter 'Testem Benevolentiae' may be considered not only for the good of America but of all civilized countries." He protested vehemently that he had no intention of casting the least slur on Ireland, "for whom I had so much esteem and veneration before knowing him personally and still more after I had the good fortune to meet him."[111]

Some French bishops—those of Nancy, Annecy, and Beauvais— "used the utmost diligence in circulating the Pontifical letter among their clergy," an action which made the Archbishop remark: "It is a relief to know that these bishops have succeeded in strangling Americanism in their dioceses." He sternly rebuked the Bishop of Annecy, whose diocesan *Review* accused him and Cardinal Gibbons of lying when in their reply to the Pope they protested that they had never held the condemned doctrines. He ridiculed him for approving Maignen's book with all its absurdities and for praising the pamphlet of Périès, who had been dismissed from the Catholic University. He reminded him that the Pontiff had expressed his satisfaction with the adhesion which he criticized, and, as evidence that the calumnies invented against him had not taken hold among the great Catholic public, he instanced the honor shown him by the Bishop of Orléans, the priests of Paris, the principal organs of the Catholic and secular press, and the many distinguished men who had done him honor. He concluded by saying: "And surely I do not recall these remembrances through vanity; but even a fool can draw from them the lesson they contain: to know that the agitation stirred up on this side of the Atlantic against the Church of the United States has not passed beyond the dregs of European thought."[112]

No situation is so bad that it does not have its humorous side. When Lorenzelli, the Papal Nuncio at Paris, heard that Ireland was coming there he was much agitated at the thought of meeting him, and, not knowing how to deal with one who seemed to be suspect, he wrote to Cardinal Rampolla asking how he should treat him. But after the Archbishop arrived he completely captivated the Nuncio, who wrote to the Cardinal lauding Ireland, telling of his goodness and his great influence in America, and hoping that between him and the cardinals there would not be ill feeling or want of confidence. He referred to the address which the Archbishop had made to the students at Auteuil in praise of the Pope, and to the high esteem in which he was held by President Loubet and M. Delcassé.[113]

Before leaving Paris, the Archbishop sent to *L'Univers* a letter in which he divided Catholics into three classes: those who wished to revive the past, those interested only in their own piety, and those eager to spread the influence of the Church by using means appropriate to the times. The first he called incomplete theologians, confounding the relative with the absolute. The second group comprises the great mass of the faithful. In days of unity, when the Gospel reigns, this attitude may suffice. But when the bonds of religious obedience are broken, and diversity of faith causes divisions in the human family, this method no longer answers to present needs. Of the third class he said:

To gain hearts and penetrate minds so as to make Jesus Christ loved and understood by men who do not belong to Him or who have no idea of belonging to the soul of the Church, to prepare among them the only bond of real union likely to bring each particular society, and human society as a whole, near to that ideal which all have—unity; to speak without ceasing in a language understood by those around us, and, in ways that circumstances, in which Providence has placed us, have opened out for us; to make the spirit of the Gospel effectively enter into the life of the individual and of the mass; to use all the avenues of society to scatter services and secure sympathies; on all grounds, social, political, philosophical, scientific, literary, artistic, to multiply points of contact with men; by the profession and practice of Catholicism, whole and entire, to establish in theory and in fact, under the eyes of public opinion, that the Church in the cohesion of her dogma, in the sense of her tradition, in the hierarchical structure of her organization, the infallible authority and sovereign magisterium of her Head, is the sole source of complete life, of right and fruitful activity, the sole efficacious agent of safe progress; that, far from being shut in a historical period or a scientific phase, the Church is normally in correspondence with every movement of human thought and action, when once these are stripped of the fictions created by abstract speculations; that the Church alone, proclaiming that all men are equally children of God, gives a sure origin and a solid basis for human fraternity, and maintains for it in the Papacy, the visible representation of Divine paternity, a positive expression; that, in a word, the Church, representing the Divine absolutism, must oppose every pretence of human absolutism, and that thus she is essentially and by her vocation the protector of the development of each one's personality, the deliverer from all servitudes, the safeguard against all oppressions; in the light of the total doctrine of the Church to recognize in the ideas and the interests which win the heart of the age, under whatever name or whatever veil it covers them up, all that, which being truly living, good, just and progressive, is by right a part of the Catholic patrimony; to claim it as such and seek its realization; and by so doing, to give confidence to all those who more or less unconsciously have any kind of bond with Catholicism, and, without holding our faith, are anxious for truth and desirous of good—such has been in days of conquest and in times of transition, the conception of all the great Popes, of Gregory VII, of Innocent III, of Sixtus V.[114]

Ireland was more prophetic than he knew, when in his Introduction to the *Life* of Hecker he asked: "Who ever tries to do something outside routine lines, against whom hands are not raised and whose motives and acts are not misconstrued?" John T. Reily developed this thought at greater length when, speaking of the great figures in the history of the Church, he said that many of them were in disfavor in their own time and among their people, persecuted, denounced, until ages afterwards their merits and deeds were recognized. "Through the same fire," he said, "has to pass every great and progressive man in the Church." Time has more and more vindicated the wisdom of Archbishop Ireland, who was half a century in advance of his age. As Reily expressed it:

It will be to the everlasting honor of prelates like Ireland, Keane and Gibbons that they have shown the world that they can be at once fervent Catholics and loyal Americans. They can afford to be misunderstood while their work prospers. But henceforth, though many assail, none will misunderstand them. By their previous efforts the danger of warring Catholic communities in America has been averted; their adhesion to the Papal letter is but an avowal of what they have always cherished.[115]

Perhaps the best word on the controversy was said by Father Tierney, the Jesuit: "Americanism was magnified out of all proportion to its importance by a clamor raised in France."[116]

Chapter 7

MISSIONS ABROAD

1. THE ENVOY OF THE POPE

When the school question had been fought out at Rome, Archbishop Ireland received from the Sovereign Pontiff a commission of the highest difficulty and importance at once to the papacy and to France. For years one measure after another had been directed against the Church, with the result that a large and influential section of the Catholics of France had viewed the Republic as the born enemy of religion. Many religious orders were expelled; the schools were laicized, some of them becoming hotbeds of infidels. There were many who longed for the return of royalty. They regarded the Republic as standing for everything they feared and hated, and the breach between the Church and State was daily growing wider. Leo XIII saw clearly the madness of the policy they were pursuing; he knew that the future of the Church lay with the people, not with dynasties, and he did everything in his power to rally the Catholics of France to the Republic. In February, 1892, he sent a letter to the French people in which he urged them to accept the Republic, to forget their differences and unite for the protection of religion against those who sought to destroy it. His efforts, however, were in vain, nullified by the enmity of the radicals and the stubbornness of the royalists. Indeed, his letter to the French Catholics seemed only to embitter their resentment, especially among the old influential families.[1] He took advantage of the presence of Archbishop Ireland in Rome to suggest that he go to Paris as his unofficial representative and, if possible, bring about a change of heart among the recalcitrants. It was an unpopular mission and one that called for consummate tact.

When the Archbishop arrived in Paris in the middle of June, 1892, he made contact with a number of prominent personages whom he knew, and some with whom he had corresponded—Vicomte Melchior de Vogüe, the brilliant author and contributor to *La Revue des Deux Mondes*; M. Albert de Mun of the Chamber of Deputies, who four years before had sent him copies of his books as a token of his respect and admiration; M. Henri Lorin, whom he had invited to accompany him to Rome and for whom he had a warm affection; M. Max Le-Clerc, who had visited him in St. Paul in 1890. These formed a committee which invited him to speak at the Hall of the Geographic Society on the subject "Conditions in America." On June 18 an audience of twelve hundred, comprising the intellectual and social elite of Paris—diplomats, authors, priests, senators, ambassadors—greeted him. Among them were Prince d'Arenberg, General Annenkoff, Paul Deschanel, l'Abbé Felix Klein, l'Abbé Louis Duchesne, and other well-known figures. Among them also were many who detested the Republic. It was not surprising that the committee asked for information about America, for, but a short time earlier, the Pope in an interview given to a French correspondent had instanced the United States as an example of happy relations between Church and State.

Vicomte de Vogüe, who presented the Archbishop, had on a previous occasion alluded to him as an apostle and a thinker, who made people understand the victories won by the great bishops of the fourth and fifth centuries, and he had gone so far as to say that, listening to him, one recalled the words of the disciples who journeyed to Emmaus: "Did not your heart burn within you as he spoke?"

The Archbishop quickly won his audience by paying a glowing tribute to France, the land of his youth, "the mother" of his ideas, to France's missionaries in America, to France's soldiers in the war that won liberty for America. He then painted a picture of the United States, of her wondrous development, the richness of her soil, her economic and industrial advance, the vast influx of immigrants to her shores, and her efforts to select and unify them into a homogeneous citizenry. He warned his audience against distorted ideas of Americans, who are not always understood by foreigners, and he spoke pregnant words, the truth of which he was to realize more fully and more bitterly some years later: "Europe has the habit of locating in distant countries, and preferably in America, whatever things it dreams of as exaggerated and terrible, whatever things it wishes to have removed from its own territories." He then went on to defend his countrymen against the charges of lawlessness, money seeking, and lack of culture. The American citizen, he said, regards the law as sacred. Sometimes he doesn't like it, but then he says: "Ah well, it is the law; we obey; in two or four years we will change it. That is the privilege of the American people—it can change its laws and its government without ever wishing to change the republic." The American people like to make money; they are energetic, enterprising; money represents for them the reward of their work; but, at the same time, they spend it as readily as they amass it. Because they had had to build cities and railroads and factories, they had not had as much leisure as the Europeans for poetry, painting, and music, but already their libraries, museums, and art institutes were assuming large proportions; and their universities were becoming world-known centers of thought and research. He defended the American woman against the charge of boldness and frivolity. In reality, he said, she is only independent, conscious of her power of self-control, and ready, when need came, to work for her living.

He next painted a picture of American democracy—a form of government in keeping with the fundamental principles of Christianity, culminating at last in the liberty of the individual and in the power of the people to govern themselves. When he turned to the situation of the Church in the United States, at once the interest of his audience was keenly alert. It is, he said, a free Church in a free State. While the adherents of the various denominations hold to their beliefs rigidly, all live in peace, according to one another the rights they wish for themselves. The Republic grants complete liberty to the Church. The priests and bishops live and toil among the people, appearing on public occasions, speaking on social and economic questions. "Our hearts," he said, "beat with love for the Republic, our tongues chant its praises with eloquence, our hands are raised to bless it and its soldiers."

And then he came to the real point and purpose of his address, saying:

As a citizen of a republic, I recognize this evening a special obligation to the country through which the approbation and the benediction of the Head of the Church have come to the republican form of government. I must give expression to the gratitude which wells up in my heart to-night for the great country which gave to Leo XIII the occasion to "canonize the republic." Heretofore when I came to Europe, I heard it whispered about that I was a dangerous man, that I believed in democracy, that I loved republics. Indeed, it was darkly hinted that I was almost a heretic. All that even friends would say to me was: "Your ideas may pass current in far away America where people are not yet fully civilized." To all this

I had but little to reply. Certainly, I had not at the service of my mind and heart the strong, proud words which are to-day upon my lips. Arriving in Rome a few months ago, I heard from the summit of the Vatican Hill: "Of all the forms of civil government which the Church has recognized, and of which she has made trial, she cannot say from which she has received more harm or more good." Just now she is resolved to make trial in France of the republic, and I, as a citizen of a republic, say to the Church: "In this experiment thou shalt succeed."[2]

And thus, without even alluding to the problem that was rending the Church in France, without saying a word of reproach or pleading for those who regarded the republican form of government as a danger to the Church, without offending in any way the susceptibilities of the most sensitive, he instilled into their minds lessons that were sorely needed. But the picture of America with its millions of Catholics loyal supporters of the government, America with its regard for the religious beliefs of its citizens, sank deeply into the minds of those who persecuted the Church in France and of those who looked upon the Republic as a standing menace to Catholicism. All this he did with an air of informality and a spice of humor and a glowing sympathy that pleased while it carried conviction. "They sat down to table," said a Paris newspaper, "accusing the Republic of France; they rose up wondering whether they ought not accuse themselves."

The address, which was received with great enthusiasm by the liberals and the younger clergy, was widely quoted in the press, which contrasted the happy conditions prevailing in the United States with the conflict raging in France; the friendly relations of the Church and State in the one with the wide gap that separated them in the other. It was an address that called for unusual daring. As Cardinal Gibbons wrote to him later: "It was a bold, a hazardous undertaking to fight for Republicanism in a foreign tongue before an audience largely unfriendly."[3] It is not surprising that it met with opposition on the part of many of the clergy, for nothing could be more opposed to their ideas and interests. After all, their support and the endowment of their churches had, in the past, come largely from the aristocrats and the conservatives, and here was a foreign bishop counseling them to forget their hatred of a government which afflicted them with odious laws and had robbed them of their resources. Were they now expected to break with their friends and accept the enemy? It was a revolutionary address, for it bade the priests, who had restricted themselves to the purely spiritual works of their parishes, to go about among the people and to mingle with them. These things the Archbishop said by implication rather than by direction, but his meaning was obvious. Eugene Veuillot, the well-known publicist, spoke of the consummate tact of one who could address an audience numbering many monarchists and not offend the sensibilities of any. He told of the bursts of applause which again and again interrupted the Archbishop. He was especially impressed by his optimism, "by the ease with which he passed from grave to gay, from pleasantries to seriousness, from oratorical flights to conversational manner, but never at any time leaving doubt that he was a bishop, a man of God."[4] *La Paix* said that the Pope could not have found a better official representative than Monsignor Ireland to show the reactionaries of France that one can be an excellent prelate and an excellent republican, but that it would be better if what he said were spoken by an authorized representative of the Church in France, and, if many priests used the same language to show that they were really interested in democracy, that they were on the side of the people dignified by its new sovereignty.[5]

The effect of the address was shown within a month. Many priests were found addressing public gatherings, one even speaking to a meeting held under the auspices of the Freemasons, and doing so with the permission of his bishop.

During the following week the Archbishop addressed the students of the Catholic Circle at their annual banquet. He urged them to take an active part in the Republic, to have for France the care, the devotion which the Catholics of America bore their country. He appealed to them to consecrate their youth, their intelligence, their enthusiasms to the cause of virtue and truth. He told them that if ever in the world youth had a glorious mission, it was the youth of France, but they must take interest in the material as well as the spiritual interests of the people. He insisted that if the Church is to win out, it must win with the people and by the people; that there was a time when the Church could be sure of the people if it were sure of the government, but that times had changed, and that those who seek to win a victory for the Church must first win the people to the Church. He held up for them the example of America, the devotion to the Republic of Catholics, who know "that if they neglect her, she loses some of her beauty and strength," and so they watch over her. And if those who stand close to her are not worthy of her inspiration, they place other sentries near her. "In this way, she is always beautiful, always young, always powerful."[6]

The priests of Paris also wished to hear the Archbishop, and through l'Abbé Delamire, the future Archbishop of Cambrai, they invited him to come to La Maison de la Bonne Presse and speak to them about his country, its priests, and the relations of the clergy to the people. In his address he indicated what he regarded as the chief defects of the French priests. He found them, he said, not wanting in zeal, love of the people, and the spirit of self-sacrifice, but aloof. They did not mix sufficiently in popular movements because they did not have a personal knowledge of their parishioners. He quoted the example of the Good Shepherd, who knew His sheep, not in a general way as a crowd but in such a way that He could give the name of each one. Every sheep knows the voice of the shepherd, and when another speaks, it says, "That is not the voice of my shepherd." He reminded them that it is not always by the supernatural that souls are attracted, that our Lord came to perfect the natural and to add something to it, and in that way win hearts. The faithful see with their eyes and feel with their hearts those who love them, and, therefore, the first duty of the priest is to make himself loved, and in turn know and appreciate his people. For that one must be in the midst of them like a brother; not by way of condescension or evident effort, but with affection and disinterestedness. The people must see that his affection is true and sincere.

Another fault which he pointed out was failure to give attention to the temporal interests which mean so much to the workman and to the little shopkeeper who often have so much difficulty in making a living. It is not sufficient to offer them happiness in heaven; they have a right to expect happiness on earth. The earth belongs to God as well as heaven, and the priest, the representative of God, should protect these interests from both points of view. He said: "The people will love us if they see that we are of their time, and that we love everything that is good in progress—that is the way to disarm our enemies."

He told them that he attended all the important meetings held in St. Paul, that they would be scandalized if they knew the kind of speeches he made, but that the people were always glad to see him. On the other hand, he was scandalized, at the international meeting held in Paris to make Sunday a day of rest, to find only one priest, Abbé Garnier. "Go out, gentlemen, from the sanctuary," he cried. "Be in church, but don't be there all the time." He created a sensation when, referring to a statement of a French priest that in certain churches of Paris three, four, five, and even eight thousand people attended, he said: "That is fine, but not so fine is the forty, fifty, and even eighty thousand who remain outside. These are the ones you must attack." He continued: "Some say: 'I say Mass, let them come, I am in the confessional, the people have only to come.' It is as if the Apostles said: 'We are in Jerusalem, the nations have only to come.' What use are the beautiful chants in the churches, the gold chasubles, solemn sermons, if the people do not come? You must go out, go into the highways and the byways. You must preach from the housetops."

He told of his custom, when on Confirmation tours, of engaging a hall and inviting everybody to a conference. The people have a right to expect the priest to be interested in them, because their life is hard. The workman goes to his shop, works long and hard for a mere pittance, returns home without being able to give his family the things they need. We must not blame him if sometimes he loses patience, because he knows that God has given the earth enough prosperity for all, but that this prosperity is held by just a few. Priests must not forget that the workman feels deep down in his soul that every man has, in justice, the right to be able to live, that God does not create men without assuring them the means of living. The priest should say to the workman: "You have the right to work and to eat. We demand this as a right and not as a gift." If we let the workman know that we want to sustain his rights, we can then speak to him about his duties. Then he said:

Go into the factories, see the awful conditions that are so often found there. See these men packed together in an atmosphere in which even an angel could not live. See their children, their young daughters, their wives broken in health before their time by deplorable hygiene and over-work, say: "In the name of Christ, in the name of humanity, this must be changed." Be the first apostles of social justice and the upholders of distributive justice.[7]

It was inevitable that he would encounter objection on the part of some of his audience. To one of these he replied frankly: "You will not, sir, ever be without voices which will preach to you prudence. As for me, I prefer to preach to you action." People do not like criticism, especially from a foreigner, and the irritation of some of the clergy was not helped by the reaction of the press. The *Temps* made comparisons between French and American ecclesiastics, contrasting the aloofness and formality of one with the affability and simple manners of the other, the priestly class and formalism of the one with the democracy and informality of the other. The Anglo-Saxon races, it said, have a love of independence and of self-government, while the Latin are enslaved to an inflexible discipline.[8]

Thus, for several days, the American prelate was the central figure in Paris. Not only did paper after paper reproduce his addresses, but they also described in detail his personal appearance, his habits, and his democratic ways. *Le Petit Journal*, for example, etched his portrait:

Tall, well-built, his face a mixture of energy and sweetness, frank and refined, his look clear and penetrating, his voice warm, sonorous as brass, his speech fluent, at times familiar, at times lofty. Simply dressed, he wears no pectoral cross or evidence of his dignity, not even a watch chain. His old-fashioned trousers and large hob-nailed shoes reveal a gentleman who does not frequent the best New York clothiers.[9]

It told of his visit to Cardinal Foulon, who asked him in amazement: "Where is your secretary? Where is your valet?" and the answer: "In St. Paul." Georges Poignant in *Le Pays* compared him to the famous Père Didon, who had to leave his chair in the University and go to the Monastery of Corbara, in Corsica, to expiate for seven years his daring words in defense of the Republic.[10]

The *Nouvelliste* of Bordeaux, on June 27, recalled the time when *L'Univers* hurled anathemas at Montalembert for having issued his famous formula, "A Free Church in a Free State," and declared heretics Lacordaire, Cochin, Dupanloup for being guilty of having faith in liberty. "But now, Mgr. Ireland has gone infinitely farther than these men. It is not the memory of Lacordaire that the language of Mgr. Ireland recalls; it is the memory of Lamennais on the eve of his fall." *Le Républicain Coutances*, on June 25, exclaimed: "What life, what vigor of action and work. For more than an hour and a half he astonished his audience unaccustomed to his frank and clear language." The *Moniteur de Rome* referred to his conference before the elite of France as a triumph. "It revealed an almost unknown nature—charm and finesse. This apostolic and winning figure has exquisite tact, smiling simplicity, language at once suggestive and strong."[11] M. Spuller, in *La République Française*, spoke of his bold, spontaneous, original way of understanding the relations between priest and people. "Never has Paris had such a spectacle—an American prelate, a prince of the Church just as much as his high-

est and most titled colleagues in Europe, who speaks an entirely
different language from that usually heard from dignitaries."[12]

Boyer d'Agen of the *Figaro*, who interviewed him in his hotel, and
who was amazed to find him occupying a simple room on one of the
upper stories, asked him if he believed in a renaissance in France, and
received the reply: "Yes, in your democratic and social renaissance."
The Archbishop said that nothing could stop the democratic movement. What element, he asked, is better suited than the democratic
to preserve the good seed which Christ plowed deep in the soil of
the multitude, and what greater tree can grow in human society than
that which the divine husbandman planted according to the wishes
of the people? The kings and emperors who survived were only
flowers that adorned this magnificent tree, but it was the fruit which
people had a right to expect. The masses, who cultivated the tree, had
now a right to garner the fruit, a right which might be defined as the
common law both in politics and in religion. The Church, he said,
needed no special privileges, for if it is the work of God in human
society no human power can weaken or strengthen it. "Free churches
in free states—that is the new code which new times impose, which
the reigning pontiff prescribes, and in virtue of which rising de-
mocracies declare open an impartial struggle, whose assured victory
will increase the prosperity and the honor of the Church and society
at the same time."[13]

Concerning this interview, he wrote to Monsignor O'Connell from
Queenstown:

What was my surprise to receive a letter from Boyer d'Agen, enclosing
an interview with me from the *Figaro*. That man is the author of *"Leo XIII
before his Contemporaries."* He came to ask me to write on the Pope some
lines for his next edition and I chatted with him for some five minutes.
Then comes that interview, of which not a thought came to my mind while
I was talking with him. I trust no harm has come from it. I am glad I got
out of Paris so soon.[14]

To a representative of *Le Temps* he expressed his conviction that
the decision of the Pope concerning the Republic was irrevocable.
"The Church of France must not remain tied to a corpse; it must
sever its cause from that of the monarchy and accept not only without
reservation but with sympathy the republican government." He could
not understand the objection to this regime, since Christianity, from
the very beginning, was essentially democratic. Democratic aspirations are found in the most illustrious doctors of the Church. The

opposition of some republicans to clericalism was due to the fact that some parties had made religion an arm of combat. In the United States, Catholics had to struggle against great prejudices but overcame them by proving their devotion to the public interest, so that now the relations between Church and State did not mean hostility, but rather understanding and mutual esteem. In France, the Concordat allowed Catholics to distinguish the political domain from the religious. He noticed the attempt in France to develop Catholic workmen's unions, in contrast with the American system, in which there were no religious distinctions.[15]

During his visit to Paris, the Archbishop went to the Chamber of Deputies and made the acquaintance of many of the members. On June 18, he was received by President Carnot, surrounded by several members of his cabinet. Soon after his arrival in Europe, he went to Liége, Belgium, where he attended a meeting of Catholics from different countries of Europe interested in social questions. He wrote to Father Caillet, his Vicar-General, of the intense confusion prevailing in France among Catholics: "The Pope pressing upon them the Republic, they in large numbers resisting respectfully but firmly. The worst feature, from all I hear, is the poor stuff usually selected for the episcopate by the Government. The great episcopate of France is rapidly disappearing and a very small episcopate is taking its place."[16]

A letter from Cardinal Rampolla, dated August 8, 1892, expressed his great satisfaction over the warm welcome the Archbishop had received in France. He said: "I have seen with pleasure that you have been received by Monsieur Carnot and that the occasion was not lacking for speaking with the Ministers and several statesmen. The Holy Father has been pleased with the regard shown to you, and he listened with interest to the account of the first stage of your journey."[17]

2. THE PANEGYRIST OF A SAINT

On the second of July, 1898, Archbishop Arthur Stanislaus Touchet of Orléans invited Archbishop Ireland to preach the panegyric of Jeanne d'Arc on May 8 of the following year. All France, he said, would be happy to see America give homage, "in your venerated person," to the greatest figure in French history.[18] This statement was not altogether accurate, for soon Touchet received anonymous letters, warning of the danger he incurred in inviting one who had been called a half-heretic. Moreover, not only had *La Vérité* and *Le Gaulois* protested, but the Minister of Worship also declared that the "Organic Articles" forbade the invitation of foreign preachers without a permission—a statement which proved to be unfounded.[19]

The Archbishop accepted the invitation and, after leaving Rome, began to prepare his discourse, completing it in the solitude of his old school at Ain. Father Alphonse Magnien, Superior of St. Mary's Seminary, Baltimore, wrote to him that he had been thinking a great deal about the coming address, that the condemnation of Americanism had made all who were in sympathy with his views and principles extremely desirous that his success should be complete, and that, therefore, he must so speak that all Frenchmen, no matter what their political views might be, should be pleased with his words.[20] This advice, however, was hardly necessary for the Archbishop, who knew that it was one of the great occasions of his career. The romance of the celebration and the consciousness that all France would be listening brought forth an eloquence which for two hours held spellbound a huge audience. When he ascended the pulpit in Orléans, the city was celebrating the 270th anniversary of the raising of the siege of the city by Jeanne. All Orléans thronged to the Cathedral, which was decked with flowers and draped with flags. A choir of five hundred voices lent solemnity to the occasion. Five hundred priests and prelates filled the sanctuary and transepts; five thousand people had only standing room, while five thousand more were clamoring for entrance. Learned men and distinguished writers like Brunetière, Gaston Paris, and François Coppée came from all over France.

After telling of his own indebtedness to France, "the country of my youth, the school of my soul," and of his early interest in the story of Jeanne, the Archbishop set the background for his theme by sketching the providential role of France in the world. The Eldest Daughter of the Church, she refined and Christianized the peoples she conquered, shattered the power of Asiatic despotism in Europe, and endowed the papacy with temporal power. From her must come missionaries to evangelize the world; with the fleur-de-lis would go the Cross; in her must be born those congregations of men and women whose works of zeal and charity would be the glory of religion. Considering Jeanne under four aspects—as statesman, warrior, woman, and saint—he drew from her story lessons whose import no Frenchman could mistake. "In her whole life," he said, "she was the embodiment of patriotism and religion. Her life and

her death spoke love of country and love of Church—the one symbol-
izing the interests of earth; the other, the interests of heaven." He
reminded Frenchmen that the historic mission of France is religious;
the historic glories of France are her works for religion. Her noblest
deeds in the cause of civilization are summed up in the words of
her sons, *"Gesta Dei per Francos"*—the works of God are done by
the Franks.[21]

The address was received with almost unanimous acclaim by press
and public. Abbé Naudet, in *La Justice Sociale,* referred to the Archbishop as a man of the vanguard, disdainful of calumnies and def-
amations, continuing his way along the road marked out for him
by God.[22] *La Libre Parole* depicted him as "a refined figure, charming and strong, in which sweetness seemed mirrored in intelligence."
It told of his remark to a friend, on leaving Rome: "I go to throw
myself, like Saint Ignatius of Antioch, into the throats of lions."[23] The
Journal des Debats spoke of his wealth of language and variety of
correctness in the use of expressions which even many French orators
did not possess.[24] Father Cuthbert, editor of the *Weekly Register,*
asserted that the address placed him in the forefront of living orators
and raised him to a level which few prelates of the Church had attained.[25]

After the panegyric, the Archbishop went to Paris, where, on May
14, he preached three times in the Basilica of Sainte Clotilde before
an audience which included the Duc de Broglie, Vicomte de Vogüe,
Georges Goyau, and M. Cochin.[26] In the words of the New York
Journal, he administered quite a shock to the ancient regime, telling
the old nobility that they were behind the times in clinging to a super-
seded and false ideal. The following evening he addressed the Cercle
Catholique de Plaisance, speaking to the workmen on the encyclical
on labor. His closing address was delivered on May 28 at Saint Pierre
de Chaillot, where in the presence of an aristocratic audience he
spoke again on social problems.[27] A representative of *L'Avenir de
Lyon* was struck by the majestic appearance of the Archbishop in his
pontifical robes and his piety at the altar. He told of the remark of
one of the worshipers: "Why, my dear, he says Mass like everybody
else, in spite of *La Vérité's* charges of heresy," and of the edifying
sermon he preached on Sainte Clotilde, in which he stressed not whin-
ing resignation but action.[28] M. Brunetière remarked how strange it
was that these democratic Christians, these Americans accused of
subversive teachings, were the only ones among the Catholics to think

of developing the social teachings of the Pope. *Le Figaro* regarded his improvisation at Sainte Clotilde as even better than his discourse at Orléans.[29]

From Paris the Archbishop went to Brussels, where, on May 21, he was entertained at dinner by King Leopold and the royal family at the palace at Lacken.[30] The king expressed his deep gratitude to the Archbishop for his reception of Prince Albert in St. Paul in the previous year and for the lessons of patriotism and religion he had given him.[31] Prince Albert paid him the unusual compliment of dining with him at the United States legation. Among the guests were the Papal Nuncio, the President of the Chamber of Representatives, the Secretary of Foreign Affairs, and many members of the aristocracy. On May 22 he preached at Saint Gudule a sermon on the Feast of Pentecost. In his audience were the Countess of Flanders, mother of Prince Albert, and the Minister of Foreign Affairs. On May 24 he addressed a large audience in the great hall of the Palais des Académies, at the request of the general Brussels Association of Catholic students. Again he had a distinguished audience—the President of the Belgian Senate, the French Military Attaché, the Secretary of the Italian Legation, the Minister of State, several representatives of the Parliament, and many priests.[32]

He also addressed the students at the University. As he entered the hall, crowded with representatives of the diplomatic corps, the scientific world, and society, the entire audience rose and cheered him. He took for his theme "The Opportunities for Youth in the New Century," a century full of problems for Church and State. Once more his eloquence and his command of French made a delightful impression.

Returning to France, the Archbishop went on to his old school at Meximieux, where, in spite of an accident which might have had serious consequences, he arrived on June 6. There he remained for ten days, administering the Sacrament of Confirmation, addressing the students, whom he urged to avoid the softness and discouragement of people who folded their arms and spent their time moaning and lamenting. Then to Belley, where he received a gracious reception from the Bishop and the canons of the Cathedral and spoke to the students of the seminary. In the church of Notre Dame at Montluel he preached twice—a homily on the Blessed Sacrament and a eulogy of Cretin.

The Archbishop spent two crowded weeks in London. On June 25 he preached at the Franciscan church in Peckham, later dining with Sir Stafford Northcote, Lord Wolseley, and other notables. The following day a reception was given for him by Cardinal Vaughan, which was attended by many more of the social elite, among them the Duchess of Newcastle, Lady Clifford, Lady Howard, Viscountess Clifden. In the evening he was the guest of the Fifteen Club, composed of Catholic noblemen and including such men as the Duke of Norfolk, Lord Clifford, Lord Arundell, and Viscount Llandaf. He also addressed the Catholic Union of England, of which the Duke of Norfolk was president, on the providential revival of the Catholic faith in England, which, he said, had suffered its greatest misfortune in the Reformation.[33] Later in the evening the Duke gave a *conversazione* at the Grafton Galleries "to meet Archbishop Ireland," an honor given only once before—to Cardinal Newman on the occasion of his elevation to the cardinalate. The company, numbering five hundred, represented much of the best and noblest in the Catholic social life of England, much that was most distinguished by birth or by eminence in politics, letters, and science. It included Cardinal Vaughan, Lady and Mr. Charles Matthew, Sir Henry and Lady Bellingham, the Bishops of Portsmouth and Emmaus, the Earl of Denbeigh, etc.

Earlier on the same day he attended a meeting on arbitration at Queen's-Hall, under the auspices of the International Women's Congress, of which Lady Aberdeen was president. On the following day, Wednesday the twenty-eighth, he lunched with the American Ambassador; on Thursday he dined at the Athenaeum Club, Lord Ripon presiding. On Friday, Dominion Day, he attended the reception given by Lord Strathcairn, the High Commissioner of Canada. On Sunday he preached at the High Mass at the Oratory. Tuesday, July 4, he was the guest of Lord Ashbourne, Lord Chancellor of Ireland, and on the following day was guest at a dinner party given by the American Ambassador.[34]

Mrs. W. Gibson, wife of Lord Ashbourne, writing to Abbé Klein said:

I have excellent news for you. The Archbishop has been feted by everyone. The Duke of Norfolk was wonderfully cordial and gave him a sumptuous reception attended by a large crowd. The sermon at the Oratory was splendid, and I was surprised to find in him so much art in his manner, which is admirably expressive and beautiful, and in his voice. He reminds me of Bossuet. I was expecting something more fiery and less finished from an artistic point of view. The impression at the meeting of the Catholic Union was very good. He met many of the principal men, Lord Halifax,

Balfour, the Anglican Bishop of Rochester, and almost all the important Catholics in the world of ideas. One of the Franciscan dignitaries, who had become very reactionary and had read an essay against Americanism at the Roger Bacon Society, at the mere sight of the Archbishop and even without the opportunity of speaking to him, was completely changed in attitude. They say that Mr. [Wilfrid] Ward wishes to write an article along the same lines as my husband's.

In the midst of all his affairs, the Archbishop found time to spend a night here. His coming to dinner was marked by a significant storm, and this atmospheric disturbance which marked his arrival did not displease him any more than the surname, "Western Blizzard" which his enemies have called him and which he does not hesitate to mention.

His piety made a great impression on us. He said Mass before 7 A.M. on the feast of Sts. Peter and Paul. And then his charming way with every servant, every little girl, his simple goodness, his enthusiam for the country—all charming traits of a great personality.[35]

The London *Weekly Register* told of his room at the Grand Hotel, which was strewn with the cards of people of all nationalities and of all shades of opinion, of the leading members of the nobility, clergy, and laity, as well as of a large number of prominent representatives of both political parties.[36]

Father Berry, the well-known social worker of Liverpool, arranged a reception for him in that city, where he was the guest of the Catholic Old Boys' Association at the Hotel Adelphi, on July 6. The chairman of the meeting, attended by the Bishops of Liverpool, Salford, and Shrewsbury, told of the Archbishop's unbroken triumphal progress through Italy, France, Belgium, and England and said that Liverpool, which was a quasi-American seaport, could not allow him to pass without a tribute of respect and grateful welcome.[37] The Archbishop also spoke at the Oratory of St. Philip and at St. Patrick's Church. To a representative of *Catholic Times and Catholic Opinion*, he expressed his appreciation of the consideration shown to him by such men as Lord Wolseley, Lord Charles Beresford, Sir Stafford Northcote, Mr. George Wyndham, John Dillon, T. P. O'Connor, and Lord Balfour, who was especially interested in the working of the Washington University. He urged Catholics to widen their qualifications for leadership and to take the places of importance which were rightfully theirs.[38]

From Liverpool he went to the Isle of Man, where he spoke briefly after Mass on Sunday in St. Mary's Church, Douglas. He then passed on to Ireland, visiting his old home in Kilkenny and delivering in Cork a lecture entitled "The People and Temperance." After the lecture one thousand men accompanied his car to his hotel.[39] On his arrival in New York on July 28, he expressed to a representative of the *Tribune* his conviction that the Dreyfus affair had been badly agitated, the real question of guilt or innocence having been lost sight of. The army was sensitive about its honor, and criticisms of it created much anger. The irritation was increased by collections taken up among the Jews for Dreyfus' defense. These, though few in number, had made themselves unpopular by their control of capital and of the press.

3. THE REPRESENTATIVE OF HIS COUNTRY

On June 11, 1900, President McKinley addressed a letter to Archbishop Ireland, expressing his pleasure on learning that he had been chosen to deliver the address on the occasion of the presentation to France by the youth of America of a statue of General Lafayette, because "no more eminent representative of American eloquence and patriotism could have been chosen and none could better give appropriate expression to the sentiments of gratitude and affection which bind our people to France."[40] The Archbishop prepared carefully for the address, writing to Count de Chambrun for material and receiving from him the titles of some books which had been produced under the guidance of the Count's uncle and published in *La Revue des Deux Mondes*.[41]

The monument was meant to perpetuate between the two great republics of the world memories equally dear to both. It was inaugurated on July 5 at the foot of the Louvre, in one of the squares of the Place du Carrousel. The ceremony was of unusual splendor; all the American ambassadors and ministers in Europe not only were registered on the program as "vice-presidents of the day" but were also present in great numbers. In places of honor were General Horace Porter, the Ambassador of the United States, the President of the Republic, M. Loubet, and his cabinet, which included such well-known names as Millerand, Delcassé, Fallières, Leggues, Deschanel, Caillaux; the Papal Nuncio, Monsignor Lorenzelli; the Minister of Japan, and many members of the diplomatic corps, as well as prominent French generals. Sousa's band played the French and American anthems. At the ceremonies of dedication and at the reception to the elite of Paris given by the American Ambassador, the Archbishop was the cynosure of all eyes. The audience must have been struck by the contrast which the scene at the monument presented. Here on the one hand were the members of the government, anticlerical, hostile, critical; on the other, the deep faith and the simple natural goodness of the Archbishop; on the one hand, Loubet carefully phrasing his words; on the other, His Grace flinging his message to the winds. To rhetoricians of democratic phraseology he showed how true believers regard democracy, and what power the Church holds in reserve for the future of modern society. This personification of the enthusiasms and the *joie de vivre* of the young Republic of the West was a revelation to these representatives of an effete civilization. As he warmed to his subject, one who appreciated the contrasts and the humor of the situation noted the reactions of the cabinet: M. Brisson gnawing on the head of his cane, M. Deschanel admiring his eloquence and seeming to marvel at it, M. Millerand applauding discreetly with his gloved hands; senators and deputies gazing at the phenomenon and perhaps making comparisons. But for the crowd it was an occasion of admiration and delight. As Georges Grappe expressed it:

> To understand him you must see him. To feel the full force of his phrases you must hear him pronounce them. It is in the open air of an inauguration that one must see him stand erect, his voice without misplaced unction, without that intonation which too often weakens the force of speech. His accent seems to invite the winds to carry his impassioned words to the farthest hearer.[42]

It is not difficult to imagine the reactions of a French audience to his opening words: "Today a nation speaks her gratitude to a nation; today America proclaims her remembrance of priceless favors conferred upon her by France. France! America salutes thee; America thanks thee. Great is her obligation; not less great her gratitude." He told of the rebellion of the colonies and their struggle for freedom, and he asked: "Was the infant nation to live and grow in strength and power, or was it to die and bear into oblivion with its name and its memory the spirit of liberty, at whose bidding it had sprung into existence? This, the awful issue cast into the scales of destiny." He depicted America as anxiously questioning the nations, wondering if anywhere were hearts to beat in response to her heart, if anywhere were hands to uphold her hand. And then he said:

> There is a land, above all other lands the land of chivalry, of noble impulse, of generous sacrifice, the land of devotion to noble ideals. The sons of this land, with souls attuned by nature to the call of high-born principles, resolved to die, if need be, that truth and justice prevail. . . . That it were mine, this morning, illustrious son of Old Aubergne, to put

into fitting words the sweet and warm love which a century ago was given to thee by America's revolutionary sires. That it were mine, this morning, to pronounce thy name with such tenderness and reverence as Americans beyond the ocean wish me to pronounce it in the fair capital of France.

He told of Lafayette's devotion to American independence, of his bravery and military skill, his magnanimity of soul and grace of character, his unselfishness. It was he who developed and maintained the sympathy of France for the United States, so that France poured into America's empty treasury the vast sums of money needed to keep an army in the field. It was France who sent to America the flower of her nobility and the bravest of her soldiers and seamen. It was the ships of France which protected our coasts, kept our ports open to commerce, and confined the British naval occupation to the port of New York. It was France that made American liberty possible in the eighteenth century.

He brought out the significance of the Revolutionary War—a war for civil and political liberty, a momentous event in the story of liberty's strugglings. Through its inspiration, peoples everywhere were quickened into a consciousness of their rights. In one form or another, democracy today enters into the life of every country of the globe, the consequence of the triumph of democracy in America. America and France are today the exemplars, the champions of the new age. The fate of republican government in the world rests with them.

In conclusion, he apostrophized Lafayette as the exemplar of true liberty:

LaFayette, here take thy stand, in France's capital city, on Carrousel's historic field, amid its thousand glorious memories. Under commission from America, take here thy stand; speak adown the coming ages; speak in America's name; speak to France and to the world; speak of America's gratitude; speak of liberty.

And he also struck a note which must have brought a nostalgia to all but the most cynical of his audience:

Gesta Dei per Francos, it used to be said from the remote days of Clovis and Charlemagne—France, the Deity's chosen instrument in the accomplishment of its highest designs for the welfare and aggrandizement of humanity. Ever in the march of religion and of civilization thou wast in the vanguard; ever thy heart was prompt to beat in response to the prayers of Charity and Justice; ever was thy sword prompt to leap from its scabbard in the furtherance of grand and magnificent ideas. France, be ever the self-same. Ever thy missionaries were the most zealous and the most self-sacrificing in uplifting the cross under sultry Southern sky or amid coldest Northern glaciers; in making all lands debtors to Christ and to France. France, be always the self-same.[43]

And thus the Archbishop retold with his most exalted eloquence the epic of the alliance that helped to bring a new democracy into existence—the story of Lafayette, of Rochambeau and Vergennes. Once more all France was stirred by the eloquence of the Archbishop from Minnesota. Once more France learned from America lessons of the utmost importance to Church and State, for he not only spoke of the grandeur of the mission of France and America but also stressed the vast responsibilities which that mission imposed. It is no wonder that paper after paper throughout France reproduced passages from the address and paid warm tribute to it. The *Figaro* said:

> After his first phrases, his audience was captivated and burst into frequent applause. When he spoke of the heartbreaking struggles of the War of Independence and the dangers America faced, he grew impassioned, and his oratory became thrilling. When he is indignant, he leans forward, grasps with his powerful arms the edge of the platform, then raises himself, impressive and haughty, his head thrown to one side, his chin thrust forward, his arms akimbo—such as the lithographs of former days represent the great orators of the Revolution. He labors some phrases, others he champs with contempt, flings forth his apostrophes, details some incidents minutely, binds together his important points, throws his concluding periods on wings of enthusiasm.[44]

The *Univers* brought into relief one aspect of the occasion—the significance of the appointment of a Catholic Archbishop to be the orator of an occasion when France and America gave to each other a new pledge of friendship. From this it drew a lesson sorely needed in a country where the government was bent on persecuting the Church and where the Church was an object of distrust to considerable sections of the people. It reproduced the whole discourse, and, in an editorial, Eugene Veuillot said: "It made the hearts of the whole audience beat in unison. Again and again Americans and Frenchmen applauded the orator enthusiastically. M. Loubet, the President, applauded. We honor and admire him, and we call him a great man and a great patriot. He is a force and a power."

The papers were enthusiastic in their comments, *La Semaine Religieuse, Le Peuple Français, La Vie Catholique, Le Figaro, L'Univers* thanking him for his words, "for which all true Frenchmen would be forever grateful," and expressing their amazement to see in France a Catholic bishop commissioned by a Protestant government—a thing which would be out of the question in their land.[45]

On his way home the Archbishop passed a few days in September in the Diocese of Belley, living over again his student years with his old comrades of the Meximieux Seminary. The priests of the diocese were gathered for their retreat at the Seminary of Brou, and the Archbishop, on the invitation of the Bishop, gave them an address, which was published textually in *La Semaine Religieuse* of Belley and reproduced in *La Vie Catholique* of Paris. More than ever, he said, the salvation of the world depends on the priestly vocation. The times in which we live, full of immense difficulties as they are for the Church, demand that every priest be a saint and an apostle. In his Meximieux days the churches were crowded morning and evening, and the processions of the Blessed Sacrament were followed in triumph by the population of country and city. But now the churches are deserted, or there is only a handful of the faithful bending the knee before the Blessed Sacrament. The journals of the nation make it clear that a life-and-death battle is raging, and if things continue as they are we are humanly speaking defeated. This, he said, is so much the better for the priest, for the fiercer the battle, the more the soldier takes courage. The true soldier cares little for the life of the camp; he loves the battle which will bring him greater glory. The greatest danger for the clergy is pessimism, despair, discouragement. Some feel that the evil is so great that nothing can be done, because the world is given over to unbelief, and that therefore they should retire to their sacristies and leave the world alone, but that is not the language that Jesus Christ used when He appeared in a world bristling with hate against virtue. He said:

Is this the language of the apostles when they rushed through the nations to bring them to the Faith? Is this the language of Francis Xavier when he landed on the shores of China and Japan? Is this the language of the missionaries in China, in the heart of Africa, in the isles of the Ocean? Everything was against them, except God; but God and his missionary can conquer. Christ has not lost his power; the Christ of yesterday is the Christ of today—the Christ of Palestine is he whose spirit reigns in the world, and the grace of Christ has lost none of its sweetness and its vigor. It is we, the intelligent instruments of this grace who lose courage. It is for us to understand the grandeur of our mission, to take in hand our hearts and warm them in the flame of this divine fire which issued from the Heart of Jesus, when he said: "I am come to cast fire on the earth."

Go, then, into the arena; you will see at once that you are in a new world; you will see that the field of battle is not that which your predecessors saw. There is no use in longing for it; it will never come back. You must put yourself in contact with this new world; you must go to the people, you must fight with the proper weapons in order to have success in this world; you must win your way by the sympathies which the world asks for. Who, today, would engage in battle with the same weapons and methods used in the Middle Ages? In this war against the enemies of God, the truths proclaimed by Jesus Christ remain unchanged and we must not suppress one iota of them; the Church of Jesus Christ with its hierarchy and its authority will remain. It is the truth of Jesus Christ which must triumph, and not the thought of each one of us; we will accomplish nothing unless Christ works with us; we always need the inexhaustible sources of his graces; we must bring to the fight a stainless life; the truths of the Gospel must in some manner be incarnate in us. The world is exacting; we are lost if we give any precept which is not exemplified in our own conduct. The priest must, above all, be a saint, in order to silence the wicked tongues that wish to turn against him.

He stressed the need of learning. It will not do to go before the world with a manual of theology, for that is a language the world does not understand. Knowledge alone is not sufficient; it must be presented in an alluring and attractive manner. Nor must we put before the world, which hungers for the solution of great problems, the food which we give to little congregations—the little devotions. He continued:

I say to you—go to your people. Know your sheep by name, salute them, invite them to come to visit you, go to visit them. If they rebuff you, don't be discouraged, make a second trip; it is for Jesus Christ you are doing it. Speak about agriculture in the country, about shops in the city, speak about the temporal interests of the people. Make use of the natural, so that having taken possession of the world in its own name, you can take possession then in the name of the supernatural.

We say to the people: come if you wish, it is your affair. No, gentlemen, it is your affair, because Jesus Christ has constituted you priests, and he will demand of you the price of these souls if you have not done all you should in order to gain them.[46]

He also spoke in Arcueil, at the school of Albert-le-Grand, which was always associated with the name of Père Didon, the illustrious Dominican. The audience was much impressed by the likeness between the two—both orators, both patriots, both insistent on the need of an active ministry. The Archbishop stressed the need of developing in the young a sense of conscience and of individual responsibility. Drawing a contrast between France of the seventeenth century and France of the present day, he asked where was the merit of being a Christian in France in olden days, when the whole atmosphere of the country was perfumed with the spirit of religion, and one could not breathe without drinking in Christian ideas. But now all was changed. And if this change was a misfortune for religion and the country in general, it was not a misfortune for the individual, for what title to salvation has a man who did his duty because he could not do otherwise? Why did so many young people, brought up in Christian homes, forget their religion after a year or two in the world? The reason was that they had never known their religion. They knew the little practices, the devotions, but they had never knelt before Christ as He appeared and spoke in the fields of Galilee twenty centuries ago. "The flowers in the forest are lovely, but we must also have the oaks, and the oaks grow strong because their roots are set deep in the ground."

Of his address *La Vie Catholique* said:

In language exquisite in its originality and powerful in its energy, he took for his theme what modern education ought to be. The previous year Père Didon had, on a similar occasion, delivered his last address on education, and all the force and splendor of his eloquence now resounded in the words of the Archbishop, with the same ardor of conviction, the same faith in the destinies of France and of the Church.[47]

M. Feuillette, who presided, excused himself for speaking after the Archbishop, saying: "One does not speak after Mgr. Ireland. When he has ceased speaking, one still listens."

On September 6, the Archbishop was decorated as a Commander of the Legion of Honor by M. Jules Cambon, the French Ambassador to the United States, who represented his government. Among those who attended the presentation in Paris were Prince Ouroussof, the Russian Ambassador, M. de Vogüe, Brunetière, General Horace Porter, the United States Ambassador, and Bellamy Storer, United States Minister to Spain.[48] In an interview with a representative of the *Figaro*, the Archbishop expressed his pleasure at the honor and his joy in seeing democratic institutions penetrating more and more into the hearts of the French people.[49] Cardinal Rampolla told Bishop Thomas O'Gorman that the Pope was so pleased with the honor which the French government had paid to the Archbishop that he ordered thanks sent to Paris by special letter.[50]

During his visit to Europe the Archbishop did not go to England, but he maintained correspondence with W. S. Lilly and the Duke of Norfolk. In his letter to the Duke, he said that it was a broad, plain fact in the geography of the world that the English language was circling the globe, and that English-speaking countries were constantly growing with speed that nothing seemed able to arrest. The minds of peoples spread over immense regions of the globe were to be reached only through the English language, and very much of the missionary work of the Church was to be done under the aegis of English-speaking countries.[51] This letter was destined to cause him trouble. Rumor was that it was distrusted in Rome as an effort to revive Americanism, a report which he ridiculed. He also found it necessary to write to Cardinal Rampolla, protesting against a statement in the *Journal de Genève* that he had sent to Norfolk a denunciation of the Doctrine of the Temporal Power and of the methods of the Congregations and of the Curia in Rome. When he arrived in Paris, he was attacked by *Le Journal,* which taunted him with his British sympathies, quoted passages from the speech which he had delivered in London on his previous visit, and said that he was not a representative of the American people at large to assist in unveiling the statue of Lafayette. In this way his enemies lost no opportunity of misrepresenting and distorting his words, and international jealousies served to complicate matters for him.[52]

4. Later Visits

Archbishop Ireland made two more visits to Europe. In 1906 he went to Rome and also to Milan, where for some days he was the guest of Count Thaon de Revel. During his stay he had opportunities to confer with Monsignor Bonomelli, the Bishop of Cremona, Marquis Visconti Venosta, the Minister of Foreign Affairs, and Cardinal Andrea Ferrari, who invited him to address the students of his seminary. He told them that if they really wished to become apostles they must have Christ in their hearts. Holiness was the first indispensable, but to piety must be added knowledge. He warned them against two excesses: the first, of those who, in order to remain orthodox, neglect the study of what is new; the other, of those who are so preoccupied with what is new that they are tempted to put in second place the old.[53]

In Rome he was the guest of honor at a dinner given by Mr. Henry White, the American Ambassador to the Quirinal. The function, which was attended by Cardinals Satolli, Mathieu, Martinelli, and Vincenzo Vannutelli, had its repercussions, for a few days later it brought a circular from Cardinal Luigi Oreglia, Dean of the Sacred College, protesting against the presence of cardinals at a dinner arranged by an ambassador to the Quirinal. When the Archbishop heard of it, he wrote to his friend, Cardinal Vannutelli, from whom he received the reply that, while it was true that the circular was issued, it was caused not so much by the dinner, which was of an absolutely private character, but by comments in the press, which tried to give the impression that the rules of conduct set down after September 20, 1870, on the subject of the authority installed in Rome, were going to be changed.[54]

The Archbishop also preached at San Silvestro a magnificent discourse, which received the enthusiastic comments of those, including the writer, who were fortunate enough to hear it. The occasion, Easter Sunday, prompted a sermon on Christianity, in which he dealt with the relations between science and religion.

While he was in France he took the opportunity of spending some time at Meximieux, where he was welcomed with all the affection which both masters and students loved to show him.[55] In Paris, Delcassé, Minister of Foreign Affairs, received him in a public ceremony and thanked him for the love he had for France. At Rouen, he was invited to speak at the Grand Séminaire, where he said: "We must act, we must not let God act alone. Certainly without His grace we are useless instruments; but let us not wait for a miracle to relieve our laziness. Your Jeanne d'Arc was not content to say 'My God, save France.' She took the sword and marched at the head of her troops. Let us say with her 'let us work, and God will work with us.' "[56]

In December, 1906, the Archbishop preached a sermon in the St. Paul Cathedral which, though widely commended in the United States, did not always meet with the same reception in France. After explaining the causes of the conflict between Church and State in that country—the law of separation, the abolishment of the Concordat, the Associations of Worship, and the atheism of the government—he gave two reasons for the anti-Catholic majorities in Parliament: the failure of Frenchmen to understand the art of governing and the action of the priests in clinging to monarchism. The masses were unaccustomed to political life, and an independent, self-argued suffrage had not entered into the popular life. All power was centralized in Paris, so that there was not a true expression of the national will. The clergy were much to blame, for they had retained, even in the pulpit, the spirit of passive obedience, inherited from old regimes. They had never learned the virtues of public life. Then, too, French Catholics were unfortunate in their leaders, many of whom remained dreamers of the past, partisans of buried political regimes. Pope Leo, who had bidden all Catholics to seek the welfare of country and Church within the ranks of loyal adherents to the Republic, had not been listened to. Monarchical ideas and plottings had done dreadful injury to the Church.[57]

It would seem as if the criticism of the clergy, though well founded, was rather unfortunate in its timing. Just then the persecution of the Church was particularly bitter, and people who are suffering do not relish the assertion that some of their sufferings are due to their own fault. The sermon led to a controversy with the Paris *Matin*, which strangely enough accused him of attacking the policy of Pius X. He cabled *L'Eclair*: "The resume of my address in the *Matin* is a lie. On the contrary I strongly sustain the Pope and I only blame the French Catholics for allowing their enemies to come to the Chambers in a majority."[58]

In 1909 the Archbishop was commissioned by the President to represent the United States at the festival of the Centenary of Lafayette in Paris. It was for him the official consecration of the ideas of his whole life and another opportunity to pay to France the tribute of his filial affection. He also passed some days at Montluel, where he sought souvenirs of Bishop Cretin, and at Belley, where he was received by Bishop Francis Labeuche, who, in order to meet him, interrupted his pastoral visits and who made him an honorary Canon of his Cathedral.[59] This time he did not stay at Meximieux, and it was with deep emotion that he saw the beloved house, whose deserted walls were beginning to crumble under the action of rain and whose courtyards were overgrown with brambles and wild shrubs. By virtue of the law of separation, the Community had been expelled in January, 1907.

In Rome he presented thirty members of the archdiocese to the Pope, preached at San Silvestro on February 7, and was entertained at dinner by Ambassador Griscom on the eleventh. While in Rome he received from Georges Goyau an invitation to speak in Paris, but he begged to be excused on the ground that his plans would not permit him to do so. "Moreover," he said, "my best judgment tells me that I shall do well to remain silent in France. I am delighted with Rome, I see much, I learn much, and everywhere I receive the best welcome."[60]

Claude d'Habloville tells an interesting incident which happened at a dinner in the Farnese Palace, Rome, on January 1, 1909. The conversation turned to the betrothal of the Duke of Abruzzi and an

American woman, which had just been broken. "So much the better," said a countess, the wife of a Roman senator. "That was not the proper kind of marriage for a prince of the House of Savoy." "And why not?" asked the Archbishop. "A citizeness of free America, born of honorable parents, blessed with the highest gifts of Providence, is at home in any court, the equal, if not the superior, of the many degenerates that fill them. The only real aristocracy is one of the soul."[61]

Chapter 8

THE SPANISH-AMERICAN WAR AND ITS AFTERMATH

┿┿┿┿┿┿┿┿┿┿┿┿┿

On the afternoon of Passion Sunday, March 27, 1898, while Archbishop Keane was preaching in the pulpit of San Silvestro, Rome, a messenger from the Vatican, bearing a letter from Cardinal Rampolla addressed to the Archbishop, was sent to the Canadian College, where he lived. Learning that he was at San Silvestro, the messenger hurried to the church and, when the preacher descended from the pulpit, handed the letter to him. It read as follows:

> The danger of a grave conflict between the United States of America and Spain cannot but profoundly stir the heart of the Supreme Pontiff, the Common Father of the Faithful. For this reason, knowing well what influence the word of Archbishop Ireland of St. Paul, Minnesota, may for various reasons exercise on the mind of the President of the United States, he has expressed his keen desire that the worthy Archbishop would take such measures as might possibly bring about a pacific solution of the problem. I hasten to communicate the wish of His Holiness to your Grace, who has close relations of friendship with Archbishop Ireland, and, uniting my own warm wishes to this needful request, I take advantage of the opportunity to profess the most sincere regards of

Your devoted servant
M. Cardinal Rampolla.[1]

Archbishop Keane immediately cabled to Archbishop Ireland the wish of the Pope that he do everything in his power to preserve peace. He followed this cablegram with two others. The first, on March 29, told Archbishop Ireland that he alone was asked and that on him was incumbent immediate and strong action so that the government would accept arbitration on the explosion of the *Maine* and abstain from intervention in Cuba. It urged him to leave for Washington at once. The second informed him that the Pope was using his influence with Spain, but that he could promise nothing until he had heard from him; in the meantime he should do everything to prevent the war.[2]

The Cuban insurrection, which began in 1895, had awakened much sympathy in the United States among a people who remembered their own struggle for independence. National indignation was aroused by the action of the Spanish governor, General Weyler, who had herded the rebels into *reconcentrados,* concentration camps in fortified towns under military command, in which thousands had perished by disease and hunger. President Cleveland, however, in deference to "our obligation to the sovereignty of Spain," refused, in defiance of the popular sentiment, to interfere in an insurrection in which both parties were equally guilty of nefarious measures that rendered life and property insecure.[3]

From the moment that McKinley entered upon the presidency, he studied the Cuban situation, and, like his predecessor, refused to extend his sympathies to the insurgents. He declined to recognize the belligerency of the rebels and their claim to independence. In this attitude he was largely influenced by the action of the new "liberal" Spanish ministry, which recalled Weyler, replaced him with General Blanco, and proclaimed by decree a scheme of autonomy to become effective upon ratification by the Cortes. The majority of the President's cabinet and some of the ablest men in Congress discouraged war. But jingoism was rampant in the land; big business, scenting the prospect of gain, clamored for annexation. The Hearst papers, with their circulation of a million and more, fomented war, publishing a letter written by the Spanish Minister, Señor de Lome, in which he had characterized McKinley as "a cheap politician who truckled to the masses." Men of great prominence—Theodore Roosevelt, Henry Cabot Lodge, Secretary John Hay, and Whitelaw Reid—were ardent advocates of war. The spirit of nationalism was in the air, and a desire that the United States should take its place among the great powers of the world. To safeguard American citizens in the riots so common in Havana, the President dispatched the *Maine* to that port. Even when this battleship was blown up in the harbor on February 15, 1898, with the loss of 258 men, the President held his ground, and, in the words of Señor Polo, the Spanish Prime Minister to the United States, he withstood the powerful sentiment in favor of the insurrection.[4]

On March 29 the President, in a proposal submitted through General Woodford, the United States Minister to Spain—a proposal which proved to be his ultimatum—called for "an immediate armistice lasting until October 1, negotiations in the meantime being had, looking to peace between Spain and the insurgents through the friendly office of the President of the United States." The Spanish ministry, far from taking to heart those diplomatic and honorable suggestions, committed itself, at a meeting held on March 31, to "propositions utterly inadmissible," propositions which extorted from General Woodford the words: "Yesterday's conference was a sorrow to me, for I have worked hard for peace." On the same day Woodford told the President that Spanish pride would not permit the ministry to offer an armistice, that he had been told confidentially that such an offer would cause a revolution in Spain. The President announced that he would now lay the entire negotiation before Congress on April 6.[5]

It was at this point that Archbishop Ireland appeared on the scene, a moment when, "if a referendum had been taken, a majority would have voted for war with Spain in order to expel her from Cuba." His first interview with McKinley was on April 1, and his first cable to Cardinal Rampolla announced that he had seen the President, who ardently desired peace and assistance to obtain it. The situation, however, tended to be beyond his control, Congress and nation urging war. The following proposals would very probably be accepted here if they were made promptly: that Spain sell Cuba for a generous sum or that it offer armistice for some months during which Spain and the Cubans could arrive at a solution. Should this fail, the final decision of the problem should be left to the sense of justice and honor of the President. Otherwise war was inevitable.[6]

On the next day, Saturday, April 2, the Archbishop cabled that he had seen the leaders of the Senate and others, that the war party in Congress was very strong and threatened to act even against the will of the President. A clear, definite proposal of armistice for six months, even without the condition regarding arbitration of the President, would be accepted.

The use of the word "assistance" in the first cablegram led to embarrassing complications. What the Archbishop meant was that the President could not do everything alone and that he expected Spain to aid. Such is the interpretation of Ferrara—that he needed cooperation on the part of Spain in order to calm the emotions of the American public, which was tremendously overwrought (*tremendamente enardecido*), or, in other words, that Spain should yield gracefully what she would later be compelled to yield under less favorable circumstances.[7] The word was interpreted in Rome—either by the Vatican or by the Spanish Ambassador to the Holy See, more probably by the latter—to mean a request on the part of the President for the mediation of the Holy See, with the result that Señor Gullon, Spanish Minister of State, so informed the representatives of the great powers. This action the Archbishop regretted, as it exposed the President to attacks from anti-Catholic bigots and made him more careful of the Archbishop. At the same time, the Spanish Minister to the Vatican, after an interview with the Cardinal Secretary, informed his government that the President was willing to accept the good offices of the Pope, and asked if such intervention would be acceptable. To this he received an affirmative answer, together with an acceptance of a truce, provided that the President, as an earnest of his purpose not to support the insurrection, would order the withdrawal of the fleet from the waters of the Antilles.[8]

On Saturday evening the Archbishop had his first interview with his friend, Senator Stephen B. Elkins, who began his journal of Archbishop Ireland's work in Washington with these words, written on Sunday April 3, 1898:

> This day has been eventful and may become historical. Last night, Archbishop Ireland of St. Paul called at 8:30 and told me that he had come to Washington under instruction from the Pope to ascertain and report the exact situation, and what could be done to prevent war between the United States and Spain. I told him that I thought that the book had been closed, the last chapter written; that unless Spain opened negotiations war was inevitable and would be declared this week by Congress. I told him that the only thing left for Spain to do was to propose an armistice on the island.[9]

The Senator also suggested that a conference be held the next morning with Señor Polo in order to ascertain if he would feel authorized to reopen the subject with his government. On Sunday morning, April 3, the Archbishop had his first interview with the Spanish Minister in Senator Elkins' home. He informed Señor Polo that he had seen President McKinley, who favored peace but who perceived no way to procure it from the present attitude of Spain. He also said that he had seen Senator Cushman K. Davis, Chairman of the Foreign Relations Committee, who had told him that war was certain—indeed, that Congress would unquestionably declare war the current week no matter what the President or anyone else might say or wish. The Archbishop and the Senator impressed upon the Minister that nothing but an advance from Spain of some kind or other would prevent a declaration of war. When the Minister asked what could be done, the

Archbishop suggested that Spain ask for an armistice. Señor Polo showed himself slow to accept this proposal, as it placed Spain under the humiliating necessity of making a concession to the insurgents. After much discussion the Spanish Minister at last agreed to ask his government to propose an armistice for six months, the Archbishop at the same time promising to telegraph the Pope to urge the Spanish government to take immediate action. The Spanish Minister then remarked that if these efforts should result in peace the conference would be historic.[10]

The Archbishop at once went to see the Ambassadors of Spain and France, requesting the former to urge his government to offer an armistice and the latter to induce his own government to insist that the government of Madrid cease hostilities.[11] The French Ambassador promised that if the armistice were offered he would seek the support of the other European powers to persuade America to accept it. But everything depended on Spain.

From this time until the declaration of war the Archbishop was in daily contact with Cardinal Rampolla, urging him again and again to procure from Spain a clear, definite proposal of armistice for six months, telling him of his interviews with Señor Polo, the Spanish Ambassador, on whom he impressed the delicacy of the situation, and with the Ambassadors of the great powers, whose mediation he had obtained. The cablegrams which passed between him and the Vatican, and which have already been published in detail, show that on at least six different occasions he stressed the gravity of the situation. Through Senator Elkins he was also in constant touch with President McKinley, to whom he conveyed the request of the Holy See that the United States withdraw from Cuban waters the fleet whose presence raised a difficult situation for the Queen and the Spanish ministry—a request which the President could not grant.

Matters were complicated by American belligerency, on the one hand, and, on the other, by Spanish pride, and also by indiscretions on the part of representatives of both countries. The request made by the Spanish Minister of Foreign Affairs to General Woodford, the American Minister in Madrid, that he cable at once to the President that "gladly yielding to the request of the Holy Father who was acting on the earnest petition of the President of the United States to intervene on behalf of the United States to prevent war, the Ministry had decided to publish an armistice," made McKinley more careful in his relations with the Archbishop, who, he feared, had used his

name in a telegram to the Pope and thus given rise to the belief that
the President had suggested the Pope's intervention. On the other
hand, Woodford sent an unfortunate letter to the Spanish cabinet
while it was in a turbulent session, demanding a reply within a few
hours. As the Papal Nuncio at Madrid told the Vatican, the ministry
would have published a decree suspending hostilities had it not been
for this unpardonable *faux pas*. Then, too, feeling ran high in both
countries, the American war spirit finding its counterpart in Spain,
where there was trouble between the Queen Regent and the cabinet,
and where denunciations of her and of the Pope were common.

Senator Elkins' *Journal* describes his frequent interviews with the
Archbishop, who labored day and night, and whose emotions alternated from despair to hope. The Senator, feeling from the beginning
that war was unavoidable, was infected with the buoyant, optimistic
spirit of the prelate, who had received from the representatives of
France, Spain, Belgium, Austria, and Russia assurances of co-operation and promises of mediation. The Archbishop's confidence was
increased by cables from Madrid to the Baltimore *Sun*, which announced that the Queen had prevailed over the military party and
that the armistice would be published, and that Woodford had declared that "everything seemed to be going the right way for peace."
Moreover, the President, who had intended sending his message to
the Senate on April 6, decided at the last moment to postpone it, in
order to give Spain time to act. But Spanish indecision continued to
be a stumbling block, and no official assurances of an armistice
arrived until Sunday, April 10, the day before the reception of the
President's message by Congress. Although McKinley announced that
the Queen of Spain had directed General Blanco to proclaim a suspension of hostilities, the Foreign Affairs Committee of the House of
Representatives adopted on April 13 a resolution directing him to intervene at once, to establish in Cuba an independent government, and
to use the army and the navy for that purpose. Still hoping against
hope, the Archbishop sent word to the Vatican of new attempts of
the pacifists and of the possibility that war might yet be averted, but
only to inform the Cardinal Secretary of State a few days later that
the die was cast for war.

Archbishop Ireland had based his hopes for peace on the armistice
and on the sympathetic attitude of the President. That attitude was
clearly brought out by James Boyle, former secretary to McKinley, in
an article in the New York *Times*. He quoted the President as saying

that the declaration of war was the greatest grief of his life, that he never wanted war with Spain and only sought more time. Spain, which at first was fiercely obdurate, was coming around and was willing to grant full measure of local autonomy to Cuba. She was only parleying for time, so as to save her face before her own people. But the pressure became too great for McKinley. Newspapers yelped for war, the demands of Congress became more and more insistent, and hotheads constantly fanned the war fever.[12]

Ireland had to encounter much misrepresentation, which sought to impeach his loyalty and which charged him with appealing to foreign pressure. The European Catholic press, sympathetic to Spain, was filled with abuse of the United States as an aggressor nation, and received support from its colleagues in this country. Typical of the attacks was an article written by Paul de Cassegnac, a French monarchist, who, in his reference to a sermon preached by Ireland on the occasion of the victory in the Spanish-American War, called the United States "The Ogre." Monsignor Ireland, he said, like the rest of his fellow citizens would have gained by triumphing with a little more modesty, and above all by not giving the credit to the intervention of God in "this atrocious American filibuster against a valiant people exhausted by centuries of glory." He compared the Americans to bandits who waylay a defenseless traveler in the corner of a wood, and he hoped that the Old World, instead of coquetting with the new, would act prudently in laying the foundations of mutual defense, so as to prevent the "giant nation" from extending its arms farther than it should. The victory of Protestants over Catholics, he continued, surely brings to an archbishop painful reservations, which, however, did not seem to bother particularly Ireland.[13] As Archbishop Keane wrote to Cardinal Gibbons: "The feeling against America in regard to the war seems to grow more intense, and even in Brussels, Mr. Storer tells me that the bitterness is very hard to bear."[14] Add to this the usual misrepresentations of anti-Catholic bigots, which were so great that the Cardinal Secretary of State found it necessary to deny charges of partiality on the part of the Holy See. "It is superfluous," he said, "to deny such foolish talk; the perfectly proper attitude which the Holy See has maintained and will maintain toward the two nations being known to all; the Holy See having no other desire than that for peace."

Archbishop Ireland naturally regretted the failure of his efforts. He wrote to O'Connell that it was due to the action of Congress in going back on the President and on all friends of peace, and to delay in asking him to undertake the negotiations, which would have succeeded had he been called in two months earlier. He felt, however, that his standing in the eyes of the country had not suffered, that it was to his credit to have worked for peace, to have been chosen for that mission by the Pope and to have accomplished so much with Spain and other countries. "Of course," he said, "now I am for war—for the Stars and Stripes—I am all right as an American."[15]

Both O'Connell and Keane tried to console and reassure the Archbishop. The Monsignor reminded him that the position in which the request of the Pope had placed him was the most important sanction given to him and to his views before the whole world. He said:

When the great law of necessity came they had to accept the man. Again, by a singular fortune amidst the universal dislike present on the Continent against America, your earnest intervention for peace contradicts many an old slander and gains you great love and esteem. Ireland the great patriot was also a great man for peace. All that in due time will do vast good, and it opens up a tremendous horizon of possibilities for you in Europe in the future.

He told of the misunderstanding abroad concerning the American character and the movement of the American government, as well as of the great sympathy for Spain. Two ideas, he said, summed up the situation as Rome saw it: the right of Spain, the highhandedness of America. All said about "humanity" was pure hypocrisy, only a pretext to gain Cuba for the Union. He and Bishop Keane had realized the great delicacy of Ireland's position as well as the great honor attached to it. Then he continued:

Now that negotiations for peace have failed, in which you did your duty as a priest, it is essential that you take your place before the people as the same old patriot and keep at the head of the movement in war as well as in peace. If you lost your hold upon the people, at the end of the struggle, some other man might be called to take your place to negotiate conclusions. The philosophic view over here of the situation is Pan Anglosaxon against the world. Eichthal says there is simply consternation in Europe at the spread of American influence. Soon, they say, America will ask a voice even in European affairs. Now you can shape the future, and do it. There is a mission for John Ireland.[16]

Bishop Keane wrote in similar strain to say that it would not have been better had Ireland remained at home, for the mission not only put him personally in his true light before Rome and America but also put the Pope and the Church in their true light. He said: "While it is true that failure is unpardonable here, as in other diplomatic centres, still you are *the man* of the situation, the one to be looked to for future aid, if only you set right their view of your having so positively promised peace almost on the very eve of war."[17] This the Archbishop proceeded to do by sending the documents which passed between him, Rome, and other centers. These Keane regarded as "most interesting and most precious." He showed them to Cardinal Serafino Vannutelli, who he said, declared himself *"simply astonished, dazed*. He didn't understand it so at all—sees that the notion of your having been a child, piping *peace* all the time, was a monstrous misrepresentation. He is still studying them & will find opportunity to use them for justice's sake."[18]

Monsignor O'Connell, who had also seen the documents, wrote:

I have gone over your diplomatic correspondence three times, and reading it now, even in the light of accomplished events, I am struck with admiration for the perfect manner in which the whole series was intoned, and the deep honesty and insight that mark it throughout. I study it in order to expound it to some eminent friends.[19]

The causes of the Archbishop's failure have been analyzed by himself in two *apologiae pro vita sua* and by the late, lamented Dr. Richard Purcell. He told O'Connell that when he went to Washington he felt that he would harm himself; that he would have remained at home had it not been for Keane's repeated telegrams. He realized that time, the essential element for success, was wanting, since the country was already on the eve of war and time was needed for calming public opinion. He had pinned his hopes on the armistice, which the President had proposed and in the securing of which foreign ministers were co-operating. He never had sent hopeful cablegrams until he had first heard from the White House. He pointed out how much had been accomplished—the postponement of the President's message for four days in the hope that the armistice might come. Everything looked propitious, for the House, which was with the President, left the use of the army and navy discretionary with him, and he knew that McKinley would not use them.[20]

When he sent the documents to Keane, he defended himself against the charge that he had misled the Vatican with hopes of peace. The only time, he said, when he was positive in his announcement of peace was several days before war was declared. To say that he had announced it two days before the war was a calumny. He was in-

clined to blame both Rome and Spain, the former for publishing in
the *Osservatore* his telegram to the effect that Americans were grateful to the Pope, the latter for giving out that the Pope was acting at
the invitation of the President. It was quite evident that both of these
announcements would stir up bigotry, of which there was an abun-
dance in America. His statement that McKinley would be glad to
have help was twisted into a petition for papal intervention. He had
never, he averred, sent a cablegram until he had discussed the matter
with the Ambassadors of France, Austria, and Spain and with Senator
Elkins, whom he had used as his intermediary with the White House
in order to avoid stirring up the bigots. Not only had he the conscience of having worked prudently and well, but he stood well with
the American public and with foreigners in Washington. "I am astonished," he said, "at my ingenuity and 'habilité.' The French Ambassador declared that I gave to all 'la formule d'action.' And now to be
misunderstood by those whom I was serving so loyally and for whom
I was risking my reputation as an American—it is dreadful." He told
of his anxiety during the last fatal week when the armistice was
delayed and of his manifestation of that anxiety in his cablegrams.
Señor Polo, the Spanish Ambassador, did not get notice of the armistice to the press until Monday afternoon, and the President's message
had been sent in the morning. When the armistice finally came, it was
the best thing for Spain, for it put America in the wrong, and it gave
immense prestige to the Pope. As far as he personally was concerned,
he did not care much whether he was blamed or not, but for the sake
of the "movement," he hoped that the Vatican would not make known
its displeasure. He accepted the war with patriotism but not with
enthusiasm, for he felt that there should not have been war, and it
was not easy to defend the position of America. His consolation was
that good would come out of it, for Spain's government of her colonies
was open peculation.[21]

Ireland's acknowledgment of the "wrong" of the war was to Keane
"painful in the extreme," as it was hard to be enthusiastically loyal to
one's country if one believed she was wrong. He, on his part, viewed
it in the light of the "higher law"; humanity demanded that Spain
should leave, as she was forced to do in the case of her other colonies.
He was proud of his country for having done a service to humanity
and to Providence. He hoped, however, that Congress and the President would keep their word and not take possession of Cuba. To go

into the "colony business" would mean that America was changing her base completely and was drifting into the militarism of the Old World.[22]

Dr. Purcell has summed up most succinctly the causes for Ireland's failure:

> The vacillations of President McKinley, aggressiveness of the war hawks, hereditary Anglo-Saxon hatred of Spain, nativist hostility to the Catholic Church, unfounded leaks that the President sought the Pope as mediator, inexperienced American ministers in European capitals, especially at Rome and Madrid, false pride of empire on the part of the corrupt Spanish regime, and intrigues of imperial Germany—all these complex factors made futile Ireland's endeavors to maintain peace.[23]

To O'Connell Ireland expressed his belief that Cuba and Puerto Rico would be retained by America. The United States, which through the Civil War had become a nation would, he said, through the Spanish War become an international power. He quoted the contrasting views of Archbishops Martinelli and Riordan concerning possession of the Philippines—the former regarding it as horrible for religion; the latter, as a blessing. He assured him that he was keeping up his Americanism, it was his *"pièce de résistance,"* and he would not let it go. He had written a long report of his mission to Rampolla and he was writing again, giving news and incidents which threw more light on it.[24]

The documents to which the Archbishop referred in his letter to Keane on May 28 included the correspondence between Rampolla and himself, as well as letters from Frederick Rooker, Bellamy Storer, and Cushman K. Davis.

Rooker wrote twice in vindication of Ireland. In the first letter, he said that he did not pay too much attention to a cablegram sent to the Archbishop by O'Connell, telling of Vatican indignation that it had been misled by hopes of peace. Rooker regarded the Monsignor as an alarmist, whose source of information was of little value, merely the *"Chiacchiere"* (cackling) of underlings in the Department of State in Rome who were hostile to the Archbishop of St. Paul. Perhaps also, he said, to the same source might be traced some of the obstacles thrown in the way. The most serious mistake, he thought, was the publication in Rome of Ireland's telegram of April 1, which caused an immense amount of ill feeling in America and was strongly resented by Congressmen. It was absurd to say that he had deceived Rome, because the last hopeful telegram was sent on the eleventh, a

full week before the joint resolution was passed, during which time
Rampolla was constantly warned that things were going badly. The
telegrams from the fourteenth to the seventeenth inclusive showed
how little Ireland assured peace. "You are right," he averred, "in
saying that it is you who have reason to be indignant. I have gone
over the whole correspondence, and I confess my surprise that at the
time I did not realize the conversations which took place on the other
side between the 1st and the 9th of April." Nor did he realize, he said,
that the intent at the start was to make this country back down as
completely as possible and that it was all a question of saving the
honor of Spain.[25]

In the second letter, Rooker told of his visit to the Austrian Ambassador, to whom he related O'Connell's story of the criticisms which
Cardinal Serafino Vannutelli was quoted as having made of Ireland
for having misled Rome by promises *biduo ante bellum.* The Ambassador showed great indignation, went over the whole history of
the crisis, and said that never in his life had he been called on to
admire a man for "indefatigable zeal and heroic courage against
odds" as he had admired the Archbishop. If people had understood
the situation they would have thought that his work was anything but
puerile. He himself had felt from the beginning that there was only a
forlorn hope, that war could not be averted, and, as early as February,
he had advised his government that it would certainly come this
year. When the Archbishop arrived, the Ambassador felt that there
was no hope; there was a moment when he caught some of his enthusiasm and half-believed that peace might triumph, but from the
eleventh of April the truth was clear to all that hope was a delusion.
He had appreciated the great risks Ireland was running, wondered
that he was willing to take them, but was most enthusiastic in his
praise of the work accomplished. He realized the opportunity given
for the charge that Catholics could not be good patriots, because they
must first obey the Pope even when his commands were not in harmony with the sentiment of the country. He had written a full account to his government with a laudatory explanation of Ireland's
work, even declaring that more had been done than he had believed
any human being could do. He placed some of the blame on the
President, who was not a leader, who had allowed himself to be
pushed beyond his depth, and who had taken office realizing that he
had gone in on a platform containing a Cuban plank. His messages

to Congress were aimless and his sending the *Maine* to Havana purposeless. Spain was to blame for her failure to realize her own unpreparedness, and her admiral for remaining in Havana. After some discussion about the probable fate of the Spanish possessions, the Ambassador shrewdly asked whether the unfavorable opinion in Rome might not have been suggested from this side, and whether relations with New York were altogether amicable. That remark recalled to Dr. Rooker's mind an article in the New York *Herald* of May 22, in which a great deal of contemptible insinuation had been used in the Archbishop's regard.[26]

Mr. Storer, writing from Brussels, related his interview in Paris with General Woodford, who gave him a history of the Vatican intervention, and in particular of the visit of Señor Gullon to the United States Embassy. On Friday, April 1, General Woodford received word of the intervention of the Vatican, and on the following day he was informed by a member of the ministry that steps would be taken that night to preserve peace. The next morning the Spanish Minister of the Colonies called and told him with utmost cordiality that he had induced the ministry to agree to the suggestions of the Pope and that war was no longer to be feared, but that final word must be left to the Minister of Foreign Affairs, Señor Gullon, who would notify him officially. When the latter arrived, he told Woodford that he was bringing the happiest news—that the ministry had instructed him to request the United States Minister to cable to the President that "gladly yielding to the request of the Holy Father, who was acting on the earnest petition of the President of the United States to intervene on behalf of the United States to prevent war, the Ministry had decided to publish an armistice." Woodford made the Minister repeat it twice, saying that it was so different a statement from what he had been expecting that he feared he had not understood, and he finally took it down from the lips of the Minister. He then sent for his secretary, Mr. Sickles, an expert Spanish scholar, and retaining almost forcibly the Minister, who was very desirous of leaving, he had Mr. Sickles translate the statement into Spanish. He then submitted both the Spanish and the English versions to M. Gullon and forced him to compare them and to declare the one to be the correct version of the other, and both to be the exact message that he desired to have transmitted to Washington. The next day he received in the most peremptory terms a positive denial that the President had ever authorized the assumption of such an attitude on the part of the United

States. He went directly to Señor Sagasta and laid before him the two versions of M. Gullon and the dispatch of denial from Washington. He then said: "This is the third time that misstatements have been made, or that at all events misunderstandings have arisen from my reliance on your Minister of Foreign Affairs. I am a plain, straightforward man who cannot and will not attempt to understand this sort of thing. It must not and shall not happen a fourth time to me, for I come to you, as head of the Ministry and I will not again receive communications through the Minister of Foreign Affairs, unless from the whole Ministry and in writing. I can not allow this matter, which seeks to put in my President's mouth statements that he says are false, to stand uncontradicted. There must come from you by tomorrow morning an official explanation, or at noon tomorrow I ask for my passports." The next morning, the sixth, he received an absolute unconditional withdrawal of any claim that the United States had asked the intervention of the Vatican. On inquiring that afternoon whether the announcement of the armistice was ready, he was informed that no armistice would ever be granted until the insurgents asked for it. Three days later, on the ninth, the ministry did decide to grant the armistice, but Polo could not, for some reason or other, transmit his message to the President until late Sunday night or Monday morning, with the result that before it came the President's message was signed and ready for transmission, with only the bare fact mentioned in it that an armistice had been decided on. The terms of it were not transmitted through Woodford for his approval; only the fact of the decision reached him, while the details were sent through Polo "with the usual world-old Spanish delay and sinuosity." Woodford was impressed with the fact that, ever since Sagasta came into power, the Minister of Foreign Affairs seemed willfully to try to break up any *entente cordiale* that existed and to be "a pebble in the machinery." He did not think that the diplomacy of the Vatican was at fault. He concluded by saying, "The Spanish Ministry was absolutely doing its best to avoid war, and the Queen absolutely sincere, truthful and upright of purpose to avoid war if possible."[27]

Senator C. K. Davis, writing to Mrs. Bellamy Storer, told of his frequent conference with the Archbishop, whose "labors for peace were most arduous and incessant. If the Armistice had been tendered one week earlier than it was, I think there would have been a settlement of all our questions with Spain without war."[28]

The Queen of Spain understood what the Archbishop had done to

save her country. She invited him to Madrid, with the assurance that
he would be met at the frontier with all the honors due to royalty.
The attitude of the royal family is shown in the following letters from
the Infanta Paz. Writing from Schloss Nymphenburg, near Munich, on
August 20, 1898, she said:

I was so enchanted to read in a German paper an extract of your sermon
taken from the N. W. Chronicle, July 15, that I cannot refrain from writing
to thank you for your noble honest words, which were a great consolation
to me in the midst of my pain.

It is time for me to explain who I am—Infanta Maria de la Paz of Spain,
married to Prince Ludwig Ferdinand of Bavaria. You can imagine how
much I suffered during this unjust war, far from my beloved country.

Would you kindly let me have the entire sermon? I should like so much
to have it.[29]

Again on March 25, 1899, she wrote:

I was very much touched with your letter. I never believed you to play
double and I will explain in Spain all the facts. Have patience with my
poor countrymen; when one has suffered so much, one is more sensitive.
I recommend you those who have to remain in Cuba, Puerto Rico and
Philippines, that they may not suffer too much under the new regime.
The monks of Philippines have been so cruelly treated.

I understand the necessity of showing the people that Cuba is Catholic.
What a pity that all Christians should not be one. It is my dearest dream,
and I work as much as I can to bring together the different creeds.

I was very much flattered that Cardinal Rampolla spoke of me.[30]

She also sent him a note of introduction to all Spanish officials, asking
that he be shown every courtesy.

When the Archbishop wrote requesting her good offices for Mr.
Storer, newly appointed Minister to Spain, she replied:

Many thanks for your letter and the good opinion you have of me. I will
send it to Silvela. It costs me an effort to recommend the Minister of the
United States. I have been looking forward with horror to the moment
when after all that has happened, the Spaniards would for politic [sic] be
obliged to smile at him. You understand surely my feeling, you know
what fatherland love is. But your voice comes in the name of God and He
taught us to forgive. It is kind to have chosen a Catholic and one who did
not want that dreadful war. When Mr. Storer sees all those poor victims,
he will have patience if the Spaniards need some time to forget. If he could
arrive with the news: "The prisoners of Filipinas are free," it would be
a good beginning.

My letter will go today to Madrid, that will show you that I am truly
                                            Your obedient child. Paz[31]

1. The Philippine Negotiations

The victory over Spain did not bring immediate peace to the Philippines. The natives, who sought a government of their own and now felt that they had merely passed from one form of domination to another, turned on their liberators. Scarcely was the ink dry on the treaty of peace before an insurrection burst forth which cost many lives and much expenditure of money. It was to be expected, too, that among many of the higher clergy and laity sentiments of loyalty and devotion to the land of their origin and to their fellow Catholics in Spain would exist. Moreover, for two generations serious friction was manifest between the natives and members of the religious orders. Thus the war bequeathed a vast problem to both Church and State, and many were the burning questions to be decided when the Islands passed under the American flag and the former relations of Church and State were suddenly severed.

For the investigation of these problems, the United States government appointed two commissions. The first, headed by Dr. Jacob Gould Schurman of Cornell, recommended that the friars be expelled, that Filipino priests replace them, and that religious toleration be guaranteed. The second, headed by William Howard Taft, published reports embodying the testimony of many witnesses concerning conditions of life in the Islands and the causes of political and religious unrest, and dealt in particular with the character of the friars, their role as government officials, their unpopularity with certain sections of the people, and the extent of their landed possessions.

The general conclusion arrived at by the commissions was that, since under the Spanish rule the friars were practically the executive officers of the government, they were as such the embodiment politically of all that the Filipinos detested and they should be replaced. As Judge Taft said:

Under the Spanish regime, whenever a civil or religious charity or school was founded and maintained, the immediate executive officers selected by the Government for the purpose of supervising and carrying on such institutions were members of the clergy. Then, too, the Augustinians, the Recollectos and the Dominicans owned 400,000 acres of land, which the insurgents were determined to confiscate to the Filipino Republic, and for which many of the tenants refused to pay rent. So great was the political enmity, hostility, towards the Friars, who opposed the Revolution of 1896, that forty of them were slain and four hundred put under arrest. The

American troops had occupied churches and monasteries, and the insurgents, to prevent the American forces from having place in which to live, had in the early stages of the war striven to destroy the churches. Add to this the fact that the Independent Filipino Catholic Church laid claim to a number of parish churches and monasteries.[32]

Although no one doubted the integrity of Dr. Schurman and Mr. Taft, and their desire to be fair, serious criticism of their findings appeared in several publications. In an article entitled "Religion and Education in the Philippines," published in the *Ecclesiastical Review*, Father Middleton accused the commissioners of favoring the enemies of the Church, of issuing contradictory statements, of making evidence fit into a preconceived judgment, of summoning as witnesses very few ecclesiastics but many of the riffraff of Manila, and, in general, of putting the Church on the defensive.[33] An article contributed to the *Sacred Heart Review*[34] by Mr. Lorenzo Markoe protested against the attitude of the commission in regard to Pious Trusts, and in particular against the closing of the college of San José by General Otis "on the ground that it was the property of the Government of the United States and held for the benefit of the people of the Philippine Islands for educational purposes." A similar question, the writer said, affected the control of the hospital of San José de Dios in Manila. He also stressed his conviction that all the members of the commission, being Protestant, with their strong Protestant prepossessions against the Church, were incapacitated by their misconceptions of the relations of the Church and her institutions to the Philippine people from drawing just conclusions as to the actual feeling of the people toward the Church and her representatives in the Islands. Similar criticism was made by Father Ambrose Coleman, who had firsthand information of the situation. He averred that the commissions were packed with anticlericals, that no evidence was taken from any natives in favor of the friars; he quoted the Bishop of Jaro to the effect that the mass of the people were not antagonistic, a statement corroborated by the Provincials of the Dominicans, Franciscans, and other orders, and told of a petition of the people for the return of the friars.[35]

The Pope saw that the only way to settle the matters in dispute was by the appointment of a commission that would deal directly with the Vatican and carry on negotiations not in the distant Philippines but in Rome itself. This idea was, however, so utterly new, so utterly at variance with American conceptions and traditions that it seemed impossible of realization. Would it not arouse all the latent bigotry in this country? Would it not put all the sects of the United States up in arms, rising in their wrath against the recognition of Rome by the government? Once more Archbishop Ireland was called upon, and by consummate tact and prudence accomplished the impossible. This was a mission which was to occupy his attention for some years, and in which both the Vatican and the American government were destined to rely heavily on his co-operation and counsel in all matters pertaining to the Philippines. The confidence which Pope Leo XIII reposed in him and the friendly relations which the Archbishop always maintained with both President McKinley and President Roosevelt marked him out as the logical man to initiate negotiations. No member of the American episcopate approached even distantly the role which he played. He was in constant communication with the Vatican, the Presidents, the heads of Philippine civil and religious administration, as the vast number of documents in his files testifies. He knew the delicacy of the assignment and the probability that he would be caught between two fires. But for him the Church and what he felt to be God's purpose were ever transcending realities. Conscious of his own integrity, knowing no fear, and having no thought for the morrow, he threw himself with zeal into the task.

His first contacts with the situation are indicated in a letter which Archbishop Sebastiano Martinelli, the Apostolic Delegate in Washington, sent in reply to a communication from Cardinal Rampolla, Papal Secretary of State. In it he told of his interview with the Archbishop, whom he was using as an intermediary to take up with President McKinley the affairs of the religious orders in the Philippines. The President, he said, had assured Archbishop Ireland that the government of the United States did not recognize Aguinaldo, who with a group of terrorists had started a rebellion; that he had given orders that the priests and ecclesiastical property be protected; that he was happy to learn from the Archbishop that the Filipinos were well disposed toward the clergy, to whom opposition came largely from Malay rebels. He also told of the efforts of the Archbishop to have on the commission appointed to make peace people sympathetic to the Church. While in the territory taken over by the government there would be separation of Church and State, the status of affairs before the war would be recognized.[36]

In May, 1901, Cardinal Rampolla sent the following communication to the Archbishop:

The Holy See has reason to be preoccupied with the religious situation in the Philippines. It believes that the time has come to settle whatever concerns the interests of Catholics in these distant islands which now depend upon the jurisdiction of the United States. The chief interest of the Holy See is naturally religious, but in order to arrive at that one cannot refuse to take into consideration the exigencies which have arisen from the sum total of new circumstances. You understand, however, that for that I must have direct relations with some one who would be in a position to let me know the wishes and the intentions of the American Government. The lack of diplomatic relations is contrary to the interests of both parties; but it is not my place to draw the attention of American statesmen to that. All I could do was merely to say a word about it to you who know several of them. If you succeed in making understood in your country what I have just indicated to you, you will render the greatest service both to the Church and to your country.[37]

The Archbishop replied that diplomatic relations were not feasible. It was a matter reserved to Congress, from which nothing could be hoped, because the opposition would be formidable. He suggested that friendly informal relations be established between the Holy See and the government; the politico-religious problem in the Philippines and Puerto Rico would give an excuse, and, moreover, Secretary Root had already taken the initiative, which it would be wise to follow up. It was the psychological moment, for the government needed the co-operation of the Holy See.[38]

Rampolla assured him that he recognized the difficulties in the way of the establishment of diplomatic relations, but all the Holy Father wished was that Mr. McKinley give to someone in his confidence the honorable mission of coming to Rome to settle Philippine affairs. It would, he said, be of great interest for both sides to have direct discussions on the details of the question, so as to prevent the agreement from being merely temporary. Perhaps the advantages gained would be so evident that even the opposition to official relations might decrease. Ireland now knew the mind of the Pope, and "his former accomplishments" authorized the Cardinal to believe that he would do his best to satisfy it as far as possible.[39]

This was followed in August by a letter of thanks for Ireland's favorable reception of the Cardinal's suggestion and of good wishes for the success of his visit to Washington, "a delicate affair calling for much prudence and patience."

For the carrying out of this commission Ireland immediately began to prepare the way. With diplomacy which by no stretch of the imagination could be called "shirt-sleeve" he made contact with Taft and Roosevelt. To the former he wrote:

I pray you to forgive me for the liberty I am taking of writing to you, without having the privilege of a personal acquaintance with you, and without having as a justification for passing beyond the limits allowed by such acquaintance any matter of importance to put before you. Of course, we are not unknown one to the other. We have devoted mutual friends at the American Legation in Madrid. In letters that come to me from that Capital your name is so frequently mentioned and your words so approvingly quoted that I feel I do know you well.

He then went on to say that he had followed with particular interest Taft's work in the Philippines, with the result that if he had had in his own hands the choice of the Philippine Commission and had searched for a candidate, lantern in hand, through the whole country, he could not have found a man to suit him as well as he, whose ideas found ready acceptance at the Vatican, and that the Holy See was ready to settle definitely the matter of the friars' property. It was not a question of formal diplomatic relations—merely a business affair.[40]

Taft replied that he approved of the proposition which the Archbishop had made to the Secretary of War concerning the sending of a commission to Rome; at the same time he expressed his regret that Ireland had not been the Delegate sent to the Islands.[41] He repeated what he had already told Mrs. Bellamy Storer—that he regarded the Archbishop's position in the United States as unique, that he had more influence with the people of his own and other churches than any other prelate, and that he was held in high esteem by McKinley and the other prominent men in the government.[42]

The Archbishop kept in touch with President Roosevelt, transmitting to him in September, 1901, the good wishes of the Pope for the success of his administration and expressing the hope that the cordial sympathy of the Pontiff would not be unwelcome to him.[43] He also received frequent communications from the Cardinal Secretary of State, who told him of the delight of the Pope that the negotiations were promising results and of his recognition of the fact that "if things are done in the way you say, it is thanks to your zeal and tact."[44] Later, he thanked him for "the diligence and eager interest" with which he was pushing the affair.[45] The Archbishop impressed upon Mr. Roosevelt the fact that the dispatching of the commission would be well received on both sides of the water, sending him a favorable article written by Monsignor Eugene Boeglin, telling him of the appointment of Monsignor Donato Sbarretti as Apostolic Delegate in the place of Archbishop Chapelle,[46] informing him that he had received from the editors of the *Outlook* and the *Independent* the promise of their support, and suggesting the names of desirable members of the commission.[47] He also made contact with Dr. Schurman, who wrote to the President suggesting the purchase by the government of the lands of the orders.[48]

The first matter to engage the Archbishop's attention was that of the Papal Delegate, who should be a man who would maintain friendly relations with the administration. Unfortunately Taft had taken a violent dislike to Chapelle, who had been in conflict with General Otis on the matter of the return of the friars to their parishes. Otis, in an interview which showed bias, had thrown the whole blame for conditions on the friars, and he was, in Chapelle's mind, beguiled by agitators, whom he seemed to favor.[49] Taft, on the other hand, said that Chapelle had become identified with the friars and had incurred the enmity of the Filipinos.[50]

Chapelle's resignation did not, however, solve the difficulty. The appointment of Sbarretti did not please Secretary Elihu Root, who objected to some of Sbarretti's actions when he was Delegate in Cuba. In spite of the cordial relations which had existed between him and Sbarretti, Ireland was forced to indicate the state of affairs to Rampolla, who informed him that Sbarretti had already departed; that he would have preferred to keep him in Rome until the arrival of the envoy of the United States, but that the Archbishop of Manila had stated that his presence in Manila was needed without delay. He would, however, merely pay a visit of courtesy to the President and would not treat of affairs.[51] Two weeks later the Cardinal, in reply to a letter from the Archbishop, expressed his regrets at the bad impression caused in Washington by the news of the departure of the Delegate but pointed out that the appointment had been made in the previous November, before the mission to Rome, and that the Pope could not now revoke the nomination. "You told me," he said, "what happened in the solution of financial affairs in Cuba. I have not details enough to answer directly to that, but the fact that Sbarretti does not have to deal with the Government is assurance that there will not be a repetition of the incident."[52] There is good reason for believing that this action of the Archbishop had much to do with his failure to receive recognition, for Sbarretti was commonly considered a favorite at the Vatican and was highly regarded in Rome.[53] It was just another case in which Ireland submerged his own feelings and interests in what he considered the higher interests of the Church.

Not wishing to do anything which might interfere with the negotiations, the Vatican yielded, and appointed as Delegate Archbishop Augosto Guidi, who sent word to the Archbishop that he would work in accord with the civil authorities and that if he encountered any difficulty he would have recourse to him, for, as he expressed it to Monsignor Denis O'Connell: "Ireland is today the man of the situation."[54]

Following his usual custom, the Archbishop kept his friend, Cardinal Gibbons, informed on what he was doing. He told him of the task assigned him by the Vatican, of the Pope's *vivo desiderio* that he protect Catholic interests in the new possessions, of his luncheon at the White House, and of the promise of the President that he would put a Catholic on the commission; also of the annoyance of the administration caused by cablegrams professing to emanate from Rome to the effect that the Vatican was hopeful of seeing a diplomatic representative of the United States paying homage to it. The President, sensitive to public reaction, was fearful lest he might antagonize Protestant organizations. More than once his relations with the Archbishop were complicated, as now, by unauthorized pronouncements and rumors completely lacking in any foundation. Later, when Taft was in Rome, a tactless representative of a French journal caused him much embarrassment by asking whether the United States government planned to establish diplomatic relations with the Holy See.[55]

The personnel of the commission as finally established consisted of Taft, General James Smith, Associate Justice of the Supreme Court of the Philippines, a Catholic, Bishop Thomas O'Gorman, and Colonel John Biddle Porter, Judge Advocate of the United States Army. General Smith at first hesitated to accept the appointment, and did so only on the insistence of the Archbishop. O'Gorman expressed himself as having received from Ireland the "perilous honor to go to Rome on Philippine affairs. Perilous, because Uncle Sam is going to insist on some things the Frati influence will not give."[56]

O'Gorman preceded the others to Rome, arriving in the beginning of May, 1902, and at once began a correspondence with Ireland, which kept him informed of the attitude of the Holy See and of the progress of the negotiations. Rampolla had said to him that he hoped there would be nothing in the instructions of the delegates tending to insist on the recall of Sbarretti, as he considered the honor and liberty of action of the Holy See engaged in the matter. At the same time, Rampolla insinuated that the execution of agreements with the commission would find another delegate in the Islands. The Cardinal was also in trepidation lest all that the press, especially the Catholic, attributed to the commission in the way of extravagant and impossible demands on the Holy See were somewhat true, but O'Gorman re-assured him.[57] A few days later, the Bishop returned to the question of the Delegate, saying that when Ireland's telegram, "Must have information about Sbarretti's journey," was shown to Rampolla it displeased him very much. O'Gorman, who was amazed how the Italians stuck to him, had to insist that although Sbarretti's going might not break the negotiations, it would undoubtedly modify the instructions unfavorably to the Vatican. The Delegate seemed to be regarded as a great man, a hero for his success in Cuba and for his personal courage in facing the threats and dangers of Cuban Masonry.[58]

The Bishop's next letter told of his audience with the Pope, who spoke of the difficult task of bringing about the commission and of Ireland's great work and services, "which were not to be forgotten and deserved regard." Leo was disposed to grant every reasonable request and intended making the reception of the delegates as solemn as possible. Satolli assured him that the Pope would surely put Ireland's name on the next list of cardinals, but O'Gorman wondered whether the Pontiff would live long enough to do it. A few days later he wrote that the other cardinals whom he had seen had acknowledged that Sbarretti's appointment was a great mistake diplomatically and that even Rampolla was conscious of the fact.[59]

The rest of the commission arrived in Rome at the end of May. On June 1 O'Gorman wrote that on the following day Taft would present to Rampolla the letter of Secretary Hay, which he thought really constituted the mission a diplomatic one, although Root, in his instructions, denied the term. Taft was regarded as masterful, and the whole commission as solid, dignified, and brilliant. Of the audience with the Holy Father, he said that His Holiness was very gracious, was altogether delighted with the letter of the President and with his gift, promised that the most liberal spirit would guide the decisions, recognized the debt owed to the attitude of Roosevelt, and twice mentioned Ireland's name and his influence in Washington as instances of the attitude of America to the Church. The Bishop also said that he did not like the instructions of Root and that he had asked Taft to cable for changes in the paragraph relating to the expulsion of the friars. He told of the deep impression the Holy Father made and of the unusual courtesy he showed the members of the commission by accompanying them to the door as they left. On the other hand, he felt that some of the demands of the government were rather exacting. When Taft wanted exclusion of the four orders as orders, O'Gorman objected, saying that the most that could be asked was the removal of the Spanish members. Agreement, which was reached on this question, made it easier for the Vatican to arrange the property question, since the orders remained and only the subjects were changed. With regard to the school problem, he had presented a memoir, pointing out that the system was the Faribault plan with some valuable improvements and suggesting that a fund to pay the catechists giving religious instruction after school hours might be provided by the Vatican from the sums which the United States would pay for lands and for war compensation.[60]

On receipt of Root's instructions the Pope replied in a friendly yet firm manner. Recognizing the American principle of the separation of Church and State, he called attention to a situation de facto—that the population in the Islands was entirely Catholic—and he expressed the hope that the government would find a way of reconciling the two systems. Regarding the religious orders, he said that "the Holy See could not give its full adhesion to all the views contained therein." Recognizing also the existence of a certain amount of ill will, the Holy See had already taken steps to eliminate it by "gradually taking measures to recall the Regulars to the life proper to their institutes, to devote themselves exclusively to spiritual ministry, and to abstain from any kind of interference in things appertaining to the civil authority." It also had the intention to introduce religious of other nationalities, but Spanish religious should not be denied return to those parishes where the people were disposed to receive them. For the purchase of the lands and the settlement of claims, the Pope thought it wiser to have them handled by the Delegate. Doubts as to the ownership of property should be settled by examination, due regard being paid to the title arising from legitimate possession. Damages caused by vandalism or by occupation by the armed forces should be settled by the Delegate and the government; the Church, however, could not renounce the right of administering Pious Trusts.[61]

The just refusal of the Pope to allow any dictation on the disposition to be made of the friars or to agree to their withdrawal was destined to rankle in the minds of the government officials and to complicate the problems of the Delegate.

Taft suggested to the Pope the form of a contract to be signed in Rome, submitting the questions at issue to a tribunal of arbitration to consist of two members appointed by the Holy Father, two by the government, the fifth to be selected by the Viceroy of the English Indies. These questions were: the price to be paid for the friars' lands and the occupation of buildings by American forces, and the disposition of educational and charitable trusts. The contract included a covenant that the members of the four great religious orders, who were all Spaniards, should leave the Islands within two years after the first payment for the lands. To this last the Vatican objected as being a matter related to the administration of religious matters and therefore not the proper subject of a commercial contract. To sign such an agreement would give offense to Spain and also give color to the charges brought against the friars. Rampolla agreed that money derived from the lands should go to the Church in the Philippines, and that priests would not be sent to parishes where the majority of the Catholics did not wish to receive them.[62]

In view of the refusal of the Vatican to enter into a contract for the removal of the Spanish friars, the Secretary of War was unwilling to enter into a contract to pay money without further investigation, and he preferred to recur to the original method of negotiating proposed by the Vatican through the Delegate, who would have authority to settle such matters.[63]

Judge Smith later expressed to the Archbishop his opinion that the Vatican made a mistake in not having the value of the lands and the damages fixed by arbitration, as he felt that arbitrators could be more generous than officials of the government.[64]

Taft, who was hostile to the friars, expressed his mind to O'Gorman. Although he wished the Delegate to be an American, he was convinced that an Italian would be selected, "because the business of the Delegate is to see to the money and to rescue it from the hands of the Orders; an Italian would have more power in this respect than an American." He hoped that Archbishop Guidi, the Delegate, would not yield to the influence of the religious. He said that he had been well received by the people, but that the friars were naturally in a very unpleasant frame of mind and were trying to get up a combination between the ultra-insurgent element, the friars, and the Spaniards, all of whom had a bitter opposition to the government. He promised to send him a copy of a pastoral letter issued by the Bishop of Cebu, "which was a pastoral against the Americans."[65]

2. THE FRIARS

Judge James F. Smith sent Archbishop Ireland the following analysis of the situation of the friars as he saw it. The major work of civilizing and Christianizing the Filipinos was done by the Spanish members of the four great religious orders. The Franciscans came to the Islands in 1577 and were followed by the Dominicans in 1587, the Augustinians in 1589, and the Recollets in 1606. Tribute has often been paid to the extraordinary work they did in educating and civilizing the native inhabitants, who, at the time of the arrival of the missionaries, were sunk in the depths of paganism and barbarism. Men of culture themselves, they looked upon the Filipinos as child-Christians and never lost their tendency to regard them as people of very limited possibilities. They failed to realize that the very education they gave them would some day engender the desire for participation in the government of their country. Moreover, not only were the friars the spiritual guides of the people; they were also officials of the Spanish government, which knew that the friars could accomplish far more than military forces in making the people loyal subjects of the Crown. As a result, the friars came more and more to be regarded by the people as agents of the government and, as such, incurred the odium of those natives who hoped to free themselves from the domination of Spain. When an insurrection was attempted in 1896, the friars were rightly or wrongly accused of giving information to the administration, with the result that some of the popular leaders, including the most loved at all, Rizal, were executed. The fury of the mob turned on the friars, who after the fall of Manila were seized and either tortured or killed. The efforts of the American government to secure their release were unavailing. Some succeeded in escaping and found refuge in Manila, sheltered by the American flag. The savagery with which the Spaniards had crushed the rebellion left a heritage of hate in the souls of the natives, in which the friars had their share. It was not strange, therefore, that the American officials in the Philippine government would form the conviction that as long as the friars remained as a source of irritation the pacification of the Islands would be extremely difficult.[66]

Mr. Richard Campbell, an associate of Judge John McDonough of the Supreme Court, Manila, in one of his frequent letters to the Archbishop said that the execution of Rizal was undoubtedly the worst political investment the friars made. General Ramon Blanco, the Governor General at the time, warned them that the execution of the little Malay would have an entirely different effect from that which they intended. As a result, Rizal became a martyr in the eyes of the people, and his picture hung on the walls of nine-tenths of the households. Campbell insisted that the opposition to the friars was not moral or religious, but political. The native "padre" was much less trustworthy, yet there was no charge against him. He regretted to say that in many instances people who owed everything to the friars—their avocation, political preferment, and even wealth—had displayed the basest ingratitude and repaid them by assailing them and by joining their bitterest enemies.[67]

Ireland also defended the orders. In an interview in New York, he said:

All the civilization that the people of the Philippines have, has been received from the priests. They are the representatives of social and religious order in the Islands. The priests will uphold this government, as they upheld the government of Spain. The Government will do well not to antagonize the priests. And I know well that it is not the policy of the Government to antagonize them.[68]

Many other factors must be taken into account in any evaluation of the friar problem. Popular antagonism was fanned and kept alive by professional agitators, either members of the Katipunan Society, a Masonic organization, or men who saw an opportunity of getting hold of their possessions, as politicians have done in France and Mexico. Municipal authorities were eager to lay their hands on the splendid edifices which the orders by their efficient administration and self-sacrifice had erected and on the treasures which they had amassed. The people, having little of earthly goods, often looked with envy on the extensive tracts of land in the hands of the friars. Add to this the fact that many members of the native clergy had not realized the ideals of the Church and were not distinguished for priestly virtues. When Aglipay, an apostate priest, taking advantage of the unrest and the confusion, started a schism and declared himself head of the Independent Filipino Church, many of them flocked to his standard. These took possession of parishes which, through the withdrawal of the friars, had been left without a pastor, claimed that the churches had been erected by the labor of the people, and refused to give them up. The

American government was convinced that the first step in restoring order was the purchase of the lands of the friars at an equitable price and the withdrawal of the friars from their parishes. General Smith asserted that the attempt of the friars to return to their rectories resulted in public disturbance and disorder. In some parishes to which they did return they were maltreated and driven out; in others, because of the popularity of individual priests, they were well received. He seriously doubted the wisdom of forcing a cleric down the throats of the natives, even though it was extremely difficult to fill his place. A priest who would not be received by the people and who was hated by them was less use than none at all.[69]

McDonough, whom at the President's request Ireland had persuaded to accept a judgeship, suggested the following policy as a solution of the friar problem: Let the government first obtain the lands and, this being done, send out word to the Philippine local officials to the effect that the friars no longer possessed governmental power—no longer were agents of "the Crown," no longer landlords collecting rents, but simply priests engaged solely in the performance of their religious duties. In this way they would be better received and more easily protected. He was satisfied that it would be many years before other priests could be got to take their places, for the friars spoke not only Spanish but also the native dialects. Moreover, there were not more than five hundred native priests, some of whom were going over to "Archbishop" Aglipay and others of whom protested against the appointment of American bishops. As a result, many were losing the faith and would ultimately be as hard to govern as the non-Christian Moros. Hence he urged the friars to come down on their prices and to reach an agreement with the commission.[70]

All through the Philippine problem Archbishop Ireland supported the government. He was convinced that much more could be effected by co-operation than by an attitude of criticism and hostility. Because of his stand, he received much criticism, which he shared with the administration. His position, however, was based on his conviction that the members of the administration were fair, and also on frequent reports which he received from priests and Catholic officials in the Islands. Chaplain William McKinnon told him that Mr. Taft was the idol of the people of the archipelago, with Mr. Luke Wright a close second, and that the abuse of them in the Catholic press in the United States had done much injury to the Church in the Philippines. He said that no sane man could deny that the feeling among most of the Filipinos was bitter against the friars and was growing. He told of the lack of real knowledge of their religion among the people and of the danger of their leaving the Church rather than accept the friars.[71] Father Francis Doherty, also a chaplain, wrote that Aglipay was winning many of the people and some of the clergy. The fact that he had the people with him, he said, was demonstrated on Good Friday, when the Independent element mustered thousands, while the friars had only hundreds. He corroborated Father McKinnon's charge that the people were not well grounded in their faith, which consisted largely of outward forms. They did not go to Mass on Sundays in any numbers, but a fiesta or procession won them in multitudes.[72] A typewritten letter of ten pages, written by Chaplain E. J. Vattman, told of his visits to various dioceses and his estimate of the situation. In the island of Cebu he was much impressed by its peace and prosperity, which he regarded as due to the Bishop, a man admired by all classes for his learning, piety, and prudence. He could not, however, say the same of the Bishop of Iliolo, who "during the four years of his episcopacy never once was seen within his Cathedral, saying that he feared for his life; he has never preached or addressed a pastoral letter to his flock; none of his priests visit him. During the recent famine, due to cholera, he has absolutely done nothing to alleviate suffering." He was astonished at the absence of men in the churches, and deplored the scarcity of priests. He did not believe that American priests would be useful, as the difference of climate, the mode of living, and above all the jealousy of native clergy would oblige them to return to the States. "The hatred of the people," he said, "or rather of the native priests, towards all friars is intense. I could fill pages with quotations and relate instances which prove this assertion beyond the shadow of a doubt." He was convinced that the friars who had left their congregations could never return, except under military protection, and that their return would be a lasting menace to peace. He was also impressed by the hostility of native priests to the American government.[73] Richard Campbell told Ireland that the Delegate had been from the beginning on the side of the commission, that the friars were defiant and refused to surrender to him their deeds and titles, which were indispensable to the final adjustment of the question. He quoted the Delegate as saying to him:

The native priests have at last thrown off the mask. They knew all along that Aglipay was only a clown, and they wanted me to give them a native bishop so that he could head this schism, but I have resisted every suggestion of the kind, and the wisdom of my course is now apparent. Sixty percent of the native priests are Katipunaros. They are enemies of the United States and are secretly working against it. How can I expel the Orders and surrender the interests of Christianity to this strange, irresponsible aggregation, who are without morals or discipline, and without any real or deep religious convictions?[74]

These documents have been quoted, not with any desire to open up old sores or to pass judgment upon them, because undoubtedly demonstrations against the friars were engineered by enemies of religion, but rather to show that Taft and Ireland had reason for believing that the situation was bad. At the same time there seems to be little doubt that the administration was often deceived. As George O'Reilly, a school superintendent, expressed it:

There is in Manila a strong, well organized and well headed anti-Catholic party. They represent nothing as far as the Filipinos are concerned. They stand around, talk brotherly love, the American spirit, and the great benefits of American Catholicism in the Islands, and then use every cowardly lever against the same Catholicism. They fought Catholicism on pretext of protecting the Filipinos from the friars, until forced to admit that there is no longer a friar question. They have used the Aglipay schism against Catholicism, and are now attempting to use the Government for the same purpose. There is no longer a friar question; the Filipinos are essentially Catholic; the Federal Party essentially anti-Catholic. Protestantism cannot clear up the situation; improved Catholicism can. Aglipay is a fraud, his movement insurrectionary, his property claims absurd.

One question remains: What is the attitude of the Philippine Commission towards the Catholic Church? It either does or does not recognize the Church as a power for good. If it does, it should stop talking nonsense and untie the hands of the local heads of the Church.[75]

Ireland, who knew that he had the reputation of being opposed to the friars, said to Monsignor Denis O'Connell: "If I am designated as the leader of the movement against the friars, it is because I obeyed the Vatican in securing the Taft Commission."[76]

Certain American Catholic societies felt that an injustice was being done to the friars, and both in the Philippines and in some American dioceses protests were registered. Meetings were held in Grand Rapids, Michigan; Atchinson, Kansas; and elsewhere. Resolutions were sent to the president of the Catholic Truth Society, Pittsburgh, and to the Federation of Catholic Societies in Cleveland. Several papers, such as the Pittsburgh *Observer*, the Dubuque *Catholic Tribune*, the *Catholic Universe*, said bitter things of the government and Ireland. These meetings caused considerable embarrassment to the government, with the result that the President, Secretary Root,

Governor Taft, and the Archbishop were kept busy giving interviews to the press. Speaking to a representative of the *New Century*, Root protested against the charge that the government had determined that the friars must be expelled. He knew, he said, that the Filipinos were unalterably Catholic, and he explained that the request for the withdrawal of the friars was made in the interests of pacification. In a cablegram to Taft he said that a voluntary withdrawal could not be considered a violation of any rights under the Treaty of Paris or any reflection upon the nation or upon the orders. The reasons for making it desirable were neither religious nor racial but arose from the political and social relation which existed under the former government. It was not the government which objected to the presence of the friars; it was rather the Catholic population of the Islands.[77]

Speaking to a representative of the Associated Press, the Archbishop expressed his satisfaction with the negotiations conducted in Rome, and he hoped that there would be among certain classes of Catholics a cessation of movements and declarations regarding religious matters in the Philippines. The direction of Catholic affairs, he said, is the business of the Pope, and not of irresponsible church societies or newspaper editors. They spoke without knowledge and without proper regard for the government. They should first have been absolutely certain that injustices had been done, and then sought a remedy by appeal to the proper officials before raising irritating clamors in public. The government was doing its best to bring order out of chaos. He quoted from a letter sent by Father McKinnon, which said that there was not a particle of bigotry in Taft's make-up. The Archbishop said:

Whatever unfair things were done were the actions of individuals and not of the Government. What stronger proof of fair-mindedness in the settlement of the religious question of the Philippines could the Administration have given than to respond graciously to the wishes of the Vatican that a messenger from the American Government should go to Rome to discuss matters directly with the Pope and his advisors? Other governments would have gone to work in their own way without a word being said to the Head of the Church or counsel asked from him.[78]

He had in mind the confiscation of the possessions of the Church in France, the expulsion of the Jesuits in Portugal by Carvalho and the sequestration of their property, as well as the confiscation of the property of the religious orders in Mexico. He pointed out that the policy of separation of Church and State, as required by the American Constitution, does not indicate hostility to religion, and he instanced the prosperity of the Church in America as indicating that it had nothing to fear from the extension of the same rule over the Philippines.

Again and again he came to the defense of the government. He told of his audience with the Pope, who expressed himself as well pleased with the relation of the government to the Church in the Islands. It gave proof, he said, of good will and showed by its acts a spirit of justice and respect for the liberty and rights of the Church. The reports which he had received from bishops and others indicated this. Difficulties were to be expected, but the Holy Father had confidence in the intelligence of the American government and people and had asked him to thank the President in his name. He also quoted Cardinal Gotti as saying that the letters he had received from several Carmelite houses told of the liberty they were enjoying under the administration, and the undisturbed possession of their properties. Cardinal Rampolla had confirmed what the Pope had said, and authorized him to say so to the American people. "The Church," the Cardinal said, "needs the cooperation of the American Government for the protection of its rights and liberties."[79]

This interview brought a group of laymen to Archbishop Sebastian Martinelli, the Delegate, with a petition of five hundred signatures and a letter asking the Delegate if he had "any official knowledge of the authority vested in Archbishop Ireland to communicate the views of the Pope to the American public," because their interests and standing as American citizens were being seriously injured by the implication that their consciences were controlled by the Holy Father in matters relating to civic functions. They also requested him to communicate speedily with the Cardinal Secretary of State to ascertain if it was the desire of the Pope to stand before the American people as a partisan of any official or of any party in American politics. This mission Martinelli refused to accept.[80]

At a meeting of the societies connected with the Cathedral of Chicago, Bishop Messmer of Green Bay and Bishop McFaul made addresses which indicated that there was no intention on their part of heeding the warning given by the Archbishop. Bishop McFaul in the course of his address made an attack upon the government and the army, saying that Catholic churches in the Philippines had been looted by the soldiers and that claims for damages to church property were being preferred. He also attacked the establishment of public schools, defended the educational policy of the friars, and said that of the nine hundred teachers sent to the Philippines fewer than twenty were Catholics. He paid tribute to the chastity and purity of the people, who were now in danger of being contaminated by the Americans.[81]

Bishop McFaul also protested to the President that Governor Taft was favoring the Federal party, which, he said was anticlerical and antireligious.[82] The President, after giving the history of the Federal party, which had been organized as the opponent of the Aguinaldian or Independence party, and after defending it against the charge of hostility to the Church, went on to say:

> Smith is a good practical Catholic. I shall find out from him at once his side of the case. Meanwhile, my dear Bishop, let me urge you, not merely in the interest of the country, but in the interest of the Catholic Church, to be cautious about committing yourself on this Filippine matter until you are absolutely sure of your ground. . . . I am continually receiving letters denouncing me because I have done too much for the Catholic Church in the Philippines. I may be mistaken, but I believe that if the policy your correspondent advocates was adopted by this Government, it would produce not merely a revolt in the Philippines but a revolt here.[83]

Roosevelt also expressed to Ireland his indignation at the attacks that had been made and at many of the petitions that came to him from Catholic orders, and even from Catholic bishops and societies of laymen. "Inasmuch as what we did," he said, "was done at your suggestion and with the hearty approval of Cardinal Gibbons, I am inclined to think, however, that most of these attacks have really been aimed at you."[84]

The President told some of the men inclined to start the agitation again that they were most foolish not to see that to make Americanism synonymous in the Philippines with the endorsement of the friars would irritate the Philippine people beyond measure, and would do more than anything else to alienate them in great masses from the Church.

Speaking in his Cathedral and having in mind the approaching meeting of Catholic societies in Chicago, Ireland denounced those who attempted to use the name of Catholicism in an arraignment of the policy of the government. He asked:

> Who are they who complain and protest? Has the Sovereign Pontiff spoken? Certainly he has not complained; rather he has been heard from in very different tones. Have the ecclesiastical authorities in the depend-

encies invoked our aid? In no instance have they acted. Where they have been heard from, as in the case of Puerto Rico and of Cuba, it was to tell us in plainest words that they had no grievance, although from irresponsible sources it had been dinned into our ears that the Church was robbed and persecuted in both those islands.

He quoted Bishop Blenck of Puerto Rico as openly rejoicing that the American flag, rather than the Spanish, guarded his diocese, and the hierarchy in Cuba as thanking God that Church interests there were settled by the government in Washington before a Cuban Parliament was allowed to sit down in Havana. Societies of Catholics, he said, are organized for purposes of their own, to secure special aid or comfort for their members. Restricted to those purposes, they are within their sphere, but they must not venture beyond such purposes. Redress could always be had for grievances as far as circumstances may allow, if it is sought through quiet methods from the government. In no other country is there a government so fair-minded as the American. Catholics should be careful lest by imprudent agitation they instill into the minds of their fellow citizens the notion that they are disposed to form themselves into a people apart, ever dissatisfied with America and its institutions, ever ready to complain. There should be, he said, no discussion of matters in the Islands, since they are the subject of negotiations between the government and the Pope. To take matters into our own hands would be to mistrust the wisdom and the good will of the Pontiff.[85]

One of the sharpest critics of the administration was Father O'Mahoney, an Augustinian. He accused the commission of trampling under foot religious liberty in the Islands, of interfering with the operations of the Church and of indifference when others interfered with them, of setting up and encouraging the Federal party, which, he said, was anti-Catholic. His public statements and his letters to President Roosevelt brought replies from Governor Taft and General Wright, who denied his allegations, stating that, far from interfering, they had gone to the verge in preventing violence or interference. General Luke Wright defended Governor Smith as a thoroughly brave, frank man, who meant what he said and did not hesitate to say what he meant. He quoted Archbishop Guidi as telling him that he had the fullest confidence in the administration's spirit of fairness and liberality toward the Church and that he was writing to that effect to Archbishop Ireland.[86] George O'Reilly regretted that the resolution

of the Catholic Society of the Philippines favoring the retention of
the friars had been used in the United States and at Rome as an important factor in the controversy.[87]

3. EDUCATION

The introduction of the American educational system into the
Philippines brought several charges and criticisms, chief of which
were proselytism, prejudiced school books, and discrimination against
Catholic teachers. Charges were made in the *Catholic Times* that
nearly all of the American teachers were Protestants, some of them
preachers, who took advantage of their position to proselyte, teaching
the natives that Protestantism brought enlightenment; Catholicism,
ignorance and tyranny; and also that Catholic teachers were refused
places in Manila and sent into the wilderness. These charges Governor Luke Wright declared untrue, insisting that teachers were
selected without reference to religion and were not allowed to preach
or teach religion in schools. He quoted the testimony of Chaplain
William D. McKinnon, member of the Advisory Board of General
Instruction, and also the remarks of the Archbishop in an address
delivered at a convention of the National Education Association at
Minneapolis in which he said that the charges of proselytism had
been investigated and proved groundless.[88]

The Archbishop, in an interview published in the *Catholic Citizen*,
said:

As to schools in the Philippines, why not, when the presence of non-
Catholic teachers is talked of, state that out of a total of 5000, 3500 are
Filipino Catholics? Why not state that Father McKinnon is a member of
the school board of Manila? And why, when mention is made of non-
Catholic teachers, allow the false impression to go abroad that many of
these were ministers and active proselyters? And why not remember that
by the law of the Islands clergymen, who are ministers in any place of
organized congregations, may three times a week teach religion in the
schools of the place, the condition that they be ministers of organized
congregations, virtually confining the privilege to the Catholic priesthood?[89]

Secretary Root expressed his mind to him in July, 1902, saying:

There is one phenomenon in this country which I hope will receive your
attention. Coincident with Taft's visit to Rome, there has come from all
parts of the country, first, a stream of letters and resolutions on the school
question in the Philippines, charges of proselyting, etc., which you met
very handsomely in your speech at Minneapolis; and second, a similar lot
of letters and resolutions based upon the idea that our Government is

making an attack upon the Catholic Church as represented by the friars. I am strongly impressed with the conviction that these agitations have not been spontaneous but have been inspired for the purpose of defeating the negotiations at Rome. I think they are doing a great deal of harm, and are liable to make the visit to Rome, which you know was designed in the friendliest possible spirit, the occasion of bitterness and hostility towards the Administration on the part of great numbers of good Catholics, who would otherwise be friendly. I hope that the leading Roman Catholics of the country, who, like yourself and Cardinal Gibbons, were desirous that the visit should be made, will do all in their power to do away with this feeling.[90]

The good intentions of Mr. Taft are shown in a communication which he sent to Bishop O'Gorman on October 17, 1902. In it he told of the resignation of Superintendents Atkinson and Moses and of the intention of the President to appoint Smith in Moses' place. Two hundred or more teachers were about to be appointed and he hoped that Archbishop Ireland would send Catholic nominations.[91] The Archbishop informed Cardinal Gibbons that he had been authorized to secure 108 additional candidates and asked for his co-operation in doing so.[92]

The situation was not helped by wild statements made by some Catholic editors. The San Francisco *Leader* of October 18 said:

The statement has been made and we know the statement to be true that Archbishop Ireland advised the Government not to appoint a Catholic on the Philippine Commissions. His reason was that he wanted all Catholic questions to come into his hands and be decided by him. He had offered his services to the Holy See as Delegate to the Philippines, and when the Pope in his wisdom sent Archbishop Chapelle instead, Archbishop Ireland used all his influence with Governor Taft to render the Apostolic Delegate's efforts null and void, and to a great extent he succeeded.[93]

The Archbishop lost no time in nailing this, and on October 22 he wrote:

I have never heretofore corrected an untrue statement made against me by the press. Silence, I have thought, is always the best answer to misrepresentation. This time, however, the misrepresentation is so gross, that I am not disposed to let it pass unrebuked. Every single word in this statement bearing on supposed acts or supposed motives of mine is absolutely and unreservedly false. How a writer who puts himself forward as a man of honor and a Christian, could pen such a statement, passes my comprehension. I ask that this letter of mine be published on your editorial page and that a marked copy of the number of the *Leader* containing it, be sent to my address.[94]

It would have been strange if some attempts at proselytism had not taken place behind the government's back, but when they were discovered, they were punished. There was the case of G. M. Palmer, who in a private letter made remarks depreciatory of the friars and repeated the old insinuations about the attitude of the Church toward the Bible. The government, after an investigation, demoted him.[95]

There is, however, abundant evidence to support the charge of proselytism and anti-Catholic bigotry. R. J. O'Hanlon wrote to the Archbishop on February 25, 1902, that the entire school system seemed to be under the control of active proselyters, that Dr. Frederick Atkinson, while perhaps fair-minded, had given the few Catholics forced upon him by the demands of the hierarchy the worst positions, that the city schools of Manila were in charge of Mason S. Stone, formerly a Presbyterian clergyman, who selected 90 per cent of his teachers from the list of Protestants, and that there were only two Catholic teachers in all the schools of Manila. He narrated the following incident:

Last week, while I was visiting the city schools, one of the teachers, not knowing my name or my religion, but seeing me in company with Rev. Supt. Stone, thought perhaps that I too was one of his kind, and told me in confidence that very many of the public school children had been induced to join the Evangelical Sunday School classes and were in regular attendance. The head of the Normal School System is another Protestant clergyman named Dr. Bryan, who is an out and out preacher and antagonist of Catholics. More than once he has occupied the platform in Evangelical meetings and denounced Catholics and recommended an active campaign of proselyting among the Catholics. Chaplain McKinnon told me that every graduate from this State or Insular Normal School entered the School as a Catholic and left it Protestant.[96]

Miss Anna Hennessy, writing in June, 1903, gave similar testimony.[97]

This state of affairs persisted in the Philippines for many years. It was remarkable, to say the least, that one superintendent of education after another was non-Catholic, and that perfectly capable men like George O'Reilly, who made a splendid record as Superintendent of the Manila schools and who carried the recommendation of members of the commission, were passed up. O'Reilly, who should have succeeded Dr. Bryan as Superintendent of Education, had proof that he had been shelved at the instance of the Reverend Homer Stunts, the Methodist Presiding Elder, the real brains of the Aglipay movement and the man in whose hands Bryan left the fight against O'Reilly when he resigned. O'Reilly said that out of the thirty-five superintendents of education in the Islands, he was the only Catholic, and this in spite of the fact that there had been at least a dozen bright Catholic young men eligible for the position.[98]

One explanation of the comparative fewness of Catholic teachers is the fact that invitations had been sent by the government to all the leading universities and colleges requesting teachers, and as these were largely secular, non-Catholic teachers were in the majority. Perhaps a more plausible explanation is that the original insistence of the government that the friars be removed left the schools without teachers, whom Catholic schools were unable to supply. But once having made the mistake, the government tried to be fair, and more than once Governor Taft wrote to the Archbishop urging him to send Catholics. This the Archbishop did as far as he was able.

General James Smith, who was Superintendent of Education and a devout Catholic, brought upon himself much criticism, both from the Catholic Society in the Islands and from the bishops. Unquestionably fair, he had, if such a thing is possible, an exaggerated sense of duty and of loyalty to his superiors, and, with a legalistic mind, he hewed to the line in the matter of the separation of Church and State and in his determination not to take religion into account in making appointments. This, while altogether admirable in the United States, where there are many denominations, could easily be pushed to extremes in a country in which almost all the people are Catholics. Moreover, he was not always tactful in handling delicate situations, and once having taken a stand he was uncompromising, and by his emphatic pronouncements caused antagonism. Archbishop Ireland supported him because of his admiration for his integrity. He succeeded Mr. Taft as Governor of the Islands.[99]

Archbishop Harty of Manila did not see eye to eye with Archbishop Ireland on the charges of bigotry. He asserted that with some notable exceptions the spirit of the Bureau of Education, of the superintendents and supervisors, was anti-Catholic. This opinion, he said, all the bishops shared with him. One professor of Roman law in Manila had so influenced his class that all of the students, with one exception, left the Church. He hoped for better things under Smith, although he blamed him for leaving all educational work to the prejudiced Barrows and Brink.[100] Smith defended himself by saying that Archbishop Harty had never made such a charge to him but, on the contrary, had spoken well of the public schools. The only charge he had heard was that made against Brink at a public meeting by the Bishop of Jaro, who, however, withdrew the accusation the following day and apologized. Barrows, he said, enjoyed the complete confidence of the parents and was popular with the people.[101]

These charges and countercharges could be pursued indefinitely without resulting in any satisfactory conclusion. They merely show the great difficulty Ireland experienced in getting an accurate picture of the school situation in the Islands and also the unfairness of the criticism directed against him. But the school situation continued to be a source of apprehension and heartache even to our day.

Roosevelt, especially, worried about the effect of the criticisms upon the political situation. He wrote to Taft concerning the agitation among Catholics caused by the negotiations at Rome. While he was prepared, he said, for attacks from anti-Catholics, he was taken completely aback by the violent attacks made by Catholics. He was inclined to think, as he said, that they were really aimed at Ireland by his enemies, who seemed to control the greater part of Catholic societies and papers. What struck him strangest of all was that the anti-Ireland, antiliberal Catholics were now strenuously insisting that it was an outrage for the United States to depart from its traditional policy in opening negotiations with the Vatican. He was inclined to regard the visit to Rome as a mistake, for the sincerity and honesty of his efforts to help the Filipinos and to do justice to the Church were evidently not believed in Rome or in America. The Catholics, he said, were especially bitter about the school business in the Philippines, where Atkinson's utterances, such as those in his *Atlantic Monthly* article, were most unfortunate. He was afraid that the party would be hurt in the fall elections, although he had confidence that ultimately the people would come to recognize the government policy at its proper value. He had tried to persuade the Church to enter into an arrangement which could be for its own financial interest, an arrangement by which the Catholic laymen in the Islands would receive Catholic priests to whom they would listen, but since the Church refused and bitterness had developed he thought it better to let the friars get along as best they could. He concluded:

Of course it is none of our business how priests get along with their parishioners. If the parishioners object to them, it is not for a moment to be thought of that we should forcibly return them to their parishes, and equally of course we can tolerate no wrong-doing on their part. Can we not let this whole matter go now and simply administer the civil government, leaving the friars and other ecclesiastical bodies to get along as best they can, as they have rejected our help. . . . Excellent Catholics in the United States insist that the best Catholics in the Philippines really desire the presence of the friars. We should have good Catholic testimony to show the contrary.

What steps should I take about getting Moses out? I think it important to put Judge Smith in. It is most unfortunate that in this friar and school controversy we have not had such a man. It would have closed the mouths of critics if what has been said by you and Luke Wright could have been said by a man of their own faith.[102]

The administration, however, brought criticism upon itself by its failure to understand the Catholic position. Speaking before the American Tract Society in Washington, in March, 1904, Taft referred to the Filipinos as "kept in a state of Christian tutelage, but not educated; not instructed in the great principle of religious freedom." He seemed to regard the schism as productive of good results, and he felt that "nothing will do these Islands so much good as the introduction of Protestant clergymen to maintain charities, schools, hospitals and Protestant churches." This statement did not at all please Rampolla, who expressed his surprise to the Archbishop.[103]

4. THE LAND PROBLEM

The problem of the purchase of the lands of the friars was a source of great preoccupation to the Delegate. The valuations placed by the friars and the government showed a difference of seven million dollars. General Smith was of the opinion that the well-understood policy of the Vatican—that all sums realized from the sale of Church properties should constitute a sacred fund for the benefit of the Church in the Philippines—had induced the religious orders to look unfavorably on any transfer of their landed properties to the State. As a consequence, he said, they had placed a valuation on the haciendas in many cases beyond all reason, and one that could not be substantiated by the amount of crop which the lands could produce. Moreover, as a matter of fact, the orders had received only 10 per cent of the crop as rent, which after the deduction of expenses for seed and for farm animals was very small. The problem was aggravated by the action of the friars in transferring their holdings to other parties and corporations in which they continued to hold an interest, and whose identity they kept secret.[104] Richard Campbell, after an interview with Archbishop Guidi, reported to Archbishop Ireland that the Delegate was much discouraged over the failure of the government to do anything about the purchase of the lands. Governor Taft finally offered six million dollars, which the Delegate regarded as so inadequate that he hesitated to present it seriously to the orders lest they laugh at his pains. He agreed with the Governor's contention that the figure of fourteen million demanded by the friars was out of all proportion to the marketable value of their property, but he thought that out of deference to him the Governor might have approached more nearly to his own conception of their true value.[105]

As a result of these and other complications the matter dragged on for more than a year. It was finally settled by a payment of $7,543,000. But there still remained a claim for damages sustained during the war by bombardment and burnings, by acts of vandalism and looting, as well as by the wear and tear resulting from the adaptation of Church buildings to military necessities. Mr. Taft refused to consider claims arising from acts of war, with the result that only a fraction of the amount claimed by the Church was allowed. This was also a matter of great disappointment to the new Delegate, Archbishop Agius, as the churches had to be rebuilt and the poverty of the natives prevented any considerable contributions. Moreover, the natives in their needs were accustomed to turn to the Church for relief, which could no longer be given because the Church treasuries were exhausted. The two and a half million dollars which the Church regarded as its due was reduced to less than half a million, to be divided among several dioceses.[106] On February 3, 1906, the Delegate appealed to Archbishop Ireland to use his influence to obtain from the government an appropriation in compensation for the indirect damage sustained. To this suggestion the President was favorably disposed and he recommended that Congress pass an act authorizing it. Unfortunately a sharp letter of criticism written to the Philippine Commission by Archbishop Harty deferred the execution of the project, the President fearing lest any recommendation made to Congress under such circumstances would expose him to the charge that he was acting under Catholic pressure.[107]

In his letter Archbishop Harty began by referring to the action of the United States Army in seizing certain religious and charitable foundations which were regarded as belonging to the Spanish government but which in reality were the property of the Church. This action he excused because it was done in ignorance of the real state of affairs. But he protested bitterly against the Philippine Commission in its proposed suit to eject the Archbishop of Manila, the Franciscans, and the sisters from possession of the Hospital of San Juan de Dios, which had been administered by the Church for 250 years. He told of his patience under the depredations of the Aglipay party, the bigotry of the Bureau of Education, and the immorality of the public schools. Now, he said, his patience was exhausted, and he planned to go to the courts for his rights. Before doing so, however, he would order to be read from more than two hundred pulpits a solemn protest. Like all threats, this one was resented by the administration and caused a suspension of kindly feelings toward the Philippine Church.[108]

As late as August, 1906, Archbishop Guidi wrote to the Archbishop expressing his great disappointment that the claims of the Church still remained unpaid and that the churches still in the hands of the Aglipayanos were fast going to ruin and were being robbed of all they contained. In the meantime he had to expend more than $100,000 in lawyers' fees. The delay was all the more difficult to endure, since the property claimed undoubtedly belonged to the Church, and the money was sadly needed for the lame, the halt, and the blind, the foundling and the orphan, who constituted the care of the Church. He refused to accept any responsibility for Archbishop Harty's letter, of which he learned only five months after it was written, but his own patience was almost exhausted. He wished that the government would treat the Philippines in the same princely manner as General Wood had treated Cuba, and he expressed his conviction that if a commission were appointed with General Wood at its head all troubles would be ended within three months. The Delegate's letter concludes with these words: "Now, my dear Archbishop, from the distance which separates us, I beg you to judge always kindly of us here, who with a Protestant Government on one side, a Spanish and native element still smarting under the new regime on the other, with strong Religious Corporations and a weak native clergy nursing old prejudices, I assure you we have no easy game to play."[109]

The government finally took steps in 1906 to settle the financial question. Writing to Ireland in March, 1906, Taft recommended a composition of the Pious Trusts by the government's retaining foundation of the Hospital of San Lazaro and releasing all claim to any power and duty to administer the other trusts. With respect to the claims of the Church for the rent of church and convent property occupied by the United States troops, and the damages arising from such occupation, the Board had reported $363,000 as a just claim.

He would have been glad, he said, if a larger amount could have been reported, for the reason that the Church suffered far greater damage than this amount represented, but the damage was inflicted not by the troops but in the train of war or by the *insurrectos*. He thought that Congress might double the amount, but he feared that one fact might militate against such action—the widespread impression that no part of the $7,000,000 paid for the lands had remained in the Islands. In his message to Congress, the President made similar recommendations, but he felt that even the amount recommended fell short of what the Church was entitled to, and that another commission, with Wood or Weston at its head, should be appointed to report the additional sum, which, if not technically legal, would be morally equitable.[110]

5. THE PRELATES

The American prelates assigned to the Philippines encountered a difficult situation and varied greatly in their method of handling the problem. Bishops O'Doherty and Hendrick, and in most instances Archbishop Harty, seemed to take the position of Archbishop Ireland that in such involved questions the greatest need was patience, and that more could be accomplished by a sympathetic attitude toward the administration and confidence in its good intentions than by criticism and opposition. Bishop Rooker, who had a particularly difficult assignment, was outspoken in his indignation. Writing to the President from Jaro on May 12, 1904, he attributed most of the trouble to the Federal party, an organization formed and fostered by the administration to develop loyalty to the United States on the part of the natives. The Federal party, he averred, covered its attacks on the Church under the cloak of opposition to the friars, and had completely deceived the government. He denied that there was a friar question, as the great mass of the people respected the friars and were willing that they remain.

Another source of trouble, Bishop Rooker said, was the determination of the natives to keep the Orient for the Orientals. They were opposed not merely to the Spaniards but to the whole Caucasian race. Unable to get rid of such white rule as had an army and riches behind it, they turned on the friars. The Katapunaros, suppressed as a political society, put on the soutane of the priest and became the "Independent Philippine Church." This they were enabled to do by the government's guarantee of liberty of worship. At once they began their depredations, seizing Church property on the plea that the people had left the Church and joined them. He denied the statement made by some officials that large numbers had apostatized, and he gave statistics to prove his assertion. He ventured to say that there was not a single town in the archipelago where 20 per cent of the inhabitants had left the Catholic faith and that there were not ten towns in the whole country where more than 1 per cent had defected. He put much blame on a circular issued by Governor Taft, which allowed those in peaceful possession of Church property to remain undisturbed. This circular, he said, caused untold trouble to the Church, as it taught the schismatics how their theft could be securely and legally done. For the recovery of property the only recourse was to the courts, with all the law's delays and costs. He held that since the municipalities, which refused to return Church property, were part of the executive branch of the government, the latter was responsible for the spoliation. The Bishop then turned his attention to the schools, and accused the native teachers of perverting the children and of filling them with hate for the Church. Thus he attacked almost every phase of the administration.[111] When Archbishop Ireland in an interview[112] expressed his satisfaction at the conclusion of negotiations for the lands and his confidence that henceforth the Church in the Philippines would be well taken care of, Bishop Rooker reproached him for his statement and told him that such utterances did incalculable harm. He repeated his conviction that all the pretended opposition to the friars merely concealed a fierce and diabolical opposition to the Church and to the Catholic faith.[113] When the Archbishop once more urged patience and confidence in the administration, the Bishop in his reply told of the many difficulties he had encountered, especially of the opposition of the native priests, who had set up a schismatic organization, but who within three months had returned to their obedience. His refusal to drive out the friars had brought complaints from the government and false and vicious accusations that he had alienated the people. He told of the tragic scarcity of priests and his hopelessness of securing any.[114]

Bishop Rooker's communication to the President brought a flat contradiction of his charges as well as the accusation that the Bishop wished the government to establish a military despotism in the interests of the Catholic Church. The Bishop, he said, was asking for suppression of the rights of the Filipinos at a time when most Catholics were demanding independence for them. He deprecated the attack on Smith, who agreed with the President that in the making of appointments to schools religion should not be taken into account.

As for the question of property, he had already taken steps to see that a special tribunal be erected to pass upon those questions at once.[115]

Roosevelt was evidently feeling the pressure brought to bear on him by the bishops, because about the same time he wrote to Ireland, asking him when he was coming to Washington, as he wished to see him. He spoke of the number of members of the American hierarchy to whom he felt indebted for services rendered to the public, but, he said, "there is none to whom I feel under such obligations as to you, for no one of them has rendered as great service to the country as you have."[116]

Still more disturbing was the government attitude on the Pious Trusts. The first of these was the College of San José, originally founded by the will of a Spaniard named Gigueros, Governor of Mindnao. The will provided that a fund which he left for the purpose should be expended for the establishment of a college for the Christian education of the sons of Spaniards in the Philippines, but that the school should be free from ecclesiastical domination, except for direction and supervision by the Jesuits. When these were excluded it came under the administration of the King of Spain, who placed it under the control of the Dominicans. The second great trust was the Hospital of San Juan de Dios, founded by the religious order of St. John but later administered by the civil government. After the capture of Manila, the control was transferred to the Archbishop of Manila. The question was whether it was now a civil trust which by the Treaty of Paris passed to the United States. A third was the Hospital of San Lazaro for lepers, first administered by the Franciscans. The government claimed it was a civil trust, as it had been abandoned by the Franciscans to the Commanding General of the American Army and was being administered by the civil government. Still another was the insane hospital of San José.

Then there was the problem of churches seized and claimed by the followers of Aglipay and by other professional agitators. Mr. Taft's position was that people in possession of churches should not be driven out, and that in such disputes recourse should be had to the courts. This placed upon the Church the task of proving its claims to such properties, entailed expenses running to tens of thousands of dollars, and resulted in protracted litigation and delay. This situation could have been avoided had the government accepted the Holy Father's suggestion made at the beginning of negotiations that the government reconcile its principle of the separation of Church and State with the *de facto* situation that practically all Filipinos were members of the Church. It seems a hardship that after 350 years of undisturbed possession, the Catholic Church should find herself face to face with a litigant claimant that grew up overnight, so to speak, and that these claims to almost half the churches in the Islands had to be laboriously and expensively threshed out in the courts.

Archbishop Ireland was undoubtedly in an embarrassing position, because the administration was not without blame. As Archbishop Harty pointed out, the proposed bill giving to the Supreme Court jurisdiction to determine the title of churches, convents, and cemeteries forcibly withheld by some municipalities and by the Aglipayan sect was unsatisfactory, because these buildings were from the beginning the property of the Church. The status of all of them was the same and, at the time when the Islands were taken over, was determined by the existing laws of Spain and the Concordat between that country and the Holy See. Bona-fide claim of a municipality to them was not possible under Spanish sovereignty, because municipalities could have no right to control over a Catholic church.[117] Although Mr. Taft believed that such properties belonged to the Church, he nevertheless felt that the grounds for claiming that they were municipal property were sufficiently plausible at least to justify the submission of the matter to a court of law. It was just another instance of the inability of a non-Catholic to understand the position of the Church. Finally, Roosevelt wrote to the Archbishop on June 3, 1904: "Taft is going to arrange for a special court to try those church property cases, which will remove the last vestige of pretext for complaint."

The advice of the Archbishop to be calm and wait was not always well received. Archbishop Harty wrote to him in March, 1906, a letter, informative, querulous, and quizzical, which makes delightful reading:

Your simplicity in expecting that the money which has been paid into the capacious purse of the Religious in the Philippines, will return to the Church of Manila or the other poverty stricken Sees, does not accord with the consummate sagacity for which I have always given you credit. The matter at present is with the Holy See. In the meantime I have come to the bottom of the strong box of Manila. The books of the Diocese show $279,000 spent on litigation in the past five years. Another is in prospect, that of San Juan de Dios Hospital and Estates.

The little municipal governments throughout the Archipelago, imitating the attitude of the Governor-General are bringing suits against the Church for possession of Church lands &c. The position I take is this: put the Catholic Church in possession of the property occupied by her for two hundred years at the time the American Government entered these Islands. Let the other party sue. This was done in Cuba under the long-headed General Wood. He called the Apostolic Delegate and said, "Make a sworn inventory of your property." It was made. The property was at once handed over to the Church. There the case ended.

I had tried for more than two years to help the Bureau of Education. I have instructed the parish priests to work in accord with the Department; for instance, if the session of the public school be held in the forenoon, to hold the Catholic school in the afternoon and vice versa. I have urged the priests to compel the children to attend the schools; my public speeches throughout the Diocese have been for the schools. The unfriendly disposition of the officials, some of them ex-preachers and missionaries, has given me annoyance beyond language. The unspeakable Barrows has published a history which is an offense to every decent Catholic. I wish to see the passing of Barrows and the personnel whom he stands for. I have written for the press a review of his book. You may question the wisdom of this action, but you are not on the ground. You should be in my position to understand conditions here. I should consider myself rash were I to judge affairs in the Archdiocese of St. Paul save through your eyes.

I hold General Smith to blame for the Bureau of Education. Human respect is his weakness. He is not big enough for the situation. He lacks tact, and in striving to please all he pleases no one. He has offended the Bishops more by the sins of omission than by overt acts. I have defended him before the Bishops and before others. With the Government here I have always given him a good word, because I like him personally.

I have confidence in our Government in Washington, but they were napping when Worcester, Ide and the two judges of the Supreme Court, Johnson and Carson, were saddled on an afflicted people. For incompetency, ignorance, narrowness and vanity commend me to this bunch of public men. Their hostility to the Church is not open but all the more to be feared.

The Filipino Judges are superior in ability and with a talent for labor. Judge Tracy is the king of the bench in the estimate of the lawyers of Manila.

We have entered upon the hot weather. The air is steamy and sticky with the closeness of a hothouse atmosphere. My principal source of diet is distilled water which I would like to share with your Grace. May we expect you for a visit? I offer you the hospitality of the Palace. The Filipinos would turn out *en masse*. The experience would be worth your while and the event in your history would be equal to the bestowal of the Cardinal's hat. Of course the press would take liberties with you, would write of your mission &c, but you would be equal to the ordeal. Come and give your friends a surprise.

Always yours with affection.[118]

It is unfortunate that the limits of this book forbid the reproduction of more of the correspondence of the bishops and of men like George O'Reilly and Richard Campbell, who had an intimate knowledge of the situation. They clear up many misconceptions about the friars, give intimate pictures of Filipino life and character, indicate the magnitude of the task faced and overcome by the Church, and throw into clear light the fundamental contrast between the views of the episcopate and the administration. Criticism was directed not so much against President Roosevelt or Governor Taft, who were regarded as actuated by high motives, but rather against those who were supposed to implement their policies. Archbishop Harty said of the President: "He has an unerring instinct for the right. He has fixed ideals and possesses the fundamental virtues—truth, uprightness, probity and courage. He is as honest as the day-light."[119] Campbell said of Taft: "He has more than realized the expectations of those who believed in him and who predicted a great success for his administration. He left here with the respect even of Father O'Mahoney, colloquially known as 'the fighting friar.' "[120] While of General Smith's integrity there was no doubt, at the same time it is difficult to free him from blame for much of the misunderstanding. Animated by fine ideals, he was also lacking in tact and disingenuous in dealing with Catholic affairs. He allowed himself to get into undignified controversies with the Catholic Society, voted against the additional money which the orders had demanded before a settlement of the land question, did not support the candidacy of George O'Reilly, who, as Superintendent of Schools, could have put an end to proselytism. He did not have to run legalistic procedure to extremes in its application or apply inflexibly the law of separation to a Catholic country, which for centuries had lived under an entirely different system. He seemed to have forgotten the dictum of Cicero: *Summum jus saepe summa est injuria.*

At the close of his term of office he sent to Ireland an *apologia pro vita sua.* Summing up his differences with the Delegate and some bishops, he said that he considered the assignment of friars to the parishes as detrimental to the Church. He opposed the suppression of civil government as a return to a military regime. He declined to consider himself in office "to do as you are told by those you represent." He refused to discharge or promote an employee solely because of his religion. He ordered that no teacher should teach religion in school or out of it, and declined to make the rule applicable to Prot-

estants and Aglipayans and not to Catholics. He refused to insert in
the bill authorizing the courts to settle the title to Church properties
a recital to the effect that the title was in the Roman Catholic
Church. To do this, he said, would be to decide the title or to influence the court. He defended his action in lecturing to employees and
officials of the government at the Young Men's Christian Association.
He defended his withdrawal from the American Catholic Society in
the Philippines on the grounds that it was not interested in the religion of the Filipino but rather in an attempt to force the Delegate
to send the friars back to the parishes. It is easy to see how this inflexible attitude made matters very difficult for the Delegate and the
bishops.[121] It is, however, only fair to add that Bishop Thomas Hendrick, who at first was dissatisfied with Mr. Smith and opposed his
nomination as Governor, completely changed his attitude after an
interview with him and found him most co-operative and ready to
correct abuses. "Mr. Smith is doing splendidly, doing simply what
the Government should have done from the first, that is, protecting
the poor Catholics in their right to practice their religion."[122]

As one leafs through the voluminous documents which deal with
the Philippine problem, one wonders how Archbishop Ireland was
able to find time to deal with them. He was in constant communication with everyone of any importance in Washington or in the Islands, and matters of great and small importance were constantly
referred to him. The many things which he accomplished and the
benefits which he gained for the Church are everywhere apparent.
While he received much criticism, he succeeded in maintaining cordial relations with the President, the administration, and the hierarchy in the Islands, and he vindicated the worth of his policy of
patience and of confidence in the government. If Archbishop Harty
and Bishop Rooker at times took issue with him, they also expressed
their admiration and affection for him. One may well ask: What
would have been the situation had there been no prelate influencing
the decisions of the administration and working for the promotion of
harmony and understanding?

Chapter 9

STANDS ON SOCIAL PROBLEMS

>|>|>|>|>|>|>|>|>|>|>|>|>|<

1. THE DEFENDER OF THE KNIGHTS OF LABOR

The growth of secret societies—Odd Fellows, Knights of Temperance, and Knights of Pythias—in the first half of the nineteenth century and the formation of labor organizations bound by secrecy—the Knights of Labor, Knights of St. Crispin, etc.—in the second half caused considerable apprehension to the episcopate, some of whom regarded them as a great source of danger to religion. Archbishop Elzear-Alexandre Taschereau, of Quebec, referred to Rome, in 1883, the question of the Knights of Labor, a society founded in 1869 by Ulrich Stephens, a Freemason, receiving the following year the reply that they should be considered among those prohibited by the Holy See. Most of the bishops felt that inasmuch as the decree of 1884 was based on the material submitted to the Holy Office by the Archbishop of Quebec, it applied only to Canada. Especially opposed to any condemnation were Gibbons, Keane, and Ireland, who knew that at the time Terence V. Powderly, the Grand Master Workman of the organization, was a devoted son of the Church and that many Catholics belonged to it.

The archbishops finally decided, at their meeting in October, 1886, to submit the whole matter to Rome, and committed it to the care of Ireland and Keane, who were going there in the interests of the Catholic University.

The memorial which the two prelates presented in Rome on February 20, 1887, stated that while there existed in the constitution, etc., of the Knights of Labor some things which might be criticized there was nothing that would place it among condemned societies—no oath in their initiation, no obligation to secrecy which would bind them in dealing with ecclesiastical authorities, no promise of blind obedience, no hostility to religion or the laws of the country. It pointed out that public injustices, such as monopolies, made self-defense obliga-

tory for the workers, which could be achieved only through association. It took up and answered various objections—association with
Protestants, which could not be avoided in a country like the United
States; lack of supervision by priests, which supervision would not
be advisable in a country composed of various sects; dangers from
atheists, communists, and anarchists, which the Knights had always
repulsed; outbreaks of violence in strikes, which, however, were common in all strikes but which the Knights had always tried to suppress.
It considered the evils that would follow condemnation—the danger
that the Church would no longer be considered the friend of the people; the probability of endangering the political power of the country, which takes sides with the masses; the risk of losing the love of
the children of the Church and antagonizing them. Moreover, it said,
the organization would last only a few years, so that action was unnecessary.

Thus within two years after his succession to the See of St. Paul,
Bishop Ireland was in Rome pleading the cause of labor. While
Cardinal Gibbons has justly received praise for his saving of the
Knights of Labor from censure, the part the Archbishop played has
never been fully recognized. The document which on that occasion
was presented to the Holy Father bears many evidences of his hand.
Through the pages of the *Northwestern Chronicle*, commonly regarded as his mouthpiece, he followed with sympathetic interest the
career of Powderly, his efforts to shorten the working week, his refusal to permit liquor dealers to enter the ranks of the Knights, his
denunciation of anarchy, and his advocacy of reform in working
hours, which would have the very desirable effect of doing away
with the necessity for Sunday work.[1]

Archbishop Ireland never had any sympathy with the efforts of
Cardinal Taschereau to suppress the Knights, and he maintained that
the decree which the latter had secured in 1884 and 1886 forbidding
Catholics from membership did not apply to the United States. He
expressed resentment of the criticism directed against Cardinal Gibbons for favoring a secret society, showed that his position was altogether in accord with the policy of the Vatican as expressed in the
encyclicals of Pius IX and Leo XIII, and promised that when the
verdict of the Holy Father came it would be received by the faithful
with complete submission.[2] It would be needless to cite the many
indications of the Archbishop's interest in the progress of the Knights
of Labor. His high regard for Powderly was to some extent due to

the latter's advocacy of temperance and to his attitude of obedience to and reverence for the authorities of the Church.

The part which he played in protecting the Knights is indicated also in the correspondence which he maintained with Monsignor O'Connell and Cardinal Gibbons. The latter, writing in September, 1888, was happy to inform him that the status of the Knights of Labor was practically settled at last in their favor. He had received from Cardinal Simeoni the official report of the action taken by the Holy Office at their congregation of August 16—that the Knights might for the present be tolerated, provided that the necessary changes be made in the statutes of the organization, in order to explain what might otherwise appear to be obscure or might be interpreted in a wrong sense, especially in those passages of the preamble to the constitution which referred to local associations, words which seemed to savor of socialism or communism, and which should be corrected.[3]

Dr. Richard Purcell has summed up in the following words the part which the Archbishop played in the protection of the Knights:

> Cardinal Gibbons had received most of the credit because of his own account in his memoirs, his reasonably complete biography, and his primacy in the hierarchy, but the more determined and frank-speaking Archbishop of St. Paul was a necessary collaborator in this matter and in other joint activities when vigorous steps were required.[4]

Dr. Henry Browne writes in similar strain:

> It is impossible to attribute complete and sole authorship to Gibbons of the fifteen-page French document which was addressed to Cardinal Simeoni under date of February twentieth. This is so not only because it was completely finished and dated so soon after Gibbons' remark that he was working on it, but also because it was in French. The Cardinal did not write that language with sufficient ease to undertake the task, and so the help of John Ireland, who had been trained in a French seminary, was undoubtedly called for at least to some extent.[5]

And Bishop Keane, speaking of the attempts made to procure the condemnation by the Holy See of the organization not only in Canada but also in the United States, says: "Pending the discussion, Cardinal Gibbons arrived, to speak in the name of all our bishops. He had us prepare a memorial on the whole labor question and on the Knights of Labor in particular, which he signed and urged with all his influence."[6]

After his return from Rome, Archbishop Ireland preached in his

Cathedral, stating the exact position of the Church. He told of its sympathy with labor as the weaker party, but he warned the Knights that in defending themselves they must not infringe upon the freedom of labor, that in their strikes they must not by force induce others who do not belong to their order to strike, or deny to others the right to work.

Cardinal Gibbons sent him a copy of Cardinal Manning's letter, containing the statement: "We little thought when we were writing about the Knights of Labor in Rome, a few years ago, that every word would be so soon published to the world by an Emperor and a Pope. This is surely the new world overshadowing the old, and the Church walking like its Master among the people of Christendom. Were we prophets?" To this the Archbishop replied: "The words are cheering, and to you who staked your name on the outcome of the problem, then rather obscure, they must have been very gratifying. You were a prophet. The people are the power, and the Church must be with the people. I wish all our Bishops understood this truth."[8]

The views of Archbishop Ireland, Bishop Keane, Cardinal Gibbons, and Cardinal Manning, which are now regarded as commonplace, were subjects of suspicion in their day. As Keane wrote to the Cardinal of Westminster: "It is no small venture to utter such sentiments in an atmosphere like this of Rome."[9] And when Manning added his defense of the Knights to that of the American prelates, Keane told him that Cardinal Simeoni, "the embodiment of timid and suspicious conservatism," would not favor its publication in the *Moniteur*, and that they could expect from him only the toleration of their ideas. He wrote: "Cardinal Simeoni, and probably others like him, link together the labor movement in America and the Home Rule movement in Ireland; and the dire colors in which poor Ireland is now being painted cast a glare of suspicion upon us too. The times are certainly critical, but we know we are advancing truth and justice."[10]

2. Pleader of the Cause of Secret Societies

Not only did Archbishop Ireland protect the Knights of Labor, but also, following his theory that "as much liberty as is at all consistent with principles should be allowed Catholics," he strove for a quarter of a century to secure toleration for those societies which, in his mind, were not hostile to the Church. At the Third Plenary Council of Baltimore in 1884 he opposed condemnation of the Ancient Order of Hibernians. At the annual meeting of the archbishops in Chicago in

September, 1893, his proposal that Catholics should not be prohibited from joining the Odd Fellows and the Knights of Pythias under penalty of refusal of the Sacraments, but should be strongly exhorted not to belong to them, won the support of most of the prelates.[11] The condemnation of those two societies and of the Sons of Temperance in June, 1894, left him and his friend, Cardinal Gibbons, saddened but still hopeful of securing a reconsideration.[12] In January of the following year, however, the Pope, in his letter addressed to the episcopate of the United States, issued what seemed to be a general condemnation of all secret societies, saying that any society which is ruled by and servilely obeys persons who are not steadfast for the right and friendly to religion can be prejudicial to the interests of individuals and the community. Therefore Catholics should shun not only those societies which have been openly condemned but also those regarded by the bishops as suspicious and dangerous. Still the Archbishop continued to hope, reassured by the statement of Monsignor O'Connell that the decree of condemnation was "practically dead aborning," and by that of Archbishop Satolli, who felt that the prohibition would later be removed if the societies were willing to remove all grounds for suspicion, and that those who already belonged would not be obliged to withdraw under grave inconvenience.[13] The Delegate not only urged him to keep in touch with the societies and to persuade them to alter whatever might be objectionable, but also had suspended the decree in response to a delegation of professional men from Fall River, Massachusetts.

Heartened by these assurances, the Archbishop gave an interview to a representative of the press, in which he stated that while the Church desired her members to keep aloof from the societies she would give all possible consideration to the difficulties of circumstances. When misrepresentations of his attitude on the decree began to appear in the European press, he wrote to the *Univers* in February, 1895, protesting against statements which, he said, were "either entirely false or a travesty on the facts."[14]

The friends of the Archbishop were divided in their interpretation of the decree and in their hopes for a reconsideration. Dr. Thomas O'Gorman did not expect that the representations of the episcopate could change the mind of Rome. The only alleviation which he could see was for the bishops to instruct their priests privately that the decree, being a *lex positiva humana*, should be tempered in its application by the general rules of theology, and that confessors should judge each case on its merits. Later, he told of a letter which Satolli had received from Rome stating that the decree must stand but leaving to him its application.[15] Cardinal Gibbons continued to be hopeful, expressing his joy that the decree had gone back to the Inquisition and his hope that the Archbishop would obtain the necessary documents and information for the Delegate.[16] Nor did Father Alphonse Magnien think that the case was as bad as the Archbishop seemed to believe, first, because those who had been strongest for the condemnation realized that they had made a mistake in publishing it and were trying to retrace their steps, and second, because Bishop Chatard had sent to his priests a *monitum secretum* which practically did away with the decree in its application to particular cases, and Archbishop Elder was thinking of doing likewise. Moreover, he felt that the Cardinal in his visit to Rome would be able to make the authorities realize that they had blundered.[17]

Far different was the reaction of Dr. Frederick Rooker, who was outspoken in his criticism of the way in which the Ireland party had handled the situation. He wrote three letters, which are the most interesting of those the Archbishop received. In the first two he said that the three letters written to Rome more than a year before, opposing the condemnation, might have been stronger, while those prepared on the other side were masterpieces, and dovetailed so well together that there was no doubt of the care with which they had been prepared. There was nothing left now but to make the best of the misfortune, as he could see no hope of a change.

Rooker's last letter, while not adding comfort or light to the situation, is such a delightful bit of sarcasm and so typical of him that it deserves reproduction in full. It was a reply to the Archbishop's protests against hardships inflicted on members of the societies.

You may be certain that things are as I write, only more so. A reversal of a decree of the Inquisition would be a novelty indeed. I don't think history records a case. The latest instructions so far from reversing it rather "rub it in" and remove to a great extent the possibility of the sort of compromise we were trying to make in order to render its application a little less disastrous in individual cases. The tears of your engineer are but a drop in the ocean of them which have already been and will be shed, but the Inquisition has watched the shedding of many other tears for centuries and "*assuetis non fit passio.*" Why should a mistake be corrected by one who has the power to enforce submission to the mistake? You speak of souls being lost by the tens of thousands. *Ipsi videant.* They need not be lost. They can obey. No soul is lost but by its own fault—by disobedience to the Church. It is true that in order to obey they may have to sacrifice all that is dear to them in this world, they may have to suffer, and starve, and see their loved ones suffer and starve, they may have to give up all elevating and refining influences and surroundings of the "natural order," they may have to stand aside and let their neighbors go on in the march toward "natural perfection," but what would it profit them to gain the whole world if they suffered the loss of their own souls? Still, there is no real necessity for their actually suffering privation and want for themselves or for their families. It is true your Engineer has lost his situation and is out of work. But it was unjust of his employers to discharge him on these grounds. Besides he can turn it to advantage and from what seems his misfortune he can reap a blessing. He can open a rum shop. He will make lots more money. He will take it, to be sure, from suffering wives and children; he will help fill the world with starving widows and orphans; but that is not his fault. The selling of liquor is not bad *"in se,"* and if those who buy it want to abuse it, that is not the fault of the seller, and he will get rich and can give money to the Church and can educate priests who will go out and teach supernatural morality to the people and keep them out of the diabolical secret societies and save their souls. You say that few men in the Dakotas will go to the Sacraments this Easter. I hear the same thing from many other sections. How foolish of them. Would they compare the blessing of the eternal salvation of their souls with the very slight sacrifice demanded of them? You say your only resource is pessimism. I wouldn't say so. It is obedience. If all the world would only obey how happy all the world would be after they are dead, and how happy those who are obeyed would be both before and after they are dead. Then would true peace and concord and happiness reign. Then would the millenium, indeed, begin.—Now that I have written this I hesitate about sending it for I see it is a sermon. But you will forgive me I know. I thank you again for your kind words about that N.Y. speech. I might be proud of it if I were a more honest man.

With sincere respect and affection.[18]

In March, 1895, Ireland urged Gibbons to "go to Rome by May 1. Go to conquer and return to us having conquered." Gibbons' visit, however, did not change the situation. He found that the Holy Office was inflexible and that, only a few days before his arrival, a letter had been sent to the Delegate urging a more explicit promulgation. Interested parties had been working with the Holy Office, representing some prelates as neglectful in this regard. However, those high in authority had suggested an interpretation which would moderate the severity of the decision. Later he learned that the decree had been issued before he reached Rome; that it had been industriously circulated that he was to plead strongly for the societies and hence he had been forestalled. He was much impressed by the amount of intrigue and deceitful diplomacy which he had found on the other side of the Atlantic.[19] Ireland must have been one of those accused of being neglectful, for a letter from Satolli in June told him of the announcement of Cardinal Monaco that he had been informed that according to some prelates the promulgation of the decree of the Holy Office on the Odd Fellows, the Knights of Pythias, and the Sons of Temperance was not obligatory. Satolli said that if he knew of any diocese in his province where it had not been promulgated, he should see that it was done.[20]

A modification of the decree in January, 1896, allowed a nominal membership in the three societies if, in the judgment of the Delegate, four conditions were fulfilled: that the society was entered in good faith, that there be no scandal, that grave temporal injury would result from withdrawal, and that there be no danger of perversion.[21]

Ireland kept up his agitation for the reversal of the decision because he was convinced that there was nothing in some of the societies that called for the anathemas of the Church. Moreover, he knew that because of their condemnation thousands of Catholics were placed in the dire alternative of either giving up social and industrial advantages which were of great importance to them, and which, they were convinced, they could enjoy without any sacrifice of conscience, or else giving up the Sacraments and the sacred advantages of their religion. In such a choice of alternatives it was to be feared that many would choose the latter, as indeed many had already done. Then, too, the reasons for the condemnation were not too clear in his mind, so that he was unable to supply satisfactory answers to inquirers, thus giving the aspect of arbitrariness and increasing the dissatisfaction of the members toward the Church.

At the meeting of the archbishops in May, 1905, he raised the question of the Knights of Pythias and spoke of the great number of Catholics who belonged to the society and of the desire of the society to be investigated. As a result, a commission was appointed to make an investigation and to report to Gibbons, who, on the strength of the reports so submitted, would urge a reconsideration in Rome. At the 1907 meeting he said that in an interview which he had had with the Cardinal Prefect of Propaganda in Rome the previous year he had found him not averse to reopening the question of the Odd Fellows and the Knights of Pythias, provided there were sufficient reasons for doing so. He also stated that those Catholics who had remained in the societies had found nothing in them to injure either conscience or faith, and that others objected to a condemnation without a previous hearing. A commission was appointed, consisting of the Archbishops of St. Paul, Milwaukee, St. Louis, and Dubuque, to whom was assigned the task of examining the advisability of petitioning the Holy See to reconsider the condemnation passed upon the two societies.[22] In August, 1908, Ireland, as chairman, submitted the report of the commission to Archbishop Diomede Falconio, the Apostolic Delegate. He stated that he had found no difficulty in obtaining from the societies their rituals and other documents, that the officials expressed their willingness to answer all questions, declaring their willingness to consider seriously any amendments which might be suggested. An examination of the documents submitted showed, Ireland said, that the aim of the societies was mutual aid for their members and their training in friendship, love, and truth; that they had no intention of contravening the duty of a member to his conscience, creed, or country; that their motives for the practice of the above-mentioned virtues were those of natural ethics, but that supernatural motives were by no means excluded; that they based all duty on their relations to their Creator, on the immortality of the soul, and on the image and likeness of God in the soul and the natural law imprinted within it. Although the officer who recited prayers was called the priest or prelate, he was not *minister cultus* in the meaning of the words of the Third Plenary Council of Baltimore. The promise of obedience was by no means absolute or blind and expressly excepted what would be contrary to creed, conscience, or country. Hence it was not the obligation condemned by the Council and the Holy See. The "mysteries" were merely signs, grips, and passwords and were only means of privacy. Their various symbols conveyed moral lessons, and their symbolic representations of historical and even sacred scenes were on a simple scale, like those of the Passion play of Oberammergau. It was, therefore, the mind of the commission that the condemnation must have been based on incorrect representations of their statutes.[23]

The following letter, which the Archbishop received in August, 1909, from Father David Fleming, the distinguished Franciscan and Consultor of the Holy Office, did not offer much hope:

I duly received the "Documents" and put them in. They will come before the H.O. in the usual way. I thought there might have been something later than 1894. It would be well if the O.F.'s could be induced to give up their *Deistic* teaching. It is directly & indeed aggressively inculcated in the Ritual of 1886.

If the "O.F.'s" & the Knights of Pythias would consent to allow *all*

Catholics to be merely *passive members*, I think we could come to terms on such a basis. I mean that their names be put on the books, their contributions accepted & help given in accordance with the rules without any obligation of being *initiated* or of assisting at the meetings. American "O.F.'s" have had a bad name for over 60 yrs & not without cause. Their hostility to Catholics was more than *academic*. Hence the difference between the treatment of the H. See of British & American "O.F.'s." I don't think you have any chance of getting any reversal or modification of the condemnation of *1894* unless you can show that some change for the better has taken place since that date.

I venture to suggest the *proviso* of 1896 as a basis of compromise. The C. Church does not want to put any obstacle in the way of Benefit Societies, but she does not want her children taught a hybrid kind of Deism by these gentlemen.[24]

This letter forecast the action of the Holy See. A communication from Rampolla to Falconio in February, 1910, stated that the Holy See had examined these societies in 1894, had found in them the bond of secrecy and *communicatio in divinis*, and now regretted that the ban could not be lifted. It suggested that the archbishops work for a change and emendation in the rules and practices of the societies.[25] On receipt of this decision Ireland bowed to the inevitable and ceased his activities.

3. The Temperance Advocate

Both as priest and as prelate, Archbishop Ireland never lost his enthusiasm for temperance, and after his consecration in 1875 he made war more desperately than ever upon the liquor traffic, denouncing it as reckless and lawless, as the most fruitful of the sources of the poverty, wretchedness, and crime that afflict humanity. Never in America was an evil denounced with more fiery eloquence than was the liquor traffic denounced by Bishop Ireland, who was soon recognized as the outstanding leader of the temperance movement, the "Father Mathew of the West." From ocean to ocean appeals poured in upon him to deliver addresses on temperance in scores of cities. Never was he more aptly called "the consecrated blizzard" than when his tempestuous eloquence and enthusiasm swept from the plains of the Mississippi to the cultured halls of Boston, swaying the minds and hearts of vast audiences with the sincerity of his convictions. Among his more noted addresses were those delivered in Chicago, Buffalo, and Baltimore. His discourse in Buffalo on March 10, 1884, brought out with relentless power the lawlessness of the liquor traffic. Intemperance he called the prolific parent of vice and crime, "inflaming the passions and appetites, breaking down the barriers of decency and self-respect and bringing chaos upon the whole moral life; the feeder of immorality, theft, rapine and murder, suggesting to the mind the thought of crime, giving the animal excitement needful for deeds of violence, and silencing conscience when the deed is done."[26]

It was largely through his influence that the Third Plenary Council of Baltimore put itself on record as disapproving the liquor traffic and as advising Catholics to seek a more honorable means of livelihood. It is not surprising that his efforts won the approval of Pope Leo XIII, who in March, 1887, wrote: "Above all we have rejoiced to learn with what energy and zeal, by means of various excellent associations, and especially through the Catholic Total Abstinence Union, you combat the destructive vice of intemperance."[27] That the campaign upon which he entered as a young priest, and which closed only with his life, helped to arouse public opinion and awakened the country to a sense of its peril, that it inspired others to become leaders in the movement, that it placed high-license laws on statute books —all this is familiar to those who are conversant with the history of social welfare in America. Less familiar, perhaps, is the fact that across the seas he was looked up to as the greatest temperance advocate of the ages. His addresses in Dublin, Cork, and Limerick rang through Ireland,[28] and his discourses in Liverpool similarly stirred the people in that great city. In his address in Limerick he appealed to the religion and the pride of the people. He stated that at the convention of total abstainers, held in Baltimore some time before, it was unanimously agreed that the Catholic who kept a grog shop was unworthy of the name. He was proud, he said, of the Irish-Americans wherever he went—they attained to the very highest eminence. But there was one great blemish on their character—the curse of intemperance. He spoke of the slums of England and America, where Irishmen and their families were simply outcasts, all because of their unfortunate thirst for drink. He referred to the days of Father Mathew, and wondered, if the spirit of that apostle of temperance passed over Ireland, what it would think of the great and sad falling away from the salutary reformation which he had effected. When he reached the Irish shores he felt, he said, that he was treading on sacred ground—a land made sacred by the blood of its martyrs, a land of piety and saintliness; but he could not help feeling sorry at the dark cloud of intemperance which so sadly dimmed its luster.[29]

In Cork, on July 19, 1899, he held an audience spellbound for two hours, his enthusiasm inspired by his love for the land of his birth and his interest in its welfare. There he stressed the fact that this was an age of the people, an age of democracy, of social reform, when the hearts of all Christians and of all true citizens went out with greater earnestness and greater warmth toward man than perhaps at any other previous period of history. In such an age the Church must work among the people for their temporal good and advancement. But what was the use of speaking to men of sin when their surroundings of poverty and misery dragged them down into crime? First they must be civilized, and removed from terrible degradations, then they are capable of hearing the promises of the Gospel. "There is," he said, "one word which tells what must be done if you would succeed in any measure for the betterment of the people—the word is sobriety. Ireland sober is Ireland happy; Ireland sober is Ireland free." After speaking of the noble qualities of the Irish people, their clearness of mind, quickness of thought, and generosity of heart, and after bewailing their loss of success due to intemperance, he cried out: "I swear before the living God so long as my hand can be raised it shall be raised in opposition to intoxicating drink."[30]

At Saint Anne's Church, Spitalfields, London, he depicted in glowing terms the nature and extent of the drink evil, and at a meeting held in the adjoining League of the Cross hall he and Father Nugent addressed an audience that filled every nook and corner. Appealing in homely phrases to their faith, their love of Holy Church, their self-interest, he said:

You, workingmen and workingwomen, you have to labor from morning to night, in summer and winter. God knows how your lot is at best a hard one. Why should you make it harder by spending your small earnings in drink? At least when you touch the little reward of your sweat and your toil, bring it home, every penny of it, and put it to good use for your children, for your wives, for yourselves, and, when possible, put a penny aside for the future, so that when God sends sickness or bereavement, you will have something on which to fall back. Do not take a penny of your hard earnings to the grog shop.[31]

Whoever reads the words of the Archbishop on that occasion—words which seemed to come surging up from a flaming heart—will well understand why he was called the American apostle of temperance.

His technique did not differ much from that of other preachers of temperance. He set forth the terrible consequences of drunkenness not only on the individual but also on his family. He painted vivid pictures of ruined homes, of poverty and pauperism, of the issue of drink in vice and crime. Where he rose superior to other lecturers was in his enthusiasm, his *saeva indignatio*, his consuming zeal, the sincerity and warmth of his thought, the sacred fire that came forth from that large heart of his.

Come to me, friends and patrons of the traffic [he said in one of his memorable perorations], to garrets and to cellars in back street and in hidden alley, whither the slaves of drink repair from the saloons, and I will show you the poor man, and the wife and children of the poor man. And while you stand aghast at the scene of awful wretchedness, I will ask you to take in hand the cause of the poor man. Come with me some morning to the Police Court and study the poor man as he is introduced from a neighboring cell by the policeman who tells the story of debauch and murderous riot. Come with me to prison, to reformatory, to poorhouse. Follow me to the pauper's corner in your cemeteries, and in pity I will beg you to protect and save the poor man. Protect and save him from the cause of his poverty, his woe, his sin—the liquor traffic.[32]

He had the common touch; he knew how to reach the hearts of his people. Perhaps the following incident in his work for temperance in St. Paul will illustrate his method:

"One day," said the Archbishop, "I met John Shortall. He was half drunk, but more than half full of good sense, and he said 'You cannot do anything in Minnesota Street.' A bright thought struck me. I said, 'John, I have been reading some interesting news from Kilkenny.' John was from Kilkenny. He said, 'Sweet Kilkenny.' I saw my opportunity. I replied, 'Will you do me a favor for the sake of Sweet Kilkenny?' 'Yes, anything,' he said. 'Very well, take the pledge for the sake of sweet Kilkenny.' His quick answer was, 'You have me.' From that day, there was in St. Paul no more pious Catholic, there was no more loving father, there was no happier man than John Shortall. Some time later he was near his end and I went to see him. He said, 'Archbishop, I am blind; I cannot see you. I pray that the light of Heaven may be upon your soul. I pray for you every day.' And he went to Heaven, he was a saint, because for the sake of sweet Kilkenny, he had taken the pledge."[33]

Ireland did not allow his enthusiasm for temperance to run to excess, but rather pursued a middle course. Although, when he spoke in St. Paul in June, 1889, he seemed to favor prohibition, he was not a prohibitionist, in spite of the efforts of his non-Catholic friends to call him such. He favored control of the liquor traffic through high license and local option. He expressed his approval of Archbishop Satolli's support of Bishop Watterson, who refused absolution to saloonkeepers conducting their business in an unlawful manner, but he felt that intemperance could not be suppressed by compulsion. In December, 1900, he joined Bishop James McGolrick in telling the Senate Committee on Military Affairs that the House amendment abolishing the canteen not only was unwise but would also tend to produce those very conditions which the champions of the amendment aimed to suppress. He regarded the canteen as a powerful factor in the protection of the soldiers from outside temptations, and any attempt to prohibit absolutely the use of liquor as a temptation to find it in illegal and harmful ways.[34] He frequently expressed his opinion on liquor legislation. Asked by a representative of the New York *Tribune* about the substitute to the Schaaf excise bill pending in the legislature, he said that he considered it the boldest attempt yet made in favor of rum supremacy, the object of the bill seeming to be to throw down the barriers erected against the liquor traffic and to give traffickers in it complete freedom of action to sell when, where, and to whom they pleased.[35]

4. The Student of Social Problems

All through his life the Archbishop manifested the greatest interest in social problems. He was elected vice-president of the National Conference of Charities and Corrections in Omaha, in September, 1887. In the Music Hall in Chicago, in April, 1888, and in the Opera House in Cork, Ireland, in July, 1899, he referred to the study of these problems as the characteristic feature of the age, and he stressed the need of social reform. The intent, he said, was to elevate the human family, to make the conditions of life more endurable, especially those of the poor, the suffering, the depraved, the victims of untoward circumstances, and the children of misery of every form.

Nor was he content to speak in generalities; he sought to find practical solutions for the problems of the workman. During September and October, 1891,[36] he preached in his Cathedral a series of sermons dealing with the encyclical on labor, and with such topics as the time to labor and the living wage. He often referred to the reckless manner in which some people spoke of the freedom of labor, as if the laborer were free to degrade in himself human nature by unreasonable expenditure of physical forces and the omission of the requirements for their renewal and preservation. He regarded the agitation in favor of an eight-hour day as a movement in the right direction. It is interesting to read the comment of the Minneapolis *Journal* on these sermons, especially the statement of the editor that the Archbishop failed to find a solution for the problem, which could be solved only by the workmen themselves, and that no permanent plan could be devised by which an employer would pay as much for a day's work of eight hours as for one of ten or twelve.[37]

Labor, he said, is honorable, the source of all wealth, the cause of all progress. The harder the lot of labor, the more it deserves respect; the heavier the burden, the heavier the debt of society to him who bears it. He deprecated the idea that it is simply an article of commerce, a merchantable commodity. It is man in action, and therefore it possesses the dignity and the rights inherent in the human person.

He spoke of the injustices of the labor market, the cruelties of modern industrialism, the evils of reckless competition and the fierce greed of gain, of soulless capitalism which places on man a value less than that of the material tool. He could see no social peace among the nations of the earth until a change came about in the economics of the world (how often we hear that remark today!). He vindicated the right of the worker to a minimum wage which would permit him to live in a manner not unworthy of a human being, a rational creature of God. Nor should the work be so oppressive as to diminish unreasonably his strength and his tenure of life. Either the wage must be sufficient, so that prudent economy may set aside a portion to meet coming necessities, or provisions outside the wage must be made by the employer, and encouraged and insisted upon by the State. Modern industrialism had either made the family impossible or had despoiled it of its sanctity and its bloom. What was needed was a wage which would enable the worker to maintain not only himself but also his wife and family.

At a banquet given at the Ryan Hotel, St. Paul, on January 29, 1890, he spoke to the toast "Employers and Employees." His introduction, dealing with the natural alliance which exists between the Church and builders is beautiful in thought and expression. He said:

The noblest works of builders are the monuments erected by them under the sky-reaching inspiration of the Church. The pride of religion and of art is the majestic cathedral, enshrining the memorial of the Last Supper. Its religious conception was the resolve to do as slight dishonor as possible to ethereal, divine beauty, while crystallizing it in material forms, and, as the edifice rose from the earth and spread upward through the air its entrancing lines, the builder, exhausting his art on every stone and every beam, made portal and window, arch and turret resonant of voices and teachings of the heavens. In medieval times builders were the Church's most loyal devotees and the objects of her special patronage, and to the union of religion with the builder's art we must ascribe the sublime temples of Westminster and Paris, of Cologne, Burgos and Milan, the despair of our more ambitious and materially more potent but less spiritual and less spiritually-minded nineteenth century.

Then, turning to his main topic, he outlined the causes operating to bring on a crisis between employers and employees—the diffusion of education, urging the working classes to think for themselves and to seek betterment of their condition; the general restlessness and love of revolutions pervading the human race; the gigantic strides of industrialism, exciting keen competition and leading to the confounding of men with machines; and an increasing greed for money. He repeated his advice to employees to strive for their rights while allowing the rights of others. He again stressed the importance of capital, the destruction of which would render labor fruitless. While his sympathies went out to the employee, whose burden is heavy, he could not justify compulsion upon fellow employees to join in a strike.[38]

In an interview with M. Jules Huret, published in the Paris *Figaro* in September, 1894, the Archbishop was asked whether he approved of the title of socialist bishop so often given to him in France. He replied that it all depended on the meaning of the word. If it referred to those who were concerned with social needs and miseries, and who sought to ameliorate the state of society, even if to do so implied a reasonable intervention of the civil power, he was willing to accept the appellation.[39]

Among the many lectures which he delivered on the relations between labor and capital, his address given before the convention of the Brotherhood of Locomotive Engineers at St. Paul, on May 3, 1894, received wide and favorable comment from the press. And on the Sunday following the close of the convention he spoke from his Cathedral pulpit to a large audience of the delegates on the contribution which religion makes to the solution of labor problems. The principles which the Gospel gives are, he said, the dignity of man, justice to others, and the rights of the family and the nation. This address attracted much attention throughout the country, stirring thought in the world of capital as well as labor. It was reproduced in large part by many influential journals.[40]

While the Archbishop had complete sympathy with the just aspirations and rights of wage earners, he did not hesitate to condemn their mistakes, and when he spoke, he left no doubt about his position or his meaning. In August, 1894, a vast railway strike in Chicago plunged the city into violence and disorder that created uneasiness throughout the whole country. It was a time when feelings ran high and when only a brave man dared to speak out. It will be recalled that President Cleveland felt compelled to send federal troops into Chicago to suppress rioting. In the midst of conflicting reactions the Archbishop heartily indorsed the President's action, and his bold and candid words again won wide attention. He said that it would be well for the principles of the Republic if city and state authorities were so prompt and firm in action as to render needless all appeal to the national executive, but that unfortunately officials are sometimes so solicitous of political interests and party considerations that they fear to offend and allow social troubles to grow until repression seems impossible. He said:

The interests and rights of labor. Often I have pleaded for them, and lovingly do I plead for them anew. I hate that view of labor which makes it a mechanical force, like the rotation of a railroad engine or a turbine, purchasable at mere market value. I must see at all times the living generator of labor—the man, my own brother and the child of the Supreme God—and in availing myself of human labor I must keep well in mind the dignity and the rights of the man. I would not respect the laborer who seeks not to enjoy all his rights and to improve his condition. But all this must be done within the lines of social order and law.

The fatal mistake which has been made in connection with this strike is that property has been destroyed, the liberty of citizens interfered with, human lives endangered, social order menaced, the institutions and freedom of the country put in most serious jeopardy. The moment such things happen all possible questions as to the rights and grievances of labor must be dropped out of sight, and all efforts of law abiding citizens and of public officials made to serve in maintaining public order and guarding at all cost the public weal. Labor must learn that, however sacred its rights be, there is something above them, one absolutely supreme social order and the laws of public justice.

To labor and capital and their relations he returned again and again, allaying the passions and prejudices that spring from the strongest of human motives and so holding the balance of justice between clashing interests that his pronouncements carried weight with both parties. Rarely was the judicial character of his mind more clearly evinced than in the article on "Personal Liberty and Labor Strikes" which he published in the *North American Review* in October, 1891, and which dealt so sanely and impartially with the most contentious aspect of a thorny question that it was referred to by judges on the bench and quoted by law journals in several states. Judge Hammond of Louisville, Kentucky, quoted the article in giving an important decision, saying: "It presents the law governing the case so accurately and tersely that I adopt it as my own judgment. No lawyer or judge has stated the principles controlling the courts in these cases more aptly, though untechnically, than the prelate."

His discourse on labor and capital delivered before the labor unions of St. Paul on Labor Day, 1903, was a model of sympathetic and impartial discussion of one of the most important problems bound up with the peace and prosperity of the nation. In 1902 in the anthracite coal strike, with 140,000 miners idle, with the schools of New York closed for want of coal, everyone knew that the Archbishop, then a member of the National Civic Federation, sympathized with the miners. Indeed, what he did to save the working classes to the Church, while it seems to be little understood, should be reckoned prominently among the beneficent services that lend luster to his life.

His attitude on the Negro problem was revolutionary. In St. Augustine's Church, Washington, in April, 1890, he said that the existing prejudice against men because of their color made him ashamed as a man, a citizen, and a Christian. Every prejudice entertained, every breach of charity and justice against a man because of color is a stain flung on the banner of our liberty that floats over us. They who compel a man, because of his color, to betake himself to a corner marked off for his race contradict the principle of justice and right established by the God of mercy. This address prompted Archbishop Patrick Ryan to say to Archbishop Corrigan that Archbishop Ireland had created a sensation by declaring that Catholics must admit Negroes to social as well as political and religious equality, and that while his enthusiasm sometimes led him too far, his purity of intention was unquestionable.[41] Monsignor O'Connell quoted a gentleman from Washington who told him that the Negroes "were strutting through the Departments with their heads in the air, and saying: 'He is the fust man that ever put the nigger in his right place.' "[42] The *Catholic Citizen* said that, in the *Catholic Negro's Complaint*, Father Slattery had shown how the Archbishop laid down the very A B C of civil and religious, political and manhood equality, but that only two Catholic schools—St. Thomas in St. Paul and St. Vincent's in Pennsylvania—admitted Negroes.[43]

Again, at the twenty-eighth anniversary of the emancipation of the Negro, in St. Paul, in January, 1891, the Archbishop advocated the blotting out of all barriers and color lines, for which he could find no reason. Not in color, which is merely the result of climatic changes; not in race, for all men are sprung from the same father and mother. He would open to the Negro all industrial and professional avenues. To the question whether the homes of the whites should also be opened to them, he replied that a man's house is his castle, the door of which no man can pass without an invitation. He had no illusions about the unpopularity of his position, which would be regarded by many as untimely. "Aye," he said, "untimely today, my words will be timely tomorrow. My fault, if there be a fault, would be that I am ahead of my day. The time is not distant when Americans and all other Christians will wonder that there ever was a race problem."[44]

Once more, at the blessing of the Church of St. Peter Claver in St. Paul, in the following year, he told the colored congregation that the Catholic Church offers them not only the fullest recognition of their rights as Christians and as men but also her power to have those rights recognized by others. He regarded the colored people as the choicest, most promising field in America for apostolic work. They who see it not are blind, he said, and they who seeing it do not embrace the opportunity have not in their souls apostolic fiber.[45]

A writer in the *Literary Northwest* asserted that the principle of the brotherhood of man was better embodied in the Archbishop than in any other prelate of this country, that men of all races and colors had his active sympathy, that he pleaded successfully with the President for the red man and offended the tender sensibility of the Southerner by his bold words for the Negro, but that in all this there was not the remotest savor of the demagogue.[46]

If Archbishop Ireland spoke out boldly on labor and color, from time to time themes of gentler strain would evoke addresses full of inspiration, and the subject of charity would touch the chords of his soul to music. In an address before the National Conference of Charities and Corrections in Minneapolis on July 16, 1886, he told of the part charity plays in the Catholic Church. He showed how prevalent it is in Catholic countries and cities, mentioning in particular Rome, in which it would be impossible to name a want for which provision had not been made "to protect helpless infancy and provide for decrepit age, to shield the innocent from temptation, and bring back the fallen from crime, to spare the blushes of shrinking poverty, to assist the exertions of struggling merit and repair the broken fortunes of honest but unsuccessful industry, to afford consolation and relief to the sick, the prisoner and the dying, and secure honors of Christian burial for the dead." He told of the common instances of heroic charity—the missionary embarking for Molokai to spend himself in the service of the lepers, the sisters leaving their convents to nurse smallpox victims, the priest rushing amid shells and bullets to console the dying. He spoke of the sacrifices made and the vows taken by the members of religious orders and the welcome which they receive from the poor, who know of their selfless life. The secret of their heroism, he said, is their faith, their love of the Savior. After sketching the work done by various religious communities, he claimed peculiar advantages for the system of Catholic charities, which secures in the service of charity that which is most valuable and most difficult to be obtained—the sweetness and tenderness of love. For it is not bread and medicine that is most prized by the indigent and the sick, it is the smile, the soft caress, the kind, hopeful word. The heart rather than the mouth must be fed; the soul rather than the body must be warmed. And all this is done without effort and with exquisite delicacy when the heart of the laborer is in his work. "Love streams from the heart and ignites all hearts coming within the circle of its influence. The little Sister of the Poor lifts her finger and a hundred querulous and quarrelsome old men and a hundred old women will be silent and respectful, while they would be unmoved before a regiment of policemen. The mere rustling of the gown of a Good Shepherd nun distills fragrance of heavenly purity amid a crowd of poor creatures from whose souls the chilling blasts of sin had seemed to drive all vestige of the divine image."[47]

Although Archbishop Ireland, commonly regarded as an unusually progressive prelate, held very conservative principles on the question of private property, which he regarded as sacred and inviolable, and had no sympathy with the views of Henry George, he did not agree with those who favored the condemnation of his books. George held that the land of every country belongs to all the people, and that private ownership has no more foundation in reason than private ownership of the air. Private occupancy, however, and use of land are right and indispensable. The rent derived from land should be used for the benefit of all and would be more than enough to pay the expenses of government, which should be met by a tax upon rent alone. Hence the name "single tax," by which his theory was known. The Archbishop did not think that there was much probability of this theory's being put into practice in the United States, and, with Cardinal Gibbons, he was convinced that George's influence was spent, and that the condemnation not only was unnecessary but would result in more harm than good by giving him an importance which he did not deserve. In this they differed from Archbishop Corrigan, who sought the placing of George's *Progress and Poverty* on the Index. Although the Cardinal, while in Rome in 1887, protested the condemnation, he was informed by Monsignor O'Connell in March of the following year that "another attempt has been made to place the works of George on the Index."[48] In the meantime the letter which he had presented to Rome the previous year had been surreptitiously published. On receipt of the news from O'Connell, he urged the Archbishop to write a strong letter opposing any action against George and telling Rome how well Gibbons' letter had been received by the American press. He also asked him to urge Archbishops Heiss and Feehan and Bishops Spalding and Marty to do the same.[49]

From time to time during 1888 and 1889 O'Connell told Ireland of his fears that the condemnation would go through. The Archbishop, in April, 1888, urged him to keep up his efforts, saying: "If he is put on, there will be a vacancy in Baltimore from a broken heart. Mgr. Preston in the *Forum* announces that he will be condemned. New York is anxious for such a measure. I am sorry that just now Rome is in a condemning mood—*vide* poor Rosmini."[50] When the matter came up again in 1894, he informed the Monsignor that he was doing his best to prevent any condemnation of Georgism and had written a long letter on the matter to Cardinal Rampolla which had been placed before the Holy Father and which had impressed him.[51] The efforts of Ireland and Gibbons ultimately succeeded in keeping George's works from the Index.

The theories of Henry George appealed to Dr. Edward McGlynn, pastor of the Church of St. Stephen in New York, who supported his candidacy for mayor of that city in 1886, and whose popularity with the poor and aid on the platform almost succeeded in enabling him to win the election. When McGlynn was advertised to speak in the campaign, Archbishop Corrigan forbade him to do so and immediately after the address suspended him from his priestly functions and later had him excommunicated. McGlynn now proceeded to organize the Anti-Poverty Society and lectured in New York and elsewhere on the theories of Henry George. Of his two leading clerical supporters, Dr. Richard Burtsell and Father Thomas J. Ducey, the former was removed from the parish of the Epiphany in New York to the parish of Rondout, the latter was forbidden to attend the Lexnow investigation into the corruptions of Tammany Hall.

Archbishop Ireland's connection with the McGlynn case was comparatively slight. In the beginning, he approved of the disciplinary action which the Archbishop of New York had taken against the Doctor, who gave much scandal by his addresses before the Anti-Poverty Society, his outspoken criticisms of his superiors, and by an open letter which he addressed to his Ordinary.[52] Later, however, his sympathy for McGlynn was enlisted by Bishop John Moore of Florida, who wrote to him in March, 1892, enclosing a copy of a letter which he had just received from McGlynn and which appeared to be very satisfactory. "For God's sake," he said, "remain in Rome until my letter arrives there, and urge them to accept the conditions. McGlynn must be relieved of all censures, and not merely of the Pope's excommunication; for that would still leave him under the Archbishop's suspension, if it has not lapsed by the terms in which it was worded." McGlynn showed no pettiness in stating the terms of his submission, and now it remained for Propaganda and the Pope to treat him as a man and not impose humiliation on him. "He is now yielding; the authorities in Rome should display generosity towards him, encourage him, make him feel that they do not seek to degrade him, and I am convinced that they will have in him a devoted and faithful son of the Church."[53]

McGlynn in his letter to Bishop Moore expressed his desire to be restored to his priestly ministry and his joy that such restoration was probable. He also stated that he was willing to go to Rome if he were relieved from all censures and invited to go. In August he called upon Ireland, who was in New York and who had the choice, as he said, "either to refuse him and embitter him, or see him and expose myself to publicity."[54] In a letter to Cardinal Ledochowski the Archbishop explained the meeting, saying that if he sinned it was on the side of charity, and that as a matter of fact he persuaded him to postpone indefinitely his Anti-Poverty discourses and await patiently Rome's action.[55]

Shortly after Archbishop Satolli arrived in 1893, he restored McGlynn to the communion of the Church. A year later McGlynn was appointed pastor of the parish of St. Mary's, Newburgh. The Delegate also insisted that Dr. Burtsell be restored to the Church of the Epiphany or given a parish of similar importance in New York.

The man who loved the workingman as none other and who devoted his whole life to his defense has paid a beautiful tribute to the work which the Archbishop did for labor. Recognizing the fact that the Archbishop was not an economic reformer in the same sense as Ignatius Donnelly, Monsignor John A. Ryan says: "I did receive from him considerable inspiration in the period (1882-1892), and much more in subsequent years." After speaking of Ireland's discourse on "The Catholic Church and Civil Society," he goes on to say: "The ideas and the love of political democracy which I learned from this and similar addresses by the great Archbishop of St. Paul in the eighties supplemented and reinforced the things that I was learning about economic freedom and economic reform from men like Ignatius Donnelly."[56] Referring to his address in Baltimore on November 10, 1889, he asserts that although the Archbishop, when he spoke of the passing of the days of princes and feudal lords, did not foresee the rise of a worse political system—totalitarianism—nevertheless what he had to say about the social question and economic injustice is still true and apposite, and he quotes the passage in which the Archbishop spoke of the existence of dreadful social injustices and his regret that Catholics were so little interested in them. He concludes with these striking words:

Be it remembered that these sentences were spoken a full eighteen months before the appearance of the great encyclical of Pope Leo XIII "On the Condition of Labor." Indeed, Ireland's statement: "Until their (the cruelly oppressed members of the wage-earning class) material condition is improved, it is futile to speak to them of supernatural life and duties" anticipated by more than forty-one years the declaration of Pope Pius XI in Quadragesimo Anno: It may be said with all truth that nowadays the conditions of social and economic life are such that vast multitudes of men can only with great difficulty pay attention to that one thing necessary, namely, their eternal salvation.

Soon after Monsignor Ryan's first book, *A Living Wage*, was published, the Archbishop told him that he had read it all, and that though he disagreed with some of his positions he agreed with many of them. As the author says: "Inasmuch as *A Living Wage* was not then regarded as excessively conservative, the Archbishop's evaluation was very significant; it reflected his fundamental liberalism and progressivism."[57]

Chapter 10

THE EDUCATOR

> ▶✦▶✦▶✦▶✦▶✦▶✦◀

A great prelate, endowed with the commission that only the Incarnate God could lay on human shoulders, to teach the nations, to guide the destinies of the Church through the tumultuous seas of time, Archbishop Ireland regarded education as the principal work of his episcopate. A profound conviction was his that the bonds of traditional religion were no longer strong enough to bind the modern world to the Church, and that the hope of religion lay not in hereditary affiliations but in a finer and deeper training of youth in the principles of the faith. He looked out upon the human scene with discerning eyes and saw the multitudes drifting through life without realizing the meaning of it. He saw the thousands torn from the bosom of religion by the shallow sophistries of the day, the loss of faith due to the failure of men to recognize the knowledge of God, the highest knowledge to which the mind of men can aspire and which demands and taxes the noblest powers of thought. And so he strove to provide for what he conceived to be the vital need of the future—religious education.

In his famous address in Baltimore in 1889, he said that an important work for Catholics in the coming century would be the building of schools, colleges, and seminaries, and, a work more important still, the lifting up of present and future institutions to the highest degree of intellectual excellence. Only the best schools would give the Church the men she needs. Modern, too, must they be in curriculum and method, so that pupils going forth from their halls will be men for the twentieth century and men for America.[1] And speaking before the French episcopate, he said that the age had its favorite theses, its ideals in science, in social progress, in liberty, in the moral and intellectual development of humanity, and every day the enemies of the Church kept on repeating that in the Church and by the Church there were no solutions adequate for these aspirations.

Archbishop Ireland's enthusiasm for education may be judged by his labors for the Catholic University of America, which must always remain deeply indebted to him. Indeed, it is hardly an exaggeration to say that had it not been for him the University as such might never have existed, or at least its founding would have been indefinitely postponed. Although the project had been approved by the Third Plenary Council of Baltimore, it met with so much opposition that it was almost abandoned. Some members of the hierarchy were indifferent—Cardinal McCloskey, Archbishop Heiss, Bishop O'Connor; some were skeptical—Archbishops Ryan and Elder; some were bitterly hostile, both to its founding and to its site in Washington—Archbishop Corrigan and Bishop McQuaid; and even Archbishop Gibbons was at times opposed and at times vacillating.

When a University Committee was appointed, Archbishop Ireland was made a member of it at the special request of Miss Gwendolyn Caldwell, who had made a gift of $300,000. At a meeting of this committee, on January 28, 1885, at which an attempt was made to locate the University at South Orange, New Jersey, Ireland held out for Washington but was outvoted. Later, however, he had his way, when the decision was left to Miss Caldwell, who supported his choice. It was he also who gave the institution the title by which it is known today—the Catholic University of America[2]—as it was he who stimulated the other members of the hierarchy to action. Restive under the lack of interest which was displayed, he wrote to Gibbons to point out that the inaction was having an unfortunate influence upon the country and that some of those who were expected to be benefactors had already passed away. He urged an immediate meeting, saying: "I feel a deep interest in the University, both for the merits of the project itself and for the sake of the Council, whose honor is staked upon the realization of all its measures."[3] How necessary was this prodding is shown by a letter which Gibbons sent to Corrigan and in which he said: "I had almost given up the idea of calling a meeting in the interest of the University, after receiving your letter, as your views coincide with my own." He also informed him that the Bishop of St. Paul "almost reproaches me for seeming inaction."[4] Ireland continued to maintain pressure, urging immediate action lest Miss Caldwell change her mind.[5]

The alignment of forces at this early date is interesting, indicating as it does the East represented by New York, Philadelphia, and

Rochester, opposing the West in the persons of the Bishops of Peoria and St. Paul. Bernard McQuaid bitterly opposed the Washington site, insisting that the University be placed in New York, but on no account south of Philadelphia. To put it in Baltimore or Washington, he said, would be to "kill the babe before it was born."[6] His antagonism to the University, as well as that of his friend Corrigan, was later to be extended to any project in which the St. Paul prelate was interested. Ireland more and more assumed the initiative, feeling that abundant time should be given to organization and hoping that the "Prelates will come to Baltimore well provided with all the necessary patience to stay until something definite has been accomplished."[7]

He, together with Bishops John Lancaster Spalding, John J. Keane, and Martin Marty, was later authorized to solicit for funds the various dioceses of the country. When Keane went to New York, he was informed by Corrigan, who favored a university in New York in charge of the Jesuits, that since he was not in sympathy with the University project "in its present shape" he could not co-operate in efforts at collecting. He was, however, gracious enough to issue for a meeting at the Xavier Union invitations which, Keane was convinced, were so worded as to guarantee failure.[8]

At the meeting of the University Board in May, which Ireland could not attend, having been called home by his father's illness just as he had reached Baltimore, Bishop Keane was chosen Rector and asked to accompany him on his *ad limina* visit to Rome in November to petition the Holy See for recognition. When a motion was made to request the Pope not to authorize the establishment of any other university for twenty-five years, Corrigan objected, declaring that he had information that the project of the University was regarded with disfavor by the Holy See, or at least by the Propaganda.[9] At the next meeting of the bishops, on October 27, a letter was addressed to the Holy Father recommending that the University always remain under the direction of the hierarchy and not of a religious order, that the discipline be placed under the control of the Sulpician Fathers, and that no other pontifical university be allowed until the next plenary council.

Ireland and Keane, who sailed from New York on October 30, 1886, had many an anxious moment in Rome. When, after waiting for six weeks without accomplishing anything, they were informed by the Secretary of Propaganda, Archbishop Domenico Jacobini, that consideration of the University would be postponed until the arrival of Gibbons, and then, in all probability, deferred indefinitely, great was

Ireland's indignation. He demanded an immediate audience with the Holy Father, who received him kindly, but who mentioned his apprehensions for the future of Georgetown University. When Ireland told him, however, of the alternate plan which had been suggested—a university in New York under the control of the Jesuits—Leo expressed his disfavor of the idea and said that the University, like the Church, must be organized hierarchically. He preferred, nevertheless, to wait until he could consult Gibbons.[10]

Meanwhile the two prelates had prepared a memorial entitled *Animadversiones Quaedam de Universitate in America Fundanda*,[11] in which they answered point by point the various objections which had been raised. The most serious difficulty with which they had to contend was the charge of bad faith on the part of some of the bishops, who were said to have signed the petition although they were not in favor of the project. This charge, which "someone had whispered," made Ireland exclaim, "Discredit is thrown on the character of our prelates for truth and honesty" and brought from him a request to the other members of the committee to forward a personal statement of their position.[12]

Subsequent events showed that the principal opposition had come from Bishop McQuaid and Archbishop Corrigan, to whom the former wrote in January, 1887: "Ireland and Keane will get answers only from those who favor the bantling they are coddling into puny existence."[13] Not only did Corrigan send a document criticizing the site chosen, the personnel, and the system of training proposed, but, as Ireland was informed, he was also responsible for the charge of bad faith.[14] It was also commonly said that the Jesuits were opposed on the ground that the University would injure Georgetown and block the plan of His Grace of New York to found a university under their direction. This charge seems to be corroborated by a letter written by Father Robert Fulton, S.J., to Corrigan in which he supplied the criticisms embodied in the latter's memorial,[15] and also by an interview "with one of the most eminent Jesuits in Rome," which appeared in the New York *Herald* some years later and in which the Jesuit was quoted as saying: "It is not exact to say that we are making war on the University of Washington, but it must not be forgotten that for a century the Jesuits have had a flourishing university."[16] The Jesuit objection was not taken seriously by the Pope or by Cardinal Mazzella, another member of the Society, who could see no conflict of interests between the two schools.[17] Monsignor Denis O'Connell, Rector of the North American College in Rome, gave the reaction of Pope Leo.

He wrote: "In speaking to Mgr. Riordan of the University the Holy Father said: '*Corrigan la voulait à New York pour les Jesuites, mais non, non. Je ne le voulais pas.*' He also said to the Rector of Laval: 'The Jesuits wanted it, but the bishops did not wish it; the bishops were right.' "[18]

The greatest danger of all came from the characteristic indecision of Gibbons. It was to be expected that Rome would not take action without consulting the head of the hierarchy, but his attitude was so indefinite that Keane wrote to him a surprisingly frank protest, and when, after reaching Rome and learning of Corrigan's opposition, he told Keane that he felt that the project would be abandoned—an opinion which the Rector was inclined to favor—Ireland, whose indignation knew no bounds, cried out indignantly against "so cowardly a surrender to so unworthy an opposition."[19] Thus Ireland had not only fostered the University at its birth but now also saved it from destruction. Gibbons' attitude changed and he threw himself with vigor into the work of securing approbation, finally seeing his efforts crowned with success.

His Grace of New York, who never wished to play when things went counter to his wishes, told McQuaid that he was disposed to resign his seat on the University Board, as "he had lost confidence in the good faith of some of the members."[20] The latter lost no time in advising him by all means to sever all connection with the University, saying: "You have been shabbily treated, and the worst is to come."[21] On hearing of his resignation, Ireland, who naturally did not wish to lose the support of the important See of New York, wrote him a letter, which reflecting his frank, open personality protested against Corrigan's opposition as manifested by his Roman representative, Miss Ella Edes, who "has never ceased in your name, and with arms furnished by you, to poison the men of Propaganda against the university project."[22]

Bishop Keane went to Europe in November, 1888, to have the statutes approved and to seek professors. In the following month he wrote to Archbishop Ireland from the North American College, Rome:

Here I am in your old room. What an aroma of pleasant memories you have left in the room, and, for that matter, in all Rome. Everyone smiles and looks happy when Bishop Ireland (as we naturally still call you) is spoken of. And the old city and its way-back-yonder officials stand as much as ever in need of the good hard honest shaking-up which you alone can give them.[23]

When the Archbishop spoke at the celebration of the Centennial of the Hierarchy in Baltimore, on November 9, 1889, he paid tribute to the University.[24] And at the consecration of Bishop Thomas O'Gorman he referred to it as "the glory of the Catholic Church in America, whose destinies were largely in its hands."[25] He was appointed a member of the committee chosen to draw up the statutes and the course of studies. He wrote letters to the clergy of the country, asking for a contribution from each of $100; he collected $50,000 in Chicago and made appeals in Maryland and Pennsylvania.

His interest in the University was intensified by his friendship for two of its rectors—Bishop Keane and Monsignor O'Connell. To the former he gave valuable aid in the organization and the administration of the school, outlining, in December, 1889, his ideas on discipline and spiritual training, urging especially meditation in common and lectures on ascetical theology, but at the same time favoring a relaxation of "Sulpitian rigidity." In the light of subsequent events, the conclusion of his letter provokes a smile: "I am tired of traveling and of speaking, and propose now to settle down at home, for a quiet old age."[26]

He gave advice on the selection of a faculty, even recommending for consideration St. George Mivart.[27] Who knows what might have been the subsequent history of that brilliant but unfortunate scientist had he been connected with the Catholic University? When friction arose in the faculty, Ireland supported the Rector in his insistence that the interests of the institution demanded the removal of the malcontents—an act from which he was destined to hear much in days to come.

He expressed himself as strongly in favor of public lectures, which, he felt, would be welcomed by people in search of truth, would train students in "the all-important art of presenting learned subjects in a popular form with correctness and elegance," and would "increase the popular esteem that would thence accrue to the University." He warned Keane of possible dangers, writing to him from Rome in April, 1892, that the worst enemy of the University was Cardinal Mazzella, who had ever a sneer for it, reminding him that the University would have to gird its loins and fight. "The whole set of the frati are down on it," he said. "Mr. Descurtins of Switzerland visited the other day the Dominicans and came back to me full of the idea that without a religious order at the head it would not last."[28]

Contention marked the birth of the University and contention dogged its steps for many years. It became involved in all of the great controversies. Professors Joseph Schroeder and Joseph Pohle were prominent Cahenslyites and took part in the convention of the St. Raphael's Society in Mainz in August, 1892, an action which set them apart from many of the other members of the faculty and showed their lack of sympathy with Keane and Ireland. Schroeder had also identified himself with Corrigan by his activity at the Convention of German Societies of the State of New York in Newark, New Jersey, and by his attitude on the school question, and had been accused of abstention from the activities of the University and of failure to contribute to the University *Bulletin*. Cahensly informed Corrigan that he had learned on good authority that Ireland during his stay in Rome "passsed unfair remarks about Dr. Schroeder and Dr. Pohle, saying that they must quit their chairs."[29] Ireland finally decided to bring matters to a head at the meeting of the University Board in October, 1897. He revealed his intention to O'Connell, to whom he wrote:

Abp. Riordan will spend a week in St. Paul on his way to Washington. He & I are hot against Schroeder; he will lead the fight. The obstacle is C. Gibbons, who talks of giving a *monitum* to Schr[oeder]. I wish you would at once write to the Cardinal a very strong letter, giving him an idea of the support we have in Germany. If Maes stands with us, I have hopes; Corrigan and Ryan will vote to gain friends—and not for the University; Williams and Gibbons will want peace.[30]

Schroeder on a visit to Rome in 1896 was said to have gained the support of Cardinal Steinhuber and the Pope. On hearing that the Board intended to force resignation, Cardinal Rampolla protested against "the unfittingness of such a measure." Two days before the meeting of the Board, Schroeder wrote to Ireland, reminding him of a conversation which he had had with him in April of the preceding year, concerning his relations with the Rector, his exclusion from the *Bulletin*, and the establishment of a German chair at the University, and recalling the satisfaction he had expressed then. He protested that in spite of an article which he had prepared for the *Bulletin*, the boycott against him became even more intense. "Lying newspaper articles," he said, "were disseminated to arrouse [sic] this belief [that he had been the cause of the boycott]." He found it difficult to understand how cultured men, priests and colleagues, would find in such newspaper claptrap justification for reintroducing into the University a situation which had become a scandal.[31]

The Board, which voted ten to four for dismissal, decided to suspend action until it could lay the matter before the Pope, who finally gave his permission after Schroeder had been persuaded to resign. To O'Connell, whom he thanked for his co-operation, Ireland expressed his satisfaction, saying: "The downfall of Schroeder is the end of anti-liberalism and of Cahenslyism, and a great defeat for Corrigan."[32] As O'Connell said, it required nerve to proceed in the fact of Steinhuber's letter and Rampolla's dispatch, "but energy saved the situation, and yours is now the only party worth counting in the American Church. I suppose you have no idea of going 'into winter quarters' now."[33] Meanwhile the Prussian Minister of Education and Ecclesiastical Affairs had appointed Schroeder to the Catholic Academy of Münster, a solution of the case which prompted Ireland to write:

> The *Germania* comments on the promptness with which the Centrum and the Prussian Minister took up Schroeder. You see, Germany is grateful to him. He was doing her work in America. He was a Cahenslyite—but the last of the Mohicans. The greatest and last battle of the war has been fought and won.[34]

Pohle left in January, 1894, to accept the chair of Dogmatic Theology at Munster.

The third member of the opposition, Dr. George Périès, who was dismissed in 1896, and who had threatened vengeance, found his opportunity in 1898, when he collaborated with the notorious Charles Maignen and attacked Americanism under the pseudonym Saint-Clement.

There were times when Ireland's enthusiasm for the University seemed to wane. When his friend, Bishop John J. Keane, was dismissed in 1896, he wrote to Gibbons:

> Of course Bishop Keane's presence in Rome will be a wonderful help. Our enemies did not know what they were doing when they had him removed from Washington. Nothing but stern courage on our part will avert disaster from us. We are timid children and we are treated as children. Our enemies are not timid. The University is dead; nothing can revive it. The Jesuits have triumphed here for good.[35]

During the rectorship of Dr. Thomas Conaty he absented himself at times from the meetings of the Board and was inclined to be critical of the administration. Toward the end of 1901 he felt that the University was in a perilous condition and that, unless matters were reformed, it would go down. He regarded Conaty's elevation a mistake and he was much relieved when he received assurance from Archbishop Patrick Riordan of San Francisco that the Rector would be appointed Bishop of Monterey-Los Angeles. His feelings were shared by O'Connell, who knew something of the state of affairs, and who seemed to think that it was impossible to erect a Catholic university which would compete with lay institutions.[36]

Ireland's interest was revived when O'Connell was appointed Rector in 1903. At the meeting of the trustees on November 12, 1902, he had used his influence to secure six votes for him, knowing that Satolli had promised that, if O'Connell were named on the list of candidates, he would be appointed. He also warned Satolli that another Conaty regime would bury the University out of sight. To O'Connell he wrote: "What a change in the panorama if you come to Washington. It will be the victory of victories for the dear old cause."[37]

When the first news of O'Connell's appointment was flashed in a cable to the New York *Herald*, the Archbishop could not restrain his delight as he realized the significance of the action both in Rome and in America. A letter from O'Connell told of his happiness also, of the congratulations he had received, even from McQuaid, and also from the American Ambassador to the Quirinal. "I am dying," he said, "to meet you and embrace you and to talk a thousand things over."[38] When the new Rector arrived in Washington, Ireland again gave vent to his joy and to his amazement at the revolution which had taken place in the temper of Rome as indicated by the appointment. He gratefully acknowledged O'Connell's assurance that there was always awaiting him at the University a warm heart and a warm room. He promised to arrive in a few days, saying: "Toward nine-thirty you will hear a rap at your door. We shall wait until meetings are over and the crowd is dispersed, to hold our *piccoli congressi*."[39]

He stood behind O'Connell throughout his administration, enthusiastically supporting the project of an annual collection to be taken up in all dioceses for the University. In November, 1901, he demanded an investigation into the investment of University endowment funds and into the financial status of the University treasurer, Thomas E. Waggaman, who, three years later, went into bankruptcy. He also attempted to add to the Board of Trustees such men as Thomas F. Ryan and Charles Schwab. He continued to make his influence felt in the institution, sometimes criticizing the faculty and once informing the trustees that he would not send any more students

The Archbishop as a young priest

Archbishop Ireland and Monsignor Denis O'Connell, Rector of the North American College, Rome

The Churchman

The Statesman

St. Paul Cathedral

because of his dissatisfaction with the kind of intellectual training they received.[40] He objected to the many outside activities of some members of the faculty and he hoped to see in force the same legislation which had been enacted in his own institutions and which insisted that professors confine their interest to their classes and refuse parish assignments on Sundays.[41]

At the time of the issue of the encyclical *Pascendi Dominici Gregis*, he was appointed a member of a special committee to examine the books in the University library and to make recommendations. He was also chairman of a committee chosen to make an examination of the curriculum of studies, finances, and student attendance. Among the recommendations which it made were the appointment of a visiting committee, which was to report each year on academic work, discipline, and other matters.

The Archdiocese of St. Paul contributed to the University some of its most brilliant professors—Dr. Thomas Shields, Dr. William Turner, Monsignor John A. Ryan, and Dr. Joseph Barron.

In education as in all things else, Archbishop Ireland translated his ideas into acts. School and college and seminary he fostered, ever striving to awaken in his people ambition to take the place that is rightfully theirs, ever insisting that education severed from religion cannot mold character or give to the country the men the country needs. The first fruit of his episcopate was St. Thomas Seminary. Bishop Grace had purchased in the Midway district a farm owned by an old settler, William Finn, and erected there an Industrial School. This building Bishop Ireland enlarged and converted into the St. Thomas Seminary, which was opened in September, 1885, for the education of both clerical and lay students. Beginning with a faculty of six and an enrollment of sixty, it grew during his lifetime to a college of more than a thousand students. It had as its first Rector Father Thomas O'Gorman. A few years later, a princely gift from Mr. James J. Hill, president of the Great Northern Railroad, made possible the building of the St. Paul Seminary, for the exclusive training of young men destined for the priesthood. Joseph Gilpin Pyle in his biography of Mr. Hill tells of some of the motives which actuated the Empire Builder in his gift. He quotes him as saying:

Look at the millions of foreigners pouring into this country to whom the Roman Catholic Church represents the only authority that they either fear or respect. What will be their social views, their political action, their moral status if that single controlling force should be removed? It is not of any more importance to the Church that young men should be educated for its priesthood than it is to the State that this undigested mass of foreign material should be dealt with by those who alone have power to mould it into new shape, the anointed agents of the only authority that it understands or will obey. This is as much a matter of good business as is the improvement of farm stock or the construction of a faultless railroad bed.[42]

The more immediate impulse, however, and the more impelling motive for the gift came from a sermon which the Archbishop preached in St. Mary's Church in St. Paul, and which Mr. Hill, who accompanied there his Catholic wife, happened to hear.

As it was the ambition of the Archbishop that his seminary should more than hold its own with similar institutions in the country, he commissioned Monsignor Denis O'Connell to search Europe for members of the faculty, the latter's correspondence during 1890 describing his efforts.[43] After calling personally on every bishop in Belgium but without success and after tramping through France and the Rhineland with similar results,[44] he was finally able to inform the Archbishop that he had secured "two first class young men, Soentgerath and Minkenbasy."[45] A little later he wrote: "If you could only get Loisy of Paris for Scripture. He is the best biblical scholar in the Church. And Himmel, a young specialist in History." He also told of having in the American College two promising students, Francis Schaefer, "who was intended for a chair in Rome," and Humphrey Moynihan, "who has a fondness for modern science."[46]

The Seminary opened on September 6, 1894, with the following faculty: Dogmatic Theology, J. G. Soentgerath; Moral Theology, A. Cestelli; Ethics, N. McCaffrey; Philosophy, John Chareyre; Apologetics, H. Moynihan; Sacred Scripture, Patrick Danehy; History, Francis Schaefer; Science, John Hartigan. On September 4, 1895, it was dedicated with all the rich ceremonial of the Church in the presence of the Papal Delegate, six bishops, 250 priests, and thousands of laymen. At the east side of the Administration Building the sanctuary had been erected, its entrance decorated with the papal coat of arms entwined with the national colors. The dedicatory services began with the celebration of High Mass. The sermon was preached by Dr. Thomas O'Gorman of the Catholic University, who spoke on the priesthood, referring to the Seminary as the nursery where are tended the saplings that are to become the sturdy giants of the forest, giving shade and shelter to the wearied children of humanity, the womb where Mother Church with her own breath and blood feeds and fashions for self-life the stalwart sons from whom must come salvation to Israel.

The celebration was continued in the evening, when the assembly hall was filled to overflowing with the leading citizens of the city of all denominations, among them the officers from Fort Snelling, the judges of the district court, railroad and state officials. The Archbishop, who was the first to speak, said:

The noblest work is the uplifting of humanity to higher planes of thought and action. Humanity is not sent upward by a mechanical process; to uplift you must educate. A most effective method to the education of the masses of the people is the education of their chieftains and leaders. No class of men in the commonwealth own that educational influence which is the appanage of the clergy. They are the official keepers and expounders of the most vital element in education—religious truth; and the authority with which this fact invests them spreads itself through countless ramifications over the whole intellectual, moral and social life.

He then enumerated the subjects which he would have taught in the Seminary:

First, theology. Whatever else the priest takes with him into the world, if he carries not in soul and in hand the Gospel of Christ, he is not a minister of Christ. The sciences—covet the aid of faith, which is a voice from the far-beyond, whereof nature is silent. Faith appeals to the sciences for confirmations of its credibility. Nature and grace intermingle, and unite in chanting to the Author of both a hymn of adoration and thanksgiving. Political economy and sociology are so akin to moral theology that I should bring them into the closest quarters with it. Literature should be called upon to unfold in seminary halls the treasure of its graces and elegance of form. Religion will teach it the lesson that beauty is the splendent reflection of truth and purity.

Dr. O'Gorman read the address of Archbishop Satolli, who said that fifty years ago Newman had spoken of the Church in the United States and its growth. Did he live and write today, how much greater would be his admiration at the present condition of the American Church. For during the fifty years the Church had made such progress as would take five centuries in other lands and ages. After speaking of the seminary as among the more efficacious means for the promotion of civic virtues, he paid the Archbishop the compliment of re-echoing the words which the latter had addressed to the priests of Paris:

Come down among men, clasp hands with them, let your ministry be a co-operation with them, in every good work with every man that offers to stand by your side in the fight against evil; live among and with your people. Draw the people in all charity, by word and example, to the sweet service of Christ. The race about you is impregnated with the spirit of liberty, industry and manly assurance, a noble field in which to work. And, priests of America, do you but add to the natural virtues of the race the supernatural virtues of your faith, and thus prepared live in the people, with the people and for the people.

Other addresses were made by Bishop John J. Keane, Fathers Humphrey Moynihan and Patrick Danehy of the Seminary. Bishop Keane, who brought the greetings of the Catholic University, said: "Among all the hearts that love Archbishop Ireland there are none who love him better than those in the Catholic University, because largely to him is due the fact of its existence." Father Moynihan, who spoke on the relations of science and religion, said: "Science leads up to the portals of the supernatural, and the human mind, wearied in its long wanderings, is clasped in religion's embrace and borne into the sanctuary of truth. Religion completes the work of science and becomes the guide of life." Father Danehy called music the gift of the Church to mankind. "When first its harmonies went up to heaven's gates, the celestial spirits listened with amazement that strains so entrancing should come from lips less ethereal than their own. Dumb canvases grew eloquent beneath her magic touch. The noblest fanes that ever bore the cross, were purely the creations of faith."[47]

Ireland not only founded the College of St. Thomas and the St. Paul Seminary, but he also kept in close touch with both institutions. The professors at St. Thomas never knew when the door of the classroom would open to admit the Archbishop, who forthwith took over the class. His special favorites were the classics—Cicero, whose rolling periods find echoes in his orations; Virgil, whose jeweled phrases he used more than once; Horace, whose urbanity, "simplicity," and grace were to him a constant delight. Patron of a de luxe edition of Horace, he loved to gather the faculty around him in the parlor after dinner and discuss his favorite passages. One still recalls his joy when Father Patrick O'Brien, a distinguished scholar, rendered *"Simplex munditiis"* as "an ingenue of neatness," or repeated the translation of an Oxford don of *"splendide mendax"* as "lying in state." If he were especially fond of such passages as *"Sunt quos curricolo pulverem Olympicum collegisse iuvat," "fortiter occupa portum," "integer vitae scelerisque purus," "aequam memento rebus in arduis servare mentem,"* or *"justum et tenacem propositi virum,"* it was perhaps because they reflected his own ideals and experience.[48] His visits were a constant stimulus and inspiration to the faculty and left them with a heightened sense of his wide culture.

His lectures to the students of the Seminary have fortunately been preserved and reproduced in both the *Ecclesiastical Review* and the *Catholic Bulletin.* On one occasion, dissatisfied with a synopsis of his previous lecture, he used the opportunity to stress one of his frequent recommendations—the keeping of a notebook—with the result that Father John Duggan of Oakland, California, kept a careful record of subsequent addresses. These notes he published in the *Ecclesiastical Review*[49] in October, November, and December, 1939. At the suggestion of Monsignor William Kerby he classified them under the headings of the priest as gentleman, scholar, saint. Beginning by insisting that the priest must be an incarnation of Christ, the Archbishop insisted equally that he must be a gentleman, for manners are but the reflection of the interior man and a criterion of it. He must be able to enter with equal ease and politeness the cottage of the poor and the palace of the prince. Of truthfulness he said that it should extend to one's enemies and even to His Satanic Majesty, for we only weaken our cause by equivocation or unfair arguments. He was undoubtedly reflecting his own experiences when he said:

We should not be the slaves of public opinion. If there is anything I am intolerant of it is the man who accuses me of bad motives. Have the courage of your convictions. Very often it is jealousy that pulls a man down. What makes some countries of Europe backward is that no freedom of scope is given to individuality. This leveling spirit may creep into any society or community of men, and we are in danger of becoming a pack of sheep. The spirit of the American which has caused such great material progress and advancement in this country, is that each man says: "I am going to do what pleases me." We must stand up for our personal rights. No man has a right to impugn our motives—to peer into our conscience. God alone has the right to judge.

In his lecture on the priest as scholar, he urged a knowledge not only of Revelation but also of the physical and social sciences, which often are arrayed against Revelation. To go forth into this unbelieving world as a defender of Christ's Revelation without a fund of knowledge and without the ability to use it with tongue and pen were a crime against God and His Church. Intellect is the only power the Church has today outside of grace. The American people admire it and, in their pursuit of the material, will pause to listen to a man of intellect. If we are not holding our people, the reason is the lack of something interesting to say. Priests have a divine message to deliver and therefore must be public speakers. There must be music, charm, and enchantment in the voice. "We must accustom our ears to the melodious rhythm of the sound of the sentence, and emotion must be reflected in the fact. If one feels what he utters, his body will correspond to his emotions." No man, he said, can be called educated unless he knows at least two languages besides his own. To fail to do so is to be guilty of narrow-mindedness or laziness.

In his lecture on the priest as saint he urged the students not to be satisfied with the speculative side of theology to the neglect of the practical. Individual acts of humility and self-denial among companions may aggregate more merit than martyrdom. From a letter written by an old missionary in China to Bishop Cretin he quoted the words: "You will gain more merit than a martyr if you live here on the mission forty years." Moral theology, he averred, is no guide to the higher life; it is often mere casuistry—spider-webbed, hair-splitting legality. Priests must have generous souls, not a selfish, groveling, earthly spirit; cold, calculating men have no vocation for the priesthood.

In his address at the Golden Jubilee of Notre Dame on June 11, 1895, the Archbishop took as his theme "The Catholic Church and Liberal Education." He lamented the tendency to pursue purely technical studies to the neglect of the liberal arts. Mind should be developed for its own sake, for truth is the life and light of the human mind. "Mind, nurtured upon truth, converting truth into its own fibre, grows and expands, takes unto itself the largeness, the sweetness, the elevation of truth, and makes man live his highest and noblest life." It is the educated mind that in all ages has advanced mankind, lifting it above sordid aims, bringing to it ennobling enjoyment, holding before it exalted ideals.[50]

At the semicentennial of the coming of the Sisters of St. Joseph to St. Paul, the Archbishop recalled the names of the first four sisters and sketched the history of the first school with its ten pupils, among whom was the future Mrs. James J. Hill. He told of the boundless zeal, the ardent faith, the unstinted charity, the holy simplicity of those early days. Describing the life of the nuns, he said:

Prayer, without the slightest dross of affections of earth, constantly ascending from virginal hearts to the Author of all goodness, to return upon this world of misery and sin in richest streams of divine grace; utter self-immolation at the foot of Calvary's cross; humility sublime in its lowliness; purity winning the very love of the Immaculate Lamb; charity like Christ's own charity in ardor and effusiveness—all the virtues of the Gospel in fullest bloom, all the fragrance of Christian holiness shedding divine sweetness through the surrounding atmosphere.[51]

Addressing the graduating class of St. Joseph's Academy, St. Paul, in June, 1901, he said that one of the great evils of the present time was that women in so-called high society were coming to regard with more and more toleration breaches of moral and civil laws committed by members of their own sex. And the great fault of American education, he said, was lack of seriousness. There was no depth of thought, no consistency of principles. An intellectual levity pervaded society, so that America was inferior to other countries in intellectual culture. He expressed his belief in the higher education of woman—an idea now commonplace but regarded as advanced in his day.[52]

In spite of the fact that his first address before the National Education Association in St. Paul on July 10, 1890, had brought a storm about his head, he addressed the Association again in Minneapolis, on July 9, 1902. This time he was on firmer ground, having chosen for his subject "Devotion to Truth; the Virtue of the Teacher." Truth, he said, is reality, and, in its plenitude, the infinite essence of God. The mind, the faculty that knows truth, makes man like unto God. Truth is the life, the light and beauty, the strength of the mind. The dignity of the teacher lies in the apostolate of truth; the office of the teacher is the priesthood of truth. Among the enemies of truth he mentioned inertia of the mind and will, passion and prejudice, and *"odium theologicum*—the most baleful of hatreds—the first of all foes of truth."[53]

At Sinsinawa, Wisconsin, on the fiftieth anniversary of the founding of St. Clara's College, on June 14, 1904, he again put forth his ideas on education, returning to his favorite topic, truth, but also stressing the need of training in goodness. "If the will," he said, "is not enamored of moral goodness, and trained to obey its laws without hesitancy, while the mind is brightened and sharpened for the battle of life, the moral force which should control the mind and bend it to serve the cause of righteousness is left undeveloped and inert."[54]

Mr. Charles M. Schwab, president of Bethlehem Steel, invited the Archbishop to address the students of Lehigh University, of which he was a trustee, "because I want the community to know what great men we have in the Catholic Church."[55] The Archbishop was unable to accede to his request at the time, but on May 14, 1913, he delivered at the University a magnificent address, redolent of Plato and Carlyle. Choosing for his subject "Liberal Education," he stressed as the need of the day leadership, the development in the halls of schools of an aristocracy of thought and action. Not only is there no incompatibility between democracy and this aristocracy of thought, he said, but this aristocracy is also the need of democracy and its salvation. Jealous as the masses of men are of coercion or imperious dictation, they yield to the magnetism of intellectual and moral suasion. Aristocracy of political power is hated; that of wealth is suspected; that of mind and of heart is courted and served. Liberal education is the salvation of democracy, for the masses are too absorbed in their immediate concerns, too limited in knowledge and foresight, to unravel the intricacies in which political and social issues are involved. They need light and guidance that their stepping be firm and secure. He showed the evils of false leadership, of the demagogue and the charlatan in the French Revolution, and the need of intelligent and patriotic leadership in America. Mindful of the intellectual atmosphere in which he spoke, he used effectively some of his favorite Horatian quotations, especially his wonted "*O navis, referent in mare te novi fluctus. O quid agis? Fortiter occupa portum.*"[56] He dealt with the problems of the Founding Fathers—their conviction that all power comes from the Creator through the people, and their desire to safeguard the exercise of that power, not directly by the people in their confused and scattered individualism, but through representatives seated in calm thought and timely research. The masses are not experts in the solution of complicated problems. They are not experts in law and jurisprudence, as they are not in art and science. They are more easily swayed by impulse than the chosen few, who counsel, deliberate, weigh arguments, as of themselves the masses cannot do. He concluded by urging the students to build up in their souls lofty ideals, to be worshipers of the true, the good, and the beautiful, to be men, never lowering their vision, never tiring in their efforts to incarnate in their daily lives the splendid realities it uncovers to mind and heart.[57]

In all these addresses one cannot help noticing how beautifully the Archbishop adapted his theme to his audience, whether he was speaking to students in a Catholic college, to sisters in their convents, to teachers in public schools, or to students in a secular university. And nowhere did he scant the claims of religion.

The Archbishop maintained to the end his interest in education, and throughout he was consistent in his attitude. The following letters, written late in life, show both his love for the parish school and his advocacy of the Faribault plan. In August, 1913, he issued a letter to the clergy and laity of the archdiocese in which he urged a Catholic school for Catholic children. Years ago, he said, the question was more or less confined to the region of theory or principle, because the consequences of the non-Catholic school had not unfolded themselves to actual vision. Now, however, such instruction as was given in the home or in Sunday school was altogether inadequate, and it was necessary to adopt the one course which would save the faith of the children—Catholic education. The whole atmosphere of the secular school, the studied absence of the spiritual, the words and example of unbelieving teachers, the aggressive warfare against the primary principles of natural religion itself—all constituted a grave danger. Thoughtful observers, outside the Catholic Church, were alarmed at the decay of religion and morals, at the infiltration of materialism into religion. "As things are going," he said, "it is the death-knell of religion, and to Catholics comes the mission to rescue America from its perils." Some parents had the illusion that the religious instruction given in lower schools was adequate, but graduation from lower schools was the time when religion should be presented to young people in its deeper and broader aspects, since they were beginning to think seriously for themselves and were, therefore, exposed to greater perils. He protested especially against the action of parents who chose schools from motives of fashion and social ambition, which were "as the kingdoms offered from the mountain-top to the Savior, the reward of adoration of Satan."[58]

A few months later, in reply to an inquiry concerning the possibility of giving religious instruction in public schools, he stated that in the present condition of public opinion he could not see any solution to the problem. A serious change would have to be made in the system, a change which would take cognizance of schools where religion is deemed to be of paramount importance. He did not ask for the appropriation of money for sectarian purposes, but a payment could be allotted by the State to result in secular education, judged by examinations. This would be simple justice, and would save the country from drifting into materialism. The plan which the writer of the letter proposed, of reading selections from the Bible, was not realizable. It would be colorless and meaningless, would impart no principle of or sanction to morals, would, by excluding the Bible as a whole, infringe on Catholic convictions, and would be useless because teachers would not be allowed to answer questions. "All things considered," he said, "America is in the presence of a fearful problem resulting from a system radically wrong—the total and imperative exclusion of religion from the schools of the country."[59]

When Father Thomas McMillan, C.S.P., published his pamphlet on *The Demand for Christian Schools*, which quoted a passage from Brownson in favor of universal education sustained by universal taxation in order to safeguard universal suffrage, Ireland congratulated him. In his reply, the Paulist referred to Ireland's recent Milwaukee address, which, he felt, would produce enduring results. "The United States," he said, "needs a strong declaration from time to time to arouse faltering brothers in our ranks, besides giving information to men of good will to assure them that an educational work has a value for the nation at large." He then went on to quote from an editorial which he had published in the *Freeman's Journal* on July 12, 1913, and which gave a history of the opposition to the wearing of religious garb by nuns teaching in public schools. Dr. Andrew Draper, he said, had the inglorious distinction of being the first school official to declare that the religious garb was a disqualification for teaching—a ruling made in 1889. After the decision of 1889, the question was again brought before Superintendent Charles R. Skinner following the constitutional convention of 1894. Finally it was forced upon ex-President William H. Taft in connection with the sisters teaching among the Indians. While his ruling sufficed to rebuke a subordinate official, there was still a doubt to be removed, and this could be done only through a supreme legal argument on the basis of the American Constitution, which would secure action by the court of last appeal at Washington. "At the battle of Gettysburg," Father McMillan said, "the garb of the nursing Sisters was no barrier to their patriotic service." He was convinced that an able lawyer could make out a strong case by showing that the Constitution does not permit discrimination against the religious preference of any citizen; that it is an act of aggression bearing on the right to life, the right to earn a living. The fitness of the sisters for teaching being assumed, who has the authority to declare that they shall not be allowed to teach the Indians? He suggested that the question of religious garb as a national issue before the federal court might be worthy of mention at the annual meeting of the archbishops.[60]

When the question came up at the fall meeting of the state high-school board in 1914, the Archbishop took an active part in opposing the plan to prohibit teaching in the public schools by teachers in sectarian garb. The movement was aimed at the nuns employed as instructors in some Minnesota schools, and when Judge Ell Torrance sent him copies of the decisions of Judges Baxter and Searles, which were unfavorable to the teaching of religion in public schools, the Archbishop, while admitting the principle upon which they acted—that in the administration of schools the right of conscience of every citizen must not be infringed—made the point that principle must not be run to extreme. "Logic," he said, "must not wind its thread-thin conclusions into situations to which hypothetical meanings, not borne out by strict facts, are supposed to attach. Speculative logic is not to be held in mind without a due regard to practical things. Too much law leads to grave injury." He showed that if the principle were applied with extreme severity, there would be no chaplains in army or navy, no chapel service in colleges, and no state function would be opened with religious exercises. Religion is a fact in the life of the people, and the State must not, for its own sake, repress it, but rather see that it takes its due place in private and public life. He quoted the words of a Congregational minister, Reverend J. W. Robb: "We have schools of education, but not of conscience, and we are bringing up a race of moral idiots"; and of Vice-President Marshall: "There is too much science in our so-called educational system and too little of God Almighty." He regretted that there should be any break in the religious peace with which Minnesota had been blessed, and he saw no gain, but rather serious loss, to the public-school system. He could see no harm lurking in the statute of the State which authorized the use of schools for religious worship or other purposes. There were, he said, many places in which the schools were the only buildings available for religious, social, or political purposes. He answered the objection that salaries paid to nuns did not go to them personally but to an institution and therefore were made to serve directly religious propagandism. Referring to the garb question he said:

The gown of the Sister tells, of course, that she is a Catholic, just as the gown of the Quakeress tells that she is a Quakeress; just as a medal or a badge tells that a woman belongs to the Christian Endeavor Society or to that of the Daughters of Rebecca. Shall we exclude from our State Educational institutions all women who dare wear such medals or badges? Shall we continue in our course and eliminate from all bureaus of public service, from all colleges and universities, all the men, whoever otherwise they be, who by the color of their neck-tie, or the form of their coats, are recognized as ministers of a certain religious organization? What the dress of a woman or of a man should be, provided it do not run counter to common proprieties —it is not of the province of the State to say.

This letter also disposes of the contention that he changed his views on the Faribault system, for he said:

In most places situations are such that no connection is to be thought of between schools acceptable to Catholics and state schools. But there are places, it seems to me, where the state schools can be so organized that without a direct violation of the principles of our school laws, the parish school will be unnecessary, and the public schools will have full and exclusive sway. Where it can be done, is it not under every respect good policy to have it done?[61]

Archbishop Ireland's devotion to religious training needs no defense. As he wrote to Father Daniel Hudson:

I have done during my ministry all in my power to the end that children and adults be well instructed in their religion. That they be so instructed is a matter of absolute necessity if they are to retain their faith and be of any value to religion. The most effective means I have been able to employ is that of careful systematic examination of candidates for Confirmation made directly by the Bishop himself. This examination has wrought a revolution in the diocese—stirring up all the amibition and energy of priests, teachers and children.[62]

And when he announced the abolition of tuition in the parochial schools of the diocese, he declared: "The Catholic school—the future will prove it beyond a doubt—is the most fruitful of all institutions for the preservation and perpetuation of the faith in this country."[63]

Chapter 11

THE STATESMAN

Archbishop Ireland was a leader in civic, national, and international affairs. The history of St. Paul and of the Northwest for half a century is his history. He grew up with the city of St. Paul, saw it expand from a hamlet of one thousand souls to a metropolitan center of a quarter of a million. Few were the civic projects entered upon without his participation and his counsel. Full of interest in whatever was afoot, he was ever eager to meet his fellow citizens irrespective of creed or position, and his own tolerant disposition discerned in others qualities of goodness and greatness. Whether it was a temperance rally, a meeting of the historical society or a historical commemoration, a charity convention, a celebration of Negro emancipation, a meeting of the Law and Order League, an agitation in favor of high license or in opposition to prize fights, his long frock coat, his vest with the three upper buttons open, his slouch hat, his rapid walk with the right arm flung out at his side and his head thrown back were a familiar sight in the streets and halls of St. Paul. As he told the Parisian clergy, he could be found everywhere, and one never knew what his next activity might be. He was, in fact, the father of the electric railway system of St. Paul. When he began buying property in the western end of the city in preparation for the expansion of diocesan institutions, he saw the need of adequate transportation facilities. Streetcar companies and influential individuals had sought for years to secure a franchise for a street railway, but in vain. Pleading his cause before the city council, he convinced them of its necessity, and so won their confidence that he was granted the right to construct and operate a railway as an experiment for one year. And so was constructed the Grand Avenue car line, which extends from the center of the city to his college and seminary in Groveland Park. While he was responsible for the conduct of the road, he operated it only in name, the money to build it being furnished by others.[1]

When an attempt was made to promote the Hall-Fitzsimmons fight in St. Paul in August, 1891, he succeeded in preventing it. Characterizing prize fighting as savagism, animalism, the pounding and beating of a man until, exhausted and disfigured and bleeding, he confesses himself conquered, he urged his audience to exert pressure upon civic officials so that the camp followers of pugilism would not be welcomed in the city.[2]

He was a moving spirit in the organization of a Law Enforcement League, which was especially aimed at enforcing the liquor laws. In an address to the League, he called laws "the sinews which link the parts of society into one compact whole, the veins and arteries through which the life-bearing blood circulates."[3]

Among other instances of his civic spirit are his speech on high license in Market Hall, St. Paul, in March, 1884, his appearance before the special committee of the Minnesota Senate in February, 1885, and before representatives of the Republican party in October, 1886, his participation in meetings of Irish-Americans interested in the cause of Parnell, in October, 1885, and his address before the National Conference of Charities and Corrections in St. Paul, in July, 1886.

When Archbishop Ireland came to Minnesota, it was a community of pioneers and Indians. He lived to see it prosperous and populous, advanced in education, charity, and the arts of civilization, with famous cities whose growth almost from a village he had watched. In that growth and construction he played an active part.[4] This vast stretch of prairie, where buffaloes roamed, his colonization scheme peopled with men and women, who brought to it the culture of the Old World and to whom his sympathetic interest in community activities brought prosperity and prominence. The spirit of the frontier seemed to have entered his soul and filled him with a love for its rolling prairies. In an address to the Army of the Tennessee at Lake Minnetonka on August 14, 1889, he gave rhapsodic expression to his admiration for "the Golden Northwest," its azure sky, its health-giving atmosphere, its rushing rivers and sparkling lakes, its prairies, and its forests.[5] He was one of the principal speakers at the first Minnesota Conservation and Agricultural Development Congress in the St. Paul Auditorium, on March 16, 1910, paying tribute to the Minnesota farmer.[6]

The interests of the commonwealth Archbishop Ireland made his own. Whether it was the opening of a new hotel, the dedication of the state capitol, the completion of a railroad, the funeral of a veteran, the reception of a distinguished guest, a tribute to a governor or an empire builder, he could be relied upon for appropriate remarks. When the Earl of Aberdeen, lately Lord Lieutenant of Ireland during the premiership of Gladstone, visited St. Paul, in July, 1887, the Archbishop made an address of welcome in approval of the acts of his official career in Ireland and of his appreciation of Irish temperament, which responds to love but not to hate.[7] At the commemoration of the completion of the Great Northern road to the Pacific, in June, 1893, he paid tribute to his friend, Mr. James J. Hill, as a magician, at the wave of whose rod "forests vanish, prairies contract their horizons, rivers are spanned. He rubs his lamp and cities arise and palaces appear, stores of wealth are revealed."[8]

A lover of America, an admirer of her institutions, a trusted confidant of her statesmen, a friend of her finest minds, Archbishop Ireland occupied a unique place among the prelates of the country. Recognized as a statesman of comprehensive views on all questions of general interest, he always took an active part in public affairs and appeared frequently upon the public platform. His sound judgment, his imaginative insight into high matters, his uncanny ability to discern the trend of events, to estimate men and measures, and to win the public to his cause enabled him to wield immense influence. In the words of Justice Pierce Butler, he was "a giant on the side of right in every crisis, in peace and war." To realize how just was the appraisal of America's leading newspaper, which said: "John Ireland is one of the Country's greatest citizens, one of his Church's greatest prelates," one has but to recall his commission to Rome for the settlement of Philippine affairs, his co-operation with the administration and his support of the government in the delicate questions involved in the acquisition of the Islands, his membership in the Lafayette Commission, his visit to France as his country's representative at the unveiling of the Lafayette monument, his selection as a member of the National Arbitration and Peace Congress in 1907, his appointment, subsequently canceled, as a member of the Hague tribunal and his dictation of his successor, his position as an officer of the National Civic Federation, and his role as labor conciliator. It is no wonder that President Theodore Roosevelt said: "Every true American should be glad that there lives in the United States so stout a champion of Americanism as Archbishop Ireland—the only bishop, by the way, in existence who is entitled to wear that badge of nobility, the button of the Loyal Legion."[9]

The Archbishop was on terms of cordiality, and sometimes of warm friendship, with all the Presidents during his lifetime, with the exception of Woodrow Wilson. President Harrison was glad to accede to his wishes in the appointment of Catholic chaplains,[10] and in the securing of a position for the son of Mrs. Esther Lowe, widow of ex-Governor Lowe.[11] At the birthday celebration of Father Sylvester Malone, the ex-President spoke warmly of the Archbishop, saying: "If we had more Irelands, we would have less sectarian rancor, and the Republic and the Catholic Church would alike be the gainers."[12]

Although Archbishop Ireland did much for President McKinley, aiding him by pronouncements in the campaigns which resulted in his election in 1896 and 1900, he did not always receive the return which he felt he had a right to expect. While the President paid him the honor of appointing him to make the address at the presentation of the statue of Lafayette in Paris in 1900, he was unable, for one reason or another, to fulfill the promise which he made to Senator Stephen B. Elkins that Ireland would be chosen as a member of the Hague Disarmament Conference, nor was he willing to comply with the requests of Bishop O'Gorman and Mr. Roosevelt that he write to the Pope a letter expressing his desire that the Archbishop should receive recognition. For these failures Ireland expressed his resentment to O'Connell and his determination that McKinley would have cause to regret his actions. When he met the President at the banquet of the Marquette Club in Chicago, in October, 1899, he maintained an attitude of aloofness. The Lafayette assignment, however, helped to heal the breach, and brought an interview given by Ireland in London, in which he expressed the Pope's satisfaction with the treatment of the Church in the Islands, a statement which gave the President much pleasure. Upon receipt of the news of McKinley's tragic death, in October, 1901, he expressed his esteem and love for him as "a true man, honest, pure of morals, generous-minded, conscientious and religious, who was brave on the battlefield in his country's peril, zealous of its glory, and unswervingly loyal to its honor and interests.[13]

The Archbishop's relations with Roosevelt and Taft were especially warm. Writing in September, 1898, the former said that he was tempted to begin his letter, "My dear Comrade," for "you are so true a comrade, so true a Democrat, in the proper sense of the word, that I feel a right of comradeship with you, both as soldier and citizen."[14]

He told Father Thomas O'Gorman that he counted the opportunity of becoming friends with the Archbishop as one of the greatest benefits he had derived from being in Washington, that there was not a man in the country who deserved better of the nation or rendered better service to the people.[15] And in a total abstinence speech which he delivered in New York in 1895, he said that he numbered Archbishop Ireland among his most valued friends. In acknowledging a letter from the Archbishop he told him in strict confidence that when he eulogized him at Carnegie Hall he was conscious of the fact that Archbishop Corrigan was within two feet of him. He said: "Now one favor from you. There is just one fight that I take even greater interest in than I do in the fight which I am now engaged in; that is the fight with the A.P.A. If you see a chance where you think an address by me would do good in that fight, pray let me know."[16]

The Archbishop's correspondence shows that he was a frequent and welcome visitor at the White House and that his advice and co-operation were often sought. Roosevelt writes at one time urging him to come to Washington as he had several things to discuss with him, and at another asking him when he could come.[17] He requests him to urge John T. McDonough of Albany to accept a judgeship in the Philippines, and later to suggest to the Judge that he be discreet in his statements.[18] He thanks the Archbishop for "all you have done not merely for this administration but for the American Republic during the past three years," and he wishes that he had five minutes to himself, so that he could pay his respects to one "whom I am proud to hail as one of the greatest exemplars of American citizenship."[19]

The Archbishop's frequent contacts with Mr. Taft during the Philippine negotiations developed a fine understanding. On his election to the presidency, Taft thanked him for all he had done, and expressed his satisfaction at knowing that many Catholics, normally Democrats, voted for him. "To find the unreasoning and un-American bigot," he said, "one has to travel far outside the lines of the Roman Church." He assured him that no one would receive a more cordial welcome in the White House.[20]

The mutual admiration of Roosevelt and Taft, so warm in the beginning, gradually cooled and ended in open hostility. Taft, who in an address before the Republican Club in New York in 1912 referred to Roosevelt's advocacy of the referendum and recall as an attempt to pull down the pillars of the temple of freedom and representative government,[21] reflected his attitude in his letters to the Archbishop.

In 1912, when running for election, he excused his going on the stump while President on the ground that he had to answer the calumnies of his adversary, whom he regarded as a real menace to the country.[22] Later, he told of the attempt of the Bull Moose to steal his electors and of his success in cleaning them out in Maryland and Pennsylvania.[23] In 1914, when he was a private citizen, he wrote that he cherished their friendship and their common view of demagoguery and political plunging,[24] and that he hoped to offset the socialistic tendency shown by many professors of political economy. He said that he respected Wilson as a politician but not as a man, because he was an opportunist of an extreme type, whose proposal to provide presidential primaries was a flagrant violation of the Constitution and a bid for radical support. He regarded the possibility of hard times as not altogether an unmixed evil, because the country, suffering from "overweening confidence and conceit of fifteen years of prosperity," felt that it could set at defiance all national laws of economy, and had a hysteria on the subject of what legislation can do. United with this emotional campaign for great happiness of all the people was a vicious looseness shown in increasing divorces and a cultivation of familiarity with subjects that in his younger days were discussed only with a physician. For all this the country must pay.[25]

Mr. Wilson was the sole exception to the cordial relations which existed between the Archbishop and the Presidents. When Father Daniel Hudson of Notre Dame sent Ireland a copy of a letter from Mr. J. C. Monaghan which stated that whatever Wilson might have written unfavorable to Catholics was written before he had any notion of entering public life, the Archbishop was not impressed, feeling that what he had written then expressed his real feelings.[26] He knew whereof he spoke, for the story goes that when he and Bishop McGolrick went to the White House to pay their respects, they were received with chilling courtesy. The sole letter, of five lines, which he received from Wilson is equally lacking in warmth.

Not only the Presidents but also other leading statesmen had recourse to the Archbishop. Senator George F. Hoar asked his advice about the seating of Senator Smoot of Utah, about the treatment of the Mormon Church in general, about the advisability of passing a constitutional amendment to exclude polygamists from office and of giving Congress authority to break up the habit of frequent divorces.[27]

The Archbishop combined the qualities of the statesman with those of the politician, and it was not always easy to tell which role he was playing. His most sensational political pronouncement was made during the campaign of 1896, when the question of free silver was being debated. Scarcely had William Jennings Bryan left St. Paul, when in response to the written request of twenty-seven businessmen of Minnesota Ireland made a statement on his position, openly declaring his adherence to the Republican platform as enunciated at St. Louis, and his opposition to that of the Democratic convention at Chicago, which he termed secession—"the secession of 1861, which our soldiers believed they had consigned to eternal death at Appomattox." Quoting the declaration made in Chicago, which denounced arbitrary interference by federal authorities in local affairs as a violation of the Constitution, and which referred to the act of Grover Cleveland in sending troops to protect national property during the Chicago riots two years previously, he termed it the old secession doctrine that states are independent of the national government. He made much capital out of a statement of Senator Tillman of South Carolina, who had said: "I come from a state which was the home of secession. It is a sectional issue and it will prevail." The Chicago platform, the Archbishop averred, threatened the country with the destruction of social order, with lawlessness and anarchy, because it attacked the courts, especially the Supreme Court, which he called the Palladium of American liberties. He inveighed against the spirit of socialism which permeated the whole movement, and which he characterized as "the international" of Europe. It was the war of class against class, as shown by the appeals made "to the common people, to the poor and downtrodden," and the denunciation of "plutocrats." He discoursed on the free-silver theory like a professor of economics, prophesying that it would bring on a financial depression beyond anything hitherto experienced.[28] In his role of prophet, the Archbishop has been, to date, only half-right. The "commune" has not arrived, but it is to be regretted that he was not alive to raise his voice, like his namesake in the desert, against the packing of the Supreme Court with men calculated to give a "liberal interpretation" to the Constitution. One can readily understand what a powerful weapon his statement was in the hands of the Republican leaders, who had 250,000 copies of it printed. The sensation which it caused may be judged from the many letters he received, one writer expressing regret for his former bigotry, another telling of a Methodist minister of Los Angeles who read extracts from it which "brought the whole assembly to their feet."[29] Needless to say, the opposition press was bitter. The *Post-Intelli-*

gencer told of the "mud batteries" of invective, slander, and abuse in the Populistic newspapers, directed against a man "who ranks among the foremost of American citizens."[30]

On returning from Europe in 1900, the Archbishop spoke of the high regard in which the United States was held abroad, and then expressed his conviction that American prestige would suffer in Europe if the Democrats succeeded in the coming election.[31]

If he spared no effort to aid in the election of McKinley, neither did he hesitate to use his influence for the advancement of Catholics, trying in 1896 to interest Senator Stephen Elkins in securing a cabinet position for Richard Kerens of St. Louis.[32] The President, who was undecided between Kerens and Judge McKenna, finally chose the latter.[33] Four years later the Archbishop tried again, reminding the President that his appointment of McKenna had given great satisfaction to millions of Catholics and suggesting that now he give Kerens a cabinet post. When, in the following year, he asked Roosevelt for a favor for Kerens, who had been engaged in a factional fight in Missouri and who now wished to have his friend Smith appointed to a government office,[34] the President answered in his brusque manner that, while he wished to pay all attention to Ireland's wishes, it would be personal politics pure and simple for Kerens to take the position that he could appoint a friend to an important office and keep him there against the wishes of every prominent Republican.[35] The Archbishop, however, did not relax his efforts,[36] and finally, with the aid of Cardinal Gibbons, secured the appointment.[37] He also used his influence to have appointed to the Quirinal such ambassadors as Henry White and William Draper, who were favorable to the Vatican. In July, 1897, Monsignor O'Connell wrote: "It was a triumph and an evidence of power to send Draper here. Everybody knows that Ireland did it, and, on their arrival here, Mrs. Draper said so plainly to Miss Jones. The impression at the Vatican was surprising."[38]

The Archbishop became involved in New York politics in 1894, when he secured the election of Father Sylvester Malone of Brooklyn to succeed Bishop McNeirney of Albany as regent of the University of the State of New York. The candidates were Father Lambert, Bishop McQuaid, Colonel George Bliss, and Father Malone, who was engaged in a bitter feud with Archbishop Corrigan. Ireland urged the Malone and Lambert forces to unite, with the result that Malone won the election—for which McQuaid never forgave him.[39] He resolved to find out the "outside clerical meddlers," among whom he suspected the prelate of St. Paul.[40] When his suspicions were confirmed, his wrath was so great that he attacked the Archbishop from the pulpit of his Cathedral, characterizing his coming to New York as "undignified, disgraceful to his episcopal office, and a scandal in the eyes of Catholics."[41] McQuaid received rebukes from Archbishop Satolli and Cardinal Rampolla.[42] Ireland and McQuaid were at opposite poles in their attitude toward the ballot, the latter boasting that he had never cast a vote, the former maintaining that the man who refused to vote deserved disfranchisement.[43] Ireland further irritated Their Excellencies of New York and Rochester by the congratulatory letter which he sent to Recorder Goff, who, he said, had done great honor to the Catholic name.[44]

The leading papers of the country denounced McQuaid's attack, calling attention to the fact that priests in New York, Milwaukee, and other cities had openly urged their people to vote the Democratic ticket, whereas Ireland had advised his hearers to vote according to their conscience. As a result he emerged from the scandalous incident with heightened reputation, the Chicago *Post* referring to him as "the one Metropolitan of all whose intense devotion to American institutions has been constantly conspicuous."[45]

The Archbishop's services to the Republican party were gratefully acknowledged, bringing a letter of appreciation from Mark Hanna in November, 1903,[46] and enabling him to block anti-Catholic measures. He used his influence to checkmate J. M. King of the National League for the Protection of American Institutions, who tried to force a plank into the Republican platform relative to the union of Church and State and the use of money for sectarian purposes.[47] For this he was attacked in King's *Facing the 20th Century* as "the most specious and deceptive foe of the public schools." He also refuted the charge of Senator Bard that Catholics offered votes in return for favorable Indian school contracts, and that he had been approached by Professor E. L. Scharf of the Catholic University with a promise of carrying a number of districts in California for him if he used his influence to bring about a continuation of the contracts.[48] In the Republican National Convention of St. Louis in 1896, efforts were made to have a plank inserted in the platform opposing any union of Church and State. Ireland wrote to Thomas Carter, National Committeeman, in June, 1896, that such a clause was uncalled for, that its adoption would be taken as a concession to the A.P.A. and would awaken religious animosity.[49] At a picnic held by the parish of the

Basilica of St. Mary in Minneapolis, on July 4, 1906, he took occasion to express his dissatisfaction with the Immigration Law, which set up a literary test for immigrants. It is a fact, he said, that foreigners who make the best citizens are often unable to read or write when they arrive, and that criminals, as a class, are well educated and able to meet such requirements. "In shutting the door in the face of the unlettered foreigner, we shut out the willing laborer and law-abiding citizen and give entrance to the skilled crook and future criminal."[50]

Archbishop Ireland's interests were not confined to the United States. He was in truth a citizen of the world, none of whose affairs were foreign to him. Whether it was the Boer War or Congo atrocities, the murder of Archduke Francis Ferdinand and his consort in Austria, the deportations in Belgium, the suppression of Irish liberty, the Russo-Japanese War, or the closing of religious houses in France, his advice and aid were sought and his pronouncements were received with respect as those of one in the secret of things. He maintained cordial relations with the rulers and representatives of many countries.

When Prince Albert of Belgium visited the United States in 1898 and made an extended tour of the country, the Archbishop met him in Washington and later entertained him in St. Paul. After his return home, the Prince wrote that his conversations with the Archbishop were among the happiest memories of his life. A letter from King Leopold, which unfortunately is almost illegible, thanked Ireland for the courtesy he had shown the Prince and expressed his own eager desire to visit the United States "to admire a great and youthful people of destiny."[51] Tarnowski, Chargé d'Affaires of Austria-Hungary, who had met the Archbishop at a dinner given at the French Embassy in honor of Cardinal Martinelli and had discussed with him the dangers of perversion to which Austrian and Hungarian emigrants were exposed, wrote to remind him of the memoir which Ireland had promised on the subject and which the Minister wished to send to his government.[52]

The arrival of a distinguished European guest was usually the occasion for the enlistment of the Archbishop's services. In May, 1902, he spoke at the dinner given by the Friendly Sons of St. Patrick for the French delegates to the unveiling of the statue of Rochambeau at Washington. Recalling the indebtedness of America to France, he said that the blood of France flowing with that of America's own children poured life into the Republic of America and left the memory of

France indelibly impressed upon her soul. Holding in his hand the flags of the United States, Ireland, and France, he said that they should be ever enfolded, for they were one at Yorktown, where they fought for the establishment of freedom. He also charged his hosts to see to it that in Washington, near the monuments of Lafayette and Rochambeau, there be erected a monument to some Irish soldier, a suggestion which was approved by the Ancient Order of Hibernians at their national convention in Denver in July, 1902, and which resulted in the monument to Captain John Barry.[53]

His relations with Jules Cambon, the French Ambassador, were particularly intimate. It was Camboon who obtained for him the Legion of Honor and who conferred it in Paris. At the Archbishop's request he used his influence with the French government to obtain greater space for the American exhibit at the Exposition in Paris in 1900. In November, 1902, expressing his regret at not being able to see him before he left Washington, he wrote to tell him of the memory he carried of the co-operation and sympathy which Ireland had so often shown him. One of his finest memories, he said, was their friendship. Writing from Berlin in May, 1909, he again said that of all his contacts in America those with the Archbishop were his dearest.[54] At the farewell banquet tendered to him Ireland was one of the principal speakers, telling of Cambon's love for America and of his influence in destroying the mistrust which some Frenchmen had of America. If America, which, he said, had not yet had the time to bring into her life the culture of civilization, had received from France something of her riches of idealism, France in turn might take lessons from America and learn the power of her industry.[55]

In 1915 Cambon wrote two letters in vindication of French policy, sending in January an English translation of the Yellow Book published by his government, the letter of Cardinal Mercier to his diocesans, articles on the martyrdom of Belgium, and the official report of the French Commission of Enquiry into pillage. He told of the efforts of the French and English to get the Germans to join with them in bringing a delay of hostilities between Russia and Austria and of their failure to receive any co-operation. Later he expressed his agreement with the sentiments of the Archbishop that a half-peace should not be accepted and that justice should be done to Belgium.[56]

The noted correspondent who signed himself "Innominato" and who wrote many brilliant articles for the New York *Sun*, on hearing of the Commission on Philippine affairs which Roosevelt was sending to Rome, congratulated Ireland on his triumph and urged him to send to the Pope and the Cardinal Secretary of State a complete account of the visit of Prince Henry of Prussia. Connecting the two incidents, he felt that the tribute paid by the Kaiser to "the incomparable power of America" made intimate collaboration with Mr. Roosevelt vital.[57]

During the Russo-Japanese War, Count Cassini, the Russian Ambassador, expressed to the Archbishop his surprise that in some quarters of the United States there existed a sentiment unfavorable to Russia, which was altogether inexplicable to him in the light of the aid which Russia had given America in the troubled period of its history. He acknowledged gratefully the encouragement which Ireland had given to him.[58]

In November, 1904, the Archbishop was the guest of honor at a dinner given by St. John Gaffney, at which were present Baron Moncheau of Belgium, Prince de Bearn of France, and Baron Schilling of Russia. A little later Moncheau thanked him for interesting Senator Spooner in the Congo affair, adding that he had hastened to make known in Brussels "the kind cooperation which your Grace has given us."[59] When stories were being published in the press concerning Belgian atrocities in the Congo, the Belgian Minister enlisted the aid of the Archbishop, who issued a statement declaring that the agitation against King Leopold had its origin in England "among fanatical preachers and unscrupulous merchants."[60] This statement brought a letter of appreciation from the Minister, M. Buisseret, who said that "Belgians can indeed be thankful and proud that men in high position and of the moral authority of your Grace rise in support of a cause so dear to them."[61] Again, in December, 1916, Baron Carton de Wiart, Belgian Minister of Justice, appealed to him to use his influence against the deportations conducted by Germany.[62] In March, 1917, the Baron again expressed his gratitude to the Archbishop for all he had done. And when the Belgian Commission visited St. Paul in July, 1917, Ireland said at a mass meeting in Como Park that the Star-Spangled Banner would never be withdrawn from battle until Belgium had been restored to its home. In his response, General Leclercq broke down, and, being unable to express himself in words, the rugged fighter seized the Archbishop in his embrace and kissed him warmly.

When in 1887 an imperial ukase in Russia compelled a hasty withdrawal of Jews from the provinces of the empire outside the Jewish zone, and it was most important for the Jews to obtain a delay in the enforcement of the ukase, Mr. Jesse Seligman went to Rome, called upon the Archbishop, who arranged for him an interview with Cardinal Rampolla, and secured the intervention of the Pope.[63] When, however, Ireland was requested in November, 1913, to add his name to a petition to the Czar, protesting against the charge that one of the Jews had committed murder for "ritual purposes," he informed Herman Bernstein that there had been delay in his reception of copies of the petition, but that he would not have signed it in any event, as he did not believe it "a proper thing to prejudge decisions of courts in Russia or in any other country."[64]

The extent to which the First World War engaged his attention is indicated by the many contacts which he maintained with leading men here and abroad. One of the first was with Mr. Roosevelt, who wrote in December, 1914, to thank him for his letter and to say: "I have always said that you represented the now almost or altogether bygone type of those great ecclesiastics who in the Middle Ages, as Chancellors, swayed the policies of great kingdoms or guided the conduct of mighty monarchies."[65] From Washington, on April 18, 1917, the Archbishop telegraphed Mr. Charles W. Ames, a prominent civic leader of St. Paul, stressing the duty incumbent upon every citizen of giving full support to the government.[66]

The Archbishop's heart went out in sympathy to the French bishops in the ruin of their dioceses, and they, in turn, had recourse to him. Cardinal Sevin of Lyon asked his aid in preventing the proselyting of the war orphans by designing Protestants, mentioning in particular the activities of Madame Dick-May, who had used the generosity of Americans for the perverting of the faith of the children.[67] Cardinal Lucon of Rheims, after reminding him of their happy relations when he was Bishop of Belley, recounted the dreadful misfortunes which had befallen Rheims, which twice in half a century had experienced the horrors of war. Many of his people, terrified by the stories of brutality related by Belgian refugees, had fled with nothing except what they could carry. Whole villages in the Ardennes had been wiped out; at Rheims, the entire center of the town surrounding the Cathedral had been burned.[68] Archbishop Touchet of Orléans recalled their conversation in Montreal in 1910 as they sat watching the Eucharistic procession. Ireland had said to him: "Be sure that we have not forgotten the ties which unite us to your country. American and French blood flowed during the early days of the American Republic; these old loves, born of a glorious past, are not forgotten." And then without thinking of any war, they both remarked: "Who knows whether these flags, whose colors now go side by side, will not grow closer in days to come?" At the time that "Who knows?" did not seem to Touchet to be very probable, but the improbable had been realized, and the flags were again marching side by side.[69]

It is amazing how people of all kinds turned instinctively to the Archbishop. Before starting out on his famous peace mission, Henry Ford telegraphed and wrote, urging him as "a representative of American democracy" to join his pilgrimage, an invitation which, needless to say, Ireland did not accept.[70] Princess Henrietta, sister of the King of the Belgians, after painting a picture of the devastation of her country, sought sympathy for her people.[71] The French Ambassador, Jusserand, concerned about the attitude of the Middle West toward France, was reassured by the Archbishop, whose opinion, he said, counted above all else.[72] In a sermon in the Cathedral in July, 1914, at a solemn requiem Mass for Archduke Ferdinand and his consort, whose assassinations led to the European war, the Archbishop severely condemned "doctrinaires, who, by work and pen, attack law and order."

Monsignor Louis Duchesne, the famous historian and a warm friend of the Archbishop, wrote interesting comments on the situation in Rome during the First World War. In January, 1915, he indicated the problem caused by the presence in the Vatican of some pro-Germans, and his joy that "the spies and the traitors had gone back to their lairs." As Italy was then thinking of entering the war, the Vatican, he said, was wondering how to maintain neutrality in a situation for which the Law of Guarantees had made no provision. There was some thought of replacing the diplomats of the Central Powers with auditors at the Rota; for the newspapers, some other arrangement would be found "which would give society a little amusement." It was hoped that France would follow the example of England and send a diplomat, but two uncompromising elements had to be taken into account—the radical Freemasons and the Italians. The "Sons of the Widow" had their eye on clericalism as much as Pius X had his on modernism; nothing escaped their anxious vigilance. Nothing, he said, would be more disagreeable to the Italians than to see the Holy See add to its diplomatic stature, and they found unbearable the idea that it would be invited to the next Peace Congress. This he regarded as childishness; the condition of the papacy was not such that she ought even to wish for a place where the Metternichs and the Talleyrands of the twentieth century would draw up agreements. But at the first news of the mission of Sir Henry Howard, Tittoni dashed quickly to the Quai d'Orsay to inquire whether France was going to do likewise. The Vatican would not cause any trouble to Italy, but from another viewpoint there was religious and perhaps political danger in this progressive confiscation of the papacy by Italy. Under Pius X the movement was already far advanced; he was a patriotic Pope. Benedict would hardly return to the tradition of Leo. The Italians, while paying court to Benedict, were gently encircling him. The Italians, he said, even the most distinguished of them, never reached the conception of the Pope as the head of the universal Church; for them he was above all and almost exclusively so the head of the Italian clergy. A reaction was necessary, and the only means he could see was the energetic internationalization of the Holy See and especially of its personnel. "But," he concluded, "I begin to ramble. May God keep you, Monseigneur, and give to your counsel, so wise, the greatest fruits."[73]

In January of the following year, while expressing appreciation for American sympathy for France, Duchesne thought it well that someone was staying out of the infernal whirlpool and might aid in bringing the war to an end through discussions. He did not feel that the Vatican was succeeding too well in keeping the scales of justice evenly balanced in its attempt to be neutral, and believed that the pontifical propositions won more applause in Germany than in France. The entire Curia, "including the dowagers," was definitely hostile. For this Metternich was responsible; the spirit of the Holy Alliance was not dead everywhere. But the opposition was confined to some little cliques, and neither the Pope nor his Secretary of State was prepared to anoint William II as emperor of the West. He did not see how the Holy See could hope to play a principal role in the conclusion of peace; everyone would see in it the advocate of Germany, vanquished or victorious. It would be better for it to "remain quiet and take refuge in prayer and in the exercise of charity." He concluded: "The air continues breathable in theological circles. Up there I am always received with the greatest cordiality. At the reception on Christmas eve, a Dominican came and offered most cordially his best wishes. It was Père Esser. Some days later I had occasion to meet at his home the Cardinal Prefect of the Index; he was charming. As for the point in question [probably the removal of his *History* from the

Index], Père Lepidi is giving it attention and has no doubt of its success."[74]

Two letters in 1917 conclude the correspondence. The first gave his reactions to Wilson's letters, "the last epistle of the apostle Wilson to the Europeans—I was going to say to the Corinthians." This, like other sacred texts, was being variously interpreted and gave rise to contradictory ideas. If the President wished to take his advice, he should be more definite in his proposals; better still, he should keep quiet for a while. The olive tree was being cultivated at the Vatican no less ardently than at the White House, the Pope working in conjunction with the President. At the moment, the Gerlach affair was causing the Pontiff much embarrassment, because it gave a hold over him to the Italian government. The time would come when the President would appear with an olive branch in his left hand and a stout club in his right. He hoped that Ireland would come to Rome soon to see Pope Benedict, who was very kind and affable.[75]

The other letter was written after America had entered the war. Thanks to the President, said Duchesne, the world had heard the voice of a people which was truly the voice of God. He regretted that the Pope, hampered by his neutrality and his diplomacy, could not have taken this role. Around him there seemed to be no idea of the importance of events. He pictured the situation to himself graphically in his way: "An archangel wearing a high hat with a starry band threatens with his lance a demon having a pointed helmet; the Pope on the side-lines makes vain gestures in an attempt to restore peace." But in a fight between good and evil the place of the Pope should be somewhere other than in the gallery where "the spectators are looking on and deploring as needs be the incidents of the fight." He saw the passing of the monarchies, a Chinese republic and then a Russian. He wondered what the future held for Christianity. "Perhaps," he said, "the Christians will wish to look into their own religious affairs. Then shall they see strange things, and the code of Canon Law should be the subject of a second edition."[76]

Another close friend, Cardinal Francis-Aidan Gasquet, also expressed his mind freely on the war situation. In January, 1915, he was confident of the outcome, for he felt that the victory of Germany would mean the destruction of the Catholic faith as a great power for civilization. "These Italian ecclesiastics," he said, "have never read the historical books and philosophical books of modern Germany, which plainly set forth the intention of the ruling powers there, their determination to have a world dominion and to impose their religion upon mankind."[77] A few months later he wrote that the destruction of the *Lusitania* had caused much feeling against the German element in the Vatican, but fortunately most of them had quitted Italy. While the Italian papers generally condemned the destruction as plain murder, the mere "regret" (*rimpianto*) expressed by the *Osservatore Romano* was altogether inadequate, as it seemed to imply that the Allies were not without blame. The Holy Father was full of sympathy, but his advisers, he thought, were very pro-German.[78]

Asked by the Archbishop in January, 1918, whether he still looked for the triumph of the Allies, he replied that he could not conceive that Providence would permit the Central Powers to win, for "it would be a victory of injustice and Lutheran principles." The Pope saw that his peace note had had its effects, and Wilson seemed to be even more pro-German than the Pope in his message.[79]

Neither the French Ambassador nor Ireland had much patience with those who were advocating peace on the basis of the restoration of the *status quo*. Jusserand said:

> Exactly, just as you say; I am with you in this awful problem from my heart. Peace, yes, but not the peace of German militarism, not the peace of absolutism, not the peace of the system that oppresses Poles, Danes, Alsatians, for which treaties are "scraps of paper," pledges a thing to be laughed at, and the violation of every law of warfare a joke. Think of the state of mind revealed by Count Bernsdorff's declaring that Belgium's attitude was "foolish." Foolish! Those poor people defending their hearths, children, altars, universities, their Louvain, their Zermonde.
>
> Peace, yes, peace as soon as possible. But no peace at all, rather destruction, than not to try to the utmost, to our last breath, the killing of the monster, Pangermanistic militarism. One in an exalted situation spoke to me the other day of the blessing of peace and of the reinstating of the *status quo*. Agreed, I answered, with all my heart. The *status quo* must include of course their bringing back our dead to life.[80]

Cecil Spring Rice, the British Ambassador, expressed his thanks for the constant sympathy and kindness which the Archbishop had shown him. He told of the appreciation of Mr. Balfour for all he had learned in his conversation with His Grace. "You will have learned from Jusserand," he said, "what the Allies think of your attitude and how grateful they are. May I add as an Irishman, I take a special pride in the great fame and influence which you enjoy in this country as a great Catholic and as a true and loyal and devoted American."[81]

Cordial relations existed also between Ireland and other British ambassadors. James Bryce wrote to acknowledge his telegram of welcome and to express the hope that "it may not be long before I have the good fortune to meet you again and have a talk over those social questions which interest us both so deeply."[82]

The affairs of France were closest of all to the heart of the Archbishop, and he followed with keenest interest the many vexatious questions which agitated it. The hostility of the government to the Church came to a head in 1889, when the Ferry ministry launched a campaign of confiscation and persecution, dissolved the Society of Jesus, and obliged other religious orders to seek authorization. The schools were gradually laicized, and the teaching of religion was banned from the public schools. The law of separation of Church and State was passed in 1905, and the appropriation for public worship (*budget des cultes*) was suppressed. Episcopal residences were left for two years, presbyteries and seminaries for five, and churches for an indefinite period, at the disposal of associations for religious worship (*associations cultuelles*) which were to be created in each diocese. Concerning these associations there was a difference of opinion among the Catholics. Some feared that they would result in an influx of laymen into the government of the Church. Others thought that this anxiety was excessive, and that the associations could be controlled by the episcopate. A general assembly of the episcopate, held on May 30, 1906, considered the question but did not divulge whatever decision they reached. In March, twenty-three Catholic writers and members of the Chambers had expressed, in a confidential letter to the bishops, a hope that the associations might be given a trial. The publication of this letter stirred up a bitter controversy which divided French Catholics. Pius X, in the encyclical *Gravissimo Officii* of August 10, 1906, prohibited the formation of any association "so long as it should not be evident that the Divine constitution of the Church and the immutable rights of the Roman Pontiff and of the bishops would be fully secure." The rigors of the controversy are indicated in the letters which Archbishop Ireland received from his friends.

His old friend, Bishop Jean Germain of Rodez et de Vabres, wrote on February 27, 1900:

I am moving in an intelligent milieu, but those who ought to help us only throw obstacles in our way. Between those who dream of the return of the past and those who dream of an impossible future, people of good sense find it difficult to walk (carry on). If we were effectively sustained in

Rome when we try, at the peril of our life, to find an escape from the thickets where all kinds of beasts of prey lie in wait for us, we would finally succeed, but while the power of the bishops is exalted the respect for this power is countermanded in beautiful and eloquent pages. The youngest escapee from the Seminary, having to clothe himself in the frock of the Assumption, gets the better of us, acts in spite of us and we have no way of curbing the madmen who have the pretension of representing the great and holy Church of Jesus Christ. In Rome we have a changed situation which must be regulated soon if our relations with the State are to be established on certain bases. The religious Orders which are multiplying and have never been so prosperous since we have been a Republic are independent both of the Bishop and the State. That gives them now a power which they never had under the old monarchy. That is the real obstacle to the action of the Bishops. For the people in the service of the old parties, who make them live in opulence, hold us under suspicion and form the opinion among the masses. This violent situation the government understands, and it will be a shame if it is left to the civil power to take the initiative in the measures which Rome should take in concert with the French episcopate.[83]

He wrote again on July 20, 1915, about the sufferings of the war, his two hundred parishes without a priest, his ten thousand wounded, thirty ambulances, his joy at the election of Benedict, his hope that in place of a Masonic government they would have a truly French and liberal one, and his eagerness to see the Archbishop.

The Count de Meaux told of his joy at the Archbishop's reception of his *Souvenirs,* but he was sad because of the harm which the extremists had done to both the political and the religious interests of France, and he regretted that they alone had been listened to in Rome, and that the advice of Floureur, a former enemy, had been taken in preference to that of Brunetière. On the recommendation of a Commission of Cardinals which included only one Frenchman, the Pope had rejected the *associations cultuelles* proposed by the great majority of the bishops of France. As a result, not only had the Church in France lost its last resources, but public worship would probably become impossible. He feared lest the action of the Pope would be interpreted as distrust of the laity. The Vatican had often submitted to the control of governments either hostile or indifferent; why then keep at a distance those who have never ceased to give evidences of devotion? "What," he asked, "will the Papacy gain by isolating itself from the Bishops; or the Hierarchy by isolating itself from Christian people?"[84]

Frédéric Boudin, founder of the Progressive Union of Catholic

Youth, formerly a neo-Christian and a student of Père Didon, writes a pessimistic letter. After the announced policy of Leo XIII he was hopeful that the evil from which France suffered would come to an end, because he saw in the alliance of Christianity and democracy the promise of religious, political, and social progress. But now, he says, the friends of the Archbishop are convinced that nothing can be done in France. He develops a theory of his own—that the Latin civilization which rules France had its origin in the sixteenth century at the time of the Renaissance, which was merely a revival of paganism; that the so-called barbarians were the new men who were civilized by the Gospel and developed in the Middle Ages on the ruins of the Latins. The evil from which Catholic nations are suffering is not the fight between the Church and the age, but the decomposition of a pagan society. To make the Latins evolve toward the inner life, the religion of the spirit, seems to him impossible. Therefore the hope of the Church lies in America, England, Germany, Switzerland, Holland, and Scandinavia, and in bringing into the organism of the Church the Protestants, who are in revolt only against the Latin spirit of the Greco-Roman world.[85]

Duc de la Salle Bokemaure, writing from Granada, Spain, told of his visits to Spain and Portugal, of his favorable impression of the King of Spain, who had frank and liberal ideas but who said that his predecessors Charles V and Philip II would have anathematized his ideas and that the Inquisition would have burned him for his liberalism. The people of Portugal impressed him as being devotedly Catholic.

Turning to the affairs of France, he lamented the breaking of the Concordat, and he believed that it would take many years to recover all that was destroyed by the separation. The masses were imbued with a Platonic religiosity rather than with a truly Christian spirit. His friend, Archbishop Edmond-Frédéric Fuzet of Rouen, said in a recent pastoral that "France was a democracy having behind it ten centuries of monarchy, looking at the State, as in the days of the kings, as the sovereign dispenser of all justice and liberty." To the extent that Catholic worship was official, the Duke said, the majority of the people tied up with it all the great acts of private life. They elected anti-Catholic Deputies, but they were baptized, confirmed, married, and buried in the Church; but they would not follow the priest in the private ways of worship when the evilly disposed government made difficulty after difficulty. That was why the majority of the bishops regretted the separation. As long as the Concordat existed there was some hope of settlement. Leo XIII would have done everything to maintain it. La Salle placed some of the blame on the religious who had been expelled, and "who took the most violent measures in the hope that the breaking of the Concordat would allow them to re-enter France and take the places of the secular clergy." The popular vote would probably support the government, and insidiously there had been created an atmosphere of opposition against the Pope and Cardinal Merry del Val.

He said that the separation was regarded as a great gamble by such men as Archbishop Eudoxe Mignot of Albi, Archbishop Jean-Augustin Germain of Toulouse, and Bishop François-Xavier Schoepfer of Tarbes. He was also impressed by the lack of unity among the bishops, Bishop François Delamaire of Périgueux urging his priests to throw themselves into politics, the Archbishop of Rouen pointing out the danger of this policy, which would result in the defiance of the voters for the political counsels of the clergy. He concluded: "I don't care to mention any name, but Your Grace knows of a Cardinal of whom we have often spoken, a man of real worth, but one who did not appear to your American eyes as a liberal, and who without change of manner might perhaps today be considered a liberal—a word to the wise."[86]

As Maisie Ward says, at the time of the Dreyfus trial it was almost the mark of a good patriot to believe in his guilt. Only a very small section of French opinion admitted any doubt that Dreyfus had been the paid spy of Germany. Many people in England and the United States felt that the trial was unfair, and held meetings to protest the conviction. When the Archbishop heard that such a meeting had been arranged in St. Paul, he declared that gatherings dealing with the sentence of the Rennes court-martial were untimely, unfair to France, and likely to breed regrettable ill feeling between that country and this.[87] Writing to the *Weekly Register* concerning the trial, Virginia Crawford said that French Catholics had to bear their share of blame for the lamentable *affaire*, but that there should be no indiscriminate censure of them. In appealing for a better feeling toward France, she said:

In support of my plea, I can quote the testimony of one whose opinion on this subject can certainly not be held suspect. I mean the Archbishop of St. Paul. Mgr. Ireland has spoken out strongly in America in favor of Dreyfus, but he has also spoken of Catholic France with the affection that only those feel for her who really know her. As it is in the cause of peace and fraternity, I feel at liberty to repeat what in a private conversation the Archbishop said to me about France when he was in London last July. He had come straight from Paris, where he had seen much of Catholic social and philanthropic activity, and he declared deliberately—and I confess my own experience entirely coincides with his—that the best French Catholics illustrate the faith in a manner unequalled in any other country. To the solid virtues of the devout Christian they add an exquisite charm and a perfection of charity which only centuries of Catholicism can give. Of this pure essence of Christianity, there is, of course, as His Grace remarked, not enough to go around; yet who can believe in the essential rottenness of a nation that can produce such incomparable fruit.[88]

Ireland wrote to Abbé Felix Klein of the interview which he had given to the press, which, he said, "while irritating some has been well received by the country and according to letters I have got has had an excellent effect." He suggested that it be reproduced in some French newspapers and "at least indirectly give the lie to our friend Périès, according to whom I am an enemy of France in America."[89] Klein replied that it had been quoted by many journals, in particular by *Le Figaro,* but that *L'Univers* had not ventured to quote it because it had a word of sympathy for the unfortunate victim of anti-Semitic prejudice. "This madness," he said, "goes on eternally. Scarcely any of the adversaries of Catholicism see impartially on this point. The conservatives have just offered General Mercier! one of those rare senatorial seats which they are able to control, and the election is practically certain."[90]

Among many appeals that came to Ireland was one from Father Columban Tyne, a Passionist, who in December, 1902, asked him to use his influence with the United States government to save St. Joseph's Church in Paris, which had been frequented by English-speaking Catholics and built and maintained with American money. The London *Times,* he said, had already protested against the spoliation of the church as something that would arouse the indignation of the civilized world, and had urged the ostracism of France by Catholic priests.[91] The Archbishop placed the matter before the United States Ambassador to France, who replied:

I saw your good friend Mr. Delcassé at once and told him what you said on the subject, knowing the respect he has for your opinions. The entire question regarding the Congregations is now before the French Parliament, and their status will depend upon the action taken by that body. Whatever may take place it does not seem to be the intention to close the Avenue Hoche Church or interfere with worship there, provided it is not conducted by a Congregation. You well know the pleasure it always gives me to hear from you, and I trust you will not hesitate to command me if I can be of service in any direction.[92]

Correspondence with Mr. Wayne McVeagh concerning the relations between Colombia and Panama, with Senator Cushman Davis concerning arbitration of the boundary dispute with Canada, with M. George Peixotto in reference to the latter's efforts to bring about an agreement between Italy and Turkey, and with Cardinal Moran of Sydney, Australia, about the relations between the political parties of that country and the Church, indicate the extent of the Archbishop's interests as well as the confidence which men reposed in his judgment. The correspondence with McVeagh treats of a so-called Colombian Syndicate consisting of Auerback, a well-known lawyer, Barr, an associate of George Perkins and Charles H. Flint, and their relations with Domingo Merry del Val, brother of the Papal Secretary of State. McVeagh told of a rumor that Speyer and Company were trying through the State Department to persuade Colombia to give them a concession to build a railway from the coast to Bogotá and to accept the building of such railway and some part of the money held by William Nelson Cromwell, fiscal agent of Panama, "the residue of the $10,000,000 diverted from Colombia to Panama in 1904, in full settlement."[93]

Peixotto, Director General of the Equitable Life Insurance Company, sent a long account of his efforts as a peacemaker, of his visit to Constantinople and Rome, his suggestion that Turkey should demand compensation on the Red Sea, a seaport in Eritrea, and an outlet on the Mediterranean and yield to Italy the lands on which Italy had raised her flag, and that Italy in turn should give up her claims to the Libyan desert.[94]

Cardinal Moran told of the victory of the Labor party with the aid of the Catholic vote. The Catholics held the electoral balance in their hands, and if the Liberals hoped to recover their power they would have to cast off their connection with the Orangemen.[95]

With regard to Canada, the Archbishop made a sensational statement at the dinner of the Minnesota Society in New York, in December, 1902. He said:

I do not want to be bellicose, but I say this for myself. As sure as fate, although you and I may not see it, the starry banner will wave mistress over all the territory from the gulf to the bay. There will be no conquest, no war. The hearts across the border are already beating with love for us, and commerce and agriculture are calling for espousals.

In its comment the Boston *Pilot* said: "When the Archbishop spoke on this question, he interpreted the hopes and feelings of 90 percent of the American people."[96]

In all these varied interests Ireland merely practiced what he preached. In Baltimore, in October, 1893, he said:

We desire to win the age. Let us not, then, stand isolated from it. Our place is in the world as well as in the sanctuary; in the world, wherever we can prove our love for it or render it a service. We cannot influence men at long range; close contact is needed. Let us be with them in the things that are theirs—material interests, social welfare, civil weal—so that they may be with us in the things that are ours, the interests of religion. Let us be with them because their interests are ours, and ours are theirs, because nature and grace must not be separated.[97]

Chapter 12

THE CHURCHMAN

▶┼◀▶┼◀▶┼◀▶┼◀▶┼◀▶┼◀▶┼◀

1. HIS ROLE AT THE COUNCIL OF BALTIMORE

The secret of Archbishop Ireland's greatness, the inspiration of his whole life, is to be sought in his devotion to the Church of Christ, and in his love of his fellowman. If ever man was enamored of the Church, of its beauty and truth, of its mission through the ages, it was he. Whether he was hearing confessions by night on a southern battlefield, or carrying help and hope to his colonists on the prairies, or fighting for souls against intemperance; whether he was speaking to the little ones of Christ in some remote parish of his diocese, or addressing the hierarchy of the United States in conclave assembled or the Catholics of France at Paris or Orléans, or those of England, Ireland, or Belgium; in all his varied activities love of the Church was the passion of his life, dominating and overshadowing all other motives and purposes.

Although not ten years consecrated, he made a deep impression at the Third Plenary Council of Baltimore in 1884, proving himself one of its master minds. In the matter of calling the Council there was sharp difference of opinion between eastern and western prelates. Cardinal McCloskey of New York, when asked his opinion by Cardinal Simeoni, was not favorable. Neither was Archbishop Gibbons, who advised its deferment until provincial councils were held as a preliminary step. The bishops of the West, however, were much in favor of it. This was especially true of Bishop John Lancaster Spalding and Bishop Ireland. Spalding, who was in Rome in January, 1883, told Ireland of the plan to call three or four American bishops to Rome for consultation and information, and then to summon another plenary council. He referred to the "old fogies" in America who were opposed to it, and to the many appeals pouring into Rome from priests against their bishops. He said that there was nothing in reason which Rome would not do for the American prelates if the chaotic condition of their views as to what ought to be done did not keep the Roman authorities in a kind of labyrinth from which it was not easy to find a way out.[1]

A few months before the Council opened, Bishop Ireland made to Archbishop James Gibbons, who had been appointed delegate, some suggestions which the latter regarded as excellent, and which, he said, he would place in the hands of the theologians so that they might receive careful attention.[2] The similarity of viewpoint of the two prelates was shown from the very beginning, both insisting that special attention be given to violations of the Sabbath and to intemperance. Ireland's leadership was manifested in his constant participation in the discussions and was also recognized by his appointment to the presidency of two commissions as well as by his assignment as one of the preachers of the Council. Among his recommendations were the appointment of a commission of bishops to draw up and have printed the routine of the visitation of parishes after the approval of the Holy See, and the examination of candidates for Confirmation by the bishop or his representative. He favored the elimination of the Feast of the Circumcision as a holy day of obligation and the cutting down of the number of holy days, on the ground that the violation of the Feast led to a violation of other ecclesiastical laws. In the discussion concerning the establishment of irremovable rectorships, about which there was much disagreement among the prelates and much reluctance to carry out the wishes of Rome, which desired that one out of every ten parishes should be irremovable, he brought matters to a head by asking the Delegate to express his mind on the subject. Gibbons reminded the prelates that such was the will of the Holy See and that nothing could change its mind; that it was also the wish of learned and pious priests, whose desire should be satisfied; that, as a matter of fact, more qualities were required of an irremovable rector, who had charge of only one parish, than were usually required of a bishop, who had charge of a whole diocese, and that it would be easier in the future to remove such rectors should they prove to be unworthy and to remove those who were already regarded as irremovable. After John Lancaster Spalding had attacked the proposed legislation, averring that if it were once passed it would never be abrogated, that the present discipline was nearer to that of the early Church, and that it was only office seekers who desired it, Ireland arose and said that he wished to free his own soul and conscience from the evils and scandals which he foresaw would come from the attempts to remove a pastor by canonical trial, for there were often causes for removal which could not be canonically proved. He knew parishes in Ireland which the pastors never dared to enter, so great was the hatred of the parishioners, and yet the bishop had no remedy except to name an administrator. Thus religion lost its force and value, as had often happened in Italy. The pastor might be a man of great sanctity and yet be a detriment to the Church. The parishioners, especially the Irish, are unwilling to testify against the pastor, no matter how unworthy he be. This the Sacred Congregation did not know, and only too easily did it listen to troublesome priests and calumniators of the bishops. He foresaw that if one out of ten parishes were made irremovable, there would be constant envy and dissension. He concluded by saying that he would not refuse to accept any law proposed, provided it would be unlawful to remove any priest without the advice of the consultors.

In the discussion on the schools he wished to have a Catholic school defined as "one which is subject to ecclesiastical authority and inspection by the bishop." He objected to the compulsion of non-Catholic students in Catholic schools to attend Mass, on the ground that they scandalized the Catholics by not kneeling during the Canon. He urged the maintenance of a strict program of studies in seminaries but did not favor insistence on music. He approved of the examination of teachers in parochial schools, including the nuns. Among things which he opposed were the demanding of money at the entrance to churches, which, he said, was a deterrent to non-Catholics, the holding of picnics at night, on Sundays, and holy days, or when accompanied with drink, and the insertion of a clause forbidding round dances, lest it give the impression that other dances were permitted. He recommended that, as in the case of the diocesan clergy, an accounting must be made to the bishop by religious for goods given to their parishes, and that buildings constructed by the alms of the people be held by the same title as the other properties of the diocese. He fought the condemnation of the Ancient Order of Hibernians. On November 10, he preached on "The Church the Defender of True Liberty."[3]

2. HIS WORK FOR THE INDIANS

The next matter to engage the attention of Archbishop Ireland was the welfare of the Indians, who were so numerous in his diocese and who were in constant danger of exploitation. When the attitude of some of the government agents toward the Indian schools gave evidence of bigotry, Ireland decided to take the matter directly to President Harrison, to whom he wrote in August, 1889, citing instances of competent Catholic teachers who had been discharged by a Reverend Mr. Dorchester from the government school at Lawrence, Kansas, on the ground that there were too many Catholics in the Indian service, and of others who had been notified that they would not be needed after the end of the month. He concluded significantly:

I am most anxious for several reasons, most of which pertain to Catholics themselves, that no check be put to the drifting of their political allegiance to the Republican party. Democratic leaders have, in the past, been careful to urge upon them that the Democratic party alone promised them fair play, and a mere pretence will now be taken hold of by the same leaders to renew and strengthen their old calumnies.[4]

To this the President replied by expressing his regret that anyone had received the impression that there was any disposition in any department of the government to allow proscription of Catholics. He had never, he said, appointed anyone to office on the grounds of his membership in any church communion, but he insisted that those holding public office should exercise it solely with reference to the public good. He justified and gave reasons for the dismissals, and urged Ireland to investigate the cases thoroughly. He also told of his appointment of Catholics to conspicuous positions, and assured him that he would always listen with the greatest respect to any suggestions which he might make.[5]

Two months later the Archbishop, writing to Cardinal Gibbons of his visit to the President and of their discussion, continued to express his dissatisfaction with the attitude of the Indian Commissioner, Morgan, of whom he wrote: "I have no confidence in him. He is a bigot and a liar."[6]

As the Indian problem continued to cause apprehension, he had interviews with Secretary of the Interior Noble, in October, 1890, and with Commissioner Morgan in August, 1891. He also gave two interviews to a representative of the St. Paul *Pioneer Press,* in which he asserted that Mr. Herbert Welch did not approve the policy of Morgan, and he quoted a letter written by Welch to Cardinal Gibbons, attacking the appointments made by the Indian Office as unfair and asking protection for two Catholics who were in danger of losing their positions. In July, 1891, Morgan wrote to Ireland protesting that the latter had misunderstood his spirit and his methods, but that their differences were no reason why they could not work in harmony in elevating and Christianizing the Indians.[7] In the following year, Morgan, instead of encouraging the Catholic apostolate, depreciated its importance. Angered by criticism from the Catholic Indian Bureau, he announced that he would hereafter deal directly with the Indians and ignore the Bureau. After another series of conferences, the Archbishop so assuaged his wrath that Morgan increased by $40,000 the aid granted to the schools.[8]

Another source of discord was the question of the right of Indians to send their children to Catholic schools. The matter came up in 1894 and again in 1896, when D. M. Browning, Commissioner of Indian Affairs, in response to a question by an Indian agent as to "whether parents of Indian children shall have the right to decide where their children shall attend school," said: "It is your duty to first build up and maintain the government day schools, and the Indian parents have no right to designate which school their children shall attend." This so-called "Browning ruling" was the subject of discussion and protest for six years. The Catholic Board of Missions took up the matter and never relaxed its efforts to secure the abrogation of the order. Ireland appeared before the Indian Commission, W. A. Jones, and the Secretary of the Interior, Ethan Hitchcock, pointing out that the Indian parents should have the right to select schools in order that the religious education of the children be directed along desired lines. As a result of his arguments, Hitchcock rescinded the ruling, and Jones issued instructions that pupils must receive religious training in their own faith, that none might change his church membership without the consent of the parents, that proselyting must not be tolerated, and that denominations large enough to constitute a representative body must have their religious sensibilities respected by being excused from the general service.[9]

There was no interest of the Church which was alien to Archbishop Ireland. In the words of a writer in the *Catholic Register and Canadian Extension*, Toronto:

> In every crisis of Church and State, it was his voice that sounded the call to action, it was he who spoke for the Church in terms which no one might misunderstand. If the motives and purposes of the Catholic Church are better known and understood from end to end of the great Republic, and if she is regarded a tower of strength in all that makes for the permanency of national institutions, the credit must be given to him who had stood forth as the mouth-piece of the Catholic body when silence would have been a mistake. The people of the United States love and ad-

mire the strong, fearless, brainy churchman, whose first thought has not been of himself, but of the Church to whose service he consecrated his life, whose dominating principle has been to break down the walls of prejudice and to make the Church known and understood by his non-Catholic countrymen. He holds the first place in the affections of his countrymen. He has made the Church and country walk hand in hand.[10]

His was a life spent in battling for every cause in which the interests of religion and country were at stake. As we have seen, early in his career he entered upon a crusade that carried his name and influence far and wide through the country and that won for him the name of the Father Mathew of the West. His work for Catholic colonization directing the stream of immigration to the prairies of Minnesota is perpetuated in hundreds of homes in flourishing parishes of the Archdiocese.

The movement which he characteristically inaugurated and which was always dear to his heart aimed at nothing less than making the Church the supreme mistress of the new age which was dawning, and which he believed was to be the most fateful epoch in history since the days when God came on earth. He strove to make the Catholic Church a vital force in the life of the nations. To millions who knew nothing of the creed or the history of the Church, it was a new thought that the Catholic Church could be the stoutest bulwark of the institutions of the Republic of the West. Indeed, the relations of Church and State he kept steadily in the forefront of his addresses, on the one hand emphasizing the duty of patriotism for the Catholics of America, and on the other hand instilling into the minds of the people at large the conviction that in religion alone lies the safety of the nation. And America listened to him, as with prophet's fire he declared that the Catholic Church has been the defender of human liberty through the ages. America listened with growing respect to the man who dared to declare with singular boldness of thought and candor of expression that the aim of Catholics must be to make America Catholic.[11]

3. His Advice to Catholics

Sensitive to the honor of the Church he loved, the Archbishop did not allow her to be maligned, and he brought to her defense his learning, his enthusiasm, and his vigor of expression. But on more than one occasion he had warned Catholics not to mix religion and politics, and he found it necessary to re-emphasize that warning in

1884, when Father Young of the Paulist Society made a public statement that, although hitherto a Republican, he now felt compelled to vote the Democratic ticket, and that in his opinion seventy thousand other Catholics would do the same. His reason was that Republicans "sustain as far as they dare the movement set on foot by anti-Catholic bigots to abridge the civic and religious liberties of Catholics."[12] The Archbishop deprecated the introduction of the religious question, which he considered to be "without foundation in reason, unjust to a large portion of our fellow-citizens, and disastrous to the Catholic Church." The Church allied to one party is, he said, narrowed in her influence, dragged down from her high pedestal of universal teacher and guide, and exposed to the hatred and opposition of both parties.[13]

Toward the end of 1900 a federation of Catholic societies was being agitated, and a meeting in New York was proposed.[14] In March of the following year, Bishop McFaul of Trenton asked Archbishop Ireland's advice about the proposed federation, which, he said, aimed at the advancement of Catholics along social, civil, and religious lines. He had already outlined several plans of federation in an article in the *American Ecclesiastical Review,* in which he said that the union would promote good will among Catholics of all nationalities, would enable them to become better acquainted, and would be of assistance in finding employment and fostering Catholic literature, etc. There was no intention of forming a political party, and grievances such as the Indian school question would not be touched upon unless by the advice and at the request of the archbishops. The advantage of the federation was that in case of public protest against injustice the voice of millions would be heard.[15]

In his reply, the Archbishop expressed his belief that at the present juncture at least the federation would be hurtful, as it might give a pretext for the revival of A.P.A.-ism. Moreover, when the federation was first proposed, the idea went out that it was to be more or less political, and denials would now be ineffective. "Indeed," he said, "your own first article helped not a little to beget this idea, and many of those who wrote or spoke in favor of the Federation, quoted the Centrum in Germany and mentioned the need of massing Catholic votes." While it was true that Catholics did not get all the political recognition they deserved, Catholic newspapers exaggerated the grievances and used them for political purposes. Even on religious and social lines the federation would lead to a race for national superiority, and it would wear a foreign aspect. He suggested that it be killed at the coming Cincinnati meeting by Fabian policy. He concluded by saying that in some things called grievances Catholics were themselves to blame, as, for example, in the matter of Catholic chaplains and the loss of appropriations for Indian Catholic schools.[16]

As time went on, however, the Archbishop looked more favorably on the Federation and addressed its meeting in Milwaukee in August, 1913.[17] There he denied the charges made against Catholicism—that it is an alien institution, opposed to state schools and influenced in politics by ecclesiastical authority. Catholics, he said, demand only rights, not privileges. While he would have America Catholic, he did not imagine that the goal was near.

Archbishop Ireland was very sensitive to the overplaying of Catholic grievances. When Cardinal Gibbons informed him, in December, 1914, that Archbishop Messmer had requested him to confer with his two colleagues in the Sacred College as to the expediency of writing a letter of protest against the atrocities which were being perpetrated in Mexico, a protest which the Cardinal felt would have no effect on Carranza, Villa, and the other bandits who were snapping their fingers at the Washington administration, the Archbishop heartily agreed with him. He considered sufficient for all purposes the letter addressed some weeks earlier in the name of the hierarchy. Messmer and his suffragans he regarded as "fussy" people, who were unconscious of American public opinion and ready to embroil the Church in difficulties of any and every kind. The President was already quite anxious over the Mexican situation; a letter from three cardinals would be too solemn a document, and, in any case, Gibbons' name was "the only one that would have any weight."[18] The Archbishop had already said from his Cathedral pulpit that the United States stood responsible before the world for the preservation of order in Mexico, and should intervene to suppress the civil disorder and the persecution of the Church.[19]

In February, 1917, Monsignor Francis Clement Kelley, President of the Catholic Church Extension Society, wrote to him of the desire of Archbishop Ruiz of Morelia, Mexico, to enlist the support of the American hierarchy for a proposed protest of all the exiled bishops of Mexico in the United States against persecuting provisions of the new Mexican Constitution. When Ruiz suggested a conference with the American cardinals, Kelley told him that "it was my serious judgment that it would be much better to consult with your Grace, as I knew that your influence with the American people was greater than any other member of the American hierarchy, and that whatever you said would receive more consideration from the general public than the utterance of any other prelate. My words were repeated to the Delegate by the same Archbishop, and he immediately agreed."[20]

When the *Ave Maria* spoke of the lack of army chaplains and used the expression "we must bombard the episcopate," the Archbishop wrote to Father Hudson, pointing out that the regiments which he mentioned as lacking chaplains were mostly volunteer regiments, to which chaplains were appointed, not by the President but by governors of states, to whom the bishops should appeal. Neither he nor Archbishop Riordan had any trouble in having chaplains appointed, and neither would any other prelate if he tried.[21]

He wrote, in January, 1907, to the Catholic *Union and Times* to defend the Associated Press from the charge of sectarian bias, saying that he knew intimately the president, Melville Stone, and his assistant, who would not tolerate religious discrimination, and that while some Catholics complained that too little space was devoted to the Church, non-Catholic enemies complained that there was too much. The offices in London, Paris, and Rome were in charge of devout Catholics, and during the illness and death of Pope Leo, orders were issued from New York that everything should be said to honor the Holy Father.[22]

He also defended the United States Census Bureau against the charge of prejudice, denying the statement of the editor of the *Ave Maria* that the department of the Bureau which had been established with the idea of showing the relative strength of the various sects had been discontinued because its results favored the Church. He said that it was still active and in the charge of two gentlemen whom he knew personally to be just and fair-minded—Mr. Merriam and Mr. North. The latter had complained to him that it was very difficult to get from bishops and priests answers to his questionnaires, so that a request for more definite information had to be addressed to the archbishops through Cardinal Gibbons,[23] in response to which they appointed a special commission to consider ways of aiding the Bureau.

When Father Robert Hughes of Mankato, Minnesota, obtained an injunction against the reading of the Bible and the recitation of prayers in the public schools of that city, the Archbishop remonstrated with him. He foresaw much harm resulting in angry discussions, bitterness toward Catholics and non-Catholics, and intensification of the social and political war which was being waged against Catholics, and ultimately laws would be invoked against the use of religious garb in schools. Moreover, in many district schools in the Diocese of St. Cloud, Catholic symbols were not wanting in schoolrooms and Catholic teaching was given. In the contention of Father Hughes, therefore, Catholics were also lawbreakers. "And then," he said, "by excluding, in public schools, everything adverse to Catholic faith, you will open wider the road for Catholic children to enter them."[24]

4. HIS AFFECTION FOR THE PIONEERS

The Archbishop's heart was always in his diocese; he harked back with pride and affection to the early days of its history, and he took pains to hand on to posterity the memory of its pioneer missionaries. At the celebration of the Golden Jubilee of the dedication of the first church in St. Paul, on November 1, 1891, he gave a history of the beginnings of Christianity in the diocese and of the dedication of the first church in St. Paul, which measured twenty-seven by twenty-two feet, and which gave the city its name. He told of the dozen settlers and their families, who lived within call of the church—discharged soldiers, ex-employees of the American Fur Company, Swiss and Canadian refugees from Selkirk, who had been compelled to leave the reservation; of Parrant, the whisky seller, who was the first settler and from whom the name pig's eye was derived. He narrated the return of Loras from France, his visit to the few Catholics at St. Peter and Fort Snelling, the joy of the inhabitants, who had never seen a priest or a bishop before, of his visit to Kaposia and his royal reception by Chief Little Crow, and of the bloody battle between the Sioux and the Chippewas. He told of the coming of Galtier to Mendota in 1840 and traced his subsequent history. He sketched the work of Father Ravoux and of Bishop Cretin, who built a new church.[25]

The tearing down of this old brick structure in 1914 afforded the Archbishop a theme for his eloquence at the Cathedral, where he said:

There are, we are told, lessons in stones and running brooks. There are lessons too in the memories of the past. You have noticed as you approached this temple this morning the old brick building hard by, uncrowned, stripped of all its ornaments, standing solitary and without beauty on the eve of its final death and burial. And yet there was a day when this old building seemed to the inhabitants of St. Paul a stately magnificent edifice. And memories sweet and tender cling around the old building, making it this morning, despite all its present unsightliness, dear and precious.[26]

The Golden Jubilee of the diocese was celebrated on July 2, 1901, the anniversary of the coming of Bishop Cretin. Pontifical Mass was sung on the grounds of the St. Paul Seminary by Bishop James McGolrick. At three o'clock in the afternoon the Jubilee Fund and Memorial volumes were presented; at four the cornerstone of the Seminary Chapel was laid by Bishop James Trobec, and the sermon was preached by Bishop Thomas O'Gorman. The Mass was attended by ten prelates, more than four hundred priests, and eight thousand of the laity. The Archbishop preached at the Mass, telling of the two priests, Vivaldi and Ledon, and the three seminarians, Fayolle, Peyragrosse, and Legendre, who arrived with Cretin, of the churches of St. Peter and St. Paul, the Mission of St. Francis Xavier—later called St. Anthony—above the Falls of St. Anthony, and the mission at Pembina on the Canadian border. He contrasted the twenty-nine churches, thirty-five stations, twenty priests, five convents, and the Catholic population of fifty thousand, at the death of Cretin in 1857, with the six episcopal sees, six hundred priests, and a population of 400,000 in 1901.[27]

On the following day, a Mass of Requiem was said in the Cathedral, followed in the evening by a grand parade of Catholic societies and a public meeting in the St. Paul Auditorium, in which addresses were made by Judge William Kelly and by two old settlers, William Pitt Murray—a non-Catholic—and Auguste Larpenteur, who had resided in the city since 1843. The Jubilee was honored by letters from Pope Leo and the Apostolic Delegate, Archbishop Martinelli.

The affection of the Archbishop for the pioneer priests is shown in the sermons which he preached at their funerals. Monsignor Louis E. Caillet, Rector of the St. Paul Seminary and Vicar-General of the archdiocese, died on Sunday, November 28, 1897, after forty years in the priesthood. He was the fourth pastor of the original cathedral parish, the builder of St. Mary's School. He was one of the seven seminarians brought from France. For many years he ministered to the spiritual needs of the family of James J. Hill, and it was the latter's high regard for him that caused Mr. Hill to devote half a million dollars to the building of the St. Paul Seminary. The Archbishop paid glowing tribute to his zeal, his energy, his fidelity, his great personal virtues, and also the worth and character of the French priesthood. He said:

When we speak of the priesthood, the humanity of the priest must be forgotten. He is the bearer of Christ's cross, the speaker of Christ's truths to the world. If today the family is intact, it is because the priest in the name of Christ has spread about it a divine charm, silencing human passions and bidding the flowers of innocence grow within its portals. If social government is able by moral force to keep men together, it is because the word of God goes out from the priest, saying that authority is divine. If we are not pitted one against another because might is right, if we are not reduced to the lot of savages fighting for every small part of their possessions, it is because Christ has conquered and lives; it is because the moral life of humanity is made to endure through the reign of Christ, through Christ's ministers, working with Christ and in Christ's name.[28]

Monsignor Ravoux, who died on January 17, 1906, was the last link binding the ancient missionary days of the Northwest with our times. He saw St. Paul when it was a scattered Indian village, and he lived to witness it the capital of a great state, and a flourishing city of 200,000 inhabitants. He had the affection not only of the members of his church but of all who knew him. Born on January 11, 1815, at Langeac in Auvergne, France, he accepted the call of Loras and was one of the clerics who came to this country with him. He mastered the Sioux language, in which he wrote a catechism. For many years he was connected with the Cathedral under Grace and later under Ireland. He published his memoirs in English in 1890, and in French two years later.

At his funeral, on January 20, 1906, the Archbishop referred to him as the symbol and the representative of all the ancient memories of the time when the sole token of civilization found a home within the military garrison of Fort Snelling or at a few trading posts. All else was forest and prairie, tenanted only by the Indian and the buffalo. He told of his wandering with the Sioux from camp to camp, of his ministrations to the wounded and the dying massacred by the Chippewas, of days without rest or without food save for dog meat, and of his refusal to eat meat on Good Friday, although almost starved to death. He praised the devotion of the early priests who came into the wilderness to speak of God to the settlers engaged in the material things of the world—the search for earthly homes and earthly wealth. "Let one thing remain with us," he said, "the faith of the old missionaries. Let the gospel which they echoed be still heard by us. Without it what is our civilization but a shadow, and how long ever will that shadow last if at the foundation of all our efforts there is no thought or love of God."[29]

If the consecration of three bishops for three new sees was unique in the history of the Church in America, the consecration of six bishops on May 19, 1910, was still more remarkable. Of it Gibbons wrote to Ireland:

The consecration of six bishops by the same prelate, at the same time and for the same province, is not only a remarkable event, but is unprecedented in the annals of the American Church. One hundred years ago, the ordination of six priests for the same diocese at one time, would have evoked sentiments of surprise and gratification; the consecration of so many prelates is an evidence at the same time of the healthy growth of the Province of St. Paul and of the unceasing vigilance of its distinguished Metropolitan. God grant that the six prelates may be to your Grace a "corona ornatissima."[30]

The events leading up to the memorable service were the resignation of Bishop John Stariha of Lead, the death of Bishops Cotter and Shanley, the erection of the two new dioceses of Crookston and Bismarck, and the appointment of an auxiliary for St. Paul. The new members of the hierarchy were Bishops Joseph Busch for Lead, Patrick Heffron for Winona, James O'Reilly for Fargo, Timothy Corbett for Crookston, Vincent Wehrle for Bismarck, and John Lawler, Auxiliary for St. Paul. The consecration took place at the St. Paul Seminary in the presence of the Papal Delegate, Archbishop Diomede Falconio, sixteen prelates, 550 priests, and Governor Eberhart and his staff.

5. THE BUILDER

As it was love of the Church that, in the days of his boyhood, called John Ireland away from "things that savor more of earth and less of Heaven," so it was love of the Church that, at a time when most men are lightening their burdens, led him to undertake tasks the fulfillment of which would be deemed the work of a lifetime for men of less ardent zeal. Although at the turn of the century a wave of church and school building swept through St. Paul, it still left a void in his heart, for the ambition which he had long cherished to build a cathedral worthy of the archdiocese still remained unfulfilled. Fitting, indeed, it was that the boy who, a half-century before, had drifted on the tide of emigration to the banks of the Mississippi, and who had watched the frontier settlement grow into a great city, should crown the metropolis of his state with a temple that for ages to come would lift heavenward the thoughts of all whose eyes rested upon its majestic beauty. As early as 1887 he began to plan it and on his visit to Europe he secured plans of prominent churches. He even had hopes that it would be completed for dedication in 1892, the

semicentennial of the dedication of the first little log chapel. But a
crop blight and financial panic intervened, and it was not until the
spring of 1904 that he was able to initiate his project. On Holy Thursday evening, putting his trust in the Providence of God, he made his
final decision. A week later he purchased property on the brow of
St. Anthony's Hill, overlooking the city. Steps were taken to remove
any building which might obstruct the view. For architect he chose
Emmanuel Masqueray, a pupil of noted French artists, a laureate
student of the Ecole des Beaux Arts of Paris, a restorer of one of the
great French cathedrals, and the chief designer of building of the
Louisiana Purchase Exposition in St. Louis. Ground was broken in
August, 1906, and on June 2, 1907, in the presence of five archbishops,
twenty-five bishops, scores of priests, and thousands of laymen, the
cornerstone was laid. Among those present was Isaac Labisonniere,
who had helped to build the first little log chapel in 1841. The contrast between the thirteen families that worshiped in the first chapel
and the thirty thousand men who marched in parade to the site of
the Cathedral was eloquent testimony to the marvelous growth of
the archdiocese in threescore years. The ceremonies were conducted
by Bishop James McGolrick of Duluth, the sermon was preached by
the Archbishop. Addresses of felicitation were made by Governor
John A. Johnson representing the state, Senator Moses Clapp speaking for the nation, Mayor Herbert Keller heralding the pride of the
city, and Judge William Kelly voicing the joy of the Catholic laity.[31]

In his sermon the Archbishop recalled the early days of the diocese,
telling of the first offering of Mass on November 1, 1841, in a chapel
twenty-four feet in length and sixteen in width, erected at a cost of
seventy-five dollars—"all that the poverty of the givers could afford."
Those were primitive days, but "fields and hillsides yielded their
treasures; skies melted down their dews and rains; lakes and rivers
opened highways to commerce; and man, great in thought, great in
strength, bade all things move and fructify." Then he launched into
one of his favorite topics—the relations of science and religion and
the limitations of the former and its inability to satisfy the highest
aspirations of man. He spoke of "an all-ruling intelligence, ever instilling into the things beneath order and beauty, ever guiding all
contingent things in power and wisdom to the ends toward which
they tend and in which alone they reach completeness." In a magnificent apostrophe he concluded his discourse:

Upward then, high upon this fair-viewing hilltop, rise, noble Cathedral;
rise in the name of Almighty God, in the name of the supreme teacher,

Jesus Christ, and day by day, night by night, speak to the people beneath and around thee: "Get thee up upon a high mountain, thou that bringest good tidings of Zion; lift up thy voice with strength, thou that bringest good tidings of Jerusalem; lift it up, fear not, say to the cities of Judaea—fear thy God. Behold the Lord thy God shall come with strength, and his arm shall rule; behold his reward is with Him and His work is before Him."

In architectural design the Cathedral is a modification of the Renaissance; that is, the classic design is so modified that it is wholly twentieth century in spirit and in purpose, yet much of the imposing beauty and dignity of the medieval churches is embodied in its composition. The general outline, like that of St. Peter's, Rome, defines the form of a cross; other reminders of the "mother of churches" are the ambulatories or aisles between the main body of the church and the surrounding chapels. But, unlike the medieval churches, the transepts are wider and the nave is shorter than those in its historic models. Like the original St. Peter's, as designed by Michelangelo, the dome surmounts the intersection of nave and transepts, making the main feature of the architectural composition. Beneath a monumental arch framing a beautiful rose window is the main entrance; above the arch is the figure of Christ surrounded by His apostles. Crowning the granite columns are two figures representing Science and Religion.

The Cathedral is notable for the number and the beauty of its chapels. In the ambulatory which skirts the apse are six shrines of the nations, dedicated to Sts. Anthony, John the Baptist, Boniface, Theresa, Patrick, and Cyril and Methodius. In the body of the church are the chapels of St. Peter, the Sacred Heart, the Blessed Virgin, and St. Joseph.

The main nave is sixty feet in width and eighty-four in height. Running parallel to it on both sides and separated from it by imposing piers are the ambulatories, twelve feet in width, giving easy access to all parts of the nave and to the chapels of the Blessed Virgin and St. Joseph. The great dome, 168 feet in height and 96 in diameter, is lighted by 24 windows. The transepts, of the same dimensions as the nave, have exquisite rose windows. The sanctuary, which occupies the whole apse, is sixty feet in width and sixty-five in length. The bronze grilles behind the altar are surmounted by full-size figures representing seven episodes in the life of St. Paul, beginning with his conversion and ending with his martyrdom. The outside dimensions of the Cathedral, which has a seating capacity of three thousand, are: length, 274 feet; width, 216; height, 294.

The Cathedral compares favorably with the best art produced in the United States. When Count Galeazzi, a noted architect in Rome, came to St. Paul with Cardinal Pacelli in October, 1936, he set out on a sightseeing tour but got no farther than the Cathedral. Returning to the Archbishop's residence just as the Cardinal and Bishop Spellman were leaving to take a walk, he exclaimed: "Would you see something magnificent, something stupendous in its beauty, go to the Cathedral." Marcel Dupré, the great French organist, called it one of the most magnificently proportioned churches into which he had ever stepped. Pope Benedict XV wrote of it: "This Cathedral has grown into a temple of such amplitude and such magnitude and such elegance of form as truly to merit to be called monumental."

Great bishops are often great church builders, and to this Archbishop Ireland was no exception. Not satisfied with constructing a magnificent cathedral in St. Paul, he planned at the same time a basilica for Minneapolis. On a block of ground fronting Hennepin Avenue, one of the main thoroughfares of that city, the Basilica of St. Mary towers above all the surrounding buildings. The ground, donated by Mr. L. S. Donaldson, one of the most successful businessmen of the city, was broken for the foundation in August, 1907, and on May 31 of the following year the cornerstone was laid by the Apostolic Delegate, Archbishop Diomede Falconio. A procession of twenty thousand Catholic men passed before him. Archbishop Ireland preached the sermon.[32]

In the center of the façade above the central tower is a rose window twenty-four feet in diameter, over which is a statue of the Assumption. The great dome, which rises above the sanctuary, is a square structure with buttressed corners carrying three windows on either side. The dome is surmounted by a cross two hundred feet above the foundation. The magnificent arched ceiling, the roomy sanctuary, fifty by sixty-five feet, the spacious nave unbroken by a single pillar— the widest church nave in the world—the lightsome windows, produce a beauty of interior in harmony with that of the exterior. In addition to the Chapel of the Virgin there are four others, dedicated to the Curé d'Ars, St. Teresa, St. Anne, and St. Anthony. The outer dimensions are: length, 278 feet; width, 120; height, 187. The height from the sanctuary floor to the dome ceiling is 138 feet; the height of the altar, which is surmounted by a nine-foot statue of Our Lady of Grace, is forty feet. The sacristy is twenty-eight feet wide by forty-five feet long. The church has a seating capacity in the pews of sixteen hundred, but is capable of accommodating thirty-five hundred.

A bronze plaque commemorating the centenary of Ireland's birth was erected in the Basilica by Monsignor James M. Reardon and dedicated by Archbishop John Gregory Murray on September 11, 1938. It shows a lifelike three-quarter face and bust of the prelate in bas relief in a sunken panel garlanded with laurel leaves. The head is well poised, the features are strong and expressive; the whole bearing is suggestive of physical strength and intellectual vigor. In the right upper corner is his coat of arms, the escutcheon displaying an erect Sioux Indian in feathered headdress and blanket, the left hand resting on the hilt of a naked sword, the right holding aloft a cross, and beneath it is the motto "Omnibus Omnia Factus Sum" (I became all things to all men). The crook of the crozier above the shield is copied from the pastoral staff carried by the Archbishop in religious functions. Below the medallion are two flags with staffs crossed— the Stars and Stripes and the Church Flag of the Army, the former a symbol of Ireland's devotion to American ideals, the latter recalling his services as chaplain of the Fifth Minnesota regiment. The lower half of the memorial chronicles the chief events of his life and concludes with the words: "A great prelate who in his days pleased God and wrought wonderful things for the Church."

6. HIS ROLE IN THE ESTABLISHMENT OF THE PAPAL DELEGATION

There was something beautiful and inspiring in Archbishop Ireland's devotion to the papacy. As has been said, "he treasured every word of exhortation, of command, that issued from the source of Apostolic Authority." His best literary work was done in defense of the rights of the Holy See, and no prelate of his day did more than he to inspire obedience, reverence, and love for the person of the Pontiff. His loyalty was shown in his co-operation in the establishment of a Papal Delegation in Washington, in the many tributes which he paid to Pope Leo XIII, in his articles and speeches in defense of the Temporal Power, and in his vindication of the Vatican policy in the Fairbanks and Roosevelt incidents.

He played a unique role in the coming of an Apostolic Delegate to the United States. When the matter of sending a papal representative was first broached, it met with very little enthusiasm on the part of the episcopacy. It had always been the dream of Pius IX, who sent Archbishop Bedini on a mission that ended in failure. Leo XIII urged it more than once on the American bishops, only to be told each time that a delegate was unnecessary, and that his presence would inflame the bigoted and encourage the insubordinate. When the archbishops were invited to come to Rome in 1883 to prepare the plans and material for the Third Council of Baltimore, which was to be convened in the following year, the Pope wished to appoint Bishop Sepiacci to preside at the Council, but at the request of the prelates he substituted Archbishop Gibbons. And at the Council, in the discussions concerning the establishment of parishes and the selection of irremovable rectors without process, the bishops were unwilling to carry out the instructions indicated in Rome in the previous year until Gibbons warned them that such was the decision of the Holy See, and that if they did not yield, an Italian delegate would be appointed who would restrict their authority.[33]

The Holy See proceeded cautiously, first sending Archbishop Satolli in 1889 to represent the Pope at the Centenary of the Establishment of the Hierarchy at Baltimore and the inauguration of the Catholic University at Washington. It found its real opportunity in 1892, when Secretary of State Foster asked the Vatican to send an exhibit to the Columbian Exhibition, which was to be held in Chicago the following year. Cardinal Rampolla granted the request, at the same time indicating the intention of the Pope to send a representative. Satolli arrived on October 12 and, on reaching New York, received all the official courtesies of the government.

Archbishop Ireland was well aware of the mind of the Holy Father. From Genoa he wrote to Cardinal Gibbons in June, 1892: "The Pope has taken occasion from our controversies to revive the talk of a Delegate."[34] After returning to this country he heard frequently on the subject from Monsignor O'Connell, who informed him in August that he had had a long conversation with the Pontiff, that all arrangements had been made for Satolli to leave in the middle of October, attend the dedication services, and return to Washington, where he would remain at the University for the first year at least. "There were," he said, "but two occasions possible, since he must go under cover of the Exposition, either the dedication or the opening next May. His instructions must be made out just now under the influence of the favorable sentiments that are dominant at present. Then those instructions and those influences will help shape all the future."[35]

It seems clear that while the Archbishop was in Rome he and O'Connell arranged with the Vatican the whole matter of the delegation, for in September, 1892, the latter wrote:

I am just from the Vatican where I communicated the news. You are a big man there today. The significance of the event is duly appreciated.

Satolli has not the official title of Delegate. His letter states that he goes on a temporary mission. He is commended especially to your care. . . . I saw the Pope yesterday. He said: "*Satolli mettera Corrigan al muro.*" This mission perpetuates your victory and gives you independence.[36]

And a year later, Ireland said to O'Connell: "His coming saved me. Our night's deliberation was divinely directed."[37]

Satolli arrived on October 12, 1892, and, after paying his respects to Cardinal Gibbons and President Harrison,[38] went to make an extended visit to Archbishop Ireland. During his stay he visited the educational institutions, St. Joseph's Academy and St. Thomas Seminary, receiving in the latter school addresses in several languages, to which he replied in Ciceronian Latin. He also pontificated in the Cathedral.

The Archbishop and his guest went together to the meeting of the archbishops in New York, held on November 16, 1892, where Satolli, after defending the position of the Archbishop on the school question, broached the subject of the desirability of appointing a permanent delegate, a suggestion received with anything but enthusiasm. When, on the following day, the metropolitans had not given an answer, he took occasion to remind them of it and hoped that they would freely express their opinion. He then withdrew so that they might discuss the matter. After some deliberation they informed him that they did not feel warranted in taking any action on so important a matter until they had the benefit of counsel with their suffragans. The mind of Cardinal Gibbons was shown in a letter to Archbishop Corrigan, in which he suggested that the Holy Father should merely be thanked for sending "so learned and excellent a representative on a temporary mission." When a few days later information reached the Vatican that neither the scholastic propositions presented by Satolli nor the project of a permanent delegation would receive united and harmonious support, a cable dispatch from Rome to the New York *Tribune* told of the surprise and vexation of the Vatican at the opposition manifested at the conference.[39]

Those who were not in the secret had erroneous views concerning the status and the powers of Satolli and expressed their opinions openly, much to their later embarrassment. Condé Pallen, editor of *Church Progress,* said that Satolli had come simply to represent the Holy Father at the World's Fair. Bishop John Lancaster Spalding, outspoken as usual, stated that the establishment of a permanent Papal Delegation would be a stupendous disaster, that the idea was mischievous and full of evil to the American Church.[40] Great must have been their chagrin when within a month word came that Satolli had been appointed permanent Delegate. O'Connell felt that some inconveniences would be involved in the appointment but that "it had to be accepted under the present stress." He told of the opposition to the Delegate in Rome, all the enemies of Satolli, Ireland, and the Pope uniting to make the mission a failure and then to proceed to make it tell on the Pope's republican policy in general. Cardinal Parocchi, he said, regarded the sending of Satolli the master mistake of the Pope. The Propaganda was indignant because it had not been consulted about the appointment; "Ledochowski broke from Rampolla and joined the Triplice." Rampolla, at first much embarrassed at the opposition, "soon took fire at hearing the truth and answered the attacks by making the delegation permanent."[41] Among the opponents he mentioned the Jesuits, but a representative of the Society of Jesus was quoted as saying: "It is absolutely false that we opposed Mgr. Satolli. Far from having opposed him, we have been his warmest friends. We are opposed to Archbishop Ireland and make no secret of it." Ireland, he said, was too fond of accusing the Society of plotting against him, and in a secret document addressed to certain cardinals had accused them of leaguing themselves throughout the world to injure him. Their hostility, the Jesuit said, was not personal—they admired his talents and character—but they objected to his ideas on the religious orders, on education, and on the relations of Church and State.[42] On the other hand, Father Salvatore Brandi, editor of the *Civiltà Cattolica*, organ of the Jesuits, told Father René Holaind that Satolli "inspired no doubt by Archbishop Ireland & Co." had written to the Pope, complaining of the opposition of the Jesuits in the United States to the Apostolic Delegation, that the Holy Father had protested to the Father General of the Society, and that he (Brandi) was ordered by the Vatican to write an article favorable to the Delegation, which he did *"in timore et tremore"* (in fear and trembling).[43]

The Delegate, who had taken up his residence at the Catholic University, was not in the country two months before attacks appeared in the press, asserting that his mission was a failure and that he would be recalled to Rome. This Ireland denied, averring that Satolli represented the Pope and that opposition to him was opposition to the Pontiff.[44] He also expressed his satisfaction when he was informed of the establishment of the Delegation, which, he said, was a complete answer to those opposed to Satolli's authority.[45] Indeed, so strong was the Archbishop's defense of Satolli that O'Connell was moved to write: "It is no longer your fight or mine, and it seems to me it would be a mistake to make it so. It is the fight of the Pope for his delegate, and you have no better time to retire. The victory remains, cannot be undone, and the laurels should not be risked for trifles."[46]

Neither did the Delegate make any secret of his friendship for the Archbishop. He paid a second visit to St. Paul in August, 1893, and, at a reception given in his honor at the Ryan Hotel, said that when he came to the United States he brought two letters from Cardinal Rampolla, one to Gibbons, the other to Ireland, and that he had heard from the lips of the Holy Father that, while holding in veneration and love all the prelates of the American Church, yet he had a special esteem and affection for the Archbishop, "whose personal fame had made the city's name like unto itself—world-wide."

But the Archbishop's friendship did not help the Delegate, who had arrived at a very unfortunate period in the history of the Church in the United States. The bitterness engendered by the controversies centering around Cahenslyism and the school question was intense, and the episcopate was sharply divided. The establishment of the Delegation was commonly regarded as a triumph for Ireland, and, if the coming of Satolli had not been popular with those bishops who were opposed to the appointment of any foreigner, his identification with the Archbishop antagonized others. This was especially true of the Archdiocese of New York and of Archbishop Corrigan in particular, who was gravely irritated by the decisions given by Satolli in the cases of some refractory priests—Fathers Edward McGlynn, Richard Burtsell, and Thomas Ducey, whom he restored to good standing without paying too much attention to Corrigan's feelings. The bitterness continued to grow in intensity, and, as happened in the case of the other controversies, this one also made its appearance in the press. To the great scandal of the people articles appeared almost daily in the leading newspapers containing attacks on Archbishop Corrigan and his suffragans on the one hand, and, on the other, on the Delegate, Archbishop Ireland, and his friends, Cardinal Gibbons and Bishop Keane.[47] The headlines screamed of the "Conflict in the Catholic Church," "The Politico-Religious Dispute," "Rumors of Church Intrigue," and "A Brutal Attack upon the Apostolic Delegate." One particularly vicious article entitled "Catholicism and Satollicism" appeared in the New York *Sun* over the signature of "An American Catholic," defending Corrigan and telling of the dissatisfaction engendered by the coming of the Delegate. To those who had long regarded the Church, its officials, and its members as a well-rounded and thoroughly disciplined whole it was difficult to understand the widespread dissension, the bitterness of discussion, and the charges and countercharges with which the air was filled. Nor was the controversy confined to America; it furnished material for many a European publication. The matter did not end with merely sensational stories of intrigue; charges of conspiracy became common. When the verdict of the archbishops on the establishment of the Delegation was slow in reaching Rome, Cardinal Gibbons was accused of purposely delaying it. Under headings of "The Catholic World Shaken by a Scandalous Plot Against Papal Authority" and "The Conspiracy Unmasked," the Sunday Chicago *Post* indicted Archbishop Corrigan, Father Lavelle of St. Patrick's Cathedral, and Father Gerardo Ferrante, the Archbishop's secretary, for having supplied articles to the press.[48] Archbishop Ireland told Cardinal Gibbons that he had seen the autograph letters of Corrigan and Lavelle, one addressed to a reporter, the other to Maurice Francis Egan, who refused, however, to be involved in the controversy.[49] He also told O'Connell that Michael Walsh, editor of the *Catholic Herald*, once an agent of Corrigan, had turned on him and given to Satolli Corrigan's letters showing his connection with the war against the Delegation. "One of the worst articles," he said, "was written by Corrigan himself, who enclosed it in a letter to Walsh, in which he told him to 'Change a few words, so that I can say that the article is not mine.'"[50]

In an interview concerning the conspiracy given to a representative of the *Evening Post*, the Archbishop said:

It is not proper for me, in my present manner of viewing things, to talk publicly on the conspiracy against Msgr. Satolli and myself. I am not the sole one attacked; the arrows winged toward me are bidden to seek higher victims, some of whom are others than Msgr. Satolli. These can care for themselves and need no word of help from St. Paul.[51]

Cardinal Gibbons and Archbishop Ryan, who had expressed sorrow for the discord in the episcopate, used their influence to bring about better relations between His Grace of New York and the Delegate, for Corrigan made a sudden *volte-face* and in August, 1893, invited Satolli to pontificate at St. Patrick's Cathedral, where Corrigan protested his loyalty, surrendered unreservedly. He considered it humiliating that it should ever become necessary to deny even the thought that he should have been disloyal.

This reconciliation took place only two months after Ireland had written to Gibbons of his visit in Chicago with Satolli, who, he said, was "confirmed in truth and grace, far more advanced in all our ideas than we are ourselves."[52] When he heard of the rapprochement in St. Patrick's he presumed that the Cardinal had arranged it, and he expressed to him his misgivings about the outcome and his fears that "many poisoned shafts would be aimed at the Delegate's ear."[53]

Archbishop Ireland basked in the warmth of Satolli's friendship for three years, but the time came when there was a parting of their ways. What the reason was, no one had been able to discover, not even the Archbishop, who, after Satolli's return to Rome, urged O'Connell to attempt to ascertain it. Was it the influence of Monsignor Schroeder of the Catholic University, was it pressure from Rome, which must have grown weary of the discord in the American episcopate, or was it Satolli's own conviction that in his identification with Ireland he had alienated many powerful and influential ecclesiastics? Whatever the cause, little by little he began to loose the ties and to recover his independence of action, so that by the time he returned to Rome he seemed to have completely gone over to the opposition. As a writer in the *Giornale d'Italia* expressed it: "When he came to America he had been filled with enthusiasm for everything American; when he left, he had become the bosom friend of the anti-Americanists, had gone bag and baggage into the camp of Mazzella."[54] O'Connell, who had noticed his intimacy with the Jesuit Cardinal, felt that trouble was brewing.[55]

The first clear indication of the change came in April, 1895, when Satolli spoke at the laying of the cornerstone of the St. John the Baptist School in Pottsville, Pennsylvania. There he said: "I am completely convinced of the sincerity of those sentiments which animate the German American Catholics." He praised them for their spirit of love for one another, said that they and their priests had become the subject of false charges and accusations, urged them to "so live among those who revile you that they may cite as your characteristic mark that you are Christians," approved of their good family traditions as well as their mother tongue, and paid tribute to their aid to education. "The German American Catholics," he said, "can point with confidence to the results which education in the parochial school has achieved."[56]

Satolli also pontificated at the opening of Forty Hours' Devotion at St. Mary's German Church in Washington. Monsignor Joseph Schroeder, who preached, made reference to the fact that the people of St. Mary's used the German language in their worship because it was the one in which they had been taught religion in their infancy, and they could better praise God in the language of their fatherland. At the dinner which followed, Satolli said he was fully persuaded that, if left to the operation of natural causes, the question of amalgamation of the various races coming to this country would solve itself without disturbance or difficulty, and that the interference by violence in either one direction or the other could only be productive of bad results and retard the solution of the question itself.[57]

These statements must have sounded ominous to Archbishop Ireland, who did not, however, have long to wonder, for actions followed words, and more and more Satolli became identified with the opposition.

The Delegate showed the state of his mind when he left the country without paying Cardinal Gibbons the usual visit of courtesy. He went first to the residence of Bishop Wigger of Newark and afterwards to the home of John D. Keiley in Brooklyn. There Ireland and O'Gorman called upon him; the Archbishop spoke his mind freely and fearlessly and "rebuked him to his face."[58] The cause of his wrath was the removal of Bishop John J. Keane from the Catholic University, an action which left Ireland aghast and scarcely able to conceal his feelings. While he gave the press a very correct interview on the incident, he said that it was probable that the Bishop would be re-elected by the Board of Trustees.[59] When Father Alphonse Magnien, Rector of St. Mary's Seminary, Baltimore, sent him a copy of the protest which Cardinal Gibbons thought of forwarding to Rome in the name of the Directors of the University, he approved of it "on condition that not one word be taken from it." Recent occurrences, he said, showed them the necessity of being frank and courageous, as Satolli was evidently determined to sustain his action toward Bishop Keane by arraigning others, Gibbons included, "and," he said, "if we lie down as cowards we shall be the others."[60] He wrote a strong letter to Cardinal Rampolla and also two to Satolli, demanding from him a denial or a confirmation of statements Satolli was said to have made concerning him.[61] Bishop McQuaid's reaction to Keane's removal was a shout of joy: "What collapses on every side, Gibbons, Ireland and Keane. They were cock of the walk for a while and dictated to the country and thought to run our diocese for us."[62] Rumors were even spread that Gibbons and Ireland might also be removed from their sees. To quiet these, Archbishop Sebastian Martinelli, the new Delegate, wrote to Gibbons that he had communicated these reports to Rome and had received word from Rampolla that the Pope was distressed by the news, and that the assertion was a lie.[63]

Attacks on Archbishop Ireland became more frequent in Europe, two defamatory articles appearing in the *Italie*. The New York *Journal* published the statement that Satolli had called him "the Apostle of Heresy."[64] *La Croix* averred that he had made *naufragium fidei*. Satolli denied the charge, and in an interview with a correspondent of the Baltimore *Sun* he told of his sentiments of profound veneration, friendship, and gratitude for the whole American hierarchy. "Without prejudice to the feelings I have towards any one else," he protested, "I have this sentiment in regard to Cardinal Gibbons, Archbishop Ireland and Archbishop Corrigan, for from these I have received special testimony of their affection for me." He then went on to say that he had visited various religious institutions, which, he knew, were working for and with the episcopate, "especially the Jesuits, who are now accused of being partisans—an accusation which is a gross calumny."[65] This interview did not achieve its purpose either in Rome or in America, the two Vannutellis not having words to express their disgust at the "whitewashing,"[66] and Keane writing from Rome that Satolli and Mazzella had opened war on Americanism.[67] Neither did the letter which Satolli wrote to Ireland and in which he said concerning his audience with the Pope:

> And among other things I wish to say that I did not fail to testify to the Holy Father how sincerely and loyally you are devoted to the Holy See and to the sacred Person of the Holy Father, with what zeal and efficiency you work untiringly for the welfare of the Church in the United States. Nor did I forget to speak in regard to Msgr. Keane, and I set before the Holy Father my opinion that at a time not far distant he repeat in ways suggestive of a father the expression of his desire (certainly not using any form of will or command) that Msgr. Keane make his decision to come and establish himself in Rome, where the Holy Father will honor him with the title of archbishop and assistant at the throne.[68]

Of this the Archbishop wrote to Gibbons, with a wry smile: "Wasn't his letter sweet?"[69] If Ireland encouraged Keane to go, he had his own reasons for doing so. He wrote to Magnien:

> Bp. Keane has recovered himself; and he is willing to be the soldier rather than the hermit. He has realized that he is disgraced, that he must fight for his honor, and for the cause which he represented. He goes to

Rome, nominally as "conciliarius," really in order to fight Satolli and
Satolli's allies. I have written to Rampolla that I will go to Rome soon after
McKinley's inauguration. I shall wait until I can go with all the prestige of
my American influence. This influence is, thank God, immense just now.

Satolli has killed himself. Stand by Bishop Keane and myself—ask
Cardinal Gibbons to stand by us, and *"Loquemur victorias."*[70]

Satolli wrote later that he had arranged for Keane to live at San
Silvestro and that he would be Archpriest and Canon at St. John
Lateran. He also said that he had explained to the Pope the meaning
of the words which Ireland had used of the religious orders. He
wrote:

I said that it was the mind of your Grace that every bishop ought to use
all care that the diocesan clergy emulate the religious in doctrine, zeal and
piety, and so every bishop should have his own subjects for the spiritual
and intellectual needs of his diocese. The Holy Father told me some time
ago that such was his advice from the beginning, when he was Bishop of
Perugia. Nevertheless, it is only reasonable and right that the great merits
of the Religious Orders be recognized and appreciated. The Pope is glad
that the newspaper controversy is over and that your Grace has good relations with the Archbishop of New York, who assured me that he had a
sincerely fraternal attitude towards you.[71]

In spite of these letters, however, Satolli did not overexert himself
for Keane, whose letters to Ireland reveal the struggle he was forced
to make for recognition in Rome. After a very satisfactory audience
with the Holy Father, he wrote:

The Pope sees that he was duped into an action whose bearing he did
not suspect. You may imagine this did not please him. Now he is eager
to repair the mischief, and so all has turned in favor of the good cause
which we represent. They appreciate also what your power now is in
America, and how important is your plan in regard to the ministers to
Paris and the Quirinal. Your getting those matters into good shape will be
of immense weight in the Vatican. So your stock never was higher, if as
high.

He also conveyed the interesting information that Satolli was *"directed* by the Pope to write the letter [to Ireland], and that was
taking things back badly for him." Keane realized the power of those
who were working against him—Ledochowski, who did not want
him in the Propaganda, the Jesuits, and Satolli.[72] He asked Ireland
to write on his behalf to Rampolla urging that the promise of a con-
sultorship be kept. Finally, through the intervention of Cardinal
Vincenzo Vannutelli, he secured the appointment.[73]

Rather formal letters continued to come from Satolli, who, in his role as Prefect of the Congregation of Studies, expressed the hope that in doctrine and in discipline the St. Paul Seminary was conformed to the spirit of the Church and solidly attached to the Holy See. After receiving a copy of the Seminary catalogue, he voiced his dissatisfaction with the program of philosophical studies, too much attention being given to the natural sciences and too little to the speculative and moral. He was afraid lest the large number of subjects studied would not allow the students sufficient time to know St. Thomas thoroughly. He concluded his letter with this amusing remark: "Finally allow me to express my amazement that on page 27, among the authors to be consulted I find the Angelic Doctor placed between Spencer and Kant, which made me think of Jesus Christ placed between two thieves."[74] His later correspondence, during 1901 and 1902, deals largely with the proposal of the American government to purchase as a residence for the American Ambassador to the Quirinal the Palazzo Farnese, for which Satolli hoped it would pay one million dollars.[75]

But again the years brought their changes, and, partly because some bitter opponents had left the scene and partly because Ireland knew how to stoop to conquer, gradually the old friendship was revived. Satolli gave indications of a changed attitude in late 1902, when he successfully advocated the promotion to the rectorship of the Catholic University of America of Monsignor O'Connell, who had formerly been dismissed from his position at the North American College. This action brought great delight to Ireland who wrote to Gibbons in March, 1903:

And so we have Mgr. O'Connell. What a revolution in the temper of Rome there is implied in this nomination. Even at this late day it is difficult for me to realize it. In a letter I received not long ago from Cardinal Satolli, in which mention is made of this change of manner in Rome, he says in explanation—"certain prelates having gone to a better life." It would look as if Satolli himself had not been in his heart so much of an enemy of ours—but had rather yielded to pressure from others, from whom he is now glad to recover.[76]

And O'Connell wrote: "It seems as if with the vanishing of Ledochowski and Corrigan the clouds begin to break."[77] Satolli not only spoke to the Pope and various cardinals in favor of the former rector and placed a memorandum in the hands of Cardinal Girolamo Gotti, the new Prefect of the Propaganda, but he also assured O'Connell that no matter what names might be placed on the list for the rectorship his would come out ahead.[78]

When Satolli returned to America in July, 1904, he again visited Ireland, and once more a reception was arranged for him at the Ryan Hotel, which was attended by thousands of people. The reception lasted two hours, during which the Cardinal, standing between Archbishops Ireland and Redwood of New Zealand, received the greetings of the citizens.[79] Thus was re-established a friendship, which lasted until the death of the Cardinal in 1910. Satolli labored unceasingly to secure for Ireland that recognition which so many hoped would one day be his.

7. His Devotion to the Papacy

Archbishop Ireland's devotion to the Holy See is also shown in the many tributes which he paid to the papacy. One of his earliest sermons on the papacy was delivered in his Cathedral on the first Sunday of December, 1887, on the occasion of Leo's Golden Jubilee. He developed at length the various facets of the personality of the Pontiff—Leo the man of his times, the wise teacher, the great teacher, the great statesman. He recounted his own reactions at an audience:

It has been my privilege to see, to study near by, to converse with Leo XIII. Delicious moments, those passed in his presence. Sitting at his side, watching the play of his grand soul upon his countenance, replying to his anxious inquiries, drawing from him words of wise counsel, I was enraptured with his sweetness of manner, his kindness of heart, and I admired in him the great master mind soaring into higher regions of thought, reading aright and at a glance the world's enigmas, understanding all its woes, solving all its problems.[80]

In the Church of San Andrea della Valle, Rome, in May, 1892, he referred to him as the real friend of democracy, encouraging the poor to better their condition and blessing all social endeavors to help the masses.[81] In his Cathedral, after his return from Rome, he preached on "Leo the Pontiff of the Age," who maintained the golden mean between ultraconservatism, which clogs the wheels of progress, and ultraliberalism, which, in its ambition to master the present, imperils principle and gives way to imprudent precipitancy of action.[82] When Leo sent a letter to the president of the European Commission of the Chicago World's Fair, the Archbishop took the occasion to pay tribute to the Pope's acuteness of mind, the depth and universality of his knowledge, his ability to go at once to the heart of a subject and to reply in concise, pregnant phrases.[83] In his address at the Silver Jubilee of Cardinal Gibbons, in October, 1893, he praised Leo's spirit of progress in bidding the age to go forward in its discoveries and inventions and in opening to the scholarship of the world the archives of the Vatican.[84] Upon receipt of the news of the death of the Pontiff he bewailed the passing of "an orb of light such as is seldom seen to dominate the high skies of the moral and intellectual firmament."[85] Finally, at the conferring of the pallium upon Archbishop Glennon of St. Louis, in May, 1905, he said that "Leo rose into the highest altitudes accessible to human genius, and with him rose into sublime mountain tops the spiritual power of Rome."[86]

Nowhere, perhaps, was the Temporal Power of the Sovereign Pontiff more grievously misunderstood than in the United States. Suspicions had to be allayed, prejudices removed, public opinion enlightened. This task the Archbishop undertook, pleading with voice and pen that, as the Catholic Church is the church of all nations, its Supreme Chieftain must be of no nation, but have a territory of his own where all nations are at home, and where no nation is master. "Will any one assert," he asked, "that it is merely a right to what is vitally essential to its life and its author, or that it was not the intention of its Founder that it should not always have that integrity of outward form and freedom of action required for the exercise of its ministry with dignity and efficiency?" Cogent reasons drawn from the mission of the Church, telling historical illustrations, testimonies cited from friend and foe drove home his powerful plea. History, he said, bears witness that whenever the Pope has been temporarily under the domination of a king or empire the church has fared ill. Nor must the Head of the world Church ever be a bishop of Italy, the court chaplain of Italy's sovereign.[87] Whoever reads the Archbishop's article on the Civil Princedom of the Pope in the *North American Review* for March, 1901, will see him at his best as an apologist and will be filled with fresh wonder at the justice of the Pontiff's claims for the independence essential to the exercise of his high office.

His wonderful tribute to Leo XIII—the tribute of a great Bishop to a great Bishop of Bishops—was worthy of him who wrote it and of him who was its theme. His matchless exposition of the Civil Princedom of the Supreme Pontiff carried light and conviction to thousands outside the Church, for whom the Temporal Power of the Pope was a stumbling block.

Even as a young priest he had defended the Temporal Power. As early as January, 1871, he organized a huge protest against the interference of Victor Emmanuel with the Pope's sovereignty. Notwithstanding a driving snowstorm, the members of the various religious and temperance societies turned out with full ranks and marched to the St. Paul levee to meet the trains from the various roads, which brought great hosts of Catholics from all parts of the state. The grand procession, numbering seven thousand men, was by far the largest that ever had taken place in Minnesota. In the Cathedral he delivered an address, in which he said:

Will you place the Pope under the sway of an earthly power, be it that of a monarch or of a sovereign people? The result—frame theories as you may—practically he will not be free. It may be his duty to denounce as wrong and immoral the acts of that power; as in times gone by, he may have to hurl the thunders of excommunication in defense of the people against a tyrant—in defense of the weakened poor against adulterous monarchs and royal robbers. Were they above him, would they not seek to stifle his voice? What efforts have not princes and powers made in the past to keep the voice of the Vatican from resounding within their borders. If they had held the Vatican itself, would that voice have at all spoken? And were the Pope, while the subject of a nation, free, how would other nations and peoples view him? With a jealous eye; his decrees would come to them tinged, in their belief, with national partiality.[88]

Again, in a sermon preached in St. Patrick's Church, Washington, on December 10, 1900, he reviewed the question of the independence of the Pope, and he prophesied that at no remote day the Italian people and Christendom at large would give back to the papacy its wonted dignity and liberty. He gave as his reasons for choosing the subject his recent visit to Rome, which enabled him to understand the situation, and also the appearance in the *North American Review* of an article in which he was mentioned as one of those who did not favor the temporal sovereignty.[89] This discourse, when reproduced in many Continental journals, notably in *L'Univers* of January 4, 1901, brought criticism from those favorable to the Italian government and praise from the friends of the papacy. The international review, *Le Papauté et les Peuples*, said of it: "Mgr. Ireland's discourse contains the most beautiful and peremptory pages on the gravity of the situation. Witness for the Pope, on the frontiers of two worlds, his voice has prolonged and distant echoes."[90] The American Consul at Castellammare wrote:

I am not given to flattery, and were I, you are not the man to receive it. I want to say, however, that your exposition of the subject is a great com-

fort to me. You clinch the whole subject when you say: "The restoration of
the independence of the Pope does not mean Italy's return to her former
condition." In other words, I take it that you mean that it is not essential
to the temporal power that the Pope should exercise jurisdiction over 23
temporalities, some of which extended into France and even into Africa.
I think your sermon should be translated into Italian and published in the
official organ of the Vatican at Rome.

The great trouble with the "Curia" is, they don't understand Americans,
and what is more, there is a certain class whom I need not mention, that
don't want us understood. The sermon, coming from one who is looked
upon as the very embodiment of American principles and at the same
time one whose voice is always heeded in Catholic matters, will make a
very necessary impression upon those who have fancied that we are quasi-
heretical. In other words, it will set us right before the Curia, and at the
same time enlighten the Government as to where we stand.[91]

8. HIS DEFENSE OF THE HOLY SEE

Archbishop Ireland came to the defense of the Holy See on more
than one occasion. When an article, signed "A Catholic Priest," attacking the papacy appeared in the *North American Review* of January, 1907, it brought an immediate answer from Ireland. The author
had shown his animus by accusing the papacy of bigotry, cruelty,
hatred of the truth, and defiance of civilization. "Thoughtful Catholics," the writer said, "have long been aweary of Pontiffs that were
great diplomats, great builders, great theologians. A great Christian
is what they have been sighing for." This first charge the Archbishop
rejected with contempt as a rehash of Carlyle and Fogazzaro, with
this difference—that Fogazzaro was dignified and respectful. The
second he answered by saying that diplomats, builders, and theologians are precisely what the Church requires. Since the Church is
not only spiritual but also temporal, the Pope must address those
who are governed and those who govern; he must argue and negotiate in order to safeguard the interests of religion, to secure for it
liberty of speech and action. As a builder he must organize the work
of the Church in the world and plan for the widening of its spheres
of influence. He must be a theologian since he must preach the
Gospel to every creature. Ireland then continued:

Since the New Testament was written, its germinal truths have been
growing, unfolding this divine meaning branch by branch, leaf by leaf,
assimilating to themselves cognate truths from every garden of human
knowledge. Christian truth has life and motion; it progresses. It is not a
dead letter, a mere archeological mummy locked up within the pages of the
New Testament.

He next outlined the doctrine of infallibility and explained the function of the Congregation of the Index, defending its action during the pontificate of Pius X in condemning Loisy, Viollet, Laberthoniere, and Fogazzaro, the decision of the Scriptural Commission on the Mosaic authorship of the Pentateuch, and Pope Pius' treatment of Bishop Bonomelli, Father Tyrrell, and the Lega Democratica Nazionale of Italy.[92] For this article Cardinal Merry del Val thanked him, telling him at the same time that persons who ought to be well informed on the subject strongly suspected that Tyrrell, if not the author of the attack, had at least inspired it.[93]

Ireland sent two other contributions on the papacy to the same review. In January, 1908, he replied to Professor Charles Briggs, who had written an article entitled "Is the Papacy an Obstacle to the Reunion of Christendom?" and in April of the same year he answered Charles Johnson's article on "The Catholic Reformation and the Papacy."

The next matter which engaged the attention of Archbishop Ireland had its origin in the visits to Rome of ex-Vice-President Charles W. Fairbanks, in February, 1910, and of ex-President Theodore Roosevelt in April of the same year. Fairbanks had requested an audience with the Pope, which was readily granted. But before the reception could take place he chose to lend his support to the Methodists, who had been conducting a vicious anti-Catholic propaganda in the very heart of the Eternal City. As a result of this affront to the Holy Father his visit was canceled. When the incident caused considerable discussion in this country, Ireland gave interviews to representatives of the press, in which he said that it was not a question of the religious affiliation of Fairbanks or of his attendance at a Methodist church in Rome for Sunday devotions. It was rather one of appearing to give the fullest approval to the work of the Methodist Association in Rome, which was an active and pernicious proselyter, and which was there not to serve American Methodists but to pervert from the Catholic faith all those upon whom it could bring influence to bear. The Methodists, he said, employed means that were anything but honorable, took advantage of the poverty of the poor in Rome, circulated and displayed in their bookstores slanders against the Catholic faith, the Pope, and the whole Catholic system. The success they achieved was not at all commensurate with the efforts and money expended. They did not make permanent Methodists of Italians and they only succeeded in detaching from all things Christian the few they perverted. One arm of their combat was to create the impression that Methodism was the great faith of the American Republic and that the Catholic Church was merely an Italian institution. To welcome Fairbanks under such circumstances would be to give the approval of America to such propaganda. Ireland was careful to say that his criticism did not apply to other Protestant denominations in Rome, which minded their own business, and of some of which the rectors were his personal friends. Nor was he attacking the whole Methodist Church, but merely the Association in Rome. He concluded by saying: "I shall be pleased to answer the Methodists at any time, I am not too old to enter a fight when the occasion requires it."[94]

These interviews brought approval from the Pope and from Cardinal Gibbons. The Cardinal told of the sense of intense satisfaction with which he had read the timely and luminous vindication of the Pope, whose action had put Catholics in an unpleasant situation and would have been followed by renewed attacks and charges of medieval bigotry and intolerance if Ireland had not exhibited the Methodist propagandists in their true light. His interviews had taken the sting out of the wound inflicted on the ex-Vice-President by making known to the American people the pernicious activity of the Roman Methodists.[95]

But only a few months elapsed before the Archbishop was called upon once more to enter the fray. This time it was the case of Mr. Roosevelt, who, on his return from hunting big game in Africa, and before his departure from Egypt, indicated to Mr. Leishman, the American Ambassador to the Quirinal, that he wished to visit the King of Italy and the Pope during his brief stay in Rome. Leishman conveyed his wish to Monsignor Thomas Kennedy, Rector of the North American College, who was informed by the Vatican that the Holy Father would most gladly receive Mr. Roosevelt, hoping at the same time that no incident would occur similar to the one which made impossible the reception of Fairbanks. When Leishman transmitted this reply to Roosevelt at Cairo, he took it upon himself to suggest that it was objectionable, an intolerable restriction on the Colonel's freedom of action, and, moreover, that Catholics would make capital of the affair at the expense of the Methodists. To this communication Roosevelt replied that while it would be a pleasure for him to be presented to the Pope, for whom he held the highest respect, and while he recognized his right to receive or not receive whomsoever he chooses, he, on the other hand, must decline to submit to any conditions which would limit his freedom of conduct. He still hoped, however, that he would be received. To this the Vatican replied that, in view of circumstances for which neither the Pope nor Roosevelt was responsible, the audience could not take place except under the conditions mentioned.[96]

Light is thrown on the whole affair by two letters which Cardinal Merry del Val wrote to the Archbishop. In April, 1910, he expressed his gratitude to him for all that he had done, his assurance that there was no bitterness in the Vatican and no ill feeling, and his regret that anyone should have attributed to himself an unworthy attitude, as he had always been a stanch friend and admirer of America. He merely did his duty, knowing that he would have to face a storm, but he was convinced that when the true facts became known, the best American opinion would do him justice. He said:

> Subsequent events and rather painful revelations of what was going on behind the scenes have only served to show with greater evidence that our judgment was not at fault and that God was guiding us at a difficult moment. It was an unfortunate circumstance, but as far as the Holy See is concerned, and given the facts, our attitude was inevitable and our duty clear.[97]

In May he indicated what the revelations were—Roosevelt's public and marked demonstrations of friendship and sympathy with Fera and the other Italian Freemasons, from whom he received and welcomed significant honors. The Cardinal wrote:

> It was so striking and eloquent that most people were convinced that I had foreseen or that I had been informed previously of Mr. Roosevelt's intentions. As a matter of fact I was not. Had Mr. Roosevelt been received by the Holy Father, and then followed up with these demonstrations, a very grave insult would have been offered to the Holy Father.
>
> As you are aware, the Masons here, especially these, are the most heinous and blasphemous adversaries of Religion, of the Holy Father &c politically, socially, and are the avowed enemies of Christianity in every way. It is precisely because the Methodists here go hand in glove with these Masons, that they are so objectionable. Hence, as a matter of fact, Mr. Roosevelt did accomplish what was just as bad or worse than showing friendship for the 20 Settembre Methodists. Many believe that he had them in mind when the hope was courteously expressed that nothing similar to the Fairbanks incident would crop up to prevent the audience, and that, as he had already taken an engagement with Fera, he could not or would not undertake to give any assurance; for, if he did not intend honoring the Methodists, he was already committed to something just as bad or worse.

I understand that Mr. Leishman is a Jew and a Freemason. Judging by the dispatches published in the *Outlook* he tried to excite Mr. Roosevelt rather than make things easy.[98]

The Cardinal's position is borne out by Salvatore Cortesi, chief of the Roman bureau of the Associated Press, who told of Roosevelt's speech at the San Carlo Opera House in Naples, in which he praised Italy for having proclaimed liberty of conscience, and for standing firmly against any interference of the Church in State affairs.[99]

When Roosevelt was in Germany, St. John Gaffney, the Consul General at Dresden, who met him and his secretary, Lawrence Abbott, in Berlin, got the impression that they were seriously worried over the incident. The ex-President tried to brazen out his action and seemed to insist that Merry del Val had deliberately invited the contretemps. Gaffney, who was inclined to throw the whole blame on O'Loughlin, quoted for him Ireland's interview, which contradicted O'Loughlin's statement that the President was just the man to go from the Pope to address the Methodists. Roosevelt praised the interview, but "in his characteristic bumptious fashion said that if he was attacked by the Catholics there was sufficient Irish in him to fight back." Whereupon the Consul pointed out that under very great provocation Catholic opinion in America had been marked with both dignity and repression—which Roosevelt admitted. Gaffney also told Archbishop Ireland that Mr. Frederick Grundy, London correspondent of the New York *Sun*, a Protestant and a journalist of the first rank, and almost the only writer to give an unprejudiced account of the incident, had expressed profound sympathy and admiration for the Cardinal Secretary of State. He hoped that Grundy, who knew the inside history of the whole affair, would present a complete account of it in its true light and thus furnish an accurate and unvarnished story, not for Catholic but for non-Catholic public opinion.[100]

Roosevelt later wrote to Ireland that he would not attempt to discuss the incident by letter, but that he would go over it in full when they met. He expressed his reactions to the *Outlook*, to Otto Trevelyan, and to Maurice Francis Egan. In the *Outlook* he said that it was his desire that the incident should be treated in a matter-of-course way as merely personal and as not warranting the slightest exhibition of rancor or bitterness. He referred to the number of close friends he had among Catholics and to the good will and sympathy existing in America among peoples of different beliefs.[101] He told

Trevelyan that he had been anticipating trouble in Rome and had been preparing for it. He paid tribute to Pope Leo, who had sent him a beautiful mosaic picture of himself as a token of his recognition of the way in which the matter of the friars' lands had been handled. Pius X he regarded as a worthy, narrowly limited parish priest, "completely under the control of his Secretary of State, Merry del Val, who is a polished man of much ability in a very narrow line, but a furiously bigoted reactionary, and in fact a good type of a sixteenth century Spanish ecclesiastic." He said that Rome offered the sharpest contrasts between radical modern progress, social, political, and religious, and the extremes of opposition to all such progress. How little Roosevelt knew of Church affairs is shown by his placing in the first class the free-thinking Jewish mayor, in the last the Vatican, and in between, the King, Fogazzaro, Abbot Janssens, and the Bishop of Cremona. While he approved of the general work of the Methodists as introducing a spirit of rivalry, which he considered good for the Church, he regarded one Methodist minister, however, as a "crude, vulgar creature, cursed with the thirst for self-advertisement, utterly unable to distinguish between notoriety and fame, and given to denunciations of the Pope." He also told of the visit of some Methodist and Catholic ecclesiastics, among the latter Abbot Janssens of the Benedictines, who, he said, expressed their entire sympathy with the position he had taken.[102] This last statement led to an amusing communication sent by Archbishop Diomede Falconio, the Apostolic Delegate in Washington, to Archbishop Ireland, in which he referred to a Roman cablegram, consisting of two parts, quoted in the press. The first part told of the disapproval of Abbot Janssens' initiative as liable to an interpretation offensive to the Holy Father and as an act unauthorized; the second said that the Vatican "did not wish Mr. Roosevelt to bracket the Pope with more or less royal personages whom he would boast of having hunted in Europe after his African hunt." This part, the Delegate said, did not come from the Vatican.[103]

When Roosevelt passed through Denmark, he visited Maurice Francis Egan, the American Minister at Copenhagen, to whom he said that there were in Rome two conflicting representatives of the Freemasons, each of whom he received with urbane politeness, at the same time assuring them that he was unalterably devoted to the cause of religion, good government, liberty, and order. Egan threw the blame for the muddle on Leishman and O'Loughlin. The latter was, he said, a very decent chap, but one "who—and it seems to be a vice with most Americans—understands nothing of etiquette or finesse." The Minister thought that Roosevelt had been led to believe that the Secretary of State might insist on other conditions—for instance, he had accepted an invitation to dine with the Mayor of Rome, who was a Jew and a Freemason. It had been suggested, he surmised, that if he accepted any condition he might be required to refuse this banquet. Egan's letter concludes as follows:

I never saw anything more frightfully bungled, and I never saw Mr. Roosevelt so concerned about anything as he was about this. He was especially desirous that you should know that he was concerned, and I was never so impressed with his regard for the regard of his Catholic friends—especially for your opinion—as I was during his talks with me here.

There are two or three Sisters for whom he has a special regard, and he seemed very much afraid that they would cut him dead because of this absurd business. I must say, at the risk of offending you who are devoted to His Eminence, Cardinal del Val, that I do think he behaved after the manner of the mayor of a small village rather than a Secretary of State to a Papal King—but I shock you.[104]

Again Archbishop Ireland came to the defense of the Holy See. In an interview granted to a representative of the New York *Herald* he said that the Methodist propaganda in Rome was so calumnious in its assaults upon the Catholic faith, so dishonest in its methods to win proselytes, that the Holy Father was compelled by the vital principles of his high office to avert at all costs the slightest movement on his part that might directly or indirectly be interpreted as abetting the propaganda or approving even by implication its purposes and tactics.[105] Needless to say, the Archbishop became the butt of attacks, to which he replied in the St. Paul *Dispatch* on April 10, 1910, and which precipitated a controversy in the *North American Review* throughout the latter half of the year. Throughout it all he was careful to insist that his criticism was not of the Methodist Church in the United States, but only of the methods employed by the Italian group. That he had the sympathy of some non-Catholics is shown by a letter which he received from Mr. William Edgar, editor of the *Bellman*, Minneapolis, who said that the situation had been made delicate by the objectionable and wholly unjustified antics of "that blatant trouble-breeder Tipple, who, in my opinion, is a disgrace to Methodism." He heartily agreed with the Archbishop's judgment concerning the character of this man's work and he promised to do all he could to encourage his removal.[106]

The controversy was resumed in May, 1912, on the occasion of the Methodist convention in St. Paul. Wild statements by Bishop Frank Bristol, that the Church had tyrannized over the people of South America by superstition; by Reverend Walling Clark, that the Bible came to Rome only with the troops of Victor Emmanuel and Garibaldi; and by Reverend William Rice, that the Church forbade the reading of the Bible, brought sharp answers from the Archbishop, who accused the Presbyterians as well as the Methodists of "pouring out, in unstinted hate, misrepresentations and calumnies against the Church." He knew, he said, that inside the walls of the conference there were many who loved peace and truth and who would fain bridle the wild tongues of their intemperate brethren "bent on the futile task of beating down the battlements of the Church." He stressed the fact that in defending the Church in South America he was defending the Church in the United States, for its doctrines and mandates are the same the world over. He regarded as an insult to the Catholics of this country the statement of a minister that their religion was "Protestantized Catholicism."[107]

The Archbishop's replies brought an expression of delight from Cardinal Gibbons, who said: "Your remarks were so timely, so clear and so triumphant a repudiation of the wild and extravagant utterances of those bishops. Would to God we had in every city so zealous and able a champion to strike a blow at an opportune moment in the cause of truth."[108]

Of the three Pontiffs who reigned during his life, the Archbishop enjoyed the personal love and esteem of two. He had always recourse to Rome with confidence that he would find there sympathy and understanding. When in 1887 he encountered opposition to the founding of the Catholic University, he demanded an audience with Leo and accomplished his mission. When foreignism threatened to disrupt the unity of the Church, when the Knights of Labor were attacked, when his school experiment was in danger, when his orthodoxy was questioned, he had recourse to the Holy Father. More than once the Vatican profited from his counsel and co-operation. Writing from Rome to Monsignor Louis Caillet, in March, 1892, the Archbishop said: "The Pope is preparing a grand Encyclical for the Catholics of America. It will give great pleasure and will be all right for the counsels given. I am at work suggesting what is to be said."[109] In the negotiations preceding the Spanish-American War, in the arranging of a commission on the purchase of the friars' lands, and in the conduct of affairs in the Philippines, he was in constant touch with the Holy See. There is no doubt that for him Leo had an especially warm affection. "The Archbishop of St. Paul," he said to Archbishop James J. Keane, "is a truly great and good man. Give him my deepest love."[110] It was he who softened the letter on Americanism and who impressed on the Archbishop that it was not aimed at him. In the incident of the *circolo*, in August, 1900, he showed him honor such as had been given to few men.

Before he left Rome in August, 1900, the Archbishop attended the *circolo* or meeting of the cardinals to felicitate the Holy Father on his patronal feast of St. Joachim. Noticing him among those present, and inviting him to come forward, the Pope remarked that, as the Archbishop was about to leave Rome to return to America, he would like to know what he would have to say to the people of the United States. Whereupon the Archbishop replied, in words of devotion and attachment, that the sight of His Holiness had inspired him with new zeal to stimulate the people of America to greater devotion and loyalty to the Apostolic See. The Holy Father then asked him what the people of America thought of the Pope and his present situation. The Archbishop answered that American Catholics, like all others, were united in lamenting that the Holy See had been despoiled of that full liberty and independence necessary for the free exercise of its apostolic mission. At the close of this impromptu address, the Pope said: "You have well interpreted my sentiments." Count Vannutelli, who narrated the incident, remarked in his Italian way: "It was twenty minutes of glory." Monsignor Benedetto Lorenzelli, Nuncio at Paris, told the Archbishop that all the newspapers and notably *La Voce della Verità* had given a marked place to his answers to the different questions that the Holy Father deigned to ask on the day of his patronal feast at the *circolo*. He congratulated him cordially on the joy that he had given to His Holiness and to Cardinal Rampolla by his visit, and the good feeling which they had manifested for him.[111]

There were those who cynically wished to think that the *circolo* incident was a prearranged profession of faith which the Archbishop was "invited" to make in the most solemn and public manner, and that it was clearly understood beforehand what he was to say.[112] But this interpretation would seem to be farfetched, as an analysis of the meeting will show. Ireland was not the only one whom the Pope invited to speak. He called to him some Maronite bishops who had come to Rome for the Jubilee year, praised their faith and their obedience to the Holy See, and told them of his intention to contribute toward the development of their college in Rome. He also questioned the Prefect Apostolic of Abyssinia, Father Colbeaux of the Priests of the Mission, concerning the state of the Catholic religion in his country and the attitude of the Negus toward Catholics. After speaking of many other things, the Pope, "knowing that Mons. Ireland was among those present, called him paternally and asked him what he was going to tell his people about his visit to Rome and what American Catholics thought of the Pope and of his abnormal condition in the government of the Church." At the end of the Archbishop's impromptu remarks, "the words of Ireland," an Italian paper says, "were received with the greatest sympathy by all present, and the Pope remained visibly moved by the sentiments expressed so enthusiastically by the illustrious shepherd of the Church of St. Paul."[113]

Bishop Mourey, Auditor of the Rota for France, congratulated him, saying that his statement had definitely put an end to misunderstandings and would dissipate national prejudices. "Your expression of high and noble candor," he said, "leaves room for no doubt, for no equivocation. You have spoken in Rome, and the case is finished."[114]

Cardinal Gibbons regarded his address at the invitation of the Pope, in the presence of the Sacred College, as an extraordinary honor. He wrote the following year:

In my first audience, the Holy Father spoke very warmly & affectionately of you. He referred in glowing terms to your address before himself & the Cardinals. "They said," he remarked, "that the Abp. was a liberal, but I told him to express his mind, & we were delighted with his words." Then continued the Pope: "Abp. Ireland said to me: When I return home, I will say more." He referred to your article with which he seemed to be much pleased. The same line of conversation took place in my subsequent interview with Card. Rampolla. You evidently retain a hold on their confidence & affection.[115]

Chapter 13

RELATIONSHIPS PERSONAL AND OFFICIAL

In addition to the correspondence already indicated, Archbishop Ireland maintained contacts with a remarkably large and interesting variety of people. One of his earliest was with Cardinal Manning, with whom he had much in common and for whom he had the highest admiration. Both were temperance advocates, deeply interested in social problems, having compassion on the multitude, liberal in their views, defenders of the Knights of Labor, opposed to the condemnation of Henry George's *Progress and Poverty*, influential in the governments of their countries. Both were critical of the religious orders and especially of the Jesuits. There is often a surprising similarity in their pronouncements, such as their denial that the spirituality of the members of religious orders is higher than that of the diocesan clergy, that the latter need not be as well educated as the former. If Ireland could say that the diocesan clergy are the principal mainstays of the bishop, Manning could say that he loved all orders, but loved more the pastoral theology which can be found in no order, that the regulars are under the *vow* of poverty, but the seculars under the *reality*. Both may have been indebted to the same source for their assertion that the loss of the faith in England was due to the action of the Jesuits in opposing the restoration of the hierarchy, an opinion which was shared by Monsignor Duchesne. Both were tolerant of those who differed from them in religion and maintained cordial relations with Protestant dignitaries, "refusing to consider Protestantism a term for perdition." In 1871, when the Prince of Wales was gravely ill Manning obtained for him the prayers of the Pope. In 1894 Ireland wrote to Gibbons: "Permit me to say that you missed a great opportunity when you did not preach at the funeral service for Carnot in Washington. Your words would have been hailed with delight in France."[1] Both were fearful of any attempt to establish direct diplomatic relations between the Vatican and their governments. If Manning "constantly frustrated" efforts to connect England and the Holy See diplomatically, Ireland told Rampolla that such efforts in the United States would stir up latent bigotry.[2] If Manning was convinced that Rome could only return to the Pope by the will of the Italian people, Ireland in the beginning deemed all agitation of the question in America unwise and fruitless.[3]

Their correspondence—slight, because the Cardinal died in January, 1892—began in April, 1887. After speaking of a letter of his in the *Moniteur de Rome* and thanking the Archbishop for his brief on total abstinence, the Cardinal said:

I am rejoiced about the "Remotio Rectorum." I hope the wording is clear and safe. I should like to be fully informed as to Cardinal Simeoni's mind about the whole policy of Cardinal Gibbons' Paper. Mgr. Jacobini ought, I think, to go with it. The state of the "New World" is not the normal state of Christendom. But it is with the abnormal state that we have to do. We must deal with facts, not with memories and lamentations. And to deal with facts we must go down into the midst of them. The Incarnation is our law and wisdom.[4]

Some months later, when the Archbishop wrote concerning a proposed congress of English-speaking Catholics, he reported that he had discussed the matter with Cardinal Gibbons, Archbishops Williams, Ryan, and Corrigan, and Bishops Gilmour, Spalding, Keane, Maes, and Marty, all of whom approved of the project. He suggested the autumn of the following year as a proper time for holding the congress, expressing hopes for great results and urging Manning to further it actively. "Let this congress," he said, "be the work of your old age, crowning so many other works in the honor of religion. The Congress of London held, it will be easy years later to hold one in Dublin or in New York." He hoped to return to Europe the following year so that he might again see and hear Manning, who had been so kind to him on his last visit. "The pleasure of my whole European voyage was to see Pope Leo and Cardinal Manning, and so great was the pleasure that I crave for a renewal."[5] Ireland always associated in his mind these two. On another occasion he said: "Once elsewhere in Europe I was in presence of a mind that seemed an image of Leo's—not resplendent as Leo's mind, but yet an image of it."[6]

The Cardinal replied that the letter gave him much consolation and that he would take the necessary steps without delay, first obtaining the sanction of the Pope. He asked the Archbishop to put down his own thoughts as to organization. "Any united act of the English-speaking races," he said, "will have a powerful effect of showing the vitality of the Church in its greatest independence and freedom, and in the face of the races of the world."[7] The congress, however, never took place, the project not being too warmly greeted in Rome.

When Ireland delivered his address at the Centennial of the American Hierarchy in 1889, he won the approval of the Cardinal. J. C. Bodley, writing to Gibbons, said: "Archbishop Ireland would have been gratified to hear what the head of the Church of England said about his sermon."[8] And a few months later Manning wrote:

I should greatly enjoy a talk with you about your grand sermon at the Centenary. Either you & I are right or we ought to be burnt. My whole reason tells me that we are right. But I may be *"sapientiae supernae ignarus,"* and yet whenever any man comes face to face with the New World, like Mgr. Satolli, he comes back repeating our words. I hear that you will come over to Europe next year. I hope you will, for I may see you—and we should have much to speak of.[9]

Speaking of Manning's books, *The Eternal Priesthood* and *The Pastoral Office,* Shane Leslie says that the Cardinal completed his trilogy by a book on the rights and dignity of the priesthood, "which never passed out of the manuscript, but which he showed to Archbishop Ireland as prospective editor. Unfortunately, while the Archbishop of St. Paul was crossing the Atlantic, the manuscript, which Manning intended to publish after his death, disappeared."[10]

As the Archbishop passed through Chicago en route to Europe, in January, 1892, he received news of the Cardinal's death. Deeply moved, he said:

By the death of Cardinal Manning, the Catholic Church loses one of its most eminent prelates, and humanity is deprived of the services of one of its warmest friends. My chief idea in making this trip to Europe was to meet Cardinal Manning and enjoy a few days' visit at his home. Now that he is dead, I feel that the principal pleasure of my trip has been lost.[11]

As we have already seen, Cardinal Gibbons first came to know the future Archbishop of St. Paul at the Vatican Council, which, as a young priest, the latter attended as the representative of Bishop Grace, but at which he had merely the role of observer. Among the first correspondence between them is a letter dated February, 1884, when Bishop Ireland welcomed Archbishop Gibbons back from Europe and congratulated him on having been designated to preside over the coming Council.[12] His magnificent discourse on that occasion established him as one of the great figures of the hierarchy and won for him the admiration of Gibbons, who said, when he visited St. Paul in September, 1887: "For many years I have been closely watching Archbishop Ireland's career. It was my pleasure to be associated with him at the last Plenary Council of Baltimore. For three weeks I studied him, and the more I studied him the more I admired and loved him. Archbishop Ireland came to you as a providential messenger sent to you by Almighty God. He has done untold good by the blessings which he has helped to bestow upon society."[13] Whatever might have been the first occasion, there was from the beginning a friendship which never faltered and which grew stronger with the years. In every controversy in which he was engaged, the Archbishop of St. Paul consulted the Cardinal of Baltimore, who saw eye to eye with him on almost every problem. Gibbons was an admirable foil for Ireland, tempering his enthusiasms with his natural conservatism, his daring with his prudence. At times the Archbishop sought approval, at times he stimulated into action one who had a tendency to "think too precisely on the event." He was careful at all times to recognize the Cardinal's position as the head of the hierarchy and he constantly deferred to him. If at times Ireland's impetuosity and his readiness to engage in battle must have disturbed the Cardinal's equanimity, the latter saw that behind it all was a passion for God and country, as well as an honesty and a sincerity of soul. More than once Ireland expressed his gratitude for the shield of his powerful influence, without which he felt he would have long since given up. Gibbons in turn was deeply touched by these acknowledgments and willingly endured the arrows of the fortune of war.

It would, indeed, be difficult to conceive of a more beautiful friendship than that which existed between the two prelates. In 1892, when attempts were made to alienate them, Gibbons wrote: "That effort will never succeed until Baltimore becomes so blind as not to see and admire honor, virtue and heroism. Fear not, be prudent & conservative in words & writings."[14] Ireland once described Gibbons as:

A man most lovable for depth of heart; distinguished for most astute human penetration, for a broad conception of the conditions of religious and civic affairs, for most surprising ability in settling disputes upon the plane for harmony and justice, and for astounding administrative qualities, either as president of a plenary council or as the head of his own archdiocese.[15]

They rejoiced in each other's success. Writing in November, 1889, Ireland said:

The Baltimore celebrations have awakened great interest among Protestants as well as among Catholics. Never did the Church stand so well before the Country as to-day. We have to thank you for all this. You have the ear of the American public as no other man in the Republic. Your words were heeded by all &, God be thanked, they are always the words that are heeded.[16]

Of Ireland's sermon at his Jubilee in 1893, the Cardinal wrote:

Your sermon is still "the talk of the town." It has evoked general admiration. Everybody that didn't hear it, seems to have read it, & some twice. Fr. Starr, a severe critic, heard you near the end of the Church, & said there was suppressed applause at the close of some sentences. I feel like sending you a heavy bill for being the occasion of lifting you up so high in the pinnacle of fame. But I believe that no money is equivalent to the glory you have achieved.[17]

Not to be outdone in compliments, Ireland said that, if there was anything good in the sermon, it was due to the inspirations which came to him thick and ennobling from his "hero," about whom it was scarcely possible to say commonplace things. He went on to speak of Gibbons' providential role in the episcopate and of the remarks of Secretary of State Walter Gresham, who paid tribute to the work of Gibbons in dissipating prejudice among non-Catholics and winning them by his conciliatory language and demeanor.[18]

When attacked by Bishop McQuaid in 1894, Ireland expressed his sympathy for the renewed strain to which the Cardinal's generous friendship was being put. "I am," he said, "so pleased that you have understood me. I can say, before God, that I had only the interests of the Church, which I desired to put above all political parties, the queen of all, the servant of none. Had nothing been said, the victors of today would have reason to hold the Church as their enemy." He was, however, coming to the conclusion that for the sake of peace it was best, as far as he was concerned, to let the Church jog her way and for him to "enter into winter quarters."[19]

The beginning of each year saw the exchange of warm greetings, Ireland writing in December, 1894, that while others spoke to the Cardinal in language more attractive and graceful, none spoke with warmer love, deeper gratitude, or more thorough appreciation than did the Archbishop of St. Paul. "In this desert of ours," he said, "so poorly tenanted with men who see beyond narrow frontiers, who put high interests above self, who have the courage of their convictions, what should have become of us, if God had not cared for the See of Baltimore by placing you in it."[20]

In January, 1908, the Cardinal wrote:

I am deeply touched by the expressions of affection and gratitude contained in your letter of Jan. 1st. I have indeed been loyal to you. I have fought your battles and made your cause my own. In doing so I have been impelled by two motives, my sense of the justice of your cause and still more by my personal admiration for you. I received many a scar in the conflict and perhaps have felt more keenly than you the sharp stings of the enemy, because I am, I believe, more sensitive. But I never faltered or hesitated for a moment because I believe your cause was right.

And now we can rejoice together after the smoke of battle has passed away. *"Forsan haec olim meminisse juvabit."* I am feeling sad at the departure of old friends. I earnestly hope that you will survive me.[21]

The friendship deepened with the years, and the expression of it became more pronounced. In December, 1912, the Archbishop wrote:

Whatever else the ravages of time, it has no power to dim the rays, or cool the warmth of my gratitude for the friendship of many years with which you have honored me, or the deep-felt and most sincere affection in which I have always held your memory and your name.[22]

The nobility and affection of the letter moved the Cardinal, who replied:

Among the very many letters of greeting I have received during the last few days there is none I esteem so much or have touched my heart as yours. It brings back old memories dating as far as 1884. Since that time, during a conflict of over a quarter of a century we both fought shoulder to shoulder against formidable opponents, and we advocated ecclesiastical measures which were then almost condemned and aroused against us a suspicion of heterodoxy—such as the separation of Church and State as we understand it in this country. But times have changed since I commended that policy (with your cordial adhesion) in Rome in 1887. Those who were then opposed to us were afterwards eager to join our bandwagon as experience has taught them that it is the only sound policy, and the sooner the Christian nations adopt it the better it will be for the Church and for the invigorating of its members.

I still cherish the hope that I shall not quit the busy scenes of this life till you receive that honor which the American people within and without the Church believe you richly deserve by your signal services to God and Country. But no new title can add to the esteem and love in which they hold you.[23]

In January, 1914, Gibbons told of the remark which Cardinal Rampolla had made a few days before his death, that he had two very dear friends in the United States—ex-President Taft and Archbishop Ireland; and he continued:

Most of your friends in Rome have passed from the busy scenes of life— Leo, Satolli, & Rampolla. But other friends still remain, the Vannutellis and Falconio. When these, however, will go to their reward, others will abide with you and will never forsake you—I refer to the American people, who will always cherish you regardless of accidental titles, and, even if those titles were conferred, would still hail you as John Ireland.[24]

A few weeks after Ireland's death Gibbons, at the celebration of his Golden Jubilee, after stating that he was the only surviving bishop of the Third Plenary Council, said:

The last prelate who has descended below the horizon of the tomb, was the Venerable Patriarch of the West, the great Apostle of Temperance, the sturdy Patriot who had endeared himself to the American people without distinction of race or religion, the man who had contributed perhaps more than any other to demonstrate the harmony that exists between the Constitution of the Church and the Constitution of the United States. Needless to say, I am speaking of John Ireland, the Lion of the fold of Juda.[25]

Monsignor Denis O'Connell, the Rector of the North American College, Rome, was a man of unusual ability. Possessing all the graces of society, he formed a large circle of acquaintances among both laity and clergy. At first the agent of the American episcopate, he became, as time went on, more and more identified with Gibbons, Ireland, and Keane. His relations with the Archbishop of St. Paul were especially warm, as is indicated by a huge volume of correspondence extending over many years. He kept Ireland informed on conditions in Rome, attended to his affairs, and assisted him in his visits to Europe. The first correspondence in the Archbishop's files dates from 1887 and deals with the formation of the new Province of St. Paul, the Knights of Labor, and the question of nationalism. Having had for many years entree to the Vatican, O'Connell knew the sentiments of the various members of the Curia, their reactions to the Archbishop's activities, and the attacks made upon him. His letters are a mirror in which are reflected Ireland's successes and failures. If in January, 1893, he congratulates him on his success on arranging the Delegation, he informs him in February, 1900, that "there is no doubt there is a very general impression on both sides of the water that you are a crushed man, and there is no doubt that all your enemies, especially the religious are working hard if silently."[26] Ireland at one time thanks him for all his efforts on his behalf, and at another rebukes him for imprudences in speech. At times their friendship seemed to suffer from strain, and O'Connell's letters became less frequent, but when the Monsignor was made Rector of the Catholic University, the old warmth was renewed and continued to the end. The warnings which Ireland had sent to O'Connell to give no interviews and to stay close to the College, as well as his protest against his interview on the South American bishops, which "was most unfortunate and led to the repudiation of Americanism," were all forgotten, and the Monsignor wrote after his appointment:

Now that the first flush of excitement is over I want to turn to you in all calmness and acknowledge my debt to you for your great part in this affair, and to offer you my most sincere thanks for it all, and assure you that I do not regard my debt as one that can be paid quickly nor in a few words. . . . I considered that the part you took in this matter gave you a right to give me guidance, and I was going to put myself at your feet and ask it. . . . I am dying to meet you and embrace you and to talk a thousand things over with you.[27]

In December, 1907, when news of O'Connell's nomination as Bishop reached Ireland, he said that he regarded the act as a great rectification of things which had happily gone forever. While he did not believe that the rectorship of the University should mean a stepping to the episcopate—for the sake of the institution—in O'Connell's case there were special considerations.[28] He undoubtedly had in mind the Monsignor's removal from the American College in 1895, which he regarded as the work of their enemies. In 1909 O'Connell resigned his position at the Catholic University and took up his work as Auxiliary to his friend Archbishop Riordan of San Francisco. After the consecration of the six bishops in May, 1910, he wrote his reactions:

The spectacle was without a parallel in the history of our own or any other national church, and only in Rome could we find a counterpart. And still how short a time since the *"piccoli congressi"* wherein were engaged the cutting away from Milwaukee and the creation of the Metropolitan See of St. Paul, and now *"pulchra matre pulchrior filia."*
The long kind letter you wrote me gave me the greatest pleasure. It seemed like old times and I lived again in the past. And truly they were

great days and the fruit of our work still endures. We could not do it now. A change has come over the soul of the city.

About the end of this month I expect to start on a visit East, and on my returning about the middle of August, accepting your welcome invitation to pay you a little visit at St. Paul. I look forward to seeing you as to a great pleasure, to see how you look, if you are ageing, to see the cathedrals, and out of the strifes "to talk the night away."[29]

One of the last letters in the file, dated Richmond, September 8, 1915, deals with the death of Cardinal Serafino Vannutelli and reveals the warmth of O'Connell's heart:

Your dear letter gave me an opportunity of opening my heart to myself for dear Card. Serafino. To those about me his death was only an item of news; to me it was the extreme of bitterness. I never mentioned it to anyone, and it was like a festering sore that had no opening. And how I loved him, not only for all he did for me or might do, but for the goodness I found in him and for the admirable image of priest and manhood that he held up to my despairing imagination. Nothing that could even approach him did I ever meet in the Curia Romana. And with him much of my interest in life went out. God grant him his reward.

Vincenzo now is about all that's left, for us the others are nearly all *"novi viri."* The Pope himself is now our oldest acquaintance after Vincenzo. I was very fond of Henri [Lorin], and I held him in great admiration. I often wondered how he was and how his feelings must have been torn. Now in the dialogues of Fenelon they can all talk it over calmly on the other side. At the dinner table of S. Sulpice, Rome, they told me in a clear voice that Boeglin was dead: *"Il est mort miserablement a Vienne abandonné de tous."*

The cathedral is only the mighty crown you placed on the brow of the great province you built up in your life time. That will last and will speak without any need of commentary.

The sun's going down and evening is coming on; let us continue the journey together.[30]

The correspondence with Archbishop John J. Keane and with Bishop Thomas O'Gorman has already been considered. That of the former covers largely the years 1897 and 1898, during his first two years in Rome after his removal from the Catholic University. It deals, at first, with his insistence that he be appointed Consultor of the Propaganda, as the Holy Father had promised, and with his efforts to disabuse the Pope of the idea that he and his friends were disloyal, and later, with the vicissitudes of Americanism. He praises highly the speech in which Ireland protested that he was fighting, not any national group, but only the "refractaires," comforts him after his failure to prevent the Spanish-American War. For him Ireland had the greatest admiration, for his learning, piety, zeal, and courage. The many years in which they had worked side by side in the interest of the Catholic University, for the Knights of Labor, for the cause of temperance, and in the controversies over nationalism and Americanism had forged bonds which grew stronger with the years and ended only in death. Ireland's admiration for him was shared by all classes of people, and especially by Cardinal Gibbons, who wrote in September, 1909, when he heard that the state of the mind of the Archbishop of Dubuque, who at the time was visiting Ireland, gave cause for apprehension:

I am profoundly grieved that a luminous mind is clouded, & that a Prelate hardly surpassed for eloquence, zeal & piety is no longer able to exercise his apostolic ministry. He was one of the most beautiful and disinterested souls I have ever encountered. I hope that the unfavorable report I have heard of him is exaggerated.[31]

All during life the two Archbishops were united, and it can hardly be said that in death they were divided, for only a few months separated their demise.

Very close bonds knit the Archbishop and his old schoolmate, Bishop Thomas O'Gorman. In addition to the letters which the latter wrote in 1902, when he was a member of the Philippine Commission, he sent others in 1914 which show him at work in the interests of his friend. In November he informed Ireland that the Pope had given Archbishop Cerretti his picture to be brought to him, that he was eager to give him recognition, was faced with the difficulty of four cardinals in North America, but would find a way out. He told of the enthusiasm of Falconio and the Vannutellis and the oral message of Rampolla, as well as the indignation of the Vatican with Wilson's handling of the Mexican situation. A few days later he listed the cardinals who expressed their desire that the Archbishop be elevated—the two Vannutellis, Falconio, Liga, Gasparri, Gasquet, and Gotti. They had told him that there was no doubt of its accomplishment, if not at once, not later than the following summer. He also gave interesting details of the last conclave:

The most furious opponent of Della Chiesa was Sevin, who wanted a continuance of the former regime and policies. Maffi & Ferrata ran for a few ballots, then were dropped, it being evident neither could be landed. Then began a struggle between Della Chiesa & Serafino, until finally Della Chiesa got two thirds exactly. When Gibbons arrived in Naples, Cerretti &

Cortesi met him at the station & informed him of the election. "Della Chiesa? Never heard of him; who is he?" So much for Baltimore's influence and knowledge of men.

His last letter again assured Ireland that his nomination was sure, that the Pope and the influential cardinals were set on it. Cardinal Agliardi had said to him: "*Le nombre quatre* is not an insuperable difficulty in view of the greater question of the coming peace in which we shall need a non-Italian personality, and Ireland is the man."[32]

Perhaps for none of the Roman cardinals did Ireland have as much admiration as for Rampolla, in whom he always found a sympathetic and understanding spirit. When in February, 1892, he sent the Cardinal a letter from St. Louis and an item in the *Corriere de Napoli* implying that the bishops in the United States were either indifferent or hostile to the Temporal Power, Rampolla told him not to worry about the articles and to have confidence in the impartial judgment of the Holy See. In August the Cardinal expressed his pleasure at Ireland's reception by President Carnot of France, and in September he recommended to him Satolli, who was coming for the Columbian Exposition. When Ireland told him of the splendid welcome accorded Satolli and the preparations made in Chicago to receive him, Rampolla wrote: "It is not difficult to recognize your hand." In January, 1893, Rampolla sent the Archbishop news of Satolli's appointment as Delegate; in January, 1895, he told him of the Pope's indignation at McQuaid's attack and of his protest. When rumors of Ireland's disloyalty to the Pope were being spread in 1895, the Cardinal assured him that neither he nor the Holy Father had any doubt about his attachment to the Holy See. Again, a little later, when some interpreted the encyclical *Longinqua Oceani* as reflecting on Ireland, Rampolla assured him that nothing was farther from the mind of the Pope.[33] These and other letters leave no doubt that an excellent understanding existed between the Cardinal Secretary of State and the Archbishop of St. Paul.

Rampolla was Ireland's choice as successor to Leo XIII, and great was the Archbishop's indignation that the Austrian veto was not rejected. It is interesting to speculate what would have been the situation had Leo XIII carried out his intention to elevate Ireland, who undoubtedly would have been a powerful influence in furthering the candidacy of Rampolla. When Ireland met Abbé Klein in Washington in 1903, he said to him: "If the Cardinals had a sense of their duty and of the honor of the Church, the veto would have brought about at once the unanimous election of the candidate who was vetoed." When Klein replied that they did not wish to elect a Pope who would from the start have against him the government of one of the most important Catholic countries, Ireland showed considerable feeling. "Give me," he said, "an antagonistic Pope, give me any kind of Pope you wish, but give me an intelligent Pope. Gibbons should have protested without hesitation in the name of the great western world."[34]

A great deal of correspondence passed between the Cardinal and the Archbishop, not only during the negotiations preceding the Spanish-American War but also from 1901 to 1903 in connection with Philippine affairs. These as well as their contacts in Rome developed mutual understanding. When Cardinal Cerretti took possession of his titular Church of St. Cecilia in July, 1926, he paid tribute to his predecessors Cardinals Sfondrati and Rampolla. Speaking of his desire to erect a monument to the latter, he told of Pope Benedict's desire that the work be completed as soon as possible, and of the words which the Holy Father addressed to him: "I shall invite myself his dearest friends, and first of all Mgr. Ireland."[35]

When Monsignor Giacomo Della Chiesa, later Benedict XV, was secretary in the office of Rampolla, he always showed sympathy and kindness to the Archbishop. When Ireland wrote to him on the death of the Cardinal, Della Chiesa replied in a singularly beautiful letter:

Among the letters of condolence which I received on the death of Cardinal Rampolla yours of December 23 has for me a character all its own. Not because it has come from afar, but because it reawakens in my soul the memory of what I heard so many times from the lips of the poor Cardinal. His Eminence was very appreciative of the service Your Grace rendered to the Church when you were the link with the White House; it is due to Your Grace that the Cuban affair came to good issue, and the visit of Taft to Leo was another evidence of the success of your negotiations. Your Grace tells me that you believe that you had the esteem of Cardinal Rampolla. I am happy to have had evidence of it always.

I am gratified for your thought of me in these sad circumstances; the good Cardinal had much affection for me and I in turn was devoted to him. As soon as I learned of his death, I went to Rome to say Mass near his coffin, and to assist at the funeral. It was then that I realized how devoted I was to him. Alas, the Church has suffered a loss, the gravity of which will be felt in times to come.

Thanking Your Grace for having made known to me in your sympathy and your sorrow for Cardinal Rampolla the new bond that unites our hearts.[36]

Monsignor Germano Straniero, who had been the schoolmate of Benedict, not only at the Collegio Capronica but also at the Accademia dei Nobili Ecclesiastici, wrote in November, 1915: "What I know is this: that our present Pope, Benedict XV, is a great friend and admirer of you."

Ireland had many other friends in the Curia—Gasquet, Falconio, Ferrata, Satolli, Cerretti, and especially the two Vannutellis. When Cerretti received notice of his appointment as Delegate to Australia, he thanked the Archbishop for his many acts of kindness and for his friendship, of which, he said, he would always feel proud. Before leaving New York for San Francisco, he wrote: *"Il piccolo mondo antico is gone and a new world is born* in which you will find yourself very much at home. I have many things to tell you which will give us matter for conversation for some time." He visited the Archbishop a little later. Writing from Sydney in June, 1915, and sending his congratulations on the dedication of the Cathedral, he regretted that the disturbance caused by the war prevented the ceremony from being *even more solemn.* "I am sure," he said, "that in normal times you would have assisted at the functions *con altre spoglie ma non sotto altro nome."* Expressing the hope that the Archbishop would come to Australia, he said that he had a room which was quite worthy to receive even the *"lion of St. Paul."*[37]

Among the letters from Cardinal Vincenzo Vannutelli is one sent in May, 1910, congratulating Ireland on his defense of the Holy See against the Methodist attacks, inviting him to accompany him to and from Montreal, where the Cardinal was to be Legate at the Eucharistic Congress, and also expressing the wish to visit St. Paul. This visit the Cardinal made in September, celebrating Mass in the Cathedral, inspecting the new Cathedral site, and visiting the Seminary, after which the Archbishop accompanied him to Omaha, St. Louis, Chicago, and Washington. Alarmed by rumors of Ireland's ill health, the Cardinal wrote in May, 1918, asking him for definite news and assuring him of his constant prayers.[38]

Not all of Ireland's relationships, however, were as pleasant as these. Apart from those whom he antagonized in his fight against Cahenslyism, his principal opponents were Archbishops Corrigan and Ryan and Bishop McQuaid. Corrigan was the central figure of the trio, aided by the former and abetted by the latter. He showed his hostility at a very early date, refusing in January, 1888, to grant Ireland permission to speak on temperance at Chickering Hall, and he maintained it to the end of his life.[39] His secret ways and his practice of working through others revolted the Archbishop, who expressed his opinion of them in very strong language.[40] His sympathy with Tammany Hall, his refusal to allow Father Ducey to take part in the Lexnow investigation of its corruption, his bitter opposition to the Faribault plan, which was a matter of internal administration in the Archdiocese of St. Paul—although he had a similar plan in New York —his constant contacts with every adversary of St. Paul, his tendentious reply to the Holy Father's letter on Americanism, his opposition to Satolli, whom he regarded as a friend of Ireland, his exultation at what he wished to regard as the condemnation of the school experiment, his encouragement to the ecclesiastical members of his household to attack the Archbishop and the Delegate, his collaboration with Brandi to undermine Ireland in Rome, are not too easy to explain. The interview which he granted Austin Ford, who sought to bring about a better state of feeling between the two prelates, is typical. After having regretted that Ireland's prudence was not always in keeping with his zeal, he said that "he never thought of the words being construed as inimical." He justifies his brandishing of the telegram at the consecration dinner of the Bishop of Ogdensburg on the ground that "he was at a loss for something fresh to say about our great Pontiff. It was not a glorification over the discomfiture of any individual, but the triumph of a principle."[41] In spite of the fact that the Archbishop's files contain copies of the letters which Corrigan sent to Michael Walsh, editor of the *Catholic Herald*, urging him to attack Ireland,[42] he assured Ford that his constant injunction had been to say as little as possible or nothing at all to the newspapers. The whole conspiracy against Satolli and Ireland was exposed in all its unsavory detail in the Chicago Sunday *Post* in March, 1893, and one would gladly pass over in silence this unfortunate conflict, which, widely publicized, shocked the people of the country, were there not the inescapable conviction that His Grace of New York was responsible for much of the grief and, one might almost say, the tragedy in the life of the Archbishop of St. Paul.

Ireland's criticism of the Archbishop of Philadelphia arose largely over the latter's attitude on the school question, and especially over his attempt to maintain that the archbishops, in their meeting in New York in November, 1892, adopted the two extra resolutions simply because when he addressed them individually they did not object to them. Ireland also learned that Ryan "had been discovered supplying the German Catholic paper of Baltimore with articles against the

Cardinal [Gibbons]."[43] The disagreement between the two prelates, however, never reached major proportions.

If the Archbishop engaged in combat with Bishop McQuaid, he evidently regarded him as a fair, open antagonist, and he did not refer to him in the bitter terms which he used in speaking of one or two other opponents. It is pleasant to record that he visited Rochester later in life and composed their differences. To Abbé Klein, who visited him in 1907, McQuaid said:

> You must not take me for an enemy of Archbishop Ireland. I have always admired his zeal; and at present we are on the best of terms. But at the time you speak of he meddled a deal too much in things that did not concern him. It was intolerable, especially for me, who have always looked upon poor Corrigan as my spiritual son. A protest was needed, and I undertook the burden of it. It did not please them in Rome. Cardinal Rampolla reprimanded me, saying that only the Holy See had the right to blame bishops. But all the same, Ireland gave up meddling in New York affairs, and left Corrigan in peace.[44]

It is significant that when Archbishop Corrigan left the scene in May, 1902, discord seemed to have gone out of the life of Archbishop Ireland, who could write later in the same year: "Farley is ostentatiously reversing in all points the Corrigan regime. He proclaims '*in plateis*' his friendship for me. McQuaid, too, is my staunch admirer. *Le monde est à rebours.*"[45]

As might be expected, Archbishop Ireland maintained a large correspondence with Abbé Klein. When a group of the Parisian friends of the Archbishop, with Henri Lorin as their spokesman, expressed the wish to see published the discourses which he had delivered in France, Klein was asked to prepare an edition as soon as O'Connell had obtained the Archbishop's permission. When the volume appeared, in 1894, the Abbé sent it to Ireland, reminding him of the words he used in Paris: "If there were no America, Oh! how I would love to be your companion in arms." Now he was collaborating in the moral, religious, and social rehabilitation of France. His words, full of life and promise, would carry to all who read them light, strength, and hope. They might surprise some reactionaries "who wish to roll Niagara back into Lake Erie," but they would call forth the liveliest sympathies of the intelligent.[46]

In April the Archbishop sent him two letters, the one private, telling him of a few ideas which he had committed to paper and which he might publish if he wished; the other, intended for publication, thanking him for his Preface, in which "not only have you grasped completely my thought, but you have also clothed it, as I could not have done, in clear and attractive words."[47]

Two months later the Abbé told of the generally favorable reception of the Archbishop's Foreword. Only the *Gazette de France* had said that Ireland would do well to keep "his socialism, his liberalism and his infinite number of heresies for the American savages." These were happy days for Klein, who could hardly believe that French opinion had made such progress. He said: "Only ten years ago, (ask M. Hogan), they would have cursed you and I would have been burned in effigy. Today, only some of those, who are behind the times, write that America is not France, and France is not America. To which I am driven to answer that they are geographically correct." Ireland's words, he averred, were enthusiastically received by 95 per cent of the Catholic newspapers. He rejoiced at an article in the *Bulletin* of the Catholic Institute, which named Leo XIII, Lavigerie, Strossmayer, and Ireland as the great men of the Church of the nineteenth century. Even the Jesuit Fathers were astonished, and it was with a very respectful tone that they reproached the Archbishop for associating the words "democracy" and "Catholicism." The intelligent laity and all the young clergy had found encouragement and light in Ireland's words; the nonbelievers were impressed—something which rarely happened in France, where Catholic books were not publicized; the independent press—*Figaro, Temps,* and *Journal des Debats*—had given the book a warm welcome, even the yellow journals had reproduced the most significant parts, and some friends had contributed important and very favorable articles.

In January, 1895, he told of his new position as director of *L'Enseignement Chrétien,* an appointment he had received in spite of some old superiors, who "crossed themselves while pronouncing the three terrible words: Lavigerie, Ireland, New Tendencies."[48]

The Archbishop, who wrote in July, 1896, to announce publication of the second volume of his addresses, spoke of the sensation caused in many parts of Italy by the Abbé's translation, of the requests for an Italian translation. "But in my opinion," he added, "our ideas would not be understood in Italy; then, too, the Jesuits of the country would be angered beyond measure."[49] In December Klein related the reaction to the dismissal of Bishop Keane from the Catholic University, and especially the sore amazement manifested by Duchesne and De Lapparent. The joy of the reactionary press, which up to that time had been opposed to the pontifical directives, was most insolent, as they cried out delightedly that Leo had changed his ideas, and they tried to find justification in what they regarded as the reversal of his policy. When the attacks made on Ireland in America were reproduced in France, Klein supplied Eugene Veuillot, editor of *L'Univers*, with documents in order to clarify the situation. Placing much of the blame on Périès and Maignen, he asked for information concerning the events which led to the dismissal of the former from the Catholic University. He told of a new Spanish version of *L'Eglise et le Siècle*, and offered to produce an Italian version. He concluded by saying: "I often envy those who can leave material matters alone. But your ideas do such great service, that it is better to make them known, in their strong apostolic spirit, and not let them be misrepresented any longer by adversaries. When that is done, we shall no longer have imbeciles against us."

Klein had translated only a few of Ireland's discourses in *L'Eglise et le Siècle*, and when he received the complete English work, *The Church and Modern Society*, his first impulse was to ask permission to translate it, but he concluded that it was better to give the extreme rightists time to digest *The Life of Father Hecker*. While the diocesan clergy and the majority of Catholics continued to be friendly, some of the religious orders, especially the Jesuits and the Dominicans, had manifested anger, and there were rumors that representations would be made in Rome. In May, 1898, he wrote indignantly of the *Imprimatur* granted to Maignen's book, and in December of the following year he told of the reception of the Archbishop's article on the Dreyfus affair. Having recovered his courage after the condemnation of Americanism, he wrote:

In spite of the reactionary wind which continues to blow, my personal position is good; the past crisis has given me more significance with the public than I deserve; and it has not tarnished my reputation for orthodoxy with the authorities. At the solemn meeting for the reopening of the Catholic Institute, before cardinals, archbishops and bishop protectors, the reporter for the School of literature praised unreservedly my new book (*Mgr. Dupont des Loges*, Bishop of Metz), with an allusion, which was vigorously applauded by the audience, to the fact that I know how to unite love of the present with love of the past.

This he related, not through vanity, but to make clear his complete recovery as a soldier, ready to place himself under the Archbishop's orders for the good fight. In the Abbé's correspondence during this time there is a strange and rather ominous silence concerning the incident of the *circolo,* which Cardinal Gibbons had regarded as a great honor. Perhaps he viewed it in the same manner as he and some others regarded the Archbishop's discourses on the Temporal Power.

Their correspondence has not much of interest until the end of 1906, when Klein expressed himself on the religious situation in France as follows:

I don't have to tell you of the ravages caused in the Church in France by the refusal to form the "associations cultuelles." They have escaped some dangers of an imperfect law only by putting themselves under the rule of laws which are much less broad and liberal. But nothing is gained by recrimination; and it is not for this reason that I am writing to you. Various priests deserving of consideration and still young write to me to learn if, in the destruction of their seminaries, they could not find in America a field for their zeal. May I have those who write to me and who seem deserving of consideration address you or one of your subordinates?[50]

Ireland expressed his sympathy with the French clergy in their sufferings, and said:

I feel it keenly. Moreover, the repercussion is felt outside of France. Here we have the painful task of explaining it as best we can, of reassuring our Catholics, and of refuting the arguments of the enemies of France and of the Church. I, who love both France and the Church, find myself in a particularly embarrassing position. But, unfortunately, I know too much and I can't speak.[51]

In April, 1907, the Abbé returned to the subject, indicating that matters had become worse. As the difficulties increased, certain spirits revealed a daring, bordering on rashness, concerning fundamental doctrines. The authorities, in turn, became so excited and baffled that they confounded the serious inquirers with the rebellious, and took for real dangers the phantoms of heresy invented by the heresy hunters whom Ireland knew so well. The effects of the rules imposed by Rome were proving more and more disastrous. The material losses, passing all imagination, were beginning to entail the suspension of religious life and of priestly recruitment. "Try to imagine," he said, "not having any legal existence, any means of establishing property or of transferring it. Before long, many of the bishops say, it will be necessary, unless we are to perish, to establish some sort of associations of the type of 1901, much less favorable than that set up by the Law of Separation." All around him he saw growing from day to day fears, suffering, collapses. The publication of the Montagnini papers had shown everyone, what some already knew, that the advice of the reactionary politicians had prevailed over that of the bishops and of the commission unanimously appointed by them. The Archbishop replied that he could read between the lines of the Abbé's letters and understand all that he said of *"la Terreur blanche."* While he was hopeful of a gradually more satisfactory state of affairs, he regarded the present condition as "Martial Law."

In January, 1908, Klein suggested a French translation of the second volume of *The Church and the Age.* He told of the sensation caused by the removal from his position in the Catholic Institute of Toulouse, of Monsignor Pierre Henri Battifol, whom he called "a scholar it is true, but such a politician," and of the fight waged around Paul Bureau, professor of the Faculty of Law of the Catholic Institute of Paris, and author of *La Crise Morale des Temps Nouveaux,* who had to write a letter of submission but retained his position. Modernists were hunted down, some professors of the Grand Séminaire were removed, but, generally speaking, the Catholic Institutes remained untouched.[52]

In December, 1911, Ireland congratulated Klein on his productivity, even if through a somewhat different orientation, and on setting his sails, like a wise mariner, in accordance with the wind currents of the moment, whose force and velocity were not to be mistaken. These he regarded as so unfavorable that he felt they would prevent his return to France.[53] The Abbé's last letter to the Archbishop, written in September, 1914, when he was chaplain of the American field hospital at Neuilly, told of the moral and religious revival in France. The weaknesses of the French spirit, he said, appeared only on the surface; at heart she was alive, hopeful, generous, resolute, and worthy of her past. All divisions had disappeared as if by magic; the worst antimilitarists had become ardent patriots, and no trace of anticlericalism existed. The national faith had blossomed all at once; soldiers and officers received the Sacraments before going to the front, and during the week the churches were as filled as on Sunday. "You must," he said, "be as pleased as we are with the choice of the Sacred College, with Benedict XV and Cardinal Ferrata. I suppose that a trip to Rome will have more attraction for you. You will also find a modest and respectful friend who will be very happy to serve you."

The correspondence of Monsignor Louis Duchesne, perhaps the most interesting of all, covers the years 1910 to 1918. When, after a long contest, Duchesne was elected a member of the French Academy in succession to Cardinal François D. Mathieu in 1910, he wrote to acknowledge the Archbishop's felicitations. Of the panegyric which, according to custom, he was to deliver on his predecessor, he said: "It is not at all easy, for, as some one here remarked, his virtues were on the inside and his faults on the outside, in relief even. The people whom I ask are well supplied with little stories, which are of little use, but they are not informed on what is necessary for the beatification. I'll have to do the best I can." Concerning ex-President Roosevelt, who had recently stirred up a hornet's nest in Rome, and who was refused audience with the Pope, he wrote:

> We do not know any more what to make of your Roosevelt. He definitely lacks culture. Too much hippopotamus, too many receptions and conferences. We'll see now whether the trusts will fall under his bullets like the poor beasts of central Africa. Perhaps we shall see him consul for life, protector, emperor. Pius X, however, will not make a voyage to Washington for the consecration ceremony. It is a pleasure, dear Monseigneur, to see you in our old hemisphere. You, at least, do not massacre rhinoceroses, and you make only very few conferences.[54]

Duchesne's book *Les Fastes episcopaux de l'ancienne Gaule,* which gave a history of French dioceses, brought a storm around his head. The appearance of the first volume in 1895 caused scandal to the traditionalists by deflating some of the claims of the churches, such as, for example, that Martha and Mary with Lazarus landed at Marseilles. In the same year he was chosen head of the French School at Rome and lived in the Palazzo Farnese. His principal work, *L'Histoire Ancienne de l'Eglise,* appeared in 1905, 1907, and 1910. These three volumes had received the *Imprimatur* of the famous Father Lepidi, Master of the Sacred Palace, but had been attacked in *L'Unità Cattolica* of Florence. Duchesne was working on the fourth volume when he received a rude shock to find, on January 22, 1912, that his book had been placed on the Index. A visitor to his studio found him with his head between his hands weeping bitterly.[55] On February 5 he made his submission and wrote to the Cardinal Prefect of the Index that as a faithful son of the Church he bowed respectfully before the decree. Writing to Ireland a few weeks before the condemnation, he said:

> While so many of the bishops pronounce maledictions upon me, it is pleasant to meet one who blesses me. It is true that he is as far removed from me in distance as he is near to me in friendship. He whose home meets my eye when I raise my head from my writings has only violent feelings towards me, which some day or other will transform themselves into some abominable condemnation. For nearly fifty years now I have

been working for the Church, not, I think, without some religious success. A suspicion enters a certain mind—voilà, I am reduced to the state of an evil beast, which must be exterminated at any price. For eighteen months the "papal" press pursues me with its wrath. The bishops of France and Italy pour a long rosary of maledictions upon my remains. They interdict me in the seminaries, in religious Orders, where not long ago I was honored by being read in the refectory—even in the presbyteries I am condemned. And that is not all. The list will end with the Index, if they do not go as far as excommunication.

"And now, oh learned man, break your head to write books." Thus spoke Poggi when he told how the rats of Monte Cassino had devoured for bread the masterpieces of antiquity. So can I say that, in another sense.

We have seen here two new American cardinals; they are not the ones we expected. One alone would have been enough, and that one neither the one nor the other. The one from New York has made a sensation by his extravagance and ostentation. It would seem that as an American and as a bishop it would have been better for him to be more reserved.

Mlle de C— and I often speak of you. I do not need to tell you that she sometimes makes remarks which are a bit daring and which certainly would not be approved by Monsignor Bressan [Secretary of the Pope].

In January, 1913, in response to the Archbishop's New Year greetings, he wrote:

How your remembrance touches me. You are indeed a great soul; neither time nor great distances can master your faithfulness in remembering your friends. They, on their part, do not forget you. We have known better times, when we could exchange hopeful thoughts. Present clouds can cast gloom over the future, but they disconcert neither friendship nor resistance to discouragement.

Of late we have had to fear for the worse. Delehaye, the President of the Bollandists, was marked out for the Index. The decree, they say, was already signed, but the Belgian Government intervened with such vigor that the danger is for the moment averted. At a time when even the *Osservatore Romano* is censured, who can remain tranquil? When will be the end of terror? Madame de Thebes announces it for this year, but the *Messagero* declares that its anticlericalism makes it a duty for it to welcome the prolongation of the present state of affairs.

You had the kindness to wish me a "Happy Christmas." Alas. At Christmas in Bethlehem there was an announcement of peace to men of good will. Now war is made upon them. I do not know whether in the depths of your Minnesota and of your many occupations in America you have time to follow European politics. It looks as if we are about to have a house-cleaning, and in little Europe strange things are happening. The sick man has become worse, and we can see the time when the sick woman will also give the doctors something to think about. Meanwhile, the eagle with the two heads is making a great fuss, but he is in a cage, or almost so. I did not fly into Egypt. It was merely a coincidence. The Minister of Public Instruction asked me to go to Cairo on a tour of inspection. I spent the month of April there. The newspapers did the rest, some of them very irreverently, for from the comparisons they made with the Gospel, the result was that Herod would be living not far from the Borgia apartments. It isn't I who used such language.[56]

In November, 1893, Leo XIII issued the encyclical *Providentissimus Deus,* which was a rejection of Alfred Loisy's Biblical theories. Loisy, in his inaugural lecture at the Catholic Institute of Paris in 1892 and in an essay published the following year, had denied the absolute inerrancy of the Bible and the Mosaic authorship of the Pentateuch. A month after the appearance of the encyclical, Loisy wrote to Ireland that what the Pope had said about inspiration did not give him any difficulty, but that evidently historical exegesis had no right to exist. Moreover, rumors of a series of condemned propositions dealing with his book on Job made it impossible for him to continue the publication of his *Biblical Review.* He did not intend to put into circulation the issue of January, 1894, which had been already printed. He doubted whether he should accept the chaplaincy placed at his disposal by Cardinal Richard of Paris, who had forbidden him to publish anything until the instruction of the Holy Office had come.

In December, 1899, Klein told Ireland of the pitiable condition of Loisy, who had been gravely ill and who was living quietly at Belle-vue after resigning his chaplaincy, and he suggested that he might send him some stipends. On receipt of these, Loisy wrote in February, 1900, to acknowledge them and to tell of the kindness of Archbishop Mignot of Albi, who had obtained permission for him to say Mass privately. He went on to say:

The time is more propitious for silent work than for immediate publication of scientific works. Attention seems to be inclined in an altogether different direction. And although there is a movement manifesting itself, the state of mind of the French clergy is altogether different from what it was ten years ago. But if progress is evident, the reaction increases. The "Etudes" of the Jesuits in Paris publishes articles which are truly insolent with ignorance, one-sided and in bad faith. A certain Mr. Micheneau has just begun a series of articles to prove that we cannot in conscience abandon the apostolic authenticity of the strictest sense of any writings of the New Testament. He has already proven that the Mosaic authenticity of the Pentateuch is of faith, and all that is said with an arrogance which would be perfectly ridiculous if we did not know that these bad pleadings sometimes serve the good better than acts which are much better warranted.

The great question is: what will happen to Catholic teaching if one admits that it can be changed on important points? To which one can answer that that will happen which has already happened more than once.

The first Christian generations believed in the imminence of the last judgment and in the parousia. The Church came to abandon that primitive eschatology and strengthened herself in so doing. For centuries people heard with absolute rigor the axiom "Outside the Church there is no salvation." Now we admit the possibility of salvation for all, and the Church is only the agent providentially destined to bring it to all men. We do not have to confuse any longer the rejection of scholastic theology with the abandonment of tradition. In one sense it is not a question of abandoning tradition; it is a question merely of understanding it better in order to interpret it better. A great many opinions which occupy or amuse theologians have nothing to lose when one corrects them. The progress of science and of criticism calls for a change in theological teaching, but neither science nor criticism demands that we act foolishly. This would be equivalent to admitting the necessity of the transformation taking place of itself. This work cannot be done by scholars alone nor by ecclesiastical authority alone. Let authority watch, correct, guide. If it strikes indiscriminately both friends and foes in its attempt to obtain silence and inaction, we know what will happen.

The case of Professor Mivart is most regrettable. His articles contain truth mixed with extravagances. It would not have been difficult to get him to disavow those, and we would have been spared the scandal of putting out of the Church a man who has long served it. Why not have pity on all misfortunes, even those of the intellect. It is not largeness of mind or heart that makes one rigorous in regard to those who are mistaken. And can we today police ideas by summary processes of condemnation in which it would seem that often everything else is condemned but error?

He gave an outline of what he intended to do. He planned a series of articles for *La Revue du Clergé Français*, a commentary on the Fourth Gospel, and a translation of the whole Bible with notes. He concluded by saying: "Your Grace, the patron of my chapel is a saint, I should say a martyr not canonized, Cardinal Newman, whose portrait an Englishman, Mr. Gibson, whom you must know, procured for me."[57]

That the Archbishop's sympathy extended to the pitiable condition of the unfortunate Loisy and not to his theological aberrations goes without saying. In his article on the Pontificate of Pius X, published in the *North American Review*, he said:

Read *"Autour d'un Petit Livre"* and tell me what is left therein of the doctrine of the Incarnation and the Redemption, what is left therein of the divine origin of the Church and the Sacraments? Either Loisy was to be condemned, or Pius X was to fold his tent and hie himself and his illusion of a divinely established Church into the nebulous regions of fable.[58]

At another time he quoted approvingly the words of a writer who said: "What they [Abbé Loisy and Abbé Houtin] are doing is to implant within it [the Roman Communion] a leaven, which, if it ever becomes active, cannot stop working until it drives out every vestige of Christianity itself."

During the Archbishop's visit to Paris in 1892 he met many of the leading figures and made many friends who wrote to him from time to time. Max Turmann of *L'Univers* and *Le Monde,* who had met him at the home of M. Paul Philippon and heard him at the Cercle du Luxembourg, and who had also urged Abbé Klein to translate the Archbishop's discourses into French, writes to him for some material on the Catholic social movement in the United States. L'Abbé Paul Naudet, director of *La Justice Sociale,* who had defended Americanism so ardently, sends him a brochure. M. Edmond Demolins, director of *La Science Sociale,* speakes of the great impression Ireland made on two of his co-workers who visited him—M. Paul de Rousiers and M. Paul Bureau—and joins his request with that of M. Firmin-Didot that the Archbishop write a Preface for a work published by the latter, entitled *The Vatican, the Popes, the Civilization and the Government of the Church,* a request which Ireland had refused. Paul de Rousiers, author of *La Vie Américaine,* who had visited him in St. Paul in 1890, when he was seeking material for his book, now sends him a copy. Henry Lasserre, author of *La Crise Chrétienne,* begs his intercession in Rome that his condemnation be recalled. The Marquis de Grasse asks his blessing on the occasion of the translation of the remains of Admiral Comte de Grasse, the companion-in-arms of Washington, Lafayette, and Rochambeau. Arthur Verhaegen invites him to address La Ligue Démocratique Belge at Liége, of which he was president. Eugène Tavernier of *L'Univers,* a nephew of Eugene Veuillot, who in turn was a brother of Louis, the opponent of Montalembert and Dupanloup, asks about the advisability of contributing some articles on the French situation to an American journal. Julien de Narfon, author of *Léon XIII,* speaking of the sad condition of affairs in France in 1908, feels that he is assisting at an extraordinary comedy, in which it seemed that the Reverend Fathers were the impresarios while still remaining in the wings (of the theater). The Pope, after having granted the bishops a plenary council which they unanimously wished, had withdrawn the permission. Roman fear of the independence of the episcopate was, he said, very flattering to the shade of Bossuet, but it showed a debatable sense of reality. What, would be strange would be to revive Gallicanism by stirring up its ghost.

The Count de Meaux, who had sent him his volume on his father-in-law, M. de Montalembert, thanks him for his appreciation of it, saying: "If he were living, there is surely no one by whom he would be prouder and happier to be appreciated than by the eloquent and valiant organ of the Catholic Church in free America." Of the Archbishop's *The Church and Modern Society* he said: "While I read it I felt that I was listening to you once more, and, though far away, I felt my soul thrill to your words." When Ireland sent his condolences on the death of Madame de Montalembert, the Count wrote: "Of all the tributes paid to her none could be in all respects more precious to the family than yours; none pictures her to us as we love to recall her, with all the memories she evoked."[59]

Among all his French friends, the Archbishop seemed to have a special regard for Henri Lorin and Georges Goyau, both of whom were interested in the social question. Lorin was a friend of Rampolla and of Pope Leo XIII, and more than once he entertained Ireland at Maule. His weekly meetings on social problems attracted a large group of fine minds. When he died in 1914, shortly after Count de Mun, with whom he had collaborated, many of the papers, especially *La Libre Parole* and *Le Figaro*, paid high tribute to his work. He had just returned from Rome, where he went to counteract the influence of the Austrian Ambassador, who, at the beginning of the war, was working against France. He enjoyed the respect and affection of Pope Benedict XV, who in his audience conversed with him for almost two hours. The Archbishop had invited him to accompany him to Rome on a visit which he hoped to make.[60]

In August, 1909, he thanked Goyau for his two volumes on Germany, which he said were rich in erudition, exact in analysis and synthesis, and altogether a masterpiece. Among other things he said: "Give your friend, Fonsegrive, a good scolding in my name for having quoted in La Quinzaine LeRoy's article on Dogma. LeRoy is certainly in error and he will drag with him to their ruin those who give him support." In January, 1912, he wrote:

I am glad that my friends in Paris do not forget me. For my part I surely do not forget them—there is always a large part for them in my memory and in my heart. I am so deeply indebted to them for the affection with which they have honored me and for the beautiful ideas in which they have allowed me to share. I have long had the intention of writing to thank you for having sent me a copy of your book *Bismarck and His Time*. What a fine history—so complete in its details, so dramatic in its composition, so correct, so poetic in its style. You have to perfection the ability to place your personages and your facts so that the mere reading of them makes one live in the midst of them, breathe the atmosphere which surrounds them, understand their motive and its consequences. When I came to the last page I was sorry that there was not a fourth volume giving the details of the reconciliation of the German Empire with Leo XIII. I imagine that your visits to the Vatican have been interrupted. You and Henri Lorin are no longer the intimate advisers, when it comes to a question of the pontifical policy towards France. Well, what can you expect? You must just wait. That is what others are doing.[61]

The Archbishop had also a special affection for Monsignor James Nugent of Liverpool, who had co-operated with him in the work of temperance and of colonization. On receiving news of his death in July, 1905, the Archbishop preached at the Solemn Requiem Mass celebrated in the Cathedral of St. Paul. Writing to Father Berry he said: "Seldom have I had a friend, to whom my heart went out so wholly, in whose soul, as I thought, I read so completely my own, whom I sought so willingly to please and to serve with unreserved loyalty. With him there went from earth the *'dimidium animae meae.'* "[62]

Chapter 14

AN HONOR UNACHIEVED

Give me the avowed, erect and manly foe
Firm I can meet, perhaps return the blow.
But of all plagues, good Heaven, thy wrath can send
Save me, oh, save me from the candid friend.[1]

Archbishop Ireland had no more devoted friends than Mr. and Mrs. Bellamy Storer. Mr. Storer was born in Cincinnati, Ohio, on August 28, 1847, and died in Paris on November 12, 1922. A Harvard graduate, he practiced law in Cincinnati until 1891, when he was elected to Congress. A man of transparent honesty and outstanding character, he won and kept fine friendships among the great figures of his time. He maintained close relationships with Presidents McKinley and Roosevelt, both of whom were indebted to him. The former spoke of him as "the most unselfish man I have ever known"; the latter referred to him and his wife as "among the few very staunchest friends we ever had."[2]

Just when Archbishop Ireland first met the Storers is difficult to say. A letter from Mrs. Storer sent from Rome in April, 1895, seems to indicate a well-established friendship. In it she tells a delightful bit of gossip about her visit to the North American College in search of an audience with the Pope, of Father Farrelly's cold reception, his amused aloofness, his faint remembrance of the Archbishop's visit to Rome some years before on "that little affair of the schools," his assurance that "private audiences are not granted to everybody," and his sudden *volte-face* when a casual visitor's greeting revealed the fact that Mr. Storer had been a member of Congress.[3] The following year, during which Mr. Storer was received into the Church, she writes from Cincinnati of her offer to Archbishop Elder of a house valued at $100,000, which, however, he did not accept.[4] Her letters reveal her desire to see her husband once more in public life. A visit to Secretary of State John Sherman brought only the suggestion of an undersecretaryship or consulship, and she seeks the advice of the Archbishop.[5] In her laudable ambition for the public recognition of her husband's ability she received encouragement from Theodore Roosevelt, then Governor of New York, who appealed to President McKinley and received from him the assurance that nobody was more appreciative of the ability and nobleheartedness of his friend Mr. Storer than he. Within a few months the President appointed him Minister to Belgium, which post he held until the end of the Spanish War. At that time he was asked to accept an assignment in Madrid, for the purpose of bringing about the renewal of diplomatic relations and of drawing up new treaties—a task which, because of the passions aroused by the war, called for fine statesmanship. After service of more than three years and the completion of the treaties, he was rewarded with the ambassadorship to Vienna, filling the office with distinction until his recall in April, 1906. After that he retired from public life.

During all these years the Storers maintained constant correspondence with Archbishop Ireland, as revealed in more than fifty letters. Mrs. Storer's letters are full of interesting and amusing small talk about Roosevelt, Taft, Leopold II of Belgium, the Queen Regent, the Queen of Spain, various high ecclesiastics, senators, etc. When dealing with men like Senator Foraker, Mr. McNutt, and General Merritt, whom she dislikes, her language is not noticeably inhibited. She characterizes John Hay as "a little man of literary talent but small calibre, ruined by opulence"; she quotes Roosevelt as referring to General Miles as "a swine, a Gadarene swine." She knows everyone of importance on the Continent, visits the Queen Mother of Belgium, who is full of indignation at the attack on *The Life of Father Hecker*, and the Queen Mother of Spain, who requests her to work for the liberation of the Spanish soldiers in the Philippines. She corresponds with Lord Halifax, whose hopes for the reunion of Anglicanism and Rome fill her with enthusiasm. She and Bellamy have breakfast at Henri Lorin's in Paris with Monsignor Lorenzelli, the Papal Nuncio, to whom she gives a copy of her article on Americanism, argues the question with him, and is happy because "it is such a triumph to have gained over a *nonce de première classe* and an intimate friend of Cardinal Satolli." She tells of her visit to the White House, of Roosevelt's childish irritation with Archbishop Ireland, with whom, he avers, the Vatican is always first, and his sudden burst of laughter when, quoting himself, she says: "Well, he is 'the only archbishop living who wears the badge of the Loyal Legion.'" For this irritation she blames Henry Cabot Lodge, whom she regards as Roosevelt's evil genius. She is indignant because a confidential letter of Bellamy's to McKinley brings only an answer from his secretary. She begs Rampolla to ask the Pope to offer prayers for McKinley's recovery, and strives to persuade the Nuncio to say Mass on the day of mourning for his death. Writing from Biarritz, she relates her farewell audience in Madrid with the Queen Mother, who refers in most unflattering terms to her uncle, Leopold II of Belgium, her surprise at finding that he is staying at her hotel, her delight at all the attentions he shows her to the great amazement and envy of the other guests. She seasons her letter with some piquant gossip about the Viennese court, and longs to escape from the heat and inaction of Madrid and the expensive entertainment of Vienna. She describes in detail her audiences with Rampolla, the polished diplomat, and with Leo XIII, who assured her that no one had been condemned in his letter to Cardinal Gibbons, but only "some tendencies."[6]

Bellamy's letters are fewer and of sterner stuff—Taft's mission to the Philippines, Roosevelt's feud with Miles, his own interviews with cardinals and the Pope. Speaking of Merry del Val, he says: "His reception and manner were all that I could hope for, Spanish grace and dignity tempered with English straightforward frankness and simplicity of manner. A most charming young man, full of zeal and ambition, and giving the impression of wide views and open ears." Pope Pius X he describes as "a man shorter than middle size, with snow white hair, and a kindly weatherbeaten, parochial face, and who laughs readily." Rampolla seems to him "bowed and broken; the disappointment and undoubtedly the sense of the world's forgetfulness of him was stamped on him, but I think in him there was and is greatness." Monsignor O'Connell he characterizes as a "clever, accomplished intriguer—but an imprudent and unsafe confidant; vainglorious of his own influence and personality."[7]

Both husband and wife were of superior intelligence, delightful, charming, cultured people, welcomed in the highest circles in Europe, utterly honest and sincere, and intensely devoted to Archbishop Ireland.

The Archbishop's letters were in kind. He wrote as one would to dear and trusted friends, giving intimate details of his interviews with Popes, cardinals, and Presidents, revealing all of his ambitions for the cardinalate, and encouraging them in their efforts to secure it. He tells them with evident satisfaction that his welcome in Rome could not possibly be better and that he is in high favor; he repeats the words of McKinley that he regarded as a great honor the Pope's complimentary reference to him and to his administration, as well as the President's assurance that he wanted to do for Bellamy the best in his power. The shade of his fellow townsman, Jonathan Swift, seems to lurk in the shadows, as one reads his minute relation of his efforts to have a suitable envoy sent to Rome for the settlement of Philippine affairs, of his ultimate success, and of his authorization to communicate the decision to Cardinal Rampolla. He is happy that Roosevelt is sending to the Holy Father beautifully bound and autographed copies of his books—including the one on hunting. He notes that the President is not altogether at ease about the future and that he would not be sorry if Hanna's rheumatism crippled completely his leg, or if the Democrats continued to worship Bryan. In 1903, he hopes that Rampolla will be the next Pope and that Merry del Val will not succeed him as Secretary of State. Of Francis Bourne, the new Archbishop of Westminster, he writes: "He is good, and nice, and kind; he will not repeat Vaughan's mistakes; but, O spirit of Manning." When his efforts to secure the ambassadorship at Paris or London for Bellamy fail, he puts on a bold front, urges Maria to be proud of her title—*ambassadrice à Vienne*—and assures her that London and Paris remain in the perspective of the future.

Like so many prominent converts, the Storers took an intelligent interest in the affairs of the Church. They followed with enthusiasm the career of the Archbishop and his brilliant contributions to the welfare of Catholicism. They felt, however, that his work was seriously hampered by the opposition of ecclesiastics in America and in Europe, and that only recognition by Rome would re-establish his influence. They were convinced that after the war with Spain it had become a matter of paramount importance that he be made a cardinal. Many non-Catholics, too, were deeply interested in this recognition, which, they felt, would give him a wider influence in the United States, and also in the Philippines, where many changes had to be made involving questions of great importance to this country and needing discussion and decisions at the Vatican. Foremost among these public men was Theodore Roosevelt. As early as 1899 he had urged McKinley to send a message to the Pope, requesting this favor. As Governor of New York he wrote to Mrs. Storer in March, 1899: "I absolutely agree with you as to Archbishop Ireland. It seems to me that from every standpoint of sound public policy, it will be a fortunate thing if we can have him made a cardinal, especially in view of what must occur in the Philippines."[8] The Governor's mental courage, however, did not always keep pace with his physical, and a few days later he hesitated about expressing himself publicly, not knowing how matters would end if he interfered directly, and fearing lest he might put himself under obligations. He favored the elevation of the Archbishop because of his liberal attitude. The administration, he said, had to guard against reactionary Catholics who might oppose the correction of abuses in the ecclesiastical arrangement of the Islands, and also against Protestant fanaticism, which would be fanned into a dangerous flame if Catholic reactionaries were put into control. While he did not wish his letter to be published, he did not object to its being shown.[9]

Again in April, 1900, Roosevelt expressed himself in similar strain, speaking of the high regard he had always had for Ireland, who represented to him the kind of Catholicism which must prevail in the United States if the Church was to attain its full measure of power and usefulness to the people. He felt that a reactionary or anti-American spirit in ecclesiastical affairs would in the long run result in disaster, just as a similar course would in political affairs, and that such a spirit would be welcomed by the bigoted opponents of Catholicism. "I may add," he said, "that the bigoted opponents of Catholicism are those who are most anxious to see the triumph within the ranks of Catholicism of this reactionary spirit, and the throwing out of men who have shown a broad liberalism and Americanism in policy."[10]

In September of that year the Storers went to Rome with Bishop O'Gorman, interviewed several of the cardinals, and were received by the Holy Father, to whom they conveyed the wishes expressed by the President, at the same time emphasizing the fact that only elevation to the cardinalate would dissipate the sad effects of the condemnation of Americanism. Rampolla they found as usual most gracious but also most diplomatic. Although their visit to Rome was without any concrete results, it pleased the President, who, as Ireland told them, attached the greatest importance to the Pope's opinion of Church matters in the Islands, and who was worried about the Catholic vote, since the Democrats were making capital out of persecutions and neglect of Catholics.[11]

Not only Roosevelt but also Taft favored the Archbishop's promotion. The latter indicated his interest in May, 1901, when he wrote to Mrs. Storer:

I share in your disappointment that Archbishop Ireland was not appointed Cardinal. The position which he occupies in the United States is unique. I think he has more influence with the people both of his own church and of other churches and with the people at large than any other prelate that I have ever known of in the United States. He is regarded as truly Catholic—in the usual sense of that word—and it is thought that he has solved the difficulty which sometimes presents itself to the non-Catholic mind, of complete loyalty, both to the church and to the country. The high esteem in which he is held by President McKinley and by all the prominent men in the Government cannot be exaggerated. I am sure that nothing would so tend to ameliorate the unjustifiable but still existent prejudice against the Catholic Church in some quarters of our country as the recognition by the Vatican of the merits of Archbishop Ireland by giving him the Cardinalate.[12]

While the Storers worked for the elevation of the Archbishop, they were also hopeful of recognition for themselves. Mrs. Storer's letters reveal her dissatisfaction with her husband's assignments. She felt that his ability and his services entitled him to something better— Berlin, Paris, or London. Madrid did not suit her health, and, after the signing of the treaty of peace with the United States, there was little to do. In Vienna, which came later, there was, she said, even less diplomatic business than there was in Brussels, and Bellamy was tiring of a life made up of social entertainments at his own expense. The Archbishop's efforts to secure a more desirable post for Bellamy were unavailing, for both McKinley and Roosevelt were more interested in making sure of their political fences and in taking care of men who deserved well of the party, with the result that one assurance after another only ended in disappointment. When the government decided to send a mission to the Vatican for the settlement of Philippine affairs, Ireland favored the selection of Storer, but the influence of Secretary of State Root prevailed and resulted in the appointment of Judge Smith.

These disappointments did not in the least dampen the enthusiasm of the Storers, who continued to use their influence in Rome in the interest of the Archbishop. They were encouraged by an interview which Ireland had in October, 1903, with Roosevelt, who told him that he had commissioned Bellamy to speak for him, *viva voce*, at the Vatican, and who seemed rather proud of having done so. The gist of this interview, which later became a matter of controversy and of veracity, was expressed more precisely a month later by the Archbishop, who quoted Roosevelt as saying: "I told him [Storer] I would not write a letter to the Pope asking for honors for you, but I said that he could go to Rome and say—*viva voce*—to the Pope, how much I wish you to be Cardinal, and how grateful I personally would be to him for giving you that honor."[13] When Monsignor O'Connell delivered this message at the Vatican, the Pope told him to say to the President that his wishes in regard to Ireland would most probably be fulfilled. Unfortunately the Associated Press got hold of the information and wired that an American prelate had seen the Pope to convey the President's message, whereupon Roosevelt's secretary, William Loeb, gave out a statement denying that the President had authorized anyone to speak for him. Evidently Roosevelt, while eager to co-operate, was not going to allow his advocacy of Ireland to hurt in any way his own ambition or to antagonize any large section of the people.

Only the extreme loyalty of the Ambassador and his wife can account for their persistent efforts on behalf of the Archbishop, for as early as April, 1901, Bellamy was convinced that the cardinal's hat would never come to him. He wrote to Bishop O'Gorman:

> To say now, as they do that the hat is sure, that it is already fixed for Msgr. is idle bavardage. Msgr. Ireland must again wait. Wait for the death of the Pope; wait for his own passing away; wait until the Greek Kalends. Mark my words, dear Bishop, Msgr. Ireland will never receive the Cardinal's hat. He is more likely to be canonized in the 22nd Century than biretta-ed in the 20th.[14]

This conviction was borne out by his visits to Rome and his audiences with the Pope and with Rampolla, who had been succeeded as Papal Secretary of State by Merry del Val, but who remained as inscrutable as ever. His wife, more hopeful, enlisted the interest of Princess Windisch-Graetz, who reported that Pius X had assured her "*sara fatto*" (it will be done).[15] Maria's letter to Merry del Val brought only the indefinite answer that the matter was of a delicate nature apart from Ireland's personal qualities, and one which the Pope must consider from many different points of view. She had her own explanation of Roosevelt's impulse to deny absolutely that he had ever sent any message—his indignation at the failure of the Vatican to accede to his request. Finally her activities brought matters to a head. Her frequent visits to Rome attracted the attention of the press, and early in 1904 items appeared in the Scripps-McKay news service and in *Leslie's Weekly* telling of her audiences. These and similar revelations thoroughly alarmed Roosevelt, who wrote to her in December, 1905, a long, "strenuous," bitter letter, in which he said:

> I am very gravely concerned at the mischievous effect your letters must have in misrepresenting the position of the United States Government. . . . I have always positively and unequivocally refused directly or indirectly to ask for the appointment of any man as Cardinal. . . . It is a matter of settled and traditional policy of this government not to interfere, under any possible circumstances.

He went on to rebuke her for taking advantage of her position as the wife of an ambassador, and he threatened the removal of her husband unless she gave assurance that her activities would cease.[16] When she scornfully refused to answer his letter, he sent in March, 1906, a communication through the Secretary of State recalling Bellamy from Vienna.

The removal of the Ambassador became the sensation of the press, which published long accounts of the incident, the denial of the President that he had sent any message to Rome on behalf of Ireland, and the interviews granted by Mrs. Storer, in which she not only denied interference in affairs of state but also quoted from White House correspondence in authorization of her actions.[17] The humiliation of the Storers, who were known and loved in many European diplomatic circles, was a source of deep chagrin to Archbishop Ireland, who regarded the suspension of Bellamy from office by a brutal cablegram as unforgivable. When Mrs. Storer expressed her indignation to a representative of the New York *Herald*, he wrote to her from Rome:

> I read yesterday your letter to the *Herald*, and with it Theodore's letter of 1900, communicated by you to the same paper. It clears the atmosphere, puts a stop to future newspaper guessings, and leaves "our friend in Washington" just where nothing more can be said by him. It was most fortunate that you were able to say that in no other letter was my name mentioned to you in connection with Roman affairs; Bellamy's mission was given and delivered *viva voce*; the President's confidence is respected, and the public is, or ought to be satisfied. Here all seems to be well understood. The authenticity of Bellamy's message remains indisputed; even admitting that the President has since declared that he wrote or said nothing officially as President, it is a fact that he made avowal of his own personal good will. . . . The President's whole conduct towards Bellamy

and you is simply inexplicable. While speaking with him I could not but recognize that there was something in his mind beyond his words, that I was unable to fathom.[18]

A suggestion from Mrs. Storer that perhaps it might be more prudent for him not to see them in Paris, if he wished still to be friends with Roosevelt, brought an indignant protest and the assurance that, President or no President, his affectionate regard for her and Bellamy would never be kept out of sight. It would be strange, he said, and something of which he would be forever incapable, if in order to please Roosevelt or Root or anyone else he feared to meet them openly.[19] But Mrs. Storer's efforts to secure from the Archbishop material which she might use in her vindication, and his efforts to pour oil on troubled waters, only resulted in irritation. He realized the futility of prolonging a newspaper controversy which already had brought enough embarrassment to those most concerned. He may also have felt that she had already given enough evidence to support her cause and that personal considerations must be subordinated to the interests of the Church, which demanded that he maintain his influence with the administration. A long, frank letter which she wrote in February, 1907, terminated the correspondence and interrupted the friendship for several years. Running through her letter is a note of disappointment that Ireland seemed to take her husband's humiliation with a certain appearance of *sang-froid.* She was especially hurt at his advice that they regard the whole incident as closed, as an affair of the past which should be buried with the past.[20] There is no further correspondence until December, 1911, when Bellamy sent congratulations to the Archbishop on his Golden Jubilee. In November, 1914, when he was in Rome, organizing for the Vatican a Bureau of Inquiry for missing soldiers, he wrote of his audience with Benedict XV, in which the Holy Father told him that he had sent Ireland his portrait through Cerretti, as a token of his respect and his great esteem.[21] Early in January, 1915, and once more in the following year, Mrs. Storer sought to recapture the old newsy manner of earlier years, but it was difficult to rebuild a friendship once broken.[22] When Monsignor Humphrey Moynihan asked her in August, 1923, for her memories of the Archbishop of St. Paul, she excused herself on the grounds that her health would not permit her to do so and that, moreover, she had given all of Ireland's letters to Cerretti. Finally, in April, 1930, she sent him the address delivered by Cardinal Cerretti on the occasion of his taking possession of his titular Church of St.

Cecilia, in which he paid tribute to the Archbishop. She added this postscript:

Today the bitterest enemies of Archbishop Ireland, in Rome and in the United States, are dead; and he lives in our memory as the greatest American patriot, whose aim was to convince the non-Catholics of America that the Church, as Leo XIII said, should clothe itself in the dominant traits of the nation—our great Archbishop Ireland is still with us—as one of the dead who speak.[28]

Unfortunately, the whole affair of the attempts of the Storers to secure recognition for the Archbishop received world-wide publicity. On his removal from the Vienna ambassadorship in 1906 Bellamy published extracts from his own and his wife's correspondence in a pamphlet sent to the President, his cabinet, and the United States Committee on Foreign Affairs, a brochure which finally made its appearance in the press. Four years later, Mrs. Storer renewed the controversy in a long letter to the Springfield *Republican*, in which she included two letters written by Ireland in the latter part of 1903. She concluded by characterizing Roosevelt as "a dangerous influence, whose power the truth alone could overcome." She also stressed the fact that his request to Pius X for the red hat was not made at the solicitation of Ireland, who heard of it, first of all, from the President himself, after the commission had been given. She returned to the subject again in 1923 in a privately printed book entitled *In Memoriam Bellamy Storer*, which contained many of Ireland's letters. Her desire to vindicate herself can easily be understood, but in so doing she inflicted cruel hurt not so much on Roosevelt as on the Archbishop. The whole episode was most unfortunate, and must have been ineffably embarrassing to Ireland. Lay open to the public the innermost heart of any man, his secret thoughts, hopes, and ambitions, and who will not know chagrin? And there is genuine pathos in the spectacle of a most devoted friendship driven by its very loyalty into excess and ending only in grief. Cynics who smile and regard it all as a concerted effort for mutual promotion forget that it was but the outcome of devoted friendship. Perhaps for a truer explanation we have to return to Virgil's "*Dux femina facti*," as also to Roosevelt's well-known impetuosity and to his apprehension lest his political ambitions be thwarted. One cannot but admire the intense loyalty of the Ambassador and his wife and regret that such devotion had so unfortunate an outcome. To them Ireland was deeply indebted for many of the important contacts he made in Europe. It was they who

opened for him the door of many a noble house, gained for him many
an influential friend: it was they who considered no effort too great
in the advancement of his cause, and brought surcease from the
labors of office by many a letter, every line of which breathed fealty
and reverence.

The Storer controversy leads naturally to the question of the
ambitions of the Archbishop of St. Paul. That he desired the cardinalate is a fact about which there can be no doubt; that in the pursuit of
it he welcomed the co-operation of his friends is well attested. Indeed, in his eyes there was something definitely wanting in one
who was devoid of ambition. It was John Morley who said:

> It is always the most difficult thing in the world to draw a line between
> arrogant egoism on the one hand, and, on the other, the identification of a
> man's personal elevation with the success of his public cause. The two ends
> probably become mixed in his mind, and, if the cause be a good one, it is
> the height of pharisaical folly to quarrel with him because he desires that
> his authority and renown shall receive some of the lustre of a far-shining
> triumph.[24]

Personal ambition, that "last infirmity of noble minds," may not be
the noblest motive which can actuate a public man, but it is usually
one of the motives, and it is a source of strength to recognize
it in oneself and in others. One may well ask how many members
of the hierarchy would not have welcomed the highest honor in the
gift of the Holy See? Ireland was merely unfortunate in that he
poured out his soul to intimate friends who should have destroyed
his letters. One wonders, it is true, at his imprudence in speaking so
frankly to a woman who was commonly known for her officiousness,
but it was the imprudence of a temperament that was essentially impulsive and frank, and one can find its only justification in the intensity of friendship. It is, perhaps, significant that his encouragement to the Storers to continue their efforts increased after 1899,
when the condemnation of Americanism must have made him all the
more eager for recognition. Then, too, zest was added to his ambition by his knowledge of the influences at work in Rome for the
elevation of His Grace of New York. He had heard many times from
Keane and O'Connell of the efforts of Eugene Kelly, Bourke Cockoran,
Bishop Gabriels, etc., on Corrigan's behalf.[25] Bishop Thomas O'Gorman, who said that "the negative result of his visit to Rome would be
to make it impossible for New York to get the Red Hat," presumed
that "strong efforts would be made to get him the honor for his Silver

Jubilee."[26] Bishop John Farley kept Corrigan informed on the results of his audience with the Pope in which he presented Philbin, District Attorney, as a close friend of Roosevelt, who "wished him to be a member of the Philippine Commission." "What we (Mr. P. and I) wanted to do," he said, "was to impress them with the sense of the President's friendship for Your Grace through his high regard for your close friend Mr. P."[27] These attempts did not succeed, however, for, as Cardinal Rampolla said on another occasion to Bishop Keane: "Rest assured that these tricks are fully understood in the Vatican."[28] Ireland protested more than once that on no account must Corrigan be made a cardinal, and, on the other hand, Bishop Messmer expressed to Corrigan his hope that St. Paul would never receive the "red hat," as "everybody would naturally consider it as an authoritative endorsement of Archbishop Ireland's policy."[29]

It would, indeed, be strange if Ireland did not have hopes. He had been regarded by many as the most influential figure in the episcopate and as one who had given valuable service to the Holy See. He had co-operated with Leo XIII in the establishment of the Apostolic Delegation in Washington, he had labored night and day to prevent the Spanish-American War, he had been the accredited agent of the Vatican in the Philippine negotiations, and he had been instrumental in sending the Taft Commission to Rome. The unofficial agent of the Pope in carrying out Leo's policy of persuading the French to accept the Republic, he was the official representative of the United States government in presenting the statue of Lafayette to France. He had defended the Vatican in the Fairbanks and Roosevelt incidents, and he had been influential in sending as ambassadors to the Quirinal such men as Henry White and General Draper, who were favorably disposed toward the Holy See. He had been told more than once that his services were appreciated in Rome and would meet recognition. No other man was more highly regarded by non-Catholics, and none had done more to make the Church known and respected in the United States. He was on intimate terms with almost all of the Presidents of his day, and his advice and counsel were constantly sought by the leading statesmen in this and in other countries. As Archbishop Patrick Riordan said:

> After your campaign in France, undertaken at the special request of the Holy Father, and the knowledge and approval of Rampolla, there was but one thing which should have been done in decency, to give you that appointment which all your friends looked for, and which was your due.[30]

Moreover, numberless expressions of opinion in private correspondence and in the press indicated the general expectancy of recognition. The Archbishop was constantly receiving letters not only from men in public life—Presidents McKinley, Roosevelt, and Taft, Senators Scott and Davis, Ambassador Kerens, and many others, who took it for granted that the cardinalate was merely a matter of time, but also from men in the highest ecclesiastical circles. Senator Cushman K. Davis of the Committee on Foreign Relations wrote in March, 1899, of the great interest aroused by the reports of his advancement, an interest expressed by those who were not of the Church but who felt that the cause of law, order, and social security would be thereby promoted.[31] As early as 1892 Cardinal Gibbons, who was most eager for the Archbishop's promotion, wrote to Rampolla that he had heard apparently well-founded rumors that Leo XIII was thinking of giving the United States a second cardinal in the person of John Ireland, and Gibbons wished to say that it would be a useful work for the glory of God and the welfare of the American Church. This, as he said, he wrote only after serious reflection. Of all the bishops in the United States the Cardinal of Baltimore did not know one whose promotion, especially in existing circumstances, was more opportune than that of the Archbishop of St. Paul, whose virtues, talents, zeal recommended him, but, as Gibbons said, especially the force he exercised on American public opinion and the favor he had with the government. The Cardinal knew that the President of the United States would be much flattered, as also Secretary Blaine, who had the highest admiration for Ireland and who gave him the warmest letters of introduction to American diplomats abroad.[32]

While he was in Rome during the same year, Ireland received a great many strong hints from both Rampolla and Ledochowski that a great honor was coming to him. When the former bade him farewell, he said with a smile: "You know, it is only until next year." Ledochowski repeated that nothing short of the great act which the Pope was preparing in the Archbishop's favor would conclusively stop the opposition to him.[33] The hopes of the two cardinals, however, were not realized. When on the death of Leo XIII in July, 1903, none of Ireland's candidates was elected to the papacy, he seemed for the moment to abandon hope, for he knew that he would not receive consideration from the new Pope, Piux X, who was no friend of the so-called liberals. He revealed his disappointment to O'Connell, to whom he wrote: "I have had my eye on Venice, and at last my fear is realized. Card. Gibbons wires me 'Pope man of God.' Well, we shall see. Present my deep regrets to Vannutelli and Rampolla. Either one would have done me for 'a man of God.' "[34] His conviction that all was over was trebled in force when Merry del Val was made Secretary of State, and his first impulse was to wish that the American public would drop his name forever from all connection with Roman news.[35] But eleven years later his hopes were revived upon the election of Benedict XV, who when secretary to Rampolla had always treated him with great kindness. Gibbons, who had hurried to Rome for the conclave, but who had arrived too late, had two audiences with the Pope, in the second of which he expressed the hope that some great recognition should be made of Ireland's eminent services to religion. Without holding out vain hopes or ignoring the weak links in the chain, he assured the Archbishop that the Pope's esteem of him was not merely academic and also that he had a number of stanch friends in the Sacred College.[36] To this Ireland replied:

Strange, as perhaps, it may seem—I am not surprised at the kindness of Benedict in my regard. Were it otherwise, he would have changed greatly from Mgr. Della Chiesa. The latter was always most gracious to me, and was always glad to make me feel he was my friend. Of course, he was the friend of Rampolla—his chosen son; and he knew, as he wrote me, Rampolla's affection for me. Of Della Chiesa it would not be said, as it could be of Sarto—*non cognoverunt Joseph*. In the letter I received from him last January he recounted at length what he knew about me—almost everything that could be known—and laid stress on words spoken of me by Rampolla.

A letter from Cardinal Falconio confirms his conversation with yourself. He [Pope] inquired about me—and that in a very loving manner.

Cardinal Ferrata is most willing to serve me. He did his best repeatedly, to commend me to Pius IX [sic—Pius X], though to his regret he met with small success.

I am no longer an exile from the Vatican—and that fact, of course, is pleasing.[37]

Again a month later he told Gibbons:

You need not fear that I become over-confident. I have been seeing for many years the weak links in chains. Nor, strange to say, shall I be over chagrined should the weak link turn out unexpected strength. Age calms ambitions, and readily anticipates disappointment. So, *fiat voluntas Dei*.[38]

On the death of Rampolla in 1913, Cerretti wrote of the Cardinal's admiration for Ireland and of the message he had sent to St. Paul through the Delegate, telling him to be prudent and to wait patiently.

And in March, 1916, the Delegate spoke of the celebration that sooner or later must take place in St. Paul.[39] Cardinal Gasquet expressed the disappointment of Ireland's many friends that they did not see him in the late consistory.[40] Cardinal Ferrata prayed God to keep the Archbishop in good health for many years for the welfare of his great diocese and for the Church "to which he had given so many and so valuable services." He referred to the noble sentiments which Ireland had expressed in their last conversation concerning the cardinalate, and which corresponded so perfectly to the "nobility of a spirit that knew how to look at human circumstances in the light of Christian philosophy." While he himself was desirous that the honor would come, he knew that others did not think in the same way, and it was therefore necessary to leave the thing to God, who would know how to find the means, if it were His will, "to recompense virtue and merit even in this world."[41] Similar regret was expressed by Cardinal Serafino Vannutelli, who said that one of his most fervent desires was to see Ireland elevated, and that he would not cease his efforts until the Archbishop entered the Sacred College "amid the unanimous applause of his fellow citizens and to the great good of Catholicism in America."[42]

Some months before Ireland's death, Cerretti told him of the way in which Pope Benedict, in an audience with the members of a Serbian mission, referred to the Archbishop as "Cardinal" Ireland. Cerretti, who was impressed by the "very significant" smile with which the Pope spoke to him later concerning the incident, explained that no consistory would be held until the end of the war, because the Holy See would have to reveal those who "are *riservati in petto.*"[43] Reference to this incident was also made by Father Francis Jaeger, a member of the mission, who later had a private audience with the Pontiff. He told the Pope that His Holiness had referred to the St. Paul prelate as "Cardinal" Ireland, and that other members of the mission had spoken jestingly of the papal infallibility as a result of the "error." "You may tell them," said Pope Benedict, "that Rome is still infallible. I know whereof I spoke. Archbishop Ireland is a Cardinal *in petto.*"

There is abundant evidence that only death prevented the realization of the hopes of these prelates. Bishop Francis C. Kelley states in his book *The Bishop Jots It Down* that when the news of Ireland's death reached Rome, he was with Cerretti, then Under-Secretary of State, who told him that the Pope had decided on the elevation.[44] At the dinner given for Cerretti when he came as the representative of Benedict XV at the Golden Jubilee of Gibbons, he said:

> If the great Archbishop of the West had been spared, he would have rejoiced to be here today; and we also would rejoice were he with us today; especially would we all have rejoiced in the future—this I may say without indiscretion—when the great Archbishop Ireland, whom the Holy Father esteemed so highly, would also have received the highest distinction within the power of the Sovereign Pontiff to bestow.[45]

And this statement is confirmed by a letter which Cardinal Gasquet wrote to Bishop Thomas O'Gorman shortly after the death of the Archbishop. He said at that time:

> I have only just had your cable here. I had, however, heard of the death of our friend, Archbishop Ireland, the day after it happened, and offered up my Mass for the repose of his soul. He is a great loss to all who knew him and to America. I am particularly sad about it, as there is no doubt that had he lived only a month or so longer he would have been created Cardinal. Since you were in Rome I have often spoken on the subject to the Holy Father and always found him most sympathetic—the difficulty was the fact that there were already three Cardinals in America. Directly I heard of Cardinal Farley's death. I came up from the country to Rome and made such an impression on him that he sent for the Cardinal Secretary of State, and it was practically determined. Alas, three days after, we had the news of the Archbishop's death. However, I believe that the Pope has authorized a statement for the Press, that he had intended to give Archbishop Ireland the hat at the next Consistory.[46]

There seems to be little doubt that in so far as it is possible for human nature to abscind from itself, the Archbishop's ambition was based at first on the opportunities the cardinalate would have given for greater service to the Church, and later, on the desire for vindication of his policies, which had been the target of so much opposition. When in 1904 he was informed that Pius X had said, "It will be done," he replied: "In view of controversies, oppositions, annoyances sure to have come from failure, in view, too, of opportunities now opened for higher and more definite work, it is well that the Holy Father said—'It will be done.'"[47] It was only natural that he should desire to triumph over those who left no stone unturned to discredit and to block him in Rome. His real mind was revealed in a letter sent to Gibbons, in which, after thanking him and expressing his sympathy for all that the Cardinal underwent in standing by him, he continued: "I can say before God that I had in view only the interests of the Church, which I desired to put above all political parties, the queen of all, the servant of none."[48] Indeed, the agitation of his friends and the constant rumors appearing in the press were often a source of great annoyance and chagrin. Once he referred to Senator Scott as "a self-constituted champion," and to St. John Gaffney as "meddling in the affair," and more than once he expressed the wish that his name would be forgotten. He said to O'Connell: "The last cable of the *Herald* was that the Jesuits were opposing my being Cardinal. Confound that Cardinal business, I am ashamed before the country. Get all correspondents to drop me, to forget that I live." He realized that his contention with the Archbishop of New York would keep the honor away from both of them, and he did not care very much, but he was in the fight and he liked to win. He said in May, 1901: "I made up my mind a good while ago that McQuaid, Brandi etc. would do the work. And now that it is done I am quite placid. Not much lost after all. But this much we must decide on; my name must never again be bandied around the world. I will say something or do something to make plain that I must never again be disturbed."[49]

Chapter 15

DEATH OF THE ARCHBISHOP

⊁⊰⊁⊰⊁⊰⊁⊰⊁⊰⊁⊰⊁⊰⊁

During the late summer of 1917 Archbishop Ireland's friends began to be seriously preoccupied over his health. The burden of his fourscore of years was weighing more and more heavily upon him. A slight illness in August was followed a few weeks later by a serious cold, which left him in a weakened condition. Unaccustomed to give much thought to himself, he refused at first to regard his illness as serious. The patriotism which characterized his whole life was true to the end, and September found him addressing a group of Marines in Rice Park and also attending a meeting in the St. Paul Auditorium on the occasion of the visit of Secretary McAdoo. But the effort was costly; he was soon forced to take to his bed, and in November his weakness had so increased that for a while his life was despaired of. His naturally rugged constitution, however, asserted itself, so that he was able once more to take up his work. His physicians did not think it advisable for him to face the rigors of another winter, and in January, accompanied by Bishops Thomas O'Gorman and James O'Reilly, he went to St. Augustine, Florida. But the warmth of the South failed to have the hoped-for result, and when he returned to St. Paul, in April, 1918, he showed so little evidence of improvement that by the end of the month his physicians again feared for his life.

Once more he rallied, so that he could resume his wonted interest in international affairs, especially in the progress of the war. But each rally was followed by greater depression of spirit and weakness, until finally the conviction grew upon him that his tenure of life was short. A week before his death, when his condition seemed to be taking a marked change for the worse, one of his physicians, Dr. Charles Greene, said to him: "I believe you've given up this fight. Is that true?" The Archbishop looked at him a moment, and then made a sign of acquiescence, a sign that he was weary of the struggle. "Won't you," said Dr. Greene, "for the sake of the hundreds of thousands who look to you as their head, make another effort to conquer?" The Archbishop smiled and nodded his head. For a few hours he seemed to make an effort to gather his strength, but there was not sufficient vitality left, and surrender was inevitable.

During the final week his death was expected almost hourly, but the extraordinary will power which characterized him throughout the eighty years of his life asserted itself again and again. He was completely unconscious for almost twenty-four hours before he died. His last nod of recognition was for Bishop O'Gorman, the companion of his childhood and his school days, and his devoted associate throughout his life. When, just before the end, this tried and true friend whispered to him: "You will soon be in heaven now," the Archbishop faintly smiled his recognition and his gratitude. Pathetically his mind seemed to turn back to the days of his youth, and when Archbishop Sebastian Messmer visited him two weeks earlier, the thoughts of the dying prelate reverted to the jolting prairie schooner which had brought him from Chicago to St. Paul.

The end came quietly a few minutes before four o'clock on the morning of September 25. At his bedside were his sister, Mother Seraphine, Provincial of the Sisterhood of St. Joseph, and her assistant, Sister St. Rose, Bishop Joseph Busch of St. Cloud, the Vicar-General of the archdiocese, Father James Byrne, and the Chancellor, Father Thomas Welch, Fathers Bajec, Reardon, Crowley, and Ryan, and Dr. Greene. And so amid the prayers and the grief of his attendants went out a life which shed luster on the American episcopate and which will ever remain a benediction and an inspiration.

Throughout the months of Archbishop Ireland's illness solicitous inquiries came from near and far during all hours of the day and night, testifying to the affectionate regard in which he was held by thousands of people of every creed, and to the position of international importance which he occupied. Among the visitors were old settlers who knew him in the early days when he was pastor of the Cathedral; veterans of the Civil War, whose encampments he loved to attend; men of affairs, who recognized the deep indebtedness of the State to his administrative ability; people in humble walks of life, who had reason to know his selflessness and his priestly zeal.

The funeral was set for Wednesday, October 2, at ten o'clock. The body lay in state in his residence, where a constant stream of clergy and laity passed in reverence. On every side there was evidence of genuine grief. The flag on the City Hall flew at half-mast until the conclusion of the obsequies, and on the day of the funeral the flag of the state capitol was lowered in respect. All business in the state and municipal departments ceased for two hours in order that the officials might attend the obsequies, and business in both St. Paul and Minneapolis was suspended for five minutes to testify to the country at large how deeply Minnesota felt its loss.

On Tuesday, October 1, the remains were borne in solemn procession to the Cathedral, where a solemn High Mass of Requiem was celebrated by the Vicar-General and attended by the children of both parochial and public schools. The sermon was preached by Father Humphrey Moynihan. All through the day and night thousands of his people came to pay their respects, while a Guard of Honor, composed of Fourth Degree Knights of Columbus and members of the Ancient Order of Hibernians, kept vigil. In the evening the Office of the Dead was chanted by his seminarians.

At an early hour on Wednesday morning people began to assemble before the Cathedral, waiting for the opening of the doors. At nine-thirty two processions started, one of acolytes, seminarians, brothers and priests, from the Cathedral rectory; the other of prelates, celebrants, and ministers of the Mass, from the archiepiscopal residence. In front of the Cathedral they joined ranks and proceeded into the church between two lines of cadets from the College of St. Thomas. Eight archbishops, thirty bishops, twelve monsignors, seven hundred priests, and two hundred seminarians took part. Reservations had been made for relatives of the deceased prelate, the diocesan sisterhoods, the Knights of St. Gregory, representatives of the Loyal Legion, the Grand Army of the Republic, Garfield and Acker Relief Corps, the Territorial Pioneer Association, Cathedral and Pro-Cathedral building committees, state and city officials, United States army and naval officers, representatives of the French High Commission, and other distinguished visitors. Governor Burnquist and fifty state officials attended with military escort; there were an equal number of city officials, as also judges of the Supreme Court, district, and municipal courts. Hamline University, a Methodist institution, suspended classes during the funeral as a mark of respect.

Pontifical Mass was celebrated by Bishop O'Gorman, assisted by Father Francis Schaefer, Rector of the St. Paul Seminary, as Archpriest, Father J. J. Howard of Springfield, Illinois, a cousin of the Archbishop, as Deacon, Father Humphrey Moynihan, President of the College of St. Thomas, as Subdeacon, and Father Alois Ziskovsky of the St. Paul Seminary, as Master of Ceremonies. The chant was sung by a choir of seminarians under the direction of Father Francis Missia. The five absolutions at the catafalque were pronounced by Archbishops Harty of Omaha, Glennon of St. Louis, Messmer of Milwaukee, Mundelein of Chicago, and Bishop O'Gorman.

It might have been expected that the Archbishop would be laid to rest in the Cathedral, which was his pride, but in accordance with his own wishes he was buried in Calvary Cemetery, that he might lie beside his predecessors, Bishops Cretin and Grace. "Let me," he said, "lie out there with my people under the green sod of Calvary. It is my wish." And his wish was respected. Most of the prelates and clergy, as well as the Governor and his staff, accompanied the body to the cemetery, where Bishop James O'Reilly of Fargo conducted the service. The funeral procession, one of the largest ever witnessed in the United States, told of the respect and admiration in which the distinguished prelate was held.

Archbishop James J. Keane, who preached the eulogy, took for his text the words from the 138th Psalm: "O Lord, Thou hast tried me and hast known me." He reviewed the achievements of the Archbishop— his service in the Civil War, his campaign for temperance and for colonization, his mission in France, his war on foreignism, his help in the settlement of Philippine affairs. He spoke of his splendid mind, his remarkable memory, his oratory, his devotion to Church and country. He said:

It would not be easy for any one to bring into orderly review the striking events of a life distinguished by such rare talents, such strenuous endeavor, such high ideals, such splendid achievement. . . . His forceful advocacy of the true principles of religious and social life won respect for Catholic ideals, and he became the confidential counsellor of several successive administrations. . . . He knew America, he understood its people, he loved its ideals, he was passionately devoted to its aspirations and hopes. America tried him and knew him. It had confidence in him, it trusted him, it honors him. His loyalty and devotion to the See of Peter was genuine, beautiful, inspiring. He treasured every word of exhortation, of direction, of command, that issued from the source of Apostolic authority. He enjoyed the confidence of successive Popes, and the deep personal love and highest esteem of at least one. . . . He preferred a great cause to his own. . . . He was a life-long, consistent, wise and uncompromising advocate and promoter of Christian education. . . . He might have become a distinguished specialist in theology, in history or in social science. . . . He was called by the circumstances of time and place not to the quiet of study

but to the active life of a pioneer bishop, of an apostle. . . . In his private
life he was a model of every priestly virtue. He was regular in everything
and in nothing more than in his religious duties and devotions. . . . He had no
great attachments save such as came of his faith. . . . The cheerful resignation, the patient suffering, the spiritual-mindedness, the Christian hope, the
burning love of God, which filled the last months, the last days, the last
hours of his life, were a fitting and due termination of the career of a great
bishop, a holy priest. He won his way to our hearts where we shall hold
him in loving gratitude and earnest prayers, for we have tried him and
known him.

As the news of the death of the Archbishop went forth, messages
of condolence and tributes began to pour into the Chancery Office
from the President and other leading men of the country, from the
hierarchy, public officials, distinguished foreign citizens. President
Theodore Roosevelt said:

I mourn the death of Archbishop Ireland. He was a great patriot as well
as a great churchman. Personally, he was an old and valued friend, and,
moreover, when with him I felt as though I were in the company of a great
ecclesiastical statesman of the old type in point of ability, and yet abreast
of modern American thought. His death is a great loss, and coming right
after the death of that other great churchman and patriot, Cardinal Farley,
it leaves a very real blank in American life.

Jules Jusserand, the French Ambassador, wrote "We mourn with
you a great prelate of noble character and a model citizen. His death
is a great loss not only for his country but for mine, where he was
so well known and admired." Tributes came from Cardinals Sbarretti,
Cerretti, Gasparri, and Gibbons. The Cardinal of Baltimore said:
"He contributed probably more than any other man to demonstrate
the harmony between the constitution of the Church and the Constitution of the United States. He was one of the most eloquent orators
and a great intellectual leader. He was a man of fascination and
magnetism which has been rarely equalled." Archbishop Giovanni
Bonzano, the Apostolic Delegate: "The monuments of his untiring
activity and zeal will assure for him a glorious place in the history of
the Church by the side of the greatest and most illustrious prelates
of this country." Bishop Gunn of Natchez: "The history of Ireland's
life is the history of the West and of the Catholic Church for the last
fifty years." Monsignor Louis Duchesne: "He knew bad days, but his
courage never failed. What friendships he leaves in mourning. It was
necessary just to see him and hear him for a few moments in order to
love him. We who knew him personally will always keep a deep

affection, sanctified now by the conviction which we have of the high recompense which he has found with God." Archbishop Edward J. Hanna of San Francisco: "He loved his country as few have loved it. He loved Christ with a love that knew no bounds. To Him he consecrated his superb talents of mind and heart. No one ever showed his courage in advancing Christ's cause and in making it loved and respected by the American people." Bishop John P. Carroll of Helena: "The mightiest leader in the American Church." Bishop Michael J. Curley of St. Augustine: "The Church universal feels a sense of loss. This republic will miss one of its noblest citizens and one of its greatest ecclesiastical leaders." Bishop Kelly, Auxiliary of Detroit: "We will not see his like again." Bishop Patrick A. McGovern of Cheyenne: "We have lost the greatest prelate of the Catholic Church in America." Mr. Frederick Underwood: "A Christian gentleman, the like of which we shall not soon see again." Sir Thomas O'Shaughnessy: "Most capable, conscientious and broad-minded, he occupied an outstanding position in the United States and was universally respected. His demise is a national loss." Nicholas Murray Butler: "America loses in him a great citizen and the Christian Church a noble prelate." Mr. James J. Walsh: "The man to whom the American Church owes more than to any other."

In spite of the fact that the minds of the French people were absorbed in the hopes of an imminent armistice, the French press paid him tribute. The *Figaro*, on September 25, 1918, said: "He was one of the great figures of the American episcopate and his fame extended into Europe. His apostolate marked one of the most prosperous epochs of the American Church." The *Journal des Debats*, on September 27, said: "The Archbishop of St. Paul has been one of the types most highly representative of that American episcopate which knows how to combine the defense of the religious and moral doctrines with which it is charged and the anxiety to make them contribute to the cementing of national bonds and the promotion of social interests; to be at once the 'nova et vetera' of its religion, its time and its country. His influence as well as his priestly action was frequently exercised for the settlement in a liberal way of the struggle between capital and labor. He had great authority, and a large part of the respect which American Catholics enjoy is due to the prestige which the Archbishop of St. Paul possessed."

Chapter 16

HIS PERSONALITY AND ACHIEVEMENT

To explore the secret of a man's personality is always a task beset with difficulties—Tennyson pronounces it the highest function of a writer—and the task grows more difficult when we have to do with a mind that was world-wide in vision and sympathy. Happily, however, a man's words are his biography; they are the expression of his mind and heart; they are identical with himself; and so it is that Archbishop Ireland's discourses and his correspondence, much of which has been preserved, furnish the surest clue to his personality—just as they are also the bond between him and thousands in every land who never heard his voice or saw his face.

His discourses reveal many of the qualities that make for greatness. To a mind in which the mingling of the ideal and the practical was as remarkable as it is rare, he united a memory that seldom forgot a fact and a will that was undaunted by difficulties. "Do not," he said on a historic occasion, "lose time in thinking of opposition," and no one ever accused him of wasting time in counting the odds when the interests of religion were at stake. With these gifts were joined two others equally necessary for men who devote their days to great causes; an eloquence that always made its appeal to reason and yet reminded one of the sweep and power of the eagle's flight, and an untiring industry—the industry required to complete the works that genius began. His correspondence reveals other endowments of a more personal character: a high sense of dignity, which was instinctive with him, a keen and kindly insight into human nature and all its ways, a feeling for the simple beautiful things of life and a faculty of thinking largely and liberally on the common things of life, a delicate perception of the word that should be spoken and of the thing that should be done, a temperament that took interest in everything. Dr. Johnson said that no man could meet Burke under a gateway, to avoid a shower, without being convinced that he was the first man in England. Similarly might one say that even a chance contact with Archbishop Ireland revealed him as a born leader of men. And yet these qualities of soul do not account for fifty years' devotion to the interests of Church and State. They do not account for toils that never ceased, for enthusiasms that never waned, for sacrifices that were never shirked. He had no patience for those who sought the sheltered paths of life, and he never issued an order which he would not gladly have carried out.

His oratory, while recalling in some degree the style and spirit of his French masters, was peculiarly his own. He had few of the devices of the finished speaker, nor did he give evidence of having studied the refinements of elocution. The timbre of his voice, at times almost harsh and discordant, added virility and power to his eloquence. Its strength and resonance made it possible for him to reach his farthest hearers. His enunciation was clear, every syllable receiving its proper value. His classical training as well as his constant devotion to Virgil and Horace gave him a sense of diction and variety in his choice of words. His delivery, at first slow and deliberate, gathered impetus as he warmed to his subject, and soon his swinging arms and his emphatic, if awkward, gestures won him rapt attention, his whole manner giving the impression of one who felt keenly the truth and worth of what he said and who lived what he preached. He aimed not at charm but at conviction, and he ended by achieving both. The incisiveness of his logic and the force of his eloquence invariably broke down every barrier in his path. A powerful physique, a dominant personality, and a magnetic presence impressed his hearers with a sense of power, so that his very appearance on a platform brought them to their feet. He had the "grand manner," which made him a tribune of the people as well as a great prelate of the Church. It was no conscious art in his words but rather transparent honesty breaking through the veil of language which captivated hearts. He interwove crisp statement, lucid thought, impassioned prose, bold flights, and purple patches in a tapestry that often held his audience beyond the usual limits of human endurance. Understanding the psychology of the crowd, he knew how to appeal to the emotions of a popular audience, who, he felt, would be impervious to carefully reasoned exposition. He spoke without manuscript, and he had the unusual ability to study his composition for an hour and repeat it almost word for word. Thus "while he was not the master of perfect oratory, he did possess in a marked degree that striking individuality of expression, that clear conception, the high purpose, the dauntless spirit, speaking on the tongue, beaming from the eye, informing every feature, and urging the whole man onward to his object— which is something greater than eloquence." If he often indulged in platitudes, in moments of great earnestness words would tear themselves from his lips and light up truth in memorable expression. Many of his pronouncements haunted the hearer: "If you dread opposition you are not of the seed of those by whom salvation is brought to Israel." "What material progress has not been able to provide is a power to control human passion." "I preach the new, the most glorious crusade." "The common! We are surfeited with it; it has made our souls torpid and our limbs rigid. Under the guise of goodness it is a curse."

His frequent use of the series construction and of parallel clauses made it easy for his audience to follow him; his fondness for the rhetorical question and the apostrophe added emotional appeal; his use of the imperative gave emphasis and point. "Leo, I hail thee, pontiff of thy age, providential chieftain of the Church in a great crisis of her history." "Republic of America, receive from me the tribute of my love and my loyalty." "Tell all this to the age, and work to make good your assertions. Bid science, beneath the spell of religion's wand, to put on brightest pinions and covet highest flights. Whisper in tender accents to liberty that religion cherishes it, and stands ready to guard it alike from anarchy and despotism." "Into the arena, priest and layman! Seek out social evils. Speak of vested rights, but speak, too, of vested wrongs." "Will self-interest take the place of duty and compel men to submit to authority?" And thus, time and again he enunciated some principle with freshness and force in an utterance of ease and naturalness.

In thinking of him as one of the great orators of the Church, we are likely to forget the sermons which he preached from his pulpit in the Cathedral, whose vaulted arches seem to echo the spirit voice of his master, Bossuet. Sunday after Sunday crowds listened to him "speaking truth in love." There was hardly any phase of Catholic doctrine that, in the fifty-seven years of his priesthood and episcopacy, he did not present clearly and convincingly to his people. His skill as a controversialist manifested itself at an early date, as is shown by the series of lectures he delivered in 1877 on the effects of Protestantism and Catholicism; in his sermons in reply to two Episcopalian ministers, Ten Broeck and Thomas, in 1878; in his reply to the Reverend Samuel Smith in 1881; in his discourses on Luther and on the influence of the Reformation on culture and progress in 1883; and in his answers to the Reverend Mr. Mabie's attacks on the Church in 1889. His doughty spirit and his dialectical ability made him a formidable opponent, and he was ever ready to break a lance in defense of the Church. Close and explicit logic, harmonized with bursts of emotional eloquence, gained him the respect of both friend and foe. His discourses were the product of careful plan and deep thought, and were characterized not only by order and meaning but also by that unction of soul which wins conviction. When he spoke in Rome in 1899, at the Church of San Andrea della Valle, the *Moniteur de Rome* said, "You do not summarize a discourse of Mgr. Ireland, as you do not analyze the word all light and flame of a missionary. Rarely has Rome resounded with accents more beautiful on the Papacy and Catholicity."[1]

His oratorical ability made him a frequent speaker at Church functions. One of the earliest of his addresses was delivered in April, 1882, at the bestowal of the pallium upon Archbishop Michael Heiss of Milwaukee.[2]

He returned to Milwaukee in May, 1886, to speak at the First Provincial Council on "Councils in General, and the Present Council," as illustrations of the authority of the Church. At the close of the Council on May 30, he addressed Archbishop Heiss on behalf of the prelates. These were the days before the storm on nationalism had burst forth, and he said: "Men of many nationalities, we have been laboring in the cause of one faith, one Lord, one baptism, actuated by the one purpose in God's honor, sinking all differences in our interest for souls and the advancement of Holy Mother Church."[3]

Archbishop Ireland was frequently invited to speak at the consecration or the installation of other prelates. In September, 1884,[4] he spoke at the consecration of Bishop Henry Cosgrove at Davenport, Iowa, and in November, 1887, at that of Bishop Maurice Burke of Cheyenne, Wyoming. At the latter function, which took place in the Cathedral in Chicago, he chose as his subject "The Church a Divine Agency of Truth and Moral Goodness." Showing the powerful action of the Church in past ages, he outlined the duties of Catholics in the present. He found fault with the inaction of clergy and laity and he asked:

Why do we priests of the Church keep so obstinately to routine methods, the mere mechanical administration of Sacraments, the reading of the Gospel and time-worn sermons on thread-bare subjects, instead of going out into the highways and by-ways, into houses and public places, compelling men by the sweet accents of love and zeal to receive our word, thinking, planning, how best we may secure a hearing from them, and with soul-reaching persuasiveness wresting them from error and sin? Why do laymen consider their duty done, when they hear Mass, go to Confession and pay pew-rent, without furthermore inquiring in deep anxiety what they may do for God and the neighbor, spending themselves in the service of religion and charity? How rare to see Catholics, clerical and lay, leaders in the moral movements of the day.[5]

One of his favorite topics was the role of the layman in the Church. Speaking in Chicago in April, 1894, at a banquet in honor of William Onahan, who had received papal honors, he said that bishops and priests have little power of themselves and must depend upon the layman. To do our work well the priest must become more of a layman and the layman more of a priest. Acting under the divine message: "Go, teach all nations," every layman has the care of his brother's soul, and he who asks "Am I my brother's keeper?" does not understand God's religion. The work of the layman, he said, is to personify in himself the Church, working out in his daily life the worth that is in him. He should have a thorough knowledge of his religion, should study the interests of Church and State, and must not confine himself to Catholic organizations, but be ready to unite with others on the platform of good morals and good citizenship.[6] He returned to the theme two months later at the convention of the Catholic Order of Foresters in St. Paul,[7] at the Golden Jubilee of Notre Dame University, in June, 1895, and again at a banquet of the Knights of Columbus in Pittsburgh, in October, 1909.[8]

In his first sermon at Notre Dame, in August, 1888, at the Golden Jubilee of Father Edward Sorin, the Superior of the Congregation of the Holy Cross, he spoke of the priesthood and its forces of good, and of the glorious freedom of the Church, which, "bound to no enervating conservatism, no old-time traditions repressing her movements, can encounter with the liberty of action which ensures success, the multitudinous problems, social and philosophic, which have sprung up from the complications of modern times."[9] Here the Archbishop was tentatively striking out themes which he was to realize more fully on other occasions. This discourse contains the motifs of his great oration in Baltimore the following year. On the occasion of the Golden Jubilee of the University in 1895 he discoursed on liberal education. He also reiterated what he had said in July, 1890—that the state must not be criticized for the exclusion of religion, but that he would work with double energy to bring the pupils under religious influence and, while doing so, would build up the Christian school.[10]

He visited Cleveland, Ohio, three times. In May, 1897, at the invitation of the Chamber of Commerce, he spoke on "Conscience, the Mainstay of Democracy," telling of the perils facing democracy, from which it could be saved only through the power of conscience, "the voice of the Lawgiver of the universe, proclaiming the eternal law of righteousness and summoning men to obey it."[11] At the dedication of St. Patrick's Church, in April, 1901, he preached on "Jesus Christ, Yesterday and Today, and the Same for Ever," quoting the tributes of Strauss, Renan, Harnack, and John Stuart Mill to Christ, showing His influence on individual and social life, and demonstrating the inadequacy of science to provide a basis for morality or to take the place of religion. Typical of the whole discourse are the following passages:

Behold our Christ. Behold Him rising above all who went before, or who came after, immeasurably higher than Himalaya's farthest reaching peak towering above the hill-tops nestling around its base. . . . Rich is He above all men in the virtues that bring upon earth the reign of the All-holy, Who is in Heaven. Ever wrapt is His mind in the thought of the Eternal Father; ever bent is His soul in doing the Father's will. Tender and merciful is He to men. "He passed by, doing good," helping the needy, comforting the afflicted, instructing the ignorant, recalling the sinner to pardon and holiness. Especially gracious is He to the lowly and the outcast, whom others so readily shun. Humble is He, yet self-respecting; patient, yet powerful; magnanimous to those who had known sin, yet jealous of God's rights and justice. In the frightful ordeal of Pilate's Hall and of Calvary's Mount, how heroic is He in strength of soul, how celestial in sweetness of temper! How forbearing towards His enemies—reviled and not reviling, smitten and not provoked to smite. It is at all times and in all circumstances the unalloyed fragrance of purest innocence and sublimest virtue that distills from His life and words; it is, as never before or since, the radiance of Heaven shedding itself upon earth.

He spoke of the long and painful groping of humanity amid clouds of dense darkness, calling, with agonizing earnestness, but ever in vain, for answers to the eternal questionings of the soul, and of

Christ's satisfying replies. Of Christ's dealing with the individual soul he said:

There came the awakening of the individual conscience, the realization that righteousness is a personal duty, to be sought because it is God's will. There came the exaltation of soul to attain union with God by longing for Him and by laying hold of Him as ideal and pattern. There came a moral beauty unheard of, undreamt of, before. There came purity, tinted as delicately as the petal of the lily; and humility, trembling in fear of vainglory and ambition, but lion-hearted where duty speaks; and sweetest and most unselfish charity for the suffering and the poor, in whom Christ was seen and succored. New virtues sprung up, to express which new words were brought into use, or new meanings given to old words; and a state of soul, a sanctity and nearness to the Divine—utterly unknown to the best and most religious of Greece or Rome, became the endowment of multitudes of men and of women. Human nature was transformed even into the very likeness of God's own life and holiness.[12]

Once more, at the Golden Jubilee of the same church in November, 1903, he took for his theme "Religion, Deepest Instinct of the Human Soul." Of the three splendid discourses, this is the most eloquent. He said:

The rising of the soul to God is the inborn instinct of the human soul. By native law the plant shut up in subterranean darkness speeds towards the light of day its restless vines ever weak and colorless until they bask in the coveted sunshine. By native law the infant reaches out its tiny hands to its mother in search of love and help. In like manner, by native law does the soul of man reach out after God.

Mounting aloft on wings of love and worship the soul rejoices in the immediate presence of supernal truth, goodness and beauty. Close to the Divine, the soul participates in the blessedness of the Divine. Ideal truth illumines its understanding; ideal goodness tempers its will; ideal beauty sheds splendor over its whole being. The soul is transformed. It returns to earth, a new entity. It still moves on earth, but it dominates earth's possessions; it purifies earth's aspirations, and in repeated flight towards the Infinite it lifts other souls to heights of inspiration and of daring otherwise beyond their ken and beyond their reach.[13]

This sermon he repeated substantially in Toledo on the following day, and again in the Church of San Silvestro, Rome, on Easter Sunday, 1906.

In his discourse at the bestowal of the pallium upon Archbishop John J. Keane of Dubuque in April, 1901, he discussed the subject of losses in the Church, stating that the estimate of the *Catholic Directory* that there were eleven million Catholics in the United States was short by three million. He returned to the charge of huge losses made by Cahensly, refuted them by the words of John Gilmary Shea and Bishop O'Gorman, and showed the utter impossibility of the loss of five million asserted by Bishop John England, who estimated the losses in the whole country by those sustained in the Carolinas, where there were few priests.[14] In March of the following year he spoke at the funeral of Mrs. William Onahan in Chicago, and in May at the Silver Jubilee of Bishop John Lancaster Spalding in Peoria, where he took as his subject "The Priesthood." Knowledge in the priest, he said, exalts his soul, enriches his mind with lofty ideas, mellows his heart to love and sacrifice, and bears him onward to sacred ambitions, whence spring great designs and the heroic courage to pursue them.[15]

Archbishop Ireland had the happiness of seeing his old schoolmate, Father Thomas O'Gorman, raised to the episcopate by Cardinal Satolli in St. Patrick's Church, Washington, D.C., in April, 1896. His sermon dealt with the institution of the apostolate and its perpetuation, the episcopate as the fullness of the apostolate, the relative roles in a diocese of the regular and diocesan clergy, and the spheres of Church and State. The Catholic Church, he said, rests her cause on its truth and beauty, but she demands liberty from the State as a sacred and inalienable right—the same liberty which other associations receive. "I am," he said, "a Catholic, I am a priest and bishop; but I am an American citizen, and I must be debarred from no rights or privileges accorded to other citizens because I am a Catholic, of because I carry upon me the insignia of my priesthood." The State must not impede and hamper the Church and close her out from the necessary opportunities to do her work, and in the separation of Church and State there must be no wild and extreme measures which would tend to make society Godless and destroy in it all moral life and supernatural hopes.[16]

One discourse in a city often resulted in the second. In Sioux City, Iowa, he delivered a sermon on the Pope and a lecture on religion, in February, 1893, and he returned to speak on the supremacy of religion, at the dedication of St. Joseph's Church, in September, 1899. He spoke twice in Loretto, Pennsylvania—at the unveiling of the statue of Father Demetrius Gallitzin, in October, 1899, and at the dedication of St. Michael's Church, in the same month two years later. He was a welcome visitor at St. Patrick's Church, Washington, D.C., speaking there on "The Refractaires" in March, 1897, on "The Temporal Power" in December, 1900, and at the celebration of the

110th anniversary of the church in November, 1904. On this last occasion he gave an interesting account of the relations between the Vatican and the French government, which at that time was persecuting the Church. He traced the history of the despoliation of the Church during the Revolution, of the Concordat which Napoleon established with Pius VII, of the later insertion by Napoleon of the Organic Articles, which placed extraordinary restrictions on the Church and which the Vatican had never approved. He told of the intention of the French government to abrogate the Concordat, and of the difficulty caused by the Bishops of Dijon and Laval, who, accused of serious offenses by the Vatican, had refused to resign or to stand trial in Rome. The conflict, he said, was the old battle of the State for supremacy and the march of secularism. Some of the causes were the inertia of French Catholics who refused to assert themselves, and the enmities between the Republicans and the Monarchists. But one should not forget the glories of France or despair of the French Church. The government was not France, and advantages as well as inconveniences would follow the rupture of the Concordat.[17]

His discourse at the bestowal of the pallium upon Archbishop John J. Keane in Dubuque in April, 1901, has been considered elsewhere. At a similar ceremony for Archbishop John Glennon of St. Louis in May, 1905, he chose as his subject the "Unity of the Church," paying tribute to Kenrick and Kain, and referring to St. Louis as the "Rome of the West."

In November, 1906, he spoke at the Golden Jubilee of St. Thomas Pro-Cathedral, Winona, and in 1907 in St. Cecilia's Church, Omaha, on "Religion the Need of Humanity"; in July, 1909, at the funerals of Bishops Joseph Cotter and John Shanley. His sermon on "The Supernatural," preached at the consecration of Bishop Edward Kelly at Ann Arbor, Michigan, in January, 1911, is considered by critics one of his most powerful. Calling attention to the growing indifference about religion, he urged greater effort to stay the progress of infidelity. "The teachings of unbelief," he said, "are fast bearing fruit. They fall on soil well fitted to germination and growth. The minds of men are so engrossed in material occupations that scant time is allowed to think of aught else than what increases earthly wealth and happiness."[18] In September, 1911, he preached at the Eucharistic Congress in Cincinnati, and in October he paid tribute to Cardinal

Gibbons at the banquet held on the occasion of his Silver Jubilee as Cardinal, of whom he said:

> The providential gift to America in the last fifty years was James Gibbons. I have differed with him sometimes as I watched Baltimore to see how things were going. I thought that perhaps his Eminence might go faster, or he might go slower, or that he might go straighter instead of taking the roundabout path, but when all was over he had given the helm the right twist.[19]

In January, 1912, he was the orator at the conferring of the pallium on Archbishop James J. Keane of Dubuque; in December, 1914, at the Silver Jubilee of Bishop James McGolrick of Duluth; and in October, 1915, at the Golden Jubilee of Bishop Thomas O'Gorman of Sioux Falls. His tribute to Bishop Richard Scannell of Omaha, who died in January, 1916, might well be a description of himself:

> To all that was low or tortuous he was the utter stranger. As he thought so he felt, so he spoke and acted, whether thereby he served or injured his own interest. The question always was, what it was that helped the great cause to which he was dedicated, what it was that righteousness and truth command. Brusque of manner, blunt of address he sometimes seemed. It was the excess of his straightforwardness of impulse, and, whatever he seemed, a moment's inspection brought to light the goodness, the comeliness of nature that underlay all outward surfacing.[20]

One of his last addresses was given at the Golden Jubilee of Archbishop John J. Keane, whose ill health had forced him to retire in 1911. When his other intimate friend, Bishop McGolrick, died in January, 1918, Ireland was too ill to preach.

Mr. Albert Shaw said that as a speaker the Archbishop reminded him of Gladstone, that "his eloquence is of a native and spontaneous quality, but is never frothy or hifalutin. His flow of language is beautifully idiomatic and lucid. His wit is an ever-ready weapon, but he does not use it cruelly."[21]

Describing his appearance at the convention of the Catholic Educational Association of America, in St. Paul in July, 1915, Father Richard Tierney, S.J., wrote:

> He came into the sanctuary, a man of heroic stature, magnificent in purple robes, and with unborrowed and unartificial dignity ascended the pulpit, stood silent for an instant and then made the great cathedral ring with Matthew, XXVII, 19, 20. From period to period flowed the eloquent discourse, a complete and accurate statement of Catholic ethics and theology on the subject of education. And it was a sincere pronouncement; the words fell burning from the speaker's lips. Now he stood erect, hands

aloft, and thundered his fine periods; again he bent swift and low in the pulpit, almost as an eagle swoops, and pleaded that Christ's children be brought up in Christ and for Christ, through schools Catholic in all ways.[22]

What can be said of Archbishop Ireland's character that will not sound like fulsome praise? There are those who consider that he was stubborn, brusque, overbold and incautious, even to the extent of being tactless and of brushing aside or crushing those who stood in his way—the faults of one who saw clearly his goal and who had complete confidence in his own judgment. He might have secured with greater patience and consideration some of the objectives which he sought, but his assurance of the truth of his cause and the strength of his convictions, as well as his eagerness to achieve his objectives, made him intolerant of delay. When he felt that the Church was in danger or that the interests of humanity were in jeopardy, he knew not hesitation. His spiritual integrity made it difficult for him, once he had decided on a problem, to temporize about the solution which he regarded as inevitable. Fears and the possibility of frustration he knew, only to disregard. To turn his hand from the plow was for him intellectual cowardice, disloyalty to duty. Because he saw farther and more clearly that the average man, time has vindicated his position. No one who has read the recent pastorals of Cardinal Suhard can help being struck by the parallelism between them and the discourses which the Archbishop delivered in Paris. Not only is there similarity in thought, especially in the advice to the clergy to mingle with their people and to interest themselves in their social problems, but there is also a striking similarity in expression. Because Ireland fought for principles, he won the unchanging allegiance of his friends. Those who admired him loved to think of him as the happy warrior, the one "whom every man in arms should wish to be."

The antagonisms which he created in his work for the Catholic University and in his opposition to nationalism followed him in the school question and in Americanism and have continued to our day. As unsuccessful politicians often accuse their opponents of disloyalty, so those whom Ireland defeated in their attempt to divide the Church in the United States into a series of national camps tried to charge him with theological liberalism. This was the policy pursued by some of his contemporaries, and it is unfortunately still followed by an occasional scribe who refuses to allow the ghost of Cahenslyism to rest and who continues to repeat the charges of Maignen, Delassus, Tardivel, and others, noted for their hatred of everything American, as well as Gisler, distinguished by his ability to find heresy every-where. We are still told that the school question and Cahenslyism are "parts of the entire complex of modernist trends later condemned under the name Americanism," and this in spite of the fact that the Pope rejected the demands of the Cahenslyites and allowed the Faribault experiment. Moreover, the Americanism of Archbishop Ireland was not condemned, but merely the ideas attached to the name in Europe. Not only, as we have seen, did the Holy Father make that abundantly clear to Ireland and permit him to blazon the fact abroad, but he also stated it definitely in his letter. For the Pontiff said: "You are aware, beloved son, that the book entitled 'The Life of Isaac Thomas Hecker,' chiefly through the action of those who have undertaken to publish and *interpret in a foreign language,* has excited no small controversy on account of certain *opinions which are introduced* concerning the manner of leading a Christian life." We still hear that the leasing of the parish schools signified secularization and that "the instigators of the scheme were less concerned with remedying an obvious injustice—the double burden of taxation—than they were with perpetuating liberalistic ideas"—in spite of the Archbishop's repeated assertion that he was simply making an honest effort to secure Catholic education in two villages where he felt that otherwise it was difficult if not impossible. He is accused of "losing sight of the lines of demarcation which eternally separate the spirit of Christ from the spirit of the world" and of wishing to reconcile secularism and religion, although he stated again and again that the Church should accept what is good in the age and reject what is evil. But no amount of inflated verbiage or of what Charles Lamb would have called "impertinent correspondencies" will ever convince anyone but a dyed-in-the-wool Cahenslyite that the Archbishop of St. Paul ever dropped one jot or tittle of the fundamental doctrines of the Church. Neither Leo XIII nor Benedict thought much of such accusations, for he enjoyed the admiration of both and he was prevented only by death from receiving the highest honors in the gift of the Holy See.

If he knew the glory of achievement, he also tasted the bitterness of failure. One who knew him intimately said:

Looking back over his career, we must admit that in view of immediate results many of his rainbows proved to be not the harbingers of sunshine but the forerunners of storms. Colonies suffered blight, movements died out, dreamed-of harmonies in Church and state turned into discord, large areas here and there refused to receive the light of his beneficent genius. But his influence in the long run has powerfully leavened the world for the better, and, although his sun has set, its light will for ages illumine the horizon.

In one phase of his administration he experienced considerable trouble—the financial. He had invested more than a million dollars in real estate, in the hope that its appreciation would enable him to achieve his lifelong ambition to build a cathedral. The depression of the early nineties found him so involved that he was forced to fall back on his eastern friends for assistance. According to report, these helped him to the extent of half a million dollars, for which he gave mortgages. Later, however, he was forced to sell many of his holdings in order to meet his obligations.

There were times when he tired of the arena, its contentions and its intrigues, and more than once he re-echoed the thoughts of his favorite *De Amicis*: "Quanto ho gia perduto di quel confidente abbandono, di quel sentimento di ammirazione facile e schietto che scattage come una molla al piu leggero tocco." (How much have I lost of that confident abandon, of that feeling of facile and frank admiration, which leaped like a spring at the lightest touch.)

He was patient and forbearing. Under the strain of ceaseless annoyances and days of deadly drudgery, under importunity and ingratitude, he was patient even unto gentleness. He gave people time to think. He was slow to hold them to their word or to force a matter to a speedy issue. Impetuous by nature, he was singularly tolerant of the mistakes no man has a right to make. Under a rugged personality there was veiled a native gentleness of soul, a spirit of forbearance Christian in its tenderness. "He could storm at times, but his storms carried no blighting hail, and the sunshine appeared afterwards brighter than before." No man was more forgiving, and forgiveness with him meant complete oblivion. At home with princes and statesmen, he loved the companionship of the lowly and seemed never so happy as when he listened to the anecdotes of the pioneer and the veteran. To a kindly sense of humor and a temperament that took interest in all the affairs of men, he joined a charm of manner, a considerate courtesy, and a gentleness of soul known only to those who came into closest contact with him.

His humanity was best seen in his own house, where he was an admirable host. Like Cardinal Wiseman, in his old age he longed to have his old friends around him and to live over with them the exploits of former days. He shared what seems to be a characteristic of great men—an eye for detail. Preoccupied with great interests, national and international, when he invited guests to dinner he would discuss with his housekeeper the courses to be served and the manner of their serving. Whether his guests were distinguished visitors or members of the faculty of one of his institutions, the occasion was always memorable. Seated at the head of his table, he had kindly attention for everyone, directing the flow of conversation along the lines of common interest. After dinner he would lead the guests into his library and seat them around a long table. There the crackling of the logs in the fireplace made an appropriate setting for his scintillating wit and his sallies of laughter. A memory that never seemed to fail revived incidents of the Civil War, stories of the early days of colonization, snatches of conversations with the litterateurs of Paris or the politicians of Washington. Without monopolizing, he would lead the talk from topic to topic, enlivening it with many an appropriate story to the music of deep-throated laughter and an occasional English equivalent for the French "*Mon Dieu.*" One thing he always expected and demanded of his company—honesty of expression; for insincerity or sycophancy he had the utmost contempt. One of his characteristic gestures was to sit back in his chair, rest his elbows on the arms, shade his eyes with his hands as he listened to the interplay of talk, suddenly resuming his wonted vivacity as some expression stimulated him to agreement or dissent. Drawing on his marvelous memory enriched with travel, wide acquaintanceship, vast erudition, and varied interests, he made his conversation always instructive and entertaining. A remarkable raconteur, his stories were always gems, full of his own inimitable wit and humor, always creating a laugh, but seldom inflicting unnecessary pain.

A great Bishop, who knew the meaning of the Apostle's words, "Take heed unto yourself and unto the flock in which the Holy Ghost hath set you to rule," Archbishop Ireland ruled his diocese with wisdom and prudence and solicitude of all the churches. Faithful to the Apostle's injunction, he labored like a good soldier of Christ. Born to rule, he rejoiced in the power that enabled him from his high station to reveal the Catholic Church in all its vast possibilities for good to humanity. How he toiled for his diocese let his works speak. Like the Homeric husbandman standing in the harvest field, gazing with satisfaction on the sheaves that ripened under his cultivating hands, Archbishop Ireland could look around upon the field to which he

devoted his life and behold on all sides the fruits of his labors—
the colonies which he planted, the parishes which he organized, the
churches which he erected, the priesthood which he trained, the
schools and colleges which he called into being, and the two great
churches—the Cathedral in St. Paul and the Basilica in Minneapolis—
which take their place among the noble temples of the world.

Above all, he was a priest, a priest devoted to his people, devoted
to God. His life was a life full of toil and care, but in the midst of
many harassing duties there was one thing he never lost sight of—the
part of the Lord's vineyard entrusted to his charge. Night and day
he worked, going from parish to parish, from one end of the state
to the other, firing others with his enthusiasms, making to all an
appeal that was rarely in vain, for the zeal that consumed him, the
transparent goodness and sincerity of the man opened hearts to him
wherever he went. His piety was simple and sincere. Men who saw
him always in the thick of things knew little or nothing of the holiness
of life that was the mainspring of his enterprises and activities. In
the midst of the affairs in which he played so great a part, his
thoughts and steps would often turn to the little oratory in his
residence. Early morning saw him at the altar, and no matter how
burdened the hurrying hours, he found time for visits to the Blessed
Sacrament. The shades of evening saw him before the altar with his
household gathered around him. He faithfully carried out in his
daily life the advice he so often gave: "Work as if all depended on
yourself; pray as if all depended on God." He was a priest in every
fiber of his being, and to no man can greater praise than this be given.
In all the varied activities of his life we see his priestly soul reflected.
The story of his life is in great part the story of all the salutary enterprises undertaken in the Northwest during half a century. His work
for colonization bespoke in a practical way his love for the Catholic
people. His work for temperance was the work of a priest who saw
in the drink evil the greatest curse that ever blighted the world. His
work for education told of the farseeing priestly vision that discerned
in higher Catholic culture the hope of the future. His work for the
promotion of the spirit of patriotism was rooted in his love for the
Church as well as in his love for the country. The priest-patriot, of
whose daring and devotion so many stories were told around southern
campfires, the archbishop who was chaplain of the Grand Army of
the Republic, did more to dissipate prejudice against the Catholic
religion than any other man in the history of the Church in this

country, with the possible exception of Cardinal Gibbons. No wonder that thousands outside the fold learned to trust the Church because of their trust in Archbishop Ireland; no wonder that Catholics the world over were proud of the great prelate, whose cry, like that of Joshua, always was "let the people go forward."

There is much truth in the remark that Archbishop Ireland strove to do in this land what Lacordaire and Schlegel and Wiseman had done in Europe—to show that the Church alone can minister to the dire needs of the modern world. At last the silent millions of our Catholics beheld one of their bishops who aroused them to the sense of the glory of their Church and the grandeur of their mission, a bishop to whom America listened with wonder and sympathy and respect. The mission of Archbishop Ireland was essentially to make the Catholic Church known and understood in the United States— a mission that will always give him a unique place among the great prelates of the Church.

Comparing him with Archbishop John Hughes, John T. Reily wrote:

Hughes passed to his reward January 3, 1864—a greater prelate than Bishop England—a man for the times—more able, active and energetic than Cardinal McCloskey—he finds in our day a comparison in Archbishop Ireland as a man fearlessly confronting present necessities, the master of opportunity, the statesman surmounting every difficulty—free from the failures and follies of the past—ambitious for the highest and best future possibilities—politically progressive, religiously progressive, representing in the truest Christian sense the highest type of nineteenth Century liberality and generosity—as Catholic as Pius IX or Leo XIII—as American as Lincoln, Grant, Harrison. Catholic men of such towering prominence in American citizenship are few in history—great in peace and great in war.

If one were to choose one dominant feature of his personality more than another, it might well be his magnetism. His very appearance on a platform brought color and light into the air. The splendid physique, the commanding presence, the massive grandeur of countenance, the rugged yet refined personality, the charming dignity of manner—the unfailing note of a highborn nature—all stamped him as a man among men. In the deeply etched lines which curved about the mouth and threw into relief the powerful jaw, in the lofty sweep of brow, in his attitude of absorption as one brooding over the enigma of life, in his habit of communing with himself and gesticulating as he walked, some found remembrances of Dante. In his aggressiveness, his will to achieve, his swiftness of decision, he has been called

Napoleonic. He has been ranked with Carroll, Hughes, and England; called "too democratic to show the princely magnificence of the Cardinal of Carthage [Lavigerie], too busy ever to acquire the literary finish of Newman, too active to wear the seer-like look of Manning." Of him a writer once asked:

What is the personality of this man whose name is an electrant wherever it is spoken? Who is so kind, so gracious, so terrible, so resistless? Who equalizes himself with laborer and potentate, and obliterates lines of caste and color? Who is the slayer of cliques and sectionalism? Whose language is vivid and dynamic as Carlyle's and direct and comprehensive as Roosevelt's? Who is the most splendid and persistent optimist of his age? Who is the poet born, a missionary bred, a soldier in action, a priest in ministration, a judge of the court of the world?

A vitalized intelligence, in his courage there is no fear, in his purpose there is no deflection. Born in Ireland, he was a citizen of the world. Located in St. Paul, his movements have shaken Europe. A defender of the faith, he has been its iconoclast. Never a man so contradictory, yet true. Never a man so dominant, more emancipated from mental heredities, more quick to perceive the right, more intrepid in accomplishing it. Never could man steer through blacker darkness to gleam of light nor fling himself against greater odds, and never was man more prescient of results.

Of him Father A. P. Doyle, Rector of the Apostolic Mission House in Washington, wrote:

His voice has been heard in Church councils, his strong hand has been at the wheel to guide its destinies. History will tell how great an influence his has been in the fostering of the marvelous growth that we enjoy. The strength and breadth of his mind was the sharing of his sympathies with the Church Universal. His practical sagacity in the administration of his great diocese was the outcome of his faith and his devotion to Church ideals, so that he moved along through the drama of these fifty years a peer among his contemporaries.

Of him Father Richard Tierney, the Jesuit, wrote:

A heart that pulsed with a thousand vital interests is stilled forever, and the country is mourning a noble man who for more than half a century upheld the priestly dignity and the honor of American citizenship with unmatched power. Soldier, patriot, Bishop, and Archbishop, the "Lion of the Northwest" was distinguished in each sphere. A fearless, godly man, keen of intellect, strong of will, a relentless yet chivalrous opponent, he left an indelible impression on all he touched, for Archbishop Ireland was a great man among the greatest men. When shall we see his like again?

In order to be understood and appreciated, Archbishop Ireland must be studied like a work of the old masters, not too near and in a proper light. As you stand at the foot of Mont Blanc, you cannot form an adequate idea of its far-flung vastness; you are too close to realize that its glittering helmet of snow rises nearly sixteen thousand feet into the air of France and Italy and Switzerland. But suddenly, as you round a curve of a mountain road, you see it from afar, across a wide-spreading valley, lifting itself up in all its massive majesty above the diminished heights and peaks around it, a glorious altar reared by nature to the living God. So is it with some favored son of our race, who, with his genius and grandeur of soul and splendor of achievement touched to new power, new beauty, by the graces of religion, is seen in his true greatness only in the perspective of time, across the widening valley of the years. So is it with John Ireland. He will take his true place only in the mind of generations to come, when, in the revealing perspective of the past, he will be seen as he really was—one of the greatest bishops of the Church in an age that called for the consecration of glorious gifts of mind and heart and of devoted allegiance to the cause of Christ and of humanity.

APPENDIX: *Liberalism*

The words "Liberalism" and "Americanism" were the occasion for much misunderstanding and were twisted by Ireland's enemies into terms of opprobrium. In a letter which Father William Kerby of the Catholic University wrote to his brother from Louvain in April, 1897, but which, unfortunately, is too long for reproduction, he said many sensible things about conservatists and liberals, the former clinging to the old and slow to admit the new, the other welcoming the new and clinging less warmly to accidentals in the old. The modern world, he said, cherishes liberty of thought, of press, of worship and of teaching, which the Church condemns because they are at variance with philosophy and revelation. The question is what attitude will the Church take toward a State built on such foundations? The liberal looks to the present and the future and accepts things as they are—the separation of Church and State in a country where there is little possibility of an ideal union. He says to himself: "The Constitution is all right, it leaves us alone. Let us be patriots. The Conservative, however, looks back to the past, shudders at the recklessness of modern states, mourns over the heresies which develop daily, and cannot love a country which cherishes what he despises." St. Paul, Father Kerby said, was a liberal; he had to fight to abolish old customs and ceremonies. Leo XIII was a liberal; he forced the clergy and hierarchy of France to accept the Republic. He then asked: "Did the Pope sanction revolution, did he deny the supremacy of Christ, did he admit as desirable the modern liberties which reason, revelation and Church condemn?" Leo saw the trend of things, however, and knew that he could not convert the world by stirring up antagonism and hate.

The liberal, he goes on to say, is at one disadvantage. Progressive, he is constantly lecturing, writing. He has new ideas, he is full of zeal, he preaches his ideas. The Conservative has nothing new to say—he is merely stationary. If he talks or writes, he does two things, no more, no less. He constantly repeats principles absolutely true and denied by no Catholic; he insinuates that the Liberal denies those principles. Monsignor Schroeder says: "It is a great heresy to deny the supremacy of Christ and Church over the modern State. Liberalism does that. No Catholic can be a Liberal." In themselves those statements are true of another kind of liberalism, but who defends them? Is it Ireland the Archbishop, Gibbons the Cardinal, Keane the Scholar? Not at all. To call them heretics is mean, contemptible and false.

Soderini refers to the American Intransigents as a closed clique, with its virtues and defects. Its virtue was in guarding jealously the integrity of its own belief; its defect was in condemning with a singular want of charity everything outside it. The "Liberal" Catholics engaged in various social and moral activities of the country, while the intransigents stood at their windows and regarded them with hostility, seeking in every way they could

387

to block their action, or at least following their initiative with a constant accompaniment of criticism and ill-will.

Louis Veuillot, editor of *L'Univers*, said that anyone in France who tried to do anything was called an Americanist. Whoever thought it desirable to accomplish any progress or to attempt a reform instead of remaining frozen in the somnolence of old practices, or to attempt to move out of the status quo, was an Americanist. One who, noting the progress of science and the growing interest in it, suggested to the episcopate to encourage in the clergy an interest in scientific studies, is suspect as an Americanist. A religious, who with the approval of her Ordinary, wishes to found a normal school in order to increase the number of students in colleges for girls, excites the horror and scandal of her adversaries, who call her an Americanist. When a group of priests and work superintendents meet in Paris to devise means of bringing religion to the workers by establishing recreation centers, they too are Americanists. Indeed, he says, it is to the credit of Americans that they have a monopoly on progress.

NOTES

The following abbreviations have been used in the notes:

AASP   Archives of the Archdiocese of St. Paul.

ACUA   Archives of the Catholic University of America.

ADC   Archives of the Diocese of Cleveland.

ADR   Archives of the Diocese of Rochester.

AUND   Archives of the University of Notre Dame.

BCA   Baltimore Cathedral Archives.

NYAA   New York Archdiocesan Archives.

PFA   Paulist Fathers Archives.

RDA   Richmond Diocesan Archives.

CHAPTER 1. *Preparations for Prelacy*

1. Little is known of Archbishop Ireland's ancestors. A mutilated letter found among his papers and dated Milwaukee, October 18, 1904, gives the result of the genealogical researches of the writer, who evidently did not impress the Archbishop, as the writer wonders whether his two previous letters were received. He said: "I frequently find both in Devonshire, Somerset and Yorkshire the name of John Ireland at an early date. The oldest record I find is of John Ireland of Hipperholme in the parish of Halifax. In those days the constable was the principal officer of the township. The record reads—the year was 1379—'John de Ireland the Hiperum constable reported John Annson, Matil. de Sculcotes, Elena de Wyloby and Richard Masohon for brewing, fined 4d each.' But alas for consistency, in 1383 John del Rokes, constable had John Ireland fined 2d 'for brewing.'"

2. T. O'Herlihy, *The Famine*, Drogheda Independent Co., Drogheda, Ireland, no date.

3. Boston *Herald*, April 21, 1895; *Catholic Bulletin*, St. Paul, September 28, 1918.

4. The names of the children were Mary Ann (child of the father's former marriage), John, Ellen, Eliza, Richard, and Julia. Ellen and Eliza became members of the Community of the Sisters of St. Joseph of Carondelet, and were later known as Mother Seraphine and Mother St. John.

5. *Catholic Bulletin*, October 2, 1918.

6. AASP, Joseph Guillot to James M. Reardon, Faribault, Minn., November 21, 1918.

7. AASP, Francis Redwood to James M. Reardon, Wellington, New Zealand, January 4, 1933.

8. AASP, copy in French, John Ireland to Canon Theloz, St. Paul, June, 1891.

9. Ireland to Perretant, St. Paul, June 1, 1913, *Bulletin Gorini*, No. 49, p. 193.

10. Ireland to Jean-Augustin Germain, St. Paul, August 27, 1915, *Bulletin Gorini*, No. 49, p. 196.

11. Ireland to Stanislas Touchet, St. Paul, August 27, 1917, *Bulletin Gorini*, No. 49, p. 197. When one of his priests made bold to ask the Archbishop why he had dined with Viviani, he replied: "There are two ways of treating men who have persecuted us; one way is by drawing them out, the other by throwing them out. Time will reveal the wisdom of the course I have followed."

12. St. Paul *Pioneer Press*, November 1, 1862, and October 6, 1912.

13. *Sunday Tablet*, New York, May 22, 1892.

14. Letter to the *Catholic Times*, August 12, 1893.

15. Utica *Herald*, October 6, 1912.

16. Humphrey Moynihan, "Archbishop Ireland," *Acta et Dicta*, Catholic Historical Society of St. Paul, Vol. VI, No. 1, October, 1933.

17. AASP, William B. McGrorty to Eugenie F. McGrorty, Camp Van Burgesrode, June 12, 1862.

18. AASP, Robert J. Burdette to John Ireland, Los Angeles, September 11, 1910.

19. St. Paul *Pioneer Press*, August 7, 1909, "Forty Years Ago Today."

20. AASP, copy, J. L. MacDonald to P. Hayes, Kansas City, August 29, 1902.

21. *Northwestern Chronicle*, May 20, 1871.

22. Humphrey Moynihan, "John Ireland," *Catholic World*, November, 1918, p. 195.

23. *Northwestern Chronicle*, July 30, October 16, December 22, 1875.

24. *Ibid.*, July 3, 1884.

25. Chancery Office, St. Paul, Martin Marty to Giovanni Simeoni, Sioux Falls, November 16, 1886.

26. AASP, Denis O'Connell to Ireland, Rome, June 24, 1887.

27. *Ibid.*, September 4, 1887.

28. *Ibid.*, March 15, 1888.

29. *Ibid.*, July 10, 1888.

30. *Northwestern Chronicle*, September 28, 1888.

31. St. Paul *Globe*, September 28, 1888.

32. *Scriptorium*, St. John's Abbey, St. Cloud, Minn., Vol. VI, No. 1, Spring, 1946.

33. ADR, Ireland to O'Connell, St. Paul, August 4, 1888.

34. AASP, O'Connell to Ireland, Rome, August 7, 1888.

35. *Ibid.*, July 23, 1889.

36. *Scriptorium*, Vol. VII, No. 1, Christmastide, 1946.

37. AASP, O'Connell to Ireland, Rome, February 24, 1889; July 13, 1889.

38. BCA, 87-C-6, clipping from the *Catholic Citizen*, Portland, Ore., January 27, 1890.

CHAPTER 2. *The Archbishop as Colonizer*

This chapter is a condensation of an article contributed to *Acta et Dicta*, Vol. VI, by Monsignor Humphrey Moynihan. He left no notes, but the sources are largely: Sister Mary Evangela Henthorne, *The Irish Catholic Colonization Association of the United States; Catholic Colonization in Minnesota*, Pioneer Press, St. Paul, Minn., January 1879; *Irish Colonization in America*, M. H. Gill & Son, Dublin, 1880; Alice E. Smith, "The Sweetman Irish Colony," *Minnesota History*, Minnesota Historical Society, December, 1928; the *American Catholic Quarterly Review*, January to October, 1900; the *Catholic World*, Vol. XXV; *American Catholic Historical Researches*, July, 1886; Mr. John Sweetman, "The Sweetman Catholic Colony of Currie, Minnesota," *Acta et Dicta*, Vol. III, No. 1, July, 1911; and William J. Onahan, "A Chapter of Catholic Colonization," *Acta et Dicta*, Vol. V, No. 1, July, 1917.

CHAPTER 3. *Defining the Role of the Catholic Church in American Life*

1. John Ireland, *The Church and Modern Society,* Pioneer Press Mfg. Co., St. Paul, 1905, I, 27.
2. *Ibid.,* I, 67.
3. *Ibid.,* I, 103.
4. Chicago *Journal,* September 5, 1893.
5. ADR, John Ireland to Denis O'Connell, St. Paul, September 5, 1892.
6. AASP, Gibbons to Ireland, Baltimore, September 16 and 22. BCA, 90-F-4 and 10, Ireland to Gibbons, St. Paul, September 14 and 19, 1892.
7. AASP, Bertha M. Palmer to Ireland, Washington, March 22, 1892.
8. St. Paul *Pioneer Press,* July 18, 1892.
9. Ireland, *The Church and Modern Society,* I, 135.
10. *Ibid.,* I, 347.
11. AASP, O'Connell to Ireland, Rome, September 25, 1893.
12. *Northwestern Chronicle,* St. Paul, June 2, 1893.
13. *Missionary Review,* June, 1892.
14. BCA, 90-Q-3, minutes of the conference.
15. ADR, John J. Keane to Denis O'Connell, Washington, October 10, 1893.
16. BCA, 92-P-5, Gibbons to Rampolla, Baltimore, October 28, 1893.
17. *The World's Parliament of Religions,* Parliament Publ. Co., Chicago, 1893, II, 1559.
18. Milwaukee *Sentinel,* October 19, 1895.
19. St. Paul *Pioneer Press,* clipping.
20. A. Houtin, *L'Américanisme,* Libraire Emile Nourry, Paris, 1904, p. 127.
21. *La Revue Bleue,* Paris, November 16, 1895.
22. *Le Matin,* Paris, September 25, 1895.
23. AASP, copy, Ireland to Felix Klein, St. Paul, July 15, 1896.
24. AASP, Carus to Ireland, La Salle, Ill., October 8, 1902.
25. Ireland, *The Church and Modern Society,* I, 163, 193.
26. Sioux City *Journal,* February 7, 1893.
27. Ireland, *The Church and Modern Society,* I, 193.
28. *Ibid.,* I, 198; BCA, 93-S-2, Ireland to Gibbons, March 4, 1895: "People were wicked enough to see in those words an allusion to His Lordship of Rochester."
29. Ireland, *The Church and Modern Society,* I, 176.
30. *Ibid.,* I, 199.
31. *Ibid.,* I, 186.
32. *Ibid.,* I, 177.
33. *Ibid.,* I, 176.
34. Chicago *Times,* October 9, 1899.
35. Ireland, *The Church and Modern Society,* II, 83.
36. Wheeling, W. Va., *Intelligence,* October 25, 1899.
37. AASP, copy of address given at Galena, Ill., April 27, 1912; *Catholic Bulletin,* May 4, 1912.
38. *Northwestern Chronicle,* March 2, 1894.
39. Ireland, *The Church and Modern Society,* II, 247.
40. Chicago *Tribune,* March 20, 1894.
41. Ireland, *The Church and Modern Society,* I, 189.
42. *Ibid.,* I, 178.
43. AASP, copy of address; also quoted in *Catholic Bulletin,* September 28, 1918.
44. AASP, O'Connell to John Ireland, Rome, April 24, 1898.

45. *Ibid.*, October 17, 1898.
46. St. Paul *Pioneer Press*, October 18, 1898; also AASP, brochure.
47. Minneapolis *Journal*, July 16, 1898.
48. *Pioneer Press*, May 11, 1898. A similar thought was expressed at the Peace Jubilee in Chicago, on October 18, 1898. AASP, copy of address.
49. St. Paul *Dispatch*, February 12, 1916.
50. St. Paul *Pioneer Press*, October 18, 1898.
51. At the Crève-Cœur Club, Peoria, Ill., February, 1911.
52. Major White, May 10, 1898; General Shields, October 20, 1914; Colonel King, February 19, 1916; General Hubbard, April 8, 1913; General Bishop, March, 1912.
53. St. Paul *Pioneer Press*, May 11, 1898.
54. Wheeling, W. Va. *Intelligence*, October 25, 1899.
55. AASP, copy of address.
56. Klein, *In the Land of the Strenuous Life*, A. C. McClurg, Chicago, 1905, pp. 332, 333.
57. Ireland, *The Church and Modern Society*, I, 180.
58. AASP, J. A. Zahm to John Ireland, Rome, May 30, 1896.
59. Ireland, *The Church and Modern Society*, I, 180.
60. *Catholic Bulletin*, August 16, 1913.

CHAPTER 4. *Resisting Nationalism in the Church*

For a detailed study of the national question, the reader is referred to two articles by Mr. John J. Meng in the *Catholic Historical Review*, January and October, 1946, and to a forthcoming study by Father Colman Barry, O.S.B.

1. AASP, James Whitfield to Dr. N. Wiseman, Baltimore, June 6, 1833.
2. A. Houtin, *L'Américanisme*, Libraire Emile Nourry, Paris, 1904, p. 7.
3. AASP, copy, *Relatio de Questione Germanica in Statibus Federatis*, September 28, 1886. Of it Keane said: "A more villainous tissue of misstatements I have seldom read." (BCA, 82-G-4, Keane to Gibbons, Rome, December 4, 1886.)
4. Daniel F. Reilly, *The School Controversy*.
5. BCA, 73-W-3, Thomas Grace to J. J. Gibbons, St. Paul, September 8, 1878.
6. AASP, printed copy of letter addressed "Monseigneur," Rome, December 10, 1886.
7. AASP, copy of the minutes of the meeting.
8. AASP, copy, *La Question Allemande dans L'Eglise aux Etats-Unis*.
9. Bishop Richard Gilmour to Gibbons: "Not a single Irishman in all the Province of Cinti [Cincinnati] with its ten bishops." (BCA, 42-4-10, December 20, 1886.)
10. *Columbia*, September 1, 1887.
11. *Northwestern Chronicle*, August 18, 1887.
12. ADR, Ireland to Denis O'Connell, St. Paul, August 18, 1888.
13. AASP, copy, Camille Maes to Simeoni, Covington, Kentucky, July 10, 1888.
14. AASP, O'Connell to Ireland, Rome, October 8, 1888.
15. ADC, Ireland to Gilmour, St. Paul, October 12, 1888.
16. *Northwestern Chronicle*, October 26, 1888.
17. AASP, William H. Elder to John Ireland, Cincinnati, October 23, 1888.
18. Elder to Gibbons, Cincinnati, December 16, 1886 (La Question Allemande aux Etats-Unis).
19. AASP, Gibbons to Ireland, Baltimore, October 19, 1888.
20. BCA, 85-G-9, Ireland to Gibbons, St. Paul, October 27, 1888.

21. Milwaukee *Sentinel,* August 18, 1887.
22. BCA, 83-J-6, William Gross to Gibbons, Portland, Ore., August 30, 1887.
23. ACUA, Ireland to Keane, St. Paul, March 3, 1890.
24. Allen S. Will, *The Life of Cardinal Gibbons,* E. P. Dutton and Co., New York, 1922, I, 501.
25. AASP, O'Connell to Ireland, Rome, June 11, 1891; also BCA, 88-U-2, O'Connell to Gibbons, June 2, 1891. O'Connell was not always a safe guide for Ireland. There was not much probability that Cahensly and Von Schloezer were working together, because the former belonged to the Center party, the latter to Bismarck's.
26. New York *Herald,* June 1, 1891.
27. St. Paul *Pioneer Press,* June 12, 1891.
28. BCA, Ireland to Gibbons, St. Paul, May 30, 1891.
29. AASP, O'Connell to Ireland, Rome, June 5, 1891.
30. *Ibid.,* June 11, 1891.
31. O'Connell to Ireland, Grottoferrata, October 20, 1891, and O'Connell to Gibbons, Rome, August 3, 1891.
32. Copy of letter, AASP.
33. BCA, 88-S-3, Ireland to Gibbons, St. Paul, July 2, 1891.
34. BCA, 88-H-2, O'Connell to Gibbons, Rome, January 17, 1891.
35. Allen S. Will, *op. cit.,* I, 528. The discourse prompted a well-known priest to write to the Baltimore *Volkszeitung:* "These men dragoon us with their Americanism."
36. AASP, copy of the minutes of the meeting.
37. AASP, Ireland to Louis Caillet, February 14, 1892.
38. BCA, 89-W-8, Ireland to Gibbons, Genoa, June 5, 1892.
39. AASP, copy, May 15, 1892.
40. ADR, Gibbons to O'Connell, Baltimore, July, 1892; also Gibbons to Corrigan, July 14, 1892.
41. AASP, Davis to Ireland, Washington, April 22, 1892. The malice in his remark was that Ganganelli was Pope Clement XIV, who had suppressed the Jesuits.
42. AASP, O'Connell to Ireland, Rome, October 20, 1891.
43. Detroit *News,* September 22, 1892.
44. AASP, clipping, scrapbook 36, p. 61. This was not Ireland's opinion, for he wrote to O'Connell from Liverpool that some French representatives of the Lucerne Conference had told him in Paris that Cahensly's memorial contained some extraordinary things. (July, 1892.)
45. ADR, John S. Foley to O'Connell, Detroit, May 7, 1891.
46. AASP, John B. Brondel to Ireland, Helena, June 2, 1891.
47. BCA, 88-R-8, William Gross to Gibbons, Portland, Ore., June 28, 1891.
48. ACUA, O'Connell Papers, John Moore to O'Connell, St. Augustine, September 30, 1886.
49. Boston *Pilot,* March 19, 1892.
50. AASP, O'Connell to Ireland, Grottoferrata, October 20, 1891.
51. ADR, Ireland to O'Connell, St. Paul, August 10, 1892.
52. AASP, John Murphy to Ireland, Pittsburgh, March 24, 1892.
53. NYAA, C-41, Peter Paul Cahensly to M. A. Corrigan, Limburg a.d. Lahn, October 31, 1892.
54. New York *Freeman's Journal,* October 1, 1892.
55. AASP, Edward Fitzgerald to Ireland, Little Rock, Ark., October 17, 1897.
56. *Northwestern Chronicle,* June 5, 1891.

57. ACUA, Proceedings of the Seventh German-American *Katholikentag*, Louisville, Ky., September 24-27, 1894, pp. 57-59.
58. William McGucken, S.J., *The Catholic Way in Education*, Milwaukee, 1934, p. 83.
59. AASP, O'Connell to Ireland, Rome, January 7, 1897; Freiburg, August 26, 1897.
60. New York *Freeman's Journal*, April 3, 1897.
61. New York *Times* article reproduced in the *Catholic Bulletin*.
62. AASP, copy, Washington, May 12, 1897.
63. Dr. Max Groesser, S.A.C., *Die deutschamerikanischen Katholiken im Kampf mit den Nativesten*. Taken from *Gelbe Hefte*, V (1928-29), 295: "*Wie ich bestimmt weiss, haben Kardinal Gibbons und Erzbischof Ireland ausdruecklich anerkannt, dass sie sich geirrt haben.*" (Courtesy of Father Colman Barry, O.S.B.)
64. AASP, Sebastian Messmer to John Ireland, Milwaukee, December 20, 1911.

CHAPTER 5. *The School Question*

For a fuller treatment of the school question the reader is referred to *The School Controversy* by Daniel F. Reilly, Catholic University of America, Washington, D. C., 1943.

1. John Ireland, *The Church and Modern Society*, Pioneer Press, St. Paul, 1905, I, 215.
2. Correspondence Copy Book, The Chancery Office, St. Paul, p. 23, dated November 1, 1890.
3. AASP, Denis O'Connell to John Ireland, Rome, August 18, 1890.
4. *Ibid.*, Grottoferrata, August 30, 1890.
5. *Ibid.*, Rome, November 15, 1890.
6. BCA, 88-D-6, Denis O'Connell to James J. Gibbons, Rome, November 24, 1890.
7. Allen Sinclair Will, *Life of Cardinal Gibbons*, E. P. Dutton and Co., New York, 1922, I, 483; Also ADR, Gibbons to O'Connell, Baltimore, September 12, 1890.
8. BCA, 88-B-2, Ireland to Gibbons, St. Paul, September 23, 1890.
9. BCA, 88-D-7, Rampolla to Gibbons, Rome, November 24, 1890.
10. BCA, 88-E-5, Ireland to Gibbons, St. Paul, December 13, 1890.
11. BCA, 88-E-8, Ireland to Gibbons, St. Paul, December (no date), 1890.
12. Daniel F. Reilly, *op. cit.*, pp. 242-247, December 30, 1890. AASP, copy in French.
13. AASP, O'Connell to Ireland, Rome, December 31, 1890.
14. ADR, Ireland to O'Connell, St. Paul, March 8, 1891.
15. ADR, Gibbons to O'Connell, Baltimore, February 3, 1891.
16. BCA, 88-J-4, Ireland to Gibbons, St. Paul, February 11, 1891.
17. St. Paul *Pioneer Press*, December 20, 1891.
18. BCA, 89-B-2, Ireland to Gibbons, St. Paul, October 17, 1891.
19. John Murphy and Co., Baltimore, 1892.
20. *Catholic World*, December, 1891, and February, 1892.
21. NYAA, René J. Holaind to Michael A. Corrigan, New York, 1891 (no date).
22. John T. Reily, *Collections in the Life and Times of Cardinal Gibbons*, II, 926.
23. *Educational Review*, July, 1891.
24. Quoted in Daniel F. Reilly, *op. cit.*, p. 123.
25. AASP, copy, Walter Hill to Charles Hardy, Chicago, no date.
26. ADR, Gibbons to O'Connell, Baltimore, April 11, 1892. There is in the

Archbishop's files a letter written from St. Vincent's Hospital where Corrigan used to rest and addressed to the Director of the *Civiltà Cattolica.* Speaking of the request of Gibbons to Ireland to explain the nature of his contract with the civil authorities it says:

"What may have been the reason of the request we are unable to say. Possibly it was that some good Catholic journals had censured the laicization of those schools, quoting the decrees of our Councils and certain pontifical declarations. Be this as it may, the report of the Archbishop of St. Paul, being in various points not in accord with what could be gathered from official documents quoted in the aforesaid Catholic papers, we expected some misunderstandings which it would take time to clear up.

"There were some who spoke openly, we might say vigorously, against such a surrender to the civil authority.

"The light of facts, as they were, came later, and other still more recent events give us the right to infer that if things had either been known or foreseen, the report forwarded to Rome, to be read by his Eminence the Cardinal Prefect, would have been quite different, nor would our manner of acting on that occasion have been interpreted as an approval of the secularization of those schools." Thus does His Grace of New York impeach the veracity of Cardinal Gibbons, Archbishops Ryan, Riordan, and Ireland. (AASP, original. Date and subscription excised.)

27. Reilly, *op, cit.,* II, 947.
28. December 14, 1891.
29. AASP, O'Connell to Ireland, Rome, November 10, 1891.
30. BCA, 89-G-3, Ireland to Gibbons, St. Paul, December 28, 1891.
31. AASP, Ireland to Louis Caillet, Rome, April 28, 1892.
32. BCA, 89-P-1, Ireland to Gibbons, Rome, February 21, 1892. Ireland delivered a defense of Bouquillon before the Propaganda on March 28.
33. AASP, original draft written by Humphrey Moynihan when a student at the American College, Rome. He and Dr. Denis O'Connell, the Rector, drew up the memorial.
34. AASP, Gibbons to Ireland, Baltimore, March 8, 1892.
35. ADR, Gibbons to O'Connell, Baltimore, March 1, 1892.
36. New York *Freeman's Journal,* April 23, 1892. For this rumor Ireland blamed Baumgarten, "a friend of Frs. Faeber and Goller of St. Louis." Baumgarten was correspondent of *Amerika* (J. T. Foley to Magnien, St. Louis, April 8, 1892).
37. AASP, March 25, 1892.
38. *Northwestern Chronicle,* March 18, 1892.
39. AASP, Ireland to Caillet, Rome, March 14, 1892.
40. *Educational Review,* May, 1892, pp. 462-471.
41. BCA, 89-F-1, John J. Kain to Giovanni Cardinal Simeoni, Wheeling, W. Va., December 17, 1891.
42. BCA, 89-G-3, Ireland to Gibbons, St. Paul, December 28, 1891.
43. AASP, Cardinal Ledochowski to Ireland, Rome, April 30, 1892. Decision of cardinals given on April 21.
44. AASP, copy, Rome, May 18, 1892; also *Northwestern Chronicle,* June 17, 1892.
45. AASP, Ledochowski to Ireland, Rome, May 30, 1892. In spite of the clearcut statement of the Archbishop that the decision permitted the multiplication of centers of educational influence, and of the reply of the Cardinal that his interpretation was legitimate, some Cahenslyites would have us believe that "the papal decree merely tolerated the two aforementioned instances,

but did not endorse them, and certainly did not sanction the extension of the plan to other schools."

46. AASP, Ireland to Caillet, Rome, February 14, 1892.
47. ACUA, Ireland to John J. Keane, Rome, April 26, 1892.
48. AASP, Keane to Ireland, Washington, April 29, 1892.
49. BCA, 89-S-3, Keane to Gibbons, Washington, March 21, 1892. "Let God arise, and let his enemies be scattered. Let not man prevail, O Lord."
50. AASP, Walter Elliott to Ireland, Montreal, March 25, 1892.
51. AASP, Gibbons to Ireland, Baltimore, August 29, 1892.
52. AASP, copy, Ireland to James Byrnes, Rome, April 27, 1892. The London *Tablet* interpreted "tolerari potest" to mean "it can be maintained." (May 21, 1892.)
53. *Northwestern Chronicle*, April 28, 1892. Father Walter Hill, S.J., wrote to Ireland: "You may remember that you showed me a note in Palmieri's *Theology* interpreting the famous editions of his work. I did not find the first edition of the work either in our Chicago library or in the library here in St. Louis University, but no matter, the fact is as you stated it. I will, when the opportunity offers, search into the inwardness of what was done." (AASP, St. Louis University, January 18, 1898.)
54. AASP, Alphonse Magnien to Ireland, Baltimore, March 31, 1892.
55. AASP, copy, Ireland to Rampolla, Rome, May 22, 1892.
56. AASP, Rampolla to Ireland, Rome, May 23, 1892.
57. BCA, 89-W-8, Ireland to Gibbons, Genoa, June 5, 1892.
58. New York *Freeman's Journal*, July 2, 1892.
59. AASP, Eugene Veuillot to Ireland, Paris, June 14, 1892.
60. Zwierlein, *Life and Letters of Bishop McQuaid*, Art Printshop, Rochester, 1927, III, 171.
61. *Ibid.*
62. BCA, 89-W-8, Ireland to Gibbons, Genoa, June 5, 1892.
63. AASP, O'Connell to Ireland, Rome, June 6, 1892.
64. ADR, Magnien to O'Connell, Baltimore, May 14, 1892.
65. BCA, 89-W-8, Ireland to Gibbons, Genoa, June 5, 1892.
66. BCA, Magnien to Gibbons, Santa Fe, N. M., June 30, 1891.
67. Ireland wrote to Father Magnien from Rome on March 17, 1892: "The feeling seems now clear of difficulties—except the *Civiltà*, which is to my mind positively devilish. . . . The Jesuits evidently make of the fight a question of life or death. . . . An acquaintance of mine stops at the S. American College—kept by the Jesuit Fathers. He tells me that the talk among the Fathers is all about Abp. Corrigan. He it is, they say, who had induced them to go into the fight on the School Question. . . . I charge most of our trouble to Abp. Corrigan, whose ambition throws him into secret alliances with all our enemies."
68. The *Review*, St. Louis, October 20, 1904.
69. ADR, McQuaid to O'Connell, Rochester, January 16, 1892.
70. RDA, Corrigan to McQuaid, New York, June 21, 1892.
71. BCA, 88-S-3, Ireland to Gibbons, St. Paul, July 2, 1891.
72. Reilly, *op. cit.*, pp. 271-276. There could be no doubt about Satolli's intention to support Ireland. On January 5, 1893, he wrote him: "*In silentio et in spe erit fortitudo vestra.*" Again, on January 15, after telling him that he had received from Rome word of the establishment of the Papal Delegation, he said: "*Quindi con fermezza maggiore di fiducia attendiam la rizaluzione della questione scholastica. Io non so qual figura nel presente e nel avvenire della istoria faciano i vescovi che si posero in linea di opposizione.*" (Therefore let

us await the solution of the school question with greater confidence. I do not know what a figure in present and future history those bishops will present who set themselves in opposition.)
73. AASP, copy, Corrigan to Satolli, New York, November 17, 1892.
74. *Catholic Standard,* Philadelphia, July 1, 1893.
75. BCA, 91-M-4, Ireland to Gibbons, St. Paul, June 13, 1893.
76. *Northwestern Chronicle,* September 28, 1893.
77. *Ibid.,* September 15, 1893.

CHAPTER 6. *The Father Hecker Controversy or "Americanism"*

1. For a fuller treatment of the subject the reader is referred to Abbé Felix Klein's *L'Américanisme,* Libraire Plon, Paris, 1949.
2. Walter Elliott, *The Life of Father Hecker,* Columbus Press, New York, 1891, p. ix.
3. *Northwestern Chronicle,* March 17, 1899, quoting the London *Chronicle.*
4. Elliott, *op. cit.,* p. 318.
5. *Dublin Review,* July, 1892.
6. PFA, Walter Elliott to Felix Klein, Washington, June 2, 1902.
7. *Hecker, Fondateur des "Paulistes" Américaines 1819-1888, par le Père Elliott de la même Compagnie.* Traduit et adapté de l'Anglais avec authorisation de l'auteur. Introduction par Mgr. Ireland, Preface par l'Abbé Felix Klein. (Paris, 1907.)
8. Published by Herder under the title: *A New Idea in the Life of Father Hecker.* Translation in New York *Freeman's Journal,* September 25, 1897. PFA, O'Connell to Klein, Freiburg, September 3, 1897: "It was deemed best to send out my paper on Americanism and, in the public mind, transfer the combat from the theological to the political issue."
9. Klein wrote to Ireland that the savants attending the Congress regarded the criticisms of Turinaz the highest praise. Paris, September 29, 1897.
10. Klein, *L'Américanisme,* p. 151.
11. Charles Maignen, *Le Père Hecker—Est-il un Saint?* (Paris, 1898), Preface to the English edition.
12. AASP, John J. Keane to John Ireland, Rome, June 4, 1898.
13. Maignen, *op. cit.,* p. 191.
14. *Ibid.,* p. 181.
15. Bernard O'Reilly, *Life of Leo XIII,* John C. Winston Co., Philadelphia, 1903.
16. *North American Review,* May, 1900, p. 689.
17. Maignen, *op. cit.,* p. 302.
18. *Ibid.,* p. 180.
19. *Ibid.,* p. 109.
20. Klein, *L'Américanisme,* p. 257.
21. *Ibid.,* p. 138. The following is the only reference to the article in the Archbishop's correspondence:
"Have you seen the last number of the *North American Review?* The article of Etheridge is excellent, evidently the best defence of the cause that has yet appeared. It could have been written only by one who was on the inside, or who at least came in contact with one who had been on the inside. The information the article contains seems to be most exact, and such as, for several details, must have been obtained only after diligent research.
"If you know the writer, give him my most sincere compliments. The allusions to different men are capital. That to Father David is wonderfully

good. I am sending you several copies—for judicious distribution." (RDA, St. Paul, May 7, 1900. To Denis O'Connell.)

22. J. St.-Clair Etheridge, "The Genesis of Americanism," *North American Review*, May, 1900, p. 683.
23. L'Abbé Henri Delassus, *L'Américanisme et la Conjuration Antichrétienne*, Desclée, Lille, 1899.
24. Jules Tardivel, *La Situation religieuse aux Etats-Unis, Illusions et réalité*, Desclée, Paris, 1900.
25. Etheridge, *op. cit.*
26. *Ibid.*
27. P. L. Péchenard, *La fin de l'Américanisme en France*, Mersch, Paris, 1901; *North American Review*, March, 1900.
28. Etheridge, *op. cit.*
29. New York *Freeman's Journal*, April 25, 1896. Dom Gasquet said in San Silvestro, Rome: "What he says respecting England is even less than the whole damaging truth—the faith was chiefly lost in England, because the Jesuits prevented the establishment of the hierarchy there." (AASP, F. P. Mackale to Ireland, Laurel, Md., January 23, 1897.)
30. BCA, 94-M-9, John A. Zahm to James J. Gibbons, Rome, May 18, 1898. Father Zahm was president of the Fourth International Scientific Congress in Freiburg, Switzerland.
31. *Franciscan Annals*, August 25, 1899. Also ADR, Cuthbert to Gibson, Sussex, March 20, 1899.
32. Etheridge, *op. cit.*
33. Klein, *L'Américanisme*, p. 291, August 4, 1898. Also *Nineteenth Century Review*, May, 1899, p. 786.
34. Etheridge, *op. cit.*
35. *La Justice Sociale*, March 11, 1899.
36. London *Tablet*, March 18, 1898.
37. Coppinger, *La Polémique française sur la Vie du Père Hecker*, Oudin, Paris, 1898.
38. Monsignor Eugène Boeglin, correspondent to Associated Press for Catholic news, wrote under the name *Innominato*. *Northwestern Chronicle*, November 18, 1898. *La Liberté*, March 2, 1899, said: "The translation gave a too philosophical twist to Hecker's doctrines."
39. AASP, Ireland to Coppinger, quoted in Coppinger to Ireland, Neuville, France, November 27, 1898.
40. New York *Sun*, clipping.
41. *North American Review*, July, 1899.
42. AASP, O'Connell to Ireland, Rome, March 6, 1897.
43. AASP, Keane to Ireland, Rome, May 9, 1897.
44. *Ibid.*, June 4, 1897.
45. *Ibid.*, January 24, 1898.
46. *Ibid.*, March 8, 1898.
47. *Ibid.*, June 4, 1898. The granting of the *Imprimatur* by the Reverend Alberto Lepidi, O.P., Master of the Sacred Palace, Rome, was regarded by O'Connell as an evidence of bad faith on the part of the Curia, which "while openly giving us smiles and fair words, had covertly given every encouragement in its power to our enemies, and never lost an opportunity of hurting us. It cherished Schroeder in its bosom, never put any check upon the false correspondence of Baumgarten. This patronage of Périès & Co. is nothing but the continuation of the same false system, and now that the Curia has publicly shown its hand, it is in order for us to ask it: where we stand and what are their intentions." He also said that Rampolla had

given orders to the Roman press under his control that Ireland's name should never appear in it, that time and again all allusions were rejected or suppressed, but that they printed everything about Corrigan. It is well to remember, however, that O'Connell was somewhat prejudiced against Rampolla, who disliked him.

48. AASP, Keane to Ireland, Houlgate, Calvados, France, July 16 and 21, 1898.
49. AASP, O'Connell to Keane, Rome, July 12, 1898; O'Connell to Ireland, Rome, July 12, 1898.
50. AASP, O'Connell to Ireland, Freiburg im Breisgau, August 28, 1898.
51. AASP, Thomas Bouquillon to Ireland, Washington, no date. "And yet," he added, "in the month of August last, the Dominicans of Fribourg proposed to our Professors (Pace, Grannan, Shahan, etc.) that they should ally themselves with them against our common enemies. I say nothing about the Jesuits.

    "Have you noticed that the *Civiltà Cattolica* has said almost nothing about the Pope's attempt at mediation? And that on the pretext that it has no information about it. Evidently these people have not spoken, so as to avoid mentioning your name."
52. BCA, 96-M-6, Gibbons to Rampolla, August 28, 1898. Rampolla replied by assuring Gibbons that Lepidi had meant no insult to any member of the American hierarchy, and that "In regard to the teachings of P. Hecker, His Holiness will himself write Your Eminence a personal letter." (Rome, September 23, 1898.)
53. PFA, Americanism Papers, 280, Keane to Lepidi, Rome, June 13, 1898.
54. *Ibid.*
55. PFA, Americanism Papers, 281, Keane to Rampolla, Rome, June 13, 1898; Calvados, July 25, 1898.
56. *Ibid.*, 284, Ireland to Rampolla, St. Paul, July 11, 1898.
57. *Ibid.*, 287, Rampolla to Ireland, Rome, August 6, 1898.
58. *Ibid.*, Ireland to Rampolla, St. Paul, August 29, 1898.
59. Frederick J. Zwierlein, *The Life and Letters of Bishop McQuaid*, The Art Printshop, Rochester, 1927, III, 246, McQuaid to Corrigan, Rochester, August 30, 1898.
60. AASP, Keane to Ireland, Washington, October 18, 1898.
61. PFA, Americanism Papers, Ireland to Elliott, St. Paul, November 6, 1898.
62. *Ibid.*, Gibbons to Elliott, Baltimore, April 14, 1898.
63. PFA, Klein Papers, Elliott to Klein, New York, February 14, 1898.
64. *Ibid.*, October 20, 1898.
65. AASP, Elliott to Dufresne, Thomaston, Conn., April 29, 1898. This was not Ireland's reaction. He said to Klein: "Well, Elliott's a better man than I am. As for me, I send him to the devil every day."
66. PFA, Klein Papers, O'Connell to Klein, Rome, November 25, 1897.
67. PFA, Americanism Papers, Ireland to Deshon, St. Paul, July 30, 1898.
68. *Ibid.*, Ireland to Elliott, St. Paul, August 10, 1898.
69. Klein, *L'Américanisme*, p. 340.
70. BCA, 96-S-8, Keane to Gibbons, Rome, November 9, 1898.
71. BCA, 96-N-4, Ireland to Gibbons, St. Paul, September 13, 1898.
72. BCA, 89-T-6, Hennessy to Gibbons, Jersey City, April 9, 1892.
73. NYAA, Brandi to Corrigan, Rome, January 2, 1899; September 3, 1898; October 12, 1898; Pappi (Province of Arezzo), July 11, 1898. O'Connell wrote to Klein: "Cardinal Rampolla protests that neither he nor the Pope knew anything of it and he promises serious action will be taken." (Klein, *L'Américanisme*, p. 247.)

74. *L'Univers*, December 30, 1898.
75. PFA, Ireland to Deshon, Rome, February 24, 1899.
76. *The True American Catholic*, February 4, 1899. Ireland complained to Baccelli, the Minister of Public Instruction, who suppressed the paper.
77. *Northwestern Chronicle*, February 10, 1899.
78. NYAA, Brandi to Corrigan, Rome, January 2, 1899.
79. PFA, Americanism Papers, Ireland to Deshon, Rome, February 24, 1899.
80. *Osservatore Romano*, January 22, 1899; *Catholic Encyclopedia*, XIV, 537.
81. AASP, copy, February 22, 1899.
82. PFA, Klein Papers, Thomas O'Gorman to Klein, Sioux Falls, S. D., March 7, 1900.
83. San Francisco *Argonaut*, April 17, 1899, quoting the *Evening Post*, New York.
84. Klein, *L'Américanisme*, p. 381.
85. PFA, Ireland to Deshon, St. Paul, March 16, 1899.
86. London *Tablet*, March 11, 1899.
87. Felix Klein, *Sans Arrêt*, Libraire Plon, Paris, 1950, p. 10.
88. Holden, "A Myth in 'L'Américanisme,'" *Catholic Historical Review*, July, 1945, p. 162.
89. PFA, Spalding to Elliott, Peoria, June 26, 1900.
90. *Civiltà Cattolica*, July 15, 1899. English translation AASP. When Lepidi informed O'Connell that someone from America in high position had informed Rome of the presence of religious Americanism in the United States, O'Connell replied: "Yes, I know it, Mgr. Messmer, Bishop of Green Bay." Messmer was in Rome in June and had matters of great importance to treat with the Pope. (O'Connell to Ireland, July 12, 1898.)
91. PFA, Klein Papers, O'Gorman to Klein, March 7, 1900. The London *Times*, September 15, 1899, said: "Corrigan addressed to the Pope a letter gleaming with a *schadenfreude* comprehensible only in the light of his previous efforts to secure the condemnation of his rivals, Cardinal Gibbons and Mgr. Ireland."
92. ADR, John A. Zahm to O'Connell, Notre Dame, March 30, 1899. AASP, Zahm to Ireland, Notre Dame, March 30, 1899.
93. AASP, Alphonse Magnien to Ireland, Baltimore, March 9, 1899.
94. London *Times*, September 15, 1899.
95. ADR, Frederick Rooker to O'Connell, Washington, March 14, 1899.
96. Taft Papers, Library of Congress.
97. Klein, *L'Américanisme*, p. 418.
98. PFA, Americanism Papers, Ireland to Klein, St. Paul, September 15, 1899. Also Etheridge, *op. cit.*
99. London *New Era*, June 24, 1899.
100. *Northwestern Chronicle*, March 17, 1899.
101. ADR, Ireland to O'Connell, Naples, March 23.
102. *Ibid.*, Turin, April 10 and 17, 1899.
103. ADR, O'Gorman to O'Connell, Brou, France, June 13, 1899.
104. Klein, *L'Américanisme*, p. 438.
105. ADR, Ireland to O'Connell, New York, October 21, 1899.
106. BCA, 97-R-5, minutes of the meeting, October 12, 1899.
107. Klein, *L'Américanisme*, p. 417.
108. Keane to Ireland, Dubuque, October 29, 1900. Only two months earlier, Ireland had written to Mrs. Bellamy Storer: "The Pope told me to forget that letter on Americanism, which had no application except in a few dioceses in France." (*In Memoriam Bellamy Storer*, p. 43.)

109. AASP, O'Connell to Ireland, Rome, February 28, 1900.
110. AASP, Paravicino to Ferrari, Milan, June 2, 1899.
111. AASP, Ferrari to Paravicino, Milan, June 3, 1899.
112. AASP, original draft of letter.
113. PFA, Americanism Papers, 299, Lorenzelli to Rampolla, July 21, 1900.
114. *La Justice Sociale*, June 30, 1899. Quoted from *L'Univers*.
115. John T. Reily, *Collections and Recollections in the Life and Times of Cardinal Gibbons*, 10 vols., Martinburg, W. Va., 1890-1904, p. 845. In May, 1902, O'Gorman wrote to Gibbons: "On all sides it is proclaimed that Americanism, which was supposed to be our defeat, has been turned into a glorious victory. We are on top."
116. *America*, October 5, 1918.

CHAPTER 7. *Missions Abroad*

1. *Journal de Genève*, Paris, June 30 and July 1, 1892.
2. Ireland, *The Church and Modern Society*, Pioneer Press, St. Paul, 1905, I, 361.
3. AASP, James Gibbons to John Ireland, Baltimore, January 2, 1897.
4. *L'Univers*, June 24, 1892.
5. H. Béranger, *L'Aristocratie Intellectuelle*, Paris, 1894, p. 93.
6. *Le Figaro*, June 26, 1892; *Journal des Debats*, June 25, 1892.
7. *Grenoblais*, Grenoble, June 29, 1892.
8. *Le Temps*, June 21, 1892.
9. *Le Petit Journal*, June 19, 1892.
10. *Le Pays*, June 22, 1892.
11. *Le Moniteur de Rome*, June 24, 1892.
12. *La République Française*, July 5, 1892.
13. *Le Figaro*, June 18, 1892.
14. ADR, Ireland to O'Connell, from the Ocean, July 7, 1892.
15. *Le Temps*, June 19, 1892.
16. AASP, Ireland to Caillet, Paris, June 28, 1892.
17. AASP, Rampolla to Ireland, Rome, August 8, 1892. Pope Leo XIII, in a public audience in July, 1892, praised Ireland for the "good work he had done for the Church in Paris." (New York *Herald*, July 19, 1892.)
18. AASP, Touchet to Ireland, Orléans, July 2, 1898. Asked why he had selected Ireland, Touchet replied: "Because we admire the fervid, virile eloquence of the Archbishop of St. Paul. He is the nearest approach to our own Bossuet that the Catholic Church has today." (*Northwestern Chronicle*, February 10, 1899.)
19. AASP, O'Connell to Ireland, Rome, February 28, 1900.
20. AASP, Magnien to Ireland, Baltimore, March 9, 1899.
21. Ireland, *The Church and Modern Society*, II, 5.
22. *La Justice Sociale*, May 20, 1899.
23. *La Libre Parole*, February 9, 1899.
24. *Le Journal des Debats*, May 25, 1899.
25. *Northwestern Chronicle*, May 26, 1899.
26. *Ibid.*, June 9, 1899.
27. *Ibid.*, May 19, 1899.
28. *L'Avenir de Lyon*, May 23, 1899.
29. *Le Figaro*, May 15, 1899.
30. *Northwestern Chronicle*, June 30, 1899.
31. AASP, King Leopold to Ireland, Chateau de Lacken, May 25, 1899.
32. New York *Herald*, May 22, 1899.

33. *Catholic Times and Catholic Opinion,* June 30, 1899.
34. London *Times,* June 28, 1899; *New Era,* July 1, 1899.
35. AASP, Gibson to Klein, Moorhurst, Holmwood, Surrey, July 7, 1899.
36. *Weekly Register,* London, July 8, 1899.
37. *Daily Post,* July 7, 1899.
38. *Catholic Times and Catholic Opinion,* July 14, 1899.
39. Cork *Examiner,* July 20, 1899.
40. AASP, William McKinley to John Ireland, Washington, June 11, 1900.
41. AASP, Count de Chambrun to Ireland, Paris, April 17, 1900.
42. *La Vie Catholique,* July 13, 1900.
43. Ireland, *The Church and Modern Society,* II, 29.
44. *Le Figaro,* July 5, 1900.
45. *L'Univers,* July 5, 1900; *Le Peuple Français,* July 5, 1900; *La Vie Catholique,* July 13, 1900.
46. *La Vie Catholique,* September 21, 1900.
47. *Ibid.,* July 24, 1900.
48. *Northwestern Chronicle,* October 6, 1900.
49. *Le Figaro,* clipping.
50. AASP, O'Gorman to Ireland, Rome, October 16, 1900.
51. AASP, copy, Ireland to Norfolk, St. Paul, February 23, 1900.
52. New York *Sun,* October 21, 1900.
53. *La Difesa,* May 15, 1900.
54. AASP, Vincenzo Vannutelli to Ireland, Rome, May 14, 1906.
55. *Bulletin Gorini,* Diocese of Belley. No. 47. Clipping.
56. AASP, Scrapbook 40.
57. *Northwestern Chronicle,* December 31, 1906.
58. AASP, copy of cable, Ireland to editor of *L'Eclair,* St. Paul, December 30, 1906.
59. Labeuche to Ireland, Belley, March 17, 1909.
60. AASP, copy, Ireland to Goyau, Rome, January 16, 1909.
61. Claude d'Habloville, *Grandes Figures de l'Eglise Contemporaine,* Perrin, Paris, 1925, p. 243.

CHAPTER 8. *The Spanish-American War and Its Aftermath*

1. AASP, original. Also Baltimore *Sun,* April 23, 1898.
2. AASP, three cablegrams, March 27, 29, 30.
3. J. F. Rhodes, *The McKinley and Roosevelt Administration,* The Macmillan Company, New York, 1922, p. 47.
4. *Northwestern Chronicle,* February 11, 1898.
5. Rhodes, *op. cit.,* p. 56.
6. Copies of this and of all other cablegrams passing between the Archbishop and the Vatican are in the writer's possession.
7. Ferrara, *Tentatives de entervençon Europea en America, 1896-98,* Havana (Biblioteca Nacional, Madrid).
8. Spanish diplomatic correspondence and documents, Library of Congress.
9. A copy of Elkins' *Journal* is in the writer's possession; it contains all conversations with the Archbishop.
10. Elkins writes: "After an introduction and exchange of the usual courtesies the Archbishop proceeded, in his vigorous and emphatic way, to state to the Minister that by direction of the Holy Father he had come from his home in St. Paul, a distance of 1200 miles, to the capital to see if something could not be done to avert war. The Spanish Minister expressed his gratification to learn of the efforts he had been making. The Minister was under

the impression that Archbishop Ireland was a Cardinal, being led to this conclusion because he thought in a matter of so much moment the Pope would call upon a Cardinal rather than an Archbishop. I explained to the Minister that the Archbishop was our great American prelate, that he had not only been a soldier, but was loyal Republican and had more influence with the Administration than any other Church authority in the United States." Ireland must have felt from the beginning that he was on a hopeless mission, for Elkins says: "After a general exchange of thought, the conference terminated, all feeling some hope but not encouragement."

11. Spanish feelings are reflected in a letter which the Spanish Ambassador in London sent to McKinley on June 8, and in which he referred to the war declared by the United States against Spain as the most unreasonable and inconsiderate of all the unjust wars contained in the annals of history. He called his attention to the following facts: The United States complained of Weyler and De Lome, and both were recalled. It demanded autonomy for Cuba and it was granted. It protested against the concentration camps and Spain not only changed its laws dealing with them but sent $600,000 to relieve the sufferers. It sent an ex parte decision on the *Maine* unaccompanied by accusation or demand for redress, and Spain expressed regret and proposed arbitration. It expressed alarm at the proposed sailing of a Spanish flotilla to a Spanish island where the ships would be ready for war, and Spain countermanded the order. It proposed an armistice with the Cuban insurgents; Spain granted it and stopped all offensive fighting. It demanded the evacuation of Cuba within forty-eight hours; Spain refused, till compelled by force, to relinquish the land she discovered and Christianized. He spoke of the injustice of not awaiting patiently the mediation of the Pope and of placing in command of a division of the army the ex-Consul General of the United States at Havana. He called General Lee and the American press the sole and effective causes of the "Present Monstrous war," and he concluded by saying: "I ask Your Excellency in your conscience to say whether all that is happening is not iniquitous, and worthy of the Incorruptible Essence proving to humanity that the strength of His Mighty Arm has not been shortened." (R. A. Rondan to William McKinley, copy in writer's possession.)

12. New York *Times*, September 1, 1912.
13. AASP, Scrapbook 50.
14. BCA, 96-H-1, Keane to Gibbons, Rome, April 6, 1898.
15. ADR, Ireland to O'Connell, May 2, 1898.
16. AASP, O'Connell to Ireland, Rome, April 24, 1898.
17. AASP, Keane to Ireland, Rome, May 24, 1898.
18. *Ibid.*, June 19, 1898.
19. AASP, O'Connell to Ireland, Rome, June 16, 1898.
20. ADR, Ireland to O'Connell, St. Paul, May 11, 1898.
21. ADR, Ireland to Keane, St. Paul, May 28, 1898.
22. AASP, Keane to Ireland, Rome, May 24, 1898.
23. Aquin Papers, No. 11, St. Thomas College, St. Paul.
24. ADR, Ireland to O'Connell, St. Paul, May 28, 1898. Ireland's remark about keeping up his Americanism was not just a boast, as some would like to regard it. It was merely a reply to O'Connell, who had written him on April 24 urging him to "keep at the head of the movement in war as well as in peace."
25. AASP, Rooker to Ireland, Washington, May 16, 1898.
26. *Ibid.*, June 1, 1898.

27. AASP, Storer to Ireland, Brussels, May 11, 1898.
28. AASP, C. K. Davis to Mrs. Bellamy Storer, Washington, May 17, 1900.
29. AASP, Infanta Paz to Ireland, Schloss Nymphenburg, August 20, 1898.
30. *Ibid.*, March 25, 1899.
31. *Ibid.*, May 24, 1899.
32. AASP, brochure of address at Notre Dame, October 5, 1904.
33. AASP, brochure, March, 1903.
34. *Sacred Heart Review*, June, 1901.
35. *American Catholic Quarterly Review*, July and October, 1905.
36. BCA, 96-H-4, Sebastiano Martinelli to Rampolla, Washington, August 23, 1898.
37. AASP, Rampolla to Ireland, Rome, May 23, 1901.
38. AASP, Ireland, to Rampolla, St. Paul, June 16, 1901.
39. AASP, Rampolla to Ireland, Rome, July 2, 1901.
40. Taft Papers, Library of Congress, Ireland to Taft, St. Paul, August 19, 1901.
41. AASP, Taft to Ireland, Manila, October 15, 1901.
42. AASP, copy, Taft to Mrs. Bellamy Storer, Manila, May 19, 1901. The writer has ignored much of Mrs. Storer's correspondence as lacking in either significance or influence.
43. Roosevelt Papers, Library of Congress, Ireland to Roosevelt, St. Paul, September 11, 1901.
44. AASP, Rampolla to Ireland, Rome, November 17, 1901.
45. *Ibid.*, December 11, 1901.
46. Roosevelt Papers, Library of Congress, Ireland to Roosevelt, St. Paul, December 8, 1901.
47. *Ibid.*, December 11, 1901. Also William H. Ward to Ireland, the *Independent*, March 7, 1902.
48. AASP, Jacob G. Schurman to Ireland, Ithaca, New York, February 6, 1902.
49. ADR, Ireland to Denis O'Connell, St. Paul, October 27, 1898.
50. AASP, copy, Taft to Mrs. Storer, Manila, January 12, 1901. Chaplain William D. McKinnon also stated that there was not hope for any change for the better as long as the present Delegate remained, that Judge Taft and General Wright were two of the broadest men that could be found, but that the Delegate showed no disposition to meet them halfway. He feared that if the Philippine situation were referred to Congress, all the scandals of the Church would be aired. He said that Chapelle, whose chancellor and secretary were friars, ignored the native priests, who retaliated by throwing their influence on the side of the insurgents. (AASP, McKinnon to Ireland, Manila, January 19, 1901.)
51. AASP, Rampolla to Ireland, Rome, March 17, 1902.
52. *Ibid.*, March 31, 1902.
53. A prelate who had intimate knowledge of the affair so informed the writer.
54. AASP, O'Connell to Ireland, Rome, October 14, 1902. Guidi was titular Archbishop of Nicaea and Auditor of the Holy Father.
55. BCA, 96-N-4, Ireland to Gibbons, St. Paul, September 13, 1898; 98-Y-9, August 25, 1901; 99-E-8, November 7, 1901; 99-J-1, January 1, 1902.
56. BCA, 99-M-3, Thomas O'Gorman to Gibbons, Sioux Falls, March 13, 1902.
57. AASP, Thomas O'Gorman to Ireland, Rome, May 4, 1902.
58. *Ibid.*, May 7, 1902.
59. *Ibid.*, May 14 and 17, 1902.
60. *Ibid.*, June 1, 1902; (AASP) copy of Root proposals.
61. AASP, copy (in French); also copy of *Formule d'Accord* of June 25.
62. AASP, copy, Taft to Roosevelt, Rome, October 5, 1903.

63. New York *Post*, September 23, 1902. AASP, copy of letter, Root to Taft, July 14, 1902.
64. AASP, James Smith to Ireland, Manila, August 29, 1902. Smith held the position of Secretary of Public Instruction. This was also O'Gorman's opinion. (O'Gorman's memorandum, Taft Papers, Library of Congress.)
65. AASP, Taft to O'Gorman, Manila, October 17, 1902.
66. AASP, Smith to Ireland, Manila, May 7, 1903.
67. AASP, Richard Campbell to Ireland, Manila, March 9, 1903.
68. *Church News*, December 24, 1898.
69. AASP, Smith to Ireland, Manila, May 7, 1903.
70. AASP, copy, John McDonough to Colonel Clarence Edwards, Manila, July 3, 1903. Colonel Edwards was Chief of the Division of Insular Affairs of the War Department.
71. AASP, William D. McKinnon to Ireland, Manila, January 19, 1901.
72. AASP, Francis Doherty to Ireland, Camp Jossman, Guimavas, May 2, 1903.
73. AASP, E. J. Vattman to Ireland, Fort Sheridan, Illinois, December 31, 1902.
74. AASP, Campbell to Ireland, Havana, July 21, 1903. Similar testimony was given by Chaplain Patrick J. Hart (Hart to Ireland, Calamba, Laguna Province, Luzon, May 18, 1901); by Father E. H. Fitzgerald, who was assigned to the Cathedral, Manila and who was an interpreter between the Bishop of Cebu and the American officials (Taft to Mrs. Storer, Manila, May 19, 1901); and by Mother Mary Joseph Hartwell (to Ireland, St. Michael's Convent, San Juan, July 12, 1904).
75. AASP, O'Reilly to Ireland, Havana, February 1, 1904.
76. ACUA, O'Connell Papers, Ireland to O'Connell, St. Paul, June 28, 1903.
77. *New Century*, July 14, 1902.
78. *Catholic Universe*, Cleveland, July 25, 1902.
79. Chicago *Tribune*, October 24, 1900.
80. New York *World*, October 25, 1902.
81. *Irish World*, August 16, 1902.
82. AASP, copy, James A. McFaul to Roosevelt, Trenton, July 28, 1903.
83. AASP, Roosevelt to Ireland, Oyster Bay, New York, July 23, 1902.
84. *Ibid.*, July 31, 1902.
85. Minneapolis *Tribune*, August 12, 1902.
86. AASP, copy, Taft to Roosevelt, Manila, September 15, 1903; Wright to Roosevelt, Manila, September 15, 1903. Wright was Acting Governor.
87. AASP, O'Reilly to Ireland, Manila, July 27, 1903.
88. AASP, copy, Luke Wright to Root, Manila, July 9, 1902.
89. *Catholic Citizen*, July 26, 1902. Also Taft Papers, Library of Congress, Root to Taft, Washington, July 14, 1902.
90. AASP, Root to Ireland, Washington, July 19, 1902.
91. AASP, Taft to O'Gorman, Manila, October 17, 1902. Smith wrote on November 14, 1902, announcing the appointment of 200 teachers and urging Ireland in the name of the Governor to supply Catholics. He said, however, that with few exceptions the Catholic teachers who had sought service in the Philippines were often drunk and inefficient. He also tried to enlist the co-operation of Archbishop Riordan of San Francisco and Father Kenna, president of Santa Clara College.
92. BCA, 100-J-5, Ireland to Gibbons, St. Paul, May 4, 1903.
93. AASP, San Francisco *Leader*, October 18, 1902.
94 AASP, copy, Ireland to the editor of the *Leader*, St. Paul, October 23, 1902.
95. Letter published in the Galena *Gazette*, October 23, 1902.
96. AASP, R. J. O'Hanlon to Ireland, February 25, 1902.

97. AASP, Anna Hennessy to Ireland, Pagsanghan, June 27, 1903.
98. AASP, Campbell to Ireland, Manila, January 25, 1904. Also August 8, 1903.
99. *Ibid.*, July 21, 1903.
100. AASP, copy, Jeremiah Harty to Doyle, Manila, May 1, 1906.
101. AASP, copy, Smith to Roosevelt, Washington, June 13, 1906.
102. Taft Papers, Library of Congress, Roosevelt to Taft, Washington, July 29, 1902.
103. AASP, Rampolla to Ireland, Rome, April 23, 1904.
104. AASP, Smith to Ireland, Manila, May 7, 1903.
105. AASP, Campbell to Ireland, Manila, July 21, 1903.
106. AASP, Augosto Guidi to Ireland, Manila, April 7, 1904.
107. AASP, copy, Roosevelt to Taft, June 29, 1906, and Taft to Ireland, June 30, 1906.
108. AASP, copy, Harty to Roosevelt, Manila, February 27, 1906.
109. At Ireland's suggestion Father Freri of St. Mary's Seminary, Baltimore, asked General Wood for information regarding the financial settlement he had made in Cuba. Wood replied that he had found the claims of the Church just and fair, that he had purchased all *censos* and *capellanias*, had paid rent on the property adjudged to belong to the Church, and some claims for damages, etc., amounting to $951,236.97. He also secured an option for five years, under which the State could purchase, at a fixed price, the real property of the Church which the State was holding. While it continued to hold the property, it paid a yearly rental of $91,027.00. (AASP, Freri to Ireland, January 27, 1903; Wood to Freri, January 5, 1903.)
110. AASP, copy, Roosevelt to Taft, Washington, March 6, 1906.
111. AASP, copy, Rooker to Roosevelt, Jaro, May 12, 1904.
112. New York *Tribune,* December 22, 1903.
113. AASP, Rooker to Ireland, Jaro, February 11, 1904.
114. *Ibid.*, August 22, 1904.
115. AASP, copy, Roosevelt to Rooker, June 22, 1904.
116. AASP, Roosevelt to Ireland, June 3, 1904.
117. AASP, copy, Harty to Luke Wright, Manila, August 30, 1904.
118. AASP, Harty to Ireland, Manila, March 17, 1906.
119. AASP, Harty to Ireland, Manila, September 6, 1904.
120. AASP, O'Reilly to Ireland, Manila, July 24, 1904.
121. AASP, Smith to Ireland, Cloverdale, Cal., July 17, 1906.
122. AASP, Thomas Hendrick to Ireland, Cebu, January 19, 1906.

CHAPTER 9. *Stands on Social Problems*

1. AASP, "La Question des 'Chevaliers du Travail,'" *Le Moniteur de Rome,* March 26, 27, 1887.
2. *Northwestern Chronicle,* March 10, 1887.
3. AASP, Gibbons to Ireland, Baltimore, September 17, 1888.
4. Richard Purcell, *Archbishop Ireland,* Aquin Papers, No. 11, St. Thomas College, St. Paul, 1949.
5. Henry J. Browne, *The Catholic Church and the Knights of Labor,* Catholic University Press, Washington, 1949, p. 238.
6. ACUA, *Keane Chronicles,* p. 16.
7. BCA, 82-G-4, Keane to Gibbons, Rome, December 4, 1886.
8. BCA, 87-J-7, Ireland to Gibbons, St. Paul, April 21, 1890.
9. Shane Leslie, *Henry Edward Manning,* Burns Oates, London, 1921, p. 363.
10. *Ibid.*, p. 363.

11. *Northwestern Chronicle*, May 13, 1892, quoting "Canonist" in the New York *Sun*.
12. BCA, 93-N-3, Ireland to Gibbons, St. Paul, December 7 and 29, 1894; AASP, Gibbons to Ireland, Baltimore, December 10 and 26, 1894.
13. BCA, 93-R-4 and 93-S-2, Ireland to Gibbons, St. Paul, February 6 and March 4, 1895; AASP, Gibbons to Ireland, Baltimore, January 12 and February 9 and 17, 1895. Fergus Macdonald, *The Catholic Church and the Secret Societies in the United States*, United States Catholic Historical Society, New York, 1946, pp. 198, 199. The reader is referred to this work for a full treatment of secret societies.
14. *L'Univers*, March 5, 1895.
15. AASP, O'Gorman to Ireland, Washington, January 10 and February 12, 1895.
16. AASP, Gibbons to Ireland, Baltimore, March 6, 1895.
17. AASP, Magnien to Ireland, Baltimore, March 26, 1895.
18. AASP, Rooker to Ireland, Washington, February 21, March 4 and 18, 1895.
19. ACUA, Gibbons to Keane, Rome, June 29, and Wörishofen, Munich, July 12, 1895.
20. AASP, Satolli to Ireland, Washington, June 11, 1895.
21. *Northwestern Chronicle*, March 6, 1896.
22. AASP, copies of minutes of the meetings of the archbishops.
23. AASP, original.
24. AASP, Fleming to Ireland, Rome, August 27, 1909.
25. AASP, copy, Rampolla to Falconio.
26. John Ireland, *The Church and Modern Society*, Pioneer Press, St. Paul, 1905, I, 270.
27. *Northwestern Chronicle*, April 21, 1887.
28. *Ibid.*, May 26, 1887.
29. AASP, Scrapbook 44, p. 22.
30. Cork *Examiner*, July 20, 1899.
31. AASP, Scrapbook 43, p. 137.
32. AASP, Scrapbook 44, p. 55.
33. Cork *Examiner*, July 20, 1899.
34. Minneapolis *Journal*, December 14, 1900.
35. AASP, Scrapbook 43, p. 156.
36. *Northwestern Chronicle*, October 16 and 30, 1891.
37. Minneapolis *Journal*, November 7, 1891.
38. *Northwestern Chronicle*, February 7, 1890.
39. *Le Figaro*, August 29, 1894.
40. St. Paul *Dispatch*, May 4, 1894.
41. NYAA, Ryan to Corrigan, Philadelphia, May 20, 1890.
42. AASP, O'Connell to Ireland, New York, May 17, 1890.
43. *Catholic Citizen*, Milwaukee, December 20, 1890.
44. *Northwestern Chronicle*, January 9, 1891.
45. *Ibid.*, December 23, 1892.
46. *Literary Northwest*, St. Paul, May, 1892.
47. *Northwestern Chronicle*, January 9, 1891.
48. BCA, 84-D-4, O'Connell to Gibbons, Rome, February 25, 1888.
49. AASP, Gibbons to Ireland, Rome, March 19, 1888.
50. ADR, Ireland to O'Connell, St. Paul, April 14, 1888.
51. *Ibid.*, February 16, 1894.
52. NYAA, Ireland to Corrigan, St. Paul, July 14, 1887.
53. AASP, Moore to Ireland, St. Augustine, March 31, 1892.
54. ADR, Ireland to O'Connell, St. Paul, August 3, 1892.

55. *Ibid.*, August 10, 1892.
56. John A. Ryan, *Social Doctrine in Action*, Harper & Brothers, New York, 1941, p. 25.
57. *Ibid.*, p. 27.

CHAPTER 10. *The Educator*

1. John Ireland, *The Church and Modern Society*, Pioneer Press, St. Paul, 1905, I, 92.
2. John Tracy Ellis, *The Formative Years of the Catholic University of America*, American Catholic Historical Association, Washington, 1946, pp. 103, 110.
3. BCA, 79-H-5, John Ireland to James J. Gibbons, St. Paul, March 26, 1885.
4. NYAA, C-2, J. J. Gibbons to M. A. Corrigan, Baltimore, April 1, 1885.
5. BCA, 79-I-8, Ireland to Gibbons, St. Paul, April 6, 1885.
6. RDA, Bernard McQuaid to John J. Williams, Rochester, April 13, 1885.
7. BCA, 79-J-9, Ireland to Gibbons, St. Paul, April 20, 1885.
8. ACUA, "Chronicles of the Catholic University of America from 1885," p. 3.
9. RDA, John J. Keane to Denis O'Connell, Richmond, May 20, 1886.
10. Ellis, *op. cit.*, p. 212.
11. BCA, 82-G-6, *Animadversiones Quaedam de Universitate in America Fundanda.*
12. BDA, Ireland to Williams, St. Paul, December 14, 1886.
13. NYAA, McQuaid to Corrigan, Rochester, January 13, 1887.
14. Ellis, *op. cit.*, p. 211.
15. NYAA, C-8, Robert Fulton to M. A. Corrigan, September 17, 1886.
16. New York *Herald*, October 13, 1893.
17. "Chronicles," pp. 6 and 7.
18. AASP, O'Connell to Ireland, Rome, November 21, 1888. "Corrigan wanted it in New York for the Jesuits, but I was not willing."
19. "Chronicles," p. 11.
20. ADR, Corrigan to McQuaid, New York, June 22, 1887.
21. NYAA, McQuaid to Corrigan, Rochester, June 23, 1887.
22. NYAA, C-16, Ireland to Corrigan, Rome, February 5, 1887.
23. AASP, Keane to Ireland, Rome, December 22, 1888.
24. Ireland, *The Church and Modern Society*, I, 92.
25. *Irish World*, April 25, 1896.
26. ACUA, Ireland to Keane, St. Paul, December 7, 1889.
27. NYAA, Keane to Corrigan, Cape May, August 2, 1889.
28. ACUA, Ireland to Keane, April 26, 1892.
29. NYAA, C-41, Cahensly to Corrigan, Limburg am Lahn, October 31, 1892.
30. ADR, Ireland to O'Connell, St. Paul, September 13, 1897.
31. AASP, Schroeder to Ireland, Washington, October 18, 1897.
32. ADR, Ireland to O'Connell, St. Paul, December 3, 1897.
33. AASP, O'Connell to Ireland, Rome, December 2, 1897.
34. ADR, Ireland to O'Connell, St. Paul, January 8, 1898.
35. BCA, 94-U-1, Ireland to Gibbons, St. Paul, December 2, 1896.
36. AASP, O'Connell to Ireland, Rome, November 25, 1901.
37. ADR, Ireland to O'Connell, St. Paul, November 28, 1902.
38. AASP, O'Connell to Ireland, Rome, January 14, 1903.
39. ADR, Ireland to O'Connell, St. Paul, April 19, 1903.
40. ACUA, Ireland to O'Connell, St. Paul, November 15, 1903.
41. Minutes of the Board of Trustees, November 27, 1906.
42. Joseph Gilpin Pyle, *The Life of James J. Hill*, Doubleday, Doran & Co., Inc., New York, 1917, I, 63.

43. ACUA, O'Connell to Keane, Paris, July 7, 1890.
44. BCA, O'Connell to Gibbons, Rome, August 4, 1890.
45. AASP, O'Connell to Ireland, Grottoferrata, August 20, 1890.
46. *Ibid.*, Rome, September 21, 1890.
47. St. Paul *Daily Globe*, September 5, 1895.
48. Translations: There are those who joy them in the Olympic strife and love the dust they gather in the course. Haste valiantly to reach the haven. The righteous man of upright life and pure. Remember when life's path is steep to keep an even mind. The man of firm and righteous will.
49. *American Ecclesiastical Review*, October, November, December, 1939.
50. *Ave Maria*, July 6, 1895.
51. Ireland, *The Church and Modern Society*, II, 279.
52. St. Paul *Globe*, June 23, 1901.
53. Ireland, *The Church and Modern Society*, II, 143.
54. *Ibid.*, II, 305.
55. AASP, Charles M. Schwab to Ireland, South Bethlehem, Penn., July 30, 1910.
56. Horace, *Odes*, I, 14. Translation: O ship, new billows threaten to bear thee out to sea again. Beware. Haste valiantly to reach the haven.
57. AASP, brochure, privately printed.
58. *Catholic Bulletin*, August 23, 1913.
59. AASP, copy, Ireland to W. A. Frisbie, St. Paul, December 9, 1913.
60. AASP, Thomas McMillan, C.S.P., to John Ireland, New York, October 2, 1913.
61. AASP, copy, John Ireland to Ell Torrance, St. Paul, May 22, 1914.
62. AUND, Ireland to Hudson, St. Paul, November 28, 1913.
63. *Northwestern Chronicle*, September 4, 1896.

CHAPTER 11. *The Statesman*

1. *Northwest Magazine*, July, 1890, p. 28.
2. *Northwestern Chronicle*, July 29, 1891.
3. AASP, Scrapbook 43, p. 20; also *Northwestern Chronicle*, October 14, 1886.
4. New York *Times*, September 26, 1918.
5. Clipping, AASP, Scrapbook 36, p. 85.
6. St. Paul *Pioneer Press*, March 17, 1910.
7. *Northwestern Chronicle*, July 14, 1887.
8. *Ibid.*, June 16, 1893.
9. *Ibid.*, December 1, 1893. He was elected a member of the Industrial Peace Commission in April, 1907. (AASP, T. L. Weed to Ireland, Washington, April 1, 1907.)
10. AASP, James Gibbons to John Ireland, Baltimore, February 17, 1888.
11. *Ibid.*, November 20, 1900.
12. Minneapolis *Journal*, September 14, 1901.
13. Brooklyn *Times*, May 9, 1894.
14. AASP, Theodore Roosevelt to Ireland, Oyster Bay, N. Y., September 19, 1898.
15. AASP, Theodore Roosevelt to O'Gorman, U.S. Civil Service Commission, Washington, March 1, 1898.
16. AASP, Theodore Roosevelt to Ireland, Police Department, New York City, August 19, 1895.
17. *Ibid.*, Oyster Bay, N. Y., August 8, 1902, July 18, 1903, June 3, 1904.
18. *Ibid.*, White House, January 2, 1903 and May 18, 1904.
19. *Ibid.*, Washington, November 9, 1904; Chicago, September 29, 1917.
20. AASP, William H. Taft to John Ireland, Hot Springs, Va., November 21, 1908.

21. Henry F. Pringle, *The Life and Times of William Howard Taft*, Farrar and Rinehart, New York, 1939, II, 966.
22. AASP, Taft to Ireland, Washington, June 17, 1912.
23. *Ibid.*, White House, Washington, August 14, 1912.
24. *Ibid.*, New Haven, Conn., no date.
25. *Ibid.*, December 27, 1915.
26. AASP, John Ireland to Daniel Hudson, St. Paul, September 12, 1912.
27. AASP, George F. Hoar to John Ireland, Washington, May 1, 1904.
28. St. Paul *Pioneer Press*, October 11, 1896.
29. AASP, E. S. Goodrich to John Ireland, Washington, November 5, 1896.
30. AASP, clipping, Scrapbook 43, p. 91.
31. Chicago *Tribune*, October 24, 1900.
32. AASP, Stephen B. Elkins to John Ireland, Washington, December 10, 1896.
33. *Ibid.*, January 25, 1897.
34. Library of Congress Archives, Roosevelt Papers, St. Paul, November 13, 1900.
35. AASP, Theodore Roosevelt to John Ireland, Washington, November 9, 1901.
36. AASP, Thomas Carter to John Ireland, Washington, June 3, 1909.
37. John Ireland to James Gibbons, BCA, 105-N, St. Paul, June 15, 1909.
38. AASP, Denis O'Connell to John Ireland, Rome, July 21, 1897.
39. AASP, Bernard McQuaid to M. A. Corrigan, Rochester, January 19, 1894, NYAA.
40. *Ibid.*, March 31, 1904.
41. Zwierlein, *Life and Letters of Bishop McQuaid*, The Art Printshop, Rochester, 1927, III, 208.
42. *Ibid.*, III, 210; also *Northwestern Chronicle*, November 25, 1894.
43. BCA, 93-S-2, Ireland to Gibbons, March 4, 1895. Referring to his statement in Chicago that the American refusing to vote merits disfranchisement, he said: "People were wicked enough to see in those words an allusion to His Lordship of Rochester."
44. New York *Tribune*, January 15, 1895.
45. Chicago *Post*, February 22, 1895.
46. AASP, Mark Hanna to John Ireland, Washington, November 14, 1903.
47. *Northwestern Chronicle*, October, 1896.
48. Minneapolis *Journal*, February 4, 1905.
49. John T. Reily, *Collections and Recollections in the Life and Times of Cardinal Gibbons*, IV, 589.
50. Minneapolis *Journal*, July 5, 1906.
51. AASP, King Leopold to Ireland, Lacken, March 4, 1903.
52. AASP, Tarnowski to Ireland, Washington, May 29, 1901.
53. New York *Herald*, May 30, 1902; *Pilot*, June 14, 1902.
54. AASP, Jules Cambon, Washington, November 26, 1902, and May 2, 1909.
55. AASP, brochure, The Grafton Press, New York, February, 1903.
56. AASP, Cambon to Ireland, Paris, January 20 and March 17, 1915.
57. AASP, Eugene Boeglin to Ireland, no date.
58. AASP, Cassini to John Ireland, Washington, March 27, 1904.
59. AASP, Moncheau to Ireland, Washington, January 17, 1905.
60. St. Paul *Pioneer Press*, January 8, 1910.
61. AASP, Buisseret to Ireland, Washington, January 16, 1910.
62. AASP, Carton de Wiart to Ireland, London, December 15, 1916.
63. *Northwestern Chronicle*, March 17, 1887.
64. AASP, Jacob Schiff to John Ireland, New York, November 21, 1913.
65. AASP, Theodore Roosevelt to John Ireland, New York City, December 11, 1914.

Notes

Notes 411

66. AASP, John Ireland to Charles W. Ames, Washington, April 18, 1897.
67. AASP, Hector Irenée Cardinal Sevin to John Ireland, Lyon, March 14, 1916.
68. AASP, Louis-Henri-Joseph Cardinal Lucon to John Ireland, Rheims, March 3, 1916.
69. AASP, Stanislas-Arthur Xavier Touchet to John Ireland, Orléans, April 10, 1917.
70. AASP, Henry Ford to John Ireland, November 27, 1915.
71. AASP, Princess Henrietta to John Ireland, Cannes, France, March 22, 1915.
72. AASP, Jusserand to John Ireland, Washington, March 27, 1917.
73. AASP, Louis Duchesne to John Ireland, Rome, January 11, 1915.
74. Ibid., January 10, 1916.
75. Ibid., February 1, 1917.
76. Ibid., April 11, 1917.
77. AASP, Gasquet to John Ireland, Rome, January 1, 1915.
78. Ibid., May 16, 1915.
79. Ibid., January 12, 1918.
80. AASP, Jusserand to John Ireland, Washington, September 10, 1916.
81. AASP, Cecil Spring Rice to John Ireland, Washington, January 12, 1918.
82. AASP, James Bryce to John Ireland, February 27, 1907.
83. AASP, Jean Germain to Ireland, Rodez, February 27, 1900; Toulouse, July 20, 1915.
84. AASP, De Meaux to Ireland, Montbrison, Loire, December 27, 1905.
85. AASP, Frédéric Boudin to Ireland, Perroy, Eure, no date.
86. AASP, Duke de la Salle to Ireland, Granada, Spain, March 7, 1905.
87. St. Paul Dispatch, September 13, 1899.
88. Weekly Register, London, September 26, 1901.
89. AASP, copy, Ireland to Klein, St. Paul, September, 1899.
90. AASP, Klein to Ireland, Bellevue, Seine-et-Oise, December 8, 1899.
91. AASP, Columban Tyne to Ireland, Paris, December 4, 1902; Chicago Interocean, January 18, 1903.
92. AASP, Hoenaboetee to Ireland, Paris, January 24, 1903.
93. AASP, Wayne McVeagh to Ireland, Washington, March 27, 1912.
94. AASP, George Peixotto to Ireland, Paris, September 23, 1912.
95. AASP, Patrick Francis Cardinal Moran to Ireland, Sydney, Australia, May 1, 1911.
96. Boston Pilot, December 30, 1902.
97. Ireland, The Church and Modern Society, Pioneer Press, St. Paul, 1905, I, 119.

CHAPTER 12.   The Churchman

1. AASP, John Lancaster Spalding to John Ireland, Rome, January 21, 1883.
2. AASP, James Gibbons to John Ireland, Baltimore, August 21, 1884.
3. Acta et Decreta Concili Plenarii Baltimorensis, a die ix Novembris usque ad diem vii Decembris, A.D. MDCCCLXXXIV.
4. AASP, copy, John Ireland to Benjamin Harrison, St. Paul, August 19, 1889.
5. AASP, Harrison to Ireland, Washington, September 7, 1889.
6. BCA, 86-U-5, Ireland to Gibbons, St. Paul, November 20, 1889.
7. Baltimore Sun, July 28, 1891.
8. AASP, J. A. Stephen to Martin Marty, Washington, July 27, 1892.
9. Washington Post, December 2, 1902.
10. Clipping, no date.
11. Chicago Tribune, February 24, 1895.
12. New York World, November 4, 1894.

13. Cleveland *Universe,* November 9, 1894.
14. AASP, Gibbons to Ireland, Baltimore, November 23, 1900.
15. AASP, James McFaul to John Ireland, Trenton, N. J., March 21, 1901.
16. AASP, copy, Ireland to McFaul, St. Paul, March 26, 1901.
17. *Northwestern Chronicle,* August 16, 1913.
18. AASP, Gibbons to Ireland, Baltimore, December 26, 1914. BCA, 110-XYZ, Ireland to Gibbons, St. Paul, December 31, 1914.
19. Minneapolis *Journal,* October 5, 1914.
20. AASP, Francis Kelley to John Ireland, Chicago, February 9, 1917.
21. AASP, copy, Ireland to Daniel Hudson, St. Paul, July 22, 1898.
22. AASP, copy, Ireland to the editor, St. Paul, January 30, 1907.
23. *Ibid.,* February 4, 1907.
24. AASP, copy, Ireland to Robert Hughes, St. Paul, May 5, 1913.
25. *Northwestern Chronicle,* November 1, 1891.
26. *Catholic Bulletin,* St. Paul, September 5, 1914.
27. Ireland, *The Church and Modern Society,* Pioneer Press, St. Paul, 1905, II, 251; *Northwestern Chronicle,* July 13, 1901.
28. *Northwestern Chronicle,* December 3, 1897.
29. St. Paul *Pioneer Press,* January 21, 1906.
30. AASP, Gibbons to Ireland, Baltimore, May 3, 1910.
31. St. Paul *Pioneer Press,* June 3, 1907.
32. *Acta et Dicta,* St. Paul Catholic Historical Society, Vol. I, No. 1, p. 117.
33. AASP, letter of Richard Burtsell to the Pope (in Italian).
34. BCA, 89-W-8, John Ireland to James J. Gibbons, Rome, June 5, 1892.
35. AASP, Denis O'Connell to John Ireland, Rome, August 3, 1892.
36. *Ibid.,* September 16, 1892. ("Satolli will drive Corrigan to the wall.")
37. ADR, Ireland to O'Connell, St. Paul, November 17, 1892.
38. BCA, 86-G-10, Ireland to Gibbons, St. Paul, August 9, 1889. AASP, Gibbons to Ireland, Baltimore, September 21, 1892.
39. New York *Tribune,* December 17, 1892.
40. St. Louis *Chronicle,* December 16, 1892.
41. AASP, O'Connell to Ireland, Rome, January 25, 1893.
42. New York *Herald,* January 22, 1893.
43. Woodstock Archives, II, A8-b4, Brandi to René Holaind, Naples, July 26, 1893.
44. *Northwestern Chronicle,* December 23, 1892.
45. New York *News,* January 15, 1893.
46. AASP, O'Connell to Ireland, Rome, August 29, 1893.
47. New York *Sun,* August 1, 1893.
48. Chicago *Post,* January 8, 1893.
49. BCA, 91-A-7, Ireland to Gibbons, St. Paul, January 8, 1893.
50. ADR, Ireland to O'Connell, St. Paul, April 29, 1894.
51. AASP, clipping, Scrapbook 43, p. 56, from the Chicago *Herald,* January 10, 1893.
52. BCA, 91-M-4, Ireland to Gibbons, St. Paul, June 13, 1893.
53. BCA, 91-S-4, Ireland to Gibbons, St. Paul, August 11, 1893.
54. *Giornale d'Italia,* August 5, 1904.
55. AASP, O'Connell to Ireland, Rome, March 6, 1897.
56. *Katholische Volkszeitung,* Baltimore, May 4, 1895.
57. *Church News,* February 1, 1896.
58. BCA, 94-U-1, Ireland to Gibbons, St. Paul, December 2, 1896: "I frightened him in my last interview in Brooklyn."
59. St. Paul *Pioneer Press,* October 5, 1896.

60. ACUA, Bouquillon Papers, Ireland to Magnien, St. Paul, November 19, 1896.
61. ACUA, Bouquillon Papers, Ireland to Bouquillon, St. Paul, November 19, 1896.
62. NYAA, McQuaid to Corrigan, Rochester, October 3, 1896.
63. BCA, 94-V-2, Sebastian Martinelli to Gibbons, Washington, December 2, 1897.
64. O'Connell urged Ireland to make the New York *Journal* prove its statement that Satolli had called him an apostle of heresy. "Of course it never can," he said, "and, if it tries, we shall have funny revelations. The Italian proverb is 'chi pecora si fa, il lupo lo mangera' (make a sheep out of yourself and the wolf will eat you)."
65. Baltimore *Sun*, November 21, 1896, Scrapbook 30, p. 41.
66. AASP, Keane to Ireland, Rome, January 1, 1897.
67. *Ibid.*, May 9, 1897.
68. AASP, Satolli to Ireland, Rome, November 5, 1896.
69. BCA, 94-U-1, Ireland to Gibbons, St. Paul, December 2, 1896.
70. ACUA, Bouquillon Papers, Ireland to Magnien, St. Paul, November 19, 1896.
71. AASP, Satolli to Ireland, Rome, December 20, 1896.
72. AASP, Keane to Ireland, Rome, December 21, 1896.
73. *Ibid.*, December 21, 1896; January 1, 1897.
74. AASP, Satolli to Ireland, Rome, August 3, 1897.
75. *Ibid.*, April 23, 1901; December 25, 1902.
76. BCA, 100-J-1, Ireland to Gibbons, St. Paul, March, 1903.
77. AASP, O'Connell to Ireland, Rome, October 6, 1902.
78. *Ibid.*
79. St. Paul *Pioneer Press*, July 14, 1904.
80. *Northwestern Chronicle*, January 6, 1888.
81. AASP, copy of the sermon.
82. Ireland, *The Church and Modern Society*, I, 399.
83. AASP, copy.
84. Ireland, *The Church and Modern Society*, I, 123.
85. St. Paul *Pioneer Press*, July 20, 1893.
86. *Western Watchman*, May, 1905.
87. *North American Review*, March, 1901.
88. St. Paul *Pioneer Press*, quoted in the *Catholic Bulletin*, January 14, 1911.
89. Washington *Post*, December 10, 1900.
90. *La Papauté et les Peuples*, January, 1901.
91. AASP, Joseph Hayden to Ireland, Castellammare, Spain, January 4, 1901.
92. *North American Review*, January, 1907.
93. AASP, Cardinal Merry del Val to Ireland, Rome, September 14, 1907.
94. New York *Evening Globe* and New York *Herald*, February 8, 1910.
95. AASP, James Cardinal Gibbons to John Ireland, Baltimore, February 9, 1910.
96. *True Voice*, Omaha, and *Western Watchman*, April 8 and May 12, 1910.
97. Merry del Val to Ireland, Rome, April 24, 1910.
98. *Ibid.*, May 26, 1910.
99. Salvatore Cortesi, *My Thirty Years of Friendships*, Harper & Brothers, New York, 1927, p. 133.
100. St. John Gaffney to Ireland, Dresden, Saxony, May 18, 1910.
101. *Outlook*, April 9, 1910.

102. Joseph B. Bishop, *Theodore Roosevelt and His Time*, Charles Scribner's Sons, New York, 1920, II, 194.
103. AASP, Diomede Falconio to Ireland, Washington, April 28, 1910.
104. AASP, Maurice Francis Egan to Ireland, Copenhagen, May 16, 1910.
105. New York *Herald*, April 5, 1910.
106. AASP, William Edgar to Ireland, Minneapolis, June 11, 1910.
107. St. Paul *Pioneer Press*, May 23 and 26, 1912.
108. AASP, Gibbons to Ireland, Baltimore, May 22, 1912.
109. AASP, Ireland to Louis Caillet, Rome, March 30, 1892.
110. *Northwestern Chronicle*, October 5, 1918.
111. Benedetto Lorenzelli to Ireland, Finistère, August 25, 1900.
112. Frederick Rooker to O'Connell, Washington, October 22, 1900.
113. AASP, Scrapbook 40, p. 74.
114. AASP, Mourey to Ireland, Amelie, Pyrénées-Orientales, August 25, 1900.
115. AASP, Gibbons to Ireland, Rome, June 20, 1901.

CHAPTER 13. *Relationships Personal and Official*

1. BCA, 93-J-4, Ireland to Gibbons, St. Paul, July 31, 1894.
2. Ireland to Rampolla, St. Paul, June 16, 1901.
3. BCA, 85-G-7, Ireland to Gibbons, St. Paul, October 27, 1888.
4. AASP, Manning to Ireland, Westminster, April 15, 1887.
5. Ireland to Manning, St. Paul, September 23, 1887.
6. Shane Leslie, *Henry Edward Manning*, Burns Oates, London, 1921, p. 366.
7. AASP, Manning to Ireland, Westminster, October 30, 1887.
8. BCA, 87-B-2, J. E. C. Bodley to Gibbons, London, January 11, 1890.
9. AASP, Manning to Ireland, Westminster, June 9, 1890.
10. Leslie, *op. cit.*, p. 343. There is no reference to this incident in Ireland's papers.
11. John T. Reily, *Collections and Recollections in the Life and Times of Cardinal Gibbons*, II, p. 189.
12. BCA, 77-N-10, Ireland to Gibbons, February, 1884.
13. *Northwestern Chronicle*, October 6, 1887.
14. AASP, Gibbons to Ireland, Baltimore, August 29, 1892.
15. Reily, *op. cit.*, VI, 1334.
16. BCA, 86-U-5, Ireland to Gibbons, Washington, November 20, 1889.
17. AASP, Gibbons to Ireland, Baltimore, October 27, 1893.
18. BCA, 92-Q-2, Ireland to Gibbons, St. Paul, November 1, 1893.
19. BCA, 93-N-3, Ireland to Gibbons, St. Paul, December 7, 1894.
20. BCA, 83-N-9, Ireland to Gibbons, St. Paul, December 29, 1894.
21. AASP, Gibbons to Ireland, Baltimore, January 2, 1908.
22. BCA, 108-U, Ireland to Gibbons, St. Paul, December 23, 1912.
23. AASP, Gibbons to Ireland, Baltimore, December 26, 1912.
24. *Ibid.*, January 7, 1914.
25. BCA, 119, October 20, 1918.
26. AASP, Denis O'Connell to Ireland, Rome, February 28, 1900.
27. ADR, O'Connell to Ireland, Washington, January 14, 1903.
28. ACUA, Ireland to O'Connell, St. Paul, December 11, 1907.
29. AASP, O'Connell to Ireland, San Francisco, no date (1910).
30. *Ibid.*, Richmond, Va., September 8, 1915.
31. AASP, Gibbons to Ireland, Baltimore, September 13, 1909.
32. AASP, Thomas O'Gorman to Ireland, Rome, November 18, 20, 24, 1914.

33. AASP, Mariano Cardinal Rampolla to Ireland, Rome, February, 1892; August 8, September 12, October 18, 1892; and January 17, 18, March 11 and 13, 1895.
34. Felix Klein, *La Route du Petit Morvandiau, Souvenirs,* Vol. V, *Sans Arrêt,* Libraire Plon, Paris, 1949, p. 229.
35. AASP, extract from the address delivered on July 6, 1926.
36. AASP, Giacomo Cardinal Della Chiesa to Ireland, Bologna, January 12, 1914.
37. AASP, Germano Straniero to Ireland, Rome, November, 1915; Bonaventura Cerretti to Ireland, Washington, April 10; December 13, 1914; and Sydney, Australia, June 4, 1915. (With other "foliage" but not under another name.)
38. AASP, Vincenzo Cardinal Vannutelli to Ireland, Rome, May 29, 1910, and May 18, 1918.
39. NYAA, Ireland to M. A. Corrigan, Baltimore, January 22 and 23, 1888.
40. BCA, ALS 91-A-7, Ireland to Gibbons, St. Paul, January 8, 1893; ADR, Ireland to O'Connell, St. Paul, August 20, 1892.
41. AASP, Austin Ford to Ireland, New York, no date.
42. AASP, copy, Corrigan to Michael Walsh, New York, November 26, 1892.
43. ADR, Ireland to O'Connell, Washington, July 11, 1892.
44. Abbé Felix Klein, *In the Land of the Strenuous Life,* A. C. McClurg, Chicago, 1905, p. 108.
45. ADR, Ireland to O'Connell, St. Paul, December 7, 1902. (The world is in reverse.)
46. AASP, Felix Klein to Ireland, copy of letter without date, sent to Monsignor Humphrey Moynihan by Abbé Klein.
47. AASP, copy, Ireland to Klein, St. Paul, April 20, 1894.
48. AASP, Klein to Ireland, Paris, June 8, 1894, and January 29, 1895.
49. AASP, copy, Ireland to Klein, St. Paul, July 15, 1896.
50. AASP, Klein to Ireland, Paris, December 5, 1896; September 23, 1897; Bellevue, Seine et Dise, December 5, 1906.
51. AASP, copy, Ireland to Klein, St. Paul, January 8, 1907.
52. AASP, Klein to Ireland, Bellevue, April 30, 1907, and January 21, 1908.
53. AASP, copy, Ireland to Klein, St. Paul, December 7, 1911, and September 15, 1914.
54. AASP, Louis Duchesne to Ireland, Rome, June 23, 1910.
55. Claude D'Habloville, *Grandes Figures de l'Eglise Contemporaine,* Perrin, Paris, 1925, p. 101.
56. AASP, Duchesne to Ireland, Rome, December 31, 1911; January 13, 1913. The reference are to Turkey, Italy, Austria-Hungary.
57. AASP, Alfred Loisy to Ireland, Paris, December 8, 1893; Bellevue, February 22, 1900.
58. *North American Review,* February, 1907.
59. AASP, De Meaux to Ireland, Paris, September 5, 1897, and April 13, 1905.
60. AASP, Pierre des Mazis to Ireland, Paris, December 27, 1914; Baronne de Boulement, Vendée, France, November 28, 1914.
61. AASP, copy, Ireland to Georges Goyau, Rome, January 16, 1909; St. Paul, August 9, 1909, and January 28, 1912.
62. *Rescue Notes,* No. XVIII, October, 1905.

CHAPTER 14. *Honor Unachieved*

1. George Canning, *The New Morality,* Stanza 36.
2. Maria Longworth Storer, *In Memoriam Bellamy Storer,* privately printed, 1923, pp. 3-5, 18, 37.
3. AASP, Maria Storer to John Ireland, Rome, April 13, 1895.

4. *Ibid.*, Cincinnati, March 8, 1896.
5. *Ibid.*, Cincinnati, January 23, 1897.
6. The quotations from the letters of the Storers and Archbishop Ireland are taken *passim* from their correspondence, AASP.
7. AASP, Bellamy Storer to John Ireland, Meran, December 9, 1903.
8. Maria Storer, *In Memoriam Bellamy Storer*, p. 42. Also copy, AASP.
9. *Ibid.*, p. 43.
10. *Ibid.*, p. 46.
11. AASP, Maria Storer to John Ireland, Barcelona, October 18, 1900.
12. AASP, copy, William H. Taft to Maria Storer, Manila, May 19, 1901.
13. AASP, copy, John Ireland to Maria Storer, St. Paul, October 23 and November 10, 1903.
14. AASP, B. Storer to O'Gorman, Biarritz, April 20, 1901.
15. AASP, copy, Princess Alexandrine Windisch-Graetz to Maria Storer, Rome, Good Friday, 1904.
16. AASP, copy, Roosevelt to Maria Storer, White House, December 11, 1905.
17. Mark Sullivan, *Our Times*, Charles Scribner's Sons, New York, 1930, III, 100-127.
18. Maria Storer, *In Memoriam Bellamy Storer*, p. 115.
19. *Ibid.*, p. 117.
20. AASP, Maria Storer to Ireland, Saranac Lake, N. Y., February 3, 1907.
21. AASP, Bellamy Storer to Ireland, Rome, November 29, 1914.
22. AASP, Maria Storer to Ireland, Rome, January 9, 1915, and Cincinnati, December 13, 1916.
23. AASP, Maria Storer to Humphrey Moynihan, Paris, August 19, 1923, and April 10, 1930.
24. John Morley, *Critical Miscellanies*, Macmillan and Co., London, 1898, I, 99.
25. ADR, O'Connell to Ireland, Rome, March 6, 1897; Keane to Ireland, Rome, March 24, 1897.
26. AASP, O'Gorman to O'Connell, Sioux Falls, November 8, 1897.
27. NYAA, John Farley to Corrigan, Rome, December 27, 1901; January 30 and March 4, 1902.
28. AASP, Keane to Ireland, Rome, April 10, 1897.
29. NYAA, Messmer to Corrigan, Luxemburg, Wis., February 7, 1893.
30. AASP, Patrick Riordan to Ireland, San Francisco, December 17, 1913.
31. AASP, Cushman K. Davis to John Ireland, Washington, March 6, 1899.
32. BCA, 89-T-14, Gibbons to Rampolla, Baltimore, April 15, 1892.
33. BCA, 89-W-8, Ireland to Gibbons, Genoa, June 5, 1892.
34. ADR, Ireland to O'Connell, St. Paul, August 4, 1903.
35. *Ibid.*, November 15, 1903.
36. AASP, Gibbons to Ireland, Rome, September 30, 1914.
37. BCA, 110-F, Ireland to Gibbons, St. Paul, September 27, 1914.
38. *Ibid.*
39. AASP, Cerretti to Ireland, Washington, December 17, 1913, and Sydney, Australia, March 23, 1916.
40. AASP, Francis Cardinal Gasquet to Ireland, Rome, January 21, 1912.
41. AASP, Domenico Cardinal Ferrata to Ireland, Rome, January 9, 1912.
42. AASP, Serafino Cardinal Vannutelli to Ireland, Rome, January 3, 1912.
43. AASP, Bonaventura Cerretti to Ireland, Rome, January 17, 1918.
44. Francis C. Kelley, *The Bishop Jots It Down*, Harper, New York, 1939, p. 90.
45. BCA, clipping, January 22, 1919.
46. AASP, Francis Cardinal Gasquet to Thomas O'Gorman, Montecassino, October 3, 1918.

47. Maria Storer, *In Memoriam Bellamy Storer*, p. 107.
48. BCA, 97-N-3, Ireland to Gibbons, December 7, 1894.
49. ADR, Ireland to O'Connell, August 13, 1892; November 24, 1893; May 9, 1901.

CHAPTER 16. *His Personality and Achievement*

1. AASP, copy of address.
2. *Northwestern Chronicle*, April 29, 1882.
3. *Ibid.*, May 23, 1886.
4. *Ibid.*, September 18, 1884.
5. *Ibid.*, November 3, 1887. In September, 1888, at the invitation of Bishop John A. Watterson, he spoke at Columbus, Ohio, on the occasion of the Ohio Centennial, and in July of the following year, at the dedication of the Cathedral of SS. Peter and Paul, at Providence, Rhode Island, he took as his subject "Religion and Science." In November he preached at the installation of Bishop Otto Zardetti in St. Cloud, Minnesota; in April, 1890, at the laying of the cornerstone of the Cathedral in Davenport, Iowa; and in November, 1891, at the Golden Jubilee of Archbishop Peter Kenrick's consecration in St. Louis. Only a month before, in Dubuque, Iowa, at the Silver Jubilee of the consecration of Bishop John Hennessy, his sermon reflected the Cahensly agitation, which at the time was in the air. While he realized, he said, that the work of transition of Catholic immigrants must necessarily take time, which he would certainly be willing to allow, he demanded in the name of religion that it be not retarded.
6. *Northwestern Chronicle*, April 5, 1894.
7. *Ibid.*, June 8, 1894.
8. *Ibid.*, October 23, 1909; AASP, brochure issued by Duquesne Council, K. of C., Pittsburgh.
9. AASP, brochure, *Scholastic Press*, Notre Dame, 1888.
10. *Ave Maria*, July 6, 1895.
11. John Ireland, *The Church and Modern Society*, Pioneer Press, St. Paul, 1905, II, 83.
12. *Ibid.*, II, 401.
13. *Ibid.*, II, 377.
14. *Ibid.*, II, 219.
15. *Pilot*, Boston, May 17, 1902.
16. *Irish World*, April 25, 1896. In the same year he delivered the eulogy at the funeral of Bishop Martin Marty of St. Cloud, and at that of Bishop Stephen Ryan of Buffalo, at whose Jubilee he had spoken three years before, and he also preached at the dedication of the Cathedral in Duluth. In July, 1897, in the Chicago Cathedral, he paid tribute to Dr. Thaddeus Butler, who had been consecrated Bishop of Concordia, Kansas, in Rome, but who had died before he could take possession of his see.
17. *Pilot*, Boston, November 20, 1904. Cardinal Merry del Val thanked him for bringing before the public the true facts of the case in the conflict of the Vatican with the French government.
18. *Catholic Bulletin*, January 26, 1911.
19. Allen S. Will, *The Life of Cardinal Gibbons*, E. P. Dutton and Co., New York, 1922, II, 736.
20. AASP, copy of address; also quoted in the *Catholic Bulletin*, September 28, 1918.
21. Albert Shaw in the *Christian Union*, May 21, 1892.
22. *America*, October 5, 1918.

BIBLIOGRAPHY

Ahern, Patrick, *The Catholic University of America, 1887-1896*, Catholic University of America Press, Washington, 1948.

Anderson, William H., *The Philippines*, Putnam, New York, 1939.

Andrews, Christopher C., *History of St. Paul*, Mason, Syracuse, N. Y., 1890.

Barry, Colman, O.S.B., *The Catholic University of America, 1903-1909*, Catholic University of America Press, Washington, 1950.

Barry, William, *Father Hecker*, Columbus Press, New York, 1893.

Beard, Charles A., *The Rise of American Civilization*, The Macmillan Company, New York, 1935.

Béranger, H., *L'Aristocratie Intellectuelle*, Paris, 1894.

Bishop, Joseph, *Theodore Roosevelt and His Times*, shown in his own letters, Scribner's, New York, 1920.

Blegen, Theodore, *Building Minnesota*, Heath, Boston, 1938.

Blount, James H., *The American Occupation of the Philippines, 1898-1912*, Putnam, New York, 1912.

Bouquillon, Thomas, *Education: To Whom Does It Belong?* John Murphy & Co., Baltimore, 1892.

Browne, Henry, *The Catholic Church and the Knights of Labor*, Catholic University of America Press, Washington, 1949.

Burns, James A., *The Catholic School System in the United States*, Benziger, New York, 1908.

Campbell, Thomas, *The Only True American School System*, Messenger Office, September, 1901.

Castle, Henry A., *A History of St. Paul and Vicinity*, Lewis Publishing Co., Chicago, 1912.

Christianson, Theodore, *Minnesota Becomes of Age*, Chicago Historical Society, 1935.

Code, Joseph, *Dictionary of the American Hierarchy*, Longmans, Green, New York, 1940.

Coffin, Charles, *The Seat of Empire*, Fields, Boston, 1870.

Conway, James, *The State Last*, Pustet, New York, 1892.

Coppinger, E., *La Polémique française sur la Vie du Père Hecker*, Oudin, Paris, 1898.

Cortesi, Salvatore, *My Thirty Years of Friendships*, Harper, New York, 1927.

Delassus, Henri, *L'Américanisme et la Conjuration Antichrétienne*, Desclée, Lille, 1899.

Delattre, A. J., *Un Catholicisme Américain*, Namur, 1898.

De Meaux, Vicomte, *L'Eglise catholique et la Liberté aux Etats-Unis*, Lecoffre, Paris, 1893.

Dennis, A. L. P., *Adventures in American Diplomacy*, Dutton, New York, 1928.

D'Habloville, Claude, *Grandes Figures de l'Eglise Contemporaine*, Perrin, Paris, 1925.

Diocese of St. Paul, *The Golden Jubilee*, Pioneer Press, St. Paul, 1901.

Egan, Maurice Francis, *Recollections of a Happy Life*, Doran, New York, 1924.

Egan, Maurice Francis, *Ten Years Near the German Frontier*, Doran, New York, 1919.

Ellinger, Agnes, *A History of the Temperance Movement in Minnesota to 1865*, Minnesota Historical Society, St. Paul, July, 1933.

Elliott, C. B., *The Philippines—The End of the Commission Government*, Bobbs-Merrill, Indianapolis, 1914.

Elliott, Walter, C.S.P., *Life of Father Hecker*, Columbus Press, New York, 1891.
Ellis, John Tracy, *The Formative Years of the Catholic University*, American Catholic Historical Association, Washington, 1946.
Folwell, William W., *History of Minnesota*, Minnesota Historical Society, St. Paul, 1924.
Forbes, W. Cameron, *The Philippine Islands*, Houghton Mifflin, Boston, 1928.
Foreman, John, *The Philippine Islands*, 1899.
Gillis, James, *The Paulists*, The Macmillan Company, New York, 1932.
Guilday, Peter, *A History of the Councils of Baltimore, 1791-1884*, The Macmillan Company, New York, 1932.
Guilday, Peter (ed.), *The National Pastorals of the American Hierarchy, 1791-1919*, National Catholic Welfare Council, Washington, 1923.
Gwynn, Stephen, *Letters and Friendships of Cecil Spring Rice*, Houghton Mifflin, Boston, 1929.
Halifax, Charles L., *Leo XIII and Anglican Orders*, Longmans, Green, London, 1912.
Haskin, Frédéric J., *The Immigrant, An Asset and a Liability*, Revell, New York, 1913.
Hecker, Isaac Thomas, *The Church and the Age*, New York, 1896.
Henthorne, Mary Evangela, *The Irish Catholic Colonization Association of the United States*, Champaign, Ill., 1932.
Hoffman, Mathias, *Church Founders of the Northwest*, Milwaukee, 1937.
Hogan, Peter, S.S.J., *The Catholic University of America, 1896-1903*, Catholic University of America Press, Washington, 1949.
Holaind, René, *The Parent First*, Benziger, New York, 1891.
Holbrook, F. F., *Minnesota in the Spanish-American War and Philippine Insurrection*, Minnesota War Records Commission Publications, St. Paul, 1923.
Holden, Vincent F., *Early Years of Isaac Thomas Hecker*, Catholic University of America, Washington, 1939.
Holmes, Frank, *Minnesota in Three Centuries*, Publishing Society of Minnesota, St. Paul, 1908.
Houtin, A., *L'Américanisme*, Libraire Emile Nourry, Paris, 1904.
Hughes, William H., *Three Great Events in the History of the Catholic Church in the United States*, Detroit, 1889.
Ireland, John, *The Church and Modern Society*, Pioneer Press, St. Paul, 1905.
Ireland, John, *L'Eglise et le Siècle*, conférences et discours de Mgr. Ireland, publ. avec une préface par l'Abbé Felix Klein, Lecoffre, Paris, 1894.
Jenkins, Thomas, *Six Seasons in Our Prairies and Six Weeks in Our Rockies*, Rogers, Louisville, 1884.
Johnson, Stanley C., *History of Emigration from the United Kingdom to North America*, London, 1913.
Kelley, Francis, *The Bishop Jots It Down*, Harper, New York, 1939.
Kittell, Ferdinand, *Souvenir of Loretto Centenary*, Cresson, Pa., 1889.
Klein, Felix, *America of Tomorrow*, McClurg, Chicago, 1911.
Klein, Felix, *In the Land of the Strenuous Life*, McClurg, Chicago, 1905.
Klein, Felix, *Le Père Hecker, Fondateur des Paulistes Américaines*, par le Père Elliott. Traduit et adapté de l'Anglais avec authorisation de l'auteur, Paris, 1907.
Klein, Felix, *La Route du Petit Morvandiau, Souvenirs*, Libraire Plon, Paris, 6 vols.
L'Americanismo, Risposta ad un Articolo dell'Opinione Liberale Sul P. Hecker, Desclée, Rome, 1898.
Lecanuet, Edouard, *La Vie de l'Eglise sous Léon XIII*, Paris, 1930.

Leclerc, Max, *Choses d'Amérique*, Plon, Paris, 1895.

Leslie, Shane, *Henry Edward Manning*, Burns Oates, London, 1921.

Lodge, H. C., *The War with Spain*, Harper, New York, 1900.

Longworth, A. L. R., *Crowded Hours*, Scribner's, New York, 1933.

Lugan, A., *Le Catholicisme aux Etats-Unis*, Letouzey, Paris, 1930.

McCaffrey, James, *History of the Church in the Nineteenth Century*, Dublin, 1909.

Macdonald, Fergus, *The Catholic Church and the Secret Societies in the United States*, Catholic Historical Society, New York, 1946.

Maignen, Charles, *Le Père Hecker—Est-il un Saint?* Paris, 1898.

Maignen, Charles, *Studies in Americanism—Father Hecker, Is He a Saint?* Rome, 1898.

Martin, Sister M. Aquinata, *The Catholic Church on the Nebraska Frontier, 1854-1885*, Catholic University of America Studies, Washington, 1946.

Maynard, Theodore, *The Story of American Catholicism*, The Macmillan Company, New York, 1941.

Myers, G., *History of Bigotry in the United States*, Random House, New York, 1943.

Newson, Thomas, *Pen Pictures of St. Paul and Biographical Sketches of Old Settlers*, St. Paul, 1886.

O'Connell, Denis, *A New Idea in the Life of Father Hecker*, Fribourg, 1897.

O'Donnell, John H., *The Catholic Hierarchy of the United States*, Catholic University of America Studies in American Church History, Washington.

O'Hara, Edwin V., *Archbishop Ireland*, Aquin Papers, St. Thomas College, St. Paul, 1949.

O'Herlihy, T. O., *The Famine*, Drogheda Independent Co., Drogheda, Ireland, no date.

O'Reilly, Bernard, *Life of Leo XIII*, John C. Winston Co., Philadelphia, 1903.

Palladino, Lawrence, *Indian and White in the Northwest—a History of Catholicity in Montana*, Wickersham Publishing Co., Lancaster, Pa., 1922.

Parrington, Vernon Lewis, *Main Currents in American Thought*, Harcourt, Brace, New York, 1930.

Péchenard, P. L., *La Fin de l'Américanisme en France*, Mersch, Paris, 1901.

Pollock, Hester McLean, *Our Minnesota*, Dutton, New York, 1917.

Pringle, H. F., *The Life and Times of William H. Taft*, Farrar & Rinehart, New York, 1939.

Pringle, H. F., *Theodore Roosevelt, a Biography*, Harcourt, Brace, New York, 1931.

Purcell, Richard, *Archbishop Ireland*, Aquin Papers, St. Thomas College, St. Paul, 1949.

Purcell, Richard, "John Ireland," *Dictionary of American Biography*, Scribner's, New York, 1932, IX, 497.

Pyle, Joseph, *The Life of James J. Hill*, Doubleday, Doran, New York, 1917.

Quigley, Joseph, *Condemned Societies*, Catholic University of America, Washington, 1927.

Reilly, Daniel F., *The School Controversy*, Catholic University of America, Washington, D. C., 1943.

Reily, John, *Collections and Recollections in the Life and Times of Cardinal Gibbons*, 10 vols., Martinburg, W. Va., 1890-1904.

Reports of the Philippine Commissions to the President, Government Printing Office, Washington, 1901.

Reports of the Taft Philippine Commission to the Secretary of War, 1902, 1903, 1904.

Rhodes, J. F., *The McKinley and Roosevelt Administrations, 1879-1909*, The Macmillan Company, New York, 1922.

Riviere, J. *Le Modernisme dans l'Eglise*, Letouzey, Paris, 1929.
Roosevelt, Theodore, *Letters*, edited by Elting Morison, Harvard University Press, Cambridge, 1951.
Ryan, John A., *Social Doctrine in Action*, Harper, New York, 1941.
Ryan, John A., and Millar, M. F. X., *The State and the Church*, The Macmillan Company, New York, 1922.
Saint-Clement, *La Liquidation du Consortium Américaniste*, Thoren, Paris, 1899.
Schurman, J. F., *Philippine Affairs*, Scribner's, New York, 1902.
Sedgwick, Henry D., *Father Hecker*, Small, Boston, 1900.
Seymour, E. S., *Sketches of Minnesota, the New England of the West*, Harper, New York, 1850.
Soderini, Eduardo, *The Pontificate of Leo XIII*, Burns Oates, London, 1934.
Soukup, Cuthbert, *The Public Speaking of Archbishop John Ireland*, St. John's Abbey, St. Cloud, Minn., 1948.
Stephenson, George, *A History of Immigration, 1820-1924*, New York, 1936.
Storer, Bellamy, *Letter to the President and Members of His Cabinet*, Cincinnati, 1906.
Storer, Maria Longworth, *In Memoriam Bellamy Storer*, privately printed, 1923.
Sullivan, Mark, *Our Times*, Scribner's, New York, 1930.
Taft, Helen, *Recollections of Full Years*, Dodd, Mead, New York, 1914.
Taft Philippine Commission to the Secretary of War, Report of War Department, 1900-1904, Government Printing Office, Washington.
Talbot, James, *Pope Leo XIII, His Life and Letters*, Garrison, Boston, 1886.
Tardivel, Jules, *La Situation Religieuse aux Etats-Unis, Illusions et Réalité*, Desclée, Paris, 1900.
Upham, Warren, *Minnesota in Three Centuries*, The Publishing Society of Minnesota, St. Paul, 1908.
Upham, Warren, and Dunlap, R. B., *Minnesota Biographies, 1655-1912*, Minnesota Historical Society, St. Paul, 1912, Collections XIV.
Ward, Maisie, *Insurrection and Resurrection*, Sheed & Ward, New York, 1937.
Welsh, Herbert, *The Other Man's Country: an Appeal to Conscience*, Lippincott, Philadelphia, 1900.
West, Nathaniel, *The Ancestry, Life and Times of Hon. Hastings Sibley*, Province Press, 1889.
Will, Allen S., *The Life of Cardinal Gibbons*, Dutton, New York, 1922.
Williams, Daniel R., *The Odyssey of the Philippine Commission*, McClurg, Chicago, 1913.
Williams, J. F., *A History of the City of St. Paul and of the County of Ramsey*, Minnesota Historical Society Collections, vol. 4, St. Paul, 1876.
Willis, H. P., *Our Philippine Problem*, Henry Holt, New York, 1906.
Worcester, Dean C., *The Philippines, Past and Present*, The Macmillan Company, New York, 1930.
World's Parliament of Religions, Parliament Publishing Co., Chicago, 1896.
Zwierlein, Frederick J., *Letters of Archbishop Corrigan to Bishop McQuaid and Allied Documents*, The Art Printshop, Rochester, 1946.
Zwierlein, Frederick J., *The Life and Letters of Bishop McQuaid*, The Art Printshop, Rochester, 1927.

PERIODICAL SOURCES

American Ecclesiastical Review, VI (1892). Nine articles on the school question.
Barry, William, "Americanism True and False," *North American Review*, July, 1899.
Barry, William, "An American Crusade," *National Review*, March, 1899.
Bellman, The, "A Power for Righteousness," September 28, 1918.

Blossom, M. C., "Archbishop Ireland," *Current Opinion,* June, 1900.
Bonghi, R., "Leone XIII Mons. Ireland," *Nuova Antologia,* August, 1894.
Brunetière, Ferdinand, "Le Catholicisme aux Etats-Unis," *Revue des Deux Mondes,* November, 1895.
Burns, J. A., "Catholic Secondary Schools," *American Catholic Quarterly Review,* July, 1901.
Burt, W., "Reply to Archbishop Ireland's Strictures upon the Methodist Episcopal Church," *North American Review,* October, 1910.
Carr, J. F., "The Archbishop of St. Paul," *Outlook,* April 24, 1909.
Catholic World, "For God and Country," February, 1939.
Civiltà Cattolica, Series 15, II, 385 (1892), "La Santa Sede e la Questione Scholastica negli Stati Uniti"; 755, letter of Ireland to *Civiltà.*
Civiltà Cattolica, Series 17, V, 513 (1899) "Testem Benevolentiae"; 641, "Leone XIII e l'Americanismo."
Civiltà Cattolica, "Un Breve di Leone X citato dai Rosiminiani," February 7, 1899.
Cunningham, C. D., "Origin of the Friar Land Question," *American Political Science Review,* August, 1916.
Current Opinion, "Roman Catholicism in America Loses Two of Its Leaders," November, 1918.
Doyle, A. P., "The Vexed Question of the Friars," *Catholic World,* September, 1902.
Duggan, J. F., "The Education of a Priest," *American Ecclesiastical Review,* CI, Nos. 4, 5, 6 (1939).
Egan, H. E., "Irish Immigration to Minnesota, 1865-1890," *Mid America,* October, 1929, January, 1930.
Etheridge, J. St. Clair, "The Genesis of Americanism," *North American Review,* May, 1900.
Fonsgrieve, Georges, "Américanisme et Américains," *La Quinzaine,* April 1, 1899.
Gibson, William, "An Outburst of Activity in Roman Congreg.," *Nineteenth Century Review,* May, 1899.
Goyau, Georges, "Appreciation of Archbishop Ireland," *Living Age,* December 21, 1918.
Holden, Vincent F., "A Myth in 'L'Américanisme,'" *Catholic Historical Review,* July, 1945.
Ireland, John, "The Catholic Church and the Saloon," *North American Review,* October, 1894.
Ireland, John, "The Dogmatic Authority of the Papacy," *North American Review,* April, 1908.
Ireland, John, "Is the Papacy an Obstacle to the Reunion of Christendom?" *North American Review,* April, 1907; January, 1908.
Ireland, John, "Leo XIII," *North American Review,* September, 1903.
Ireland, John, "The Life of Bishop Cretin," *Acta et Dicta,* Catholic Historical Society of St. Paul, July, 1916, 1917, 1918.
Ireland, John, "Memoir of Rev. Lucien Galtier," *Minnesota Historical Society Collections,* III (1874).
Ireland, John, "The Methodist Episcopal Church of America in Italy," *North American Review,* July, 1910; September, 1910; January, 1911.
Ireland, John, "Personal Liberty and Labor Strikes," *North American Review,* October, 1901.
Ireland, John, "The Pontificate of Pius X," *North American Review,* February, 1907.

Ireland, John, "The Pope's Civil Princedom," *North American Review*, March, 1901.

Ireland, John, "Right Rev. Mathias Loras," *Catholic World*, September, October, 1898.

Ireland, John, "Theobold Mathew," *Catholic World*, October, 1890.

Ireland, John, "Very Rev. Samuel C. Mazzuchelli, *Acta et Dicta*, July, 1915.

Keane, John J., "America as Seen from Abroad," *Catholic World*, March, 1898.

Klein, Felix, "The Religious Congregations and the French Government," *North American Review*, February, 1904.

Kunkel, R., "Spanish Friars in Philippines," *Catholic Mind*, October, 1943.

Literary Digest, "Archbishop Ireland's Address on Labor," September 16, 1893.

Lovelace, Maud Hart, "A Face in the Crowd," *America*, January 18, 1930.

Markoe, Lorenzo, "A Golden Jubilee in Minnesota," *Ave Maria*, July 6, 1901.

Martin, Hyppolite, "L'Américanisme," *Etudes Religieuses*, July 20, 1898.

McAvoy, Thomas, "Americanism, Fact and Fiction," *Catholic Historical Review*, July, 1945.

McAvoy, Thomas, "Americanism and Frontier Catholicism," *Review of Politics*, July, 1943.

Meng, John J., "Cahenslyism: The First Chapter," *Catholic Historical Review*, January, 1946.

Meng, John J., "Cahenslyism: The Second Chapter," *Catholic Historical Review*, October, 1946.

Moynihan, Humphrey, "Archbishop Ireland," *Acta et Dicta*, October, 1933.

Moynihan, Humphrey, "Archbishop Ireland," *Catholic World*, November, 1918.

Moynihan, Humphrey, "Archbishop Ireland's Colonies," *Acta et Dicta*, October, 1934.

O'Gorman, Thomas, "The Educational Policy of Archbishop Ireland," *Educational Review*, May, 1892.

Onahan, William, "A Chapter of Catholic Colonization," *Acta et Dicta*, July, 1917.

Outlook, "Patriot and Priest," October 9, 1918.

Outlook, "Religious Conditions in Our New Island Territory," August 26, 1899.

Parnell, Charles S., "The Irish Land Question," *North American Review*, February, 1880.

Péchenard, P. L., "The End of Americanism in France," *North American Review*, March, 1900.

Purcell, Richard, "The United States of America, the Irish Immigrant, the Famine and the Irish American," *Irish Ecclesiastical Record*, LXVX (1947).

Rassegna Nazionale, "The Temporal Power," May 1, 1901.

Reardon, James, "The Catholic Total Abstinence Movement in Minnesota," *Acta et Dicta*, July, 1909.

Roddis, Louis H., "The Last Indian Uprising," *Minnesota History Bulletin*, February, 1920.

Ruffoni, G., "Le Teorie di Mons. Ireland," *La Scuola Cattolica*, Milano, Serie II, Vol. IX (1895).

Schaefer, Francis J., "Archdiocese of St. Paul," *The Catholic Encyclopedia*, XII, 366-369.

Schaefer, Francis J., "History of the Diocese of St. Paul," *Acta et Dicta*, July, 1915.

Smith, Alice, "The Sweetman Irish Colony," *Minnesota History*, December, 1928.

Smith, John Talbot, "Archbishop John Ireland," *Dublin Review*, January, 1921.

Snell, Merwin-Marie, "Pen Pictures of the American Hierarchy," *Independent*, April 27, 1893.

Storer, Maria, "Archbishop Ireland and the Hat," *North American Review*, April, 1921.

Sweetman, John, "The Sweetman Catholic Colony of Currie, Minnesota," *Acta et Dicta*, July, 1911.

Tablet, The (London), "Father Hecker," March 11, 1899.

Taft, W. H., "Political Parties in the Philippines," *Annals of the American Academy of Political and Social Science*, September, 1902.

Velasquez, "Archbishop Ireland," *Literary Northwest*, May, 1892.

Vernon, S. M., "The Methodist Episcopal Church of America in Italy," *North American Review*, August, 1910.

Vernon, S. M., "Rejoinder to Archbishop Ireland," *North American Review*, October, 1910.

Vieillard, "A Great American Churchman," *Nation*, September 2, 1915.

White, James, "For God and Country," *Catholic World*, February, 1939.

Other sources of information on the Life of Ireland are the *Minnesota Historical Society Collections*, the *Minnesota Historical Bulletin*, *Northwestern Chronicle*, *Irish Standard*, *Boston Pilot*, *St. Paul Pioneer Press* and *Dispatch*, *Minneapolis Journal*, *New York Times*, and *New York Tribune*.

INDEX

Abbelen, P. M., 55, 57, 59, 60, 63
Abbott, Lawrence, 313
Aberdeen, Lady, 149
Adalbert, Prior, 17
Adams, quoted, 20, 21
Adrian, Minn., 27
Agen, d', Boyer, 144
Agius, Archbishop, 202
Agliardi, Antonio, 78, 329
Aglipay movement, 188, 189, 190, 191, 198, 203, 206, 207
Aguinaldo, Emilio, 179
Ahern, Patrick, xii
Albert, Prince, of Belgium, 148, 264
America
    Arbishop Ireland on, 137-38, 139, 140
    as example of happy relations between Church and State, 137
    feeling against, in Spanish-American War, 168, 169
    Lafayette and, 153
Americanism, 47, 62, 74-75, 379, 387-88
    controversy on, 18, 56, 106, 108-35, 158, 303; (background of, 104-5)
    ecclesiastical and political, 108
Américanisme et la Conjuration Antichrétienne (Delassus), 112
Ames, Charles W., 267
Ancient Order of Hibernians, 214
Animadversiones Quaedam de Universitate in America Fundanda, 237
Annenkoff, General, 137
Anti-Poverty Society, 232
A.P.A.'s, 48
Apologia pro Vita Sua (Newman), 107
Apostolic Delegate; see Papal Delegation, establishment of
Arenberg, d', Prince, 137
Aristocracy of thought, 250
Arkins, John, 7
Arundell, Lord, 149
Ashbourne, Lord, 149
Aspirations of Nature, The (Hecker), 106
Associated Press, defense of, 287
Associations cultuelles, 272, 273, 336

Atkinson, Frederick, 197, 198, 200
Augustinians, 177, 187
Austin, Horace, 11
Avoca, Minn., 28-29, 30

Bajec, Father, 363
Balfour, Arthur J., 150, 271
Ballufin, 5
Baltimore, Third Council of, 33-34, 279-81, 296
Bard, Senator, 263
Barron, Joseph, 243
Barrows, John Henry, 43
Barry, John, 265
Barry, William, 107, 115
Barse and Company, 24
Battifol, Pierre Henri, 337
Baudelaire, Pierre Charles, 104
Baxter, Judge, 253
Bearn, de, Prince, 266
Becker, George L., 23
Bedini, Archbishop, 295
Belgium, Archbishop Ireland's visit to, 148
Belley seminary, 4
Bellingham, Sir Henry and Lady, 149
Benedict XV, 100, 269, 270, 271, 273, 294, 330, 331, 337, 343, 353, 358, 359, 379
Benedictine controversy, 16-17
Bennett Law, 82
Beresford, Charles, 150
Bernsdorff, Count, 271
Bernstein, Herman, 267
Berry, Father, 150, 344
Bigotry, 48, 91, 93, 282
Bishop, General, 51
Bishop Jots It Down, The (Kelley), 359
Bismarck and His Time (Goyau), 343
Blaine, Secretary, 357
Blanco, Ramon, 163, 167, 188
Blenck, Bishop, 195
Bliss, George, 262
Bodley, J. C., 321
Boeglin, Eugene, 64, 84, 89, 98, 115, 182, 327
Bonney, Charles, 40

427

The Imprimatur is hereby granted for the printing of *The Life of Archbishop John Ireland* by Right Reverend Monsignor James H. Moynihan.

☩ John Gregory Murray
Archbishop of Saint Paul

October 17, 1952